Adventure Guide

Bolivia

Adventure Guide

Bolivia

Vivien Lougheed

Assisted in research, writing and survival
by John Harris

HUNTER

HUNTER PUBLISHING, INC,
130 Campus Drive, Edison, NJ 08818
732-225-1900; 800-255-0343; fax 732-417-1744
www.hunterpublishing.com

Ulysses Travel Publications
4176 Saint-Denis, Montréal, Québec
Canada H2W 2M5
514-843-9882, ext. 2232; fax 514-843-9448

Windsor Books
The Boundary, Wheatley Road, Garsington
Oxford, OX44 9EJ England
01865-361122; fax 01865-361133

ISBN 1-58843-365-X

*This and other Hunter travel guides are also
available as e-books in a variety of digital formats
through our online partners, including
Amazon.com and Netlibrary.com.*

Cover photo: Man in reed boat © Pete Oxford, naturepl.com
All interior images by Vivien Lougheed, unless noted.
Index by: Nancy Wolff

Maps by Kim André © 2004 Hunter Publishing, Inc.

1 2 3 4

www.hunterpublishing.com

 Hunter's full range of guides to all corners of the globe is featured on our exciting website. You'll find guidebooks to suit every type of traveler, no matter what their budget, lifestyle, or idea of fun.

Adventure Guides – There are now over 40 titles in this series, covering destinations from Costa Rica and the Yucatán to Tampa Bay & Florida's West Coast and Belize. Complete with information on what to do, as well as where to stay and eat, *Adventure Guides* are tailor-made for the active traveler, with all the practical travel information you need, as well as details of the best places for hiking, biking, canoeing, horseback riding, trekking, skiing, watersports, and all other kinds of fun.

Alive Guides – This ever-popular line of books takes a unique look at the best each destination offers: fine dining, jazz clubs, first-class hotels and resorts. In-margin icons direct the reader at a glance. Top-sellers include *The US Virgin Islands, The Cayman Islands* and *Aruba, Bonaire & Curaçao.*

Our **Romantic Weekends** guidebooks provide escapes for couples of all ages and lifestyles. Unlike most "romantic" travel books, ours cover more than charming hotels and delightful restaurants, with a host of activities that you and your partner will remember forever.

One-of-a-kind travel books available from Hunter include *The Best Dives of the Bahamas; Golf Resorts; Cruising Alaska* and many more.

Full descriptions are given for each book at www.hunterpublishing.com, along with reviewers' comments and a cover image. You can also view pages and the table of contents. Books may be purchased on-line via our secure transaction facility.

Acknowledgments

My first acknowledgment goes to my husband, John Harris, for his acceptance of my obsession for travel rather than him. He claims that he is content to be a possession rather than an obsession. His never-ending attention to my comfort and security and his attention to the fine details of English grammar have made this book possible.

My next acknowledgment is to Kim André who, even through sleepless nights and endless piles of kid-work, managed to promptly answer my many questions. Her enthusiasm and support are what make the collaboration of book writing as pleasant as traveling.

Paige Pedersen is always with me on my journeys, sometimes in person and always in spirit.

There are others in my life whose voices I often hear when I'm in the desert or jungle looking at things like tarantulas, leaf-cutter ants, capybaras or dung beetles. They are Craig and Carl Blanchard, Levi Chamberlain, Jake MacDonald and Seb Harris. When I'm sticking my crampons into the ice of a glacier or crossing a raging river, I often hear Robin and Kelsey MacDonald encouraging me to chance a next move.

I would like to thank Patricia Martinez who translated any Spanish that was too difficult for me to understand. Without her, critical information may have been misrepresented.

When we became homesick, Barry and Joy McKinnon brought us some fresh adventures, among which was an escape into Peru during the War of Taxation. They also brought us some Canadian humor delivered with a Canadian accent.

A writer can never complete a book without the help of the people in the host country. I would like to thank Sonia Cruz and Oscar Crispe from Copacabana for giving us so much insight into the Aymara culture. Rick de Rave and his partner Margarina kept us fueled with their cappuccinos while advising us about things like the dangers of gringos driving in Bolivia or boats that ply the waters of Lake Titicaca.

Thanks to Pieter de Raad and his wife Marga Van't Hoff for their hospitality, endless leads and the rhubarb jam that gave John spiritual rejuvenation halfway through our journey. He liked Marga's legs, too.

I thank Jerome and Lillian Luis in Tupiza for their information about the area and especially about Butch Cassidy and the Sundance Kid. I thank Hanne Inners for her skill with horses that helped make me look like a seasoned cowgirl.

Louis Demers in Sorata is an inspiration for everyone who visits that area and his dedication to Bolivian tourism is unsurpassed. Things in the mountains change rapidly, but Louis kept me informed on all the latest trail information.

Manuel Español from Santa Cruz gave me more information about the Pantanal than I could have gathered in a month of travel there. He was eager to help and paid scrupulous attention to detail.

I would like to thank Susan Bryan and Andrew Watts, a couple of young Canadians, who helped us on a horrific hike out of Tupiza. They boosted my morale. Thanks also to Harry Muller, now known as Piraña Harry, for his humor and understanding when on the Yacuma River with us.

Alex Shand, who runs SpeakEasy in La Paz and is part of the editorial team for Llama Express, has supplied me with countless details on Bolivian politics and history. I hope she becomes the first female mayor of the city. Her information was supplemented by details from the now-defunct *Bolivian Times*, thanks to the cooperation of Peter McFarran and his wife Wendy. Thanks to Tomer Weingram, a volunteer at Villa Tunari animal shelter, for the corrected details he gave me about the shelter. Due to roadblocks, I was unable to get into Villa Tunari.

Thanks to Martin Recardo in Cochabamba for his recommendations about good places to eat in the city. I would also like to include Norma David Peña and David Carbonell for their contributions about places to visit, many of which have never before been described in guidebooks or tourism publications.

Elva Alfaro in Sucre helped me make more informed recommendations about travel in the Potolo area. Rick and his Dutch partners at Joy Rider took us on a great cycling excursion out of Sucre, and fed us excellent cappuccinos and breakfasts.

I also want to thank Dr. Hugo Barrios and his wife Damiska for their help and assistance in the mountains. Their jeep and driver were a great help, too. Without them we would not have seen some of the climbing sites that we saw around La Paz and Sorata.

My final acknowledgment goes to Eunice, who shared her intimate knowledge of adventure destinations and possibilities.

I am sure there are many more people I have forgotten to mention. For that I apologize. You know who you are. When I'm back in a few years to write the next edition, grab my notebook and write your names in block letters.

Contents

APPENDIX

INDEX

■ Maps

Introduction

Bolivia is a land-locked country with a smorgasbord of land-scapes. There are tropical jungles in the Amazon River Basin and bleak but beautiful deserts on the Alti-plano. These are a photographer's dream. The Andes Mountains, with four of the world's highest peaks, of-fer some of the best hiking, climbing and caving in the world. Lake Titi-kaka and its surrounding area al-lows the amateur anthropologist/ historian to explore the ruins of the

ancient Inca and pre-Inca civilizations. The only thing missing in Bolivia are ocean beaches.

Hubert Herring, in *History of Latin America*, called Bolivia the Tibet of the Americas. I agree with him if comparing the cultural richness of the two countries, but Bolivia is much cleaner and has far less poverty than Tibet.

Bolivia is a country rich in people. The native Aymara (eye-MAR-a) and Quechua (KAY-chew-a) live their lives as they have for centuries, tending sheep and llamas, weaving garments or planting fields on the steppes, going to market on specific days and teaching their children traditional ways. The Indian ladies, in their bowler hats, full skirts and tassled shawls, are beautiful. The bowlers, evidently, owe their existence to some British salesman with an eye for new fashions.

I love to walk in the Andes and hear the romantic music from a shep-herd's pan flute wafting through a valley. I love to sit in the market and talk with a local lady proudly sporting her best bowler hat. I like to ask about products I have never seen before. With those ladies who seem in-terested, I like to talk about myself. I use my broken Spanish with a funny accent and, when they laugh at me, I laugh too. I've discovered my ankle length red dress to be a big attraction with both the bowlered ladies and their men, who never fail to admire it. My hiking boots, on the other hand, are frowned upon. The Indian ladies wear pumps. I like to taste the strange foods and watch the reaction of Bolivians watching me.

The more Europeanized residents of the cities are friendly too, but wary about the judgments travelers will make of their country. Once they are sure quick judgments are not forthcoming, they'll talk openly about the problems of one of the continent's poorest countries, one of Latin America's most corrupt, and one of the world's least known.

Since Bolivia is such a diverse country, each district offers different kinds of adventures. For example, in the Andes, hiking is a must, but in the Amazon River Basin travel by boat is the only way to go. Some places have exceptional archeological sites, while other areas are especially interesting to birders and photographers. I recommend that everyone enjoy at least one activity that involves learning about the weavings made by indigenous people. Reducing your activities to suit your time frame will be the most difficult part of planning your trip to Bolivia.

Sucre is Bolivia's capital, but La Paz, perched at 12,000 ft/3,632 m above sea level, is the largest city in the country and the seat of government. It sits in a natural bowl three miles/five km in diameter that was carved out of the mountains by a river thousands of years ago. Today the river trickles through the bottom of the valley, carving its path at a much slower pace. It is thick with sewage and industrial sludge, one sight you want to avoid.

In La Paz, as in Santa Cruz (soon to be the country's largest city), accommodations and restaurants can be luxurious or simple. Museums are plentiful and the treasures are well displayed. Movies are usually Hollywood fare with Spanish subtitles; cultural shows, especially Andean bands, are abundant, but jazz bars can also be found. All towns and cities have Internet cafés.

On the other hand, because Bolivia is a developing nation, it does not have the advanced infrastructure common in North America or Europe. The roads, most of which are unpaved, can be deplorable, especially during rainy season. The buses are slow and crowded, often carrying freight or livestock in the aisles and under the seats. The trains are slow and run on narrow gauge, resulting in a teeter-totter ride. Buying a ticket, which must be done on the same day you ride, can sometimes take longer than the trip itself.

The La Paz, Copacabana, Oruru, Sajama roads are well paved. Roads to and from Tarija, a prosperous city, are nightmares, as is the Santa Cruz to Villamontes road. Travelers who are weak in the stomach or afraid of unprotected 1,000-foot/300-meter sheer drops off blind curves should fly, which is cheap and comfortable.

And of course there is the La Paz/Coroico road, the main route from the seat of government through the Yungas to the Amazon. Coroico is coffee country. The area also grows bananas and other exotic fruits, so movement of these items along this horrendous road is heavy work. Due to the number of trucks and buses that go over the ledge each year, the route has been named by the Inter-American Development Bank the most dangerous road in the world. Also known as the Road of Death, it has become a major attraction to Kamikaze mountain bikers. Or to people like me, who prefer to be in control of their own fates and book "gravity assisted" rides with a back-up van carrying the luggage.

Crime, although usually petty rather than violent in nature, does occur and tourists are most often the target. However, of all the Latin American countries, Bolivia is considered the safest. I have never been accosted, although I have been approached by phony National Police. I told them to buzz off and they did.

Health care in Bolivia is varied. Some villages have no medical facilities at all, but Cochabamba has a sophisticated teaching center that attracts students from both Brazil and Argentina. When sick, the patient must purchase everything from meals to needles. Nothing is included with the doctor's fee other than the expertise of the doctor. Cities have up-to-date clinics and laboratories with personnel trained in North America or Europe. In Sajama, the village at the base of the highest mountain, I found a well-equipped clinic with oxygen for altitude sickness. However, in three days I never found anyone there – no staff, no patients.

Large parts of Bolivia are empty or nearly empty. The country has the second-lowest population density in the Western Hemisphere, with just under three people per square mile. (Guyana has the lowest.)

For the adventure traveler, there are outfitters who offer exciting trips to remote areas, though most of them do not have the high-tech gear to which Europeans and North Americans are accustomed. I recommend you bring some of your own gear, especially if climbing. English is not common; survival Spanish is essential and, if you're going to remote areas, a few words in Quechua or Aymara would be of great help.

In summary, if you want to try something different than what you have at home and are willing to give some of yourself in return, you will have one of the most exciting experiences of your traveling life when you come to Bolivia.

History

POST COLUMBUS HISTORICAL TIME LINE	
1538	Spanish conquer Bolivia.
1545	Cerro Rico is discovered and Potosi becomes the largest city in South America.
1824	Bolívar liberates Bolivia.
1836-39	Bolivia and Peru unite, but are separated after war with Chile.

POST COLUMBUS HISTORICAL TIME LINE	
1879-84	War of the Pacific when Bolivia's access to the Pacific is lost.
1900-14	Tin becomes an important commodity, big industry and unions develop and some Bolivians become rich.
1903	Large area of Amazon Basin lost to Brazil.
1932-35	Chaco War; Bolivia loses territory to Paraguay.
1952	Revolution results in social and economic reforms and a social democratic government comes to power.
1967	Che Guevara killed in Bolivia.
1971-85	Unstable period featuring a series of political coups and military governments.
1986	Tin market collapses.
1989	Jaime Paz and Hugo Banzer share power so they can make more social and economic reforms.
1980s to the present	DEA attempts to eradicate the growth of coca – used in everyday life of the people as well as in cocaine production.

■ Before the Spanish

Scientists have two basic theories about the arrival of humans on the American continent. The oldest theory, which is being questioned by some, is that people migrated, while the oceans were lower, over a land bridge (Beringia) between Asia and Alaska. As ice from the glaciers that covered huge areas of North America melted, people migrated south, following herds of wild animals.

The second theory that is gaining popularity among anthropologists is that people from Asia came across the land bridge and then sailed down the Pacific coast. Some found places to their liking, so they stayed and started communities.

Whichever theory is correct is not as important to us as the fact that there is proof of human existence on the American continent as early as 12,500 years ago. Monte Verde in Chile is the oldest archeological site so far discovered. The Kennewick man, found in the United States, carbon dates back about 8,500 years and a site at Tierra del Fuego on the tip of South America also goes back to about the same period. Generally, archeological studies are continually moving the earliest dates of human occupation back into the distant past.

Although evidence is sparse, it is believed that farming/fishing societies in the Bolivian highlands were firmly established about 3000 BC (5,000 years ago). Agricultural life gave people time to develop sophisticated societies with strong governing bodies, tax systems, music, art and science. This in turn gave them time to trade with groups living hundreds of miles away. The highland people of Bolivia were especially known for their weavings made from llama, alpaca and vicuña wool, which they traded for fish and foods grown by the lowland peoples of the coastal valleys.

Records show that by 1200 BC pottery was being produced and intricate figurines depicting life in the highlands were painted onto the clay. With the abundance of metals on the Altiplano, copper and silver were soon mined and worked into tools.

By 600 BC the first known **Andean empire** was established at **Tihuanaco** (tee-wan-A-koa), then located on the southern shores of Lake Titikaka. The water has since receded and the remains of Tihuanaco are now 12 miles/20 km from the lake. The Tihuanaco people were a sun-worshiping kingdom; they believed that they were direct decedents of the sun god whom they called Inti Taita.

Inca legends state that the Inca originated from a white-haired tribe who migrated to the Cuzco area from Lake Titikaka. Some anthropologists believe that those living at Tihuanaco were the predecessors of the Inca.

At its peak, it is estimated that 100,000 people were living at Tihuanaco. Remains of the city show that its construction required advanced engineering skills. Most of the city walls and buildings were made of cut stone blocks held in place with copper pins, making the use of mortar unnecessary. The earthquake-proof structures were adorned in gold-covered sculptures. The entire city also had extensive plumbing systems.

The roadways around Tihuanaco were mostly cobbled and the irrigation methods allowed the dry desert to produce vast quantities of food. The Tihuanacans traded with those living as far to the east as El Fuerte near Samaipata, as far south as central Chile and as far north as Ayacucho in Peru.

Then, for some unknown reason, around AD 1000-1200 the civilization collapsed. That is, remnants of Tihuanaco society moved towards Cuzco.

The resulting migration is believed to have led to the beginning of the **Inca** civilization at Cuzco in present-day Peru. Only small pockets of people continued to eke out an existence on the Altiplano of Bolivia. With the passage of time, three major ethnic groups developed from these people. They are the **Aymara**, the **Uru** and the **Quechua**. The Aymara occupied the areas south of Peru and northern Chile; the Uru became poor landless workers throughout the Altiplano; and the Quechua inhabited the Cuzco area and became the first large group conquered by the Inca, who adopted the Quechua language.

After the Incas built a strong administrative center at Cusco, the Bolivian Altiplano became an extension of the kingdom and was known as **Kollasuyo** (koy-a-SOO-yoo). Although the people living in Kollasuyo fell under the basic rule of the Inca, they remained mostly autonomous, keeping their customs, language and religion.

Though the Inca brutally suppressed any who opposed them, basically they acted as benevolent rulers, wanting only to employ and tax the people of Kollasuyo. The natives worked as miners, construction laborers and soldiers.

> **NATIVE INTEREST:** *If traveling near Sajama or Ulla Ulla national parks, you will see pre-Columbian (AD 1200-1550) grave towers, called* **chullpares***, belonging to the early Aymara culture. These towers, made from stones, are about 10 ft / three m high and eight ft / 2.5 m in diameter. Each tower contains the remains of a prominent person who lived in the nearby community. The resident corpse is called a "mallku" (MAY-koo).*

As time went on, there were a few rebellions between the groups living in the highlands and the Inca rulers from Cuzco had to settle the disputes by sending in Quechua soldiers and administrators. The activity caused a lot of animosity so that, when the Spanish arrived in 1532, it was easy for them to turn one group against the other. This eventually resulted in the fall of the entire Inca civilization.

The only people in Bolivia who were able to resist Inca rule were those living in the Amazon lowlands. Those groups, who today inhabit about two-thirds of Bolivia's land, were able to remain autonomous not only from the Inca, but also from the Spaniards.

■ Conquest and Colonization, 1532-1809

Francisco Pizarro and **Diego de Almagro** started their explorations of South America with the financial and influential help of a priest named Hernando de Luque and with the blessing of Charles I, King of Spain. Pizarro and Almagro rapidly conquered and looted the Inca empire. The early phases of conquest were facilitated by civil war among the ruling Inca.

As Pizarro was still sailing down the western coast of America, the sons of a recently deceased Inca king, Huayna Capac, were fighting over the succession. Atahualpa, the bastard son of Huayna Capac, defeated and imprisoned his brother, Huascar, the rightful heir to the throne. But, Atahualpa, after declaring himself king, failed to consolidate his power with his own people. Thus, when Pizarro and Almagro arrived, they had no problem turning the Indian factions against one another.

Pizarro's most notorious and remembered act against the Inca occurred on November 16, 1532. Pizarro called a meeting for himself and the Inca ruler, Atahualpa, at the Spanish camp in Cajamarca. About 5,000 Inca came and stood, unarmed, in the village square. Not a Spanish soldier was to be seen. A priest read out the "requerimiento," while a Quechua man translated for Atahualpa. The "requerimiento" was a document that the King of Spain required his soldiers read to a group of people before conquering them.

After reading the document, the priest handed Atahualpa a Spanish bible. Understanding the request for submission, Atahualpa threw the book onto the ground in contempt. Pizarro's hidden army then attacked the Inca, killing about 2,000 men. Pizarro took Atahualpa prisoner.

However, Atahualpa was imprisoned in comfort, as was the right of captured nobility according to the law of Spain. While Atahualpa was in prison, the Spanish killed his brother Huascar. Some historians suspect that Huascar was killed on the orders of Atahualpa.

It didn't take long for Atahualpa to learn about the Spanish love for gold, so he cut a deal for his own release. He said he would trade one room the size of his prison cell full of gold and a second room full of silver in exchange for his life. Pizarro agreed and Atahualpa had his messengers bring the bounty. Pizarro and his men couldn't believe their luck. They were now all very rich men. However, Pizarro didn't keep his part of the bargain. After receiving the treasure, he charged Atahualpa with inciting treason among his followers and sentenced him to death. He was given the option of being burned at the stake or baptized and then strangled. He chose strangulation.

The death of Atahualpa turned out to be a bad move for Pizarro. The Indians, who no longer trusted Pizarro, could not be ruled peacefully. Realizing this, Pizarro moved quickly, using heartless methods to capture Cusco within a year of his first meeting with Atahualpa. Pizarro then had the city looted, the Indians tortured and the tombs, palaces and temples stripped of their treasures.

In an attempt to keep Indian rebellions down, Pizarro made **Manco Capac**, the youngest son of Huayna Capac, a puppet ruler. But, Manco, along with one of Atahualpa's generals, was soon killed by the Spanish. This final act solidified the Indians' distrust in Pizarro. They again rebelled. Almagro, who had been setting up house in Lima, came to the assistance of Pizarro.

The Indian rebellions were ruthlessly put down. Thousands of lives were lost, most of them Indian. Once the Indians were under control, the two Spaniards, Pizarro and Almagro, couldn't agree on territorial rights. Within two years of Manco's death, Pizarro felt so threatened by his compatriot that he ordered Almagro executed. Pizarro then kept tight control of his conquered subjects across an expanse that included everything from Cusco to Lake Titikaka, down the Altiplano beyond present day Santa Cruz and west to Chile. The territory was called Upper Peru.

Pizarro also built an administrative city at La Plata, now Sucre, so his army could be close by to quash any rebellions in that area.

But Pizarro didn't rule for long. Within three years of Almagro's death, Almagro's followers had Pizarro executed. His burned bones were shipped down to the thriving center of Lima and eventually entombed in the underground crypt of the cathedral. The year was 1538, just six years since the Spanish had entered the area.

Pizarro's brother, Gonzalo, then became ruler of Upper Peru (today's Bolivia). The Indians continued to rebel and eventually, under the leadership of Almagro's mestizo (mixed Indian/Spanish blood) son, had Gonzalo Pizarro executed.

Spain finally realized that the men in the hinterland of the New World were not capable of governing and so sent a delegation of colonial rulers with **Viceroy Antonio de Mendoza** from Mexico into Upper Peru. They were to control the area from a new vantage point. The new settlement, called La Paz, was in the heart of Aymara territory. Within a short time La Paz became the most important commercial center in the country.

By the early 1560s, most of the highlands of Bolivia were under control of the Spanish and the natives were placated. Only one small pocket of people remained a problem. The **Chiriguano Indians** living in the Chaco area south of Sucre resisted colonization. The Spanish strengthened the military center in Santa Cruz, close to the wild frontier. From there, they thought they could control the rebels but, much to their surprise, they were not successful. The Chiriguano remained independent.

The Spanish were not concerned about Upper Peru simply on political and military grounds. They had the problem of exploiting and controlling a new source of immense wealth – Cerro Rico, at Potosi.

■ Potosi Period

 A Quechua legend, originally told by a traveling trader, tells us about silver being discovered at Potosi's Cerro Rico long before the Spanish arrived. However, when the Spanish discovered the rich veins of glitter that virtually burst from the mountain's side, they invaded and occupied the area in great numbers. It was 1545.

The Indians of the region were forced into mining for the Spanish. They were treated miserably and overworked. They suffered malnutrition even though the area was rich in food production. By 1560, as a result of the poor conditions and the usual devastation caused by European diseases, there was a severe labor shortage. By this time, the surface silver had depleted and the miners now needed to go underground, an expensive method of extraction that resulted in less profit.

When the manpower became desperately low because of Indian resistance, the colonialists (under the encouragement of Viceroy Francisco de Toledo), used the pre-Columbian taxation system to obtain free labor. The tax, called *mita*, required that adult men spend one out of every six years in the service of their ruler. This meant that the men were away from their families, which only added to the strong resentment already felt against the Spanish.

It was believed that the Spanish could have paved a road from Potosi to Spain with the mined metal. In fact, the word *potosi* became a synonym for rich or wealthy and turned out to be a cliché used by everyone in America and Spain. By 1650, Potosi was the largest city in the Western Hemisphere, home to over 160,000 people.

As they had to dig deeper for silver, costs became higher and the male Indian population continued to decrease. The Spanish brought in Negro slaves to supplement the manpower. These men died even faster than the Indians because they were unaccustomed to the cold and the altitude. About six million men died in the mines during this period. By the early 1700s, mining at Cerro Rico declined and only a small amount of bullion was being shipped to Spain.

The next hundred years resulted in many Spanish settlers making America their home rather than just a place from which to extract wealth. As a result, a distinct class system developed. Settlers born in Spain, Castillanos, were at the top. Whites born in the New World, Creoles, were next. They were followed by mestizos (mixed Spanish and Indian blood) and, finally, the Indian and Negro at the laboring bottom. Struggles for power were common among the rich, as were pockets of rebellion among the poor. Integration between the indigenous groups was practiced and encouraged. Catholicism spread and melded into the old Indian beliefs to make the religion acceptable. Coca, once used only by the ruling Inca, became a poor man's substitute for adequate meals and the only comfort in the impoverished life they led. Those of Spanish descent born in America rebelled against colonial rule.

■ Napoleon

In Europe, Napoleon overthrew the Bourbon Dynasty in Spain. Many Spanish subjects living in America sat low and waited to see what would happen in their homeland. Some were loyal to the new Spanish king and his promises for reform. Some saw Spain as hopeless and wanted independence.

While Napoleon was strutting around Europe, Carlota, the overthrown king's sister, ruled an area of South America that is now part of Brazil. She ruled with her husband, John. Some people of Upper Peru (Bolivia) believed the promises that these two offered for a better administration and started working towards home rule.

Finally, an independent group of radicals living in Upper Peru demanded independence for the country. The conflicts and struggles for independence culminated in street riots, the first of which occurred on May 25, 1809. The riots were brutally put down by the Spanish.

In July, **Pedro Domingo Murillo** led another revolt in La Paz demanding the independence of Upper Peru. By November, Cochabamba, Oruro and Potosi had joined the rebellion. The revolt was squashed by the Spanish but Upper Peru was never again fully controlled by Spain.

Argentina, also trying to obtain independence from Spain, used Upper Peru as a battleground against the Spanish. Rebellions occurred consistently throughout the country until finally, **Simón Bolívar**, a Creole born in Caracas, Venezuela, led rebellions against those supporting Spain.

■ Independence

 Born of an aristocratic family, 22-year-old Bolívar visited Europe and watched elaborate ceremonies performed by the rich. In disgust, Bolívar vowed, "I will not give rest to my arm or my soul until I have broken the chains which bind my fatherland to Spain."

Bolívar also visited America, where he studied the approach used by the revolutionists there to keep the 13 colonies united into one federation. Bolívar finally won independence first for Venezuela and then Colombia. He set up democratic governments in these new states before following his friend and colleague, Antonio José de Sucre, to Ecuador where, together, they defeated the Royalists. The three northern states were united and called the Republic of Colombia. This was in agreement with Bolívar's beliefs that a united South America would be free of internal strife and able to resist any unwanted influence from Europe. Bolívar saw the emerging power of the USA as an example of how a number of colonies could unite into an irresistible federation. He called his one country Grand Colombia.

While Bolívar and Sucre worked from the north, General José de San Martin began liberating territories in the south. From Argentina, he crossed the Andes and went into Chile then up to Lima, defeating anyone who was a Royalist. The two liberators eventually had a meeting in Ecuador, after which San Martin returned to Argentina while Bolívar continued to fight for independence.

Sucre and Bolívar headed east to Junin and Ayacucho, where they captured the last of the viceroys and liberated Peru. Sucre continued to the Altiplano, where he quickly got rid of Spanish supporters.

Bolívar then set up a government in Upper Peru and produced a constitution. He was rewarded with the position of being the first titular chief executive of the new country and, to honor him, the people named the country after him. It was 1825.

The first constitution provided Bolivia with four legislative chambers, a complicated administrative system and a president for life who, of course, should have been Bolívar. But troubles were brewing in Colombia and Venezuela because of Bolívar's absence, so he returned, leaving Bolivia to the hands of Sucre, who became the first president. The capital city, La Plata, had its name changed to Sucre in honor of the first president.

But in the north, the task of a united Colombia was too great for Bolívar to handle. In April, 1830, after the split of territory and the formation of Colombia, Venezuela and Ecuador, Bolívar resigned. Ill from tuberculosis, impoverished and bitterly disappointed, he then learned of the murder of his good friend. Sucre had left Bolivia to attend a unification conference in Ecuador. After the conference, he was assassinated. Bolívar died that same year, in December, in the village of Santa Maria, Colombia.

However, the pattern for rebellion was set in Bolivia. It was constitution, revolution, new president, new constitution and revolution again. Today, the people of Bolivia, although most gentle in day-to-day matters, still can and often do produce an effective demonstration or revolution at a moment's notice.

▪ Post Independence

In 1829, **Andres Santa Cruz** succeeded Sucre as president; he lasted more than 10 years. His main goal was to unite Peru and Bolivia, which he did, but the country was soon split up by Chile and Santa Cruz was forced into exile.

The next 40 years were unstable, with many presidents taking power and producing just about as many new constitutions. One of the most notorious of these opportunists was **General Mariano Melgareja**, who ruled as a dictator from 1864 to 1871. Known as the "scourge of God" by his enemies, he earned this name due to a number of different acts. He abolished the Indians' communal agricultural system and made it easy to confiscate Indian lands.

He then offered these lands for sale at bargain prices, making them available only to the richer, white population. The land was often purchased by ruthless landlords who, in turn, enslaved the Indians.

Besides being the scourge of God, Melgareja was a drunk. During one of his drunken brawls he traded a huge parcel of land in the Amazon Basin for a horse and the right to use the Amazon River to reach the Atlantic. He is also credited with tying a British ambassador naked to the back of a mule and sending him on his way because the ambassador's drinking abilities were not up to par with Melgareja's.

At independence, Bolivia had twice as much land as it has today, but that land has been taken by surrounding countries, usually after a war.

The first war took place between 1879 and 1883. It was called the **War of the Pacific**. Initially, Bolivia owned the Atacama Desert and a long strip of Chilean coastline, including the port of Antofagosta. However, once it was learned that the Atacama Desert was rich in nitrate and copper deposits, the Chileans decided they wanted it. After four years of battle, Bolivia lost the war and its only ocean access. As compensation, the Chilean government built a rail line between Oruro and Antofagosta that was completed in 1892, plus they gave the Bolivians free access to the newly formed port of Arica. But Bolivia never forgot the insult. The nation stands united on the desire to get back the lost land. This is such a passion that Bolivia still maintains a navy that waits for the time when they again will have ocean access. You can see the navy base on Lake Titikaka.

Eduardo Avaroa, a hero from the War of the Pacific, is remembered as saying, "Surrender? Only when you give up your grandmother!" A lot of Chilean grandmothers must have been turned over, because on March 23rd, Bolivia surrendered. It is also the day Avaroa died. Today, that date is celebrated by Bolivians who make a vow to reclaim the land.

Bolivia is presently involved in on-and-off negotiations with Chile for the rights to put more gas/oil pipelines over the mountains to the sea. Chile is not very cooperative.

■ The 20th Century

 The first 20 years of the 20th century saw a rise in the standard of living in Bolivia due to the boom in tin mining. Low taxes and a good rail system drew foreign investors and world markets brought high prices. **Simon Patiño**, an Indian born in Cochabamba, was one of the local men who benefitted from the tin boom. Born a poor peasant, Patiño's entrepreneurial skills and the tin mines eventually made him one of the richest men in the world.

Paraguay controlled a large portion of the **Chaco Boreal**, a flatland covered mostly with scrub brush. The climate in this region is humid and hot in summer, but cold and windy in winter. Standard Oil of New Jersey went into the area in the early 1920s to explore for oil. Up until that time, Paraguayans used the land to produce coca that they sold in great quantities to neighboring Argentina.

In the early 1930s, Paraguay and Bolivia – both land-locked countries – wanted control of the Paraguay River that flows into the Atlantic Ocean. They needed access to an ocean port to make export more economically viable. Also, Bolivia thought it could get control of the promised petroleum wealth of the Gran Chaco. This was the start of the **Chaco War**.

On June 15, 1932, the Bolivian army attacked Paraguay at Fort Vangaurdia. The advantage the Paraguayans had was that the men readily went to war to protect their country from the aggressors, while the Bolivians had to be conscripted to fight. Most Bolivian soldiers were Indians from the Altiplano who wanted to be at home tending their corn crops rather than fighting in the malaria-infested Chaco Boreal.

The war lasted three long years and took the lives of over 100,000 men. Most of the deaths were from malaria and infection, rather than from gunshot wounds. Bolivia again lost and Paraguay took about 75% of the Chaco that had previously belonged to Bolivia.

 For an excellent story about the Chaco War, see Augusto Cespedes' short story called **The Well**, published in the book **Fat Man from La Paz** (see *Recommended Readings*, page 519).

After the Chaco War, discontent was running rampant throughout the country. The tin boom didn't significantly benefit the poor and the Chaco War showed the lack of leadership.

In 1936, **Colonel David Toro**, a socialist, led and won a revolution. He organized labor and nationalized Standard Oil's holdings in the Chaco area. The following year, **Colonel German Busch**, a hero of the Chaco War, overthrew the government and became the leader. He abolished tenant farming and set up some controls over the mining industry. Busch remained in power for two years, implementing reform – until he committed suicide.

Busch was followed by a military regime led by **General Carlos Quintanilla**. Then, in 1940, a democratic election brought **General Enrique Peñaranda** to power. But democracy didn't seem to bring the people what they wanted. Discontent continued and the people moved toward the left wing philosophy of governing. Numerous left wing parties were formed, with the **Nationalist Revolutionary Movement** (MNR) being the most successful. They advocated better conditions for Indians and less power for mining companies. The MNR, in 1942, disclosed to congress the massacre of striking miners, along with their wives and children, by government forces.

The MNR led and won a revolution the following year that made **Major Gualberto Villarroel** the head of state. They worked hard at improving the conditions for the Indian people, but this pitted them against the tin barons. The resulting conflicts, plus the drop of the tin market after World War II, caused a rash of riots. In La Paz, mobs grabbed Villarroel and hanged him from a lamp post in Plaza Murillo, the city's center.

There were a few more leaders during the next six years. **Mamerto Urriolagoitia** was the president in 1951 and, when his period of leadership expired, an election was held. This resulted in the MNR getting the majority of votes, but Urriolagoitia refused to turn over the government. Instead, he put a military junta into power. The tin boom lasted until 1952, when miners' unions actually overthrew the army, setting up the socialist MNR government and putting Paz Estensoro into power. The mines were expropriated from foreigners and made into national holdings. The big estates were broken up and land was distributed to the peasants. Patiño had sold some of his holdings before this happened.

The MNR went into a frenzy of reform. They gave the Indians the right to vote. They passed an agrarian reform law and divided up large parcels of property owned by hidalgo (a man belonging to the lowest rank of Spanish nobility) landlords and gave them to the Indians. Education was made available for the poor, medical clinics were established and cooperatives were set up so profits could go to the producers. In the next few years, the MNR developed roads and built hydroelectric dams. They also financed a sugar mill and a cotton-growing project, mostly in the eastern part of the country, around the Santa Cruz/Cochabamba area.

The years from 1952 to 1964 were the most politically stable in the history of Bolivia. It became the great hope of communists around the world attracting Ernesto Che Guevera to try to stage a revolution. On the other side of things, Klaus Altman (alias Barbie) entered Bolivia and set up shop as the resident consultant to various Bolivian, Chilean and Paraguayan presidents on torture and interrogation.

Inflation due to corruption, falling prices in tin and no foreign investments led to troubled times for the MNR. They were finally overthrown by a military junta and a period of oppressive rule followed.

In 1966, **General Rene Barrientos Ortuno** became president. He is remembered for bringing in the army to suppress a military revolution led by Guevara. It was under Barrientos's command that Che was killed and planted under the tarmac of an airstrip in southern Bolivia.

When Barrientos died in a plane crash in 1969, a period of insurrection began that led to a succession of 19 presidents (13 of whom were generals), and seven military juntas being staged. Only two presidents actually completed full term. Some leaders were in for as little as six hours. Two juntas were in power for one day; another was in for a few hours.

Congress appointed **Lidia Gueilar** as interim president in 1979, but when the elections were held the following year they resulted in a no-majority government. Congress then tried to appoint the leader of the Unidad Democratica y Popular (UDP) party as president, but a military coup led by **Luis Garcia Meza Tejada** and backed by the drug cartels took over instead.

Garcia Meza was thrown out of government in 1981 and, after an attempted coup the following year, he went into hiding in Brazil. He was later charged and convicted of genocide, treason and human-rights abuses, which won him 30 years behind bars. At the time of his trial he was still in Brazil but finally in 1995 he was extradited back to Bolivia where he started serving his sentence.

In 1989 **Jaime Paz Zamora** took office after a democratic election. This was the beginning of the latest stable period where all the presidents to follow were democratically elected. The most notorious of these were **Hugo Banzer Suarez** of the Accion Democratica Nacionalista (ADN) party, **Jaime Paz Zamora** of the MNR and present day president **Gonzalo Sanchez de Lozada**. Banzer managed to survive 13 coup attempts between 1971 and 1978 and then won a democratic election in 1997. His main aim was to rid the country of coca production. He died of cancer before this was accomplished.

If you ask Bolivians about their government, they will usually say that Bolivia's real government is in Washington. Or they will talk more specifically about government by the International Monetary Fund (IMF), the World Bank (WB) and the World Trade Organization (WTO). This is because Bolivia, since World War II and except for the period of MNR rule, 1952-64, has been scrambling for access to world markets and for development money.

Support from the three international agencies depends on Bolivia opening itself to business. Restrictions on foreign investment and ownership must be removed, government subsidies for local businesses must go and government-owned enterprises must be sold off. Taxes on businesses must be low. Labor rights must go (a process called "flexibilizacion").

Bolivians once shrugged it all off, knowing that any benefits would be far in the future and would go first to the whiter *hidalgo* class that runs things. The example of Argentina helped keep Bolivia to the WB/WTO agenda. But the Argentinean economy collapsed in 2001-2 and patience is running out.

I experienced the resulting tensions during my latest visit to Bolivia. The event, which took place mainly around the Plaza Murillo in La Paz, was quickly dubbed the "War of Taxation" by local media. The IMF wanted the Bolivian government to improve its credit rating by making interest payments on its loans. It suggested an income tax. Only about 1/8th of Bolivians earn wages, and most of these are civil servants, so the IMF wanted them to pay the tax. Unfortunately, the police are a big part of the civil service. On February 12, 2003, they went on strike and started marching toward the legislature. The army standing guard at the palace stopped the march. A shootout occurred, with police finally being driven out of the plaza. Thirty-three people died, over half of them civilians caught in the crossfire. Once the locals realized that the police were out of commission, they began looting. The looters tried to steal as much as possible from the shops and unprotected bank machines. And they tried to destroy as many government records as possible.

When the riots were over two days later, we saw a lot of pockmarks on the buildings around the plaza. Numerous bank machines were torn apart. Two colonial buildings were burned out and the Vice-Presidential building was badly damaged. On the Prada, the Minesterio Desarrollo (Ministry of Development) was gutted.

Throughout the event, tourists were in no danger; hotel owners kept them inside. Outside of La Paz, people went on a sort of public holiday. Since no one could go anywhere, we all partied and watched events unfold on TV. I consumed my first *chicha* (locally made corn beer) at this time.

Government

Bolivia is a republic with the seat of government in La Paz and the Judiciary seat in Sucre. The first constitution was adopted on November 19, 1826 and was re-drawn and re-adopted numerous times. The newest constitution was drawn up on February 2, 1967 and revised in 1994.

The president, who is the Chief of State, is elected for five years and he is the head of the democratically elected party. **Congress** is then appointed by the president. If a party does not get 50% of the vote, congress chooses and appoints the president. This is done by secret ballot and the candidates are the leaders of the three leading parties.

National Congress is made up of the Chamber of Senators and the Chamber of Deputies. The 27 senators (three from each department) and the 130 deputies are elected by popular vote or appointed for a period of five years. The 1996 amendment to the constitution now allows for 65 deputies to be voted in by popular demand and the rest nominated by party leaders. The National Congress convenes for 90 days every year.

At present, the four major parties in Bolivia are the **National Revolutionary Movement** (MNR), the **Movement of Revolutionary Left** (MIR), the **Movement to Socialism** (MAS) and the **New Republic Force** (NFR).

There are nine departments in Bolivia and these are divided into 112 provinces. They are further divided into sections and then cantons. Each department has a prefect appointed by the president and a legislature elected by municipal councilors. Elections are held once every five years.

> **DEPARTMENT KNOW-HOW:** The nine departments of Bolivia are Beni, Chuquisaca, La Paz, Cochabamba, Oruro, Pando, Potosi, Santa Cruz and Tarija.

Bolivia is ruled by Spanish law and is under Napoleonic code. It is compulsory for everyone to vote at the age of 18 if married and age 21 if not married.

The National Congress appoints Supreme Court judges for 10-year sessions. Each department also has a district court that looks after minor infractions of the law. The Supreme Court has five justices for criminal law and five for civil.

The **military** consists of an army with about 25,000 men and 36 light tanks, a navy of 3,500 men (1,700 of these are in the marines) and an air force of 3,000 men, with 37 combat aircraft and 16 armed helicopters. The air force was first established in 1923 with 4,000 men.

There is conscription for men at the age of 19 and the men must serve for 12 months. The army looks after six regions in the country and the navy patrols Lake Titikaka and the Beni, Bolivia and Paraguay rivers. In the event of a war, over two million men are available for service.

The **police** consist of the National Guard and the Tourist Police. The Tourist Police employ many women.

Economy

▪ Debt

 Bolivia is in a state of permanent debt. More is spent on servicing that debt than is spent on health care. Foreign investment is minimal. There was a surge of it when government corporations (i.e., railways, telephones, electricity) were privatized, but the end result was failure (most rail lines were closed). Also, Bolivia's history of labor militancy (MNR in 1952) still scares off corporations. Fundamentally, after the tin markets collapsed, there was nothing left in Bolivia that anyone wanted, although there are promising signs of oil and gas reserves in the Santa Cruz/Villamontes area. Bolivia has been self-subsistent in petroleum for some time and there are signs now that it could soon become an exporting country. Most Bolivians are subsistence farmers. Some made it big in coca production, but that is now over. There is an "informal sector" of street vending and sweat shops producing imitation brand-name clothing. **Tourism**, while still minimal, is becoming a major source of moveable income.

Jeffrey Sachs, long-term US advisor to the Bolivian government, summed up the Bolivian economy in a statement to the *New York Times*: "I always told Bolivians, from the very beginning, that what you have here is a miserable, poor economy with hyper-inflation. If you are brave, if you have guts, if you do everything right, you will end up with a miserable, poor economy with stable prices." That is now pretty much what travelers will find in Bolivia.

During the 1980s, 70% of the population was living far below the poverty line. But thanks to a half-stable government, elimination of some of the corruption and a genuine effort to improve life for the people, that is changing. Today, with 2.6 million people in the labor force, there is an unemployment rate of about 7.6%. However, there is still a large number of under-employed people.

■ Industry

Bolivia's **Gross Domestic Product** (GDP) is about $25 billion, or $977 per person. Statistics make it appear that the GDP has stayed the same over the years but in fact, due to the devaluation of the boliviano and increased inflation, the GDP is lower. Of the entire GDP, 16.5% comes from agriculture, 35.5% from industry and the rest comes from services.

Bolivia's agricultural industry produces soybeans, coffee, cocoa, cotton, corn, sugar cane, rice, potatoes and lumber, with soy being the largest export. In the Santa Cruz area the farmers are able to grow two crops of soybeans a year. Quinoa, a food of the Incas, is grown in the Altiplano. The government is trying to make this a viable export also.

Industry includes mining, smelting, petroleum production, tobacco, wood, food and beverage production, handicrafts and clothing. Bolivia also has natural gas, zinc, lead, tin, antimony, tungsten, silver and gold for export. The soy, natural gas, zinc, gold and wood bring in about $1.5 billion a year. However, the import costs for capital goods, raw materials, chemicals, petroleum and food are close to $2 billion.

In 1985 the international tin market dropped and inflation ran so high that the government introduced its **New Economic Policy**, which incorporates the advice of Jeffrey Sachs, the World Bank and the World Trade Organization. It includes de-restricting foreign trade, abolishing price controls and subsidies, freezing wages and privatizing state-owned industries. The privatization was actually capitalization, where investors got 50% of the stake and management control. In return, they ensured capital expenditures to the value of the enterprise.

Bolivia has also become a partner in a number of common market agreements. The first was a free trade treaty with Mexico and some countries farther south more than a decade ago. In the subsequent agreement signed in 1993, Bolivia became a member of the **Andean Community** that includes Peru, Equator, Colombia and Venezuela. The United States signed the **Trade Preference Act** with Bolivia that resulted in tariffs only on leather and clothes going into the States. There is also a separate agreement with Peru that permits duty-free transit of imports and exports through the Desaguadero border crossing so that Peru can have access to the Atlantic via Bolivian roads and rail systems.

Because of the large amount of natural gas Bolivia produces, about 30 million metric cubic meters (40.5 million cubic yards) a day, a pipeline going through Brazil to the Atlantic was built and another to Arica, Chile was added shortly after. These lines, used for exporting the gas, have helped improve the economy of the country.

Three out of the four leading **banks** in Bolivia ran into financial problems in 1995. They were restructured under new owners and are now stable. Today, Banco Sol has 30% of Bolivia's banking customers. One of the reasons that Bolivian banks do well is that most borrowers pay their bills. However, investors and depositors are not protected by any government insurance (the government is talking about implementing some type of insurance in the near future). This reputation for paying debt includes not only the small peasant farmer borrowing from the local bank, but also the government itself which, because of its habit of paying on time, often receives soft loans or forgiveness of debt from the international community. For example, in the late 1990s the United States reduced 67% of Bolivia's debt. Today, the national debt is about $5 billion and is owed to foreign governments and multilateral development banks.

Coca has been a billion dollar contributor to the economy in the past, but the government, with the encouragement of the United States, is trying to eradicate the export of the plant to places like Colombia where it is used for cocaine production. Only coca grown in the Yungas is used for domestic purposes, while any plants grown in the Chapare region are reportedly used for cocaine production. The DEA is active in Bolivia, digging up and defoliating crops and searching buses to prevent the movement of precursor chemicals. This causes unrest among coca-growing *campesinos*, or *cocaleros*, as they are called. Regularly, Bolivian highways are blocked by the *cocaleros*.

YOU'RE HOW OLD?

The old age pension, or Bonosol, was introduced in 2003 and everyone over the age of 65 will receive 1,800 bolivianos (US $240) per year. The plan, originally set up in 1997, is privately managed and individually funded. The biggest hurdle now is how to establish the age of people who have never registered their birth.

As the economy stabilizes and the standard of living improves, Bolivians look for new ways to earn a living, including **tourism**. Bolivia is new at the game. This was obvious to me when I tried looking at hotels; often I would be refused entry because the owners were suspicious of my motives. However, there are far more tour agencies in Bolivia now than there were five years ago and some hotels are offering things like private bathrooms and hot water from tanks rather than electrical units attached to the end of shower heads. These changes in services stem from the demands of tourists.

Chilean and (until the economic collapse) Argentinean tourists have been making Bolivia their vacation destination for years. Now, Europeans (there are sometimes more Dutch in Bolivia than there are in Holland) and North Americans are discovering the country. It is what Guatemala was 25 years ago, unspoiled and a delight to visit.

Trade unions have been legal for over half a century. It was the 50,000 workers who held a strike in Bolivia to demand land reform and the nationalization of the mining companies that eventually resulted in changes being made. The demands were met in 1952 after a period of revolution. The struggle of the unions was a great stage for revolutionists like Che Guevera, who came to help.

Today it is legal to organize and bargain collectively. Laws supporting labor unions were last amended and ratified in 1973. Today, about 50% of the working force belong to the **Bolivian Labor Federation**, which is an affiliate of the World Federation of Trade Unions. However, even today, the public sector is legally not permitted to join unions, although most do without penalty. Also, labor laws are not favorable to unions. Protests and brief wildcat strikes are common, but prolonged picketing doesn't seem to happen.

Happy Bolivian children.

People & Culture

■ Cultural Groups

 The **Aymara** and **Quechua** indigenous groups make up more than 55% of the population. These people were here long before the Inca and many still practice the traditions of their ancestors. The Aymara and Quechua occupied the lands as far north as Colombia and as far south as southern Chile and Argentina. The indigenous people of Bolivia are a big attraction for tourists.

The **mestizo** or cholo, as he is called in Bolivia, is part European and part Indian. These people make up 35% of the Bolivian population. The rest is made up of **Europeans**, mostly Spanish from the early settlers, but also those who arrived in the last 150 years from places like Germany, Yugoslavia, Asia and North America. Many minority groups are also represented, including Chinese East Indians, Japanese and Africans, whose ancestors were brought as slaves to work in the mines of Potosi.

LOCAL LINGO: Yuraqsiki, literally translated, means "white rear-end," or gringo, in the Quechua language.

Of the many tribes and groups who are in the minority, there are the Tacana, the Pano, the Arauco, the Chapacura, the Guarani and the Botocudo, who are all, in turn, made up of smaller tribes. Most of these groups live in the Amazon Basin.

Quechua proverb:
It is better to die while standing than to live on your knees.

These tribal groups were matrilocal, which means that after marriage, the man moved in with his wife's family. They were also patrilineal and patriarchal, which means that, no matter whose house they lived in, the oldest man in the house was the boss and the children followed their father's lineage of ancestry.

SPANISH NAMES 101

Spanish names have a first or common name and then two family names. The first family name is the main one and is from the father, while the second one is from the mother's line. When speaking of a person, the common name and the name of the father is mentioned. For example, with the name "Hugo Banzer Suarez," Hugo is the common name, Banzer is the father's name and the one most used. Suarez, the mother's name, is added to the other two when formality dictates it.

The Aymara and Quechua were farmers and sheep or llama herders and lived in the higher valleys of the Andean Mountains or the Altiplano that sits between two mountain spines, the Cordillera Real or Eastern Cordillera and the main spine of the Andes or Western Cordillera. The split of the main chain starts in Peru and re-forms again in the southern tip of America, and the altiplano sits in that mountain embrace. The two groups have distinct and separate languages. It is commonly suggested that the Aymara sound more guttural. The two seldom intermarried.

NATIVE BAGGAGE: The Aymara/Quechua rendition of the backpack is called an **awayo**. It's a colorful length of cloth in which babies, children or a number of parcels are wrapped, strung across the shoulders and tied at the front. The awayo is worn by both men and women. Today cotton, machine-made awayos are being worn instead of the traditional home-spun wool ones.

Catholicism was introduced to Bolivia by the conquering Spaniards. The Indians integrated the new religion with their own. This resulted in a belief that honored Pacha Mama (Mother Earth), along with Christ and the Virgin Mary. Most villages have patron saints who are regularly paid respect with celebrations that include drinking of *chicha* (corn beer) dancing and music. Dances are especially important in Aymara celebrations and vary from one place to the other. The devil is naturally important to miners who work in his turf and is known as Tio (Uncle). There isn't the same feeling about the devil that prevails among Europeans. For the Indians, if you work on the devil's turf, you pay him your respects.

MOTHER EARTH

Pacha Mama, or Mother Earth, protects all living things, including plants, but when angered she is cruel and causes droughts, floods, pestilence, accidents and any other hardship she can think of. To keep her happy, people offer her coca leaves or a sprinkle of alcohol before they go on a trip, plant or harvest a field, drive a car or give birth to a child.

Both the Aymara and the Quechua spin and weave cloth from wool or llama and alpaca hair. These same types of weavings have been found in tombs or wrapped around mummies that date as far back as 3000 BC. The cloth and the clothes made from the weavings are warm and practical for the cold climate of the Altiplano.

Traditional Andean music is still played by shepherds tending their flocks in the mountains. The instruments used include pan flutes of every conceivable size, drums and the chorango, a ukulele-styled instrument traditionally made from the shell of an armadillo.

The Indian women of today wear traditional dress. This includes a multi-layered skirt, an apron (sometimes), a shawl (often of exquisite design embroidered with pearls and beads) and a hat, usually a bowler (called a *bambin* in local lingua). The other most common outfit seen on women is a black woven dress with a wide skirt embroidered at the hem. The sleeves are just past the elbow and the neck is high. These dresses are accompanied by a weaving worn either hanging at the back from a woven belt or around the shoulders, kept in place with a pin. This outfit is also accompanied by a hat, usually a felt one that looks like a bowl (rather than a bowler). However, there are an increasing number of women replacing their expensive bowlers for baseball caps. All the women wear their hair in two braids that hang out below their hats and down their backs.

SAFE SHAWL

Silver pins, called *topos*, are made in the shape of spoons and worn by Quechua ladies to fasten their shawls.

For the most part, Indian men of Bolivia wear Western-styled clothes. However, you will find a few with colorful, hand-woven ponchos and their heads crowned with a leather form-fitting hat.

Geography

■ Land

 Surrounded by land, Bolivia is bordered on the north by Peru and Brazil, on the east by more of Brazil, on the south by Paraguay and Argentina and on the west by Chile.

N

BRAZIL

Guayaramerin

Cobija Riberalta

PERU

BOLIVIA

Rurrenabaque

Trinidad

NORTHERN FOOTHILLS

Coroico

Copacabana

La Paz Cochabamba

Santa Cruz

Puerto Suarez

Oruro Sampaipata

SOUTHERN FOOTHILLS

WESTERN CORDILLERA

CORDILLERA REAL

Sucre

Potosi

Camini

Pacific Ocean

Uyuni

Tarija Villamontes

Tupiza

PARAGUAY

Villazón

CHILE

San Pedro
de Atacama

ARGENTINA

NOT TO SCALE

© 2004 HUNTER PUBLISHING, INC

LOFTY LANDS

Bolivia is about 800 miles/1,300 km wide and 900 miles/1,500 km long. Much of its land sits above 10,000 ft/3,000 m in elevation, but a lot is below 330 ft/100 m in elevation.

Although landlocked, Bolivia is one of the most geographically interesting countries in the world. It is home to the six highest mountain peaks in the Andes, all of which stand over 20,000 ft/6,000 m. It has part of the highest navigable lake in the world. It has the richest silver mine ever discovered and the largest salt lake on the planet. It also has the highest volcano on earth and the highest archeological site known to man. It has the Altiplano, the rich platform of land where most Bolivians live. And then it has part of the Amazon Basin, with mighty rivers like the Beni, the Madre de Dios and the Mamore flowing into the Madeira, the second greatest tributary of the Amazon. Finally, Bolivia has the sparse dry deserts of the Chaco, rich in oil and good for canola production on large corporate or Mennonite farms.

The Andes provide a spectacular backdrop for hikers.

The northwestern ridge of the Andes is known as the **Apolobamba Range** and is a group of peaks that include such features as Bolivia's longest glacier. The glacier runs six miles/11 km down the southwest face of the region's highest peak, **Mt**. **Chaupi Orkh**. The Apolobamba Range forms the border between Bolivia and Peru. It is difficult to access and is rarely visited.

The southeastern ridge of the Andes, angling off the Western Cordillera north of Lake Titicaca, is the most prominent and accessible range. It is known as the **Cordillera Real**. Many of the more accessible peaks that beckon from a height of around 16,500 ft/5,000 m are not far from La Paz. Six of the major peaks reach a height of over 20,000 ft/6,000 m and **Mt**. **Illimani** is even higher, sitting at 22,000 ft/6,700 m. On clear days, it overshadows La Paz like a god.

TOUGH TERRAIN

The Cordillera Real has one section that runs continuously at a height of over 20,000 ft/6,000 m for a distance of 100 miles/160 km. At their widest point these mountains form a formidable barrier about 120 miles/200 km long.

The third ridge is a tiny speck of mountains, a single vertebrae, just south and east of La Paz in the direction of Oruro that is called the **Quimsa Cruz Range**. Often visited, the range is a mere 25 miles/40 km long and nine miles/15 km wide. It has glaciated peaks in the south and granite spires in the north, with mining roads running close to both the glaciers and spires. The roads make visiting these mountains quite appealing, especially to rock-climbers who gravitate to the granite spires.

Between the two major spines of the Bolivian Andes, the Western Cordillera and the Cordillera Real, is a dry plain, the world's largest, called the **Altiplano**. Starting at Lake Titikaka, the Altiplano runs 490 miles/800 km to the south. Some geographers believe that the Altiplano is a dried lake bed and that Lake Titikaka is the shrinking remnants of the ancient lake. Standing at 11,000 ft/3,660 m above the sea, the Altiplano has been cultivated to grow high-altitude crops like potatoes, barley and quinoa. Half of the nation's population lives in the Altiplano, the main theater of Bolivia's history.

EARLY MEDICINE

Archeologists have discovered that quinoa was cultivated as early as 5800-4500 BC in the Ayacucho Basin of Peru and the people traded with those living in places as far away as southern Chile. Quinoa has many essential amino acids, including lysine, as well as iron, calcium and vitamins A, B and E.

Sloping off the Cordillera Real, just north of La Paz and descending northwards toward the Amazon, is the **Yungas**, with its rich rainforest. In the Yungas, the steaming jungles of the Amazon send humidity toward the snow-capped mountains of the Cordillera Real. As soon as the moisture-laden air comes in contact with the brisk mountain air, it causes a thermal inversion and turns to rain. This happens about 300 days of each year. The plentiful rain encourages a variety of lush plants, such as coffee, sugar, coca and tobacco to grow in abundance.

Because of the rains and the huge drainage area of the Altiplano, major rivers flowing down these slopes offer spectacular whitewater rafting and kayaking.

The **Amazon jungle** is a different world altogether, with isolated pockets of people, lush vegetation and numerous rivers that eventually flow into the Amazon River. It also has some of the few remaining virgin forests in South America. During rainy season, the Amazon is a quagmire of non-absorbing earth where residents are often forced to travel the roads by canoe rather than motor vehicle.

Sloping off the Eastern Cordillera to the east are the **Colinas** (Foothills) that are less precipitous than the Yungas. These descend to the Gran Chaco, and include large temperate valleys like those holding the cities of Cochabamba, Samaipata and Tarija.

A desert-like terrain is just one of the landscapes Bolivia offers.

Finally, there is the **Gran Chaco** area in the southeast of the country near the Paraguayan border. Temperatures in this part of the country average 99°F/37°C. It is in places a dry, inhospitable land and, except for a few desert animals and the odd cactus or small bush, it is sparsely populated. In other parts of the Chaco it can be humid and infested with dengue and malaria-bearing mosquitos. The largest settlement in the Chaco is **Camiri**, which proudly holds the record for the nation's highest recorded temperature at 126°F/52°C (although Villamontes, a few hours to the south, claims the same). Because of the small human population, the Gran Chaco has some of the rarer animal species, such as the jaguar and peccary. The biggest draw to the Chaco was the discovery of oil and gas.

Santa Cruz sits between the Amazon and the Chaco. It is the real capital of the Eastern Amazon and the Gran Chaco.

■ Water

 Water covers 58,000 square miles/150,000 square km, 14% of Bolivia's total territory. That, of course, is in dry season. In the highland basin is **Lake Titikaka**, which alone covers 2,500 square miles/6,600 square km. The **Desaguadero River**, the main waterway in the highlands, is 235 miles/380 km long and flows from Lake Titikaka to Lakes Popoo and Uru Uru.

Uyuni Salt Lake on the Altiplano covers 4,200 square miles/11,000 square km of land and is the largest salt mass in the world. The main tributary to the Uyuni Salt Lake is the **Rio Grande de Lipez**. The second-largest salt lake in the highlands is **Coipasa**, which is fed by the **Lauca** and **Saboya rivers**. Although there are many small lakes in the highlands, those most often visited are the **Colorado**, the **Verde** and the **Celeste**.

The **Pantanal**, east of Santa Cruz, is the largest wetland in the world and covers an area of 81,000 square miles/210,000 square km, much of it underwater during rainy season.

The **Amazon Basin** covers over eight million square km of land, 44% of South America's territory. It spreads across Bolivia, Brazil, Colombia, Ecuador, Guyana, Peru, Surinam and Venezuela. Bolivia has 280,000 square miles/722,000 square km of that basin. Except for the Acre River, all Bolivian rivers from the Amazon Basin flow into the **Madera**, which in turn flows into the Amazon. The Madera River is fed by the **Mamore**, the **Madre de Dios** and the Beni.

The **Itenez** (also called the Guapore) and the **Mamore rivers** collect most of the runoff from the Bolivian savannas and jungles of Santa Cruz, Beni and Cochabamba districts. The Beni River collects most of the runoff from the Andes and its tributaries are often used for whitewater kayaking or rafting.

In the southeast, **La Plata Basin** has many small rugged rivers that are tributaries to the **Paraguay** and **Pilcomayo rivers**. These two waterways flow into the **Rio de la Plata**, which runs through Paraguay and down to the Atlantic Ocean. This basin is the fifth largest in the world and has a rich ecosystem.

Climate

Temperature and precipitation are almost totally dependent on altitude. The higher one goes, the colder and drier it gets. Generally speaking, the rainy season is from January to March throughout the country, except in the Amazon and Yungas, where it runs from September to April. The cloud forests of the Yungas get about 200 inches/5,000 mm of rain annually, while the southwestern highlands receive four inches/100 mm.

The overall effects of altitude are modified by **El Niño**, which appears every four to seven years. In 1997-1998, El Niño caused severe drought in mountain areas and led to increased glacial recession. On the other hand, when La Niña appears (as she did in 1999-2000), the highlands suffer severe snowstorms, avalanches and hurricanes.

The highlands and mountains can be dry and cold and the nights are always cold, often below freezing. During wet season, this region is damp and cool in the morning, hot and dry during the day, dry and cool in the evening and freezing again at night. In winter, nighttime temperature can drop to -13°F/-25°C with a wind chill temperature of -40°F/-40°C.

The cloud forests of the Yungas and Colinas sit between 3,290 and 11,500 ft (1,000 and 3,500 m) and are always hot and humid. During rainy season it rains every day, all day. In the tropical lowlands of the Amazon and La Plata Basin areas, it is hot and humid in dry season, with average temperatures of 80°F/27°C. However, in rainy season there are torrential downpours that cool the temperatures drastically.

The Gran Chaco area is always hot and dry.

■ Temperatures

The following chart gives temperatures for three common elevations. This will give you an idea of what to expect in other places with similar elevations. It is also good to remember that the colder winter temperatures are in June, July and August and the warmer summer temperatures are in November, December and January.

AVERAGE TEMPERATURES & HUMIDITY							
	LA PAZ 3,625 m		COCHABAMBA 2,550 m			CONCEPCION 500 m		
	High	Low	High	Low	Hum	High	Low	Hum
JAN	17°C/63°F	6°C/43°F	24°C/75°F	12°C/54°F	63%	30°C/86°F	19°C/66°F	78%
FEB	17°C/63°F	6°C/43°F	24°C/75°F	12°C/54°F	67%	30°C/86°F	19°C/66°F	84%
MAR	18°C/64°F	6°C/43°F	25°C/77°F	11°C/52°F	63%	30°C/86°F	18°C/64°F	81%
APR	18°C/64°F	5°C/41°F	25°C/77°F	8°C/46°F	57%	30°C/86°F	17°C/63°F	73%
MAY	18°C/64°F	3°C/37°F	25°C/77°F	4°C/39°F	52%	28°C/82°F	15°C/59°F	75%
JUN	17°C/63°F	1°C/34°F	23°C/73°F	1°C/34°F	49%	27°C/81°F	13°C/55°F	75%
JUL	17°C/63°F	1°C/34°F	23°C/73°F	2°C/36°F	45%	27°C/81°F	12°C/54°F	71%
AUG	17°C/63°F	2°C/36°F	24°C/75°F	4°C/39°F	44%	31°C/88°F	13°C/55°F	74%
SEP	18°C/64°F	4°C/39°F	26°C/79°F	8°C/46°F	43%	33°C/91°F	16°C/61°F	64%
OCT	19°C/66°F	5°C/41°F	26°C/79°F	10°C/50°F	44%	31°C/88°F	17°C/63°F	68%
NOV	20°C/68°F	6°C/43°F	26°C/79°F	11°C/52°F	69%	31°C/88°F	19°C/66°F	78%
DEC	18°C/64°F	6°C/43°F	26°C/79°F	12°C/54°F	59%	30°C/86°F	18°C/64°F	78%

LOCAL LINGO: *Surazos* is the Bolivian term that describes the cold winds of Patagonia that blow into the area and cause the temperatures to fall drastically within a short period of time.

Plant Life

Bolivia's numerous different environments produce a huge variety of plants. The **Altiplano** is a grassland known for its **puna**, a spiky grass eaten by cameloids. The **cloud forests** are located where the cold mountain air comes in contact with the moist warm air of the Amazon. This is usually around 8,200 feet/2,500 meters. The Amazon and parts of the Gran Chaco offer **jungle** with dry woods like the mahogany being an important species.

FANTASTIC FLORA FIGURES

Bolivia has over 2,500 species of lichen, 1,950 to 2,500 species of trees, 1,200 species of moss, and 1,500 species of ferns.

It is beyond the scope of this book to even just list all the plants you could see here. If your interests lie in exploring the country for its diverse fauna and flora, purchase a guide book and head out.

■ In the Highlands

 The **Queñua** tree is a twisted, knurled species that grows at elevations up to 17,000 ft/5,200 m. It has red peeling bark and tiny leaves. This rare tree can be seen on the slopes of Mount Sajama.

Puma grass grows as spiky clumps in uncultivated fields of the Altiplano. The plant can grow up to three feet/one meter in height and diameter. The seeds are found in the stems and the roots are tough and fibrous. Those using traditional methods for farming burn this plant in potato fields and use it as fertilizer.

The **totora reed** that grows on Lake Titikaka (and a few other places in Bolivia) belongs to the same family as the papyrus. It grows 10 ft/three m above the level of the water and is used in the construction of the traditional boats and houses and to feed cattle. When planting the totora reed, the roots are cut and placed in muddy water at the edge of a lake. It can be harvested for the first time after a year and three times a year after that. When harvesting, the reed is cut 5 ft/1.5 m below the water line.

Yareta trees grow in clusters at about 13,000 ft/4,000 m above sea level. Because of the high resin content in the leaves, they are used for fuel.

A cactus called the ***jacha quiriu*** (huge stake) in Spanish (I was unable to find the English or scientific names) grows up to 33 ft/10 m in height and is used to make furniture. The plant is also dried, carved and placed over doorways or along stairways to bring good luck.

Puya raimondi is a giant bromeliad belonging to the same family as the pineapple. The raimondi is considered one of the most ancient plant species on the planet and grows as a rosette with tough waxy leaves that cluster up to seven ft/two m in diameter. It takes 100 years to mature before it flowers. The flower is a huge spike that can be 33 ft/10 m high and is covered with about 20,000 flowers. The plant flowers once, for three months, and then it dies.

■ In the Lowlands

 There are over 2,000 species of trees and orchids in the lower areas of Bolivia. Of them all, the rubber tree and the mahogany are the best known.

Mahogany trees grow well over 80 ft/25 m, with foliage that offers a great amount of shade. The trunk has a red, scaly bark and there are four to eight leathery leaves on each branch. Tiny white flowers appear in clusters and bear a pear-shaped fruit that has noticeable grooves along its length. The fruit produces wing-shaped seeds.

Rubber trees are actually a wide variety of plants that produce a milky liquid in the roots, stem, branches, leaves or fruit. This liquid, called the latex, contains globules that can be treated to form what we call raw rubber. You'll see boats going up and down the rivers of the Amazon Basin buying rubber from the jungle residents who collect it.

Orchids are so very beautiful, although most are actually parasitic and grow on a host plant. Orchids are members of the most highly evolved plant groups on the planet. There are about 25,000 species worldwide. Their evolution has resulted in thick leaves that hold moisture. Some of the flowers are highly perfumed, such as the vanilla orchid.

Bromeliads or **air plants** are similar in appearance to orchids. Bromeliads can grow at elevations as high as 8,200 ft/2,500 m and in any terrain from rainforest to desert. They are also like orchids in the way they gather nutrients and moisture in their leaves; their roots are only for anchoring, not for gathering food. Some bromeliads may be as small as one inch across, while others grow to three feet/one m. The pineapple is the most commonly known bromeliad.

Coca production dates back to 3000 BC. The leaf, called *hoja sangrada* (sacred leaf) by the Inca, has been used not only to decrease the sensation of hunger and cold and the symptoms of altitude sickness, but also for ceremonial purposes. It was given by Inca royalty to the gods. More recently, Coca-Cola used it originally for flavoring and the medical profession used it as a local anesthetic. Finally, the production of cocaine began and grew to an estimated US $150-$300 million in Bolivia alone. Colombia and Peru earn even more from the illegal export of cocaine.

Coca & The Drug War

A Peruvian, Dr. Carlos Gutierrez-Noriega, in 1947 indicated that coca chewing caused a negative attitude toward the superior (Spanish) culture. His lobbying resulted in a team of experts appointed by the United Nations to examine the plant. Their report condemned coca, saying that it was "noxious and the cause of racial degeneration." Its immediate eradication was recommended. Not much happened until 1961, when a program was put in place to follow the recommendations. But this, too, was on a small scale and production did not cease. Bolivia became the second-largest grower after Peru and the second largest producer of cocaine after Colombia. Most of that cocaine hits the streets of American cities.

Finally, the United States started its drug war and gave aid money so the farmers could grow replacement crops. The US then trained military men to recognize and eradicate the plant.

But there is a positive side to the coca plant that some governments try to ignore. The Department of Agriculture at Harvard University analyzed coca for nutritional value and found that it was high in calories, protein, carbohydrate and fiber. It also contained calcium, phosphorus, iron and vitamins A, E and B. A few years later, an anthropologist at Indiana University studied the plant and suggested that coca, chewed after dinner, may help regulate glucose metabolism and enhance the digestion of carbohydrates at high altitudes. These two reports gave the Andean people something with which to fight the eradication programs.

After farmers blockaded roads and conflicts between *cocaleros* and police left 10 dead, the government compromised and permitted 74,000 hectares/30,000 acres in the Yungas to be used for coca production. The rest of the farmers, when their crops are eradicated, are given $2,000 each to grow alternative crops, such as coffee, corn, rice or quinoa. The only legal market in Bolivia for the distribution of the coca plant is in Villa Fatima in the Yungas. Each week, enough leaves pass through the market to make a ton of cocaine. However, the only purchasers are registered retailers who take the coca to other areas of the country to be sold for cultural ceremonies and chewing.

One of the reasons farmers in the Yungas are permitted to grow coca is that they still use traditional ways to plant, fertilize and harvest the leaf so there is little environmental damage. But farmers in the Chaco and Chapare areas, where eradication is practiced, are not skilled at traditional farming. Many are displaced miners who, after the collapse of tin on world markets following World War II, looked for other ways to make a living. They chose to grow coca, using chemical fertilizers and insecticides, and burning jungle to grow the plants. Besides the loss of wildlife habitat, the chemicals dumped into the rivers have caused tremendous environmental problems.

As the drug problems in the United States increase, the US Drug Enforcement Agency becomes even more intent on eradication. Production was estimated to be down 33% in 2001 and 60% in the last five years (33% in the last year).

There is another philosophy about the eradication of the coca plant. Wade Davis in his book *One River*, feels that the American attempt at eliminating the plant has little to do with controlling the drug trade, but is rather a war on the culture of the Andean people. Today, there are many in Bolivia who agree with Davis.

For travelers, the drug war causes three problems. There are the roadblocks as *cocaleros* protest eradication, bus and baggage searches for "precursor chemicals" used in cocaine production and a general dislike of *gringos* due to heavy-handed actions of the DEA and army. This is especially evident in the Trinidad, Santa Cruz and Cochabamba areas.

Animal Life

Like the flora, animals vary according to the elevation. There are 322 species of mammals, 1,358 species of non-migratory birds, 257 species of reptiles, 166 of amphibians and 550 species of fish. With a little work, you can see most of the species you want to see. And when a tour agent says that you will see certain birds, plants, animals and insects, he is usually telling the truth. This is especially true in the Amazon area. I was promised pink dolphins, howler monkeys, capybaras, cobras, anacondas, caimans, turtles, egrets, eagles, tarantulas and so on. I saw all of them on a three-day boat tour out of Rurrenabaque on the Yacuma River.

■ In the Highlands

The most common animals are the three cameloids – llamas, alpacas and vicuñas. **Llamas** live at altitudes up to 18,000 ft/ 5,500 m and are used as beasts of burden, for food and for wool. You can get llama meat in cafés, especially in La Paz. The meat is tasty, tender and low in cholesterol. **Alpaca** are smaller than llamas and have smaller noses. Their wool is also finer and thicker. Products made from alpaca wool are of better quality, but not necessarily warmer. Alpaca like to live near streams and grassy plains. **Vicuña** are small and short with long necks. Between the Apolabama region and Sajama National Park, there are 8,000-9,000 of these animals. The numbers are low because Vicuña were hunted almost to extinction. Although they are quite curious, they are also cautious. When you spot one, keep still and it may come closer.

Vezcachas are rabbit-like rodents that jump. They have long fuzzy tails and live in colonies among the rocks located near streams. Related to the chinchilla, these animals can usually be spotted at sunrise or sunset.

The **Andean bear** is a rare and endangered animal that lives near the tree line. At one time, it was hunted for meat and fat as it was believed that this food cured diseases.

The **puma** is a night hunter and is rarely spotted. Also called the mountain lion, cougar or panther, it is a bit smaller than the jaguar. Its main source of food is the deer, an animal that is abundant in Bolivia. When hunting, the puma strikes with lightening speed and can jump 25 ft/7.5 m in one leap.

The **Andean fox** looks like a coyote in color and size. It hunts guinea pigs and mice and is often seen on the Altiplano.

The **armadillo**, an insect-eating mammal with a bony-plated shell, was used to make the *charango*, a small instrument similar to a ukulele, and is now an endangered species. (You can still see *charangos* in the market made from armadillo shells; please don't purchase them.) The armadillo has simple rootless teeth at the back of its mouth and is able to eat snakes, chickens, fruit and eggs. It also likes to munch on the odd scorpion.

Of the 120 birds that live in the Altiplano, the **condor**, with its 10-foot/three-m wingspan, is the most impressive. It is black with a bald red head, white neck and white on the tops of its wings. The condor can weigh up to 45 lbs/20 kg. It is the national bird of Bolivia. The **caracara** is another large bird common to the Altiplano. This scavenger is black and white with a yellow beak.

Flamingos are abundant near lakes. Their color is dependent on algae, which they consume. The more algae, the pinker the birds become.

The **rhea** lives as high as 11,500 ft/3,500 m and as low as 1,300 ft/400 m. It resembles an ostrich, minus the tail feathers, and stands just under seven ft/two m in height and weighs 45-60 lbs/20-25 kg. It eats insects, plants and small animals. The males sit on eggs laid by several females. The eggs take between 35 and 40 days to hatch and weigh just under two pounds/one kg.

Hummingbirds can live up to 16,500 ft/5,000 m. Their body temperature drops from 102°F/39°C during the day to 27°F/15°C during the night and the heart rate drops from 1,200 beats per minute to 40. Some hummingbirds in Bolivia grow to a fairly large size.

BLIND FROGGIE

The *Telmatobious culeus* belongs to the Leptodactylidae frog family. It is endemic to Lake Titicaca and was first identified by Jaques Cousteau, the famous French oceanographer. The frog grows to 45 to 60 cm (17-24 inches) in length. It is a night hunter and is believed to be blind. It obtains its oxygen from water through extra "fingers" that are quite vascular. The high flow of water allows for optimum oxygen consumption so lungs on this species have not developed. Because it is good eating, the frog has been hunted almost to extinction.

As for insects, spiders, butterflies and ants, Bolivia has enough to keep entomologists happy for years.

■ In the Lowlands

The **coati** is a tree-climbing mammal related to the raccoon. It has a long snout (tipped white) and an even longer tail that is usually the same length as its body. It keeps its striped tail high and, as it walks, the tail swings from side to side. Coatis are social animals and the females often travel with their young in groups of up to 20. When a group attacks a fruit tree for nourishment, it can devour the entire crop in a few minutes. A full-grown male stands about 10 inches/25 cm at the shoulder and will grow to about 1.5 ft/.5 m long. An omnivore, the coati hunts both in the day and at night and eats just about anything. You stand a good chance of seeing one moving along in tall grass or along rocky hillsides.

The **peccary** is a pig-like creature that has been around for 40 million years (according to fossil finds). It weighs about 50 lbs/23 kg and travels in herds of a few individuals to as many as 300. The peccary has two distinct features. One is the smell it exudes from a musk gland on its back whenever it feels irritated. The second is its amazing nose, the tip of which is flat and reinforced with a cartilaginous disk that can lift logs and dig underground for roots and insects. A true omnivore, the peccary will eat anything from poisonous snakes to cactus. Peccaries have no fixed mating season. The female usually gives birth to one or two young about the size of a full-grown rabbit, and after only a couple of days the offspring are ready to take their place in the herd.

The **ant bear** or the great anteater is known for its lack of teeth. Instead of teeth, its elongated head has a small hole about the size of a pen. Its tongue, which can extend up to 19 inches/48 cm, whips out and snatches up termites and other insects. The ant bear's front toes and claws curl under so it seems to be walking on its knuckles. It stands about 24 inches/60 cm at the shoulder and is (including tail) about seven ft/two m long. The female gives birth to one baby that stays with her for an entire year. The infant is often seen riding on its mother's back. The anteater is inoffensive and usually runs (and swims) away from perceived danger.

Skunks are found anywhere from northern Canada all the way down to Patagonia. Related to the weasel, this striped, furry critter is well known for its defense mechanism – spraying a horrid perfume up to a distance of 11.5 ft/3.5 m. The skunk aims for the eyes of its enemy, and the liquid it produces causes temporary blindness. A night hunter, the skunk comes out of its den when the temperatures cool and forages for insects, larvae, mice and fallen fruits. Skunks mate in spring and have litters of five or six young that are ready to look after themselves after about two months. Their life span is around 10 years.

The **tapir** or mountain cow is related to the horse and rhinoceros, but it is unique in the fact that it is the last surviving ungulate with an odd number of toes that bears its weight on the middle toe. It was named from the Brazilian Indian word meaning "thick," referring to its hide. This short-haired animal stands about 4 ft/1.2 m at the shoulder and weighs around 600 lbs/275 kg when fully grown. It has a trunk-like snout that grabs leaves from aquatic plants or forest foliage for food. An excellent swimmer, the tapir can stay underwater for long periods of time, especially when hiding from its worst enemies, the jaguar and puma. Don't get too close to a tapir's rear end. He pees straight out back at high velocity.

Howler monkeys make a horrid growling sound that will spook the hell out of you. And that is what it is meant to do. This leaf-eating primate has a long grasping tail and little facial hair, except on its chin. Its skin is black and its jawbone protrudes to accommodate the bladder-like resonating chamber found in the throat. It is this chamber that allows the monkey to make the frightening racket it does. Howlers live in troops of no more than 10 and have one dominant male leader. Once a troop is formed, all members eat, sleep and travel together. Howlers weigh up to 25 lbs/11 kg and mothers nurse their young for about 18 months.

The **spider monkey** is not as common as the howler, nor is it as noisy. Spider monkeys have grasping hands that have no functional thumbs and a grasping tail that is hairless at the end. These five "hands" allow for great maneuverability. Spider monkeys travel in bands of 20 to 30 that will attack threatening invaders. They use fruits and branches as weapons, and have been known to urinate on enemies walking below.

The **capybara** is the world's largest rodent, weighing about 120 lbs/55 kg. You will find them wallowing in mud at the edge of Amazon rivers, wiggling their tiny ears while enjoying the sun. Young ones are often eaten by caimans, which live in the same areas. Capybaras are my favorite jungle animals. I have an overwhelming urge to take one home and build it a pond and large exercise wheel.

Pink and grey freshwater **dolphins** are considered the most intelligent of the five dolphin species. The only predator this mammal has is man. The dolphin grows up to 10 ft/three m in length and weighs in at 200 lbs/90 kg. They have a gestation period of between nine and 12 months and sexual maturity is determined by size, rather than age. This dolphin has a hump on its back. Because of its special fusing at the neck, it can turn its head 180°. This mammal is friendly and fun to play with, but because it is endangered, I urge you not to touch.

Geckos eat insects, especially mosquitoes, and can be seen on walls throughout the Amazon. They were once thought to be poisonous by the locals.

There are close to 1,400 birds in Bolivia. You will not be disappointed if taking a birding tour. The most sought-after bird in the Amazon is the **blue-throated macaw**, which can be seen along the rivers out of Trinidad.

The most common fish are the **pacu**, **surubi**, **palometa** and **piraña**. There are also snakes, lizards, turtles, frogs and caimans along the rivers and in the jungles. Wildlife is abundant.

National Emblems

■ National Anthem

Bolivians, a favorable destiny
Has crowned our vows and longings;
This land is free,
Your servile state has ended.

The martial turmoil of yesterday
And the horrible clamor of war
Are followed today, in harmonious contrast,
By sweet hymns of peace and unity.

Chorus
We have kept the lofty name of our country
In glorious splendor,
And on its altars we once more swear
To die, rather than live as slaves.

This innocent and beautiful land,
Which owes its name to Bolivar,
Is the happy homeland where men
Enjoy the benefits of good fortune and peace.

For the sons of the great Bolivar
Have sworn, thousands upon thousand of times,
To die rather than see the country's
Majestic flag humiliated.

Chorus

Eternal praise to the brave warriors
Whose heroic valor and firmness
Conquered the glories that now
A happy Bolivia begins to enjoy!

Let their names, in marble and in bronze,
Transmit to remote ages
And in resounding song repeat the call:
Freedom! Freedom! Freedom!

Lyrics of the national anthem were written by Jose Ignacio de Sanjines

■ National Flag

The flag of Bolivia has three horizontal stripes. The top is red and represents the blood shed during the battle for independence; the center is yellow and represents gold or prosperity for the nation; the bottom is green and symbolizes the home of the people. In the center of the flag sits the country's coat of arms with 10 stars depicting the nine states plus the lost maritime district that was taken by Chile. The coat of arms covers 9/10ths of the yellow stripe.

■ Coat of Arms

The coat of arms that appears on the flag and all Bolivian coins has a llama in the center. During one of the battles for independence, the Indians were in a field waiting for the Spanish to arrive. The Spaniards arrived on horses and charged, but stopped when they saw that there were no people, only llamas, on the field. The Spaniards left. This saved the lives of the Bolivian people who were hiding behind the llamas.

■ National Flower

The **Kantuta** is the national flower and it has the same colors as the flag. The chalice-shaped flower has a red cup with a yellow stem that attaches to the green plant.

THE KANTUTU LEGEND

This is an Inca love story. A king, while on vacation, brought his favorite daughter, Kento, to Copacabana where they rested before going to Isla del Sol. Kento fell in love with a peasant, but knew that marriage would never be permitted between the two classes. The night before Kento and her father left for the island, the daughter snuck out to meet her lover for what she thought would be her last time. The night was dark with no moon or stars to light the way. She fell into a crevasse and died. Where her body was found a new and strange plant had started to grow. The people called the plant "kentuta pankara," which means "the flower of Kento's house."

■ National Bird

The **condor** is the country's national bird.

■ National Tree

Bolivia probably hasn't gotten around to naming a national tree, but the **Breadfruit Tree** is on the coat of arms. The breadfruit is a member of the fig family and grows up to 60 ft/20 m. It produces an edible round melon that weighs up to 10 lbs/4 kg. The meat of the melon tastes similar to chocolate and is used mostly for flavoring.

TREE OVERBOARD

In 1787 Captain Bligh found the breadfruit in Hawaii. He decided to plant the fruit in the Caribbean and took 1,000 shoots with him on his journey. The plants sucked up so much water that Bligh had to ration his men in order to keep the plants alive. The men soon rebelled and sent Bligh and the plants adrift in a row boat. How they became abundant in Bolivia is unknown.

■ National Animal

The **llama** is the national animal and is proudly shown on the coat of arms. It is used as a beast of burden, for its dung-fuel, for meat and for wool.

Bolivia's Top Destinations

 I have many favorite things to do in Bolivia. The following are ones that I feel you should make every effort to experience while traveling the country.

1. UYUNI – Tour Uyuni Salt Lake and Lago Colorado (page 248).

2. COPACABANA – Hike Isles del Sol (page 184) on Lake Titikaka.

3. SAJAMA – Climb the highest mountain in Bolivia and then soak in the hot springs close to the village (page 210).

4. TUPIZA – Take a horse tour around the badlands and canyons of the area (page 333).

5. RURRENABAQUE – Take a river trip to spot capybaras and anacondas (page 502).

6. SANTA CRUZ – Eat, visit the Jesuit Missions and then eat some more (page 444).

7. SAMAIPATA – Tour El Fuerte, a pre-Inca ruin (page 374).

8. SORATA – Hike around/to Illampu (page 270).

9. YUNGAS – Travel the Road of Death by bicycle from El Cumbre to Coroico, located in the rainforest of the Yungas (page 117).

10. AMBORO NATIONAL PARK – Try to identify at least 100 of the 830 birds already known to inhabit the park (page 369).

11. POTOSI – Visit the silver mine and mint (page 232).

12. SUCRE – Visit the dinosaur tracks in the cleanest colonial city in South America and then purchase chocolate that is reputed to be better than Swiss (page 299).

13. LA PAZ – Visit Tihuanaco Archeological Site (page 149) and the Gold Museum in town and eat at the fabulous cafés (page 103).

14. ORURO – Take in the most traditional Carnival in Bolivia. This occurs the week before the start of Lent, which is always 40 days before Easter. (See page 214.)

Travel Information

Facts at Your Fingertips

PRESIDENT: **Gonzalo Sanchez de Lozada**, elected after Jorge Fernando Quiroga Ramez took over from Banzer on August 8, 2001, when Banzer was diagnosed with terminal lung/liver cancer. Sanchez was ousted in October, 2003.

VICE PRESIDENT: Carlos D. Mesa Gisbert. At time of appointment he was 37 years old and the youngest Vice President ever to take office.

OPPOSITION LEADER: **Evo Morales** is the most controversial and colorful politician, leader of the *campesinos* generally and, more spe-

cifically, the *cocaleros*. He is also the first Indian to be elected into the Bolivian parliament. He almost defeated Sanchez for presidency when negative comments made by the US ambassador gave him a huge sympathy vote. The split vote resulted in a vote in parliament which he lost by a hair.

SIZE: 424,163 square miles/1,098,581 square km, with 20% desert, 40% rainforest, 25% pasture, 2% arable land and 2% water. The remaining 11% is mountainous.

POPULATION: 8,150,000 – 15% Spanish, 30% Quechua and 25% Aymara and 30% other.

CAPITAL: Sucre is the capital city, but the seat of government is in **La Paz**. Lhasa, Tibet and Potosi are the only major centers in the world that sit higher than La Paz. Lhasa is 237 ft/72 m higher, and Potosi is 1,530 ft/465 m higher. La Paz stands at 11,924 ft/3,625 m above sea level.

DISTRICTS: The nine districts are Beni, Chuquisaca, Cochabamba, La Paz, Oruro, Pando, Potosi, Santa Cruz and Tarija.

INDEPENDENCE DAY: August 6. One of the most common street names in the towns and cities of Bolivia is 6 de Agosto.

LANGUAGE: Spanish is the predominant language spoken in the cities. **Quechua** or **Aymara** is spoken in the countryside and in small mountain villages.

AUTHOR TIP: A word glossary for the Indian languages is quite helpful if traveling independently into isolated areas. Although some Aymara and Quechua people speak Spanish, it is their second language and, if it is yours too, confusion is bound to occur. For a smattering of Aymara, visit www. aymara.org/english/index.php; for some Quechua, go to gibbons.best.vwh.net/index.html.

EDUCATION: Schooling is compulsory for children between ages seven and 11. Those with the funds and desire to continue may take three years of intermediate and four years of secondary education. Secondary education can be a general or a specialized education. High school graduates may continue at the University of Bolivia or enter one of the many private institutions. Cochabamba is renowned for its medical schools and has students from other countries specializing in the study of tropical diseases.

The literacy rate is 75% in Bolivia. You'll notice school kids moving to and from various locations throughout the day. Elementary students attend from 8 am to noon, secondary students from 12:30 to 6 pm and adults go after 6 pm.

LIFE EXPECTANCY: Males live to an average of 60 years and females live to 62. The infant mortality rate is 124.4 per 1,000 births. Nutritional deficiency affects 70% of the population. Sanitary conditions are poor, especially in rural areas. Only 23% of the population has drinkable water, 15.6% has electricity and 1% has a sewage system.

GDP: US $977 per person, per year. The unemployment rate is 7.6%. Bolivia is an agricultural society: 60% of the population are farmers – they produce 23% of the GDP. Only 15% of agricultural products are exported. Of the industrial production, 20% is silver and tin, 36% of which is exported.

NATURAL RESOURCES: Tin, natural gas, petroleum, zinc, tungsten, antimony, silver, iron, lead, gold and timber are the main resources. Bolivia is rich in mineral deposits. Forests cover 138 million acers/56 million hectares.

HUMAN RIGHTS: Human rights violations do occur, although there have been no political assassinations in recent years. Most abuses occur between the military or police and the *cocaleros* living and growing coca in the Chapare region. The government is obligated to stop production of the plant, while the farmers insist on growing it. Conflict is often violent, resulting in death. Incarceration can occur for months and even years before a suspect is brought to trial.

The **police force** does not have a good reputation. The government does not complete or force investigations into alleged abuses in the jails, so once the police become involved, there is almost no law. More than 30% of the people in prison have been waiting for trial longer than the sentence they would have received for the accused crime. **Gay rights** demonstrations always result in harassment of both protestors and bystanders.

Newspapers are not permitted to criticize the government or the Catholic church and all quotes must have a name attached. Violators are subject to two months in prison.

There is wide **discrimination** against women, indigenous people and Afro-Bolivians. Sixty-two percent of women experience domestic violence at least once in their lives; rape is under reported. Four out of five illiterate people are women.

An estimated 800,000 children between the ages of seven and 14 hold jobs to help support their families.

On the bright side, women of reproductive years receive free **medical care**, as do all children under the age of five. However, it is unlikely that this care is timely or consistent in any individual case. Cleft palates and club feet, for example, are seldom treated unless payment is made.

Prisons in Bolivia are harsh, overcrowded and often life-threatening for those without access to money. In San Pedro Prison in La Paz, there are between 8,000 and 12,000 prisoners in a space that was designed to hold only 5,000. To use a cell, prisoners must pay between $20 and $5,000. The small, less-expensive ones measure 3 x 5 x 6.5 ft (1 x 1.5 x 2 m), with no ventilation, no lighting and no beds. Some prisoners must sit up to sleep due to lack of space, and their diet causes serious anemia. Medical care is unavailable unless one has money. If a prisoner is troublesome, he may experience a cell fire – an accident, the guards will say. Children under the age of six are permitted to live with incarcerated parents. At present, there are 665 children in San Pedro Prison. Because many would end up living on the street, they continue living in the prison after age six.

There is wide corruption in the **judicial system** due to low wages and the class system. Everyone is given the right to assembly – and Bolivians use this right often.

PARKS: Bolivia's 37 parks cover 17% of the country's total land mass. Fifteen of the parks have full-time wardens. Parks are administered by the Servicio Nacional de Areas Protegidas (SERNAP) in La Paz. Most parks require an admission fee and usually foreigners pay more than locals. This fee is collected near the parks' entrances.

These are not protected parks in the American or European sense; the land can be used for farming, ranching, logging and hunting. And although there are park land rules, they are seldom enforced. In Santa Rosa, I saw a pile of caiman carcasses along a waterway. The reptiles had been killed for their skin, which is used to make shoes and purses. There are not enough rangers to prevent poaching.

Travel Information

CURRENCY: The boliviano is the Bolivian currency. At time of writing, it was exchanging at B 7.50 to US $1. Each boliviano is made up of 100 centavos. The boliviano bills are printed in denominations of 10, 20, 50, 100 and 200. There is also a five boliviano bill, but that is being taken out of circulation. The inflation rate is presently at 10%, making the boliviano one of the most stable currencies in Latin America.

When to Go

■ Seasonal Considerations

 Anytime is the best time to go to Bolivia. The winter months run from June to September and present clear skies and cold crisp days in the higher elevations. Rainy season, from November to March, is warmer but travel on the mountain roads can be treacherous and impossible in the Amazon. Peak climbing season during the winter months may require a few days leeway in your itinerary because the good guides are heavily booked. Festivals cause crowding on buses and airlines, so avoid travel during those times. Prices are low all the time.

■ National Holidays & Celebrations

 Bolivia has many celebrations and, although many are specific to a region, most are held throughout the country. If you are here for an extended period, you are certain to encounter at least one of them. Below is a compilation of holidays that are held throughout the country. Additionally, each district has its own celebrations, which are reviewed in the regional chapters.

■ JANUARY

January 6. **Dias de Reyo** (Day of the King) takes place in the main plaza and is celebrated with young people dancing in the square, while the older ones look on.

January 24. **Alasista** is a celebration also known as the Festival of Abundance, where many people climb to the stations-of-the-cross and pray for good fortune. They pray to Ekheko, an Aymara/Inca God.

■ FEBRUARY

February 1, 2 and 3. A week-long celebration for the **Virgin of Candeleria**, when the virgin's identity is re-asserted. The first and second days feature music and dancing. The third day is celebrated with a bullfight.

Near the end of February, 40 days before Easter, is **Carnival** throughout Latin America. It is a week-long event. Wednesday to Saturday features street dancing, with participants wearing costumes and masks. On Friday, everyone is forbidden to dance or drink alcohol. Saturday is water-fight day and no-one is spared. In fact, the water fights start about a month before Carnival and escalate until they culminate during Carnival. *Globos* (balloons) half-filled with water are sold in the streets and thrown at everyone. Monday the people plant flowers as a symbol of spring. Tuesday is called *challa*, and it's when everything in the house is blessed by a sprinkling of alcohol. This is the last day of the celebrations. *Las Chutas* is the action of making fun of the Spanish and this is done during the entire week.

The most traditional Carnival is held in Oruro, where the world-famous parade takes place along with the not-so-famous *globos*-throwing games.

■ **MARCH**

March 23 is the **Dia del Mar**, which honors Eduardo Avaroa, a hero from the War of the Pacific who gave the "surrender your grandmothers" speech. Avaroa was born in San Pedro de Atacama on October 13, 1838. March 23 is when Bolivia lost its land by the sea to Chile and is the day Avaroa died. During the celebrations there is a parade with government officials, peasants and children vowing to reclaim the lost land.

Semana Santa is at Easter. The date changes each year, but it is always held at the end of March or beginning of April. Many people from around the country make a pilgrimage (called a *perigrinacion*) from La Paz to Copacabana, a distance of 97 miles/158 km. *Perigrinos* start walking on Good Friday, often in running shoes. When they finally arrive in Copacabana, they are a sorry sight. Because Christ died on the Friday, *perigrinos* are permitted to steal food from fields with no repercussions on the first day. Often, people do the pilgrimage only once in a lifetime, but some do it once every three years. In addition, there are 125 boats with 25 people in each that pass through the Strait of Tiquina. On Saturday, *peregrinos* confess all their sins and climb the stations of the cross before parading to the cathedral, where they are blessed for their sacrifice. New vehicles are decorated with flowers and blessed. This occurs every Sunday all year long in Copacabana, but during Semana Santa it is extra special.

Travel Information

There is no alcohol consumption on Saturday, but on Sunday a church service is followed by lots of feasting. Copacabana is one of the best places to be during Semana Santa.

■ MAY

May 1 is **Labor Day**. All government offices are closed, and many Bolivians also close their shops and private businesses.

May 27, Dia de la Madre, or **Mother's Day**, is celebrated with football (what North Americans call soccer) matches. I am certain these are exactly what women would want on their special day! In the wars of independence, after the men were killed in some places, the women fought and won. Mother's Day honors the women who participated. Maybe the women should be playing football on this day.

■ JUNE

June 5 and 6 is the birthday of **Manco Capac**, the first male Inca ever born, according to legend. He was created along with Mama Huanca. Their birth spot (one of three) is on Isla del Sol at the large table-rock. The day is celebrated in many towns with parades and football.

June 23 is the **Dia de San Juan Bautista**. This is when everyone builds a fire in front of their house to celebrate the longest night and coldest day of the year. Fire (the first element) is believed to clean the land. When put out with water (the second element) fertility of the crops is enhanced. People also do a ceremonial cleansing where they wash their faces and bodies in ice-cold water. Some throw lead or steel into a glass of water and have their futures told. Everyone prays for health, fertility and prosperity.

July 15-17 is the **Dia de la Revolution**. This celebration is in honor of Pedro Murillo, a freedom fighter who, during a demonstration led by opposing forces, was hanged in the main square in La Paz. During this celebration, there are 16 parades and 17 lanterns, or *faroles*, put on display. There is also a mock bullfight at which everyone shares in a show of "killing the bull," who is usually the most inebriated man in town.

■ AUGUST

August 5 and 6 is **Independence Day**. Since 1825 Bolivia has been freed from Spanish rule, which warrants a huge celebration.

■ NOVEMBER

November 1 and 2 is Todo Santo or **All Saints Day**. This event is celebrated at the cemetery. Special breads and candies are cooked, often in the shape of a skull, and offered to the spirits of ancestors. This celebration is practiced everywhere in Latin America.

▪ DECEMBER

December 24 is **Christmas**. It is celebrated with family and children, who go from door to door playing music and receiving small gifts.

December 31 and January 1 is **New Year**, celebrated with parties and fireworks.

What to Take

▪ Required Documents

 To enter Bolivia a **passport** valid for six months after your entry date is required. You will be given a tourist card valid for 30 to 90 days. Do not lose the card as it must be returned to Immigration when you exit the country.

Citizens from Western countries do not need a visa for short stays, and most are given an automatic 90-day stamp when they arrive at the border or airport. Sometimes, officials give only 30 days. If that's not long enough for you, it can be extended at Immigration in La Paz, Calle Camacho #1433, open from 9 to 12:30 pm and 3 to 6 pm. However, with the cost ($25 per month of extension) and the time spent in the Bolivian bureaucratic quagmire, it is easier to leave the country and return a day later. You will be issued a new tourist card with another 30 days on it. I do not know how many times you may exit and re-enter Bolivia before they suggest you take up permanent residence.

It is the law that you must carry **identification** at all times.

> **SAFETY WARNING:** Be warned that tricksters pretending to be the National Police may demand your identification (passport) and then ask you to follow them because of an inconsistency. They get you into a vehicle and then rob you. The best thing to do is carry a photocopy of your passport and one of your entry stamp/tourist card and use those as identification.

Anyone overstaying their tourist card limit will be subject to a fine of a dollar a day at Immigration, or $5 a day at the airport. This is an inexpensive fine, but you may miss your flight, which could be costly.

Dept. of Immigration, Calle Camacho #1433, La Paz, is open from 9 to 12:30 pm and 3 to 6 pm, Monday to Friday.

For general information about Bolivia, go to www.boliviaweb.com.

Embassies & Consulates

Embassies and consulates are well represented in La Paz. See the *Appendix* for a list. If your country has a consulate or embassy here, I suggest that you register with them. I do this with the Canadian Consulate for every country I visit. Whenever there is trouble in the area, they contact me with advice. I also know that if I lose my passport or run into any other problems, they have my signature. It cuts down on the need for proof of identification later (when your passport, for example, has gone missing).

■ Packing List

 Bolivia has a large indigenous population that is strong in Catholic faith and in adherence to tribal custom, so conservative dress is essential. Like the women of the country, I wear a skirt that is calf length and a blouse with sleeves that cover my arms at least to the elbow. On the other hand, the Ladinos (the white population) do wear North American-styled clothing and provocative dress is often seen in urban areas. Most businesswomen wear skirts or dresses. Except in the Amazon area, shorts are not common. The men of Bolivia usually wear jeans or slacks with long-sleeved shirts.

You will need a warm **sweater** or jacket for evenings, especially in the higher elevations of the Andes and the Altiplano. If traveling during rainy season, take rain protection and a **jacket** – it does snow in the mountains.

An **umbrella** is good at any time of year. It keeps both the sun and the rain off, and serves as a nice little defense tool in the event of an unwanted attack, especially by dogs. Take your umbrella on any Altiplano hikes. The sun doesn't feel hot, but UV rays burn quickly.

In the jungles of Bolivia, a **cotton skirt** is far cooler than pants or shorts. Men should wear loosely woven cotton clothing. During rainy season, locals wear gumboots as a protection against water on the ground that is laden with parasites. Look to see what the locals are wearing and follow suit.

A **money belt** should always be a natural-fiber pouch worn around the midriff under your clothes. Natural fiber is far more comfortable in the heat than synthetic fiber. Inside the belt, keep documents in plastic bags to protect them from damage by sweat and rain. Always place money, credit/ATM cards and travelers' checks in different places, so if you are robbed you will have some mad money to live on. Belts like the kind used to hold up pants are available with zippered pockets sewn on the underside. These are comfortable and inconspicuous. Money must be folded lengthwise and placed in the underside pockets.

Tiny pockets can be sewn into your clothing – in the hem of your skirt or the cuff of your shirt. Sports bras worn by women that have the water bottle containers in the back are excellent for hiding money and cards. Pin or Velcro the bottle containers shut so the money or cards won't work their way out.

A **day pack** is far more convenient to carry than a handbag. It is also harder to pickpocket or snatch. In cities, on buses or crowded places like markets, wear your day pack at the front, with the waist strap done up. That way, your hands can rest on the bag while you walk. In this position, it is almost impossible for pickpockets to access the pack. Carry only the money you need for the day in your day pack and the bulk of your money in your money belt or elsewhere. If you keep your camera in the pack, it is easily accessible and can be slipped in and out quickly. Never wear your camera around your neck when touring in cities. The camera can be grabbed and the strap sliced in a couple of easy motions. If wearing a jacket, wear it over your pack.

It seems to me that a map is really hard to follow if you don't have a **compass**. They are not heavy and you need not buy one that can do triangulation measurements. A simple one will do.

Should you be stuck in a hotel room facing the front street or over a bar, **earplugs** are essential. Often, in the country, the roosters crow and dogs bark all night.

A **first aid kit** should include things like mole skin, Advil, bandage, antihistamines, topical antibiotic cream, Band Aids, prescription medicines and malaria prophylactics.

A **hat** is essential and everyone wears one. It keeps the strong sun off, shades your eyes and protects you from the rain.

Photocopies of passports and other documents should be kept somewhere other than with your passport. When traveling with someone, I give the photocopy to my companion. When traveling alone, I leave a copy at home with someone I can contact quickly if need be. Memorize your passport number. Keep a record of the numbers on your traveler's checks and record where and when you cashed them. If they are stolen, you have a record to give the company that issued them. Keep important addresses and phone numbers in two places, just in case you lose one list.

In our technological age you may also scan your passport (and any other information you find valuable) and e-mail the scan to your traveling e-mail address (i.e., Yahoo or Hotmail). This way, you always have a copy available.

AN UNUSUAL WEAPON

A friend of mine, a poet, was walking in downtown Lima (in Peru) and his wife was attacked by robbers. Barry was carrying a guidebook and, when he saw what was happening, he attacked the robbers using the spine of the book. The robbers got away with nothing and Barry's wife was not seriously hurt.

Reading material is expensive and bus trips are often long. I like to carry thick anthologies of short stories. As I finish each story, I rip it out of the book and give it to a local who is learning English. I also like to read books written about the country and by writers from the country I am visiting. The stories have more relevance when read at their place of origin. See *Recommended Reading*, page 519, for suggestions. Unless you're fluent in Spanish, always carry a **Spanish dictionary** and a list of conjugated verbs. A phrasebook is useful too.

A **sleeping bag** is advisable if you are planning trips into high areas. If going to the Altiplano, even with a tour group, the accommodations will be rustic and a warm bag could be essential. If hiking in the Andes, a bag is vital. Purchasing a bag in Bolivia is difficult, but you can rent them from some outfitters. Take a light down bag and keep it in a plastic bag to protect it from moisture. I always put some mothballs in my sleeping bag when traveling. When I use it on rustic straw mattresses, the tics and fleas tend to avoid me.

Camping gear should be brought from home. Climbing gear, especially, must be brought with you as our standard of care for ropes and biners is much different than the standard in Bolivia. However, this is changing and some companies have top-quality equipment that they know how to maintain.

If you are able, bring an old tent, sleeping bag, therma-rest, stove, pots and good quality outdoor clothing. Use them and, before you leave, sell them at a bargain price to outfitters who are trying to improve their equipment. Or trade them with a favorite person for something you would like to take home. Giving equipment away may lead locals to expect such gifts from other travelers, so a trade or sale of some kind is always better.

Electricity is 220 volts. If carrying appliances, purchase a converter in your own country. Although they are available in Bolivia, they are heavy. Often, it is easier to purchase appliances like immersion heaters in Bolivia. Those using computers should carry a good surge protector.

A **flashlight** is useful and often essential. Batteries are readily available.

FIDO FRIENDLY

Traveling with a dog is possible in Bolivia. Dogs are permitted on public transportation and allowed into restaurants and hotels, provided they are under your control. Bolivians indicate that dogs have had all their shots and are free of rabies by tying ribbons or scarves around their necks.

Health Concerns

Bring with you anything you may need in the way of prescriptions, glasses, orthopedics, dental care and batteries for hearing aids. Things like vitamins, bandages, antihistamines and topical creams are readily available in the cities and are not expensive. If you become sick, contact your consulate for recommended doctors and medical clinics. They can usually put you in touch with doctors who speak your language.

Medical treatment is cheap in Bolivia. Minor ailments are better treated in local clinics and paid for on the spot, rather than going through an insurance. If you plan on climbing or taking buses along dangerous routes, travel insurance is recommended. I have used **RBC Travel Insurance** ($1 a day for a period of six months) because their policy will pay for hospital/doctor bills without my doing any paperwork. The insured person must contact them (at a 24-hour, toll-free number) as soon as an injury or sickness occurs and RBC looks after the costs. To check out more options, a good starting place on the Internet is www.internationalplan.com.

For official government updates on outbreaks, advisories and more, visit the **Centers for Disease Control & Prevention** run by the US Health Department at www.cdc.gov.

■ Doctors & Clinics

Some hotel doctors are very expensive, usually $40 per visit, plus the cost of medication. Choosing a clinic used by a trustworthy local is an alternative that runs less than $10 per call.

AUTHOR EXPERIENCE: I needed a doctor after leaving the Amazon and went to one in Cochabamba. My Spanish does not encompass most medical terms. The doctor had a computer that could translate from Spanish to English and back. With such modern technology, a doctor who speaks your own language may not be necessary.

You may also contact the **IAMAT** (International Association for Medical Assistance to Travelers) clinics. The information reported in this section is taken from either IAMAT or World Health Organization publications. If you feel so inclined, please become a member of IAMAT and send them a donation. Their services are invaluable. Some of the money they raise goes toward a scholarship program that assists doctors in developing countries to train in more developed parts of the world. For addresses in your country, visit www.iamat.org.

■ IAMAT Clinics

Iamat Center, Edificio Servimed, 5th floor
Calle Baptista, Cochabamba
☎ (591-4) 423-1504 or (591-4) 423-3884

Clinica San Pedro, Calle Aurelio Melean S-154
Has 10 coordinators, all with a specialty.
☎ (591-4) 423-1504

IPPA La Clinica - High Altitude Pathology Clinic
Ave. Savedra 2302, La Paz
☎ (591-2) 224-5394 or (591-2) 222-2617; zubieta@bolnet.bo

Clinica Angel Foianini, Ave. Irala 468, Santa Cruz
☎ (591-3) 336-2211 or (591-3) 336-5577

■ Common Ailments

 The following website, run by the IPPS Clinic (above) has excellent information about dealing with **high altitude sickness**. If going directly to La Paz from a low altitude, read the recommendations and do what is suggested to make your arrival and stay more comfortable. Go to www.geocities.com/zubietaippa.

High altitude sickness, or *soroche*, can affect anyone, regardless of physical condition or age. According to altitude studies in Nepal, it is usually young people who suffer from the sickness. As a rule, older people move more slowly, thus giving themselves more time to acclimatize. Also, young people tend to ignore the early symptoms.

Serious altitude sickness is always possible if you ascend above 10,000 ft/ 3,000 m quickly. The atmospheric pressure at Potosi, which is about 1,650 ft/500 m higher than La Paz, is half of that at sea level. It is often assumed that if you were at high elevations on previous trips and felt no side effects, you will have no problems on your next trip. This is not the case. There is no rule that can predict your body's reaction to a substantial elevation change.

Know the symptoms of *soroche*. If you suspect you may be affected, descend immediately to an elevation where the symptoms disappear.

- The first symptom is shortness of breath and a racing pulse even with small amounts of exertion. Tiredness and lack of appetite are common, as is a mild headache. Other primary symptoms are insomnia, irritability, dizziness, muscle aches, nausea and water retention in the face, hands and feet.

- Secondary symptoms include a severe headache and/or a persistent cough. The headache is an indication that water is starting to accumulate on your brain. A cough may indicate that water is accumulating in the lungs.

- Tertiary symptoms include confusion, inability to sleep lying down and a loss of coordination that causes staggering. At this point going to a lower elevation, or getting to a hospital where oxygen therapy can be administered, is essential.

- The final stages of *soroche* are unconsciousness and then death.

When arriving at a high elevation, drink lots of water (four liters or one gallon a day) and stay away from alcohol. The rule is to drink enough water so that you pee clear. Keep stimulants like coffee at a minimum as they are dehydrating. Do not take tranquilizers, sleeping pills or other medications that slow down the breathing rate as this is counterproductive to acclimatization. For the first few days, do little except to take short slow walks and eat light foods. When you feel fine, start moving toward higher elevations or more strenuous activity.

Drugs may be taken to counteract altitude sickness. Acetazolamide can lessen symptoms by increasing the breathing rate. Dexamethasone can reduce major symptoms long enough for very ill people to be taken to a lower elevation and/or seek medical help.

If you are not able to acclimatize after about a week of slow walking and lots of water drinking, do not fret. Head for the lowlands of Bolivia and then return to the higher elevations slowly, spending a few days in a town or village about 1,000 ft/300 m higher than the previous one. Do day-trips to higher elevations, then go back down to sleep.

Bolivia has such diverse landscapes and interesting places to visit that going to lower and then higher elevations should present no problems. If you are visiting only La Paz and you can't acclimatize, then head home or go lower before you die.

You should also be aware of the condition of your traveling companions. There is always a tendency to ignore symptoms and, once confusion and lack of coordination occurs, the sick person is no longer able to help him/her self. Someone must step in. Locals recommend coca tea for altitude sickness. Since I drink it all the time, I like to think it works, but I don't know for sure.

Hypothermia can occur even when the temperatures are not below freezing. If you become wet and are in the wind, especially at a high elevation, hypothermia is a possibility. The symptoms start with shivering, which grows more severe – at which point the person often refuses to admit he is cold. Once confusion and loss of muscular control (staggering) occurs, the person can no longer help himself and intervention is required. Warm the person by putting him/her into a sleeping bag, out of the wind and rain. Small sips of warm water or tea can be administered, but never alcohol. If the person becomes unconscious, a doctor is needed.

Fevers & Worse

Malaria, transmitted by mosquitoes that bite at dawn and dusk, is a possibility at elevations below 8,000 ft/2,500 m. A prophylactic is crucial unless you are going only to La Paz, Oruro and Potosi.

Bolivia has both chloroquine-responsive and chloroquine-resistant malaria. Anyone traveling near or through the Amazon Basin must use a chloroquine-resistant prophylactic. See your doctor or the IAMAT reports for the type of protection you will need. Do not use outdated information.

Mephlaquine is the recommended prophylactic against chloroquine- resistant malaria. One person in 15,000 may develop side effects (severe paranoia, panic attacks or eye irritations) from mephlaquine. Most people have little or no reaction to the drug.

In the event that you develop a fever while in Bolivia, for no explicable reason like a cold or flu, especially if you are in or have been in the jungle, you should treat the condition as if it is malaria. Some forms of malaria are lethal, so immediate attention is imperative.

In case of a fever, a person between 45 and 60 kgs (100 and 125 lbs) should take five mephlaquine tablets within 24 hours. Larger people should take one tablet for every 10 kgs (five lbs) of body weight over 60 kg (125 lbs). The tablets should be taken in three separate doses of two tablets, two tablets and, finally, one tablet, eight hours apart. If vomiting occurs within 30 minutes of ingestion, a half-dose should be taken.

If you experience ringing in the ears, reduce the dosage until the noise goes away. Get to a doctor or clinic as soon as possible. The possibility of malaria should be considered for up to three months after leaving an infected area.

Dengue fever is transmitted by a mosquito that bites during the day, rather than at dawn and dusk like the malaria-infested mosquitoes. Dengue fever causes severe headaches and severe pain to the joints and muscles. The aches are accompanied by a high fever. The disease lasts about a week. The most important thing you can do when infected with dengue is drink lots of water.

A first-time infection of dengue will not be the hemorrhagic kind, but a second bout increases the chances of hemorrhagic dengue and the chances of death are much greater. The most notable sign of hemorrhagic dengue is small red dots on your skin. This is caused from the capillaries underneath breaking and seeping blood. You will die without good medical care. In Bolivia, signs are posted whenever dengue is a threat.

CAUTIONARY TALE

While traveling on the Mosquito Coast a few years ago, I met a lady who had refused to take a prophylactic for malaria, thinking (I believe) that the medicine would be harder on her than the disease. She caught the disease. Her tremors were so severe that they ripped all the muscles in her legs and arms. I met her six weeks after the fevers subsided and she was hobbling along with a cane, still not healthy enough to head home.

To help protect against malaria-bearing mosquitos, spray or soak your clothes and sleeping gear (including net or tent) with Permethrin solution. Protection lasts for up to three washings. The recommended dose is 20 mls of Permethrin (13%) in two liters (one pint) of water. For tents and mosquito nets, spray the item with a solution of 10 mls in two liters of water. Permethrin can be purchased in any garden shop that sells pesticides. If traveling for a long time, carry Permethrin concentrate and dilute it only when you need it.

During early morning or at dusk, when mosquitos are most active, keep exposed skin covered. Repellents laced with DEET are recommended. Although traces of DEET have been found in the livers of users, it is still better than getting malaria. Using a sleeping net in infected areas is highly recommended.

Yellow fever is present in all the jungles of South America. Though inoculation is not required for entrance to Bolivia it may be required for re-entry to your own country. Inoculation, good for 10 years, is recommended if you want to avoid a lengthy stay in quarantine. Children must also have a certificate of inoculation, but it is not recommended to inoculate children who are less than one year of age. This means you should not take children under one year of age into the infected areas.

Routine inoculations common in your home country should be up to date. Besides these, immune globulin is recommended against **viral hepatitis** and inoculation against **typhoid fever** is suggested.

If traveling to the Apolobama area or along the border between Peru and Bolivia north of Lake Titikaka, inoculation against **plague** should be considered. Talk this over with your doctor.

Travel Information

LLAMAS TO THE RESCUE

Llamas were used by the Quechua to drive off diseases. One year, the Indians of the Altiplano were suffering from plague. In an attempt to stop the deaths, they loaded a black llama with the clothes of the plague-stricken people, sprinkled the llama with alcohol and sent it into the mountains to carry the pestilence away.

Typhus may be present in areas that have poor sanitation. Vaccine against typhus is no longer available. Use mothballs or Permethrin for protection against infected fleas and don't stay in dirty hotels. Tetracycline is the recommended antibiotic – it kills the disease completely.

Rabies is still a threat here. Of the 2,100 cases of dog bites on humans tested during 1997, over 1,400 were rabid and of those six people died. Rabies causes acute encephalitis. The virus is transmitted through the nervous system from the saliva of an infected animal. Incubation after the bite is anywhere from three to 12 weeks and death is usually seven days after clinical symptoms become evident. If you are bitten by an animal, go immediately to a good clinic where a prophylactic will be administered. This is not a disease that can be ignored. A study done in Santa Cruz found that male dogs tested positive for rabies more often than females and dogs from poorer urban areas were more likely to be infected.

Bugs & Critters

Worms and **parasites** are a big problem. Keep your feet free of cuts and open sores so that worm larva or parasites cannot enter. Wear sandals or neoprene booties when showering and closed shoes or hiking boots when outdoors.

If staying in budget hotels, keep your sleeping gear in mothballs during the day. The odor repels bed bugs and fleas. You will find that bed bugs do not cross that smelly barrier no matter how succulent the impending meal is. The mothball smell dissipates within a short period of time.

The **Tumbu fly** is an insect that transports its eggs into its host by way of the mosquito. Once the egg is in its host, it hatches and lives under the skin. However, the fly must have air. If you have a red swelling that sort of looks like a mosquito bite and you look closely you may see a small hole in the swollen area. Keep the hole covered with petroleum jelly to prevent the fly from breathing. Without air, it dies.

A HARD LESSON TO LEARN

Watch the locals and follow their example as much as possible. I went into the Amazon jungle to get some guava. The locals were collecting only the fruit that had fallen to the ground, but I saw a ripe fruit hanging from a tree. I climbed the tree and picked the fruit. That night I started to itch uncontrollably and the next morning I looked like I had smallpox. I went to a doctor and he informed me that I had picked up a tree parasite. It took three months of scrubbing with a sandpaper-like cloth, rubbing in creams, and popping pills to rid my body of the critter.

■ Water

 Drink treated or bottled water. Eat at places where locals are eating. If they remain healthy, you should too. If the sanitation looks dubious, don't eat salad – have some boiled soup instead.

Although tap water is considered safe to drink in the major centers like La Paz or Cochabamba, I don't drink it. Water in small hamlets is a potential hazard. Bottled water is available, and affordable, throughout Bolivia in both cities and most villages. Some isolated villages may not have bottled water, in which case you should treat the tap water with purification tablets.

The best way to treat water is to boil it for 10 minutes. However, remember that the boiling point of water in La Paz is 86°F/30°C and water must boil for at least 10 minutes to get rid of any infections. Immersion heaters can be purchased for a dollar in La Paz. With this system, I was able to make first-class filtered coffee in the mornings (I carry good coffee and filters) and a cup of herbal tea at night while relaxing in my room. Some travelers boil water and fill their own bottles.

> **AUTHOR CONFESSION:** I confess that I sometimes feel guilty about my immersion heater and coffee. I am using expensive electricity that my hotel may not have budgeted for, and I am not adding to the economy by purchasing water or coffee. However, my morning coffee is sacred and safe water is crucial.

If traveling in the mountains or any other area where creek/lake water must be used, I suggest you use a chemical such as iodine for purification. There is also a tablet available that has silver (as opposed to iodine) as a base, which makes it far more palatable. Chlorine bleach can also be used as a purifier. It is the least effective of chemicals, but the most available and can be purchased anywhere in Bolivia.

Water filters take a long time to process the water and they do not filter out all organisms that could cause problems. They are also much heavier than chemicals.

Money Matters

Bolivia is inexpensive to visit. By comparison, the cost of visiting Peru is double that of Bolivia and costs in neighboring Chile are about the same as in North America. For a comparable meal or hotel room in North America, you'll pay about four times what you can expect to pay here. Depending on your plans, daily expenses should be less than $25 for basic travel, food, accommodations and a beer or two. A frugal backpacker can travel on $10. If climbing or trekking in the out regions with a tour company offering an all-inclusive package, the cost will be $50 to $100 a day (climbing costs a bit more than trekking). Taking a jeep tour around the Salar or a boat trip down the Tuichi River will run $20 a day.

For the most part, Bolivians are honest, although I have met many hotel owners who try to squeeze more money out of foreigners, money changers who add hidden charges and tour operators who promise more than they can produce. Use the prices in this book as a guide only. Bartering may get a lower price, but if you are traveling during a festival in high season, prices will be higher. Be certain to clarify the fee for services. Even when taking a taxi, be certain that you and the driver agree on the cost for your ride before you get into the taxi. I always ask someone on the street or at the hotel what the fare should be. I found most taxi drivers honest.

All prices in this book are in US dollars. Because inflation is at 10% a year, it is unreasonable for me to use bolivianos. For each restaurant, hotel or tour agency, I give my personal impression, followed by a brief review. My impressions may have been influenced by who I saw and how they treated me. Once you have used the book for a while, you will have an idea as to what events and experiences interest me and what level of service impresses me. I like to bargain when it is clear that the seller expects it. I love the bargaining banter of the markets where high prices are sometimes tossed out to tourists just to see what happens. The ladies welcome the subsequent exchange as much as they would welcome a higher price. I bargain for hotel rooms, too. Restaurants have fixed prices.

■ Banking/Exchange

 There are numerous banks and money exchange houses, although some smaller towns (Copacabana) are sadly short of these services and other towns (like Riberalto and Guayaramerin) have none.

Some hotels in smaller places will exchange **traveler's checks**, but usually only if you are staying there. Banks don't usually exchange traveler's checks, but money exchange houses do (look for the Casa de Cambio signs). They are open from 9 am until 1 pm and then again from 4 to 6 pm. Neither banks nor money exchange houses are open on Sunday. There is often a cost that can go as high as 10% for exchanging traveler's checks and it is not possible to get a receipt that specifies the commission. This is because they know the commission is illegal. Some hotels, souvenir shops and tour agencies will take traveler's checks but, again, there is a cost. Ask before you make a deal.

You should always carry a few US dollars in cash in case you need fast money. The dollars can be exchanged for local currency anywhere, even in the smallest of villages.

American dollars or traveler's checks in American funds are the easiest to exchange. British pounds, German marks and Spanish pesetas are also readily accepted. Euros will become common soon, I am sure.

There are numerous **ATMs** in major cities and ENLACE machines are hooked into MasterCard, Cirrus, Maestro, Visa Electron, Plus and Visa systems. Bolivian banks that are hooked into ENLACE are Banco Nacional de Bolivia, Banco Santa Cruz and Banco Redito. Bisa ATMs also network with Plus. ENLACE, however, seems to be connected to the highest number of systems. The cost of exchanging money by an ATM is about $1.50 per transaction (rather than by percentage like traveler's checks) but some are as high as $3 per transaction. This service charge should be checked with your own bank in your home country. Most ATMs offer the option of being operated either in English or Spanish.

If your bank offers Internet banking, consider setting up access before you leave home. This means you can access your bank statements from any Internet café and see any charges made for ATM transactions. Most banks require that you register while in your home country.

Because the electricity is sporadic, occasionally the machine will cancel out in the middle of the transaction. If this happens, your card will be returned without explanation. Wait a minute and attempt the transaction again. Should your card be gobbled up and not returned, each ATM has an emergency number posted on the machine. English is often spoken at this number; if it is not, ask your hotel owner to help.

Major **credit cards** can be used to obtain cash from bank machines and they can be used in high-end hotels to pay for your room. Some places may charge an extra commission for using VISA/MasterCard/American Express. Report this to your VISA credit card office in your home city or call the international office at ☎ 800-336-3386, http://mastercard.com. The extra charge violates the contract agreement between the credit card companies and the merchant. American Express is not widely accepted in Bolivia at present. However, if you have a problem using their cards, place a collect call to them at ☎ 801-945-9450.

> **SAFETY ALERT:** When taking money from a machine, do so during business hours at a location inside a building. This reduces the risk of robbery or fraud by someone watching nearby. Street machines are seldom guarded.

If a machine takes your card, regardless of which company you deal with, or if you have any other problems, go to the ATC-SRL office on Avenida Camacho, in the Santa Cruz Bank Building, 11th floor, ☎ 231-4410, to report the incident. (See *Communications* for dialing instructions.)

In the event that you run out of all financial resources and need money sent from home, try one of the many Western Union offices around the country (there are 18 in La Paz and 20 in Santa Cruz). There are 110,000 Western Union agencies in 185 countries in the world. They are reliable and much quicker than any bank, although they may charge a lot for the service. In Bolivia, ☎ 800-10-5057.

You may occasionally encounter moneychangers on the streets, especially in places close to borders. The changers offer a peso or two less than Casa de Cambios for cash and are a good option if official change places are closed or far away. The changers exchange only dollars or currencies from neighboring countries.

■ Taxes & Tipping

There are no taxes on food or hotels, although some restaurants charge a 10% service charge. There is a **user fee** at bus stations and airports (for buses, it is 50¢; airports charge up to $2 for domestic flights and $25 for international flights).

Tipping is not the norm, although those accustomed to working in tourist haunts are starting to expect it. As anywhere, tipping should be at the discretion of the customer. I always tip for good restaurant service. The amount is always between 25¢ and $1.50, depending on the cost of the meal. Taxi drivers do not expect a tip, but if the service is good I tip (usually one boliviano, 13¢) and it is always appreciated. Hotel personnel should be rewarded if you stay in a place for a few days and if they cheerfully clean your room. These people make around $3 or $4 a week, so a small tip helps them out a lot. Baggage handlers at the airport usually get between $1 and $1.50, depending on the amount of baggage.

Going Metric?

To make your travels a little easier, we have provided the follow-ing charts that show metric equivalents for the measurements you are familiar with.

GENERAL MEASUREMENTS

1 kilometer	=	.6124 miles
1 mile	=	1.6093 kilometers
1 foot	=	.304 meters
1 inch	=	2.54 centimeters
1 square mile	=	2.59 square kilometers
1 pound	=	.4536 kilograms
1 ounce	=	28.35 grams
1 imperial gallon	=	4.5459 liters
1 US gallon	=	3.7854 liters
1 quart	=	.94635 liters

INCHES

CENTIMETERS

TEMPERATURES

For Fahrenheit: Multiply Centigrade figure by 1.8 and add 32.

For Centigrade: Subtract 32 from Fahrenheit figure and divide by 1.8.

CENTIGRADE		FAHRENHEIT
40°	=	104°
35°	=	95°
30°	=	86°
25°	=	77°
20°	=	64°
15°	=	59°
10°	=	50°

Travel Information

Dangers & Annoyances

Every country in the world has its robbers and petty thieves, whether you are in the polite society of Japan or the northern wilds of Canada. If you hang out in the slums of a large city where you are unknown, if you are staggering drunk in a back alley, if you trust a stranger to hold your cash while you run to the washroom, if you leave your pack or camera on the seat of your bus while you go for a *salteña*, you are going to have a sad tale to tell.

■ Common-Sense Precautions

Be aware of your surroundings. If you think you are being followed, go into a store or knock on someone's door. Make certain that expensive items like your camera or Rolex watch are out of sight. Carry only a bit of cash in your pocket and a larger amount in your money belt. Leave the rest in the hotel safe.

Be inside at night or take a **taxi** back to your room if you have been out late. Don't be **drunk** in public – it makes you an easy target. Don't get mixed up in the **dope** trade. The mandatory sentence for possession of cocaine is eight years. Remember that Latin Americans generally regard drug-taking as a sign of first-world decadence. They hate it. And Bolivia, due to the DEA, feels it is getting kicked around because of the indulgences of First World cocaine addicts.

Women should walk with confidence. If you appear frightened or lost, you are a target. Don't walk alone in non-populated places or along secluded trails.

In the event that you are grabbed or accosted in any way, create a scene. Holler, scream, kick and fight with all your might. However, if you are approached by someone with a weapon, let them have it all. Being dead or seriously maimed isn't worth any possession, including your virginity.

La Paz can be dangerous. With the average person from El Alto earning about $32 a month, money is in short supply. Your obvious wealth is a temptation. Most **robberies** are not violent. Personally, I found the hassles of Sucre worse than those of La Paz.

There are a few **pickpockets** in the larger urban centers. In Copacabana, where pickpocketing during festivals is notorious, the Bolivians swear that it is Peruvians who come to target unsuspecting tourists.

Another common place for pickpockets is along Calle Santa Cruz, just below San Francisco Square in La Paz. The street is crowded and the pickpockets like to separate tourists from one another and then go after their packs. Also look for quick-handed thieves at the bus station area around El Cementario.

A common trick to get you off guard is to have someone pour something onto your clothes or pack and then offer to clean it off. While they are cleaning your clothes, they are also frisking your pockets and bag. Move away from any such scene.

THE LATEST SCAM

You are approached by another "tourist" and asked directions or just engaged in conversation. The "tourist" claims to be from a neighboring country, which explains his accent and appearance. A second man will come up, flash an official "National Police" card and ask to see passports. The first "tourist" will readily turn over his passport; the idea is that you will do the same. If you refuse, the "police man" will offer to take you to the police station where you will feel safe turning over your passport. He will call a taxi on his cell phone. Before he gets to that stage, tell them where to go under no uncertain terms (I use strong profanity) and walk away quickly. Get into the nearest shop or hotel. These people are often armed and are considered dangerous. Their aim is to mug you inside the car.

The police in Bolivia wear uniforms and do not use taxis. You will meet plain-clothes Immigration officials at airports, bus and train stations. They will ask to see passports, often while the police are rummaging through your bags.

■ Emergency Assistance

Should you be robbed, report the incident to the **Tourist Police**, Plaza del Stadium, Olympia Building #1314, ☎ 222-5016. You should make a report to your consulate or embassy. This is important, as most embassies inform other travelers of the latest scams. The police will investigate irregularities in prices with tourist agencies, hotels, shows or car rentals and will fill out forms that will allow you to claim the loss on your insurance. The chance of retrieving your goods, however, is almost nil.

The tourist police wear green uniforms (the army wears camouflage green) and can be seen walking the streets. However, my experience is that any police person will give a foreigner assistance in the event of a problem. They are also good for directions.

Communications

■ Telephones

Bolivia's country code is 591. To call Bolivia from the US, dial 011-591, then the local number. To call the US from Bolivia, dial 1, plus the area code, plus the number. To call Bolivia from Canada, dial 011-591, then the number. To call Canada from Bolivia, dial 1, plus the area code, then the local number. If you are calling Bolivia from Great Britain, dial 00-591 and then the number. If you are calling Great Britain from Bolivia, dial 1, 44 (the country code), then the telephone number.

When in the country, only the city number and regional number are required. City numbers must be dialed only if calling from another city. La Paz's city number is 2. Regional numbers have seven digits.

For information, dial 800-10-4040. There is no charge for this service.

You may make a call from your hotel, from the telephones on the street or from the **Entel** and **Cotel** offices. If calling from the hotel, you'll pay almost double. Public phone booths require a calling card that can be purchased in 10, 20, 50 or 100 boliviano ($1.50 to $15) denominations. You may also call from a phone on the street that is like a private phone and usually on the counter of a street vendor's stall. This telephone is for local calls only and costs one boliviano (13¢). Calls from these phones automatically cut off after two minutes, at which time you will have to pay another boliviano to reconnect.

The author on a payphone in Santa Cruz, where booths are shaped as birds.

Locals calls are free from the phone offices. For long distance calls, the phones are often connected to a computer and display the time and cost as you talk. If you do not know a telephone number that you wish to reach, you must connect to an international operator to get it. If you know the country number, the area code and the telephone number you are trying to reach, you can call direct. The cost of phoning North America is $1 per minute and Europe is about $1.50 per minute.

■ Media

 The Llama Express, Avenida Arce 2131, Edificio Illampu, 10th floor, ☎ 244-1307, is an English-language paper that comes out once a month and is loaded with useful information for tourists. It contains travel reports, travel advice, restaurant reviews and entertainment listings. This free paper came to life to replace the much more elaborate *Bolivian Times*, a good weekly paper that has been bought by one of the dailies and is no longer in print. *Bolivia Touring* is another English/Spanish newspaper directed at tourists. This one allows you to read in Spanish and check your understanding by re-reading the article in English. It comes out on the 5th of every month and is distributed in tourist haunts in La Paz, Cochabamba, Sucre and Potosi and in major centers in Chile and Peru. If you have questions or comments, reach them at ☎ 241-4319, boliviatouring@megalink.com.

There are five daily newspapers in La Paz. All are in Spanish and cost around 50¢ each.

Bolivia has 125 **radio** stations, most of which are privately owned. I found none in English. Except for local stations, **television** is usually delivered by cable. There are 48 TV stations and all are in Spanish. English cable TV is available in a few hotels.

■ Real Mail & E-Mail

 Internet cafés are as common as shoe shine boys. Those cities that do not have cable connection charge about $2 per hour for Internet service, which is often slow. However, you can use the computer at a lower rate if not on line. Those with cable connection charge less than 50¢ an hour and the service is fast. If you want to connect your laptop to a cable outlet, go to an Entel office, where the hook-up charge is $4.50 an hour.

Postal service is fairly reliable. The cost to send a postcard or lightweight letter to North America is 50¢ and double that to get it to a country in Europe. It's best to send parcels from larger cities. If sending something valuable, insure and/or register it. There are also courier services like FedEx, UPS and DHL that cost about $30 to North America and more to Europe.

To receive mail, have it sent to "lista de correos" (the poste restante) in any large city. The mail is held for three months and in order to collect it you must have your passport for ID. The mail should be addressed to you, and then "Post Restante, Correo Central, City, District," with "Bolivia" clearly written on the envelope.

Culture Shock

Public affection is not uncommon in Bolivia. Young lovers can often be seen kissing, holding hands or hugging on a park bench. Anything beyond that is usually kept private.

Homosexual relationships exist, but public displays of such affection are dangerous. Homosexuality is treated as a perversion. In 2002 a group of lesbian feminists were filming a TV series on sexuality in Bolivia. The police beat and kicked the actors and tear-gassed the spectators. Many people suspected of being gay have been murdered or harassed. The constitution states that everyone has the right to a private life, but this means little.

There are a few organizations in Bolivia that promote equality for lesbigays. **Dignidad** was formed in 1980 in Cochabamba and in 1994 the first gay-day celebration was held. In 1995 the **MGLP**, a gay rights organization, was formed, and then **Mujeres Creando** for women was established. But members of these groups are often harassed.

Special needs travelers will find it difficult to travel here. Sidewalks are barely safe for walking with hiking boots, never mind trying to maneuver a wheelchair. The roads are mostly cobblestone, so crossing intersections is difficult. Wheelchair accessibility in hotels and restaurants is nonexistent.

At crosswalks or corners, pedestrians get no respect, even if they are in wheelchairs or have canes. However, police will help people cross if they notice that help is needed.

There are no communication services available for the deaf. Vision-impaired people use white canes and ask the same question (such as, "Is the light red?") until someone stops to give assistance. However, traveling with a seeing or hearing companion could make the trip an exceptional experience.

Traveling with **children** is always a positive in Latin American countries and Bolivia is no exception. There are many playgrounds and children's museums and hotels and restaurants can also be found that are clean and comfortable enough for little folk. Airlines give children under 12 a discount of 50%, but if they occupy a seat on the bus they pay full fare. Places like Dumbo's offer children's portions for meals and have play rooms.

Seniors will have to take common-sense precautions. Crossing roads could be a problem, as the traffic seems to aim at pedestrians; stoplights and crosswalks mean nothing, even if police are present. Use taxis and, on longer trips, hire a jeep rather than use public buses. LAB and AeroSur offer discounts on flights for anyone over 60.

Begging is as common in Bolivia as it is in any area in North America. Often, mothers with children will encourage their youngsters to hit up a tourist (they have the reputation of being a soft touch). However, there are genuinely hungry people who need a handout. This must be at your discretion. There are a number of ways to deal with this problem. You can purchase and carry food to give to people. You can allow yourself a daily budget and give no more than that amount. A friend of mine liked to have a beer at night, so he would purchase a beer at a *tienda* close to the hotel. The bottles required a deposit. When he returned the bottle, he left the deposit with the *tienda* attendant for her to give to whoever needed a handout, or he would give the bottles to a hungry-looking kid. Doggie-bags are common in most upscale cafés. I often had my leftovers put in these and gave them to a poor-looking family on the street.

Shoe shine boys in Bolivia wear face masks and have designated territories. In La Paz they are organized and have the opportunity to take some schooling. The government gives them ID (the kids pay for it) and the police resolve turf disputes. Although the syndication of these kids is not perfect, it is making life for them much better. The boys do a good job, offer a good service and usually don't hassle tourists much.

Shopping

■ Local Delights

Bolivia is known for its **Andean weavings**, pieces of material made from either llama, alpaca or sheep wool (vicuña wool is rarely used). The wool is hand-dyed and hand woven into designs that date back to times before Christ.

Indigenous people wear their weavings and make more to sell. There are co-ops to help the people in the outlying areas get a fair price for their work.

These days, it is rare to find a weaving that has been naturally dyed. Most textiles are woven on a heddle loom, set outside the home of the weaver. The other loom commonly used is the back-strap loom. Bolivian textiles have four selvedges because they use a continuous warp. After the threads are set up and the weaver starts, patterns are worked in by picking up the warp threads of different colors.

WEAVING A YARN

You will often see an Indian woman sitting with a spool in her hand, spinning wool or llama hair. This is the first stage of the spin. Next, two of these thin strands are combined to form a thicker strand. This is then dyed before the yarn is again spun. This process is unique to Bolivia. The third spinning is called the over spin, which produces a crepe twist, a yarn that is both strong and elastic.

Weaving designs indicate the social status of the weaver. The colors and positions of the stripes are usually artistic preference. Images of deities and mythical characters also appear on many pieces. Some of the more common figures are the llama, the condor and the puma.

If you want to purchase a weaving, distinguish between factory-made and hand-made pieces. Factory-made weavings are taking over the market and hand-made pieces are becoming harder to find.

> **LOCAL LOVE:** In the highlands, men make belts for their wives or girlfriends on a lap-loom.

Instruments, such as pan flutes, pipe flutes, charangos (ukulele-styled instruments) and drums, are found everywhere. One of my favorites is the musical rattle made of goat hooves. If you want to purchase good quality instruments, buy them from a reputable store in La Paz or Sucre. See recommendations under *Shopping* in these cities.

> **AUTHOR NOTE:** Be aware that charangos made of armadillo shells cannot legally be taken into North America or most European countries. The armadillo is a protected species.

■ Antiques & Silver

 Bolivia is inundated with new and old antiques. It is illegal to export any genuine antique without special permission. There is one shop in La Paz that sells good quality items not seen in the general market. Things like miner's lamps and saddle stirrups found in the market, although not classified as antiques, also make interesting souvenirs.

Buying silver in Potosi is a must. There are many designs copied from colonial days, plus some new items like souvenir teaspoons and letter openers. The purer the silver, the softer it is. The price for a nice letter opener is about $5.

LLAMAS OF BOLIVIA

The most famous constellation in the southern hemisphere is called the Southern Cross. Among the Quechua Indians who live on the Altiplano of Bolivia, the four bright stars and accompanying smaller stars represent a mother llama with her young (called crea). The Quechua weave a pattern, which conforms in part to the configuration of the Southern Cross. It is woven into the piece of material worn by the women for carrying children on their backs. The weaving is done with llama wool that has been colored by dies extracted from local plants.

The llama, because of its importance to human existence on the harsh Altiplano, also has become the focus of ceremonial life for the Quechua. Besides being a beast of burden, the llama, like the sacred cow of India, offers its excretion for fuel, and its hide for leather. Llama wool is spun and woven. Llama milk can be used whole or processed into a long-lasting cheese. Although llamas are not raised for food, after a llama's death the meat is eaten and the bones are carved into tools. No wonder this creature is so highly regarded.

As beasts of burden, llamas made trade between the people of the high Altiplano and the Pacific coast possible. After carrying loads of up to 100 pounds for hundreds of miles, the llamas were rewarded for each journey with earrings made from tufts of red sheep wool. One tuft was added for each completed journey. This tradition continues today, though the journeys are usually shorter.

The importance of llamas is also recognized in ceremonial practices. For more than 3,600 years the natives of Bolivia have made llama fetishes of stone, wood, wool and quinoa paste. These fetishes promote fertility, prosperity and downright good luck. Each year during festival time, they are carefully wrapped in a woven cloth and placed on the altars or buried in special areas. The following year they are unearthed, washed in *chicha* and rewrapped in a clean cloth. Prayers are said and then the fetishes are sprinkled with alcohol and re-buried in *panchan mama*, mother earth. For example, if a Quechua man wanted his female llama to successfully give birth that year, the man would bury a fetish in the llama's corral.

In the event that unfavorable influences from the Gods cause a mother llama to abort, the fetus is dehydrated and buried under the corner post of a newly constructed house, thus guaranteeing luck to the habitants of the new home. Llama fetuses are available at special stalls in the markets.

Travel Information

Food

Bolivian food is not distinctive, but the food is very good. There are llama steaks, *pico de la macho*, flan or *Para Ti chocolates*. I like to pick up fresh vegetables, homemade cheeses and crusty buns in the market and eat them in my room. I like the market cafés that specialize in specific meals or special soups, always hot and spicy. Street vendors serving their specialties like sausages or *salteñas* are worth a 10-minute wait. And restaurants like the Rincón Español in La Paz and Casa de Camba in Santa Cruz make French cuisine look almost second rate. I have had some of the finest Chinese food, steaks and pastas served up with Chilean or Argentinean wines by waiters in suits. There are also night clubs like Thelonius that make it worthwhile sitting up until midnight listening to first-rate jazz and digesting.

I also eat in the *tiendas* where the buses stop. Watch what you buy – see where the locals are flocking to and follow them. I suggest that you try things even if you don't have a clue as to what they are. That is what travel is all about. For the most part, you will be pleasantly surprised.

■ Meals of the Day

 Desayuno (dez-ay-OO-no) is the word for breakfast. My favorite is a fried egg placed inside a *panacita* (crusty bun) with a banana con leche (milk shake). Bolivians do breakfast in the street *tiendas*, with the big item being the *salteña* (see decription below). At the North American café-clones like Alexander and ice cream shops like Dumbos, you can get bacon and eggs or fruit with yogurt and granola.

> **WARNING:** Bolivianos do not eat toast and when they make it for tourists, the results are always disappointing. They use some sort of wonder bread and toast it on one side. My husband smuggles *panacitos* into places like Alexander to eat with his bacon and eggs.

Almuerzo (al-moo-ER-zo) is the main meal of the day, served from noon until two. Special restaurants make *almuerzo del día* for a reasonable price, usually just a couple of dollars. A typical *almuerzo del día* will consist of a lemonade or another type of drink made interesting with spices, a soup with noodles, meat, vegetables, French fries, and a dessert. Not all places serving *almuerzo del día* are the same. Sometimes black, red or blue potatoes are substituted for the fries. Sometimes the dessert is nothing more than a dish of gelatin. In smaller centers (away from La Paz), the *almuerzo* will be more traditional. In La Paz, the main course will be more like North American meals. There is almost always a sign outside the door of the restaurant advertising what is being served that day.

Cena (SAY-na) is supper and is usually a light meal served well after seven in the evening. Trying to get supper before seven is like trying to get a bus to depart on time.

■ Foods – The Good, the Bad & the Tasteless

Panacitas are fresh crusty rolls that are excellent eaten with some fruit or cheese. The rolls are so tasty you need no butter.

Mate de coca is a mild tea made with coca leaves and enjoyed by everyone. It is believed to stave off altitude sickness. This may be because of some chemical in the coca or because you are getting some of the four liters of water you should be drinking every day while acclimatizing.

Chicha is a beer brewed with aysuma and waltaco varieties of yellow corn (there are about 220 varieties of corn grown in Bolivia). *Chicha* is believed to be a drink of the gods. When made with a black corn, it is drunk while eating strawberries and cinnamon ice-cream. In small towns, *Chicha* bars have white flags flapping from poles outside houses.

WELCOME TO THE FAMILY, LLAMA

Upon arrival home after a long journey, lead llamas are given *chicha* that is placed in a special bowl called a *kerus*. These wooden bowls are always decorated with a llama, carved from wood and glued into the center of the bowl. Besides sharing the drinks of their owners, llamas are also considered family members and are often given family names.

Coffee in Bolivia is usually called *distilado*, but there is also a lot of Nescafé, so watch out. *Distilado* is a syrup that is made by pressurizing fine ground coffee through a device similar to an espresso machine and warmed on a stove. If a café has a cappuccino machine, the staff will often water down an espresso and serve it as regular coffee. This is quite good.

Usually you will receive a pot of hot *distilado* and have to add your own milk and water to it.

Salteñas are a pastry stuffed with meat and vegetables (the filling varies). They originated in Salta, just across the border in Argentina. They are Bolivia's original fast food and everyone eats them all the time. Fall in line. Some are good, some nondescript and some delicious. McDonalds couldn't compete with them.

Laguas is a tasty corn soup.

Escabeche are pickled vegetables used as a side dish or sometimes stuffed inside a sandwich.

Chejchi is a speckled gray and white corn that is toasted and eaten with butter. This corn can be picked up from the street vendors.

> **LOCAL LINGO:** If eye contact is made by someone eating when you walk through a restaurant, say *Bien Provecho* (bee-YAIN pro-BEY-cho) to them as you pass. The term is equivalent to *bon appétit* in French.

Pique a la Macho is a spicy stew cooked with Bolivia's special sausage and served over French fries. It can be good or bad, but most cafés know how to prepare it well.

Choclo is a white, large-kernel corn that is boiled on the cob and, in season, sold everywhere. It's good to keep you occupied on a bus, eating the kernels one by one.

Yucca is a root vegetable similar to potato. It has a stringy texture.

Potatoes need no explaining. However, the Andes has over 250 types of potatoes. Walk through the market and look at the different colors, sizes and shapes – you may not recognize some of them. They are served freeze-dried, fried, boiled, mashed, ground or raw. They can be white, red, yellow, black, blue or green and every shade between. The freeze-dried ones are the worst.

Surubi is a fresh-water catfish that is usually served grilled. It is excellent, as is the bonier **dorado**.

Llaucha paceña is a doughy cheese-bread sold at bus and train stations especially. I got the best I've ever had at the train station in Santa Cruz.

This is an excellent snack when catching an early train or bus. They are sold in bags containing about a dozen for a couple of bolivianos.

Tamales are made from cornmeal stuffed in the center with spiced meat and/or vegetables, rolled into a banana leaf and baked. They are usually made for fiestas.

Humitas are made with sweetened corn rolled into a banana leaf and steamed or baked.

Rellenos are a wheat flour pancake stuffed with cheese and deep fried. They are excellent and can usually be found in the markets.

Quinoa is a grain that grows at high elevations. It is high in protein and is often cooked in soups and stews. The plant comes in red, green or yellow and has clusters of grain along the upper portion of the stem.

Haba is short for *habichuela*, or bean in English. You will see it often growing in the fields – the flower is white and the bean is green and hides behind the leaves.

Singani is distilled wine produced in the Tarija area. Singani is the base for the cocktail called *chuflay*. It's excellent, but potent.

Changa de pollo o de conejo is a soup made with chicken or rabbit, potato, peas, beans and green onions. (*Conejo* means rabbit.)

Sandwich de chola is a roast leg of pork sandwich.

Chicharron are pieces of fried pork sausage cooked with *chicha*.

Lechon is roast suckling pig.

Papas a la huancaina are potatoes with cheese, boiled eggs, tomatoes and olives, topped with a peanut sauce.

Selecting a Place to Stay

■ Value & Pricing

When I describe places to stay, I make comments like, "The rooms have Inca beds." This sounds silly for those not familiar with Bolivia. However, an Inca bed is one that is hard as stone. Carpets are often dirty or moldy, so when I say a place has tile, that is good. The importance of a closet in a room will be appreciated after staying in a few rooms that have no place to put things. The electrical showers are freaky for Westerners so, whenever possible, I make it known if a water tank is actually in use. Also note that just because the price is high, it does not mean the quality is as well. For example, in Oruro, generally the prices are high and the quality is low. Read the descriptions carefully before choosing to stay someplace, especially if arriving late at night when you are unable to look around.

Be aware that sewers are not able to flush out toilet paper, so in every bathroom there is a garbage can where used toilet paper must be deposited. If your room has not been cleaned for a day, your garbage has not either. If this happens, place your garbage can outside your door and use a plastic bag.

To assist in planning, I have provided a dollar rate with each hotel description. The dollar signs represent the following rates.

HOTEL PRICES (US $)

Per person, per day, unless noted otherwise.

$. . . . . $2-$5

$$. . . . . $5-$10

$$$. . . . . $11-$17

$$$$. . . . . $18-$25

$$$$$ . . . . Over $25 (rates specified)

■ Types of Accommodations

Bolivia has numerous names for accommodations, each indicating to some degree the quality of room you will get. Here's a quick rundown.

- **Alojamientos** are basic with an Inca bed, heavy blankets and not much more. They usually, but not always, have shared bathrooms with hot showers. Depending on quality, a room costs between one and two dollars per person.

- **Residenciales/Casas de Huespedes/Hostels** are usually much better in quality than *alojamientos*. You should get a clean room with the choice of a private or shared bathroom and hot showers. These places often offer laundry facilities and have restaurants or kitchens attached. The cost runs anywhere from $5-$25 per person.

- **Hotels** are usually a bit higher priced and offer anything from dirty and drab to luxurious. Prices vary accordingly but seldom did I find a hotel room costing more than $50 for two per night.

- **Motels**, for the most part, are heavily secured places that rent rooms by the hour. Guess what happens there. The one across from the Villamontes bus station, when I went there, asked how long I wanted the room for. I said 24 hours. The proprietor looked at my husband with great admiration. Once I caught on, we went elsewhere.

∎ **Pensions** are for locals only and are boarding houses that do not rent rooms.

Getting Here

∎ By Air

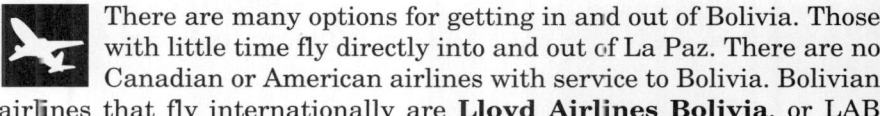

There are many options for getting in and out of Bolivia. Those with little time fly directly into and out of La Paz. There are no Canadian or American airlines with service to Bolivia. Bolivian airlines that fly internationally are **Lloyd Airlines Bolivia**, or LAB (☎ 300-337-0918 in US, 800-10-3001 in Bolivia, www.labairlines.com), **TACA** (☎ 800-525-8780, www.taca.com) and **TAM** (☎ 244-3487, www.tam.com.br).

Flying directly into La Paz is expensive and you run the risk of altitude sickness. It is much better to make your way up to this elevation slowly. If you do not have the time, a flight from Lima (Peru) or from Santiago (Chile) to La Paz is about $200. **Lan Chile** (☎ 800-735-5526, www.lanchile.com) and **Aerolineas Argentinas** (☎ 591-2-235-1711, www.aerolineas.com) also fly into La Paz. The other option is to fly into Santa Cruz via La Paz.

American Airlines, Pl. Venezuela #1440, Ed. Hermann, ☎ 235-3804 (local) or 800-433-7300, www.aa.com, now has daily flights from Miami direct to La Paz and Santa Cruz. The price, depending on the season, is about $600 for a return ticket. In my experience, American is an excellent company. I once had problems going to Venezuela due to a revolution and American looked after my safety first and then had the grace to refund my money.

Although we give airline contact numbers throughout this book, it is not advisable to work directly with an airline in Bolivia. One should go to a travel agent if purchasing a ticket.

∎ By Car

Driving into Bolivia is not recommended, but some people still do it. The roads are bad and you must have a four-wheel-drive vehicle and excellent Spanish skills to navigate the paper requirements. You must also have registration, insurance and a bill showing the value of the vehicle. Once in the country, every town has a control post and you must have papers permitting you to pass. If the papers are not in order, the bureaucratic quagmire starts. Also, the police, who are poorly paid, know you have money. Although many are honest, there are always some who will try every type of extortion possible to improve their incomes. It's worth noting that most ex-patriots who live in Bolivia do not drive because of the police hassles.

If you decide to drive, an International Driving Permit is required. If coming in with a motorcycle, it is best to cross during the early part of the day and not during the weekend. The paperwork takes a lot of time to process, partly because officials are not certain what to do with you.

Gasoline is available from international companies at all major centers. The national company is **YPFB** (Yacimientos Petroliferos Fiscales Bolivianos). In the back country and small villages, unleaded fuel may still be hard to come by.

■ Other Options

Consider flying into Santiago, Chile or Lima, Peru and then busing it into Bolivia. This gives you time to acclimatize. Others who are traveling the latest Gringo Trail that starts in Rio de Janeiro, Brazil, cross the continent from east to west, going through Bolivia to either Chile or Peru. These people usually travel by bus and boat. From Rio, you can travel to the Brazilian Pantanal and come into Bolivia at Puerto Suarez. Remember that travel through the Pantanal is cheaper in Bolivia than it is in Brazil.

Those with lots of time travel from Venezuela down to Brazil. Usually they bus to Manaus on the Amazon River and then catch a boat coming up the Madera. They eventually land in Guayaramerin.

You can also bus it up from Argentina or Paraguay.

■ Border Crossings

Tourist cards can be obtained at all border crossings and at both the La Paz and the Santa Cruz international airports. Do not lose this card, or you will be fined. If you overstay your visa (the time on your tourist card), the (negotiated) fine is $40, plus $10 in local currency. These fines take time to negotiate and process.

Crossing the Peruvian border at **Kasala** is no problem. Peruvian customs officials are far more difficult to deal with than those in Bolivia.

The **Desaguadero** crossing from Peru is often held up with transport trucks. This is a duty-free zone for the transportation of Peruvian goods to and from the Atlantic, so you may wish to avoid this crossing.

If coming or going to Brazil, the crossings are located at **Puerto Suarez** out of Santa Cruz and **Guayaramerin** in the northern Amazon area. I found officials here pleasant and easy to deal with. One official gave me 90 days when I was entitled to only 30.

There is one crossing into Argentina at **Villazon**, south of Tupiza and another at Yacuiba, south of Villamontes. This road goes down to Salta. Crossing into Argentina is smooth, easy and efficient. There are two roads going into Chile, one just south of Laguna Colorada and the other west of Sajama.

Crossing into Chile may be done just out of Sajama National Park at **Tambo Quemada** or east of Laguna Colorada on the **Uyuni Salt Lake** trip. I have not heard of difficulty crossing this border and it is done often.

Not many people cross from Bolivia into Paraguay. If you must, cross the Gran Chaco by bus or boat it through the Pantanal. Buses leave from Santa Cruz and travel down to Asuncion. Boats can be hired in Puerto Suarez to go into Paraguay. I heard of only one person who had problems with crossing from Paraguay. He couldn't get an entry stamp coming in and, when it was time to leave, he couldn't because he wasn't actually registered as being there. He eventually ran across the border to the Bolivian side where the guards let him in even though he didn't have the required stamps in his passport.

Bolivian border guards cannot extend visas; they can only issue new ones. Some people are eligible for 30 days, while others receive 90 days. This rule is stipulated by the government and changes constantly. At present, Canadians get 30 days, while Americans and Europeans get 90.

If you have questions or complaints about the border guards or the process, ☎ 0-800-3007, a toll-free number.

There are money-changers on both sides of all borders. Be aware that there are counterfeit Peruvian one-sole pieces being passed by changers at Kasala to tourists leaving Bolivia. Once in Peru, you will be unable to unload them. Ask a local to identify the difference between a legal coin and a counterfeit.

There are also basic bathroom facilities available at the borders. Drinks, *empanadas* and a few trinkets are offered for sale by street vendors.

If traveling from Peru to Bolivia, do not buy a ticket from Puno to La Paz as you will sit for a few hours in Copacabana waiting for your connection, even though there are other buses going to La Paz. However, it is highly recommended that you spend a few days in Copacabana.

Travel Information

■ Outfitters Who Do All the Work

 There are companies in Europe and North America who will arrange your entire trip. They meet you at the airport, take you on your tour, negotiate all accommodations, transportation and meals and, at the end of your stay, deliver you back at the airport. Some of these companies can also be hooked up with for one of their tours before you head out on your own. The following are a few of the better ones.

Kon-Tiki Tours & Travel, 940 Lincoln Road, Ste. 322, Miami Beach, FL 33139, ☎ 305-673-0092, 877-566-8454, www.kontiki.org, will take care of all your needs for short but interesting trips that are ecologically sound and culturally sensitive. You can go birding with them into the Amboro National Park and on the same trip into the Serrania Volcano area. They offer an Amazonian Safari around Trinidad where you will see capybaras, caimans, monkeys and, hopefully, the blue-throated macaw. Another birding trip goes into the Amazon rainforest, the Chaco woodlands and the Cerrado open pampas. Kon-Tiki also offers a trip to a remote area out of San Borja. This is a demanding excursion with a fair amount of hiking that is rewarded, of course, with lots of wildlife sightings. Popular tours include a visit to Madidi National Park for up to eight days or kayaking on the Mamore River for a week. The cost of these all-inclusive packages is just over $200 per day, per person, assuming you can live with a roommate in the hotels. If you want your own room, the price goes up. You must pay only your exit tax at the airport and, of course, any tips.

Andean Summits, 710 Calle Prolongacion Armaza, Sopocachi area of La Paz, ☎ 242-2106, www.andeansummits.com, is the best company for climbing/hiking activities. In business since 1992, Andean offers climbs for anyone from the curious with minimum skills to the intense climber who wants maximum technical difficulty. Besides helping you bag a high peak, Andean will take you rock climbing in places that are not usually explored by outsiders.

For trekkers, Andean covers routes that go to elevations over 16,500 ft/5,000 m with a gain of over 3,300 ft/1,000 m per day. This would be an arduous trip and acclimatization is necessary before starting. However, they also take people on the less difficult treks.

Andean Summits is affiliated with Gravity Assisted Mountain Biking, allowing you to customize your trip by adding a few days biking.

The guides have been trained and certified by groups like the German Alpine Club and The National Ski and Alpine School of Chamonix. All are members of the Bolivian Mountain Guides Association and some have had more than 25 years of experience in the mountains. There is one guide for every three or four people and one guide for every two people on technical climbs. The cooks, porters and muleteers are local people who are experienced and skilled at their jobs. The meals are exceptional.

Tours include round-trip transportation from La Paz, mules and porters, cooks, full board, specialized guides, common camping equipment (including two-person tents) and common climbing gear (including live ropes, ice screws, snow stakes and slings). Although they don't supply boots, crampons, ice axes and harnesses, these can be rented in La Paz. They do not provide your booze either.

Astronomical Tours, 149 NW 00 Highway Warrensburg, MO 64093, ☎ 888-734-0311, www.astronomicaltours.net or www.astronomicaltours. net/astrotours.htm, runs a specialized tour for star gazers and astro-photographers. Once a year they travel to a village on Lake Titikaka where they sleep most of the day and look at the heavens all night. The cost for a one-week, all-inclusive tour from Miami is less than $2,000 per person, including airfare. You may bring your own telescope, but luggage is limited to two bags of no more than 65 lbs/30 kg each, plus one carry-on of 45 lbs/20 kg. A certified doctor accompanies the trip in the event of altitude sickness among the star-gazers.

This company can include people of all levels of interest and understanding, from the curious outdoors person to the professional astronomer. During the tour you will learn about the Aymara and their understanding of the constellations. Serious astronomers are able to enjoy southern celestial objects not visible from the northern hemisphere such as the large and small Magellanic clouds, the *omega centauri* cluster and the *eta carinae* nebulae. Due to the high altitude and dry climate, vision is clear.

Explore Bolivia, 2510 N. 47th Street, Suite 204, Boulder, CO 80301, ☎ 303-545-5728, www.explorebolivia.com, has some excellent outdoor adventures. Their combination kayak/hike trip includes three days paddling around Lake Titikaka, visiting ruins and camping in secluded coves. The second leg of the trip includes a week-long hike through the Apolobamba region where the Kallawaya Medicine men live. This company looks after everything once you arrive in Bolivia. Their gear is North American quality and the food they provide is better than anything you would be able to prepare. I noticed when I did the Apolobamba hike alone, I had to do a lot of scrambling in La Paz to get together some reasonably good and lightweight food.

This company also offers a longer kayaking-only trip around the lake, as well as excursions specializing in climbing, birding, mountain biking and fishing that include terrain in the jungle and/or in the high Andes.

GAP Adventures, 19 Duncan Street, Toronto, Ontario, M5H 3H1, Canada, ☎ 800-465-5600, www.gap.ca, has a reasonably priced, 11-day tour called the Bolivian Discovery, that starts in La Paz and includes Sucre,

Potosi, Uyuni and Tiahuanaco or Chacaltaya. The cost is $683 for 10 days and their tours take a maximum of 12 people, with an average of eight or nine in each group. They cater to people in 22 countries, so there's usually a mix of cultures. Small groups allow for some flexibility with the itinerary. This company was able to get me a cheaper flight into La Paz than I was able to find.

GAP hires mostly Canadian leaders and has a bilingual guide who lives in Bolivia all year. Being Canadian, they have a relaxed way of traveling (I worked with them in Belize) so you get some free time to explore on your own or read a book if you prefer. They also understand the need to explore the local culture, food and customs so they support locally owned businesses. GAP also works with NGOs such as Conservation International, International Eco-tourism Society and the Charles Darwin Foundation. These partnerships keep the company up to date on the latest philosophies about conservation.

GAP also offers trips to the isolated Pantanal area with the largest wetland complex in the world. New species of fish and plant life are still being identified here. The World Wildlife Federation has declared the Pantanal an area of special concern.

For the more adventuresome, GAP offers a longer 146 days of touring from Lima, Peru through Bolivia and down into Chile. I highly recommend looking into this company if you want everything done for you.

Wildland Tours, 3516 NE 155th Street, Seattle, WA, ☎ 800-345-4453, www.wildland.com, offers tours that are ecologically sensitive and physically challenging. Wildland has been recognized by both *Condé Nast Traveler* and *National Geographic Adventure Magazine* as a company that follows the guidelines of ecotourism. One tour includes hiking across the Cordillera Real and over three passes at about 15,000 ft/4,600 m. It begins near Sorata and ends in the Apolobamba area. For acclimatization, they hike around Isla del Sol. For a grand finale, you spend your last night in La Paz at the luxurious Paris Hotel. The cost of this tour is about $150 per day.

Wildland also goes into Noel Kempff Mercado National Park in the eastern outback. This nine-day tour includes hiking, birding, picture-taking and seeing some of the country's unique landscape. Because of its isolation, this park is rich in wildlife. The cost is around $250 per day.

Footprint Adventures, United Kingdom, ☎ 01522-804929, www.footprint-adventures.co.uk, has a combination kayak/hike trip that takes 15 days, starting with your arrival in La Paz. They paddle around Lake Titikaka for two days and then head on foot from Sorata through villages such as Kukoyo and Waraco, and then on to Checapa Valley and Alta Khota. They eventually end at Condoriri. Sorata, where the hike starts, is at 8,500 ft/2,600 m elevation and the route goes up as high as 16,500 ft/

5,000 m. You will hike up and down for a few days, always staying above 13,000 ft/4,000 m. On the approach to Condoriri, you climb to 18,750 ft/5,700 m, where Juri Khota Lake is located. This is an amazing trek and if you want everything done for you British-style, check these guys out. The per day cost of $100 includes kayaks, English-speaking guides, cooks, camping equipment and mules that will carry up to 45 lbs/20 kilos of luggage. Not included in this rate are your high altitude clothing, sleeping bags, insurance or headlamps. I would assume alcohol and tips are not included either.

INFORMATION SOURCES

Government Tourist Offices, except for the occasional one that I mention in connection with certain cities, are not worth visiting. The workers have no material to share with tourists and less interest in giving information. Most seem to have been hired because they are related to someone important. It is best to get information from tour agencies. They have a vested interest in promoting their area and usually do so enthusiastically.

Getting Around

The standard of public transportation is not what most North Americans or Europeans are accustomed to. There are 25,100 miles/41,000 km of roads in Bolivia, 75% of which are dirt and gravel, in bad shape, and can be dangerous if they are in the mountains.

But conditions are improving. In 2002 the World Bank gave Bolivia a $77 million loan with no interest and the International Development Association gave them an additional $284 million at a low interest rate with 35 years to repay. The money was to be used for road improvements. One of the deciding factors for the loans was that there are about 1,000 fatalities a year due to road accidents.

Bolivia's rail system features 2,300 miles/3,700 km of narrow-guage track. During the last national transportation survey it was learned that the railway carries 535 million tons of freight and 2.4 million people per year. Passenger trains pass through major centers about twice a week, but it is the route between Oruro and Uyuni that is most often used by travelers.

■ Air Travel

Both La Paz and Santa Cruz have international airports and there are 12 domestic airports with paved runways throughout the country. Unpaved runways like the one in Rurrenabaque, for example, during rainy season cause delays in flights due to wet landing strips. The capital cities in all districts have paved runways.

Lloyd Airlines Bolivia, LAB, (Av. Camacho # 1456-60, La Paz, ☎ 800-337-0918 in US, 800-10-3001 in Bolivia, www.labairlines.com) offers a $300, five-stop ticket that must be used in 30 days. Fares when flying without the five-stop ticket are also low. For example, from Riberalta to Trinidad is $72 each way for a 1¼-hour flight; La Paz to Sucre is $62.50 each way for a 50-minute flight. There is no discount for purchasing round-trip tickets. Lloyd gives a discount for married couples, but they must have the same last name on their passports or show a marriage certificate. Lloyd also gives a 20% discount for anyone over 60 years of age. For this you must show your passport.

AeroSur (Av. 16 de Julio # 616, La Paz, ☎ 231-3233 or 336-7400, www.aerosur.com) is Lloyd's competition. Their service is excellent, but their prices are higher. A flight from Sucre to Cochabamba is $42 and it takes 35 minutes. A flight from Tarija to Santa Cruz is $98 and takes 50 minutes. AeroSur offers many of the same flights and discounts as Lloyd and, in addition, they reach some outback places that Lloyd does not.

TAM, Transport Air Militar (Plaza Estudiante #11931, La Paz, (☎ 244-3487, www.tam.com.br) is the military airline that also takes civilians into the places they service. TAM and Amaszonas Air, for example, are the only airlines going into Rurrenabaque or San Borja. A TAM flight from La Paz to Rurrenabaque costs $46.50 each way, a good deal considering that you are avoiding the Road of Death (see page 117). The only drawback with TAM is that you could get bumped from a flight if urgent military affairs dictate that a fat general needs your seat.

SAVE (Calle Federico Ziazo, La Paz, ☎ 212-1548) is a small company that flies between La Paz and Trinidad, between Trinidad and Cochabamba and between Santa Cruz and Puerto Suarez. I flew to Trinidad with them and found them excellent. We were low enough to be able to see the earthworks at the Llanos de Mojos.

Amaszonas Air (Av Saavedra #1649, Miraflores, ☎ 333-8263) is a small airline that does most of the transporting of passengers in the Amazon Basin to places that have only small landing strips.

■ Buses, Trucks & Taxis

 Micros are small vehicles (usually Toyota vans) that carry up to 25 people city-wide and cost 30¢ per person. They go to any part of most cities.

Minibuses are actually vans that carry 12 passengers, cost 30¢ to 50¢ per person and go anywhere in the city. Some run directly from downtown to the airport. These are safe and high quality. When these buses go out of the city, they are called *trufis*.

Colectivos are taxis that carry four people legally and go anywhere in the downtown areas of larger cities. *Colectivos* cost about 45¢ per person. A ride, not the price, must be negotiated. You put your hand out, the driver stops, you yell where you want to go and he either lets you in because he is going in that direction or he leaves you standing because he isn't.

Taxis cost around 45¢ per person within city limits and they transport only your party. I found taxi drivers to be some of the best people in Bolivia. Only once in seven months did I have a driver try to charge more because I was a gringo. But I always knew the price in advance.

From the airport in La Paz a private taxi to downtown costs about $7. A minibus caught just outside the airport door costs 60¢. If you arrive after a long flight, I recommend you take a taxi to your hotel, especially if you do not know the city.

There are over 100 bus companies in La Paz alone. Long-distance buses called *flotas* usually have numbered seats for passengers who leave from the originating station. Once out of the bus terminal, others may get on and stand in the aisles. If you wish to avoid this, book with a more expensive company. In the areas without a major terminal, buses are often crowded. Occasionally, they have sacks of corn or quinoa in the isles and the odd duck or chicken in the luggage rack.

Because there are lots of bus accidents, there are also many rumors about drivers being inebriated. I have seen only one driver take a drink and that was during the Christmas festivities. It seems to me that it is easier and maybe cheaper when it comes to insurance claims to blame a driver (especially if he is dead) for an accident rather than the bus. The poor roads and the fact that little maintenance is done on the vehicles, only repairs, contribute to accidents. Most long-distance bus travel is done at night and many roads going through the mountains are narrow, winding death traps.

All passengers boarding buses that are leaving from a bus terminal must pay a 25¢ tax before being permitted to board. Usually, the tax ticket, once you buy it, is pasted onto your bus ticket. However, occasionally when there is no tax booth a girl will stand at the door of the bus and collect the tax. She will give you a receipt.

Trufis are small buses that go between villages. They don't go much farther than 60 miles/100 km, at which point you can catch a second *trufi*.

Camiones are trucks that transport human cargo along with everything else from silver to beer. This is the most inexpensive way to travel, but with low cost comes low comfort and you may be subject to weather. If going up from lowland areas, you should have an extra item of warm clothing to put on with each thousand feet gained. Always ask locals as to the price of the rides or watch and see what they pay. There is no fixed fare, but it is usually about half the price of the bus. Occasionally, foreigners will be refused rides in the backs of trucks. If the trucks are full, the locals, who are the steady customers, come first.

You may catch a bus or truck either at the bus station or at the police post on the edge of town. If you go to the police post you give up almost all possibility of getting a seat. The only advantage is that you pay less.

■ Driving

Driving your own vehicle or renting one is not recommended. The police will not let you through check points without fines for papers that they may claim you are missing. In order to pass, you will have to pay graft. See *Getting Here*, page 77, for more details. However, if you must rent a vehicle, I have listed a few places in the appropriate chapter.

Bicycles are difficult to use because of the high altitude and narrow roads. Although some die-hards still enjoy cycling as a means of transportation, I don't. However, cycling as a sport is different. I have included bicycle tours in regional chapters.

Motorbikes are available for rent in Sucre and the company (Joy Rider) provides a guide to accompany you on a tour (see page 315). The guide is primarily there to get you around or through the checkpoints. Prices for these tours are most reasonable. Additionally, some American companies rent motorbikes at a cost of $2,000 per month.

■ Boating

There is one boat company that transports tourists between Puno, Peru and Copacabana on Lake Titikaka. See *Copacabana*, page 172, for that information.

GENERAL DIRECTORY

■ AIRLINES

Aerolinas Argentinas	☎ 235-1624	www.aerolineas.com.ar
Amaszonas Air	☎ 333-8263	
American Airlines	☎ 800-433-7300 or 235-3804	www.aa.com
AeroSur	☎ 231-3233; 336-7400	www.aerosur.com
Lan Chile	☎ 800-735-5526 or 231-7108	www.lanchile.com
Lloyd Air Bolivia	☎ 800-337-0918 (US)	www.labairlines.com
	☎ 800-10-3001 (Bolivia)	
SAVE	☎ 212-1548	
TACA Airlines	☎ 800-535-8780	www.grupotaca.com
TAM	☎ 244-3487	www.tam.com.br

■ OUTFITTERS & TOUR OPERATORS

Andean Summits	☎ 242-2106	www.andeansummits.com
Astronomical Tours	☎ 888-734-0311	www.icstars.com
Explore Bolivia	☎ 303-545-5728	www.explorebolivia.com
Footprint Adventures	☎ 01522-804929	www.footprint-adventures.co.uk
GAP Adventures	☎ 800-465-5600	www.gap.ca
Kon-Tiki Tours/Travel	☎ 305-673-0092/877-566-8454	www.kontiki.org
Wildland Tours	☎ 800-345-4453	www.wildland.com

■ CAR RENTAL COMPANIES

Kolla Motors	☎ 241-9141	www.collamotors.com
Localiza	☎ 244-1011	
American Rent-a-car	☎ 7720-0367 (cell)	
AdMo-Tours	☎ 245-1660	www.adno-tours.com

■ EMBASSIES

For foreign embassies within Bolivia, see page 518, in the *Appendix*.

■ EMERGENCIES

Tourist Police	☎ 222-5016	
US Center for Disease Control & Prevention		www.cdc.gov
Visa/Mastercard	☎ 800-336-3386	www.visa.com
		www.mastercard.com
Western Union	☎ 800-10-5057	www.westernunion.com

■ USEFUL WEBSITES

www.boliviabiz.com

www.bolivia.com (Spanish language)

www.bolivia-internet.com (Spanish language)

Travel Information

La Paz & Vicinity

*Altitude: in town, 11,916 ft / 3,632 m; at the airport, 13,392 ft / 4,082 m.
Population: One million-plus*

Introduction

La Paz is not a big city on the world scale, but it is certainly one of the more interesting ones. Built in a bowl created by the Choqueyapu River, the upper parts of the city stand 1,645 ft/500 m above the lower sections. Unlike any other city in the world, the richer neighborhoods are located at the lower levels. This is partly due to the fact that it is warmer and easier to breathe at the lower altitudes. Also, the pinnacles and spires of conglomerate rock and

clay that have been sculptured by wind and water make a dramatic backdrop for those living below them. The higher up the bowl one goes, the more unstable the land becomes and the more likely a landslide will occur.

The plazas, squares and Prado are well kept in La Paz and even in the depth of winter plants are tended to help make the city attractive. Street cleaners are out every day and local merchants regularly wash the area in front of their shops. On a clear day, Mount Illimani, a snow-covered monolith, can be seen as a sentry towering over the city.

MURURALA MYTHOLOGY

Illimani has three main peaks. The northernmost peak is 21,500 ft/ 6,500 m high, the central and southernmost peaks are about 21,000 ft/6,200 m. Nearby is Mount Mururala, a snow-covered mountain with a flat top that stands below Illimani. Mythology claims that Mururala was at one time a tall and vain giant. But Illimani threw a stone and yelled, "Sarjami!," which means "be off with you" in Aymara. The giant's head rolled across the Altiplano and came to rest near two sisters. The head became the mountain now called Sajama, Bolivia's highest peak, and the sisters are the volcanoes, Parinacota and Pomerata.

La Paz

National Congress, Plaza Murillo.

The restaurants of La Paz offer both an exotic and ethnic smorgasbord for visitors. Hotels can be found tucked between artisan shops and street *tiendas* that are selling everything from mounted tarantulas (not considered endangered) to silver soup tureens. The nightlife is peppered with everything from Andean pan flute music to jazz bars featuring world-famous players to wild discos and secluded piano bars.

More than half of the one million people living in La Paz are of pure Andean descent and many of them are in the streets promoting the arts of their culture or selling the produce of their relatives. The markets around Plaza San Francisco and Plaza Murillo bristle with fresh produce, hand-made artifacts and factory-produced junk. Every tour in the country can be booked through an agency in La Paz or the city can be visited solely for shopping or cultural events.

Getting Here & Around

■ By Air

Lloyd Air Bolivia and AeroSur fly to most places in Bolivia. Destinations not covered by these two companies are serviced by TAM, SAVE and Amaszonas Air (see page 87 for contact details).

Between them, these airlines provide numerous flights from La Paz. There are four flights a week to Cobija, 32 flights a week to Cochabamba, two flights a week to Guayaramerin, three flights a week to Puerto Suarez, two flights to Riberalta, 22 flights a week to Rurrenabaque, one daily to San Borja, 56 flights a week to Santa Cruz, 11 per week to Sucre, four a week to Tarija and three a week to Trinidad.

Approaching La Paz by plane, you will have one of the greatest views of your life. Ice-covered mountains surrounding the city glisten and the tin roofs of houses shimmer in the sun. Red rock and clay pinnacles around the valley contrast with sleek modern high-rise buildings.

The airport has two cafés, a cappuccino bar, souvenir shops, a tourist information office and a bookstore. The coffee bar, Alexander, is part of a chain with three other locations in the city. This is Bolivia's Starbucks, with a café menu. Upstairs in the airport, Burger King offers Nescafé and their familiar menu of burgers.

You will have to use public transportation to reach the hotel area. The airport is in El Alto, a place that is considered unsafe for tourists. A minibus (50¢) located just outside the airport doors goes on a freeway down a steep slope and along Avenida Santa Cruz, the city's main street. You must know where you want to get off, and then you must carry your baggage to the hotel. A taxi ($7 for up to four people) will take you all the way to your hotel. This is a fixed rate, with no room for negotiation.

TAM (☎ 244-3487, www.tam.com.br) has an airport beyond the international one at El Alto and it offers the only service to Rurrenabaque. A taxi to this airport from town is $5.50 for up to four people. The airport tax is 75¢ per person.

Often, TAM must cancel flights because their planes can't handle difficult weather conditions or wet landing fields so common in the jungle. Occasionally, they will land in Reyes, just a short bus ride from Rurrenabaque. If they offer you this alternative, it is a good one. If they cancel a flight and you can't make the next one, they will refund your money. The flights can be rocky. They do not pressurize the cabins and to protect your ears they supply cotton batten. Security is not intensive.

There is a restaurant (check your change), a very cold waiting area and an Inca Tour Agency office at the TAM hanger, along with a couple of small kiosks and usually someone selling things like chocolate bars, gum or newspapers.

■ By Bus

 If arriving by bus you will arrive either at the main bus station on Avenida Guachalla #494 and the corner of Calle Sanchez Lima, ☎ 241-6545, or the Cementario, which runs along Heroes del Pacifico. It is a 45-minute walk from Cementario to San Francisco Plaza and less than half an hour from the main terminal to the plaza. Taking public buses with luggage is difficult and dangerous. A taxi will cost about 50¢ per person.

The main bus station has 39 bus lines that service the country. There is one bus a day to Arica, Chile, 24 to Cochabamba, one to Iquiqu and one to Llallagua, 35 to Oruro, four to Potosi, 20 to Santa Cruz, four to Sucre, five to Tarija, one to Tupiza, three to Yacuiba and one to Uyuni.

For the most part, you can show up whenever you are ready and wait for the next run. However, for trips with just one or two buses per day, it's best to purchase a ticket at least a day in advance.

■ By Car & Motorcycle

Private vehicles with drivers can be hired to go anywhere you may wish to go. The cost ranges from $50 to $80 per day. I found **Huayna Tours** to be excellent (Calle Sagarnaga #398 at Illampu, ☎ 245-6717, berrios@mail.magalink.com). Their driver was cautious and courteous and the vehicle was in good shape. Jeeps are safer than buses for some routes.

Rentals

I don't recommend driving a car, but if you must, there are some reputable rental companies. Insurance is a must. Third-party liability coverage, although not compulsory, is highly advisable, despite the cost.

Kolla Motors, Calle Rosendo Gutierrex #502, between Sanchez Lima and Ecuador, ☎ 241-9141, www.kollamotors.com, has been in business since 1973. Most of the vehicles are fairly new, but when I asked about prices I got no response.

Localiza, Hotel Radisson, ☎ 244-1011, reserves@localizabolivia.com, has everything from a small Suzuki Swift to a Vagoneta Toyota Prado. Prices vary but a middle-of-the-list vehicle, such as a Vagoneta Suzuki Gran Vitara, rents for $68 a day with 92 miles/150 km at no charge and $420 per week with 643 miles/1,050 km at no charge. Localiza also has offices in Santa Cruz, Cochabamba and Tarija.

American Rent-a-Car, Avenida Camacho #1547, ☎ 7720-0367 (cell), has eight options of 4x4 vehicles. A Toyota jeep costs $70 a day with 122 miles/200 km at no extra charge. A Toyota Hilux truck is $60 a day or $400 a week, with up to 200 km/125 miles a day or 1,350 km/850 miles a week included in the price.

AdMo-Tours, Calle Illampu #815, ☎ 245-1660, www.adno-tours.com, rents motorcycles in Bolivia and Chile. You can get one with or without a guide. They have Honda XR 200R, Honda NT 400 Falcon, Honda XR

600R and 650R and Honda 750 Africa Twin. Without a guide they run $60 and $100 per day, $380 to $600 a week. With a guide the cost is $90 to $130 a day, $550 to $820 a week. For $100, they will handle all the paperwork and insurance needed to go to Peru or Chile. You must be 23 years old, have a valid and unlimited national motorcycle license and payment must be made by check or credit card. If reserving a motorcycle, you must pay four weeks prior to rental date. Cancellation fees are minimum $100 and no-shows are subject to full payment.

History

La Paz was originally a stop-off place for silver caravans going from Potosi to the coast. Mostly, the caravans stopped to dump passengers or llama skinners who got sick. Life in this outpost must have been pretty boring until some young officer decided to try his hand at gold panning and came up with a bundle. The city started to grow.

Peace was never a lasting thing in Bolivia, mostly because the Indians were treated so badly. The Spanish greed caused no end of hardship for locals and struggles for power continued among the Spanish. **Pedro de la Gasca**, the ruler of the area, beat the ruthless **Gonzalo Pizarro** at the battle of Saxahuana on April 9, 1548. In celebration, Gasco ordered **Alonzo de Mendoza**, who presided over the area now called Bolivia, to build a new city to honor this event.

On October 20, 1548, Mendoza declared the city of Nuestra Señora de la Paz to be that place. The specific site he chose was Laja, located on the Altiplano above the valley where land was barren and winds were fierce. It didn't take long – just three days – for the inhabitants of the city to move down into the valley of the Choqueyapu River where it was warmer, where there was fresh water and where the soil was rich enough to grow food. The city, its name shortened to La Paz, started to grow. Just over 100 years later there were over 500 Spaniards living in La Paz, on the river's west side, and twice as many indigenous people living on the opposite side of the river.

Within the first year, **Juan Gutierrez Paniagua** was hired as the city planner. His greatest achievement was the design of Plaza Murillo (then called La Plaza de los Españoles). The government buildings and the cathedral were placed on the square.

■ Turbulent Times

 From the time of its inception to present day, there have been many uprisings in La Paz. The first involved the native population, who became tired of the oppression imposed on them by the

Spaniards. Their long history of rebellion began. **Tupac Katari**, an Aymara, in 1780 led an army into La Paz. They held the city under siege for 109 days, during which time they burned and destroyed many of the buildings. Men on both sides died in great numbers. The Spaniards sent an army strong enough to force the Aymara to retreat. However, within a short time, the Aymara returned. They dammed the river with the idea that it would be released with enough water to flow down to the valley in a huge torrent and kill everyone below. The dam broke on its own and did cause some damage, but not enough to cripple the town. Peace again came to the city, but trouble lay below the surface. Discontent throughout the country came as the people wanted independence from Spain and La Paz again suffered through the struggle. By the time Bolivia became an independent country, La Paz had close to 50,000 people.

But even after independence, quiet times didn't stay. There were battles between Sucre and La Paz as both wanted to be the center of government. A compromise was reached with Sucre remaining the capitol and the judicial center, while La Paz became the seat of government.

The next major event was the **Revolution of 1952**, when the government gave in to pressure from the MNR socialist party, representing *campesinos* and miners, to redistribute land and control the mining industry. When this happened, many displaced tenant farmers moved to La Paz.

The latest event, dubbed the **Tax War**, occurred in February of 2003. At that time 33 people were killed in the streets of La Paz when the military started firing on striking police who had stormed the legislature. Hundreds were injured, stores were looted and government buildings were burned. The police were protesting a proposed income tax that to them seemed unfair.

Services

■ Useful Numbers

Ambulance, ☎ 118

Fire, ☎ 119

Police, ☎ 237-7385

Hospital, ☎ 222-9180

The **telephone office** is on Avenida Ayacucho #267, between Calle Camacho and Calle Mercado. It's open from 7:30 am until 10:30 pm daily. This is the main office; smaller offices are dotted around the city. Booths here are hooked up to a computer so you can see a digital display with your time and charge.

■ Communications

 The **post office** is on Avenida Mariscal Santa Cruz and Calle Oruro. It's open 8:30 am to 8 pm, Monday to Friday, and 9 am to 7 pm on Saturdays. Postage fees are about the same as in North America or Europe.

Photocopy shops are everywhere. A large business that has many machines will charge 25¢ for one 8x11 form, while a small company may charge as little as 15¢.

Hacker's Internet Service, Avenida Sopocachi #2241, ☎ 212-0396, is in the plush area of town. The machines are fast and easy to use. There are as many Internet cafés in Bolivia as there are shoe shine boys, so finding a machine is never difficult. Prices vary according to service providers. If the service uses telephone lines, the average cost is $2 per hour; if there's a cable system, the cost is 50¢ an hour.

■ Laundry

 Laundry service is usually offered at hotels. There are also laundromats in town. The following are good and located near the tourist hotels. **La Famelia Laundry**, Calle Tarija #340, ☎ 239-2943, 8 am-6 pm, charges by the kilo and does a good job. Unlike many laundry companies in town, this one opens on time and has things ready before your agreed time. **Lavenderia Maya**, Calle Sagarnaga #339, ☎ 248-5639, charges by the kilo and will deliver your clothes to your hotel. They offer same-day service.

■ Maps

 Maps are available from the government office on Avenida Bautista Saavedra in Miraflorez, open 8:30 to noon and 2:30 pm to 4:30 pm. (Another office, located on Calle Juan XXIII, on a dead-end street off Calle Rodriguez, between Calle Linares and Murillo, does not supply maps for trekkers, even though other guidebooks may direct you there.) **Guzman** (☎ 273-3124, rguzman@acelerate.com) are the best Bolivian-made maps. A topographical map of Sajama, for example, costs $6. **Tu Musica**, Calle Sagarnaga #189, shop 17, ☎ 231-9162, has Berndston & Berndston maps, some trekking and climbing maps, road maps, Guzman maps and city maps.

■ Medical Centers

 UNIMED, Avenida Arce #2630, is a large association of general practitioners and specialists who charge $7 per visit. They patronize a laboratory across the street, Lab-tek, Avenida Arce and Campos, Edificio Illimani, #4, ☎ 243-1988. I think the lab needs some quality control training. I witnessed a patient take in a fresh stool sample to be tested for parasites. The lab stuck it in the fridge until late in the day, by which time the bugs had died. The patient continued to get sick and had to be treated by a doctor who, because of the faulty lab tests, didn't know what he was treating. If you need testing, have your doctor insist that the work be done when it is brought in. Blood tests run about $5 and stool examinations are $8.

Dr. Luis Jesus Garcia, Calle Chichas #1222, in lower Miraflores, ☎ 224-2974, is a general practitioner who has been trained in Europe. He is often recommended by the hotel administration. He will insist on coming to your hotel room and will charge $40 per visit, a steep fee for Bolivia. However, he speaks English well and gives fairly good service.

■ Outdoor Adventure Clubs

 If you are serious about climbing or skiing, you may contact either of the following clubs and go with locals. Contacting them gives you an "in" to places not mentioned in guidebooks and so not inundated with tour groups.

Club de Montañismo Halcones is actually based in Oruro at Casilla #179, cmh_oruro@yahoo.com (I could not obtain a phone number). Halcones translates into hawk or falcon, and this is a hang gliding club. A lot of their gliding is done around Lake Titikaka.

Andino Boliviano, Calle Mexico #1638, Casilla de Correos #1346, ☎ 232-4682. This organization registers solo hikers and climbers. During ski season, they will also go up to Chacaltaya to ski. They hire a van if the numbers warrant it. Foreigners are welcome.

Gravity Assisted, Avenida 16 de Julio #1490, ground floor of Edificio Avenida, ☎ 231-3849, www.gravitybolivia.com, gravity@unete.com, is for cyclists. If you would like information on places to cycle, to have your bike fixed, to purchase parts and to get information about weather, altitude or safety conditions or just to hang out with other cyclists, this is the place.

Hash House Harriers is for hashers (runners), www.lapazhash.com, ☎ 279-1524. A sister group in Santa Cruz offers a group run, followed by a dinner/party (see *Adventures on Foot*, page 116, for details).

Festivals

Make an effort to be in La Paz for one of their special festivals and you will be well rewarded. The people are friendly and you are invited to join in the fun. Besides the big events listed here, most Saints' days are celebrated with traditional food and drink. Dates for these events can be obtained from the tourist office on the Plaza Estudiantes, at the south end of Avenida Santa Cruz.

■ Alasita

 Alasita ("buy from me" in Aymara) is held in honor of the god of fertility, happiness and prosperity. Known as Ekeko ("dwarf" in Aymara), he is a miniature doll, a stout smiling guy loaded with everything from money to musical instruments to food, from coca leaves to vehicles – anything that a living person may want. According to tradition, Ekeko, carrying the objects desired, should be purchased at noon on the 24th and blessed in a ceremony that uses alcohol, confetti, paper streamers and candy. He should then be blessed again with holy water. The hope is that the items your Ekeko carries are what you will be blessed with the following year.

> **WHAT MORE COULD A MAN WANT?**
>
> Originally, Alasita was a celebration by the Aymara of the spring equinox and was in honor of the coming crops. The Spaniards changed the date of the celebration to the end of January for whatever reason. In retaliation, the Aymara made the festival into a mockery of the Spaniard's greed by creating Ekeko and loading him up with every conceivable item that could be purchased.

The event starts during the final week in January and lasts for two weeks. During this festivity, the city holds the largest handicraft fair in the country. It takes place in the grounds of the old zoo, across from the open-air theater. Ten thousand merchants play host to almost 100,000 visitors during this fair. They come from as far away as Argentina and Peru, bringing everything from horses, llamas and alpacas to handicrafts. Besides purchasing items such as weavings, jewelry, leather goods, wood carvings, books, paintings, sculptures and crystal, you may get to taste some specialty dishes of La Paz such as *chairo*, a freeze-dried potato cooked in a lamb soup, or *plato Paceño*, with corn, cheese, beans and potatoes cooked together.

La Paz

■ Carnival

 Carnival, held 40 days before Easter, is good here, although the best celebration is in Oruro. In La Paz, the event goes for four days with parades, drinking, eating, blessings and dancing. Spectacular costumes are worn in parades and there's music from the country's diverse cultures. On the Tuesday, Ch'alla is held, in which possessions are blessed by sprinkling a little wine made specially for the event. Goods include houses, cars and other items of value. People decorate their houses with streamers and sprinkle confetti on friends. Everyone visits and shares *chicha*.

The big thing during Carnival is to douse friend, foe and tourist with water. No one is spared. The most popular strategy is to fill a balloon with water and launch it at someone. Market ladies fill and sell buckets of *globos* all day long. Standing on a balcony with a bucket of water ready to dump is also common. During Carnival, rain gear is essential.

DEADLY GLOBOS

Some protestors are trying to have *globos* abolished because people have been injured and killed by them. During the 2003 Carnival, 11 people were killed in La Paz from the over exuberance of the festivities, although not all deaths were caused by the throwing of *globos*.

■ Gran Poder

 Gran Poder (Great Power), held in June, is almost as extravagant an event in La Paz as Carnival is in Oruro. First held in 1939 as a candlelight procession in the El Alto area and featuring a statue of Christ at the head of the line, it has grown to include all La Paz residents. Although it is no longer a candlelight event, Gran Poder is celebrated with a parade, costumes, dances and fiesta-type activities.

One dance satirizes the lords of long ago doing the minuet, but the costumes are bastardized imitations from the time of Philip II. Other costumes are imitations of court dresses from the 17th century. One popular dance is the Waca Tokhoris (dancing bulls), where a stuffed bull's head and dried bull skin is put on and then covered with traditional clothes. The bull is accompanied by a milk maid carrying a tin jar, typical of the old milk vendors. The two figures dance through the streets. But it is the Dance of the Devil that is most popular because of the elaborate costumes. The devil, or *tio*, is the guardian of Bolivian mines. He receives offerings of *chicha*, coca leaves and cigarettes in exchange for safety and prosperity in the mines. During the festival, he is the featured dancer.

Other dances are performed in memory of tribes no longer alive and still other dances celebrate the grape and apple harvests. The parades go through the downtown area of La Paz, ending on Calle Camacho.

The date of this fiesta changes yearly (though it always takes place on a weekend) so you must check with the tourist office or your hotel owner. If you are unable to attend the actual event, you may take in the practice session that occurs the weekend before.

■ Smaller Events

 September 28 is **World Tourism Day**, where promotional booths are set up along the Prado. There are also events like cooking competitions. Tickets to tourist events are raffled off.

October 20 is the day La Paz was **founded**. You can read about the city's history above, but it's more fun to come and join the parties and parades.

The **Festival of Todos Santos** takes place on November 1 and 2. Locals bring special cakes, breads and candies to the cemetery and offer them to their ancestors. It is believed that the spirits come back to earth at noon on the first and return to the beyond 24 hours later. The living people also place plastic wreaths, flowers and ribbons on the tombstones. This event often features a band.

Over a million people call La Paz home. (Photo courtesy of Joy MacKinnon)

La Paz

Sightseeing

■ City Sights

→ **City Tours** are offered by a number of companies and I recommend them for first-time visitors. They usually run for a couple of hours in the morning and again in the afternoon, with a break in the middle of the day. The cost is around $10 for the day. English is usually spoken or piped through an audio system that you hear with earphones. All city tours will take you to the richer parts of town to see modern-day Hidalgo homes, past the golf course and through the Valley of the Moon. Along the way are a few other interesting buildings and monuments. The other half of the day is used to visit one of the Miradors, plus the center of town and its historical buildings. One of the companies runs the tour on a double-decker, British-styled bus. If you sit on top – where you look like an exhibition piece – you get good views. Those prone to motion sickness should choose an ordinary bus.

Vesty Pakos Zoo, just past Valle de la Luna, is the world's highest zoo. It houses 63 species that include snakes, birds, llamas, lions and even a jaguar. The zoo sits at 10,740 ft/3,265 m in an attractive landscape. The animals have spacious quarters and the care given them is fair. However, as with many zoos, money is scarce. The 50¢ admission hardly covers the birdseed needed for one parrot for one day. The zoo is open from 10 am to 6 pm daily. To get there, take a bus from Plaza Estudiantes to Zoologia. At time of writing, the veterinarians affiliated with the zoo were trying to get an "adopt the animal" program going so outside interests could help improve the facilities and the life of the animals.

1. La Recoleta
2. Cathedral
3. Santo Domingo Church
4. San Francisco Church
5. San Pedro Church
6. San Calixto Church
7. Cemetery, local buses
8. Teatro al Aire Libre
9. Calle Jaen Museums
10. Museo Tambo Quirquincho
11. National Art Museum
12. Museum of Ethnic Art & Folklore, Museo de Arte Sacro
13. Presidential Palace
14. Coca Museum
15. Casa of Marina Nuñez del Prado
16. Natural History Museum
17. Museo de la Revolution National
18. Textile Museum
19. Children's Museum, Cable Car
20. Templete Semisubterraneo
21. Valle de La Luna
22. Mallasa National Park
23. Campo De Golf
24. Vesty Pakos Zoo
25. Obsevatorio de Aves
26. The Prada
27. The Witches Market
28. Mercardo Negro

to Mirador Andino
Jach'a Apacheta &
Bus Terminal

La Paz
Sights

HUNTER PUBLISHING

© 2004 HUNTER PUBLISHING, INC

Mirador Killi Killi

Mirador Parque Laykakota

Mirador Monticulo

1200 FEET
400 METERS

to Mirador Andino
Jach'a Qullu

■ Historical Churches

Most churches are open all day and visitors are welcome as long as they don't disturb services. There is no charge for this, unlike Peru where one must pay to visit historical churches.

San Francisco, on the plaza of the same name, was the inspiration of Francisco de Los Angeles. Construction was completed in 1549. The original building was of mud brick, but it crumbled under a heavy snow fall. The replacement was built between 1743 and 1753 of stone from the quarry in Viacha. The outside of the church is designed in mestizo-baroque that includes mythological creatures, pumas, fruits, birds and flowers that are integrated with ornate European design. Over the entrance is a carving of San Francisco himself, welcoming the peasants to prayer. The interior is ornate and has a gold altar, numerous paintings and richly dressed statues.

At the top end of the plaza is a stone carving known as ***Pucara***, where meetings (usually political) are held and hundreds of people gather. The carving represents the melding of all Bolivian cultures.

Santo Domingo on Calle Ingavi Yanacocha was completed in 1760 and, like San Francisco, is a mestizo-baroque design. By 1760 the design was nearing the end of its popularity. **San Pedro Church** on Plaza Sucre, built in 1790, has a façade that shows the end of the baroque period and the beginning of the neoclassic style.

For examples of neo-gothic architecture, visit the **San Calixton** church on Calle Pichincha near Avenida Jaen. It was built in 1882. **La Recoleta,** on Avenida America between Calle Pando and Plaza Alonzo de Mendoza, was finished in 1894 and is also an example of neo-gothic architecture.

The **Nuestra Señora de La Paz Cathedral** on Plaza Murillo was started in 1831 and completed in 1925. It sits next to the palace that is guarded by men in antique red uniforms. The cathedral is an imposing structure known mostly for its stained glass windows. Set on a hill, its entrance on Calle Potosi is 39 ft/12 m lower than the main entrance on the square. The interior features Corinthian columns at the entrances and five naves in all.

■ Architecture

Templete Semisubterraneo is across from the stadium at the end of Avenida Bolívar. This is a reproduction of the temple at Tihuanaco. At one time the main statue was the original, but that was moved to the Archeological Museum and replaced with a reproduction.

The **Presidential Palace** on Plaza Murillo is also called Palacio Quemado (Burnt Palace) because of the many fires the building has endured in the past. Most were set in rebellion against the presiding government. The Spanish, in 1810, hanged Don Pedro Murillo for treason in the square now bearing his name. Then, in 1946, a mob of angry women, mostly widows, grabbed President Gualberto Villarroel and hanged him from a lamppost in the same square. He was held responsible for the deaths of their husbands. There is a statue of Villarroel in the square commemorating his life, rather than his death. Outside, the guards dressed in colorful uniforms have a difficult time not smiling when you take a photo. They have a ceremony every day at dusk to remove the flags from the flagpoles across the street.

Adventures

■ Adventures in Culture

If you want a panoramic, colorful, and unique view of Bolivian history, culture, and artifacts, a visit to this group of four museums is a necessary and well-spent morning or afternoon. To reach the **Calle Jaen Museums**, walk up Calle Jaen to Avenue Sucre to the Museo Costumbrista. Purchase your $2 ticket here; it's good for all four museums – Museo Costumbrista, Museo del Litoral, Casa de Don Pedro Domingo Murillo, and Museo Metals Preciosos Pre-Columbinos. The museums are open Tuesday to Friday, 9:30 am to noon and 12:30 to 2:30 pm, and on weekends, 10 am to 12:30 pm. On Saturday there is no admission fee.

La Paz

Museo Costumbrista, Calle Jaen and Calle Sucre, ☎ 237-8478, shows La Paz and Bolivia in an array of pictorial representations of historic events, landscape paintings, photos, sculpture and ceramic doll displays. The six- to eight-inch dolls are boxed in glass cases and depict Bolivian life in various contexts: carnivals, rural life and historic struggles. The execution of de Murillo in 1810, for instance, is displayed in three scenes laid out in a glass case 16 ft/five m long. There is lots of color, detail and craft in this unique and imaginative way to tell a people's story.

Museo de Litoral, Calle Jaen #798 (no phone), showcases Spanish army uniforms, military scenes in watercolor, displays of swords, pistols, rifles, antique historical maps and life-size mannequins chronicling the war with Chile in 1884 when Bolivia lost its sea connection to the rest of the world. If you go to Copacabana on Lake Titikaka, you will see the remnants of the Bolivian navy: a few sailors, a few boats and, as one sailor humorously boasts, a large fleet of Bolivian submarines.

Museo de Metales Preciosos Pre-Columbinos (Gold Museum) at Calle Jaén #777, ☎ 237-1470, is a comprehensive precious metal museum showing pre-Columbian gold, silver and copper work. In one room, you enter a safe 12 inches thick that contains gold medallions, bracelets, earrings and beautiful gold headdresses inlaid with lapis azure stones. Needless to say, the few friendly guards here carry guns.

Casa de Don Pedro Domingo Murillo, Calle Jaen #790, ☎ 237-5273, is a museum that holds a collection of colonial furniture, textiles, glass ware and household bric a brac – typical possessions of the colonial classes. Interestingly, this museum was once the home of Pedro Murillo, who led a revolution in La Paz in 1809. For history buffs tracing Bolivia's 188 revolutions, see the painting *The Execution of Murillo*.

Museo de Instrumentos Musicales, Calle Jaen #711, ☎ 233-1077, holds a vast array of unimaginable instruments. The pan flute and its distinct sound symbolize the music of Bolivia, and here you will see the instrument's multiple types and sizes; one set of flutes (aerophonos) is taller than a man. The hundreds of guitars on display range from standard shapes, to one odd invention with five necks that circle the sound box. The drums are wonderful, wonky and out of round, with llama hide heads complete with hair. This incredible range of unique instruments, from the ancient to the conventional and contemporary, is of interest for its surprise, range and novelty. Admission is 75¢, a bargain.

The above museum profiles were written by Barry McKinnon from Canada.

National Art Museum, Calle Comercio, on the corner of Socabaya near Murillo Square, ☎ 237-1177, is open Tuesday to Friday, 9 am-12:30 pm and 3-7 pm, Saturday and Sunday, 10 am-1 pm. Admission is 50¢. The museum is located in a colonial structure built in 1775 by an official, Don Tadeo Diez de Medina. He was the Hearer of the Audience of Charcas, a position in the government similar to Speaker of the House in British/Canadian parliament. Construction materials used are lime, stone and brick. The building is square, three stories high and has a central patio. The arched walls surrounding the patio form hallways that are decorated with wood benches and large old vases.

It was inaugurated as a museum in 1964, and the religious art is dominated by paintings of Potosi's Mellchor Perez Holguin (1660-1735). Born in Cochabamba, Holguin moved to Potosi early in life and spent all his time in his adopted city. His paintings are of the Hispanic-American baroque style and his first works are in the Banco Central in La Paz. He started by painting for rich Pososi families, like the house of Micaela del

Castillo, but soon moved on to painting religious characters. All of his characters have definite indigenous features, rather than European.

The second school of art represented is in the Rollao style from the Lake Titikaka area. The greatest artist from that school was Leonardo Florez, a mestizo who worked around 1680. His painting, the *Adoration of Shepherds*, was reproduced on one of Bolivia's postage stamps.

Cecilio Guzman de Rojas and Arturo Borda, whose works are also featured in the museum, are credited with changing art in Bolivia. Guzman, born in Potosi, is known for his indigenous style, while Borda's subjects were always about the city of his birth, La Paz. Borda was also a respected author. These men worked in the first half of the 20th century. Another artist represented here is Marina Nuñez del Prado, who has international acclaim and a museum of her own in the city.

The most prized painting in the museum is the *Virgin of Peregrina*, the virgin saint of wanderers or pilgrims. This painting has a wall all to itself with soft lighting that seems to enhance the features of the virgin.

A large collection of 20th-century art includes a gown worn by a woman friend of Fujimoro, a recent president of Peru. Apparently, Fujimoro and the woman came to La Paz and danced together so that photographers could capture them on film. At the foot of the case holding the dress are copies of the photos.

The museum sells books in English or Spanish about Bolivian art.

Museum of Ethnic Art and Folklore, Calle Ingavi #916, on the corner of Jenaro Sanjines, ☎ 235-8859, had a photographic display of Javier Hinojosa when I was there. Displays change monthly. The photos I saw were black and white representations of Maya ruins in the Yucatán, Mexico. The display was well-lit and allowed plenty of room for each piece. The rest of the museum, located in a house built in the late 1700s, contains weavings and dolls. The weavings are from different regions and are laid out in drawers below an antique weaving from the same area. You'll see many variations of each style. I couldn't see enough. There's no entrance fee. If you go to just one museum, make it this one.

La Paz

POETIC LICENSE

Poet Jaime Saenz was born in La Paz in 1921 and by 1955 was an accomplished novelist, essayist and poet. He was influenced by Germans such as Nietzsche, the philosopher, and Wagner, the musician. As a poet, his work was considered dark, but he claimed that in order to understand the light, one needed to know dark.

Museum of Natural History, Calle 26, Cota Cota, ☎ 279-5364, is open Monday to Friday, 8:30 am-12:30 pm and 2:30-6 pm. It contains specimens of plants, animals, rocks and fossils from all around the country. A visit to this museum will give you an idea of how diverse the natural environment is.

Casa of Marina Nuñez del Prado, Avenida Equador #2034, ☎ 232-4906, displays sculptures by this famous Bolivian artist, teacher and sculptor. Born in La Paz in 1910, Nuñez studied art at the National school of Fine Arts and taught sculpture at the university. In 1930 she won the Best Execution of the Year award and her reputation was established. In 1936, she won a gold in Buenos Aires as the best foreign artist; in 1938 she won another gold at an international exhibition in Berlin; in 1946 she won an award in New York. All in all, Nuñez has won 20 international awards and had a public square named after her. Nuñez was married to Jorge Falon, a well-known Peruvian writer. She died on September 9, 1995. Her house in La Paz became the museum. It's open Monday to Friday, 9 am-1 pm.

The Children's Museum, also called Kusillo Museum, is on Mirador Laykakota on Avenida del Ejercito, ☎ 244-4311. It's open daily, 10:30 am-6:30 pm, and costs 75¢ for kids and $1 for adults. This interactive museum allows children to experience hands-on activities related to the culture of Bolivia. The area for preschool kids is dedicated to physical activities, while older children do scientific explorations concerning the human body. The plaza area is dedicated to nature and environmental technology. As well, there is a section on AIDs, sexually transmitted diseases and TB. There are fiber optics and a giant kaleidoscope for all ages to enjoy. The green area displays medicinal plants. Peter McFarren and his wife Wendy are involved in this project. They had consultants from numerous Western countries help with the museum's building. Some of the financial assistance came from the Dutch government.

Next to the Children's Museum will be the **Museum of Bolivian Arts and Culture**, also an inspiration of Peter and Wendy McFarren. This museum will be built with the help of the Smithsonian Institution. It will feature pre- and post-Colonial art, including feather art, textiles, masks and instruments. Also on display will be the excellent photos of indigenous people taken by Peter McFarren. (This museum is scheduled to open in the near future.)

A **cable car**, El Fenicular, is located at the Kusillo Plaza below the Kusillo Cultural Complex that includes the plaza, artists shops (not yet open) and the museums. You can take the cable car either up or down for 15¢ or you may buy a ticket to the entire complex for $1. This cable car, which opened its tracks in October, 2003, sits at 3,600 m/11,800 ft, making it the highest in the world, superseding the one in Switzerland by 144 m/472 ft. The cars are powered by electricity and will hold up to 20 people or 1,500 kg/680 lbs. They travel at a rate 1.2 m/4 ft per second.

The Coca Museum, Calle Linares #906, open Monday to Friday, 10 am-noon and 2-7 pm, charges foreigners $1 and locals 25¢ to enter. As you go in, you'll be handed a pamphlet (English language) describing the history of coca. Take a seat and read it before you look at the exhibits, so you are able to get the most out of your visit. This is a private museum that will grow as it receives more objects. Just outside is a wooden press used to compress coca leaves so they remain fresh while in transit. The displays inside cover the uses and abuses of the coca plant and how these came into being. The most interesting display shows the process of making cocaine from coca leaves. There is also information on the plant's nutritional value and its medicinal uses.

The **Textile Museum**, Calle Linares #906, open daily, 10 am-7 pm (closed noon-2 pm), charges a $1 entry fee. The museum is not strictly a textile museum as it has Inca artifacts and hats, as well as Spanish military decorations. The main display includes looms and aguayos (the cloth used as a baby carrier or backpack) dating back to before the colonial period. Some of the weavings are 13 ft/four m long – it takes a woman all day to weave two inches/five cm of the material. There is also a collection of artifacts from Tihuanaco.

Museo Nacional de Arqueologia (Archeological Museum), Calle Tiwanacu #93 on the corner of Federico Zuarzo, Monday to Saturday, 9 am-noon and 3-7 pm, Sundays, 10 am-1 pm. Entrance fee, $1. This museum is set in a building that has been designed to look like the pre-Columbian temple found at Tihuanacu. The carving of Pacha Mama (Mother Earth) stands 24 ft/7.5 m high and weighs 17 tons. Inside is a collection of artifacts from all around Bolivia, although the majority are from the Tiahuanacu culture.

Museo Tambo Quirquincha, Calle Evaristo Valle, ☎ 239-0969, is open 9:30 am to 12:30 pm and from 3 pm to 7 pm during the week and then from 10 am to 12:30 pm on weekends. This is a permanent exhibition that has early photos of La Paz. There are art works from the colonial and republican periods plus masks, sculptures and oil paintings. There is also a permanent collection of contemporary plastic art.

Museo de la Revolution National, Plaza Villarroel, is open 9:30 am-12:30 pm and 3 pm-7 pm during the week, and 10 am-12:30 pm on weekends. It costs 15¢ to enter and view the murals painted by famous artists who lived during the revolution of 1952.

Museo de Arte Sacro, Calle Socabaya #432, is open 9:30 am-12:30 pm and 3 pm-7 pm during the week, and 10 am-12:30 pm on weekends. Admission is 45¢. The museum contains religious art from the 16th and 17th centuries. There is a permanent exhibition of paintings, plus sacred ornaments, silver and furniture used by bishops of La Paz. It is a rich museum and most of the garments worn by the bishops, with their silver and gold weaving or embroidery, were done by nuns sitting in cold stone rooms constructively passing their time while thinking about God.

■ Adventures on Foot

Around Town

El Prado is the main street in town. Walking El Prado with its throngs of people is a must. There are the large colonial houses and five-star hotels to admire. Starting at the more affluent end in the south, near the higher-priced hotels, it is called Avenida 16 de Julio. The street changes to Avenida Mariscal Santa Cruz that has, near the north end, the famous San Francisco Church and plaza built in 1549. Continuing north, the name of the street changes to Avenida Montes. Branching off El Prado at the San Francisco Church is Avenida Sagarnaga, also known as "tourist street," lined with shops and vendors selling everything from llama fetuses to weavings and popcorn.

The **Witches Market**, on Calle Linares between Sagarnaga and Graneros, has objects, like llama fetuses, needed by locals who practice traditional ceremonies. There are herbs and spices, wines and amulets. A walk-through is a must, but ask permission to photograph.

Above the Witches Market is **Mercado Negro** that covers hundreds of blocks going toward El Cementario. This is where you purchase anything from food to motorcycle parts and dog collars or tutus for ballet. It makes for interesting walking. Each section covers a specific thing – electrical parts are in one area, while women's shoes and skirts are in another. The flower section is beautiful; I often wander through and purchase flowers for my hotel room. A large bouquet seldom costs more than a quarter.

Hiking

MIRADORS: There are numerous miradors, or lookout points, in La Paz from which to see the city. **Mirador Monticulo** is on Calle Salazar, five blocks up from Plaza Isabel la Catolica that sits on Avenida Arce. Monticulo is also half a block from Plaza España, up a road that takes vehicles. At the bottom of the hill is the Contemporary Art Museum. The hill itself is a favorite place for lovers.

Mirador Templo Andino Jach'a Apacheta is on a hill above El Alto. Take a bus to Villa Victoria and have the driver point out the direction of the hill. This is the highest point in the city and was a lookout point for people living in the area for centuries. If you are lucky you may find a local person burning incense and coca leaves to Pacha Mama (Mother Earth).

> **SAFETY ALERT:** Since this point is in El Alto, please do not go alone. There are many warnings from people in the main part of town about the dangers of El Alto. I have never had a problem, but I have seen pickpockets working at the cementario bus stop.

Mirador Killi Killi is in Agua de la Vida at the end of Avenida La Bandera and is an excellent lookout point. To get there, take a minibus from Avenida La Bandera and Calle Colon (Colon runs one block downhill from the palace on Plaza Murillo) to the top. The park has an arch in which you can frame the city for photographs. This is an easy place to reach and, if walking, you can be sitting on a park bench on the hill in about 45 minutes. The hill was first used as a lookout point by the military back in 1871 and it was occupied by the revolutionists during the 1952 uprising. It is visited on organized city tours.

Mirador Andino Jacha'Qullu is a tiny hill and park in the suburb of Nuevo Potosi in the west end of town, off Calle 3 de Mayo. To walk here is tricky, as the route has many curves and turns. Take a taxi instead. The advantage of coming here is that it offers a different view. The hill is an important ceremonial center of the Andean culture. In 1781, it was used by Tupac Katari during one of the country's many wars.

Mirador Parque Laykakota on Cerro Laykakota is in the Santa Barbara zone and is known as Witch Hill. "Layka" in Aymara means witch and "Kota" is hill. This is where the new Children's Museum and the Museum of Bolivian Arts and Culture are located. The park offers a good view of the city.

CHIARKOTA LAKE: Lago Chiarkota can be visited as a day trip from La Paz. The bus going past Refugio Huayna Potosi will let you off at the hamlet just before. From there, walk the road past Lake Tuni to the dam. A track goes toward Condoriri (up) and climbs from 13,000 ft/4,000 m at the dam to 18,000 ft/5,400 m at the lake. A few signs show the way. It takes three to four hours to walk to Lake Chiarkota and another two or three to get back down. This trip is offered by many tour agencies. Usually, you need to gather a few people to make it viable for a tour company, but you may also hire a local guide and go independently. The guide will cost $25 per person, per day. It is most pleasant, if you like cold and have gear, to spend the night at the lake.

VALLEY OF THE MOON: Valle de la Luna is six miles/10 km from the center of La Paz and can be reached by joining a tour or by taking micro bus #11 or minibus #231 or 273 to Mallasilla. These buses can be caught at Plaza Belzu on Avenida Mexico in San Pedro. Tell the driver where you want to go and he will point the way as you disembark. Because of the

La Paz

terrain, wear good shoes/boots and carry water. City tours that stop here are offered by many companies in La Paz.

The hillside features a maze of clay canyons and pinnacles that have been sculpted by wind and rain. Narrow trails through the landscape take about an hour to walk. If on tour, you will get about half an hour to visit the valley. There is also a cactus park just before the entrance. The park overlooks a gorge and has paths leading around numerous types of cacti. There is even an example of the hallucinogenic San Pedro cactus. The city tour does not stop at this park.

As you continue up the road you will come to **Parque National Mallasa** with its bird observatory and, across the road, the zoo area. The road passes under natural stone bridges and past Chulpani's Red Hill. There is no mistaking which hill this is. From Mallasa one can see across the river to the highest golf course in the world (see below).

DEVIL'S TOOTH: Muela del Diablo is a huge volcanic plug sticking out of the landscape to a height of 13,000 ft/3,950 m. The area is a popular picnic destination and can be reached by taking minibus #288 or #207 to El Pedregal from Plaza Belzu on Avenida Mexico in San Pedro. Tell the driver where you are going and he will let you off near a small cemetery. Several trails go to the right; follow the one that obviously leads to the village. From there, go to the left for .3 miles (about half a kilometer), to the foot of the rock. Climbers are occasionally found on the east face.

VALLEY OF THE SPIRITS: Canyon de Palca, or Valle de Animas, is a deep canyon that was carved by the Rio Palca centuries ago. To get there, take a bus going to Huni from Plaza Belzu on Avenida Mexico in San Pedro. Or take a bus to Ovejuyo and then a second *trufi* toward Huni. Your hike will end in Palca and getting back to Huni and finally La Paz will require either good timing for buses, a taxi or a hired jeep with driver who will wait for you (depending on how many people are in your party, this may be the best option). Check with your bus driver as to when the last bus leaves Palca. This route may be done from Palca to Huni, if there is a bus going to Palca first. Once in Huni, follow the main road through the village and into the valley. Mt. Illimani is constantly in view. Continue for 1½-two hours until you see the river (without much water) on your right. Follow it toward the canyon, filled with huge pinnacles and wind-carved conglomerates. The trail continues along the bottom of the canyon to a natural obelisk. Just past the obelisk is a rock that has the appearance of a human hiding in a cave. The rock is called the hermit of the canyon. Continue along the canyon to its end and climb to your left up to the village of Palca. This is a long day-hike. Be certain to carry water, wear good shoes and have a snack in case it is a long time before you get back to La Paz. If you are unable to get to Tupiza for hiking, this is a good second best.

CHACALTAYA: Skiing on the world's highest ski hill, Chacaltaya, just 23 miles/37 km from the city, is a must for ski buffs who are in the area from February through to April. Hikers, of course, should go up any time. Chacaltaya, which means cold in Aymara, is 17,800 ft/5,400 m high and the ski run starts just below the summit and goes 2,300 ft/700 m down the steep tongue of a glacier.

The tow that you must hook onto is a bit of a mystery requiring a PhD in engineering to use. It was first put onto the hill in 1939, is the only one in Bolivia and the one closest to the equator. It was built using an old car engine.

While the road here was being built, the contractor was killed in an avalanche so the locals believed that this was a vengeance from the mountain Gods for the sacrilege of disturbing the mountain. No other lifts have been built in Bolivia since.

GOODBYE GLACIERS

With present weather conditions, the glacier is melting at a rate of 20-33 ft/six-10 m per year, so it won't be too long before the hill is out of commission for skiing. A French team from the Institut de Recherche pour le Developpement is studying the condition of three glaciers here, including Chacaltaya. The Zongo Glacier near Huayna Potosi loses three ft/one m of depth and 33 ft/10 m of length every year. The run-off from these glaciers is the basic water supply for La Paz.

To get there during ski season, **Club Boliviano**, Calle Mexico #1638, Casilla de Correso #1346, ☎ 232-4682, will take a bus up on weekends if numbers warrant the trip. Alternately, you must hire a vehicle through a tour agency for the two-hour trip to the parking lot.

On foot, it is a half-hour to the chalet above the parking lot and another hour to pass the first false summit before finally reaching the top. From there you can see Lake Titikaka, Illimani, Maururata and Huayna Potosi. The air density here is only half of what it is at sea level.

Entrance fee to the ski hill is $1.50 per person.

During high rains, the road up the mountain becomes impassable. Chacaltaya is a cycling destination for those who want a fast brake-gripping rush down from the summit. See page 118 for details.

Club Andinos, ☎ 231-2875, a mountain hut near Chacaltaya, has both private rooms and dorms, although there are no private bathrooms. You should have a warm sleeping bag if staying on the mountain overnight. You may also purchase meals at the hut during ski season. If you eat at the lodge, a sandwich or a piece of cake will cost about $1.50 and pop is

La Paz

$1. As an alternative, it has been reported that you may go to the research station down the hill and try to get a room. The accommodations at the station are a bit warmer than those at the hut. I have not stayed at either place.

CHORO TRAIL: The Choro Trail runs from El Cumbre to Coroico (instead of the quicker cycle trip along the Road of Death) and follows a pre-Inca trail that takes three to four days to cover. You may take this trip back from Coroico on a horse (see *Coroico*, page 283, for details). There are outfitters who will include this section of the trail but they start in Tuni and the hike would include going from a pass near Mount Condoriri instead of El Cumbre. It is not advisable to walk from Coroico to El Cumbre because the trail is so steep. Going into Coroico is bad enough.

You will need a tent, sleeping mats, food for three days (at least), water tablets, shorts and rain gear. You must have good boots and pack, a compass (although the only direction is down), first aid kit and a walking stick. Plan to go either with a tour group or hire a guide. A guide knows the way, knows where to sleep and get water, and can talk to locals who may be curious about you or opposed to your passing.

The trail from El Cumbre starts in the grassy Altiplano, passes down to lush jungle vegetation and finally to cultivated coffee and corn fields. It starts at 15,789 ft/4,800 m and you drop to 4,934 ft/1,500 m within three days of walking. The descent is brutal and your shins will ache with fatigue once you arrive in Coroico. Rain is always a problem in an area where two climates meet, and here you will feel the effects of the cold Andean air as it collides with the heat of the Amazon. In fact, it creates the excellent growing climate of the Yungas.

To get to trailhead, take any bus from Villa Fatima going toward Coroico and get off at the pass (El Cumbre) beside a little lake. Even easier is to take a taxi, which can take four people who can then share the cost.

The trail begins just beyond the statue of Christ on the hill across from the lake. The descent follows a well-defined trail paved with stones long before the Spanish arrived. This is the toughest section of the hike as it is steep and usually wet and your pack is the heaviest it will be along the route because of your food. Stop often and eat. The first night you should stop at Challapampa, sometimes called Achapalla Pampa. It is 4,276 ft/ 1,300 m lower than trailhead and it will take approximately six hours to get there. Locals will expect to be paid for providing a campsite.

The Altiplano vegetation is left the following day and the lush rainforests become obvious. Once across the Choro River there is a long, dry walk to the Rio Jacu-Manini, nine miles/15 km from Challapampa. However, the descent is not as steep as the previous day's. The next stop is Sandillani, where a camping area is available. (Your guide may be able to suggest better places to stop than I have; take his advice over mine.) In Sandillani there is a place to stay in a garden, tastefully tended by an elderly man. The heat will start to take its toll now, as Sandillani is at 6,579 ft/2,000 m above sea level.

From Sandillani a cobbled trail leads to Villa Esmeralda where the road to Chairo passes through coffee fields, fruit orchards and vegetable gardens. There is a place to eat, purchase supplies and generally freshen up in Chairo. It is another 10 miles/17 km to Yolosa, just below Coroico. This is a long way to walk after your arduous descent into the Yungas. However, hitching from Chairo is not a disgrace. Once at Yolosa, you can catch a bus or truck going up to Coroico another five miles/eight km into the Yungas, where you will undoubtedly spend a few days recuperating.

CHACALTAYA TO ZONGO PASS: This one-day hike takes you through barren but beautiful landscapes over to Huayna Potosi. From there you can either return to Chacaltaya or have a hired vehicle drive over to the Refugio at Huayna Potosi and pick you up. This hike should be done only by those who have acclimatized. From the pass, on a clear day you can see Lake Titikaka, Illimani and Sajama, the highest mountain in Bolivia.

 Chacaltaya has numerous walks. If you're interested, check out ***Trekking in Bolivia*** by Yossi Brain, Andrew North and Isobel Stoddart, published by The Mountaineers, Seattle, WA (1997).

TAKESI TRAIL: This trail goes from the San Francisco Mine just out of La Paz (below Chacaltaya) to the village of Yanacachi, a colonial town with the oldest church in the Yungas. This is the Inca Trail of Bolivia and is popular with both locals and tourists – so popular, in fact, that it is often crowded. Almost the entire trail, about 18 miles/30 km, is stone laid by those living in the area even before the Inca arrived.

The trail starts with a three-hour grunt up to Apacheta Pass at 15,000 ft/ 4,650 m, the highest point on the trek. From there you leave the Altiplano and start down toward the Yungas, following the canyon. Within two or three hours you will be at Takesi Village, elevation 12,000 ft/3,600 m. That is a quick down! The village has traditional stone and straw huts. There are numerous camp spots beside the Takesi River another hour or so past the village.

The second day you follow the paved Inca Road that has the remains of some sewer systems built at the same time as the road. The construction is worth examining, and imagining how it was done. By lunch you should be at Cacapi and into the rainforest. The elevation here is 8,550 ft/ 2,600 m. The rest of the day involves an undulating walk to the Chojlla Mine, just 650 ft/200 m lower than Cacapi. The ups become a pleasure after the steep down done the day before. You can poke around the mine a bit. From there it is two hours to Yanacachi and the end of the hike. Or, you may continue for five or six hours to Mocori and the luxurious Tamampaya Hotel. I did not make it that far, so I have no idea what the costs or conditions are.

YUNGA CRUZ TRAIL: The Yunga Cruz Trail goes from Chuñavi to Chulumani, the capital city of the South Yungas. This is the least popular and most difficult of the three trails going down into the Yungas from La Paz. The upside is that you will encounter fewer people. It is a rugged trail passing some dramatic country and interesting villages.

To get to Chuñavi, hire a jeep. There are buses, but service is infrequent and conditions crowded. They reportedly leave from Villa Fatima daily at 9 am and the trip takes six or seven hours. Once at the village, there are numerous hiking routes.

 For detailed information, purchase *Trekking in Bolivia* by Yossi Brain, Andrew North and Isabel Stoddart, or hire a guide from a tour company.

Climbing

For those into climbing, the **Andes** of Bolivia offer three peaks over 20,000 ft/6,000 m that are not extremely technical. The tour companies that assist in climbing adventures are all highly skilled and able to offer world-class trips. In fact, some people who have never climbed before have bagged Huayna Potosi and acquired a life-lasting addiction.

Most companies prefer that you bring your own gear (harness and helmet) while they provide the group gear (like ropes and biners). Acclimatization is essential so plan on being in La Paz for a few days before going up. Companies like **Andean Summits** (☎ 242-2106, www.andean-summits.com) offer packages that include acclimatizing. They do a couple of days paddling around Lake Titikaka and then climb two 16,500-foot/5,000-m peaks before attempting the ascent of Huayna Potosi, the most popular climb in the country. For more detailed information, contact one of the tour agencies.

 Read Yossi Brain's book, *Bolivia, A Climbing Guide*, published by The Mountaineers, Seattle, WA.

Huayna Potosi in the local Aymara language means "the one who came from rocks." This mountain is the one most often climbed by foreigners and one of the world's most visited "six-thousanders." It was first climbed by R. Dienst and O. Lohse from Germany and Austria. There are two approaches to this mountain, the east and the west face. The east face starts at the dam, just past Refugio (a great place to stay, owned by Dr. Hugo Barrios from Huayna Tours, who assisted Yossi Brain in writing *Bolivia, A Climbing Guide*). Base camp, called Campamento Argentino, is at 18,000 ft/5,500 m and is reached just two hours after your arrival at the Huayna Potosi Glacier. There are three alternatives for the approach to the peak. The first and most popular follows the ridge, the second, longer route goes to the bergschrund (a crevasse formed where a glacier pulls away from the mountain) before ascending the ridge. Those doing the west face will climb the largest face in Bolivia. It's 3,300 ft/1,000 m high, with pitches around 50° and some as steep as 70°. This route is more for the strong, with lots of stamina, rather than the technically skilled.

Snow and ice conditions determine your times and sometimes your route. This mountain should not be climbed during rainy season due to the possibility of avalanches. Your guides will advise you as to the best routes to take depending on the conditions.

CONDORIRI: Condoriri climbs start with base camp at 15,300 ft/4,700 m above sea level beside Lake Chiarkhota, once described by Hans Irtle as "fairy-like." Irtle also said that the peak known as Cabeza de Condor (part of this group) was the Matterhorn of Bolivia.

From the base camp you can climb a total of 13 peaks that are over 16,500 ft/5,000 m and each peak has a number of routes. If you have a month, you could, in peak season, climb a new route every day. This group of mountains is difficult to reach, so either a private jeep or a tour company must be hired.

PAQUENA ALPAMAYO: This is the most popular of this group of peaks. Apparently, when you are sitting in base camp, the mountain looks more daunting than it is. However, the ascent is more difficult than the descent.

ILLIMANI: "Shining One" in the Aymara language, is the highest mountain in the Cordillera Real, standing at 21,000 ft/6,400 m. Because it can be seen from La Paz it is often referred to as the guardian of the city. Illimani is actually a group of seven peaks, first ascended in 1877 by a Frenchman, Charles Weiner, who had at that time gone higher than any other human in history.

Pico Sur is the highest peak on Illimani. Its normal route is also its easiest and most often climbed. **Pico Norte** and **Central** can be added to make the rarely attempted five-peak traverse. This is the most impressive mountaineering expedition possible in Bolivia. These traverses all require at least three nights at an altitude of over 20,000 ft/6,000 m.

Hikers can walk up to the base camp at 16,500 ft/5,000 m, while climbers go one better, to Nido de Condores, the Condor's Nest, at 18,100 ft/5,500 m. The views up here are second to none.

The **Quimsa Cruz** group of mountains has at least 80 peaks, many unnamed, that can be climbed. The peaks run between 16,000 and 19,000 ft (4,900 and 5,800 m) in height. Because these mountains aren't as high, they are often ignored by climbing elitists. This is both a pity and a blessing. It is a blessing because it leaves the mountains for those wanting to find new routes, and it's a pity because the elitists miss some of Bolivia's most spectacular rock.

The northern side, often referred to as **Bolivia's Chamonix**, has a number of spires that beckon those preferring rock to ice (the south side, of course, is covered in ice). The other nice thing about this area is that it is accessible by bus or truck and there are usually campsites close to the peaks.

Golf

Mallasilla Golf and Country Club, Calle Casilla #4306, ☎ 274-5124, www.boliviagolf.com, opened in 1912 and is the world's highest golf course. It has a 6,900-yard, 18 hole course sitting at 11,000 ft/3,300 m. The par 72 course attracts visitors from around the world mainly because of its elevation. Its par-3, 12th hole, known as the Lunar Hole, requires a shot of at least 130 yards to clear the 50-foot drop over the moon-like landscape. Because of the elevation and light air, judging the distance is difficult. The course is located near the Valley of the Moon and can be seen from the road going there.

Running

Hash House Harriers is a club of runners who have a fun run about once a month. This is undoubtedly the highest hash in the world. Runs are usually held on a Saturday, 11 am-3 pm. After a run, hashers often have a down-down (they down a few beers) and a pot luck dinner. Here's how a hash run works. There is a fixed route that the runners must follow. However, they don't know what the route is or what the markers are. They start running (someone tells them the direction to head) and as they figure out the markers and are able to follow them, they holler "on-on" and everyone follows. This is done at a jogging pace. When the run is finally over, everyone congregates for a few hours of socializing. In La Paz, contact Gary "Tin-Balls" Neale, ☎ 279-1524, www.lapazhash.com.

■ Adventures on Water

 Hotel Gloria at **Urmiri**, ☎ 239-1489, www.gloria-tours-bolivia.com, is just two hours (51 miles/83 km) from La Paz and has a natural spa and hot springs. The water runs consistently at 72°C down the side of the mountain into three pools. Other than resting, walking from Cumbre Pilar down to the resort (about 1½ hours), eating and drinking, there is nothing to do except pamper yourself. The hotel is part of the Gloria chain and offers some rooms with private pools. There is also a massage parlor, sauna, a pool with a waterfall and a restaurant that serves vegetarian food along with the standard fare. A single room runs $18, a double is $37 and a triple is $55. Note that it is cheaper to take three single rooms than one triple. Meals cost $2.50 for breakfast and $6 for lunch or supper. Since I did not stay here, I can't give you an honest assessment of the food or the rooms.

The spa specializes in treatments for skin problems, excess weight, gout and arthritis. The staff also works with people who have suffered physical trauma or injury, giving physiotherapy and assisting with exercises in the hot springs.

You may visit the resort and hot springs on a day tour from La Paz. Contact Hotel Gloria in La Paz and book a round trip in their van. They need a minimum of six people to make the run ($7 per person, round trip). The cost of using the hot springs and spa depends on the services you use.

■ Adventures on Wheels

 ROAD OF DEATH: The cycle from El Cumbre near La Paz to Coroico in the Yungas, along the Road of Death, is a popular seven-hour, hand-numbing, downhill thrill. I say hand-numbing because this is a brake-gripper; you drop almost 10,000 ft/3,000 m in just under 60 miles/100 km. When I reached the bottom, I could hardly hold a beer. The restaurant owner handed me a straw.

North American-made bikes can be rented in La Paz and the best company to work with is **Gravity Assisted Tours** (☎ 231-3849, www.gravitybolivia.com). Their bikes are top quality and well maintained. Gravity was closed for Christmas when I visited so I booked through the tour office in the Milton Hotel, who linked me with Inca Tours. Their bikes were terrible, although the brakes worked.

With all companies, a guide and support vehicle comes with the price, as do helmets, bright-colored vests and gloves. Repair, rather than maintenance, is the rule, so be aware that the bike you get may not be super-safe.

Some of the cliffs along the road drop 2,300 vertical feet (700 meters) and there have been many deaths. Most have involved buses, but bikers have died because of faulty equipment. Tour agents are notorious for telling you everything you want to hear just to get your business. Once you are on your way, you sometimes find that they have not delivered what they promised. My bike had derailers, but they were frozen into the one gear. My husband's brakes froze at one point and he skidded into the cliff. It could easily have been in the opposite direction. During our trip, there were three flat tires and one bike had to be retired because it just wouldn't go. After the trip got going I also learned that we were charged $41.50 (because we wanted good bikes of the highest quality) and everyone else was charged $35. There was no difference in the bikes and they were often exchanged between the riders so we could each experience the thrill of a different mechanical problem.

However, the ride of death was excellent. The cold mountain air from the pass soon hits the warm moisture wafting up from the Amazon. The vegetation goes from bleak Altiplano grasses to rich jungle forests. The glaciers disappear and streams get larger. And it all happens very quickly.

Once we hit gravel, a short distance from El Cumbre, it became tougher because we had to dodge potholes, pull over while vehicles passed and pass under waterfalls or swerve around small landslides. The road in spots is no more than a 12-foot-wide (four-meter) ledge. Vehicles going downhill must drive on the left so that when passing another vehicle the driver can see out of his window how close his tires are to the edge of the road. Many have misjudged this distance and lost their lives, as the roadside monuments confirm. Vehicles (including bikes) going down are less maneuverable than those coming up. Uphill travelers must give the right-of-way by pulling over.

LABOR OF LOVE

As you cycle toward Coroico, you will meet one young man who directs traffic. He is in a dangerous spot where drivers can't see what is coming and he uses a plastic paddle, red on one side, green on the other, to signal traffic and catch the coins tossed at him for his services. He is there because he lost his entire family when the bus they were riding went over the cliff as it was backing up to allow passage of an oncoming vehicle.

After you finish cycling, you end up at Yolosa, a junction where the Road of Death continues to the Amazon and another route goes up to Coroico. Your back-up vehicle will take you to Coroico. Those who want to continue to Caravani and Rurrenabaque may do so by public transportation.

CHACALTAYA: This ski hill (see above, page 111) is another cycling spot, with several descent routes back to La Paz. Again, **Gravity Assisted Tours** probably provides the safest tours, but check out others too. As the years pass, the locally-run tour offices will learn to give the services required by foreigners. The ride from the peak of Chacaltaya is very steep along scree and boulders, following a few lesser peaks before it starts to drop along walking trails and mining roads and ending in the Zongo Valley. This trip is only for the experienced mountain biker and can be done only when the road conditions going to the ski hill allow it.

ZONGO VALLEY: The Zongo Valley Cycle starts on the pass just past Huayna Potosi's Refugio and the spot where climbers access the Huayna Glacier. It follows the Zongo River down into the Yungas, descending rapidly from 15,000 ft to 5,000 ft (4,600 m to 1,500 m) in less than 21 miles/

35 km. It's not as steep or as difficult as the Chacaltaya run, and can be split into two days. The first day runs from Huayna Potosi to the Zongo Valley along a road that is steep to begin with but soon levels a bit and undulates to Zongo Village, where you can camp. The following day, you will be driven up to Chacaltaya and, from there, cycle into La Paz.

WAL`LATA PASS TO SORATA:** You can cycle into Sorata from Wal`lata Pass on the road between Sorata and Achacachi. This is an excellent ride taking only four hours to drop 4,300 ft/1,300 m. The views of Illampu make the trip well worth it. Some make the claim that it is better than the Road of Death. The ride is shorter, the views are more dramatic and there is only one place where the road hangs on the edge of a sheer cliff. **New Milenium (☎ 245-1660, nmas@caoba.entelnet.bo) is one company that takes cyclists along this route. The cost for the cycle there, an overnight in Sorata and the shuttle back is just $100.

■ Adventures on Horseback

Horseback riding is offered by **Sky Bolivia** (see *Tour Operators*, page 122) and can be enjoyed along a four-hour route to the Rio Abajo, which is 40 minutes by car from La Paz. The same company also offers a six-hour tour starting at Mallaso, passing Muebla del Diabla, Valencia and on to Wuay Wuasi. This follows the Choqueyapu River in part. You may also go from Valencia to Illimani and back, passing Tawapalca and Cohoni on the way. For this overnight trip you would need a sleeping bag.

■ Adventures of the Brain

ABC Spanish School, Calle Lenares #980 Apt. 202, ☎ 772-62657 (cell), www.studyspanish-lapaz-bolivia.tk, is owned and operated by William Ortez, who has been teaching Spanish for 10 years. He offers both beginner and intermediate levels, with flexible hours – even seven days a week. One advantage of being in this school is that the classes are often small, which gives more one-to-one time. Watching a class, I found that he geared his teachings to the needs of the students, rather than following a strict curriculum. One student was in La Paz to play the world's highest golf course, so golf vocabulary filled the sentences being practiced. Visit the website, take the on-line test and go directly into the skill level you need.

The costs, which include all materials needed for study, are as follows: 21 hours, three hours per day, $115; 28 hours, four hours per day, $155; 30 hours, three hours per day, $160; 40 hours, four hours per day, $215; 45 hours, three hours per day, $235; 60 hours, four hours per day, $315; 60 hours, three hours per day, $300; 80 hours, four hours per day, $400.

William can also arrange for accommodations with a family in the center of the city, with breakfast included, for a total immersion experience.

Accommodation prices are as follows (lunch or dinner are $2 extra): One week, $50; two weeks, $100; three weeks, $140; four weeks, $185.

Reservations for classes and/or accommodations can be made in advance.

The **SpeakEasy Institute**, Avenida Arce #2047, ☎ 244-1779, www. speakeasyinstitute.com, speakeasyinstitute@yahoo.com, offers courses in Spanish, Quechua and Portuguese for everyone from the beginner to the advanced student. The institute uses native Spanish speaking teachers and specializes in courses for professionals and "quickie" courses for survival. Their style of teaching includes regular testing, so the possibility of failing is minimized. SpeakEasy is part of the i-to-i international school that teaches people how to teach English as a second language. It's an efficient system.

There are two types of classes, one for the professional and the other for the general traveler. However, most classes are tailor-made for the individual. Courses run from one week to eight weeks and you have the option of staying with a family.

By the end of the first week, the beginner student should be able to give and understand general information about family, work and personal pleasures. By the end of the second week, past tense is introduced and reading the newspaper is encouraged. By the end of the fourth week, professionals should be able to make occupational comparisons and join in group discussions. The more general course focuses on travel-related issues. Intermediate students will learn past and future tenses, discuss movies and/or books and report what people say. The traveler will be able to write a letter of complaint.

Advanced students hone up their grammar, discuss political events and generally make their opinions understood.

Courses involve four hours of instruction daily. If a room with a host family is chosen, the fee includes room, two meals, laundry, trips to interesting places around the country and airport pickup. The costs of these courses, home-stay included, are $260 a week, $480 for two weeks, $700 for three. For courses without home stay, costs are $220 for one week, $400 for two and $620 for three.

The institute is involved with the publication of *Llama Express*, the English-language newspaper loaded with helpful and up-to-date information for tourists. If you need assistance on other matters, everyone at the institute speaks English well and is willing to answer questions.

NEEDY CHILDREN

The institute helps needy children, of which there are many in La Paz. If you are leaving the country and have clothes that you do not want to take home, please have them cleaned and delivered to the institute. Alix Shand, the coordinator, will see that they get onto needy bodies.

■ Tour Operators

Anyone climbing should go to **www.mountainguides.com**, which has an excellent equipment list.

Transturin, Calle Alfredo Ascarrunz #2518, Sopocachi, ☎ 242-2222, www.transturin.com, offers day tours and overnight trips in a catamaran to Isla del Sol on Lake Titikaka. This tour can be started in La Paz and end in Puno or Copacabana. See *Copacabana Tour Operators*, page 173, for more details.

Gravity Assisted Mountain Biking, Avenida 16 de Julio #1490, ground floor of Edificio Avenida, ☎ 231-3849, www.gravitybolivia.com, has made a reputation as the best company for downhill bike trips. They have US-made Kona race bikes with Hayes disc-brakes and Shimano v-brakes. All bikes have either front or full suspension. Gravity maintains their bikes, rather than just repairing them. Their guides are English speaking, first-aid qualified and addicted to riding. Gravity was also recommended in the *South American Explorer* in the fall and winter, 2002 issue. The writers of the article did the Road of Death (see page 117) and loved it.

The company offers 16 one-day rides and 10 multi-day adventures. The one that appeals to me the most is the trip around the Salar de Uyuni for five days. But they also do single-track trails about three times a week.

I like this company because safety is such an issue and because they are so much fun.

American Tours, Avenida 16 de Julio #1490, Edificio Avenida, main floor, ☎ 237-4204, www.america-ecotours.com, is across the hall from Gravity and the two compete for first-class quality. The company has been around for over five years in Bolivia and 25 years throughout the world. It has teamed with Andean Summits, offering high-quality climbing and hiking trips in the Andes. The two companies are excellent and Andean Summits has one of the best reputations in South America.

American Tours offers climbing trips, hiking excursions and cultural/ecological tours. Mountaineering trips include Huyna Potosi, Illimani and Pequeño Alpamayo in the Condoriri area (this has the lowest elevation, at 16,000 ft/5,400 m). The climbs are minimum to moderate in technical

La Paz

difficulty and the company insists on one day of acclimatization and practice before going up. After this, guides will give instruction and solve technical difficulties while on the climbs.

Hiking trips can be from three to eight days and cover different degrees of difficulty, and there's also an interesting overnight trip to Sajama that offers some hiking, but also a lot of transportation time.

The cost of hiking with this company depends on the number of participants. To climb Huayna Potosi and Charquini costs one person almost $500. If four people go, the cost drops to $236 per person. For trekking the Choro Trail, one person pays $467, but four participants pay $159 each. The most expensive (and exciting) trek on offer goes into the Apolobamba area (Pelichuco to Charazani). The fare for one person (taking a private jeep) is $1,535; if four people go (using public transportation), they pay just $331 each for the entire week. Trips include a guide, a cook, all meals and, if climbing, common climbing equipment like biners, ice screws, ropes and snow stakes. Porters and animals carry only common equipment during treks, so be prepared to carry your own gear. Food goes on the animals.

Andean Summits, 710 Calle Prolongacion Armaza, Sopocachi area of La Paz, ☎ 242-2106, www.andeansummits.com, works with a few agencies in Bolivia like American Tours and Gravity Assisted. See *Tour Operators Who Do All the Work*, page 80.

CombiTours, Calle Illampu #734, ☎ 245-1626, combicop@ceibo.eltelnet. bo, offers trips to Oruro's Carnival for $36 per person. You depart at 5 am, have breakfast and arrive at your reserved seat in Oruro by 8:30 am. You enjoy the festivities and return to La Paz at 6 pm. This is one of the best ways to see Carnival as you get to see the festivities and miss most of the alcohol consumption. This company provides everything, including a rain poncho to protect you from the *bombos* (water-filled balloons).

EBA Transtur, Calle Carlos Medinacelli #1120 (zona Cristo Rey), ☎ 242-2430, has a special trip to the Oruro Carnival for less than $50 for a complete day. You leave La Paz about 5 am and, after a quick breakfast, head out to Oruro. They have seats beside the Presidential Palace. The price includes a box lunch, some beer, service of a guide and a rain jacket. If you want to spend three days in Oruro, EBA will make reservations at the Gran Hotel Sucre for two nights for $215 per person. That price includes the cost of the seat at the Carnival.

Sky Bolivia, Calle Sagarnaga #367, ☎ 231-3254, www.skybolivia.com, offers horse trips near La Paz. Trips can last four hours, six hours or overnight. They also have a trip down the River Guanay to Rurrenabaque, one of the newer adventure trips in Bolivia.

Milton Tour Agency, Calle Illampu #1124 on the corner of Calle Calderon, ☎ 236-8003, www.khainata.com/hotelmilton, hmilton@ceibo.

entel.bo, is located in the Milton Hotel. This use minibuses that hold 32 people each. They offer a tour to Copacabana with an overnight on Isla del Sol and then a trek up to the stations of the cross in Copacabana before returning to La Paz or going on to Peru. The cost is $50 in high season and $45 in low. This is an all-inclusive trip.

They also offer the Road of Death bike tour to Coroico from El Cumbre just out of La Paz for $45 in high season, $40 in low. This trip includes transportation to El Cumbre, a hot lunch, helmets, gloves and a bike with 18 gears and wide tires. Some things they promise are not true. For example, the bikes may have 18 gears, but usually only one or two work. Be certain that you check your bike before getting on it.

Alba Tours, Calle Sagarnaga #139, ☎ 231-3052, offers a 3½-hour city tour with an English-speaking guide for $13. It also has trips to the Valley of the Moon and then to the Templete Semisubterraneo, in front of the stadium. The stone artifacts are copies of the originals that once sat there but have now been sent to the archeological museum. From the stadium, the tour goes to Mirador Killi Killi for views of the city and then to Muela del Diablo or the Devil's Tooth. It passes through colonial streets to Plaza Murillo, where you visit the National Art Museum and the traditional Ethnographic Museum. The tour ends at the witches' market. This is an excellent excursion that allows you to see some of the dramatic landscapes around La Paz.

Biking to Coroico is also offered for $35. Alba supplies bikes, gloves, helmet, lunch and a support vehicle. If you take the option to stay in Coroico, rather than come back, they will deliver your luggage.

This company has a minivan that goes to Copacabana, Puno, Arequipa, Tihuanaco, Chacaltya, Coroico, Rurenabaque, Uyuni or Cusco. If you feel uncomfortable taking local buses, this is a good alternative. The difference in cost is minimal.

Toñito Tours, Calle Sagarnaga #189, office 9, ☎ 233-6250, www.bolivianexpeditions.com, specializes in trips around Uyuni and the salt lakes. All-inclusive, four-day tours cost $110. Note that "all-inclusive" *excludes* transportation to or from Uyuni. Toñito is a family-run company that also offers custom one- to five-day tours by private car.

Vicuña Tours, Calle Sagarnaga #366, ☎ 231-0708, www.victoursbol.com, offers numerous excursions. The city tour costs $21 per person; Tihuanaco is $15; a walk around Chacaltya will cost $15; and two days and one night at Lake Titikaka costs $68.

High Camp Bolivia, Sagarnaga #189, office 101, ☎ 231-7497, highcampbolivia@hotmail.com, specializes in hiking and climbing in the Andes and has an excellent reputation. Owner Gonzalo Jaimes is a member of the Guiding Association of Bolivia and a rock and ice instructor. The company has decent equipment available for rent, including Italian

(Ferrino) tents, the new-styled plastic mountain boots for climbing, Inca foams, Vau De tents (I had a Vau De pack for years and found the quality exceptional), some good clothes, bags (North Face), ropes, harnesses, stoves (butane) and lamps. This company will also do custom trips; contact them for specifics.

This company, which works with Andean Summits, requests about a week to prepare summit trips to some of the higher peaks. Fees include guides, meals and transportation. Their prices are as follows, with a minimum of two people: Chaguini, one day, $140; Huana Potosi, two or three days, $350; Illimani, four days, $450; Condoriri, four days, $850; Sajama, four days, $725; Illampu to Ancohuma, seven days, $1,230.

Pachamama Tours, Calle Sagarnaga #189, ☎ 231-9740, pachamama@ mail.megalink.com, are interested mainly in private tours even though their advertising says otherwise. A private trip to Uyuni for four days costs $340, including a driver and interpreter, plus all meals and accommodations. The company also goes to Copacabana, Rurrenabaque and Santa Cruz. The cost of a private tour with everything included is about $250 per day. However, a trip to Copacabana with an overnight visit to Isla del Sol costs $98. On this tour they stop at the Sun Temple and the Inca Fountain and introduce you to people in a native community. Your guide will speak English. Their top-priority tour includes three days in the Amazon's Madidi National Park and a night at the luxurious Chalalan Ecolodge out of Rurrenabaque. The cost for this is just under $400.

Inca Land Tours, Calle Sagarnaga #213, ☎ 231-3589, www.inca-landtours.com, specialize in the Amazon, although they also offer tours to other places (all you need to do is ask). They have two camps out of Rurrenabaque – one in the jungle and the other in the *pampas*.

Trips to the *pampas* are via jeep from Rurre to Santa Rosa on the Yacuma River and then by paddle power for three hours. You set camp, have dinner and do a night hike. The next day is spent searching for anacondas, capybaras and monkeys. In the evening you may fish for pirañas or swim with freshwater dolphins. All is included in the price which is $25 per day, for a minimum of three days.

Also offered is the jungle trip that goes up the Beni and then the Tuichi River. Remember that hikes into the jungle are more for bird and plant lovers, as most jungle residents are not seen during the day.

Accommodations for both trips are in dorms that hold 10 people. Each bed has a mosquito net. There is also a dorm that has partial wood walls and a foundation. The cost for this accommodation is $35 per day (during low season, the prices drop by $5). The local guides speak their own language and Spanish, not English. However, you can hire an English-speaking translator for $5 per day.

Inca Land Tours is struggling with eco-tourism. Some clients want animals caught so they can be touched, but scientific research has shown that wild animals are traumatized by this. Note that cobras and anacondas cannot be seen unless they are caught. Feeding wild animals is also discouraged because the animals are inclined to stop foraging for themselves. If you wish to help preserve Bolivian wilderness, put pressure on fellow travelers to comply with the latest ecological practices. This will force companies like Inca Land Tours to offer only "no-touch" tours.

Buho's Tours, Calle Sagarnaga #242, ☎ 247-1577, buhostours@entelnet.bo, has three classes of bicycles for rent to use on the Road of Death trip to Coroico. A hi-tech US-made bike rents for $45; Italian bikes cost $39; and Chilean ones are $35. All the bikes at Buho's have spring suspension, but the Chilean ones have only front disc brakes operated at the handle bar. The Zongo Valley trip ($35) starts just beyond the Refugio lodge (see Huayna Tours, below) at the base of Huayna Potosi and goes to a dead-end road in the Yungas. You can also rent bikes and a guide and cycle to the Valley of the Moon or Devil's Tooth. The cost for that trip is $28 per day. Buho's also runs traditional non-biking trips to Tihuanaco, Chacaltaya and Copacabana.

Trek Bolivia, Calle Sagarnaga #392, ☎ 231-7106, www.trekbolivia.8k.com, specializes in trekking. They have French-, German-, Japanese- and English-speaking guides. However, all trips are cheaper with a Spanish guide. This company has been trekking in the area since 1998. The six-day hike they offer in the Apolobamaba area between Pelechuco and Curva costs $280, with a minimum of two people. It starts in Curva and goes up to Pelechuco. A three-day hike from Condorini to Chacape is $180 per person, with a minimum of two people. The first night is spent at Lake Cheracota; the second day is spent crossing a 16,440-foot/5,000-m pass and ending at Liveñosa Lake; the third day you come out. This is an exceptional hike and one with a lot of challenge, yet not too long. Gear and transportation is extra. This company offers other treks and, through their website, helps coordinate groups and thus keeps costs down.

New Horizon, Calle Sagarnaga #388, ☎ 231-6274, has three types of bikes that can be used for the Road of Death cycle trip. The best rents for $45, 2nd class is $35, and the cheapest is $30. The guide is a bike mechanic, but extra bikes are also carried just in case a problem arises that can't be fixed. This company was recommended in *Natura Magazine*. This is one of the rare companies that practices maintenance. The crew is Peruvian, so specialized trips run to Machu Picchu, though not by bike.

Huayna Tours, Calle Sagarnaga #398 at Illampu, ☎ 245-6717, is run by Dr. Hugo Berrios and his wife Damiska. Anyone who climbs in Bolivia will come upon Dr. Hugo somewhere. Although they offer all the tours offered by other companies, their specialty is climbing. They will take

La Paz

climbers to any peak in Bolivia, but Hugo's specialty is Huayna Potosi. He knows every rock and grass blade on that mountain.

Hugo has a lodge at the base of Huayna Potosi that is a true refuge (called the Refugio) after the grueling trip to the summit of the mountain. The lodge is at 15,600 ft/4,800 m and the summit of Huayna Potosi is 20,000 ft/6,000 m. A bus goes to the Refugio every day so non-climbers can also enjoy this rustic place perched on the mountain.

Before going up any high peak in Bolivia, you can take **lessons** at Hugo's climbing school. This is highly recommended if your skill level is questionable.

Huayna Potosi is not a technical mountain, yet it is still a challenge. If you go with Huayna Tours, you will have good teachers, guides and porters. A two-day trip is only for those who are already acclimatized and experienced in climbing. Three- or four-day excursions are recommended for those needing some acclimatization, practice and lessons. All equipment is supplied, including plastic boots, ropes, tents, helmets and pitons, etc. They also provide experienced guides/porters. Edwin Molina is a guide who works for Huayna; he also worked with Yossi Brain when he was writing his climbing guide. Edwin is experienced and good. Hugo Barrios, a native of Bolivia, helped Yossi Brain find and describe many of the routes published in Brain's book about climbing in Bolivia.

The two-day Huayna Potosi climb costs $100. Any additional days cost $20 more per day. The six-day Apolobamba hike from Pelechuco to Charazani can be done for $250 per person (there must be more than two people in your group).

Should you need a private jeep (because you don't want to travel the roads by bus) this is the best place to rent one with a driver. The vehicles are in excellent shape, the driver is skilled and the price is the best in town.

ACCLIMATIZATION AWARENESS

Acclimatization is often difficult for those between 14 and 19 years of age because brain and lung tissue has not yet fully developed so adaptation to this drastic change is slower.

ACELA Tours Ltd, Mariscal Santa Cruz at Socabaya, in the Galaria Handal Center, 2nd floor, office #29, ☎ 240-8125, is a good agency for flights either in Bolivia or to other countries.

Andes Amazonia Travel Agency, Calle Sagarnaga #189 on the 2nd floor, ☎ 231-8313, offers many different tours, but their prices are way out of line. A bike trip to Coroico costs $100 per person. A jeep to Sorata costs almost double what other places charge. The man I spoke with (I didn't tell him I was writing a book) seemed uninterested in what I wanted and he had no interest in bartering.

Tocando el Cielo, ☎ 279-1440, has a double-decker bus running city tours. The cost is $15 per person for a three- to four-hour tour that is offered in the mornings and the afternoons. Your ticket is good for two days, so you can do half one day, and half the next. The circuit has two sections – the first is to the south end of the city plus the Valley of the Moon, and the second includes the city center and Mirador Killi Killi.

To catch the bus, be at Plaza Isabel la Catolica just before 8:30 or 10:30 am for the morning tours and 2 or 4 pm for the afternoon tours. You can purchase your ticket on the bus. The first morning tour does the downtown circuit plus one of the miradors and the second one goes to the southern area of town plus the Valley of the Moon. Afternoon tours start with the southern area and the second bus does the downtown. A media system offers translations into English, German, Spanish, Italian, Portuguese or French. The view from the upper level is great, but I felt I was on display. This is not the tour to take if motion sickness is a concern.

Magri Turismo Ltd, Calle Capitan Ravelo #2101, ☎ 244-2727, www.bolivianet.com/magri/, specializes in custom tours for groups. I watched one of their guides, Nelly Nogales, working with a couple from the United States and was impressed with both her English and her knowledge of the sites. If you want to do only specific things and have a time frame that is tight, this may be the way to go. The company also offers trips to some of the far reaches of Bolivia. Should you wish to visit Sucre, the Jesuit Mission Churches, Potosi or the Salar of Uyuni, you can join an organized tour or book a private one. A big draw is that Magri practices sustainable tourism. On Isla del Sol they have an eco-lodge (La Estancia) that is highly recommended. For lodge details, see page 188.

New Milenium Adventure Sports, Calle Illampu #815, ☎ 245-1660, nmas@caoba.entelnet.bo, offers two excellent trips. One is a 14-day hike down Rio Yariapu in Madidi National Park to Rio Tuhichi, where you float on a *callapo* (traditional raft made by the Tacana) to Rurrenabaque and then do another tour on the *pampas* looking for anaconda and boas. Depending on the number of persons, the trip can be as much as $1,350 per person or as low as $789. The other trip is a one-week excursion in the Apolobamba area that starts in Pelechuco and ends just below Viscachani Pass. The cost is $850 per person with only two people. Of course, the price goes down when more people are included. New Milenium takes cyclists on the great glide into Sorata. It takes four hours and is by far the best way to get to the mountain village, with excellent views of Illampu en route.

Crillon Tours, Avenida Camacho #1223, ☎ 233-7533, 1450 S. Bayshore Drive, Miami, ☎ 888-8484-222, www.Titikaka.com, looks after the tours and hotel at Huatajata on Lake Titikaka. In business since 1958, Crillon is dedicated to giving first-class tours to other places too, like the Uyuni Salt Lakes and Santa Cruz. They also have a special star-gazing tour.

International Mountain Guides, Ashford, WA 98304, www.mountainguides.com, offers a great trip that includes a package of climbs up Huayna Potosi, Illimani and Sajama for $3,000. This price does not include booze or your journey to and from La Paz.

Paititi Travel, Avenida 6 de Agosto, Edeficio Santa Teresa, #106, ☎ 244-0586, offers most of the tours that other companies do. However, they have a photographic interest. Their owner Javier Palza Prudencio is the author/photographer of the book *Fantastic Parade*, which has photos of dances for all regions, cultures and festivals of Bolivia. Born in 1956, Javier is a self-taught photographer who, for this book, took over 15,000 exposures during a 10-year period. It was by accident that he discovered his unique technique of photographing at a very slow speed in order to capture the essence of Carnival dancing. If photography is your thing, contact this agency.

Places to Stay

There are many hotels in La Paz and the only place I do not recommend staying is in El Alto. Most of the *aljamientos* up there are whore houses (if you want a whore it is safer to pick one up at Plaza Estudiantes) and I did not check out any of the hotels in that area. For the roughest, but not necessarily the cheapest, hotels I looked at the ones in the Mercado Negro area.

The better-class hotels are in the southern end of the city. Most tourists with a moderate budget stay in the Sagarnaga area. Reservations are not usually needed. If one hotel is full, the one down the street will have a room. If you are going to keep returning to La Paz and have a favorite place to stay, certainly make a reservation. When I did this, I was never asked for a deposit.

HOTEL PRICES (US $)
Per person, per day, unless noted otherwise.
$ . . . . $2-$5
$$ . . . . $5-$10
$$$ . . . . $11-$17
$$$$ . . . . $18-$25
$$$$$ . . . . Over $25

■ Inca Campesino Class

 Hotel Scala, *Calle Union #425 between Calle Chiquisaca and Avenida America, $, no phone*. Clean and off the main thoroughfare, this hotel is quiet, comfortable and has personable staff. Private bathrooms and hot-water showers are available, but there is no restaurant. This is a family-run business and the owners will take very good care of you.

Pachamama Residencial, *Pasaje Juan XXIII #32 between Illampu and Sagarnaga, ☎ 212-0645, $*, has large rooms with large windows. Each room has a couch, a TV and a closet. Some feature hardwood floors. Only one room (that is a bit drab) has a private bathroom. However, there are just three rooms on each floor and one bathroom, so you don't share with many. The owners are friendly, the price is low, and the location quiet and central. You can safely leave things here while you travel around the country. The Pachamama is a real deal for those on a budget.

Posada El Carretero, *Calle Catacora #1056 between Avenida Yanacocha and Junin, (no phone), $*, has rooms without private bath. The place is acceptable and there is a kitchen for the guests to use, a book exchange and laundry service.

Hostal Señorial, *Calle Yanacocha #540, ☎ 240-6042, $$, one block from Plaza Murillo*. Bedrooms have high doors, wood floors, TVs, closets, crooked mirrors and dim lighting. The unisex communal baths have two or three toilets and the same number of showers. A kitchen with plates, pots and a gas stove is available to guests.

LA PAZ ACCOMMODATIONS	
ACCOMMODATION	PHONE
Alcala Apartment Hotel ($$$$$)	☎ 241-2336
Alojamiento La Riveira ($/$$)	☎ 235-1887
Angelo Colonial Hostal ($$$)	☎ 212-5667
Arcabucero Hosta Inn ($$$)	☎ 231-3473
Condeza Hotel (S)	☎ 231-1193
El Rey Palace Hotel ($$$$$)	☎ 241-8541
Gran Hotel Paris ($$$$$)	☎ 220-3030
Hostal Republica ($$)	☎ 220-2742
Hostal Señorial ($$)	☎ 240-6042
Hotel Alem ($$)	☎ 236-7400
Hotel Continental ($)	☎ 245-1176
Hotel Dynastia ($$)	☎ 245-1076
Hotel España ($$$)	☎ 244-2643
Hotel Europa ($$$$$)	☎ 231-5656
Hotel Garcilazo ($$)	☎ 245-3075
Hotel Gloria ($$$$$)	☎ 240-7070
Hotel Happy Days ($$)	☎ 231-4759
Hotel Ritz ($$$$$)	☎ 243-3131
Hotel Scala ($)	no phone
Hotel Sucre ($$)	☎ 249-2038
Hotel Tauro ($$)	☎ 246-2172
Hotel Torino ($$)	☎ 240-6003
Max Inn Hotel ($$S$$)	☎ 249-2247
Milton Hotel ($$)	☎ 236-8003
Naira Hostal ($$$$$)	☎ 231-1214
Pachamama Residencial ($)	☎ 212-0645
Posada El Carretero ($)	no phone
Radisson ($$$$$)	☎ 244-1111
Residencial Colonial ($$)	no phone
Residencial Rosario ($$$$)	☎ 236-9542
Sagarnaga Hotel ($$$)	☎ 235-0252

La Paz

1. Calle Sagarnaga: Naira Hotel & Café, Lak Smi Vegetarian Restaurant, Happy Days Hotyel, Alem hotel
2. Calle Illampu: El Lobo Restaurant, Dynastia Hotel, Rosario Hotel & Restaurant
3. Calle Linares (north): Pepe's Coffee Bar, Layq'a Café
4. Calle Linares (south): Les Pot Pourris de Gourmets, Angelo Colonial Restaurant

PLACES TO STAY
5. Continental Hotel
6. Milton Hotel
7. Radisson Hotel
8. Hotel Gloria
9. Rey Palace Hotel
10. Ritz
11. Hotel Paris
12. Sagarnaga Hotel
13. Torino Hotel
14. Hotel Scala
15. Pachamama Residencial, Condessa & Arcabusaro
16. Posada El Carretero, Hostal Señorial
17. Hotel Tauro, Hotel Garcilazo
18. Hotel Sucre, Max Inn Hotel
19. Hostal Republica
20. Angelo Colonial Hostal
21. Hotel España
22. Alcala Apt. Hotel
23. Hotel Europa

PLACES TO EAT
24. Chifa Amy
25. Café Cuidad
26. Café Colon
27. Wall Street
28. Alexander Coffee Shop
29. Confieteria Club de La Paz
30. Café Berlin
31. Café la Terraza
32. Surucachi Restaurant/Dumbos
33. La Casa del Corregidor, Cevichon
34. Rincon Español, Shian Restaurant
35. Giussani's Restaurant
36. Beatrice Italian Restaurant
37. Wasamama Restaurant
38. Don Vittorio
39. Dumas Café
40. Seoul Restaurant
41. El Gaucho
42. La Fiesta Restaurant

NIGHTLIFE
43. Mongos
44. Coyote
45. Diesel National, Thelonius, Bizzarro

La Paz
Hotels,
Restaurants,
Nightlife

1200 FEET
400 METERS

to 22

Residencial Colonial. *Avenida Tarija #210 on the corner of Murillo, (no phone) $$.* The hotel's 14 small rooms are carpeted and have skylights to make them bright. Towels and soap are supplied and the beds are soft. A fully supplied kitchen is available for guests to use. The Colonial is clean and located in an attractive old building. It has rooms with and without private bathrooms. There are communal bathrooms on each floor.

Hotel Torino, *Calle Socabaya #457,* ☎ *240-6003, $$.* The desk clerk was not interested in showing a room, so I don't know what they are like. There is a luggage storage, book exchange, and a restaurant on the main floor. The Torino is a lovely old building just half a block from Plaza Murillo and half a block (in the other direction) from Alexander Coffee.

Hotel Tauro, *Calle Isaac Tamayo #628,* ☎ *246-2172, $$,* is located on a street going toward the cemetery near Mercado Negro. It's a dump and the prices are so far out of line it is not worth looking at.

Hotel Garcilazo, *Isaac Tamayo #560 on the corner of Garcilazo de la Vega,* ☎ *245-3075, $$,* is an enclosed building also in the Mercado Negro area. Its rooms are overpriced – $6.75 for a room with bath but only a cold-water shower. For a hot shower you must go across the hall to the communal bath. Bedrooms are big and fairly clean. There is cable TV.

Hotel Dynastia, *Calle Illampu #684 near the corner of Graneros,* ☎ *245-1076, $$.* This hotel has moved a bit upscale in the last couple of years by putting in a new entrance and upping their prices. Rooms are large and clean, with a communal bathroom on each floor and hot water for showers. Those with private bath also have TVs. With six stories and no elevator, be prepared to hike to the top floor, where it is quiet (the climbing is good for acclimatization). There is a restaurant in the hotel, but it is seldom open for business. I found that since this hotel has appeared in other guide books, the staff has become indifferent to offering good service.

Hotel Happy Days, *Calle Sagarnaga #229,* ☎ *231-4759, happydays@ metalink.com, $$.* Located in the center of the tourist shopping area, Happy Days is run by a woman who will not put up with any hanky-panky, so it is fairly safe for a single girl. The carpets are dirty and the beds hard. I think it is overpriced.

Hotel Sucre, *Calle Colombia #340 on the Plaza San Pedro,* ☎ *249-2038, $$.* The 24 rooms are set around a common courtyard that has flowers in the center. The floors are polished hardwood and the rooms have high colonial-style doors. There is a bed, cupboard, table and chair in each room, plus a window that opens onto the courtyard. Although some of the corners are chipped, the place is clean and the staff makes one feel welcome. There is an Enlace ATM next door.

Alojamiento La Riviera, *Calle Tarija #325,* ☎ *235-1887, $ / $$ (TV costs $1.50).* There is a nice reception area and a kitchen for guests to use.

Rooms are basic and the beds are Inca. For a lower-end option, La Riviera is not bad.

Hostal Republica, *Calle Comercio #1455 and Avenida Bueno,* ☎ *220-2742, marynela@ceibo.entelnet.bo, $$,* is set in a colonial house that once belonged to one of the many presidents of Bolivia. Rooms are clean, the garden and courtyard are appealing and the staff members go out of their way to make you comfortable. Besides being a pleasant place to stay the hotel has a money exchange service, laundry, Internet, safe-deposit box, luggage deposit and parking. They also offer transportation to the airport.

Hotel Alem, *Calle Sagarnaga #334,* ☎ *236-7400, $$.* The Alem is clean, friendly and inviting. It has rooms with and without private bathrooms. The rate includes a continental breakfast.

Milton Hotel, *Calle Illampu #1124, corner of Calle Calderon,* ☎ *236-8003, www.khainata.com/hotelmilton.com/, $$,* has glittering hardwood floors at its entrance. Its 50 rooms are located on five floors and a terrace at the top offers a view over the city. Large rooms have private baths, cable TV, nice curtains, closets and counters. Some have chairs. A few rooms are a bit tattered. You may leave luggage and there is a place to leave valuables too. The rate goes up with each floor, and a single person must pay the same price as two people. Prices also go up during peak season. A continental breakfast is included in the price. Breakfast, if not staying at the hotel, costs less than a dollar per person. This includes juice, coffee, bread and eggs. Laundry service is available and there is a tour agency. The staff is pleasant.

Hotel Continental, *Avenida Illampu #826 on Plaza V. Juariste Eguino,* ☎ *245-1176, $,* is a clean hotel/hostel with spacious rooms that come with or without private bathrooms. It's a member the International Hostelling Association.

■ Inca Merchant Class

 Arcabucero Hostal Inn, *Calle Viluyo #307, between Calle Velasco and Linares,* ☎ *231-3473, $$$.* The Arcabucero is in a cheery colonial building with clear glass over the central courtyard that now holds a small bar and restaurant. The restaurant serves mainly breakfasts. Bedrooms are clean, with carpets, a phone, a small desk and dresser. Each room has a window that either overlooks the courtyard or the street. Antiques in the sitting areas and original art pieces around the building make it interesting and homey. The owner, a Bolivian, speaks perfect English. The 10 rooms are cleaned daily and the front door is kept locked – as a guest, you must ring the bell to enter. This is one of my favorite places in La Paz.

Angelo Colonial Hostal, *Mariscal Santa Cruz #1058*, ☎ *212-5667*, *hostalangelocolonial@yahoo.com*, *$$$*. This clean and friendly place is on the main drag and features antiques throughout and original art on the walls. The bedrooms, with glass doors and wooden shutters, circle a courtyard that has been closed off to hold an Internet café. It is the only place in town with a printer (the cost is about 5¢ per page).

Sagarnaga Hotel, *Calle Sagarnaga #326*, ☎ *235-0252*, *$$$*, has rooms with and without private bathrooms. The price includes a continental breakfast. Located close to San Francisco Church, it is popular with the backpackers. I felt the staff was a bit aloof, but the place looked clean.

Condeza Hotel, *Pasaje Juan XXIII #190, Illampu and Sagarnaga*, ☎ *231-1193*, *$$$*, has single, double and triple rooms. Continental breakfast is included and some English is spoken. There are seven floors and an elevator. Each average-size room has wood floors, closets, telephone, TV and a tiled bathroom. The hotel's restaurant charges way too much. It cost me $4.25 for two eggs, dry toast, one glass of juice and one syrup-like coffee. Use the restaurant only if staying here.

■ Inca Royalty

Residencial Rosario, *Calle Illampu 704*, ☎ *236-9542*, *$$$$*. Rooms with a private bath cost 40% more than those without. Accommodations cluster around a courtyard that is comfortable and appealing. I think the rates are high, but they do include a good buffet breakfast at the on-site restaurant. A tour agency in the hotel caters to climbers and a sauna caters to sore muscles. The owners have a second establishment in Copacabana and they will readily transfer you from one place to the other. This is a clean, safe and convenient place to stay.

Hotel España, *Avenida 6 de Agosto #2074*, ☎ *244-2643*, *www.hotel-espana.com*, *$$$$*, is on the main street heading toward the better part of town. The large rooms (single, double or triple) have private baths, telephones and a TV. Rates include a continental breakfast and Internet access. There is a restaurant, laundry, beauty shop and garage.

Gran Hotel Paris, *Plaza Murillo*, ☎ *220-3030*, *www.granparishotel.com*, *$$$$$*, was built in 1911 and its elegance has grown with age. It has everything from single rooms to suites that overlook the plaza. The rates include an American buffet breakfast. Each large room, tastefully decorated, has a full bath, with everything included – shampoo, hair dryer, bath beads, fluffy towels, soap and toilet paper. Set in a colonial mansion, the hotel has high ceilings and wide hallways. Each floor has a sitting area and the rooms have fireplaces, personal safes, a rich wood writing desk and bed lamps. Accessories, like curtains and carpets, are coordinated, and all rooms have small balconies. The suite has a sitting room and a sleeping room. The doors to the rooms are operated with electronic entrance cards. Artwork on the walls is mostly petit point and the chairs are tapestry. An entertainment hall often has professional performances with tickets costing around $10. This place is a nice treat, but even if you can't stay, try to get here for a steak dinner ($5), a glass of wine and a concert. Rates: $85 single; $110 double.

Max Inn Hotel, *Avenida Sucre #1494 on Plaza Mariscal Sucre,* ☎ 249-2247, *portalesip@kolla.net, $$$$$*. The Max has a large foyer and nice halls. The rooms are of moderate size, with bright lights, carpets, mini bars, cable TV and fans. Bathrooms feature hair dryers and small tub/showers. There is also a garage. Breakfast is included. I wasn't all that impressed with the staff, nor were they with me. They seemed suspicious when I wanted to look around. The hotel offers a 2½-hour city tour for $2. Rates: $35 single; $47 double; $54 triple.

Naira Hostal, *Sagarnaga #161 across from Plaza San Francisco,* ☎ 231-1214, *Hnaira@ceibo.entelnet.bo, $$$$$*. Located in the center of the tourist area, across from San Francisco Church, the Naira is a convenient place to stay. The large, clean rooms are built around a central courtyard. Although the place is well kept and the showers are clean, I found a few paint chips along the baseboards. Hot water is supplied from a tank. There is laundry service and a safe for valuables. A restaurant, coffee/bakery shop and an Internet café are on site. Avoid the travel agency downstairs as it is not equipped to handle anything other than booking a tour with another agent. Rates: $25 single; $32 double; $42 triple.

Hotel Gloria, *Calle Potosi #909,* ☎ 240-7070, *www.hotelgloriabolivia. com, $$$$$*, is part of Bolivia's rendition of a chain hotel. The one in La Paz has a fairly well-kept lobby, but the rooms have seen better days. All 90 rooms have private baths, central heating and cable TV. Rates include breakfast and transportation to and from the airport. Parking is available and the hotel is located in a convenient area just up from the Prado and very close to Alexander Coffee (go there for breakfast, rather than eating at the Gloria). Other amenities include a money exchange service, Internet access, safe deposit boxes and laundry service. Just outside the door is an Enlace ATM. The staff is friendly and helpful. Some spoke English. Rates: $45 single; $55 double; $68 triple.

Alcala Apartment Hotel, *Calle Victor Sanjines #2662 on Plaza España, in Sopocachi,* ☎ 241-2336 or 241-1113, *alcalapte@zuper.net, $$$$$*. These classy apartments are in the ritzy area of town where many consulates and upscale restaurants are found. Each has two bedrooms and two bathrooms. The tiled kitchens (floor and counters match) are fully furnished, dining rooms have tables that seat up to eight people, and the living room couches are of soft brocade. Each suite has a fireplace. There is room service, a garage, an in-room safe, cable TV and a business room. The on-site restaurant provides your complimentary continental breakfast, as well as other meals. This hotel prefers long-term guests. It's a super place for four people to use as a base while touring Bolivia. Plus, it's near all those great cafés in the south end of the city. Rates: $50 single; $60 double; $70 triple; $80 quadruple.

El Rey Palace Hotel, *Avenida 20 de Octubre #1947*, ☎ *241-8541, www. hotel-rey-palace-bolivia.com, hotelrey@caoba.entelnet.bo, $$$$$*, comes complete with doorman and elevator music in the halls. Each room has a king-sized bed (some have two) a radio, phone, cable TV, air conditioning, a safe, hair dryer, bidet, Jacuzzi bath, shampoo, soap and telephones in the bathroom and the bedroom. A mini-bar is stocked with good wine. The high-quality wood closets, colonial furniture and plush carpets are an added draw. Buffet breakfast is included in the price. The hotel also has a business center and Internet access at no extra cost. Single rooms are just a bit smaller than doubles. A discount is offered to those staying more than one night and you may have a room for just the day at the discounted price of $30. Weekend prices are much lower than during the week. There's a restaurant and a quiet piano bar. The staff speak English and some speak French Canadian.

Honeymooners can take the huge Geraldine Chaplin suite, complete with a red velvet couch, a few red velvet chairs trimmed in gold and a gold-trimmed mirror. Personal attention is this hotel's specialty, and they send birthday cards to guests who have stayed there in the past year. The hotel is conveniently located only one block from the Prado. I noticed that even the elevators were clean, unscratched and worked without groaning. Rates: $95 for a suite for two; $70 single; $30 for day-use only.

Radisson, *Avenida Arce 2177*, ☎ *244-1111 (toll-free US 800-333-3333), www.radisson.com/lapazbo, $$$$$*. All 239 rooms in this giant chain hotel have private bathrooms. There is everything on site that any five-star hotel has anywhere in the world, from coffee shops to magazine stores to hairdressers to swimming pools. Often, the hotel holds public concerts. Even if you are not staying, it is nice to visit, sit in the foyer and use the well-supplied bathrooms. Dual pricing is practiced here; locals pay less. Rates: $94-$100 for two in a room; $212-$225 for two in a suite.

Hotel Ritz, *Plaza Isabel la Catolica #2478*, ☎ *243-3131, www.hotel-ritz-bolivia.com, $$$$$*, has suites to suit all tastes. Located in the better part of town near the Bridge of the Americas, this hotel has British-styled décor (complete with John Peel paintings) and British-style reserve. The suites are large and well decorated and the price includes an excellent buffet breakfast. The starting rate is $121 and it goes up to $177 for two people. However, due to different plans and promotions available, they offer up to 47% discounts (weekends are one of the best times to get a deal). Rates: $121-$177 for two people, depending on the room.

Hacienda Villa-del-Sol, ☎ *274-0008, www.villa-del-sol.com, $$$$$* is an award-winning, five-star hotel that has one-, two- or three-bedroom suites. Located near the golf course, it looks like a North American walled city. The award it won was for the best constructed hotel in La Paz. Each suite has 60 channels on the cable TV, a bar, balcony, telephones, Internet connection, safes and a wood-burning fireplace. This is luxury.

Hotel Europa, *Calle Tiahuanacu #64*, ☎ *231-5656, $$$$$*, is a five-star hotel complete with large rooms, excellent service, sauna, restaurant and bar. Rates: $144-$152 regular double; $163-$172 large double.

Places to Eat

Gastronomic fairs are common and should be taken in if you are in town at the right times. The first one, held in June, features pork. Participating restaurants (usually associated with big hotels) offer a selection of their best pork dishes. The second gastronomic fair is in July, where freeze-dried potatoes (*chairo*) and *plato paceño* (dishes commonly made by the people of La Paz) are the specialty. The third fair takes place in August and features foods specific to different departments in the country. The last festival is on October 20th, La Paz Day, when all foods specific to La Paz are featured. Although you still pay for the food, the fairs provide you with an opportunity to taste dishes not commonly found on restaurant menus.

■ Coffee, Desserts & Breakfast

Alexander Coffee Shops have five locations in La Paz and one in Santa Cruz. The ones in La Paz are on Calle Potosi #1091, ☎ 240-6482; on Avenida 16 de Julio #1832, ☎ 231-2790; on Plaza Avoroa, Avenida 20 de Octubre #2463, ☎ 243-1006. This last location is also a bar that's popular in the evenings with both locals and tourists. The fourth one is in Zona Sur is on Calle Montenegro and Avenida La Cheviña, ☎ 277-0465. You'll also find an Alexander kiosk at the airport, ☎ 281-0240, that opens by 7 am. Alexander serves filter coffee and great cappuccinos for 75¢ a single and $1 for a double. Newspapers are available for reading and there's an upstairs overlooking the street at the Potosi location. The chain serves one of the best breakfasts in town, as long as you order the items individually. The toast that goes with the breakfast is terrible. Get a croissant instead, or smuggle in a crusty bun from the market. The carrot cake is excellent, as is the strawberry cheesecake. This is not a place to miss. Open 8 am to 11 pm, Monday to Friday, and 9 am to 11 pm on weekends.

Confieteria Club de La Paz, *Calle Camacho and Mariscal Santa Cruz* ☎ *212-6265,* has décor from the 1930s with wood walls part way up and photos of the city before World War II. This was once a meeting place for the famous Klaus Barbie, alias Klaus Altman while he was in La Paz. Barbie was a Nazi war criminal who worked as a consultant to the government leaders from the 1960s to the 1980s. He was also close to Stroessner (Paraguay) and Pinochet (Chile). His specialty was unlawful arrest, torture and murder. Today, there are no known consultants sitting in the pleasant restaurant that serves cappuccinos with thick sweet cream and pastries that are just as rich. This was also a favorite haunt of Bolivian poets Hector Borda and August Cespedes.

Oasis Café, *Calle Linares #947*, offers a breakfast from 8 am. For $1.50 you get toast, butter, eggs with ham, juice and coffee or tea. Computers with Internet access are available.

Torino Hotel/Café, *Calle Socabaya #457*, serves cappuccino and great pastries – like lemon pie and scones – that are famous. It offers a lunch buffet for less then $2. This includes a salad bar, soup, main dish (vegetarian meals included) and desserts. The *almuerzo* (main meal) is available from Monday to Friday, noon to 3 pm. This is a good deal for the hungry. Internet access is available on almost a dozen computers. This is a popular restaurant for meeting other travelers. However, the surly waiter is still there three years after we first fought with him. The coffee is not nearly as good as at Alexander's, and the breakfast can be matched by any *tienda* on the street.

Café La Terraza, *Avenida 6 de Agosto #2296*, ☎ *764-3313*, *Avenida Montenegro Bloque B #5 in San Miguel*, ☎ *799-5695*, *or Avenida 16 de*

LA PAZ RESTAURANTS

Those restaurants without a phone are not listed here.

EATERY	PHONE
Alexander's Coffee Shops	4 locations
Armonia Vegetarian Restaurant	☎ 241-2858
Beatrice Italian Restaurant	☎ 241-7198
Burger King	2 locations
Café Berlin	☎ 220-0696
Café La Terraza	☎ 764-3313
Cevichon	☎ 231-1889
Chifa Emy	☎ 244-0551
Confieteria Club de La Paz	☎ 212-6265
Don Vittorio	☎ 244-0758
Duma's Café & Bar	☎ 244-2089
Giussani's Restaurant	☎ 242-2945
Gran Hotel Paris	☎ 220-3030
La Casa del Corregidor	☎ 236-3633
Lak Smi Vegetarian Restaurant	☎ 221-3048
Layq'a Café	☎ 246-0903
Les Pot Pourri des Gourmets	☎ 154-0082
Maphrao-on Tai Restaurant	☎ 279-3070
Pepe's Coffee Bar	☎ 245-0788
Pizza Napoli	☎ 220-4090
Pollo Pinocho	☎ 244-1979
Profumo di Caffe	☎ 231-3824
Reineke Fuchs	2 locations
Residencial Rosario	☎ 236-9542
Restaurant Angelo Colonial	☎ 236-0199
Restaurant Rincón Español	☎ 243-5306
Restaurant Surucachi	☎ 231-2135
Rey Arturo Dining Room	☎ 241-8541
Ritz Hotel/Duke's Restaurant	☎ 243-3131
Roman Palace	☎ 775-72102
Seoul Restaurant	☎ 243-1361
Torino Hotel/Café	☎ 240-6003
Wassamama Restaurant	☎ 243-4911

Julio along the Prado, is a chain popular with Bolivian yuppies. Their chocolate cake is good and the coffee is okay. The service was slow.

Profumo di Caffe, *Plaza San Francisco #502*, ☎ *231-3824*, is open daily from 8:30 am to 8 pm and has excellent pastry to go with a midday cappuccino or expresso. The coffee is as good as the pastry.

Residencial Rosario, *Calle Illampu #704,* ☎ *236-9542*, offers a buffet breakfast with fruit, yogurt, dollar-size pancakes, Wunderbread (that you can toast) and granola for $2.50. The egg sandwich I had was inedible, but many foreigners choose to start their day here.

■ Snacks & Lunches

Paseo Café Colon, *Avenida Camacho #1372 and Loayza,* ☎ *214-8992,* has nice décor that includes photos from the early 1900s. The food, however, is sparse and ordinary and the coffee too strong. A New York sandwich consisting of bacon, lettuce, tomato, cheese and a smattering of French fries on the side cost $2. However, CNN television in Spanish was clear.

Wall Street Café, *Avenida Camacho 1363*, serves good burgers and falafels and draws a middle-class Bolivian clientele. The atmosphere is pleasant and the service excellent, but prices are a bit high. The café opens at eight every morning except Sunday.

Café Berlin, *Calle Mercado #1377 and Loayza,* ☎ *220-0696*, is an upscale place that attracts successful businessmen. I found the coffee average, the lemon pie too sweet, the apple pie bland, but the atmosphere attractive and the staff pleasant. Prices were a bit high.

Romano's, *Calle Santa Cruz #260, inside the Galeria Alexis, #5 (no phone)*, specializes in Italian foods and pastas, although they do make some international dishes. The place is tiny, but friendly and open seven days a week. If you have a meal here, you get 50% off your Internet costs. They had three computers when I was there.

La Fiesta, *next door to Angelo Colonial Hostal on Mariscal Santa Cruz #1060*, gives bad service, so I never got to taste the food. The waiters seem to avoid foreigners, perhaps because of perceived language difficulties. With other good places to patronize, I suggest leaving this one to Bolivians.

Naira Restaurant, *Calle Sagarnaga #161, at the very lower level of the building*, has long wooden benches set along wooden tables. Entertainment is available late, after 10, for a cover charge of $5. The food is good but portions are small. However, the upstairs coffee shop and Internet café are excellent. Any and all of the baked goods are recommended.

La Paz

Restaurant Surucachi, *Avenida 16 de Julio #1598 along the Prado*, ☎ *231-2135*, has been around almost as long as La Paz itself. The restaurant is in an elegant old building that has many rooms on two floors. Meals are huge and reasonably priced. (Chicken soup at $3 sounds like a rip-off, but you get half a chicken plus a hard-boiled egg, rice, vegetables and potatoes all served in a soup tureen.) The *almuerzo* is probably one of the best in Bolivia and the main course changes daily. Surucachi is open every day, 9 am to 10:30 pm. The service is as good as the food and the place is patronized exclusively by Bolivian professionals and me.

Pizzeria Napoli *on Murillo Square #1131*, ☎ *220-4090*, has single slices of pizza laden with cheese for just over a dollar. Or try a triple-decker ice cream served on a waffle cone for just under a dollar. A family-sized pizza to go costs $6. Although the place is tiny, it is clean and the service is pleasant.

Dumbos, *across from Surucachi on Avenida Santa Cruz*, is the local hang-out for ice cream served as creative food art, for pastries laden with delicious things we are not supposed to eat and even for substantial food like fries and hamburgers. This is an "in" place for the young, up-and-coming Boliviano. As usual, the coffee is only so-so.

El Lobo, *Calle Illampu and Avenida Santa Cruz #411*, is an upstairs restaurant that has a good buffet at economical prices. Their specialty is Middle Eastern cuisine.

Lak Smi Vegetarian Restaurant, *Calle Sagarnaga #213*, ☎ *221-3048*, offers a great Indian-style *almuerzo* for $1.25. They serve many of their meals on a *talli* tray that contains six or eight containers with spiced foods, yogurt and rice. The rice is balled with your fingers, dipped into one of the foods and popped into the mouth. Specialties are things like puri, massala, chapattis and samosas (which, I feel, leave a bit to be desired).

Pepe's Coffee Bar, *Calle Jimenez #894 off Avenida Linares*, ☎ *245-0788*, is a tiny place that serves good meals. I had a toasted veggie sandwich for $2 and the banana milkshake I ordered was so thick I could hardly suck it through the straw. Take your pick from cappuccino, espresso and other non-alcoholic goodies. Pepe's was exceptionally clean on my visit and it's one of the few places in La Paz that offers take-out coffee.

Burger King, *Avenida Ballivian #312 and Calle Calacoto*, ☎ *279-6867*, *Calle Socabaya and Avenida Mercado*, ☎ *240-8593*, *or at the International Airport*, ☎ *282-5255*, has not been run out of town by local restaurants yet (MacDonald's has already left). If you want a touch of home, a clean bathroom, air conditioning and a burger for $3, then Burger King is the place.

Restaurant Oriental, *Avenida 6 de Agosto #2179, (no phone),* has good Chinese food though the choice is limited. This clean restaurant is upstairs and its large windows overlooking the street allow you to sit, enjoy a meal and surreptitiously take photos of the locals below.

Pizzeria Morello, *Edificio Illampu, across from Hotel La Paz*, serves delicious homemade pastas and pizzas. They also serve traditional *salteñas* (stuffed pastries) and *almuerzo* for lunch.

Armonia Vegetarian Restaurant, *Avenida Ecuador #2286,* ☎ 241-2858, offers an excellent buffet *almuerzo* from noon to 2:30 pm daily. It is one of the few vegetarian restaurants in Bolivia. I found that people here still find the concept of vegetarianism – like the desire for hot showers and freshly-roasted, filter coffee – a touch weird.

Cevichon, *Calle Murillo #1165,* ☎ 231-1889, has the best and most varied menu of ceviche in Bolivia. The dining room is small, with décor a secondary concern. The first concern is the food and they carry every type of ceviche imaginable. The ceviche *piscado* (fish), enjoyed with a beer, is an excellent meal. A large plate of ceviche and a beer is under $3. This is a good spot for either lunch or supper.

Pollo Pinocho, *Avenida Arce #2132, Illampu Building,* ☎ 244-1979, despite its name, is not Italian, but Korean. Its spicy soup is worth stopping in for. This restaurant was reviewed and recommended by Sophie Livall in the *Llama Express*. Open 9:30 am to 10 pm.

■ Fine Dining

 Restaurant Angelo Colonial, *Calle Linares #922,* ☎ 236-0199, is a classy place decorated with antiques and candles, often in candelabras. The food is good, too, but the service is slow. They serve only small beers and the cost is $1.25 per bottle (a large one elsewhere is usually $1). A moderate-size dish of delicious chicken with mushroom gravy was $4.50. The Angelo also has an Internet café, post office, a telephone office and a seldom-open tourist information office. Reservations should be made if arriving after 7:30 pm. The décor, the convenient location and the food are all draws.

The **Rey Arturo Dining Room**, *Avenida 20 de Octubre #1947,* ☎ 241-8541, *www.hotel-rey-palace-bolivia.com*, is as classy as the rooms in the hotel. It has a good international wine selection, linen on the tables, hardwood floors, stained glass windows and international dishes costing anywhere from $3.50 to $10. The Rey Piano Bar, a little place open from 5 pm to 1 am, is a nice spot for a drink and quiet conversation away from the bustle of the street.

Les Pot Pourri des Gourmets, *Calle Linares #906,* ☎ 154-0082, is in the same building as the coca and textile museums. The restaurant is a great find. For $2 they serve a choice of four meals that include soup, entrée and dessert. The menu allows for either a full or half-portion. A large bowl of garlic soup for a dollar is a good deal. Other dishes offered by this unique restaurant are *locro oreño*, squash cooked in pastry with a sprinkling of cheese on top. This dish is from the Santa Cruz area. *Pukacopa* is a pastry filled with cheese and onion and in Oruro, where it originated, it is eaten with or as dessert. The lemon pie is the best in town. Pot Pourri is open 7:30 am to 10:30 pm but, because Bolivians don't generally eat a big breakfast, service in the morning can be slow.

La Casa del Corregidor (House of the Magistrate), *Calle Murillo #1040,* ☎ *236-3633*, near the lawyers' area of town, is an upper-class joint that requires reservations in high season. You will often find lawyers' wives lunching or dining here. Entrées run from $3.50 to $4.50 and the meal of the day is $6.50. Try the excellent onion soup, made with a smattering of oregano and wine. The shish kebab I had satisfied my protein requirement for a week. Plates are artistically presented and the waiters are attentive. The dining room has beamed ceilings, large chandeliers and a fireplace. The background music is just that – in the background. Live entertainment is presented every night except Sunday. La Casa is a treat.

Layq'a Café, *Calle Linares #897,* ☎ *246-0903*, has large beers and a salad bar that costs $3.50 for as many refills as you wish. But it's the huge meal of llama steak cooked with onions and tomatoes, for $6.50, that is their best offering. Llama has a mild flavor – much milder than beef – and a fine grain, just a bit coarser than organ meats. Any self-respecting meat-eater should try it at least once. Don't come to Layq'a's for for breakfast – it took almost an hour to get a small cup of luke-warm coffee that cost $1.

Reineke Fuchs, *Calle Jauregui #2241,* ☎ *244-2979, or Avenida Montenegro and Calle 18, San Miguel,* ☎ *277-2103, www.reinekefuchs. com*. A visit to one of these upscale restaurants is a must. I had pasta stuffed with spinach, drizzled with béchamel sauce and sprinkled with parmesan. It was the best-tasting pasta dish I've had anywhere in the world. The price was $4. They carry the largest variety of German beer in the country and claim to have 28 varieties available almost all the time. The waiters are attentive and friendly. When we were ready to leave one night after 9 pm, the bartender made certain we had a taxi and told us what we should pay for it. Open Monday to Saturday at 6 pm.

Gran Hotel Paris, *Plaza Murillo and Bolívar,* ☎ *220-3030*, built in 1911, is situated on the main square in town. Its elegant restaurant offers an *almuerzo* Monday through Thursday and a suckling pig baked in a brick oven on Friday. The cost for lunch of the day is about $6 per person.

El Gaucho Restaurant, *20 de Octubre #5696 and Central, no phone,* is an upscale Argentinean steakhouse that appears to be a little hole in the wall but is actually quite big inside. It has an impressive wine selection to complement the steaks cooked to perfection. Music – often Argentinean folk songs – is played at a reasonable volume and the service (waiters wear black tie and jackets) is commendable. All this is quite a contrast to the soccer posters that decorate the walls. The salad bar offers mostly sliced fresh veggies (not really salads) and the Argentinean wine we had was dry and excellent. Our total bill, that included steak, was $33 for two people. It was well worth the treat.

Chifa Emy, *Avenida 20 de Octubre #927, on Plaza Av*aroa, ☎ *244-0551,* is attractive, clean and inviting. An extensive menu offers more than 170 dishes, most costing between $3 and $5. Servings are huge (I put my excess in a doggie-bag and shared it with street beggars) and the food is excellent. If you are looking for good Chinese food, this is the best place in town. It's open Monday to Sunday, 11 am-3 pm and 6-11 pm (on Friday and Saturday it stays open until 1 am, and on Sunday it closes at 10 pm).

Los Lobos, *Avenida Aranjuez*, is 20 minutes from downtown by taxi (don't confuse this restaurant with El Lobo on the corner of Illampu and Santa Cruz). This upscale eatery offers excellent meat and seafood dishes in a comfortable garden setting. Meals run about $5.

Ritz Hotel, *Plaza Isabel la Catolica #2478,* ☎ *243-3131, www.hotel.ritz. bolivia.com,* has an excellent buffet breakfast on weekdays in the Oak Room. It is a bit expensive ($4 per person), but worth the price. Selections include fresh fruit, yogurt, buns, pastries, eggs, pancakes, sausages, bacon, cereals, coffee, fruit juice and toast. On the same premises is **Duke's Restaurant**, which specializes in Argentinean beef, Italian pasta and the house dish, Tablita Ritz. The *tablita* consists of an oak plank that carries a fillet of beef, chicken and/or sausage served with potatoes and covered with a choice of two sauces. This is a very classy place to dine.

Restaurant Rincón Español, *Calle Hermanos Manchego #2550, between Pedro Salazar and Avenida Arce,* ☎ *243-5306,* is by far the best restaurant in La Paz. It has just 12 tables, so reservations are essential. The specialty is seafood, but everything, including steak and salad bar, is excellent (the steak can be cut with a fork). The seafood stew had clams, shrimp, octopus, fish (and a few things I wasn't sure about) done in a tomato sauce and served in a hot pot. As I looked around, I noticed that many locals had ordered the same dish. The atmosphere is romantic, the service is top notch and I highly recommend at least one meal here. There is a small bar you can sit at if you have to wait for a table. Open at 7 pm.

Giussani's Restaurant, *Calle Fernando Guachalla #659 in Sopocachi,* ☎ *242-2945*, specializes in Italian food. The atmosphere is pleasant. Open Monday to Saturday, noon-3 pm and 7 pm until everyone is gone, and on Sunday, 12:30-4 pm.

Beatrice Italian Restaurant, *Calle Sanchez Lima, #2158,* ☎ *241-7198,* is a tiny, intimate and tastefully decorated restaurant. The menu lists seven types of pasta dishes with a choice of nine different sauces. The main course is served with fresh, hot garlic bread and the dessert menu is tempting. At under $5 per meal, it's well worth a visit.

Wasamama Restaurant, *Avenida Arce and Pinilla #2557,* ☎ *243-4911,* is behind Jalapeños and is the best (maybe the only) Japanese restaurant in town. Of course, their specialty is sushi and they make all kinds. But the sushi that made them famous is the trout.

Don Vittorio, *Avenida 6 de Agosto,* ☎ *244-0758,* cooks the best pizza in town. Service is fast, the price is right and the food abundant. The restaurant is small, so you may have to sit at an outside table, on the street.

Dumas Café and Bar, *Avenida Arce #2390 on the corner of Belisario Salinas,* ☎ *244-2089,* has such good gourmet food that it has been recommended in the *Gourmet's Guide* and *El Pais* from Spain. It serves fish from the mountains and Lake Titikaka, plus seafood and meats. The *pejerrey*, a fish from the lake, is the best dish. Dishes have either a French or a Spanish flare. Open daily, 9:30 am to 11 pm.

Maphrao-on Tai Restaurant, *Calle Claudio Aliaga #1182,* ☎ *279-3070,* offers hot and spicy Thai foods that are excellent. It's open Tuesday to Saturday, noon-3 pm and 7 pm to midnight, Sunday and Monday, noon-3 pm.

Seoul Restaurant, *Calle Campos 232, between Avenida 6 de Agosto and Avenida Arce,* ☎ *243-1361,* serves typical Korean foods that are good to taste and milder in flavor than most Chinese dishes. They don't offer dog, a specialty of Korea that I actually tried one time. Open Monday to Saturday, noon-10 pm.

The Roman Palace, *Calle Santa Cruz #266A,* ☎ *775-72102 (cell),* is a pizzaria that has ravioli, spaghetti, fettuccine and calzone. They have other things too, but these are their best meals. Prices are reasonable. Open 9 am to 11 pm, seven days a week.

Shian Restaurant, *Calle Hermanos Manchego #2586, no phone,* is set in a classy two-storey building in the plush area of town. Seafood is their specialty. Open Monday to Friday, 11:45 am-2:30 pm and 6:45-11 pm, and on Sunday until 3 pm.

Nightlife

Like any international city, La Paz has everything from a symphony orchestra to a jazz bar with international musicians. Most shows featuring musicians playing traditional music, called *peñas*, are in the tourist area. Head to the south end of town for the more international entertainment. If you understand Spanish, live theater is a must. If not, movie theaters offer American movies in English with Spanish sub-titles. La Paz is not a dangerous city, but I do recommend taking a taxi home after spending a night on the town.

■ Live Music, Bars, Pubs & Discos

 Thelonious Jazz Bar, *Avenida 20 de Octobre,* ☎ *242-4405*, is a tiny place that opens Tuesday to Saturday at 7 pm, although things rarely get going before 10 pm. There's a cover charge of $5 and drinks are not cheap, but the music is excellent. Thelonious is the kind of jazz club you would find in New York: a long rectangular bar, seating space for about 100, round tables with candles, and walls covered with photos of jazz musicians. We arrived to the sound of a hip 15-piece band of local musicians led by the Danish saxophonist Anders Anderson. These local cats, as they say, swung like crazy with a superb mix of familiar and complex original tunes. This was top-rate jazz music you might not expect to hear this high up and far away from the major jazz centers. (Review by Barry McKinnon)

La Cueva del Jazz *(The Jazz Cave), Calle Murillo #993, 2nd floor,* has a six-piece jazz band called Danilo's playing every weekend. The cover charge is $3. I did not visit this bar because every time I went they were closed. However, the club honors the famous Bolivian composers, Danilo Rojas (piano), Gustavo Valera (sax), Ben Chambi (drums), Oscar Valera (drums), Oscar Cordova (quena) and Rulos (Latin percussion).

Huari Peña Restaurant, *Calle Sagarnaga #339,* ☎ *231-6225*, is a pub that has live traditional music specifically for the tourist. It's a good show that you can enjoy with Andean food. The cover charge is $6 and the show starts at 8 pm, seven days a week.

Peña Bolivia, *Sagarnaga #189,* ☎ *231-6827*, is competition to Huari Peña and, for a dollar less cover charge, is much better. The hall is bigger and the food – things like llama kebab, lamb cooked in wine and spiced chicken – is good. The show starts daily at 8:30 pm. I came here years ago; longevity in this competitive society says a lot. The band I heard was good and showed a lot of interest in the audience.

Los Escudos Peña Restaurant, *Avenida Mariscal Santa Cruz #1201, on the corner of the Plaza of the Obelisco in the Club de La Paz,* ☎ *231-2133,* has grand shows of international quality. The cover charge of $5 includes your first drink and the meal of the day can be ordered for $10.

La Chopperia, *Calle Pichincha #662,* is an antique pub near the tourist area of La Paz. It serves everything from juice to coffee to beer and special cocktails.

Malegria, *Calle Goitia #155*, ☎ *244-0983*, is open daily from 7:30 pm and is another swinging pub/disco in La Paz. It's one street behind the Prada and is always crowded with young people enjoying the best nightlife in the city. There is a $1 cover charge.

Café Ciudad, *Plaza Estudiante #1901*, ☎ *244-1827*, is open 24 hours a day, perfect for a middle-of-the-night snack. Pastries, sandwiches, salads and ice creams are the primary fare, but they also serve alcoholic drinks.

The Diesel National, *20 de Octubre #2271*, is a funky place patronized by the young traveling crowd who want to dance and drink until dawn. Even if you don't want to party all night, you will find that the décor is an interesting attraction. Open Monday to Saturday at 7:30 pm.

Coyote Bar, *Avenida 20 de Octubre #2288*, ☎ *277-2856*, is a small but popular place to hang out, drink and meet the Bolivian version of the yuppie.

Bizzarro Alternative Club, *Gualchalla and 20 de Octubre*, has two lounges – the Electric Floor and the Electronic Lounge. They open at 7 pm and have a Girl's Night on Friday where the girls get drinks at half price. Friday and Saturday nights feature Bizzaro DJ shows and performances.

Mongo's Rock Bottom Bar, *Calle Hermanos Manchego #2444*, offers international foods and lots of loud music for dancing. Once the miners' bar, it has been taken over by young professionals, foreign tourists and ex-pats. The food is good and there are discounted prices for drinks during happy hour. Open weekdays at noon and on weekends at 6 pm.

Dead Stroke Pub Café and Billiards, *6 de Agosto #2460*, ☎ *243-3472*, offers the combination of billiards and music. Open daily except Sundays at 5 pm, with a happy "hour" from 5 to 9 pm.

La Casa del Tapado, *Calle Batallon Colorados*, is open Monday to Saturday from 3 pm until late. This is the new artists' hang-out that has over 200 pieces of original art donated by 130 Bolivian artists. Some are from the Fundacion RISCO and others are students from the Academia Nacional de Bellas Artes and UMSA. The three-room house has an auditorium, a bar in the motif of a mine, and a café with live music. The theater has presentations from the El Pequeño Teatro in La Paz and by the Cine al Margen. Come here to support the arts.

Scaramush Bar, *Calle Fernando Guachalla #521*, ☎ *242-1440*, is a cozy downstairs bar with lots of wood and polish. Live music, often jazz, is presented on Thursday and Friday nights. This bar was reviewed by Andrew Revel of *Llama Express*. Open Monday to Saturday, 6:30 pm to midnight.

■ Soccer Games

Football, or soccer, is an addiction here and even the youngest kids can be seen kicking a ball. If they don't have a ball, they make one out of a stone wrapped in a sock. At present, the three top teams are the **Bolívars**, the **Oriente Petrolero** and the **Strongest**. If you are a fan, watch the *Llama Express* for game times or check at the tourist office on Plaza Estudiantes.

Shopping

There are so many shops from which to choose it seems unfair to list only some here. You can purchase good-quality weavings from street vendors and you can get some shoddy stuff in shops with good displays. My advice is if you see something you like, and can afford it, buy it. Regardless of how much you pay in Bolivia, the price at home will be about 10 times as much. In La Paz, you may find better prices at shops that are a little away from Calle Sagarnaga, the main tourist spot. I also encourage you to purchase something from one of the co-ops throughout the country in support of their work with the local people. Shops open around 9 am and close for siesta during the afternoon. They re-open around 4 pm and stay open until 9pm. There are a few shops that stay open during siesta.

■ Local Crafts

El Dorado Collection, *Calle Linares #892,* ☎ *246-0269 or 245-2646,* is open from 9:30 am to 7:30 pm. They specialize in fine silver products and Alpaca sweaters. The sweaters are of high quality and unique designs.

Artesanias Wara, *Calle Sagarnaga #131,* ☎ *231-6674*, carries Jalq'a weavings, including the prized belts. Those made from alpaca are so tightly woven that they appear to be painted. Prices are high, of course. The store also carries ceramics and leather goods that have weavings worked into them.

Artesania Curmi, *Calle Linares #958,* ☎ *241-5024*, sells Bolivian textiles and a good collection of bags. I didn't find much to buy as stock was low, but if you do buy something, they will ship the goods home for you.

Wiphala, *Calle Linares #906,* ☎ *237-1805*, has good prices on unique hats from all areas of the country.

Artesanias Quechua, Calle Sagarnaga #340, ☎ 231-8218, has masks, wood products, games and children's clothing. They offer a good price on the ceramic chess sets that have one team as Inca dressed in traditional dress with llamas (instead of horses) and funeral towers (instead of castles). They play against the conquistadors. The chess sets are good discussion pieces.

Inti Illimani, *Calle Linares #890,* ☎ *281-6832,* has excellent wool and alpaca carpets at reasonable prices. The carpets are large, with unique designs, and the owner will go out of her way to show her products. A 6.5 x 10-foot/2 x 3-m carpet costs about $40 if made from wool, and $70 if made from alpaca.

Artisan San Francisco, *Plaza San Francisco #498,* ☎ *237-3723 hoskgale@caoba.entelnet.bo,* is on San Francisco Square adjacent to the church. Selling high-quality products at high-end prices, this company will export for you. If traveling for a long time, this is a good option.

Co-ops

Inca Pallay, *Calle Linares,* is a co-op center selling quality indigenous products at a fair price (for the crafts makers). Started in 1986 by two Chilean anthropologists who wanted to help the indigenous communities around the Sucre area, the program has done well. The co-op opened the Textile Museum in Sucre as well as some museums in smaller centers. They have shops in Santa Cruz, Sucre and La Paz and support workshops for those living in the rural communities to help them make quality products. At present, the co-op has over 1,200 weavers, both men and women, working in 26 workshops throughout the country. Although not all artisans belong to this group, I encourage you to purchase something, no matter how small, in support of the cause.

■ Jewelry

Tourist Shop, *Calle Sagarnaga #235,* ☎ *233-4144*, has silver and gold handcrafted jewelry in interesting designs. Prices are not low.

Another interesting jewelry shop is **King's Store**, *Calle Loayza #261, between Camacho and Mercado streets,* ☎ *220-1331.* They have a second shop in the south end.

■ Packs, Maps & Books

Kaypi Artesanias, *Calle Sagarnaga #189, shop 18,* has North Face backpacks and day packs, as well as Lowe Alpine packs. A large pack goes for about $120 and a small one is $50. Always remember that if the deal sounds too good to be true, it probably is. Some packs made in Bolivia carry "borrowed" labels. The packs I saw appeared to be of good quality, but you should examine the merchandise closely.

Tu Musica, *Calle Sagarnaga #189, shop 17*, ☎ *231-9162*, has Berndston & Berndston maps, some trekking and climbing maps, road maps and city maps. They also carry better class Andean music CDs, including those by Fernando Jimenez and Awatiñas, traditional Andean musicians. Tu Musica also has posters, books (some of which are in English or German) and videos of Bolivia. The owner speaks fluent English. This company was closed after the tax riots when looters damaged the building. Since they have no e-mail, I do not know if they have reopened.

Maps can also be purchased directly from Viviane and Ricardo Guzman, ☎ 273-3124 or 7725-1197 (cell), who have the best detailed maps of the country. Ricardo's father was the cartographer.

■ Antiques

 Javier Nuñez de Arco Antique Shop, *Avenida 16 de Julio #1615*, ☎ *211-6661*, is a fairly large shop with real antiques (as opposed to those sold on the street that are often just five weeks old). Nuñez de Arco, a famous Bolivian photographer, has a collection of photos that were originally Arthur Pasnansky's. Pasnansky was a photographer who in the 1940s convinced the archeological society that Tihuanaco was older than they thought at the time. He also wrote the book, *Tiwanaco; the Cradle of American Man*, a copy of which Nuñez de Arco holds. If for no other reason, go into the shop and purchase a collection of photos that have been reproduced as postcards – not to send, but to keep as souvenirs. They show Bolivia as it was 60 to 70 years ago. You are not permitted to take antiques out of the country.

Day Trip

■ Tihuanaco Archeological Site

 Tihuanaco ruins, the most impressive in Bolivia, are located near a small village of the same name just 43 miles/70 km along a paved road from La Paz. You can stay overnight at either the hotel or one of the smaller *alojamientos* in the village. The site itself takes a few hours to cover and for the two museums add another hour or two, depending on the depth of your interest.

About 21 miles/35 km from La Paz, on the way to the ruins, is the village of **Laja**, where the original La Paz was supposed to be constructed. Once the builder, Alonso de Mendoza, realized how cold the Altiplano was, he moved the city to its present site. The church here was the first built on the Altiplano. It was reconstructed in the late 1600s, at which time the mestizo baroque design was added. This is a lovely building, similar in its outer design to the one at San Jose de Chiquitos on the mission circuit. It is the only thing of interest in the village.

Getting to the ruins from La Paz is easy. Go to El Cementario and take one of the *trufis* that leaves every half-hour for the village of Tihuanaco. If you are interested in Laja, get off the bus and visit that village before catching the next bus going to Tihuanaco. The bus may be full when it arrives at Laja so be prepared to stand. It takes about 1½ hours to reach Tihuanaco from La Paz and another 15 minutes to walk from the village square back to the ruins. Returning from Tihuanaco, you can either go to the square and wait for a bus or flag one down along the road that passes the ruins. The last bus leaves for La Paz at 7 pm.

AYMARA LINGO	
Haya Marka Aru	Language of distant towns
Pachamama	Mother Earth
Supaya	Bad spirit
Huaca	Temple
Yanacona	Priest
Yatiri	Consultant for health and danger
Mallkus	The big boss
Kallaway	Highly respected doctor exempt from enslavement
Kopocamayo	Writer
Amauta	Wise man
Pallapalla	Guard

History

The civilization that once used the Tihuanaco ruins as their ceremonial center started building the city around 600 BC and the decline, believed to have been caused by drought, didn't occur until AD 900. The site, during its peak, covered 1,040 acres/420 hectares and the surrounding lands occupied by those with allegiance to the city covered 231,660 square miles/600,000 square km.

Some archeologists believe that Tihuanaco had as many as 115,000 people in the city itself and another 250,000 people working and residing in the surrounding countryside. The country people farmed grains, herded llamas and built one of the longest paved roads in pre-Columbian history. They also traveled and traded as far away as the coast of Peru. From findings there, it has been deduced that the Tihuanaco people were more advanced in pottery, astronomy and math than the Inca ever were.

TERRACES TELL A TALE

Archeologist Alan Kolata, from the University of Illinois, went in 1986 with a team to Luqurmata, just out of Tihuanaco, and discovered extensive terracing. Some fields measured 658x4.5 ft (200x15 m). They were covered first with coarse gravel and rock, then by a layer of clay. On top of the clay was fine gravel, above which was black topsoil. The second layer, of clay, was there to hold water. For irrigation, the farmers built channels and redirected water from the Catari River. Irrigation ditches were strategically positioned to get the maximum sun exposure to warm the water and produce an algae that was used as fertilizer. Warmer water was an attractive environment to water fowl. These birds were used for their meat and eggs. Today, scientists are studying ancient agricultural methods with the hope of reintroducing them to make present-day production more economically viable. The discovery of these terraces and channels made Alan Kolata believe that at one time the farmers were able to grow and store enough food to support a huge number of people. Prior to this discovery, it was believed that only about 20,000 people lived at Tihuanaco.

It is also believed that Tihuanaco once sat on the shores of Lake Titikaka, but, due to drought, the lake receded, leaving the city almost 10 miles/ 16 km from the water. It was because of this drought that the entire civilization had to move.

Exploring the Ruins

The ceremonial center of the city, believed to have been constructed in the 5th century BC, is worth a visit. At the city's peak, an outer wall had friezes that were either partially covered in gold or painted bright colors. People of this time were dressed in finely woven clothes, with jewelry and precious metal pins and carefully combed hair. Appearance was important; numerous mirrors have been found at the site. The heads of Tihuanaco residents were rather pointed. Boards were placed on the heads of in-

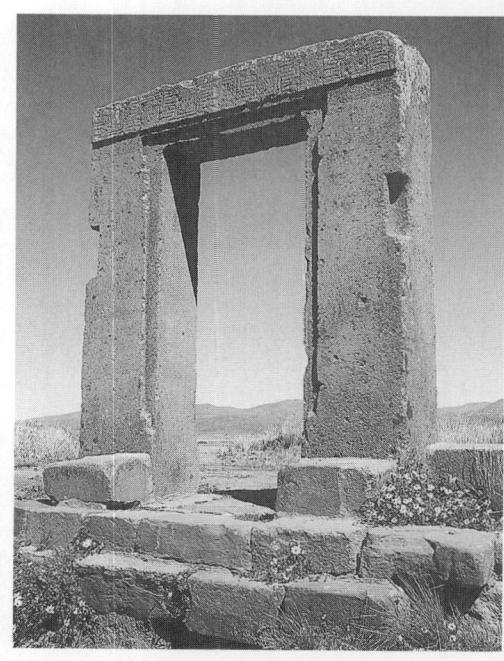

Door of the Moon.

La Paz

fants (one at the back and one at the forehead) so the soft bone grew back from the nose. The boards remained on a child's head until around five years of age. This custom was identified through the examination of skulls found in the area.

Visitors to the city had to cross the moat and call to the guards through a hole in the stone. The sound reverberated to a listener inside the gate who would then give the visitor permission to enter. Though the moat is gone, you can still whisper through the hole and have your companion hear you on the opposite side of the courtyard.

To enter the sunken court of **Kalasasaya** you must go down a wide stairway made from a single block of stone. The sandstone used here came from a quarry six miles/10 km away, but the andesite used in other parts of the city came from about 60 miles/100 km away. Some of the stones weigh as much as 150 tons.

The heads that decorate the temple beside Kalasasaya are believed to be the trophy heads of sacrificed enemies. The sunken patio is called the Semi-Subterraneo and was first described in 1903 by Franciscan missionaries, but it wasn't until 1932 that it was excavated by Dr. Wendell Bennett. The heads make great photo subjects; each is different. Three other temples surrounded Kalasasaya, but little remains of them today.

The huge monolith, excavated by Bennett at Tihuanaco, was moved to the center of La Paz, in a square across from the football stadium. However, it has now been replaced and moved to the city's archeological museum. It stood 24 ft/7.3 m high and was given the name "Bennett Monolith."

Along one side of the main ruins are small mounds that have a lot of stones missing. You may find some of them in the church on the plaza in the town of Tihuanaco and some on the railway bridge nearby.

CAN I CHANGE YOUR MIND?

The royalty of Tihuanaco used willka, red hallucinogenic seeds that were imported from the deserts along the coast and were then ground and snorted during religious ceremonies. They also used mescaline to alter their minds. The most extreme hallucinogenic used was the ayahuasca vine. This was administered as an enema.

Another archeologist, Dr. A. Posnansky, studied the site for 50 years. He believes that the people living here were a religious cult who worshipped the god of the sky and of thunder, Viracocha, whose image is represented in the bas-relief in the Gateway to the Sun. Beside him are warriors wearing masks and messengers wearing masks with condors on them.

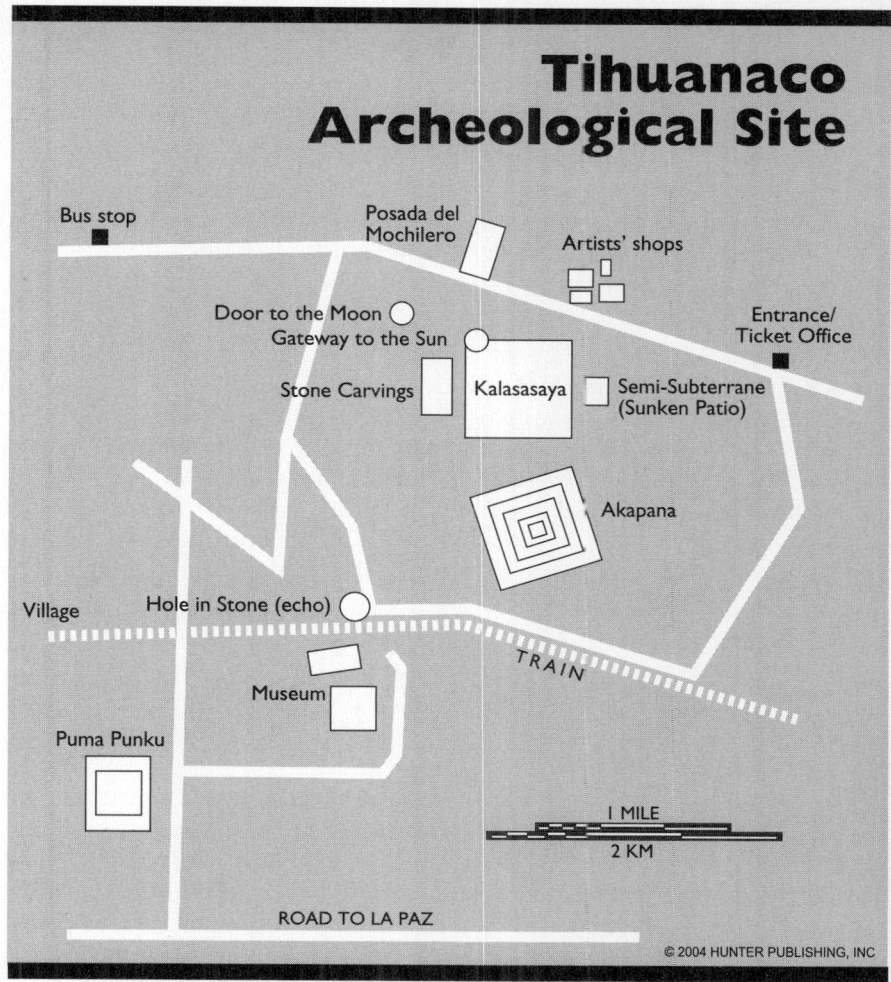

The **Gateway to the Sun** is cut from a single block of stone that is 9.8 ft/ three m high and three m wide and weighs about 10 tons. Through this gate is the carving of a regal figure, dressed in royal robes, carrying two scepters topped with condor heads. During the spring and fall equinox, the sun shines through the gate onto the figure. Today, during the spring equinox, Aymara priests come here to make offerings to their gods and watch through the gate as the sun rises. This is the Aymara New Year and once the sun has risen the priests and others join in celebration with music, dancing, rituals, food, coca and *chicha*.

The mound to the south of the Kalasasaya temple is the **Pyramid of Akapana**. It has seven levels, all of which were at one time faced with stones, some carved. The pyramid is believed to have been built in the image of the surrounding mountains and was used for ritual offerings. Only some stones remain intact, but the view from the top is worth the climb. The pyramid stands 92 ft/18 m high and each side is 375 ft/114 m long.

If you continue to circumnavigate the ruins you will come to a much smaller gate called the **Door of the Moon** (Puerta de la Luna), also made of stone. This is a peaceful place, with wildflowers growing through the doorway, a good place to rest. A tiny **museum** is open 9 am-6 pm daily. It is well organized, with areas dedicated to ceramics, textiles, gold and silver carvings, carved stones found in the area and seashells taken from the lake.

Puma Punku is a second mound 1.2 miles/two km from Tihuanaco. Walking away from town and toward Lake Titikaka, cross the tracks, pass the museum and keep going. The name Puma Punku means the **Gate of the Puma**. It is smaller than Akapana and about 200 years newer. The construction of this pyramid is interesting, like a Lego-block structure. Each stone weighs about 15 tons and some are up to 100 tons. These quarried stones, the largest in South America, interlock to form the walls and floors that were once covered with gold and carvings.

The **Posnansky Museum** is to be opened in the near future and will be located near the ruins. The famous Bolivian photographer, Javier Nuñez de Arco, has dedicated 30 years to collecting, restoring and reproducing the photos and writings of A. Posnansky (1873-1946), who came to Bolivia twice. He first visited in the late 1800s, when he operated a cargo boat on the Amazon River. When the war between Bolivia and Brazil broke out, Posnansky escaped to Europe. He returned in 1903 and stayed, photographing life. He was fascinated with Tihuanaco and, like Graham Hancock, believed that Tihuanaco was much older than people thought. Posnansky wrote the book, *Cradle of American Man*, a huge tome published in 1945. An accomplished artist, Nuñez will have opened this museum by the time you purchase this book. Ask in Tihuanaco when you arrive. If it is open, the photographs are well worth seeing.

Places to Stay

La Posada del Mochilero, ☎ *289-8544, $$$*, is across from the exit gate of the ruins on Camino Antiguo. An attached restaurant has *almuerzos* at reasonable prices.

There are some basic places to stay on the plaza and a few places to eat. The restaurants beside the museum are expensive.

Shopping

Artisan stalls are set around the square and museum. There isn't as much here as in La Paz, but if you are altruistic and want to support the local economy, purchase something.

LA PAZ - GENERAL DIRECTORY

■ OUTDOOR ADVENTURE CLUBS

Andino Boliviano . . . . ☎ 232-4682

Club de Montanismo Halcones . . . . . no phone . . . . based in Oruro

Gravity Assisted . . . . ☎ 231-3849 . . . . www.gravitybolivia.com

Hash House Harriers . . . . ☎ 279-1524 . . . . www.lapazhash.com

Mallasilla Golf & Country Club . . . ☎ 274-5124 . . . . www.boliviagolf.com

■ TOUR OPERATORS & OUTFITTERS

Alba Tours . . . . ☎ 231-3052

ACELA Tours Ltd . . . . ☎ 240-8125

American Tours . . . . ☎ 237-4204 . . . . www.american-ecotours.com

Andean Summits. . . . . ☎ 242-2106 . . . . www.andeansummits.com

Andes Amazonia Travel Agency . . ☎ 231-8313

Buho's Tours . . . . ☎ 247-1577

CombiTours . . . . ☎ 245-1626

Crillon Tours . . . . ☎ 233-7533 . . . . www.titikaka.com

EBA Transtur . . . . ☎ 242-2430

Explore Bolivia . . . . ☎ 303-545-5728 . . . . www.explorebolivia.com

Footprint Adventures . . . . . . ☎ 01522-804929 . . . . www.footprint-adventures.co.uk

Gravity Assisted Mountain Biking . ☎ 231-3849 . . . . www.gravitybolivia.com

High Camp Bolivia . . . . ☎ 231-7497

Huayana Tours . . . . ☎ 245-6717

Inca Land Tours . . . . ☎ 231-3589 . . . . www.incalandtours.com

International Mountain Guides ☎ 360-569-2609 . . . . www.mountainguides.com

Magri Turismo Ltd . . . . ☎ 244-2727 . . . . ww.bolivianet.com/magri

Milton Tour Agency . . . . ☎ 236-8003

New Horizon . . . . ☎ 231-6274

New Milenium Adventure Sports . ☎ 245-1660

Pachamama Tours . . . . ☎ 231-9740

Paititi Travel . . . . ☎ 244-0586

Sky Bolivia. . . . . ☎ 231-3254 . . . . www.skybolivia.com

Toñito Tours . . . . ☎ 233-6250. . . . . . . www.bolivianexpeditions.com

Tocando el Cielo . . . . ☎ 279-1440

Transturin. . . . . ☎ 242-2222 . . . . www.transturin.com

Trek Bolivia . . . . ☎ 231-7106 . . . . www.trekbolivia.8k.com

Vicuña Tours . . . . ☎ 231-0708 . . . . www.victoursbol.com

LA PAZ – GENERAL DIRECTORY

■ LANGUAGE SCHOOLS

ABC Spanish School . . . . ☎ 772-62657 . . . www.studyspanish-lapaz-bolivia.tk

SpeakEasy Institute . . . . ☎ 244-1779 . . . . www.speakeasyinstitute.com

The Altiplano

Copacabana/Lake Titikaka

Altitude: 12,533 ft / 3,810 m
Population: 7,500

Copacabana, tucked into a sandy bay on Lake Titikaka, is often bypassed by those going to or coming from Peru. This is a pity. Not only is the area aesthetically exceptional, but the hiking is as challenging as it is interesting, with pre-Inca and Inca ruins to enjoy. On weekends, Lake Titikaka is host to every kind of water vehicle possible (except the obnoxious Jet Ski,

and I am sure those will come in time). According to the *Guinness Book of World Records*, the highest kayak/skin dive in the world was done in this lake. But if watersports – *cold* watersports – are not your thing, you can always walk the beach looking for the Telmatobius frog. It is easy to spot because it is about a foot long.

The area is also a wetland with enormous amounts of aquatic vegetation and numerous bird species, like the cormorant and the heron.

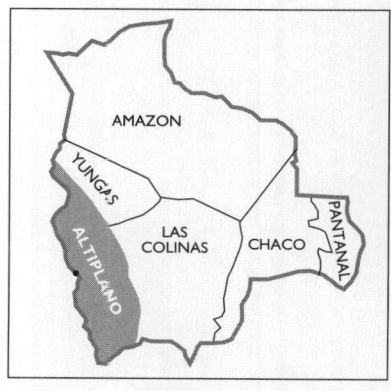

AYMARA LINGO: Copacabana comes from two words. "Kgupac" means beautiful blue; "Kgawana" means "that you can see."

Isla del Sol and Isla de la Luna have been pilgrimage sites since the days of the Chirpa, who preceded the Tihuanacan culture by almost a thousand years. There is convenient transportation from Copacabana to Isla del Sol and Isla de la Luna, the holiest islands, according to Tihuanacan and Inca legend. Today, religious pilgrimages arrive in Copacabana rather than on the islands but still it is the lake more than the beautiful cathedral that seems to be the draw for most foreigners.

There are ruins worth seeing both in town and on the islands. Accommodations and restaurants in Copacabana are excellent and the people are friendly. The only drawback is that money-changing services are poor. If you come from Peru, this can present a problem.

Bolivia owns about a third of the lake, which is 116 miles/190 km long and, depending on the source of information, 37-49 miles/60-80 km wide. It covers 2,550 square miles/6,640 square km and averages between 330 and 660 ft deep (100-200 m), but is 1,000 ft/300 m deep near Isla Soto on the northeast shore. The rain and snow melt from the Cordillera Real feed the lake through 25 different rivers and the outflow goes down Rio Desaguadero to the salt lakes of Uru Uru and Poopo, just south of Oruro. The surface temperature of Titikaka is 57°F/14°C, not very high for water that has been basking in the sun for over two million years.

Copacabana is the home of Bolivia's most venerated statue, the Virgin de Copacabana. Samana Santa (Holy Week) attracts many pilgrims who walk here from La Paz to pay homage to the virgin.

Barley, quinoa, potatoes and corn are grown on the area's terraced farms and fish farms are abundant on the lake. Llamas and alpacas often watch as you pass by, as do the locals who are still curious about foreigners.

This fish farm is one of many on Lake Titikaka.

TAXES PLEASE

A 25¢ tax is imposed on all visitors coming into Copacabana. It is collected on the highway as you approach the town. This is a legal municipal tax ordinance that falls under section CXIII, item 142, of Bolivian law. It nets the municipality a lot of money, especially during special events, and helps pay for keeping the area aesthetically attractive. The tax is paid by everyone, including Bolivians who do not live in the town.

■ Getting Here & Around

 A bus from Copacabana to El Cementario bus area in La Paz costs $2, plus 25¢ to cross the Straight of Tiquina. Buses are available on Calle 16 de Julio along Plaza Sucre. They leave every two hours between 7 am and 7 pm and take three to four hours to reach La Paz. For the most part, the views are good and the highway paved. Buses to Copacabana operate during the same hours.

If you're going to Sorata, get off the bus at Huarina just after the ferry crossing and catch a *trufi* going north to Achicachi and then another going on to Sorata. You can also take a *colectivo* to La Paz. The time is about the same as a bus, but the comfort and cost is less.

Consider staying at the lake if you would like to see some of the other islands or hang out at a resort with mostly upper-class Bolivians. To do this, travel from Copacabana to the Straights of Tiquina and then stay at Tiquina, Huatajata or Huarina.

Taxis go from Copacabana to the border town of Kasani and charge $1 per person. These go when full and there are lots of them.

■ History

Lake Titikaka and its islands have been an important place for thousands of years as the ruins from past civilizations indicate.

In Tihuanacan language, "titi" means puma or mountain cat and "kaka" means rock. It is believed that, first, the lake was created when the Sun God filled the area with tears after pumas ate his children. Another story claims that Viracocha, the Inca God, rose out of Lake Titikaka and created Isla del Sol and Isla de la Luna so the world would have light. He then made Manco Copac and Mama Huaca, the Adam and Eve of Bolivian legend. After they started multiplying, Viracocha taught his creations how to farm and build houses. Then he sailed off, leaving them to deal with the World Bank and Drug Enforcement Agency.

Altiplano

After Viracocha left, the Aymara, and later the Inca and their Quechua allies, settled around the lake.

Another legend has the god Viracocha (meaning Lake's Foam), after seeing the beauty of the lake, creating a community of people and animals to live by the lake. Later, Khunu, a powerful god, saw the degradation of humans so he sent a drought to rid the earth of the godless creatures. This is in agreement with the belief that the lake shrunk from where Tihuanaco sits to its present size. Geographers theorize that the lake once covered the valley all the way down to Uyuni and that Lake Poopo was part of Titikaka.

BEND ME, SHAPE ME ANYWAY YOU WANT ME

Local legend has it that Lake Titikaka has three parts. The part belonging to Peru is shaped like a puma, the center is shaped like a condor and the area below the Straights of Taquina is like a man praying.

Once the Spanish took over in Peru, Copacabana became a safe place because there was no reason for the Spanish to invade. Trade between Lower Peru and Upper Peru (Bolivia) went around the lake, not across the straights of Taquina and past Copacabana. It was too far from civilized society and there was no gold in the area. Instead, the area was left to early religious zealots. **Christianity** was brought to the region in 1530, and the first church was erected by 1552. Locals converted to **Catholicism** and then struggles for power started and involved various sects of Catholicism.

Francisco Tito Yupanqui, an artist and direct descendent of Inca royalty, was living in Copacabana during the time of religious struggles. One night he had a vision of the Virgin Mary dressed in elegant robes, carrying a child. In honor of the vision he made a clay model of her and placed it on the church altar. Locals in authority took it down, saying it was not good enough. Yupanqui tried making other reproductions of the Virgin but none was good enough, so he went to study at the reputable art school in Potosi. After a few years, he carved another Virgin out of wood and took it to La Paz where the church leaders again rejected it. The carving was kicked and broken, but Yupanqui salvaged the work and, with the help of a priest from San Francisco Convent in La Paz, restored the statue. It was then transported to San Pedro de Taquina and leaders there wouldn't allow it to go farther. They wanted the Virgin in their village. **Don Geronimo Marañon**, a powerful lawyer, saw the Virgin and insisted that she be the patron of Copacabana. The struggles continued until finally, on February 2, 1583 the Image of the Candelaria Virgin (as she became known) arrived in Copacabana. She had been smuggled in by those opposing the priests living in San Pedro de Taquina.

Miracles were soon accredited to the Virgin. This made the creator of the image, Francisco Tito Yupanqui, a happy man. The vision he had seen so many years before finally ended where he believed it should – with the Virgin on the altar in the church in Copacabana.

The Virgin stands 33 inches/84 cm high and is made of maguey wood. Her hands, arms and face are ceramic. In her left arm she carries an indigenous boy-child and in her right a gold candle. There is also a gold cane hanging from her left arm. Both the child and the Virgin have gold and silver crowns decorated with precious stones. The aura around the Virgin's head contains the sun, moon and 12 stars. She is adorned with jewelry – necklace, bracelets, rings and earrings – all heavily decked with semi-precious and precious stones. The belt she wears around her waist was given to her by Augustinian followers. The ruby imbedded in the belt is two inches in diameter. Imbedded in her foot is the Bolivian flag.

VIRGIN MIRACLES

One of the rings found on the Virgin's finger was given to her by a gambler who had bet and lost all his money except for the ring. When he tried to place it on her finger, she spread them so the ring would fit properly.

Another miracle occurred in 1616. Alonso de Escoto was a poor immigrant from Spain who wanted to make his fortune in the new world but had bad luck. He prayed to the Virgin, asking for her help, and then walked off with her earrings and two silver chandeliers. When he got to Arequipa, Peru, he sold them. With a small fortune in hand, he decided to buy a winery, but the volcano that year ruined all the wine. One proprietor with whom Escoto was negotiating said that instead of buying the land, Escoto should take the wine-vinegar and sell it in Lima. Escoto agreed. When the casks were uncovered in Lima, he found that the liquid had become wine of the highest quality, rather than vinegar. He sold it for a huge profit and quickly returned to Copacabana. On February 2, 1618 he returned to the cathedral and placed in the sanctuary, in front of the Virgin, a silver chandelier that contained 365 lights and weighed 650 pounds.

There are more stories of miracles performed by the Virgin and I am certain there will be more miracles to come. Because of her reputation, in 1925, the Virgin was crowned the Bolivian Queen and Copacabana became the most important pilgrimage site in the country.

■ Services

The **Entel telephone office** is on Calle Murillo (just down from the Emperador) and up from the cathedral.

Altiplano

The **post office** is on Plaza 2 de Febrero just down from the tourist office.

The **Police** are next to the post office on Plaza 2 de Febrero and on the opposite side of the square from the cathedral.

The **hospital** is on the edge of town going toward Horca del Inca (signs indicate the direction). The phone number is ☎ 118.

The **bank** on Avenida 6 de Agosto, close to Plaza Sucre, charges a 2% commission for travelers' checks. However, being a bank, they are closed on weekends, holidays and by 6 pm every day. There is usually a line here.

A money-changer at Tienda Avenida 6 de Agosto on the corner of Calle 6 de Agosto and 15 de Julio, across from Plaza Sucre, sells many items and advertises the changing of travelers' checks. He plays on tourists not knowing the currency or the language very well. When I was there, he agreed to pay the same rate as American Express with no commission charges, but when he gave us the money, he took $20 commission. We called him on it and he just walked away laughing.

American Express on Calle 6 de Agosto charges no commission. They are not open on Sundays and holidays, and often open quite late in the mornings.

The **tourist office** is on the Plaza 2 de Febrero just past the police station. They have some information, but seem reluctant to share it with travelers.

■ Festivals of Copacabana

 Festivals are fun. If you are in the area during any of the following festivals, join the locals. Samana Santa is the festival that has the most interesting ceremonies as pilgrims walk all the way from La Paz to Copacabana for the celebrations. Although Carnival is celebrated here and throughout the country, Oruro is actually the best place to be for that event. For a list of all festivals celebrated in Bolivia, see page 46. Copacabana is special for Samana Santa and for the celebration around the Virgin of Candeleria. For more information about festivals, see page 46.

Alasista is held on January 24th to celebrate fertility, happiness and prosperity. Ekeko is the honored god. In Copacabana, people walk up to the Stations of the Cross and pray for good fortune.

The **Virgin of Candeleria** is celebrated February 2nd-4th. The first and second days are celebrated with music and dancing. The third day there is a bullfight. This is the most important event in the town because of the Virgin's reputation for performing miracles.

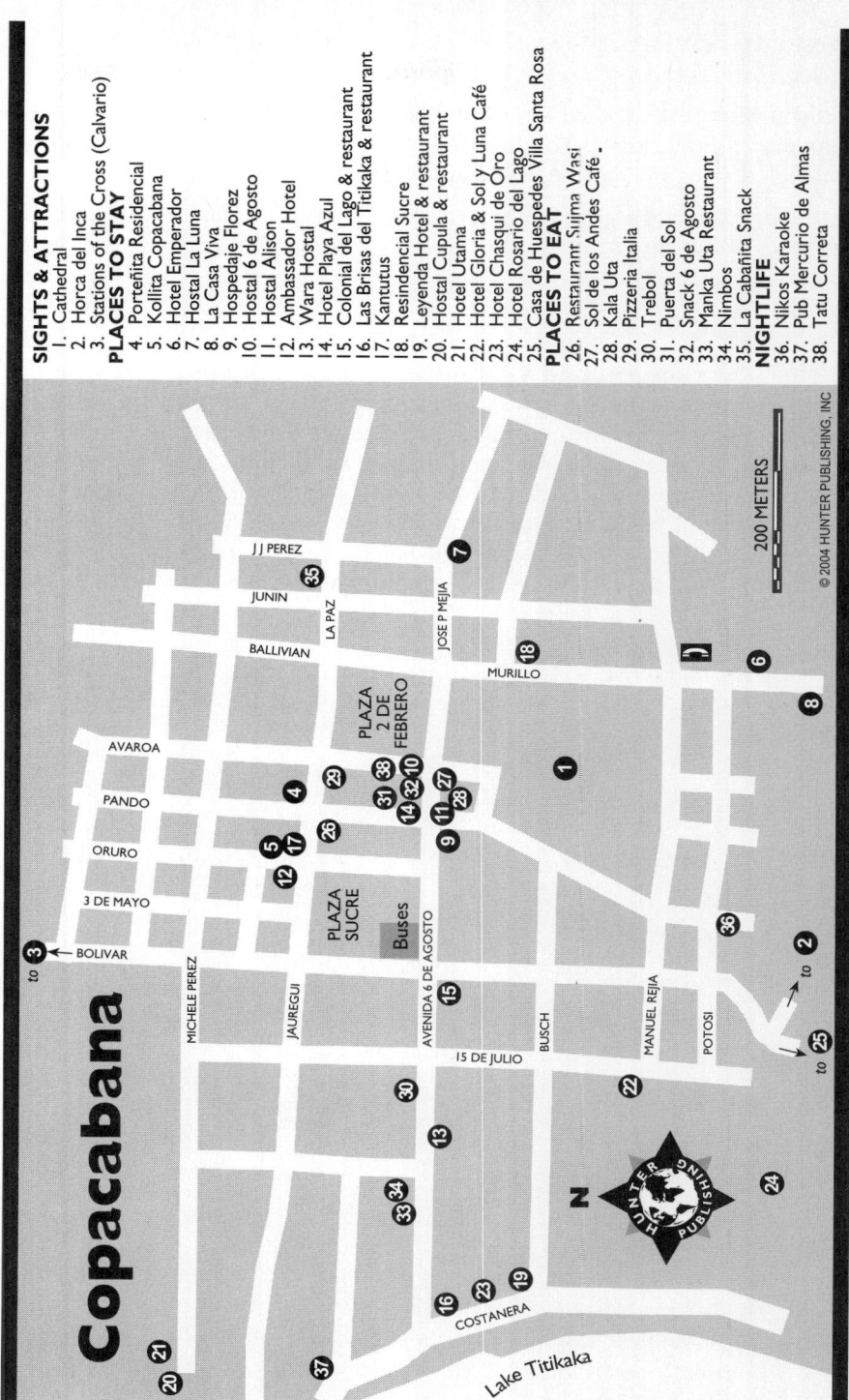

Copacabana

SIGHTS & ATTRACTIONS
1. Cathedral
2. Horca del Inca
3. Stations of the Cross (Calvario)

PLACES TO STAY
4. Portoñita Residencial
5. Kollita Copacabana
6. Hotel Emperador
7. Hostal La Luna
8. La Casa Viva
9. Hospedaje Florez
10. Hostal 6 de Agosto
11. Hostal Alison
12. Ambassador Hotel
13. Wara Hostal
14. Hotel Playa Azul
15. Colonial del Lago & restaurant
16. Las Brisas del Titikaka & restaurant
17. Kantutus
18. Residencial Sucre
19. Leyenda Hotel & restaurant
20. Hostal Cupula & restaurant
21. Hotel Utama
22. Hotel Gloria & Sol y Luna Café
23. Hotel Chasqui de Oro
24. Hotel Rosario del Lago
25. Casa de Huespedes Villa Santa Rosa

PLACES TO EAT
26. Restaurant Sujma Wasi
27. Sol de los Andes Café
28. Kala Uta
29. Pizzeria Italia
30. Trebol
31. Puerta del Sol
32. Snack 6 de Agosto
33. Manka Uta Restaurant
34. Nimbos
35. La Cabañita Snack

NIGHTLIFE
36. Nikos Karaoke
37. Pub Mercurio de Almas
38. Tatu Correta

200 METERS

© 2004 HUNTER PUBLISHING, INC

Lake Titikaka

Altiplano

Carnival is at the beginning of Lent (40 days before Easter) and is celebrated throughout Latin America. See page 46.

Dia del Mar (Day of the Sea), March 23rd, is when the death of Eduardo Avaroa is remembered. The navy's fleet sits in Copacabana, so celebrations here are a bit more elaborate than in other places.

Semana Santa is at Easter. Pilgrims walk from La Paz to Copacabana. See page 46 for more information.

■ Sightseeing

The **Copacabana Cathedral** was first, in the 16th century, a mud and brick structure. But after the Virgin of Candelaria started performing miracles, she needed a better home. The present building, with tiles on the Moorish-styled domes, was completed, according to some authorities, in 1820. However, according to five sources that I tried, the building was started as early as 1589 and completed as late as 1820. I suspect construction began around 1610 and was completed within 50 years, with re-construction and add-ons until 1820 or so.

The wooden entrance doors, carved by locals, are immense and worth looking at. The interior is not huge, but the altar and front are ornate and decorated in gold. The attached museum is open only on Sundays from

Intricately carved doors welcome you to Copacabana Cathedral.

8:30 am until early afternoon. I have never managed to go inside. The square in front of the church is a spacious and peaceful place to sit. The square outside the church walls is always full of vendors selling everything needed for the blessing of the vehicles, the blessing of humans or the burial of church members.

To the side of the cathedral is the entrance to the Candelabria, a dark, stone-walled room where people come to ask for miracles. The walls in the first section of the room (that gets light from the street) are covered in words of hope like "walk, money, Volvo, food." Some scratchings are long, while others are one-word requests. At the far end of the room are candles that you can light before speaking directly to the Virgin.

■ Adventures on Foot

BANDARINAS DE INCA: Hike to Bandarinas de Inca on Cerro Copacate, where there are rock paintings, some ruins, a marriage rock and an old hacienda. The rock paintings have been vandalized, but university students are restoring them. If taking a bus/taxi to the trailhead, this is a half-day excursion, but if walking all the way from town and stopping at the Inca tunnel, allow a full day.

To get there by vehicle, take any bus/taxi going to Kasani, the border village just five miles/eight km from Copacabana. Get off at the Km 42 sign. There is a school and an abandoned airport at the stop. Walk east up the gravel road. When you come to the first adobe hut just in from the road, look at the mountain to the north. The gully with the vegetation in it is your destination. Beside the house is a sign indicating your route (it was not yet installed when I was there). In the house lives Gregorio Ramos Kantuta who is knowledgeable about pre-Inca culture. He will guide you to the baths, the rock paintings and the temple for no charge, but a donation would be appreciated. Ramos has a generous heart and he is proud of the area's history.

After getting off the bus, take the first trail on your right, off the gravel road, and follow it up. At the end of this trail, go left. Follow the trail (it swings left) until you come to the remains of an adobe hacienda on your right.

You can go inside and snoop around. The estate was owned by a Spaniard who mistreated and enslaved local Indians until they rebelled. Seeing that they were too strong for him to fight or control, the man abandoned his estate and moved back to Spain. Who he was or when this occurred is unknown. The story probably goes back only as far as the land reforms of 1952, and the man may have had most of his land taken from him by the government and distributed to the locals.

Altiplano

Continue past the hacienda along the trail and turn left at the end of that trail. Within 20 feet the rock paintings come into view. They are ochre in color and depict the Inca flag.

From the paintings, turn right off the trail and continue past the paintings up the mountain where you will find some ruins of bathing pools and footings for temple walls. It is believed that rich Inca came here to worship and to bathe. You can see how the water may have flowed from one shallow tub down to the next. Probably rocks and mud were used to block the flow of the water and fill the pools.

To go to the wedding rock, return to the rock paintings and continue around the mountain. Stay high, but always on a trail. When you are on the back side of the hill you will see two bright, rust-colored arches. This is where some Inca would come years ago to perform their marriage ceremony. Do not walk farther into the valley where homes can be seen. The people living there do not want visitors. A few years ago there was a dispute as to where the highway should go and these people didn't get what they wanted, so they are a bit hostile to outsiders. Return as you came.

INCA TUNNEL: The Inca Tunnel apparently goes through the mountain, under Lake Titikaka and opens up again at the ruins of Pilcocaina. Although the tunnel is impressive, the walk there is the best feature of the hike. This is especially true if you do not have the opportunity to do more hiking in the region. You will pass terraced fields being worked by the owners. There are also a couple of old stone houses that are interesting to look at. The walk from Copacabana should take no more than half a day, unless you combine it with the walk to the Bandarinas de Inca. Exploring both would take a full day.

To get there, walk up Calle Murillo, on the east side of the cathedral, as far as Calle Felix Rosa. At the corner, jog a bit to the right and then the left to continue uphill. You pass a kind of landfill to your left and a wall to your right. Follow that trail all the way around the side of the mountain. It is walled for some of the way. When you are on the south side, continue into a fairly large eucalyptus grove until you come to an abandoned house made of squared stone. This is a ruin from Inca or maybe even Tihuanaco times. There is a second house above it, also abandoned. Just past the bigger house is an opening in the mountain with water trickling out. Peer inside. A flashlight would be useful. The floor and walls have been paved with rocks. Some believe that the tunnel goes all the way to Isla del Sol and was constructed by the Inca. Others believe that the tunnel is from colonial times and was made for mining purposes.

INCA LEGEND

Inca legend, as told to me by an Aymara family, Sonia Cruz Condori and her husband, Oscar Quispe Yavi, who live in Copacabana, is that a man entered the cave after the Inca abandoned it. When he was part-way in, there was an earthquake and the man was hit on the head with a rock. He became crazy and never regained his sanity. This was warning for others not to enter the cave. Apparently, the tunnel has been sealed off at the other end. Also, some of the pools in the cave are deep.

YAMPUPATA PENINSULA: Yampupata is the village at the end of the peninsula that is just northeast of Copocaban town site. The peninsula reaches into Lake Titikaka and almost meets Isla del Sol. Many people like to visit the island by renting a reed boat at Yampupata and paddling across. This takes about 40 minutes if there is no wind. Taking a motorboat – available at the end of the peninsula for $2 per person – takes about 15 minutes. A rowboat costs $1.50 an hour. If you want someone to do the paddling/rowing for you, the cost is higher.

Consider staying at Hostal Yampu (see below) in the village of Sicuani (nine miles/15 km from Copacabana). This would allow more time to explore the peninsula. Sicuani is close to the trail leading to the stone village of Zampaya. If you want to spend time in a yet undiscovered place, this peninsula is worth visiting. The owner of the hostel, Jose Quispe, is friendly and knowledgeable.

To get there, take public transportation from Copacabana to the end of the peninsula and walk the 12 miles/20 km back along an almost flat road. If you walk there, getting back may be a problem as most vehicles do not travel that road after dark. A private taxi from Copacabana will cost $10 for up to four people. A truck leaves for Yampupata from Calles Junin and Copacabana every Monday, Tuesday and Saturday between 11 am and noon (when full). Buses leave on the alternate days and cost 75¢ per person. You can also hire a boat to go to the peninsula for $3.50 per person. Contact **Faustino Hillatarco** at the clock on the main square across from the cathedral in the mornings and he will take you over. To walk here from town, go along Calle Junin and down the hill, past the soccer field.

Altiplano

It's 2½ miles/four km from Copacabana to **Kusihata** where a small museum contains an Inca skull found near the baths. It is five miles/eight km to **Chani**, where there are nice views, and six miles/10 km to Henchaka and the Grotto of the Lourdes. The grotto is a small cave in the side of the mountain. It can be seen from the road, but if you happen to miss it, ask a local to point it out. **Titicachi** is at the eight-mile/13 km point and is another spot for views of the lake. As you walk, you will notice the stone and clay houses are clean and in good repair and the fields are tended. Trout farms dot the lake and people are generally well heeled.

Sicuani (sic-WAN-ee) is nine miles/15 km from Copacabana. Hostal Yampu is basic and costs $1.50 per person. Outhouses on the property were built by CARE Bolivia. Jose Quispe Mamana, wife Margarita and son Renoldo run the place. They are presently building a reed hut for showers and will build a reed museum in the future. They also build and rent reed boats to take onto the lake. Three boats are available for anyone wanting to play Inca. If his boats are occupied, head to Fautso Paye (a local "character") just up the road. The cost to rent boats at either place is $1.50 per hour. Jose's place offers meals at reasonable prices. Lunch, for example, is about $1 and includes rice, salad, meat/fish (usually trout) and potatoes. Jose is pleasant and can teach you a lot about the use of reeds for building.

Sampaya can be reached by following a trail up the mountain from Sicuani. It's a beautiful stone village (good for photography) with no amenities except a few *tiendas* selling snacks and drinks. The people in Sampaya are friendly and, if lucky, you may see them doing something special. I was fortunate enough to observe a funeral. Ask José in Sicuani where the path that leads to Sampaya is located.

The final three miles/five km will take you to the village of **Yampupata** where you can tent on the beach for 75¢ per person. There is an outhouse available but no other amenities. If passing through, the cost of using the outhouse is one boliviano (15¢). I couldn't tell if these rules and prices were local policy or the whim of some local guys I met who needed money for *chicha*. A boat association here controls the cost of boat rentals. It also keeps operators going out sequentially so that everyone gets a turn to earn some income. A boat to the Isla de la Luna costs $10 for up to 10 people. For a really quiet night, stay at the basic hostel on Isla de la Luna for $1.50 per person. You may also be able to stay with people in the village for about the same price. A *tienda* in town sells pop and biscuits.

TRONO DEL INCA: The hike to Trono del Inca starts by walking up Calle Potosi to its end. Turn right and then left again onto the road to La Paz. You will see seven stone carvings on your left that are believed to be seats of the sun. The niches in the stones are believed to have held numerous figures covered in gold. The seats were once used for council meetings of the leaders. The abstract designs carved onto some of the

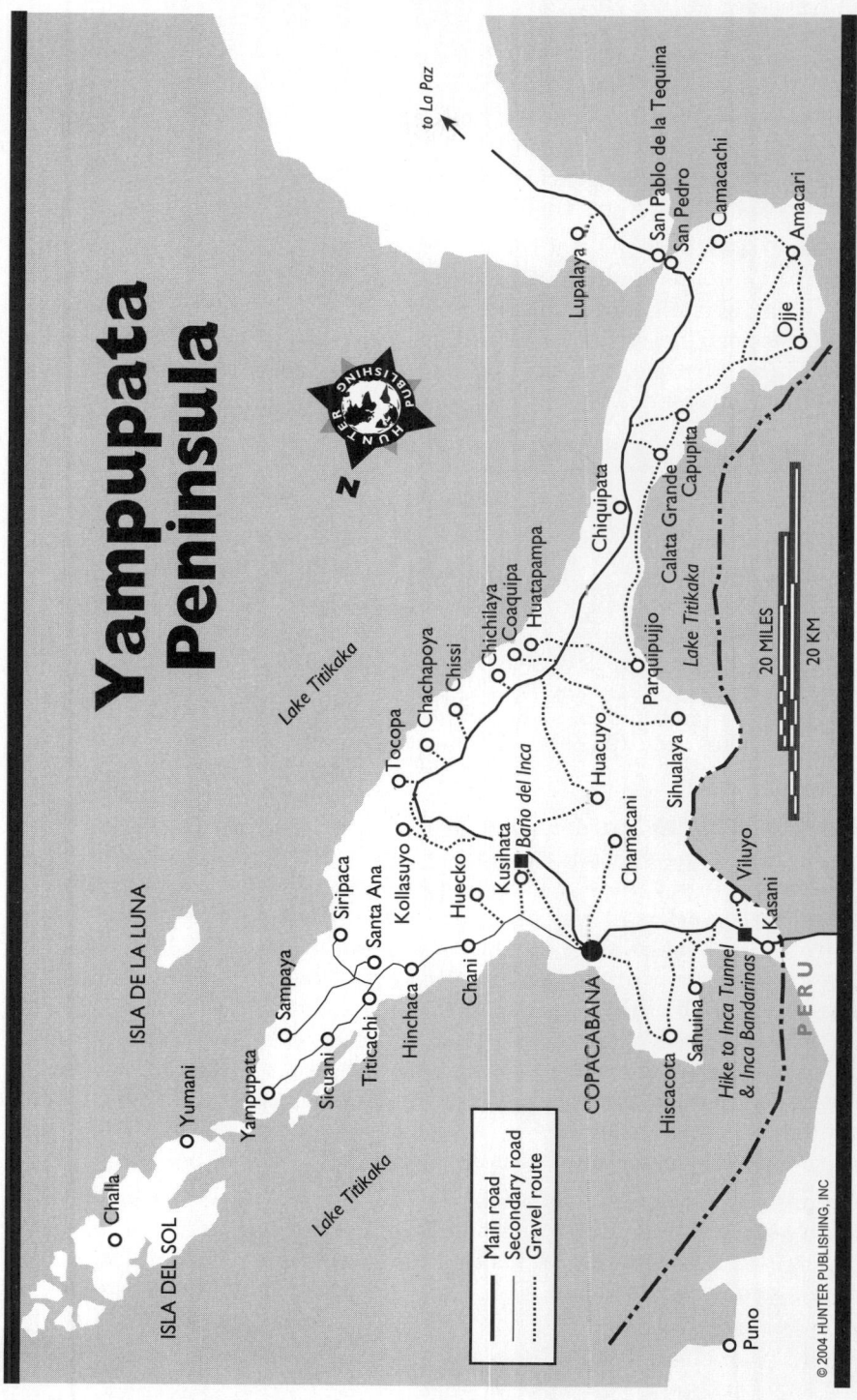

Yampupata Peninsula

Main road
Secondary road
Gravel route

ISLA DEL SOL
ISLA DE LA LUNA

Challa
Yumani

Lake Titikaka

Yampupata
Sampaya
Sicuani
Siripaca
Titicachi
Santa Ana
Hinchaca
Kollasuyo
Tocopa
Chani
Huecko
Kushita
Chachapoya
Chissi
Chichilaya
Coaquipa
Huatapampa

Baño del Inca
COPACABANA
Huacuyo
Chamacani
Parquipuijo
Chiquipata
Sihualaya

Hiscacota
Sahuina
Viluyo
Kasani
Calata Grande
Capupita

Hike to Inca Tunnel
& Inca Bandarinas

Lake Titikaka

Lupalaya
San Pablo de la Tequina
San Pedro
Camacachi
Amacari
Ojie

to La Paz

PERU

Puno

Altiplano

20 MILES
20 KM

Lake Titikaka

© 2004 HUNTER PUBLISHING, INC

rocks require imagination to understand. It was once believed that the large stones represented smaller versions of the mountains and contained the souls of people now dead. Continue walking another 660 ft/ 200 m and you will find a huge stone with a seat carved into it. This is the Trono del Inca, or the Inca Throne. Aymara priests come here during the winter solstice in June to celebrate the Aymara New Year. The fee to enter three sites – this one, the Baño del Inca and Horca del Inca – is $1.25.

INCA BATHS: Baño del Inca, or Kusihata, can be reached by walking toward Yampupata out Avenida Junin, past the football field. A carved stone barrel is filled by a natural spring. It is believed that visiting Inca kings stopped here to bathe. Considering the temperature of the lake water, it is no surprise. A museum near the baths contains some archeological objects found near town.

TINY TALENT

An artist from Copacabana by the name of Juan Gutierrez became famous for painting miniatures. Because he didn't have all the finer tools of a painter, he used bird feathers and rabbit hair to make paintbrushes and he used the back of his hand as a palette. In 1925 he received a gold medal from the Centennial of the Republic Committee for a picture of Sucre and Bolívar in two lockets. Then in 1942 he received 500 bolivianos (a large sum at the time) for painting the portrait of Salamanca surrounded by eight departmental shields and the Virgin of Copacabana in a pendant that was only 1.5 inches/four cm in diameter.

HORCA DEL INCA: Horca del Inca is also called Intiwatana. It's on top of the hill at the opposite end of the bay from the Stations of the Cross (Calvario). To get there, walk along Avenida 16 de Julio and, before you leave town, work your way up the trails to the hilltop. Intiwatana was an astronomical observatory for the Inca and/or pre-Inca. In 1978, Oswaldo Rivera from the National Institute of Archeology of Bolivia studied the site and arrived at this conclusion. Before his discovery, it was believed to have been a place of punishment. However, Rivera found that during the first hours of the morning at the summer solstice, the sun illuminates the entire monument. During the winter, a single sunbeam lights only the center of the crossbeam on the lentil. There are parts of walls visible that were used to separate the sacred areas from the public ones.

A climb to the top is recommended for views and acclimatization. On top, the most noteworthy object is a natural stone doorway with a stone lentil. There is $1.25 ticket cost for visiting the three sites – Horca del Inca, Inca Baths and Torono del Inca. There are ticket sellers at all three sites.

STATIONS OF THE CROSS: Calvario, or the Stations of the Cross, can be reached by heading uphill along 16 de Julio until you reach a small church. Often, there are ladies selling goods at the square beside the church. Continue toward the lake, again uphill. The top is splendid and often used by the Kallawaya for ceremonies that blend Catholic and pre-Christian beliefs into a ritual. You may be lucky and be there when a Kallawaya is having a spiritual purification ceremony (for me, climbing the hill was purification enough) or you may even be able to have your coca leaves read. Like Intiwatana, Calvario should be climbed at least once while in Copacabana. The two hills can be climbed in one day. Then you can celebrate your Catholic/Aymara religious purity by having a good meal and a bottle of wine in town.

■ Adventures on Water

There are seven companies along the beach who rent equipment for about the same prices. Choose the one with the best life jackets. Some were pretty solid when I looked at them.

Association Union Marinas, ☎ 862-2078, near the dock at the end of Calle 6 de Agosto, rents water vessels for use on the lake. Pedal boats for four people cost $3 for a half-hour, $4 for one hour and $10 for the day. A rowboat for two people is $2 for a half-hour and $3 for one hour. A two-

Pedal boats line the shore of Lake Titikaka.

man plastic kayak costs $1.25 for a half-hour and $2 for an hour. Be aware when taking a vessel out onto the lake that winds can make it difficult to get back to shore. You can also get up to 10 people together and rent a motorboat to go to Isla del Sol and back for $25. A half-day trip goes to the south end of Isla del Sol and to Isla de la Luna. If the water is rough, you many want to do this rather than taking the bigger, cheaper boat that often has too many passengers. One advantage of choosing the Association Union Marinas is that their workers are trained to notice if you are in trouble and can take a motorboat out to get you.

Some agencies offer a few days kayaking/camping around the lake. See *Tour Operators*, below.

You can also take a boat to Yampupata and then follow an Inca Trail to Sampaya. See **Faustino Hillatarco**, on the main plaza in front of the cathedral, for transportation. For a description of the Yampupata Peninsula, see *Adventures on Foot*.

■ Tour Operators

 Titikaka Tours, Avenida 6 de Agosto #2, the last kiosk nearest the dock, ☎ 862-2060, www.titikakabolivia.com. Tickets can be purchased at almost any hotel or tour office in town. The cost to go to both the islands for a full day on a big boat is S7 per person and $2 for half a day. If walking on Isla del Sol, the full-day cost drops to $3 per person (because you don't use the boat to reach Isla de la Luna). A full-day trip leaves Copacabana at 8:15 am and goes to Callapampa at the north end of Isla del Sol, where you have two hours to visit the Gold Museum, Footprints of the Sun, the Sacred Rock and the Chenkana Ruins. For a description of the sites, see Lake Titikaka section, page 183.

For those hiking to the south end of the island, after visiting the above sites you continue on the trail along the island's spine to Yumani, where the boat will be waiting. While crossing the lake, the first mate of the boat gives a great speech about how much trouble tourists are, especially when they miss the boat. He explains that, in fact, it is not his problem but yours if you miss the boat. So, don't miss the boat.

Near the dock at the south end of the island is the Mil Gradas (Thousand Stairs) where the Fountain of Inca is located.

I recommend taking a day for this excursion, including the hike, as there is not that much to see on Luna, and it is a long boat ride.

The half-day tour runs from 8:15 am to 12:15 pm and the afternoon tour runs from 1:30 to 6 pm. The half-day tour goes to the south end of Isla del Sol and to Isla de la Luna.

The proprietor of this company, Walter Poma, also has a catamaran that can be hired for $200 a day or $100 for half a day. It holds up to 40 people and offers bathrooms and a bar, as well as lots of recorded music that's played on the stereo.

KNOWING YOUR BOAT

Titikaka Tours has three double-decker boats that hold up to 50 people, even though there is a rule somewhere saying that they are not to carry more than 25. Although the captains are experienced in sailing, there are no rescue plans in place nor are there radios. The life jackets are not in view of passengers. As a guest, you can insist on life jackets and/or refuse to travel on an overloaded boat. This would make things safer. However, there has never been an accident with any of these boats and it is the most popular way of seeing the islands.

Transturin, Avenida 6 de Agosto, ☎ 242-2222, www.transturin.com, has the only direct bus from La Paz to Puno and back. Transturin's pricing is scaled similar to airlines, with discounts for last-minute deals and special one-time offers, while some advance bookings may cost much more. As an example, a tour to Isla del Sol on a luxurious catamaran costs anywhere from $55 per person for a day trip to $213 per person for an overnight stay on the boat and a drop-off (or pickup, if going the other way) in Puno, Peru.

Transturin takes customers to unique island events that are not open to the general public or other tour groups. You'll see a ceremony performed at the Inca Apus and Achachilas Altar by a group of Kallawaya, traditional healers whose culture is pre-Inca or Tihuanaco. They talk about traditional medicines and healing rituals. Groups also stop at the exclusive Inti Wata Underground Museum that has archeological pieces found on the island, some ancient mummies and a clay Ekako, the God of Abundance. With this tour, you will also ride in a traditional Inca reed boat (now powered by a motor rather than rowed by slaves) from the south to the north end of the island. En route you visit a traditional Andean home where weaving techniques are shown, traditional foods are served and Inca agricultural methods are demonstrated.

SAFETY ALERT: An overloaded ferry was crossing the lake at night and a bus slipped off the boat. Those who were sleeping on the bus died. Occasionally boats catch fire but this too is very rare. Generally speaking, boat travel on the lake is accident-free.

Grace Tours, Avenida 6 de Agosto and Calle 16 de Julio, ☎ 862-2160, offers full- and half-day island tours. A full-day trip costs $3 per person. The boats are fairly decent. This company prefers to take customers by boat to both islands (as opposed to you taking the boat to the north end of Isla del Sol and walking to the south end).

Alba Tours, Avenida 6 de Agosto #450, ☎ 230-6499, offers first-class transportation to Peru and Chile. Their newest day tour goes around Isla del Sol starting and ending in La Paz. The trip leaves La Paz for Tihuanaco and Copacabana where they do a short paddle to the village of Sicuani on the peninsula. The next day they paddle to Isla del Sol and camp overnight. The following day they return to Sicuani where they board a van and leave for the Apolobamba region. This company also offers a kayak-only tour.

Explore Bolivia, 2510 N 47th Street, Suite 207, Boulder, CO 80301, ☎ 877-708-8810 or 303-545-5728, www.explorebolivia.com, offers a two-day kayaking trip around the lake that is combined with a hiking trip in the Apolobamba region. It leaves La Paz for Tihuanaco and Copacabana, where there's a short paddle to the village of Sicuani on the peninsula. The next day brings a paddle to Isla del Sol and a night camping. The following day returns you to Sicuani, and from there you leave for the Apolobamba region. There is also a kayak-only tour.

Prices, depending on the numbers, are between $1,600 and $2,200 for the combination two-week tour and between $625 and $825 for a five-day paddle around the lake. All equipment and food is included. Explore Bolivia has knowledgeable guides and good equipment. Their reputation has awarded them coverage with both *Outside Magazine* and the Discovery Channel.

US-based **Nature Quest**, ☎ 800-369-3033, www.naturequesttours.com, offers a six-day kayaking trip around the lake. They go from Copacabana to Sicuani on the peninsula and then over to Isla del Sol and Isla de la Luna. From there they head to the Straights of Taquina and the north shore of the lake, where few tourists travel.

UK-based **Footprint Adventures**, www.footprint-adventures.co.uk, has a combination kayak/hike trip that takes 15 days, starting in La Paz. They paddle around the lake for two days and then head on foot from Sorata to Kukoyo, Nengruni, Chearoco, Waraco and on to Checapa Valley and Alta Khota, ending at Condoriri. This is an amazing trek. If you want everything done for you in British style, with things like pith helmets and afternoon tea by the glacier, check out these guys.

■ Places to Stay

 Copacabana has many places to stay and the only time getting a room could be a problem is during Samana Santa. Be aware that electricity can go off at any time as electrical storms in this area can be fierce. Most of the hotels have candles for emergencies, but you should always carry a flashlight.

HOTEL PRICES (US $)

Per person, per day, unless noted otherwise.

$	$2-$5
$$	$5-$10
$$$	$11-$17
$$$$	$18-$25
$$$$$	Over $25

Inca Campesino Class

Porteñita Residencial, *Calle Gonzalo Jauregui and Panda,* ☎ *862-2006, $.* Rooms have clean floors and private bathrooms with hot water from an electrical hookup unit, but the beds are bowed and some rooms have no windows. A few rooms without baths are less expensive. A clean patio is decorated with plants. There are 23 rooms with 85 beds in all. Laundry is 75¢ per kilo and there is a garage.

Kollita Copacabana, *Calle Gonzalo Jaurequi and Oruro,* ☎ *862-2020, $,* has rooms for $3 per person. Those with private bath and hot-water showers cost $5. Accommodations are basic and there are better deals elsewhere.

Hotel Emperador, *Calle Murillo #235,* ☎ *862-2083, $,* has been made popular because of the person who runs it, Sonia Cruz, who keeps her hotel spotless. Rooms, a few of which have private bath, are located around a central patio. Washing clothes is facilitated by a sink just for guests. There are common showers with water that is electrically heated – for some reason, the hot water works best in the lower-level showers. Towels and toiled paper are included in the price, but there are no seats on the toilets. There is a luggage deposit and breakfast can be served to your room if booked ahead.

Hostal La Luna, *Avenida Jose P Mejia and Oruru, no phone, $,* has eight basic rooms with private bath and wood floors. The building overlooks the Inca hill and the hostel is quiet. Laundry is 75¢ per kilo. There's a small eating area and breakfast Americano with eggs costs just over a dollar. A simple bun with coffee is 75¢. Across from La Luna is a video game place where the local kids spend their allowances.

La Casa Viva, *Calle Murillo and Felix Rosa, $.* Sonia Cruz made the Hostal Emporador what it is and now she has her own tastefully designed place across from the Emperador. The entrance is nicely decorated with a dining area off to the side and a sitting area where guests can visit. The Casa's three floors have 15 rooms – 10 with private bath – with wood floors that are complemented by boldly colored walls and huge windows. The halls are wide and the doors are high, made especially for Westerners. Bathrooms feature tile and showers with hot water. A roof-top terrace has an undercover area in case it rains. Sonia supplies towels and toilet paper. This is one of the best deals in town.

Hospedaje Florez, *Avenida 6 de Agosto,* ☎ *862-2117, $*, is just 1½ blocks from the main square. Some of the 13 basic rooms have single beds (that are actually three-quarter size). Electric water heaters are used in the showers. The family who owns the hotel is friendly. There is a roof-top terrace that has tables and chairs and a good view of the lake. Meals can be ordered from the restaurant and eaten on the terrace. Security is good; there is someone at the desk 24 hours a day. Laundry, done by hand, not by machine, is 75¢ a kilo.

Hostal 6 de Agosto, *Avenida 6 de Agosto,* ☎ *862-2292, $*, has basic carpeted rooms with large, private, tiled baths. Most rooms have small writing desks and one even has a skylight of sorts (the covering is yellow fiberglass). The restaurant is small, but the service is excellent and the food is good.

Hostal and Restaurant Alison, *Avenida 6 de Agosto, $,* is a new hotel so they don't yet have a phone (phone lines are inherited, so it could take years before they get one). The hostal has a safe deposit, laundry service, and restaurant. Rooms are clean and have hardwood floors. They are well off the street and therefore are quiet. Run by Corina Alijo, an Aymara lady, the hostel's restaurant has Aymara influences that are countered by her husband's Playboy pin-ups. The clay oven, rather than being used for cooking, has an electric heater inside. You can exchange money here.

Ambassador Hotel, *Calle Jaurequi,* ☎ *862-2216, $*. Large rooms are available in this hotel but the bathrooms are a bit shabby. The single beds are actually three-quarter size. However, a "room" for four people was actually two rooms. There is a garage, nice flowers and a patio with a small chapel at one end. The large sitting area where guests can gather is a bit dark. Laundry can be done for $1.50 a kilo. Rumor has it that the owners are a bit stand-offish.

Wara Hostal, *Avenida 6 de Agosto,* ☎ *862-2346, $,* below the Colonial, is popular with the younger crowd. It is clean, bright and close to the lake, but the beds are not all that comfy. There is a choice of private or communal bathroom (there is only one for all the guests who don't have one in their room). Laundry service is available. A restaurant on-site (but not associated with the hotel) serves an excellent breakfast for $1.50. However, the owner was a real grump, barking in English at me and in Spanish at his help.

Inca Merchant Class

Hotel Playa Azul, *Avenida 6 de Agosto*, ☎ *862-2283, playaazul@ latinmail.com, $$*. This colonial hotel has rooms set around a central patio. Although it's more than 50 years old, the building has been well maintained and is beautiful inside and out. Rooms are clean and come with tile bathrooms, reading lights over the beds, carpets and closets. Local art is interspersed around the building, making it bright and cheery. Playa Azul offers an all-inclusive rate and people who opt for this get a larger room.

Colonial del Lago, *corner of Avenida 6 de Agosto and 16 de Julio*, ☎ *862-2270, titikakabolivia@yahoo.com, $$,* is a colonial-styled building that has been well maintained. All rooms are clean and have large windows, closets, tables and a view of the lake. Some bathrooms have been artistically designed to utilize all available space. There are 38 rooms, 25 with private bathrooms. Complimentary breakfast features eggs, toast and jam served in the garden. The owners offer a $1 discount to their guests for the boat ride to Isla del Sol and Luna.

Las Brisas del Titikaka, *Avenida 6 de Agosto*, ☎ *862-2178, $$,* faces the beach. There are new tile floors in the halls and carpets in some of the rooms and wood floors in others. Most bedspreads are a bit glitzy (pink satin that has had the beauty washed out of it). Some rooms have access to the balcony and all have TV. There is a money exchange, private parking and Internet service.

Kantutas, *Avenita Jaureque and Bolívar*, ☎ *862-2093, $$,* is a tastefully designed hotel across from Plaza Sucre. It is named after the national flower of Bolivia and is almost as beautiful, featuring red brick and white plaster. Although I wanted to stay at the hotel, I seldom found a staff member around. There are 22 rooms with hot showers, private baths and TVs. The hotel is exceptionally clean, has excellent décor and a private restaurant. There is also a roof-top terrace offering views of the city and the lake.

Residencial Sucre, *Calle Murillo #228*, ☎ *862-2030, $$,* has rooms built around a central patio dotted with flowers. They have tiled bathrooms, carpets, closets, toilet seats and a TV, but no view. It's not a great value, but the price includes continental breakfast and use of a reed boat. The owner is pleasant, but has some sons who are rumored to help themselves to guests' stuff. Although just a rumor, it is a persistent one. I wouldn't let it stop me from staying here, but be careful.

Leyenda Hotel and Restaurant, *Avenida Costanera and Busch*, ☎ *862-2288, leyenda63@yahoo.com, $$*. The hotel has five rustic rooms (one has a balcony) with comfortable willow furniture and private baths. Lake views are excellent and it is nice to sit on the balcony, watching the evening light change. When negotiating the price, be certain you do not

Altiplano

misunderstand. In fact, get the price in writing. We ended up paying double what I expected, and my Spanish is not that bad.

Hostal Cupula, *Calle Michel Parez #1-3,* ☎ *862-2029, www.hotelcupula. com, $$$,* is up the hill just below the Stations of the Cross. It's run in European style by Amanda and Martin Strather, who built with an Egyptian motif. It is popular with foreigners. There are 17 rooms of every variation: single, double, with or without bath, with or without view. The price starts at $10 for a single without bath and goes up to $32 for the honeymoon suite. Hot showers are available all day and a fully supplied guest kitchen is kept as clean as the rest of the hotel. Hammocks are peppered around the well-kept grounds that are laden with flowers. There is a library and a book exchange with many German books. Hot water bottles will be supplied if you need one. Paintings on the walls are by local artists and are for sale; negotiate the price with the owners, who speak English (the staff is still reluctant to speak it). An excellent vegetarian restaurant open to all is open every day, 7:30 am to 3 pm (except Tuesday) and 6 to 9:30 pm. For example, pancakes with apple and chocolate go for $2, a good salad costs $1.50, and a trout dinner is $4.

Hotel Utama, *Calle Michael Perez, just before the Cupula,* ☎ *862-2013, $$$.* Utama means "home" in Aymara and the Aymara owners try to make their guests feel as though they have entered the family home. The colonial-styled building has unique décor and rooms set around a central courtyard that will soon have a stone fountain. Beside it will be a table with fruit and tea for guests (you are in an Aymara home). All rooms have private bathrooms, tiled and clean. The large rooms have just been re-painted and redecorated and feature hardwood floors and bold colors on the walls, with sitting areas that have comfortable lounge chairs and scatter rugs. Each has an original mural painted by a local artist. There are plants in every room and views of the lake or the cathedral. All rooms are non-smoking – if you want to smoke, look in the halls for an alcove with the mural that has a man laying down with a cigarette in his mouth. This is the smoking place.

Breakfast, included in the price, is the best in town, featuring eggs, fresh juice, coffee, pancakes, cereal, fruit and coffee served by a friendly waiter wearing a white jacket and tie. Mineral water is supplied in the rooms at no charge. There is also a museum with artifacts from Aymara *campesino* life – ploughs, tools, weavings, a working clay oven, clothing, and kitchenware. The museum gives a good sense of country life in the Andes. The small shop contains locally made items for sale at reasonable prices.

Inca Royalty

Hotel Gloria, *16 de Julio,* ☎ *864-0707, www.gloria-tours-bolivia.com, $$$$,* is part of a chain with hotels in Copacabana, Coroico, Urmiri and La Paz. This location caters mostly to tours. Rooms overlook the lake and are clean and spacious, though other areas (like the games room, balcony and halls) could use some sprucing up. There are large windows in the rooms and decorative tile in the bathrooms, but the hall carpets are grotty. There is cable TV in each room and mineral water is supplied daily. A continental breakfast is included. The dining room and bar tables have fresh linen. Lunch ($4) includes salad, soup, main meal, dessert and tea. Suppers are à la carte, with trout being the most popular dish. The games room has fooze ball and ping pong. The grounds have pretty flowering plants. No English is spoken.

Hotel Chasqui de Oro, *Avenida Costanera #55,* ☎ *862-2343, $$$$$,* means "gold runners." During Inca times messages were written on paper, sealed with gold and delivered by runners. This new hotel on the beach is decorated in colonial Spanish design and is run by a quiet, unassuming man. The spacious rooms have wood floors and tiled bathrooms. The hot water comes from a tank, which means it's not available between 1 and 5 pm. Rooms have writing desks, closets, mirrors and satellite TV, and the better ones have huge bathrooms with both tubs and showers. Even the single rooms are exquisite. Accommodations are always a comfortable temperature because they catch either the morning sun at the back or evening sun in front. Patios and balconies dot every corner of the building and there's a restaurant on the premises. This is a first-class establishment. Rates: $30 double; $20 single. Breakfast is included.

Hotel Rosario del Lago, *Rigoberto Paredes and Costañera,* ☎ *862-2002, caoba.entelnet.bo, $$$$$,* is run by the same people who own the Rosario in La Paz. This upscale hotel offers solar heat, good service and clean, well-kept rooms. Rates: from $15 single to $50 double, per person.

Casa de Huespedes Villa Santa Rosa, *Avenida Peru #4,* ☎ *862-2134, daniel@kolla.net, $$$$$,* is a classy place on the edge of town along the highway leading to the Peruvian border. It's set on a hill in a forest of eucalyptus trees away from the road. Its five double rooms and three suites are tastefully decorated with rich wood furniture and extras like bed lamps and tiled bathrooms. There is also a sauna on the premises for those cold, high-altitude nights. Rates: $40 single; $45 double; $50 for a suite for one or two people.

▪ Places to Eat

Restaurant Sujma Wasi, *Avenida Gonzolo Jauregui #127,* ☎ *862-2091,* has an indoor seating area and a patio that gets the warm afternoon sun. The tablecloths are woven Andean-style and the décor is inviting. Even if you don't want to eat, come to read the translation from Aymara to Spanish to English on the menu. A popular breakfast consists of quinoa flour pancakes with homemade jam, bananas, nuts, raisins or honey and fresh fruit juice. I also recommend the granola with fruit and yogurt. A large serving of Sujma Wasi salad has lettuce and onion plus Roquefort cheese, nuts, apples, olives and parsley. These dishes cost about $2 each. A large bowl of homemade soup is about $1. A huge plate of *pique de macho*, a local dish of stewed meat, sausage, tomato, pepper, onion, cheese, boiled eggs, olives and parsley, costs just over $3. Bolivian wine is available at $1.25 a glass or $7-8 a bottle and a large beer is $1.25. They offer special Andean drinks – like *chuflay*, *yungeño* and *singani* sours – for $2.25 each. Singani is a distilled low-quality wine that makes a powerful liquor. Chuflay is a drink made with Singani and lime juice. Yungeño is a concoction that tastes like something between straight singani and a chuflay.

Sujma Wasi, once a hotel, is run by a local family. There's an ancient well in the courtyard and the place is dotted with artifacts. The fireplace crackles in the evenings, a nice touch.

Alfanet, *Avenida 6 de Agosto, next to the Colonial Hotel*, is an Internet café that serves coffee and cake while you do your e-mail. It has comfortable working desks with PCs for 75¢ for 15 minutes; $1.25 for 30 minutes; $1.75 for 45 minutes; and $2 for an hour. The time is computed and recorded on a small box at the bottom of the screen. Remember to sign off so the calculated time stops. There are two pool tables in the next room, English-language videos for rent and nice art on the walls. Alfanet is owned by the couple who own the Café Sol y Luna.

Colonial Restaurant, *corner of Avenida 6 de Agosto and 16 de Julio,* ☎ *862-2270, titikakabolivia@yahoo.com,* is open 7:30 am to 10:30 pm. There's an indoor dining room, or you can eat out in the garden. The trout dish is a dollar less than most upscale places around town and it's delicious, cooked with lots of garlic, an herb claimed by many mountain people to help with altitude sickness. For $3 you can have the trout with rice, fries and salad. In the morning they serve large pancakes with chocolate and fruit for $1. I often dream about this dish when I am at home.

Sol de los Andes Café and Internet, *Avenida 6 de Agosto,* is upstairs and has six machines with lots of working space and bright light. A nice touch is that they serve candy with Internet rental. The machines are fast and fairly new.

Café Sol y Luna, *in the same building as Hotel Gloria, Calle16 de Julio (no phone), solyluna@post.com*, has a branch in La Paz. The coffee shop/bar has jazz playing from CDs. It's a really good place to hang out in the evenings when your requests, from the printed list, will be played. There is a two-for-one book exchange and the owner Rick Derave speaks English, Dutch and a host of other languages. His Argentinean wife, Margarina, makes a cappuccino that is second to none in Bolivia. The cost is 75¢ for a small and $1 for a large; a glass of Bolivian wine costs the same. Open hours are 6 pm until whenever. This place is popular with foreigners who like to hang out.

Kala Uta, *Avenida 6 de Agosto #115*, ☎ *862-2862*, is a popular vegetarian restaurant. Their *almuerzo* (less than $2) comes highly recommended by a number of people who really like to eat. A la carte dishes usually include nuts, quinoa, whole grains and/or yogurt.

La Cupula, *Calle Michel Parez #1-3*, ☎ *862-2029*, is another vegetarian eatery with excellent food – the lasagna is especially good. I have been enjoying meals here for over four years and have never been disappointed. The restaurant overlooks the lake and has tables outside on a balcony. There is often music, and the atmosphere lends itself to leisurely meals.

Restaurant Brisas, *Avenida 6 de Agosto and Calle Costanera*, ☎ *862-2033*, also overlooks the lake. A sunset drink and dinner is recommended. The house specialty is *trucha criolla*, a spicy trout dish with tomatoes, for about $3. Portions are large.

Pizzeria Italia, *Avenida Jauregui #140 beside Residencial Solar*, ☎ *862-2009*, is the best place for pizza in town. Pizzas come with thin crusts and thick toppings. This restaurant has branches in Sorata and Rurrenabaque, too.

Leyenda Restaurant, *Avenida Costanera and Busch*, ☎ *862-2288*. Located on the beach, Leyenda has great décor and a relaxing garden. The hamburger with fries is excellent, but the service is slow.

Trebol, *Avenida 6 de Agosto, just below the Colonial Hotel*, is a tiny place run by an older lady who works hard to give you what you want. Her portions are small and she serves one thing at a time, but her friendliness, desire to please and the quality of food make up for the lack of speed. A *trebol* is a three-leaf clover in Spanish.

Puerta del Sol, *Avenida 6 de Agosto near plaza Sucre*, ☎ *862-2232*, is a bare-bones place next to the Plaza Azul hotel. The café has a patio with umbrellas, a clay oven that is often used and good food. We had spicy mushroom soup served with hot buns for 75¢. The *almuerzo* costs about $1.50. However, change is a problem, so bring small coins/bills with you.

Snack 6 de Agosto, *Avenida 6 de Agosto*, ☎ *862-2114 or 862-2430*, specializes in vegetarian food and has both indoor and patio seating. The service is good and the people are friendly. The fries were crisp and fresh (not from a frozen package). *Café distilado* is about 30¢, and an omelet with salad, potatoes and rice runs about $3. The portion is enough for breakfast, but not for dinner. Pancakes, depending on what you have with them, cost up to a dollar. Choose from chocolate, fruit, ham, cheese, banana and /or yogurt. The chef offers *pejerrey* (a fish) in place of the ubiquitous trout. One pleasant note: There is a toilet seat on the toilet in the washroom.

Manka Uta Restaurant, *Avenida 6 de Agosto*, ☎ *862-4941*, is close to the lake and has live music every evening starting at 8 pm. The restaurant has small tables with candles held in locally produced candleholders and with chairs covered in sheepskins. The ambiance is great, and so are the waiters. The restaurant opens at 7:30 am for breakfast and will make a box lunch to go. Pizza or spaghetti cost $3 and a beer is just over a dollar. The bar is heated at night – at this elevation, heat is often important. If the music isn't to your liking, try next door at Nimbos.

Nimbos, *at Avenida 6 de Agosto on the corner of Zapana #684*, opens from 7:30 am to 11 pm and often has local bands. The restaurant décor is attractive and cosy. If the electricity goes out, the candles placed on each table will light the room, the propane stove will cook your food, and the 1980s music that plays when there's no band will go off. For $2 you can have a complete meal – an appetizer, soup, main dish and dessert. I had onion rings , soup and trout and was too full to eat dessert. This is an excellent place to eat. Come early as it is popular, but be sure to have change or small bills.

La Cabañita Snack, *Avenida Gonzalo Juarequi #125 at Oruro,* ☎ *862-2194,* is nicely decorated with woven tablecloths and reed wall coverings. Servings are large and the food is always freshly cooked. A full supper costs about $2.

■ Nightlife

 Nikos Karaoke, just off Avenida 6 de Agosto and one street below the cathedral, is the "in" place for disco. The floor is painted cement and the dance section is lined in tinfoil, which makes the place a bit tacky. There is a good mike for anyone wanting to sing. The lounge area has 25-30 chairs and the bar is well stocked. When I asked for phone and address information the owner told me to buzz off, so I did.

Pub Mercurio de Almas is on Avenida Costanera along the beach just below the navy base. This is a pleasant stop with good music and good drinks. Happy hour runs from 8 pm to midnight, but the place stays open later. Mercurio often has live music. Meals are available, but I never ate there.

Tatu Correta, Avenida 6 de Agosto and Oruro, is an intimate bar that will and does stay open until 3 am as long as the customers are having a good time (and spending money, of course). The prize of the house is the Tatu Correta milkshake made with milk, eggs, chocolate and cognac. It's often light on the milk and heavy on the cognac.

Sol y Luna, Calle 16 de Julio, solyluna@post.com, is a popular place for foreigners to hang out, listen to the music, have a few drinks and chat up other travelers.

■ Shopping

There are numerous little shops in Copacabana selling all the usual things from weavings to knitted socks. The dolls sold in the stalls around the church are a very good deal, much cheaper than any in La Paz.

Street vendors selling jewelry that is laid out on a piece of weaving or cloth are not, for the most part, Bolivians. They are traveling salespersons and their route runs from Ecuador to Argentina. Their goods are handmade and sell for fairly reasonable prices as long as you barter. A belt should run $15 and a silver ring decorated with abalone shell sells around $3.

Bazar Agar, Avenida La Paz and Junin, has cameras, video tapes and all manner of batteries, including lithium batteries. They also have non-expired film such as Advantx or Elite Chrome (ASA 200) for $6, Agfa or Konica slide film, 36 exposures,100 ASA, for $2. They carry only a limited supply of Fuji film.

■ Trips on Lake Titikaka

Isla del Sol is the main island that is accessible from Copacabana and is the primary attraction of the area. The most sacred rock on the island is Inca Rock, at the north end. This is where Viracocha is believed to have created his two humans, Manca Copac and Mama Huaca. A carving on the rock shows the bearded god Viracocha with a puma beside him. The Chincana ruins are near the island's north end. To the south are the Pilcocaina ruins. Isla del Sol also has numerous minor ruins long forgotten.

There are many ways to visit the island. If you go by boat and walk from the north to the south, you will miss Isla de la Luna because crossing over to it after walking Isla del Sol would take too long. You could, of course, go on a different day. If you want to go to all the ruins on the two islands, you can go by boat but miss the island hike. Some people choose to overnight here in order to see and do it all. There are numerous places to stay. Most are fairly simple and inexpensive.

> **AUTHOR TIP:** You should bring extra snacks you may want as the cost of these things on the island is far higher than the mainland. Meals, too, cost a bit more.

Altiplano

Lake Titikaka

Rosaspata

PERU　　**BOLIVIA**

N

Camata

Puerto Acosta

Escoma

Tacacoma

Isla del Sol

Humacha　Sorata

Isla de La Luna

Achacachi

Yampupata

Copacabana

Huarina

Juli

Tiquina　Huatajata

Yunguyo

Pt. Perez

Pomata

Isla Suriqui

Batallas

Taraco

Desagüadero

Tihuanaco

to La Paz

Tambillo

60 KM

40 MILES

© 2004 HUNTER PUBLISHING, INC

To use the public toilets will cost one boliviano. If you have an aversion to paying for this luxury, hide behind a rock somewhere along the trail. Don't leave toilet paper behind – slip it into a plastic bag and carry it out.

Hiking Isla del Sol

The seven-mile/11-km trail takes three to four hours to complete. It is a groomed pathway that makes for easy walking. The highest hill you'll encounter is 13,000 ft/4,000 m. There are actually two trails from which to choose. One climbs high almost right away and stays on the ridge, while the other starts near the shore and undulates along the island's entire length. The most popular route is the upper one, and that's the one I describe here. The lower one takes almost twice as long and is definitely twice as difficult. Boat schedules are based on people doing the upper trail. We'll leave the lower trail to more adventuresome hikers who, if they become lost, can always climb to the upper trail.

The island is vegetated and farmed in places and has many sheep and llamas grazing in the meadows. You will see short-winged grebes floating along the lake and there's a good chance of spotting other birds like the pipit and the tinamou. Looking across the lake to the north, the city on the distant shore is Puno, Peru.

Always dress appropriately.

- Wear a hat as the sun coming through the thin atmosphere is strong and will burn you. There is no shade and the cool air at this altitude fools you into thinking you're safe.
- Wear good walking shoes as the distance is fairly long.
- It is also best if you bring a lunch so you can stop at a good view point and enjoy the scenery while eating. There are a couple of *tiendas* along the way selling pop, crackers and candy.

After crossing the lake and while approaching the island, the boat passes some ruins and a set of stairs coming down into the water. On the way back at the end of the trip, the boat will pause here and the first mate will ask if anyone wants to go up. No one ever does. Most are "ruined" out and/or tired from hiking. The stairs lead to Pilcocaima.

The next thing you see is the Mil Escoladas or Mil Gradas and Inca Fountain, the staircase and baths that are almost invisible against the rocks and under the trees. This is where you will end your hike. The boat doesn't stop here until the return trip later in the day. Instead, it

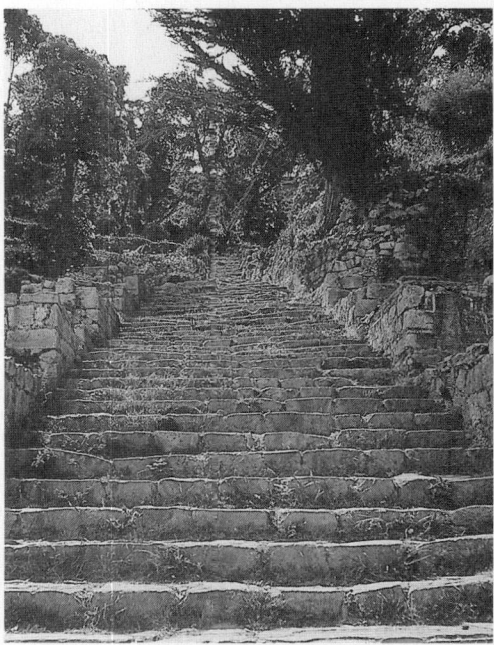

Mil Escoladas.

stops farther up the island, at Cha'llapampa, the village at the north end.

Rules from the Empire of the Sun

Ama Suwa, Ama Quella and Ama Llulla.
(Don't steal, don't lie, don't be lazy.)

Once off the boat, some Spanish/Aymara-speaking guides take visitors up to the ruins, explaining in Spanish the legends surrounding the sites. Their explanations are excellent, but if you don't understand Spanish, continue on your own.

Head up the hill toward the **Gold Museum** (75¢) and then the ruins. The price of the museum includes the entry fee to the ruins. However, in the spring of 2003, there was a dispute and the museum was closed. Apparently, it will reopen once some kind of agreement has been reached about the management of the museum. Because of this, there may be no charge posted and the guides may ask for a small donation at the end of the tour.

The museum displays artifacts, some of them gold pieces, found at the city of Marka Pampa that was once on the edge of the island but is now 26 ft/eight m under water just off the north shore. Three islands are visible from the north side of the island: Chullo, Koa and Pallalla. Marka Pampa is between them. The city was excavated in 1992 and the finds put into the museum.

The museum's most precious displays are the gold pieces found inside carved stone boxes. There's a medallion, a cup, a puma and a figure of a woman. They are not very big, but the workmanship is excellent. The stone boxes are so well made that the gold never became wet during all those years under water.

After the museum, the trail passes through a stone doorway with an impressive stone lintel on top. From there, follow the trail up the hill, past a school and around and above a couple of bays. Watch for dung beetles on the trail cleaning things up. They push chunks of dung backwards to their storage place.

Just as the trail starts to go down, veer to the right into the first yard and the Piedra Sagrada (**Sacred Rock**), an upright piece with some carving on it. Across from the rock but within the same yard is a low table that is believed to have been the sacrificial table where a living creature's heart (sometimes human) was cut out and left for the gods.

Return to the main trail and continue to the back of the island where there is first a ticket booth and then a huge round stone table with stone stools around it. This is the **Ceremonial Table**, which some believe was also a sacrificial table. The Inca brought humans, gold, silver, shells and animals there to appease and thank the gods for whatever reason, be it drought, floods, sickness or prosperity. The Aymara guides will encourage you to rub your hand on the table in order to extract some energy

Boats wait to load up at Isla del Sol.

from it. This way you will be able to complete the hike to the south end before the boat leaves.

Behind the table is another Sacred Rock, a rust-colored one, which is supposed to show the face of Viracocha with a puma beside him (use your imagination). On one side of the rock was, at one time, a basin that held *chicha* left by the Inca for their gods. The most significant ceremonies held here celebrated the summer and winter solstices.

The **Chincana ruins** are just beyond the table. The word "Chincana" means a place to get lost. When looking at the ruins you will find many hiding places and rooms with false doors. If the ruins don't interest you, continue along the trail to your left at the ticket booth.

The ruins are believed to have been residences of people working for aristocrats who came to the island on vacation. They are impressive, with their tiered quarters and labyrinth of passages. To appreciate the ruins, spend at least an hour here.

Those not hiking the island return to the boat from the ruins. Those continuing to the south end go up the trail that veers to the right just after the sacred table.

The grunt now starts and continues for about an hour. But there is no reason to rush. The boatman says he will leave at 4 pm sharp, though I

Altiplano

have never seen him take off before 4:30 pm. However, you shouldn't tempt fate. If the boat does leave without you, the cost of returning to the mainland is about $40 per boat that will take up to 10 people.

There are *tiendas* at around the 3.6-mile/six-km point that have tables and chairs. You'll go by spots where you can take photos of girls with llamas, men weaving, women with kids, kids selling stones, to a trail that leads to the hamlet of **Playa Challa**. An unnamed guesthouse on the beach here looks like a great refuge for a quiet few days. Just beyond the beach is the village of **Challa**, where the ethnographic museum is located.

You are now at the apex of the island, more than half-way to Mil Gradas and the village of Yumani, where the boat will be waiting.

Places to Stay

Descending the steep part toward the dock and Mil Gradas (Thousand Steps) you will see many places to stay. Most are basic and clean, but if you want a bit more luxury, at the top of the island before coming down is **Puerta del Sol**, $. It has 15 rooms in a two-storey, mustard-yellow (symbolizing sun) building and charges $3 per person (with private bath and carpeted floors).

Near the Mil Gradas and the Inca Fountain is the **Inti Marka Hostal**, $, which rents basic rooms without a private bath for $1.50. It costs $1 extra for a hot shower. The rooms are clean, with cement floors, and there is an equally clean restaurant that serves full dinners for $2. **La Casa de la Yumani**, ☎ 7-193-4427, $$$, is run by an Argentinean known as Ricardo. His place is tiny – just four rooms, but all with private bath. It's clean and tastefully decorated. Rooms cost S20 for a couple. This is definitely the most upscale place on the island. Ricardo can help you hire a boat to travel around the island by water. To get to his place in the upper section of the town, ask in the village. Everyone knows where Ricardo's place is. **Hospadaje de la Playa**, $, is an adobe brick building just above the lake near the north end of the village. The views are excellent, but the showers cost extra. Should you wish to use the bathroom, the cost is one boliviano for non-guests.

La Estancia is an eco-lodge run by Magri Turismo Ltd, in La Paz. The cost to stay here is $59 for a single, $88 for a double and $122 for a triple. This price includes breakfast and either lunch or dinner. This lodge is working with NGOs to help promote sustainable tourism and has restored the pre-Inca terraces on the property that are believed to be over 500 years old. The cabins are of adobe brick with thatch roofs in keeping with traditional aesthetics. However, inside they are modern and comfortable, with wood floors, tables and chairs, large windows and solar-powered electricity. Each cabin is named after a local plant and has a drawing of the plant outside.

This lodge uses local drivers, maintenance men, porters, boat services, restaurants, and so on, to help improve the economy. In turn, they teach the workers what the foreigner expects in quality of goods and services.

> **CAN YOU SWIM?**
>
> If someone falls into Lake Titikakca, it is traditional to leave them there as an offering to Pacha Mama. Remember this when you are on the boat.

Boating the Islands

If not hiking, you will see everything (including the Chincana ruins) before returning to the boat, although your time will be limited. From Cha'llapampa, the boat goes to Isla de la Luna across the way. Much smaller, the island is just 1.8 miles/three km long and barely one wide. During the reign of the Inca, the island represented the moon, female counterpart of the sun. It also had a nunnery that held the Virgins of the Sun. These women, chosen for their beauty, made *chicha* and wove cloth to be used in the religious ceremonies. The island was called Coati which, according to some linguists, means the place for elected women.

From the 1930s to the 1960s, the island was used to hold political prisoners. There was little left of the nunnery or the main palace at that time, but the prisoners were forced to reconstruct the 35-room building. From the ruins, it was learned that the palace was built in typical Aymara fashion, suggesting that the area was used before the Inca came. However, it was also learned that the doors were made in Inca style. This suggests that the site was used by both cultures, one reconstructing the remains of the previous one. Today, fewer than 50 people live here.

Straights of Tiquina

Straights of Tiquina is a narrow channel of water on Lake Titikaka. The crossing of the straight is on the Copacabana-La Paz highway. There, boats take people and barges take trucks, cars and buses across the lake. In any other country there would be a highway bridge here and the two villages on each side would be quiet fishing communities. As it is, they are busy pit stops. The two villages are **San Pablo** and **San Pedro de Tiquina**. San Pedro is on the Copacabana side of the straights.

There is one small, basic *alojamiento* in San Pedro along the street at the far side (away from the water) of the plaza. The restaurants around the plaza serve good trout. The ferry that takes the people across to San Pablo de Tiquina is not the flat-decked barge that takes the bus across (don't worry about any baggage under the bus; it will be safe so long as the barge stays afloat). Once on the opposite side, there is time to purchase a pop or run to the public restroom before the bus arrives on its barge. The cost to cross on the ferry is 25¢.

The plaza beside the ferry ticket booth on the San Pablo side is interesting and sports a number of objects like a boat, a llama, and a hut – all made out of tortora reeds. The public restroom (half a boliviano) is just off the square, past the left side of the building opposite the ticket booth.

Huatajata

Altitude: 12,533 ft / 3,810 m
Population: fewer than 1,000

Huatajata is a tourist resort where richer Bolivianos come to enjoy the lake, eat fish, drink beer and do what tourists the world over do at resorts. There are numerous hotels opening along the lake, but the big one is Inca Utama (see page 194), with 65 rooms, two restaurants, a spa and a cultural complex called the Andean Eco Village.

■ Getting Here

Take a bus (*floata*) or a micro (*trufi*) going to Copa from La Paz, or vice-versa, and get off at Huatajata. The five-star Inca Utama hotel is a little way down the lake from the restaurants and cheaper places. A hydrofoil travels between Huatajata and Puno, Peru. Transturin (see *Copacabana*, page 173) offers catamaran service to this part of the lake, though you'll need to make special arrangements with them.

■ History

Originally, Huatajata and the island of Suriqui became known for the reed boat, ***Ra II***, built there for Thor Heyerdahl's Kon Tiki Expedition in the 1970s. The skilled boat builder, Paulino Esteban, has since become an international hero. The building and sailing of these boats has been repeated by boat enthusiasts all over the world and the legend of the original expedition is still big here.

■ Adventures in Culture

In order to find any of the places mentioned below, ask at one of the many restaurants along the lakeshore, or take a taxi.

Andean Eco Village stands next to the Inca Utama Hotel. It's a reconstruction of an Inca Village as it may have looked hundreds of years ago, with mud huts, reed mattresses and boats, and clay ovens. Women weave and men cultivate the fields much as they did in ancient times. There are mortuary towers and typical huts with straw roofs like those still used in some parts of the Altiplano. You can paddle a reed boat out to the floating island that features displays from the pre-Inca Urus Chipaya culture.

HEAVYWEIGHT VESSEL

A reed boat that is 49 x 16 x 7 ft (15 x 5 x 2 m) will weigh 15 tons when the reeds are dry. In the water, it will sop up liquid and gain more weight. A boat of this size requires 1.5 million reeds for its construction.

The **Alajpacha Observatory** is part of the Andean Eco Village. It has a telescope from NASA that is the second-strongest in Bolivia. This is a popular destination for star-gazing tours that are into astrophotography and, whether on tour or not, everyone is welcome to use these facilities. Because of the altitude, the exposure time when photographing the stars is cut almost in half and because the weather is usually dry with clear skies, this is a prime spot to star gaze. The observation pad has electrical power in both 110 and 220 voltage plus 12 volt DC power and the two house scopes are 10- and 12-inch (25- and 30-cm) Starmasters. Due to the cold night-time temperatures in the Altiplano, the observatory has warming rooms with heat lamps.

Stargarden Foundation from the United States has recently held their Inter-hemispheric conference with the Astronomical League to share their information about the sky. Other star-gazing organizations are also doing this.

WISH UPON A STAR

Tunupa, an important Aymara god, is believed to control meteorological activities. He became subordinate to Viracocha only after the Inca arrived. Tunupa's friend, Illapa, controls the weather. For star gazers, it is important to know that these two gods should be fed lots of *chicha* in order to keep the skies clear and the meteor activity level high.

The **San Pablo Museum** was moved to Huatajata from Sicriqui a few years ago. This tiny museum, located beside the Inca Utama Hotel, contains objects found around the lake that pertain to the Inca and Tihuanacan cultures. The main focus seems to be archeological items from the Altiplano, although there are some pieces from the colonial period.

Altiplano

The **Kallawaya Museum**, also part of the Inca Utama, shows different herbs and how they are used in the ancient healing practices of the Kallawaya. Once you have learned how to cure your ailments, go through the last room of the museum where a Kallawaya man will bless you and read your coca leaves. As long as there is no line for blessings, he can also let you know if the cures you chose were the correct ones.

BOAT BUILDING, REED STYLE

To learn the process of boat building with tortora reeds, visit the home of the Limachi Brothers or contact the Catari family, who helped with the building of Heyerdahl's boat for his expedition. Expedition Kotamama also got a boat from the Catari family, and both expeditions involved the collaboration of the two families. The Kotamama Expedition involved a group of international scientists who took a reed boat down the Mapiri River, the Caca River, the Beni and the Madira to Manaus in Brazil.

The latest expedition is the Viracocha Expedition that will have people sailing all the way to Australia by 2007, covering 9,798 miles/16,000 km on an educational, humanitarian and ethnographic adventure. This same group completed one expedition in 2000 from Chile to the Easter Islands.

The reeds are picked in October and take four to six weeks to dry. Boat building is possible after mid- to late December.

■ Adventures on Water & Foot

Touring the Islands

 Kalahuta is an island surrounded by tortora reeds. The few people who live here reside in stone houses with straw roofs. The big draw is a visit to numerous *chullpas*, or burial towers, used by pre-Inca cultures. Residents believe that the towers are on the west side of the island because that is where the sun sets, representing the end of a life. Each tower has a door that faces the west, which supposedly allows the spirit to leave and continue on its journey. It is also believed that if you remain by the towers after dark, spirits will steal your soul, leaving your body on earth either dead and without a spirit or as a crazy person, someone who has obviously lost his spirit. If any travelers try this, please inform me of the results.

Because the island was once under water, fossils and snail shells are embedded in the rocks. There are also some large ants that bite like hell if you disturb them by moving rocks.

Suriqui Island is where Thor Heyerdahl came to build his reed boat. It has a few houses beyond which are terraced fields growing the year's food. Boats built by early civilizations usually had a puma or other fierce animal at their bows to show strength and protect the sailors from dangers on the waters.

Pariti Island is the third island near Huatajata that can be visited. It's a fishing island, and anglers may be able to join locals for a day's work.

To get to the islands, go to Hostal Inti Karka and book with the **Catari Brothers** or ask at the restaurants about tours offered by **Paulino Esteban**, who helped build Heyerdahl's boat. Regardless of who you book with, the cost to visit three islands is $50 for a boat holding up to eight people. A trip to just one island runs about $20, depending on how long the captain waits while you tour.

■ Tour Operators

Astronomical Tours, 149 NW 00 Highway Warrensburg, MO 64093, ☎ 888-734-0311, www.icstars.com/astronomicaltours, offer a specialized tours for star gazers and astrophotographers. Once a year they travel to Lake Titikaka where they sleep most of the day and look at the heavens all night. The cost for a one-week, all-inclusive package from Miami is less than $2,000 per person. See their company profile in *Outfitters Who Do All the Work*, page 81.

Explore Bolivia, 2510 N 47th Street, Suite 204, Boulder, CO 80301, ☎ 303-545-5728, www.explorebolivia.com, has some excellent outdoor adventures. The combination kayak/hike trip includes three days paddling on Lake Titikaka, visiting ruins and camping in secluded coves around the lake. See my review of their services on page 81, under *Outfitters Who Do All the Work*.

Crillon Tours, Avenida Camacho #1223, ☎ 233-7533, www.titikaka. com, is the company that arranges everything if you wish to stay at Inca Utama hotel or participate in any of their first-class tours on the lake. Their specialty is activities around the lake, in Huatajata and the Andean Cultural village.

■ Places to Stay & Eat

Inti Karka, ☎ *231-5058, $*, is the three-storey building on the lake owned by Maximo Catari. Plain rooms with a bath cost $5 per person (you'll pay a little less without a bath). The restaurant of the same name serves lots of trout.

Altiplano

HOTEL PRICES (US $)

Per person, per day, unless noted otherwise.

$....................................	$2-$5
$$...................................	$5-$10
$$$..................................	$11-$17
$$$$.................................	$18-$25
$$$$$................................	Over $25

Hostal Lago Azul, *$ (no phone)*, just up the lake from Inti Karka, also has rooms with bathrooms for $5 per person. The place is clean and the owners friendly.

Inca Utama, *on the lake*, ☎ *235-0363; advance reservations, contact Crillon Tours,* ☎ *233-7533, $$$$$*, is a five-star spread with 65 rooms that cost anywhere between $90 and $150 a night. The hotel has everything close at hand, including a massage parlor, a restaurant and bar, a museum and live entertainment. It also caters to star gazers who use the high-powered scope at the Alajpacha Observatory (see above, page 191).

Hotel Titikaka, ☎ *231-0545, $$$$*, also on the lake, is not quite as plush as Inca Utama, but it certainly has more than most need, including an indoor pool, sauna and racquetball court. Rooms are clean and fairly large.

Hotel Raices Andinas, *Km 86 along the highway,* ☎ *237-4556, $$$*, is another five-star resort offering all the luxuries you could wish for.

Places to eat are found along the shore of the lake and trout is the specialty. (By the time you leave Lake Titikaka, you will have had your fill of trout.) Most places have similar menus with similar prices. A dinner will cost about $4 per person.

If going to or coming from Sorata, Atchicachi or the Apolobamba region, **Huarina** is where the road meets the main highway between La Paz and Copacabana. There is not much of interest for the traveler, but should you become stuck here for any reason, there are places to eat and an *alojamiento* in the village.

Puerto Perez, on the opposite side of the bay from Huarina, has one five-star tourist facility called **Complejo Turistico Las Balsas**, ☎ *244-0620, $$$$$*. It's 40 miles/65 km from La Paz and 4.3 miles/seven km from Puerto Perez. Each room has a balcony overlooking the lake, air conditioning, safe deposit box, TV, tub, shower and rich hardwood furniture. The hotel has a restaurant, sauna, spa, bike rental, boat tours, racquetball court, a pool and a boat dock. This is a place where the rich gather. Rates were not supplied.

Achacachi

Altitude 12,533 ft / 3,810 m
Population: 7,900

Achacachi is an Aymara market village and the crossroads for those going to Sorata or the Apolobamba, where Pelechuco, Curva and Charazani are located. Others go from Achacachi along the north shore of Lake Titikaka and end at Puerto Acosta on the border with Peru. Although villagers in the area have a reputation for being a bit more radical than most, the town is friendly and welcoming if you need to stay the night. In times of strife, this village is best known for the effective road blocks it is able to put up and maintain for long periods of time. At the present, life is *tranquilo*, but just a few years ago tourists were blockaded in Sorata for over a week.

■ Getting Here

 Buses travel from La Paz to Achacachi daily starting at 5 am. You can also get onto a bus, *trufi* or shared taxi at Huarina. Those going to the Apolobamba or Sorata often hire a jeep in La Paz and stop in Achacachi for breakfast/lunch or a quick look around.

Buses go to Sorata from La Paz. They leave every two hours starting at 6 am; the last bus leaves mid-afternoon. Buses leaving Sorata start around 5 am and continue until mid-afternoon. Two companies service this route: Larecaja and Unificado Sorata.

Buses go to Pelechuco in the Apolobamba only on Wednesdays. A jeep costs $250 from La Paz and will carry six people and gear with ease.

■ Adventures in Nature

 Achacachi has a **wetland** on the edge of town where the rare giant coot has been spotted numerous times. Birders can also see ducks, cormorants, herons, teals and Andean coots.

■ Places to Stay & Eat

 Alojamiento Maya, *Calle Sucre #17*, ☎ *7154-7667 (cell), $*, is run by Juan Verastique. Rooms are small and simple, but certainly clean enough and all have shared bathrooms. There is a slightly more upscale place across the street, but it doesn't have the ambiance of the Maya.

The Maya also has a restaurant where set meals are served. Other meals can be purchased at the restaurants around the square. Only set meals are available. Achicachi is not geared-up for tourists.

Apolobamba Region

The only reason travelers go into this area is to hike/climb or raft in one of the most remote parts of Bolivia. **Pelechuco**, at 11,842 ft/3,600 m, has a village medical post and one basic cheap place to stay. While here, you can rub shoulders with the Kallawaya, the naturopaths of the Andes, who were traveling doctors long before the Inca came looking for cures. Today, Charazani, Amarete, Chari, Pelechuco and Curva are the most important centers for the Kallawaya culture.

Madidi National Park covers a total of 4.5 million acres with a variety of ecosystems unparalleled for their abundant wildlife. Vicuñas are seen grazing and Andean foxes will cross your trail while you are hiking. The estimated bird list is reported to be well over 1,000 species.

The village of **Pelechuco** is not modernized, although there is a hotel on the main square where you can sleep and eat. It has no showers or running water and electricity is available only a few hours a day. The owner will serve dinner and breakfast – the same meal for everyone. Although some purchases can be made in the village, most food needed for hiking or climbing should be brought with you. The medical post is usually open.

Pelechuco's most popular fiesta is on July 25, the day the village was formed. This is a fun day with ladies dancing in the streets, skirts flying and men doing their usual sipping of *chicha*.

Curva has no hotels or restaurants, but finding a spot to pitch a tent is easy. Ask around. Generally, people are friendly. The village has some small shops and a school of medicine for Kallawaya, although it does not operate all the time because the doctors are traveling and taking their young protégés with them. Buses leave Curva twice a week. If that doesn't suit your plans, walk to Charazani and make your base there.

Charazani has one hotel, the **Inti-Haus** (no phone), located on the main street. It's operated by Claudio, a retired journalist who also seems to be the unofficial town mayor. A few smaller *alojamientos* can be found on the square. Charazani does not have electricity or running water, but the hot springs are just a 10-minute walk down the road. Across the street from the Inti-Haus, Doña Sophie serves meals. She will make only one type of meal per day and you must order four hours in advance. She often serves different groups at different times, as she has only one table, so she may hurry you along. "Quiete y come!" (shut up and eat) was her constant message to us. Her food, like her humor, is excellent.

Charazani, in one of the most remote areas of Bolivia.

■ Getting Here

 To get to Pelechuco you must hire a jeep or catch the once-a-week bus from La Paz. Depending on road conditions, the trip can take up to 24 hours. A jeep will cost $250-$400 (Huayna Tours had the cheapest I could find and their driver is exceptional) and it can carry up to six people with gear. The journey takes less than 12 hours by jeep. On the return, the driver may take on locals from Pelechuco heading south. You can also try getting to Pelechuco by truck, but that trip could take a week in itself.

The bus from La Paz leaves the cemetery bus area on Wednesday mornings at 8 am and it can take anywhere from 14 to 24 hours to reach Pelechuco. The cost is $7. The bus is crowded and those with climbing/hiking gear may find it difficult. Buses return to La Paz on Friday or Saturday, depending on the festival situation and the number of people going out.

A bus goes to and from Charazani once a day. The bus going to La Paz leaves around 7 pm and often takes about 15 hours to get to the city. You must catch it at the square and purchase tickets ahead of time. The buses go only at night and you will share the aisles with everything that can possibly be sold in a market, plus kids. The bus takes its time, but when you catch glimpses of the hair-pin turns and unguarded vertical drops along the road's edge, you will appreciate the driver's caution.

■ Services

There is no electricity or water. For a shower, you should head to the hot springs. This is an isolated Andean hamlet that was here before Inca days because of the hot springs.

■ Adventures on Foot

Hiking

ISKANWAYA RUINS: The Iskanwaya Ruins date back 800 years to the Mollo Culture. To reach them you can hike from Pelechuco for four days. Or you can stay in Aucapata and hike out to the ruins, but that's only for the dedicated archeologist or serious trekkers. Most people take a jeep to Ulla Ulla on the road between Charazani and Pelechuco and then cross a pass and descend into Aucapata (7,566 ft/2,300 m). From there, you can walk up to the ruins that sit on the edge of a cliff overlooking a river.

In 1913, Erland Nordenskiold, a Swedish anthropologist, came to Bolivia with his wife Olga and together they found the ruins of Iskanwaya. Nordenskiold drew a map of the site and concluded that the ruins were the fortress of Cuzcotuyo that is mentioned by Sarmiento de Gamboa in his journals from the late 1500s. The ruins were again mentioned by Bernabe Cobo in a historical document published in 1653. However, since Nordenskiold's expedition, other scientists and laymen alike have identified other fortresses in the area that could also be the fabled Cuzcotuyo.

But early documents from the 1500s state that there were three fortresses in all: Dilava, Conyma and Cuscotuyo. In 1994 Ari Siiriainen and Martti Parssinen, two Finnish archeologists, went into the area and found all three and they surmised that Iskanwaya was definitely one of the three. However, there are other forts along the north shore of Lake Titikaka that could also be part of a chain of fortresses. Because of trade with the people farther north, these outposts may have also been used as trade centers.

At one time the ruins had 75 buildings made of slate, mortar and mud. The people living here were skilled in gold carving and ceramic pottery. They also developed large aqueducts and holding ponds for agricultural purposes.

PELECHUCO TO CHARAZANI: The hike from Pelechuco to Charazani is considered difficult because it crosses one 16,440-foot/5,000-m pass and requires descending steep shale slopes. Trekkers also have to sleep at high elevations. But the trail goes into secluded valleys, often along pre-Inca roads that pass through terraced fields of peas, wheat, corn and beans. You will see shepherds playing pan flutes while tending their animals. You will pass through Kallawaya territory and, if they are feeling generous, you will go with no trouble. However, if the ancient doctors have run out of patience you may have rocks thrown at you, as I did. I understand that we were one of the first groups to go through this area, so maybe some locals didn't really want us around. One of our

group needed the skills of the doctors by the time the stones stopped flying, and we decided that the Kallawaya needed to create some patients to cure. Dress appropriately and do not photograph the locals.

Should you choose to do this six-day hike from Pelechuco to Charazani or to Curva, you will see some spectacular country, lots of llamas and vicuñas, and will experience the thrill of being the only traveler for hundreds of miles. The trail passes through the Mapiri National Park and the Ulla Ulla National Reserve that was declared a biosphere reserve by UNESCO for its plants. This area also has the most condors in all the Andes.

Snow-covered mountains provide a magnificent backdrop for hikers.

HIKING BACKWARDS

Although some books describe the hike from Charazani, I suggest starting in Pelechuco and ending at Cherazani because of the transportation situation. It is easier to hire a jeep or catch the bus to Pelechuco, than it is to sit in Pelechuco waiting for transportation after completing a six- or seven-day hike. You have better bartering power when going in. If you are waiting to go out, the drivers know you will pay much more just to be gone. Also, Charazani has developed hot springs that will be appreciated after the hike.

Because of the high altitude and the types of camp stoves and fuel available for rent in Bolivia, choose food that takes little cooking time. Canned meat is good, as are crackers, hard cheese and granola-type cereals with powdered milk. Cooked potatoes will last a few days. Dehydrated soups with some carrots and tinned meat are great meals. Carrots can be crunchy and still good. Trying to cook pasta at a high altitude results in a pot of wall-paper paste. Bring lots of bread, but plan on eating it during the first few days. Chocolates, nuts and raisins are all available in the markets and give energy when needed. You can purchase things like tin bowls, cups and utensils in the market in La Paz. Carry out your empty tins, regardless of what locals do.

In Pelechuco, you can hire a guide with horses, mules or llamas to carry some of the supplies. Ask people on the square – usually there is a clan of local men sitting on the benches watching you. Our guide was named Marcellino and, except for taking off during the stone-throwing event and re-joining us a couple of hours later, he was good. Topographical maps of the area are poor, so a guide is highly recommended unless you are skilled in the Aymara language.

Be prepared to feed your guide and let him use other things like sleeping bags, tents and warm clothing. It gets very cold at night on this hike. Marcellino had no sleeping bag so we put him with my husband in our tent and I joined two other girls in their tent.

LOVING THE LLAMA

At maturity, a pack llama receives the *kawra pankara*, or llama flower, a string of woven wool that is attached to the hair on the llama's shoulders and on three consecutive places along its spine. Because they carry larger loads, male llamas are adorned with bigger llama flowers than females and the lead llama is always dressed in a rich head covering.

The average cost of a guide and two horses is $80 for the week. Try to have some gear available to give or sell him at the end of the week; usually you will have gotten to know him quite well. However, before you start the hike be certain that it is clear what is expected. Some things that should be clarified are the time to rise and quit, who does what chores, how far the guide must go and who negotiates passage through villages. We assumed Marcellino would go all the way to Charazani, but once he got above Curva he wanted to return home. When we insisted that he go all the way he pouted. We eventually let him go at the church three miles/five km above Charazani.

Some Quechua or Aymara words would be helpful as the guides from Pelechuco speak Spanish as their second language and misunderstandings are probable, especially if Spanish is also your second language.

If your guide uses pack animals, try to have a day pack with you for essentials. Pack animals move at a different speed than you, so your gear may be miles ahead or behind. I also get nervous when I see too much of my expensive equipment disappear over a hill.

You can also book this hike with a guide from La Paz. (See *Tour Operators* in the La Paz chapter, page 121.)

RIO YARIAPU TO RURRENABAQUE: The route along Rio Yariapu to Rurrenabaque should be done as a guided hike. It starts in Madidi National Park and ends at Chalalan, just out of Rurre. Madidi Park was created in 1995 and covers 4.5 million acres of cloud and tropical forest, lowlands and savannah. This land is drained by raging rivers and dotted with pristine lakes. It is reported to have almost 1,000 bird species and 44% of the new world's mammal species. There is also a plethora of amphibians.

The hike starts with a couple of days of difficult jeep travel from Charazani to Apolo and then on to Machua. From there, the hike starts and seven hours later and 987 ft/300 m lower you will camp at Toma Alta. Another seven hours of walking will bring you to Piñalito, where birds such as falcons and papagayos are seen, as are capybaras and howler monkeys. The next few days you will descend into jungle with dense vegetation and along the way, pass Mamacona, Palo Grande, Eslabon and Pico Plancha. Just when walking becomes a bit much, you will reach the Tuichi River. The rest is a float, except for the rapids.

Once in Rurrenabaque you will have a few days in which to visit the *pampas* and maybe see an anaconda, cobra or boa constrictor. New Milenium Adventure Sports in La Paz offers this hike with local guides and porters (at least one of whom speaks English), all river transportation, cooking and camping gear (except for sleeping bags and backpack). Park fees are extra. See *Tour Operators* in the La Paz chapter, page 121, for details.

Climbing

Cordillera Apolobamba peaks can be accessed either from Pelechuco, Curva or Charazani. Although they are all around 18,000 ft/5,500 m, thousands (according to Yossi Brain) have not been climbed. The first mountaineering expedition to go into the Apolobamba was in 1957. If hiring a guide service, I would suggest Huayna Potosi in La Paz because Dr. Hugo, who helped Yossi Brain with a lot of the routes he describes in his book, is experienced in this area. Hugo is a local who speaks English fluently and who played in the mountains from the time he could tie a rope. See the La Paz section, page 125, for information on this company.

Chaupi Orco, the highest mountain in the Apolobamba at 19,700 ft/ 6,000 m, is on the Peru/Bolivia border. To get to the base of this mountain you must take mules from Pelechuco and hike for two days. It takes another day to get to the glacier and yet another to reach the summit. There are two routes up this mountain, with the east ridge joining the main route close to the top. You can ascend the main route and return by the east ridge. There is an approach from the southwest also, but it is longer.

Palomani Grande is the second tallest mountain accessible from Pelechuco. It stands at 18,977 ft/5,769 m and can be climbed in one day. Three routes are described in Brain's book, with one having a 60° section of incline with most of the route at a 50° incline.

Ascarani is north of Pelechuco. In 1969 a Spanish team explored the mountain, making 19 new ascents during the one expedition. Those who have climbed Ascarani give it high praise. Isolation. New ascents. Rock and ice. Thin air. The best of scenery.

There are also five compelling peaks in the **Katantica Central** near Pelichuco, but it is beyond my scope to give any description of the actual climbs. Purchase Yossi Brain's *Bolivia: A Climbing Guide*, or work with the guides available in La Paz.

■ Adventures on Water

 A **Tuichi River** expedition is difficult and follows in part the trail of the now cult figure Yossi Ghinsberg, an Israeli who, with three companions, was exploring the Tuichi (without the help of experienced guides). He lost his raft when it capsized while going over a high waterfall and was missing for over a month. They still haven't found the bones of two of his companions, though Ghinsberg himself was rescued. Ghinsberg's book is available in Rurrenabaque.

The rapids that make up the Tuichi are powerful and the water volume can be extreme. The jungle is thick and wildlife abounds. Traveling through is a wild adventure. This trip is offered by Explore Bolivia (☎ 303-545-5728, www.explorebolivia.com) with skilled and experienced staff. As in any third world country, you can always find a local willing to act as a guide if you pay the cash. However, I would suggest that you be careful as they still haven't found the bones of Ghinsberg's friends.

It takes three days by jeep to reach Santa Cruz del Valle and another two-day trek with mules to reach the Tuichi River put-in spot at 3,355 ft/1,020 m. You will drop a total of about 2,300 ft/700 m during your descent to this river. It is not until day six of your journey that you actually are able to paddle. The first day on the river starts with a mild float that passes rocky beaches before throwing you into Surprise Canyon, where the rapids get bigger, going from a class II to a class IV the farther in you go. As you drop, the temperature gets warmer and the rapids appear more frequently. You then leave the canyon and float alongside the rolling hills of the Asariamas Valley.

The following day you will encounter large rapids that require technical moves to get through to San Pedro Canyon. The river becomes faster, narrower and more dangerous, moving from an average class III up to a class V. That night is spent in the canyon where monkeys and exotic birds are your only companions. The next day is an exploration/rest day when you can hike up the Ipurama River or just rest and prepare for the rush to come on the following day.

The canyon turns into a gorge and the rapids turn into class III and IV as soon as you leave camp. Those are the quiet ones. Next is the Gate of the Devil, class V, and the Gate of the Sun, class IV, the two stretches of hell that give the Tuichi its reputation. Those not skilled enough to be safe can portage these rapids.

The following day is a float by comparison, with a few class II and III rapids before the river widens and finally joins the Beni. The paddling section of the trip is over and wildlife viewing becomes the main focus as a motorized boat takes you down to Chalalan Lodge in the jungle, not far from Rurrenabaque.

Some of the above river run was described by the boaters of Explore Bolivia.

HERBAL HEALERS

The Kallawaya are naturopathic healers who have passed on healing traditions from father to son since before the Tihuanacan civilization began. They have their own language and have traveled from Ecuador to Patagonia both learning from others and healing. At the age of six or seven a boy learns how to collect and store plants. As he gets older he learns what plants are good for what ailments and how to relate to the patient so that he can prescribe a treatment that covers not only the physical but also the emotional aspects of the body. Most Kallawaya know the use of about 300 herbs, while the specialists know as many as 600. Women Kallawaya act as midwives and treat gynecological disorders. In the valleys between Pelechuco and Charazani, the Kallawaya inhabit six of the villages you will pass.

■ Tour Operators

Explore Bolivia has a combination kayak/hike trip that starts with a pick up at the airport in La Paz. From there you tour the Tihuanaco ruins and go on to kayak Lake Titikaka for three days. The kayaking includes a visit to the ruins on Isla del Sol. The last week of the trip includes the Apolobamba hike. If you like everything done for you, this is a good option. Explore Bolivia also runs a two-week trip down the Tuichi, following in part the footsteps of Yossi Ghinsberg.

Altiplano

Huayna Tours, Calle Sagarnaga #398 at Illampu, ☎ 245-6717, berrios@ mail.magalink.com is run by Dr. Hugo Berrios and his wife Damiska. Anyone who climbs in Bolivia will come upon Dr. Hugo somewhere. The company offers all the tours available with other companies, but their specialty is climbing. They will take climbers to any peak in Bolivia.

THE ALTIPLANO

Altiplano means high plain. It is high, but it is not a plain. In fact, it consists of volcanos, salt flats, dry rock formations and rolling hills. In Bolivia, the Altiplano runs from Lake Titikaka all the way to the Chilean border, a total of 551 miles/900 km, and it is about 122 miles/200 km wide. The climate is cold and dry and the vegetation is sparse. The grasses are spiky tufts that are tough to touch and unpleasant to sit upon. The trees are few. Quenua trees, which grow at elevations of up to 17,100 ft/5,200 m, are typical alpine trees. Because they are slow-growing, they are very dense and twisted.

Animals of the Altiplano are usually of the camel family, although the highland fox is common. Birds are abundant and interesting. One, the rhea, is related to the ostrich and can be found in large numbers in Sajama National Park. There are others too; the egret, the ibis, the flicker and the mockingbird are often seen.

The landscape of the Altiplano is exceptional. The climate can be bitter cold and the dryness can be irritating. But usually the temperatures are cool, even when the sun is out.

This information was provided, in part, by Tim Miller of Explore Bolivia.

Patacamaya

Patacamaya is a truck stop on the main road between La Paz and Oruro. It is also the junction where you branch off to go to Sajama or on to Tambo Quemado on the Chilean border.

■ Getting Here & Around

Take any bus going east toward Oruro from La Paz. I used Atlas Bus to Oruro and they made me pay the full cost even though I was going only to Patacamaya. Later, I used Trans Salvador from Patacamaya to Oruro and they charged only part of the fare.

Buses going to Oruro stop at Patacamaya for a few minutes and it is usually easy to get a seat. The road is paved and in excellent shape. It is a major route for travelers heading out of Bolivia and into Chile.

If you're hungry, go to the Quirquincho restaurant. They make a great fried egg sandwich for 25¢ and coffee for less than a dime. The toilets are clean (although a long way out back) and the owners pleasant.

If you are coming here from Sajama, the mini-bus often leaves before 7 am, so you may not have time for breakfast. In that case, stopping in Patacamaya to eat is essential.

The mini-van to Sajama leaves the main road in Patacamaya daily at 1 pm. Be early so you are assured a seat. The driver I had did not charge for my bags when I went to Sajama, but he charged $1 for each bag when I returned. The one-way fare is $1.25 and the ride is three to four hours. Before going to Sajama, the mini-van goes all the way to the border town of Tambo Quemado to let off and pick up passengers at the border before returning to Laguna and Sajama. Should you be going to or coming from Chile by this route, there are basic places to stay in Tambo Quemado. There is also a large restaurant with a bar attached. Those staying at the border for the night may want to patronize the bar.

Those going into Sajama can get off the bus at Laguna and tour the church while the bus goes to the border. Make it clear to the driver to pick you up on his way into the village. The road into Sajama is mud, stretching for seven miles/12 km with not a twig for shade nor a trickle of water to drink.

If you get stuck in Patacamaya for the night, there are two *alojamientos* on the main road. They are both basic, clean and cheap.

Some people take a bus from La Paz going to Chile and get off at Laguna and the turnoff to Sajama. This means a 7.3-mile/12-km walk along the dusty road with almost no chance of a ride. The sun is dangerous at that elevation, so I really discourage walking in. But if you must, be sure to have a hat, some food and lots of water. It is a boring walk, but you can look at the mountain as you trudge through the sand.

■ Adventures on Wheels

 The road between the Sajama turnoff and Patacamaya is an archeological zone for the first 18 miles/30 km or so out of Patacamaya. Three areas have funeral monuments similar to those at Sillustani, Peru. These were built long before the Inca empire was established. The site closest to Patacamaya is exceptionally well preserved, the second is showing wear, and the third, called Pukara de Monterani Archeological Site, on the opposite side of the road from the other two, is excellent. The government is doing some restoration to these structures and Expedition Kotamama, a group of international scientists, spent a few days examining these ruins.

When the Tihuanaco civilization collapsed due to drought, the people formed small groups and migrated around the Altiplano. Many lived near or on the flat-topped mountains and built forts for protection against invading groups. Monterani is such a site. The mountain stands at 13,500 ft/4,050 m and has stone terracing and some burial towers left from that civilization.

Near the 100 Km sign along the road is a canyon with wind-sculpted rock that is excellent for exploration. If possible, take a tent and camp. Close to the Km 125 sign is a river with more interesting rock formations and a deep canyon. If camping, you can get off the bus and walk in. I do not know the water situation; assume you need to carry it. The alternative is to hire a jeep in Sajama or Patacamaya to get to the canyon.

If coming from Chile, the river with rock formations is between Km 45 and 50 and the canyon is at Km 75. The archaeological zone starts at Km 125.

The village of **Curahuara de Carangas** has a church that is fondly called the Sistine Chapel of Bolivia due to the huge wall murals inside. The paintings are reproductions of the Last Supper, the Final Judgment, Noah's Ark and Adam and Eve leaving the Garden of Eden. They were all done by Ciriaco Acuña in 1876.

The village of **Lagunas** is at the turnoff to Sajama and if you don't want to go to the border and back (and don't mind standing or crouching in a loaded *trufi* for the last seven miles/12 km) you can get off at Lagunas and have the driver pick you up later. In Lagunas, the 18th-century church has frescos, oil paintings and an altarpiece that is more interesting than anything you'd see at the border town of Tambo Quemado.

Sajama

Altitude: 13,815 ft / 4,200 m
Population: 200

Sajama stands at a majestic 21,846 ft/6,549 m and is the highest mountain in Bolivia. The village of the same name is reminiscent of Tibet. It has the same mud brick huts, lack of electricity, high altitude and barren landscape. The entire mountain and village forms the Sajama National Park. The village is small and, when there are few tourists here, only one restaurant serves meals. If you need a meal, you will be sent to the place cooking for that day and there will be little selection.

There are a few places to stay, but they are basic with outhouses and communal cold-water taps for washing. Be certain to eat only food that is hot and drink water that has been purified. If purchasing bottled water, make certain the bottle has not been opened.

In winter (June, July and August) temperatures in Sajama can fall drastically to well below freezing. A warm sleeping bag is essential, along with some long-johns and warm hat. That is for sleeping. For daytime, a down jacket is highly recommended. In the summer (November, December and January) the temperature usually falls to around zero at night, but the days are warm enough to wear a cotton shirt and skirt or pants.

Sajama is one of the author's favorite places in all of Bolivia.

There are hot springs nearby and lakes teeming with wildlife. Mount Sajama is waiting to be climbed and three base camps make good destinations for hikers. A hill just out of the village is interesting to climb for the views. There are the Two Sisters Volcanos to visit and canyons on the main road (see above) that landscape photographers should not miss.

In my opinion, Sajama is one of the most exciting places in Bolivia to explore and those who miss it have missed a lot.

■ Getting Here

See *Patacamaya* section, above.

■ History

 Sajama National Park was created on August 2, 1939 and was the first protected area in Bolivia. It covers an area of 217,000 acres/120,000 hectares and abuts the Lauca National Park in Chile. The mountain (volcano) itself stands at 21,500 ft/6,550 m and the area above 17,000 ft/5,200 m is covered in snow and ice year-round.

People have lived in the area for much longer than history can tell. The church is believed to be built over some pre-Columbian ruins and the landscape is dotted with burial towers like those seen on the road between Patacamaya and the border.

■ Services

 The **park office** is at the entrance to the village. You must stop in before entering the town and, as a foreigner, pay $1.25 entry fee no matter how long you stay or what you do. Locals pay 75¢. The park office has some maps, a few photos and some dusty critters on display. The stuffed condor has been robbed of his royalty as he sits in the corner staring at a stuffed puma that also needs re-crowning. Maps of the mountain are not available for purchase at the park office.

There is a clinic in town, but often it is closed with nobody there. It has equipment to deal with altitude sickness. If you are in serious need of medical help and no one is around, go to the park office. They will find the medical staff.

Long-distance **telephone** calls can be made from the booth at the park office, open 8 am to 7 pm daily.

Jeeps with driver cost $20 for two people and $35 for four people for six hours. Ask at the park office or at Restaurant Parinacota (on the square in town) for information about vehicles.

■ Sightseeing

 The **cathedral** in the center of town is a mud-brick construction believed to be over 200 years old. It is a photographer's paradise. Whether the church and mountains behind are captured in the morning dawn or evening dusk makes no difference. The place is worth a visit. The village, too, is interesting and fun to photograph. The colors are stark, the landscape rugged and the clay ovens picturesque.

You can walk to geysers, a lake and hot springs, but not all in one day. If you have a tent, there is excellent camping near the geysers. If not walking, ask your hotel owner about a tour. The usual recommendation is for a full-day tour, but a half-day is more than enough.

■ Adventures on Foot

Hiking

GEYSERS: The geysers are five miles/eight km from town. Take the road past the church, across the creek, and up the valley on the other side. There are actually 130 pools in the area, some hot enough to boil eggs. The geysers erupt often and the colors of the landscape are interesting. Some of the plants seem as if they are from another planet, just because they are so green in such a barren landscape.

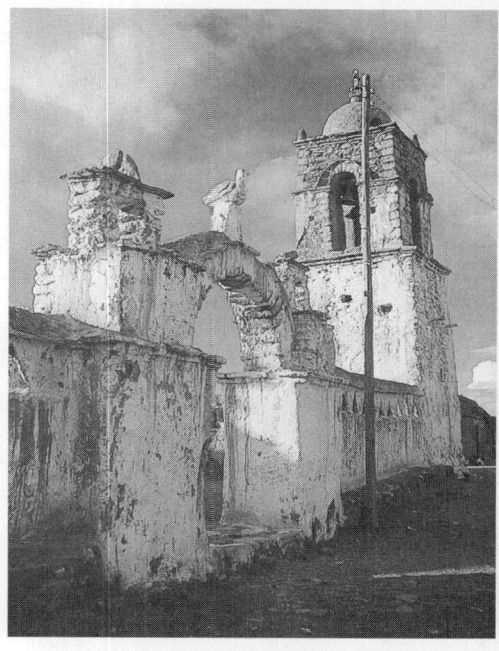

CERRO COMISERIO: A walk to Cerro Comiserio will help with acclimatization. Take the stone-lined trail behind the park office and head up the hill. The walk allows for excellent views of the entire valley plus a better view of Sajama volcano. If you are acclimatized, it will take an hour to reach the hilltop; if not, it will take three.

Sajama is a photographer's dream.

Climbing

SAJAMA: The summit of Sajama is 21,846 ft/6549 m and sits 8031 ft/2349 m above the village. It takes two days to reach the top and return. Sajama is often referred to as Bolivia's Chimborazo.

The first day of climbing is spent getting to one of three base camps, depending on which ascent – the north or the south – is to be climbed. At 4 am the following morning, the ascent is started as the summit should be reached before noon (the descent takes until almost dark). The climb is not very technical and may be attempted by those without too much experience or skill. The big factor is acclimatization.

If going up the north side late in the season, you may encounter the *nieve penitentes*, a field of ice crystals, some of which grow to a height of 10 ft/three m. If climbing the south ridge, there is enough room at the high campsite for about six tents.

Altiplano

There is enough equipment for rent at the park office for 10 people. It costs $10 per day. Four guides are available in the village and it is recommended that you use one. Juan Caballero has reached the summit of these mountains 33 times, so his skills are respected. Reynaldo is also highly recommended. A guide costs $50 per day and his fee can be shared by a group of climbers.

TWIN SISTERS VOLCANOS: Parinacota and Pomerata, along the Chilean border, can be seen from town. Parinacota is a perfectly shaped volcano and the slog up to the summit is more labor-intensive than technically difficult. Once at the top, regardless of which route you choose, you will find yourself at the rim of the crater looking down at least 329 ft/ 100 m. Although not as classic in shape, Pomerata is more technically challenging. The routes are long and the descent can be confusing. The summit of Parinacota stands at 20,822 ft/6,330 m and Pomerata is at 20,467 ft/6,222 m.

■ Adventures on Water

There are two sets of **hot springs** near the lake. You will probably need specific direction (or a guide) to reach them. The springs are on the same road as the lake, but the turnoff is before the lake. **Kasilla Hot Springs** are five miles/eight km past the pink hotel to-

This is where a local lady asked the author, because of her dark skin and peasant dress, what she was doing with a gringo *(her husband).*

ward the lake. The second hot springs, used mostly by locals, are half a mile/1 km farther along. They are smaller, cleaner and hotter.

If you can get someone to show you where the guide Ronaldo's place is, the springs are just past there on the creek. You must use the tuffed alpine grasses to hide behind when changing clothes or going to the bathroom.

■ Adventures in Nature

To get to **Sajama Lake**, walk or drive past the pink hotel for about three miles/five km. The area is rich in bird life, especially flamingoes. Lots of rheas (called *suri* by locals) hang out near the water and the curious but cautious vicuña are everywhere. The lake is not as comfortable a place to camp as the geysers.

> ## BIRDERS LOOKOUT
>
> The *Soca cornuda* is a black bird with a yellow beak that lives only in high Andean freshwater lakes. It builds a nest by putting water vegetation into a mound and then perching on the mound. There are many at the lake.

Along the road to the lake signs lead to **base camp #1**. Close to the base camp road is another road that leads to the **quenua forest**. Quenua grows as a dense and twisted tree with red peeling bark. It does not grow very high, maybe 10 feet or so, but is the toughest tree on the planet.

The second base camp is reached from the road between Sajama and Laguna. There is a sign for that one also. The third base camp is reached off the main highway between the Chilean border and Laguna at the turnoff to Sajama. There are also two other hot springs along that road.

■ Places to Stay

The pink building on the edge of town was to be a plush hotel built by Spaniards, but after spending $100,000 they ran out of money. The townspeople aren't anxious to see it open, as it will take tourist dollars away from locals.

There are places to stay around the square and along the main street. All are basic. Ask at the park office who is taking in guests on that particular day. Someone will always accommodate a foreigner. The cost is $1-$1.50 a night.

The **Eco Turismo Tomarapi** is reportedly open now and can accommodate up to 20 people at $25 per person, breakfast included. This was in a state of construction when I was there, but it is a brick hotel with thatch roof and private baths in each room.

On the square, **Restaurant Parinacota** has at least one room for rent. It's considered the best in town, with painted walls and a propane light. The Asian-style toilet is in a mud brick hut across the yard. Water is from a cold-water tap in the courtyard. Solar power generates electricity in the restaurant.

Oruro

Altitude: 12,197 ft / 3,708 m
Population: 200,000

Oruro is an odd town. If you stay by the bus or train station, you will not get a good sense of the community. If you stay in the center of town for a day or so, your impression will change. Hotels here are either badly overpriced or they are deplorable dives. Since comfort and environment influence the impression you get of a place, in Oruro it is better to pay a bit more for a hotel and enjoy the city.

Oruro is best known for hosting the most traditional Carnival in the country. It occurs usually in February, but can be as late as the beginning of March, depending on when Lent, which is 40 days before Easter, occurs. An interesting aspect of the celebration is that the dancers are mostly Hidago and the musicians are mostly Indian. Read more about Carnival below.

Oruro is also the place where in 1952, Bolivia's main, full-scale revolution occurred, when the miners' union and their allies defeated the army and established a socialist government in La Paz. The town is peppered with statues and memorials to the revolution.

■ Getting Here & Around

 The train station is on Calle Velasco Galvarro and Aldana, ☎ 527-4605. Go there for information about schedules and reservations.

Going south, the express train leaves for Uyuni on Monday and Thursday at 3:30 pm. The slower train (Wara Wara) leaves Sunday and Wednesday at 7 pm.

The train arrives from Uyuni on Wednesday and Sunday at 6:25 am and Tuesday and Thursday at 8:25 am.

To get a ticket, some people line up as early as 5:30 am. Others make reservations a week in advance. The company does not sell tickets in advance, only reservations, so you still have to wait in line to get your ticket.

(I waited in line for three hours during low season.) The cost to Uyuni is $5 for third class and $10 for first. There is little difference between the two. However, the train is the easiest way to get to Uyuni.

The bus station is about 10 blocks from the city center and a taxi there costs about 50¢ per person. La Paz buses go to Oruro every hour from 5 am until 10 pm daily. There is a 25¢ tax for using the bus station. Buses from Oruro to La Paz leave on the same schedule, every hour, all day. It is a four-hour ride to La Paz.

Buses going to and coming from Tarija stop on Avenida Ejercito at the east end of the city.

■ History

 Oruro's history lies in the tin and copper mines in the hills surrounding the city. Founded on November 1, 1606 by Judge Manuel Castro de Padilla at a time when silver was the big draw, Oruro's extraction of that metal continued until the 1800s when the city's focus changed from silver to tin. Shortly after the tin boom, copper became a lucrative metal and that too was taken from the hills in huge quantities. In Oruro, miners were treated slightly better than they were in Potosi, but the work was still hard and dangerous. This slowly and painfully led to the establishment of unions.

By the 20th century, there were three powerful mine owners in Oruro – Patiño, Aramayo and Hochschild. Patiño was a local Indian from Cochabamba who was poverty-stricken during his youth. He married a lady from Oruro and together they started amassing their wealth. He worked in the mines and eventually purchased one of his own. It became quite lucrative. Being a good businessman, Patiño didn't keep all his money in mining. He diversified and eventually became one of the richest men in the world. Because his wealth came first from the tin mines, he never lost his dedication to the area. Patiño's houses (more like palaces) in Oruro and Cochabamba are open to the public. One can also see evidence of the work of the Patiño Foundation, set up after his death by his grandchildren to promote education and art in Bolivia.

Before these men became rich and powerful, Oruro was the country's second-biggest city, behind Potosi. The economy was driven by mining. In 1780-81 a rebellion led by Tupac Amaru and joined by both mestizo and other indigenous discontents, caused many deaths in the Spanish upper class. But confusion occurred and soon the indigenous groups were turning against the mestizos. It all came to an end when the Spanish army entered the city and did away with the troublemakers.

During the War of Independence the economy in Oruro declined, as did the population, and it wasn't until after the turn of the century that silver again became a profitable commodity. During World War I tin was needed and that market stayed high until the end of World War II, as did copper. During those days, Oruro prospered. The tin went to the allied side despite general sympathy for Germany in both wars.

Oruro miners led a full-scale revolution in 1952, defeating the army in pitched battles and putting the left-of-center MNR in power. The mines were nationalized and land was seized from the owners and redistributed. Monuments in Oruro commemorate this struggle with grand statues of miners wielding rifles.

However, after the miners' strikes and the land reforms, the mining profits again dropped. The price of tin plummeted after World War II, and the mines were nearing depletion. Today, there is little to drive the economy except Carnival, which is world famous. The place doesn't seem depressed, though. Just a bit run down, with lots of abandoned buildings and rail yards.

■ Services

 The **telephone office** is on Calle Bolívar across from the tourist office. It opens at 7:30 am and closes at 10 pm daily.

The **post office** is on the corner of Calle Adolfo Mier and Avenida Pdte. Montes.

Internet Bolívar on Calle Bolívar #687 has numerous machines, but they are slow. In general, Internet connection in Oruro is poor.

The **police office** is on Calle Bolívar, a block west of the square.

The **hospital** is on Calle Potosi and two blocks west of the train station.

The **tourist office** is just off the plaza on Calle Bolívar. It is a tiny kiosk that has some brochures and items of interest. However, do not arrive just before coffee break, lunch, siesta or closing or you will be given the bum's rush.

■ Carnival

Carnival celebrations are a combination of pre-Columbian and Catholic rituals. Basically, it is a show of good against evil, with good always winning. Carnival was first celebrated in 1789 when it is believed that the Virgin of Socavon fought the devil and liberated Oruro. Through music and dance the people of Oruro re-enact this myth.

Today, the Carnival is celebrated in four days of festivities for most places and a week in Oruro. During these celebrations, hotel prices rise and finding a room upon arrival is not possible. Renting in a private home is not usually an option either. Friday night seems to be a warm up, with some street dancing and partying in preparation for the real start the next day.

The Saturday before Ash Wednesday is called **Jeska Anata**, or the Entrada de Carnival. The costumes are elaborate and the devil is always prominent. Prior to Catholicism arriving in Bolivia, the Aymara believed that the devil and the lords of the underground were not particularly evil, just dangerous and to be appeased.

The parade goes for 1.8 miles/three km along Avenida del Folklore and ends at the Sanctuary of the Virgin of Socavon. Here, 40 groups of dancers and musicians enter the church on hands and knees and crawl to the altar. They take off their masks of serpents, spiders and the devil and pray to the Virgin for things like health, wealth and love. Personally, I'd ask the Virgin for stamina. At the church, they also promise to dance in the Carnival for three years running. The Virgin, always compassionate, is believed to grant many wishes. After the dancers are blessed, they put their masks back on and return to the streets where they dance, sing, drink and party for four days.

Carnival sees 37,500 dancers and musicians all dressed in expensive and elaborate costumes. Some of the masks cost well over $200 to make and the sequined dresses are equally as expensive. Each dance group must have its own band – which can cost anywhere from $700 to $1,000 for the day – and each day of the Carnival requires the dancers to wear a different costume.

There are different dances too, but the **Devil's Dance**, or Diablada, is the most popular and prominent. The dancers gyrate down the street oozing sexuality for the entertainment of the 400,000 visitors that come to watch and for the TV cameras that send the event to TV tubes all over Latin America. But watching is not all the visitors do. They throw water and spray shaving cream. Some stand with buckets of water on their balconies and throw it over when someone passes beneath. A lot of people get very drunk.

Occasionally, the festivities get out of hand. In La Paz in 2003, 11 people were killed and hundreds injured by *globos* (balloons filled with water). We watched the run-up for Carnival in Sucre and one person was knifed to death – gang warfare evidently spilled into the festivities.

The best way to enjoy Carnival is to join a tour from either Sucre or La Paz. That way, you are there for the events but miss all the drink-fests that seem to start shortly after sunset.

Sunday is the big day for the devil when he seems to be winning in his struggle with guilt. It is also when water bombs and shaving cream are most often sprayed and thrown. Spectators who are not covered in plastic ponchos are doomed and foreigners had better expect to participate.

Altiplano

Monday is called the Day of the Devil and the Dark Ones. This day demonstrates the struggles between the devil and positive forces with good winning over. The devil symbolically loses his powers.

Tuesday, called Martes de Cha'lla, is usually the most important day for families and almost all businesses are closed. Everyone decorates their homes with streamers and balloons and pays tribute to Pacha Mama (Mother Earth) by sprinkling wine in the corners of rooms. They also throw fire crackers on the roofs of their houses to ensure good luck and prosperity for the coming year.

Most things that reach perfection are practiced and Carnival is no exception. The first hint of Carnival starts on the first Sunday in November, when the dancers and musicians go to the Sanctuary of the Virgin of Socavon to give thanks for the opportunity to participate in the event and to ask small favors. December and January finds the revelers every Saturday parading in the main streets with a bit of drinking practice thrown in. Numerous marriages take place during the pre-Carnival events. In fact, there are so many brides on the square or driving around in decorated cars, it looks like a group event. Photographers are everywhere.

Two weeks before Carnival the party speeds up and the Sunday before Carnival in Oruro is almost as good as the real thing. If you can't get seats or a room during the main events, try the Sunday before.

Remember, you will be expected to join in. For **music lessons** on the guitar, charango (like a ukulele), baterea (a percussion instrument), saxophone or piano, contact the tourist office on Calle Sorea Galvarro. They continually offer courses, some of which span only a few days.

■ Sightseeing

Churches

There are 130 churches, temples and chapels in the Department of Oruro. Half of them are colonial structures, many of which incorporate both Indian and Spanish symbols. For example, there are pumas sitting close to saints or Amazonian plants beside thorns.

Iglesia de Santo Domingo on Calle Montes and Avenida Copacabana was built in 1918 and is located beside the Mercado Fermin Lopez. The indigenous art on the outside of the building is excellent.

The oldest church in the city is **San Miguel**, built in the 1500s and located one block north of the open-air theater. Called the "parish of the natives," the church originally offered services in both Aymara and Quechua languages. San Miguel has walls 3.3 ft/one m thick. During the winter solstice, the light of the rising sun comes through the door and hits the altar.

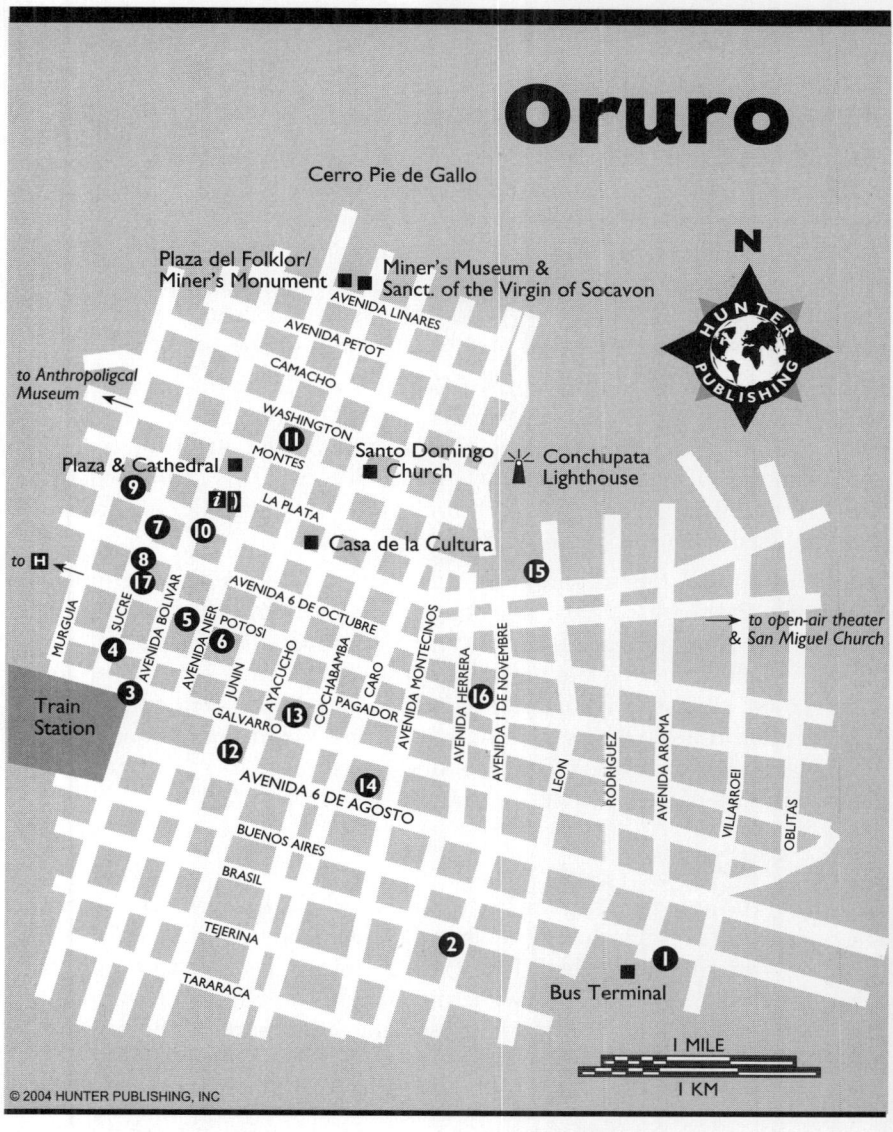

Oruro

Cerro Pie de Gallo

Plaza del Folklor/
Miner's Monument ■ ■ Miner's Museum &
Sanct. of the Virgin of Socavon

AVENIDA LINARES

AVENIDA PETOT

CAMACHO

to Anthropoligcal
Museum

WASHINGTON

MONTES

⑪

Santo Domingo
■ Church

☀ Conchupata
Lighthouse

Plaza & Cathedral ■

⑨

LA PLATA

⑦ ⑩

to Ⓗ

⑧

⑰

■ Casa de la Cultura

⑮

AVENIDA 6 DE OCTUBRE

SUCRE

AVENIDA BOLIVAR

⑤

POTOSI

④

⑥

MURGUIA

AVENIDA NIER

JUNIN

AYACUCHO

COCHABAMBA

CARO

PAGADOR

AVENIDA MONTECINOS

AVENIDA HERRERA

AVENIDA 1 DE NOVEMBRE

to open-air theater
& San Miguel Church

③

⑯

Train
Station

GALVARRO

⑬

⑫

AVENIDA 6 DE AGOSTO

⑭

LEON

RODRIGUEZ

AVENIDA AROMA

VILLARROEI

OBLITAS

BUENOS AIRES

BRASIL

TEJERINA

②

TARARACA

Bus Terminal ■ ①

1 MILE

1 KM

© 2004 HUNTER PUBLISHING, INC

PLACES TO STAY
1. Hotel International Park
2. Hotel Bernal
3. Aljamiento San Juan de Dios &
   Residencial San Salvador
4. Residencials El Express, San Miguel &
   Real, & Hotel Restoria
5. Residencial Gloria
6. Palace Hotel
7. Hotel Sucre
8. Hostal Hidalgo & Hotel Monarca

PLACES TO EAT
9. Salteñas Potosinas
10. Oggies - Super Hamburguesas
11. Gupers Restaurant
12. Churrasqueria Parrillades
13. Ametaura Restaurant
14. Nostalgias Restaurant
15. Plaza Rancheria

NIGHTLIFE
16. Wara Karaoke & the Flamingo Bars
17. Bar 77

San Francisco Church on Calle Bolívar and Soria Galvarro was started in 1610 by the free slaves who survived their lives in the mines. It was not completed until the 17th century. The church was originally built only for the slaves, with the financial assistance of the Sisters of Mercy.

The **cathedral** on Calle Alfredo Mier and La Plata was built by Jesuits in the early 1600s, but its importance was replaced by the Sanctuary of the Virgin of Socavon, five blocks west of the central plaza. The first cathedral was destroyed and this second one was built in baroque and renaissance styles. The main chapel is built in the shape of a cross (not so unusual for Catholic churches). After the first church was demolished, its stone bell tower was relocated to the Sanctuary of the Virgin.

The Sanctuary of the Virgin of Socavon is the home of the patron saint of miners, a female counterpart to St. Michael. On the ceiling are paintings of her holding a sword as she defends the city from a dragon and a snake. The first sanctuary was built in 1781 and housed the Nuestra Señora de Copacabana, but she was moved to Copacabana and was replaced with the Virgin of Socavon.

The building also has an image of Mary with two cherubs that appeared by miracle in the late 1800s. The church was built on top of an Uru ritual center and over a mineshaft that is now a museum. The mineshaft at one time was believed to be the hiding place of Chiru, the Aymara version of Robin Hood, who stole from the rich to give to the poor. When he was shot by police, he repented any sins he had to the Virgin and, as soon as he died, Mary's image appeared. This story is recounted in one of the stained glass windows of the church.

City Sights

In front of the sanctuary is the huge **Plaza del Folklor** where the culmination of events occurs during Carnival. There is also a kids' cement slide that goes from the top of the hill down to the plaza. It is fun to watch them wear out their pants within two runs. Beside the slide you will see pilgrims climbing the stairs often on their knees to the top of the hill that is flounced by a white cross.

Opposite the grand slide is a monument commemorating the miners and their part played in freeing Bolivian workers. It depicts a tunnel with an ore car, tracks and some miners with their hands raised in victory.

Behind the monument is a market where *rellenos* are the most popular dish sold. They are a wheat-flour pancake stuffed with cheese and then deep-fried. Yum. The hill behind the sanctuary is **Cerro Pie de Gallo** (Chicken-Foot Hill) and should be climbed (follow the steps) to get an excellent view of the city.

On the corner of Ayacucho and La Plata is the **courthouse**. Of course, the appropriately named Calle La Plata is lined with lawyers' offices.

The **Lighthouse of Conchupata** is on Avenida Herrera and Calle La Plata. Although it is in disrepair at the moment, this was where, on November 7, 1851, the first Bolivian flag was raised. The leader of the city, Manuel Isidoro Belzu, did the honors.

There is a market area, Mercado Golozinas, around and behind the train station at the end of Avenida 6 de Agosto. Vendors sell everything from furniture to safety pins, but little that would interest the visitor.

The **Puentes Español** spans a natural causeway on the road to Pisiga on the Chilean border and Toledo on the way to Pumiri. The bridge was first built so that mule trains carrying silver to the coast could operate during rainy season when the rivers are high. On the way back, the trains carried mercury so the gold could be extracted from the rock.

■ Adventures in Culture

The **Religious Art Museum** (no phone) is on the upper floor of the Sanctuary of the Virgin and contains religious items made in honor of her. It's $1.50 to enter the church that displays many objects left after miracles were performed, the mineshaft and the art museum. There is a small gift shop at the Sanctuary beside the ticket wicket.

The mineshaft, now called the **Etnografico Museo de Mineros**, is far more interesting than the art museum. Miners feed Tio Diablo cigarettes and small amounts of alcohol, plus they decorate him with streamers and balloons. In return they get Tio's protection and guidance to the big ore-producing veins. At the opposite end of the mineshaft are artifacts from the early mining period in Oruro. Many of these are from the mine offices; I especially liked the old lead print machine and grandfather clock.

The **Cultural Museum of Simon Patiño** (no phone) is on Calle Ayacucho and Avenida Soria Galvarro, one block up from the street of the lawyers. The building was constructed in 1899 and made into a museum in honor of Patiño in 1970. It was originally his home but then the building was given to the university. Since universities and schools in Bolivia operate on almost no money, Patiño's home is pretty much the way it was left, with the addition of a lot of dust.

Altiplano

SIMON PATIÑO

Born in Cochabamba in 1860 of poor peasant stock, Patiño married Alvina Rodriques who was from an Oruro peasant family. They had seven children.

Simon struck it rich in iron and tin and become one of the richest men in the world. He sold most of his iron to the Germans during World War I. During the second World War, he remained loyal to the allies, although the Germans got lots of sympathy from the general population.

Patino was known to pay his mine workers well, but otherwise he didn't contribute much to the poor. After becoming wealthy, he built the French-styled house in Oruro. I assume he considered the French to be the most refined people in the world. In actual fact he was like many self-made wealthy people in that they become ostentatious in an attempt to look refined.

Some of the museum's more interesting objects are French-design tapestry chairs, a silver carving of Atlas holding a horn, and a chair joined at the arm but facing in two directions (you have to see it). The smoking room has paintings on the ceiling of women smoking. I wonder if Alvina smoked. Numerous oil paintings grace the walls, often featuring Patiño or his wife, but seldom the children. The music room has an automatic orchestra that played from perforated paper like a player piano. There are three pianos in all, a Victrola, and some good Turkish statues (that the museum guide insisted were French). You'll also see some marble and bronze statues and short brocade chairs upon which ladies sat to do needlework. The games room has a snooker-type table with only two pockets at the side and a number of orifices at one end. There are also teeter-totters and two-seater rocking chairs. Patiño's mining room has expensive scales and numerous photo negatives of his mining operations. There's a saddle collection, a private chapel and pharmacy with some impressive vessels. The carriages that were used by the family are in the public library on the main floor. One carriage required 10 horses to pull it (Patiño insisted that they be white).

A guided tour costs $1. Open hours must be guessed at; I went when it was closed but they took me around anyway.

The **Anthropological Museum** (National Anthropologo Museo of Eduardo Lopez Rivas) is in the south end of the city on Avenida España. A taxi costs just under a dollar for two people and a micro costs 15¢. Take the micro marked "sur" and tell the driver where you want to get off. The museum entry fee is 50¢. The displays here are excellent and include mummies found in the tombs on the road to Sajama as well as skulls that show how earlier people flattened the head of rich children for aesthetic reasons. One skull is from an encephalitic child and another shows bore holes where doctors may have tried to release pressure for the patient. There are a few weavings, some stone carvings and a fairly good collection of Carnival masks, costumes and old Carnival photos. This is a very good museum; if you are in Oruro for even a day, it should be taken in.

The park adjacent to the museum is well kept and the trees are labeled with local, family and scientific names. Behind the park and museum is a zoo, which I did not visit.

The **Mineralogical Museum** (no phone) is at the Technical University at the south end of town. To get here, hire a taxi for 50¢ per person. Upon arrival, look for someone with a key to open the doors. The interesting displays include about 7,600 specimens in all. Dr. Herzenberg first started the collection in 1975 and those first collected specimens are still in the museum. They include minerals – some in crystalline form and some with petroglyphs – and rocks of every type found in the hills around the city. The museum is well set up and worth a visit. The museum building was designed by a graduate of the university.

■ Adventures on Water

 OBREJAS HOT SPRING: Obrejas Hot Spring is 15 miles/ 25 km from town. A taxi here will cost $3 for up to four people, or you can catch a small bus on Calle Caro and Avenida 6 de Agosto (50¢, 45 minutes). It costs $1.50 for use of the pool; you can also rent private cubicles for a family. Water from the volcano is constantly being circulated, so it is always fresh. The minerals in the water are supposed to help those with arthritis.

There is a resort at Obrejas for those needing more than one hot dip in the cold climate of the Oruro area.

In the village near the hot spring is a newly opened Anthropological Museum (no phone number available). It is just 1,000 ft/300 m from the Obrejas Resort, an obvious landmark in the village, and can be visited on weekends only. One display shows items found in the Paria Basin close to Oruro. The museum is broken up into different time periods. One section covers 8000-2000 BC with items from the pre-ceramic period made of animal skins and fruits. The second period, 2000 BC-AD 400, features items from Oruro, Tihuanaco and the Desaguadero River area, such as anthropomorphic carvings and weavings, as well as model circular buildings. The collection has items used in early agricultural and fishing practices. All time periods leading up to the Colonial period starting in 1532 are covered. Entry fee is 45¢ for nationals and 75¢ for foreigners.

CAPACHOS HOT SPRING: The pools here are filled only once a day, so they aren't quite as clean as those at Obrejas. Capachos is seven miles/ 12 km from town and you can get here either by bus or taxi (the same way as Obrejas). Individual cubicles are available for families or skinny dippers.

■ Adventures on Wheels

ROCK PAINTINGS: Cala Cala, a tiny village 12 miles/20 km east of the city, has pre-Columbian rock paintings and carvings of llamas and sheep in pastures. The date of the paintings is unknown, although the scientists suspect them to be about 2,400 years old. They are on a huge rock about three stories high where a walkway and viewing platform have been built. This is a worthwhile excursion.

On **Fiesta of the Señor de Lagunas** (September 14), women who have been married more than two years and have not had kids make a pilgrimage to the fields near Cala Cala. Those wanting a daughter place a rose on the field and those wanting a son place a cala lily. The pilgrims are guaranteed a child within a year. I was assured by one woman that this pilgrimage works – it did for her.

To get here, take a taxi ($7 for up to four people) and ask the driver to let you off near the rock paintings.

PUMIRI ROAD TRIP: The Pumiri tour requires that you hire a jeep for the day. Although you could village-hop on *trufis* and shared taxis, delays in villages with few or no hotels could result in some unpleasant evenings. With your jeep driver, head toward the village of Pisiga on a road going toward Chile. In **Toledo**, your first stop, is an old adobe brick church built in the shape of a cross, and an interesting cemetery close by. Note the high-quality thatch roofs on houses here. Continue to **Corque,** where there's an old church built during colonial times and two *chulpas*, or funeral pyres. One is in fairly good shape. The next stop is **Turco**, where the baroque church, built in the 16th century, is worth looking at. It has numerous oil paintings and an altar covered in gold leaf. You have the option of staying in Turco before moving on to the enchanted city of Pumiri, 12 miles/20 km past Turco. Now in a protected archeological zone, Pumiri's rock formations inside the city make it easy to understand why it is referred to as the enchanted city. At the entrance are two *chulpas* and then two rocks, one that looks like a puma and one like a condor. As you go inside the ancient city, the remains of old walls and some houses can be seen around a tiny plaza. The view over the Altiplano from here is impressive and in the soft light of day's end, the ruins are spectacular for photography. There has been little archeological exploration done at the site. However, it is believed to be a place that three civilizations have used for ceremonial and living/fortress purposes.

After Pumiri you pass **Titiri**, where the highest quality Bolivian wool and alpaca carpets are made. If you want to purchase any of these items, do so in Titiri. The carpets are of such quality that they are exported to Europe and North America. **Cosapa**, the next stop, has a colonial church of interest, but it is weavings that are of most interest. Again, the quality is high, the cost still fairly low. **Capilla** is where the road joins the main road between Sajama and Patacamaya. There are basic places to stay in Capilla.

LOST CITY OF ATLANTIS

Jim Allen wrote an article for the magazine *Atlantis Rising*, in which he gave strong argument that the Altiplano of this area was the fabled country of Atlantis. Some of his arguments were that the Desaguadero River and the flat-topped plateaus of this area have the same dimensions as the geographic descriptions of Atlantis. The other argument is that oracalcum, a mixture of copper and gold, is found only in the Andes and this metal was supposedly found in Atlantis.

Archeologists have been poking around the area and one group who worked along the Desaguadero River between Lake Titikaka and Poopo found 30 hilltop fortresses. There are also numerous *chulpas* (some still with bodies inside), secret underground tunnels and rock walls with double-walled entrances. Dr. Oswaldo Rivera has been working in the area for close to 20 years now and believes the civilization that lived here was a warring group who occupied the region from around 1150 to 1475 and disappeared when the Inca came.

The adventuresome who have a tent and some food can certainly explore this on their own.

Lake Poopo is fed by the waters that run down the Desaguadero River from Lake Titikaka. Poopo covers over 965 square miles/2,500 square km. Often, there are flamingos and other water fowl in the shallow areas. The lake is best seen from the train going to Uyuni.

■ Tour Agency

 EBA Transturs, ☎ 242-2426, ebatrans@ceibo.entelnet.bo, have worked in 2001 with Dr. Allen from the magazine *Atlantis Rising*. The group toured through the villages described in the Pumiri road trip, above, and compiled an argument to support the fact that the Altiplano generally and this area specifically is the fabled Atlantis. For an interesting excursion, see these people. Their English is excellent.

A two-day tour goes from La Paz or Oruro to Toledo, Corque, Turco, Pumiri, Ciudad de Piedra, Titiri, Cosapa and on to Sajama before returning to La Paz or Oruro. The cost, $172 per person with a minimum of four people, includes transportation, one night in a hotel, a bilingual guide and all your meals. Longer tours are offered at negotiated rates. For example, a three-day tour with a stop in Sajama costs $280 per person with a minimum of four people and includes two nights in hotels.

Altiplano

■ Places to Stay

HOTEL PRICES (US $)

Per person, per day, unless noted otherwise.

$	$2-$5
$$	$5-$10
$$$	$11-$17
$$$$	$18-$25
$$$$$	Over $25

Residencial Gloria, *around the corner from the palace, on Avenida Potosi near Bolívar,* ☎ *527-7250, $,* has 13 rooms in a lovely old building that has been well kept and polished clean. The halls are bright and dotted with plants, and the rooms large and clean with high ceilings, wood floors and big windows. A small cafeteria sells snacks and drinks. The front door is always locked and you must ring the bell (*tocar el timbre*) to enter. This is where I stay while in Oruro.

Residencial El Expresso, *Calle Sucre #261 and Velasco Galvarro,* ☎ *527-4315, $,* is at the low end for quality, but the rooms do have TVs.

Residencial San Miguel, *Calle Sucre #331* ☎ *527-2132 $,* charges $4.50 per person for a small room with bath. There are carpets in the rooms and rather glitzy bedspreads and curtains. However, the place is okay.

Residencial Real, *Calle Sucre #401,* ☎ *527-4722, $,* is another basic place to stay. Rooms have private baths and TVs and there is a parking area. The owners will exchange dollars, but not travelers' checks.

Alajamiento San Juan de Dios, *Avenida Valasco Galvaro,* ☎ *527-7083, $,* is across from the train station. It's basic, but clean.

Residencial San Salvidor, *Avenida Valasco Galvarro, just up the street from the San Juan,* ☎ *527-6711, $$.* Although this big hotel has been remodeled, it is already slightly worn down. Few tourists stay here.

Hotel Bernal, *Calle Brazil #701, across from the bus station, no phone, $$,* has a friendly staff and clean rooms. Consequently, it is usually full. The new place across the street from the Bernal is equally as good, but charges more. Other than these two, I'd skip the rest of the places around the bus station because they are either overpriced or deplorably drab.

Sucre Hotel, *Calle Sucre #510 and Avenida 6 de Octubre,* ☎ *527-6800, $$$,* is a grand old place with friendly staff that keeps the hotel spotless. Room rates include cable TV, a telephone and a buffet breakfast. The wide halls feature original oil paintings on the walls, the floors are wood and the furniture is of good quality. Hot water comes from a boiler tank in the central courtyard and you must use cold water to get the right temperature. Rooms without private bath are small and located a fair distance from the communal bath. The hotel does not supply towels, nor is much English spoken. The Sucre will give you a comfortable stay.

Hostal Hidalgo, *Avenida 6 de Octubre #1616, around the corner from the Sucre,* ☎ *525-7516, $$$*. Although it doesn't have the elegance of the Sucre, it certainly is a good deal. Rooms come with private or shared tiled baths, cable TV, carpet, chairs and tables. This hotel is much better than most for the price.

Hotel Monarca, *Avenida 6 de Agosto #1145,* ☎ *725-4300 or 725-4222, $$$,* has moderately sized rooms with cable TV and hot water all day. There is a restaurant on site and underground parking is available. I found the management friendly and helpful.

Hotel Restoria, *Calle Sucre #370,* ☎ *525-8001, $$$,* has single, double and triple rooms of moderate size, with night tables, cable TV and telephones, but the lighting makes them appear a bit drab. The baths are tiled and have separate shower stalls. English is spoken and breakfast is included. The old building has had quite a bit of care given to it and is a good alternative to the Sucre.

Palace Hotel, *Calle Adolfo Mier #392, on the corner of Potosi,* ☎ *527-2121, smpalace@cotear.com, $$$$,* has singles, doubles and triples. The well-kept rooms, although not overly large, have writing desks, an electric heater and private baths. The toilet seat fits and is bolted on, and there is hot water all the time. If you get a double room with two beds, you may be lucky and get the one with two rooms joined by a small foyer. The price of the room includes breakfast and secure parking is available.

Hotel International Park, *Calle Rajka Bakovi over the bus station,* ☎ *727-6227, $$$$$,* is an overpriced, upscale hotel that charges $30 for a single with private bath and $45 for a double.

■ Places to Eat

 Salteñas Potosinas, *Calle Galvaro #6150,* has well-stuffed *salteñas* for 15¢ each – an excellent snack. *Rellenos*, fried dough stuffed with cheese, can be purchased in the markets near the miner's museum on Plaza Folklore. *Chicharon* (sausage) is served on Sundays only and is a great delicacy in Copacabana and Oruro. The other special dish is *langua peqanti*, tongue stew, which sometimes includes other "special" meats.

Churrasqueria Parrillades, *Avenida 6 de Agosto #1259,* is a good eatery to try the reasonably priced sausages for which Oruro is so famous.

Oggies, *corner of Calle Bolívar and Avenida,* is popular with locals for *almuerzo*. This consists of potatoes, rice, a slab of meat, soup, buns, and a pastry for $1.25. Don't look up at the ceiling as the view is bad. The once elegant pink, satin curtains that decorate the walls are also a bit dusty, but the oilcloth on each table is serviceable.

A better *almuerzo* in a cleaner environment can be enjoyed at **Ametauna Restaurant**, *Calle Sonia Glavarro #1367*, ☎ *525-7703*. My *almuerzo* here consisted of a fresh salad, a soup spiced with a delicious blend of flavors, rice, potato and meat balls (this changes every day) and a dessert. It was excellent and the cost was 80¢ per meal. This place was the best I found while in Oruro.

Super Hamburguesas, *in front of the Entel building just up from Oggies on Bolívar,* is the popular Bolivian rendition of McDonald's, only this is 10 times as good. Super Hamburguesas has a second location at Avenida 6 de Octubre #5379. This restaurant has a lot of fresh vegetables that can be added to a hamburger or just eaten as a salad.

For the best hamburger go to **Plaza Rancherea** on Sundays at noon. It is on the corner of Calle Sonia Galvario. In a makeshift *tienda* vendors cook *churrascos* and serve them in a bun that has been partially dipped in the cooking oil. The bun is filled with freshly shredded veggies. This meal costs only 65¢, but plan on waiting at least 20 minutes because the lines are so long. You can also get a plate of *churrascos* with rice and salad at the same *tienda* for just under a dollar a plate. When you arrive at the plaza, just look for the crowd. That's where to eat.

Bravo's Pizza, *Bolívar between 6 de Octubre and Potosi,* has good pizza – a 12-inch veggie costs $3.50. Mugs of warmish beer are served with a huge head, so you either sip foam or have to wait. If you are a beer drinker, ask for a small glass and pour your own.

Gupers, *Calle Junin and Pdte Montes*, ☎ *525-3815, is up one block from Plaza 10 de Febrero.* This popular place specializes in sweet and sour chicken. The restaurant also serves salads spiced with herbs.

I often used to go to **Govindo's Restaurant** run by the Hari Krishna, but it was not open on my last visit. Nor was the pub next door, the La Jaula. They may have been closed for renovations or just closed for good.

Nostalgias Restaurant and Lounge, *Avenida 6 de Agosto #1145,* ☎ *525-4300,* is a large area that serves *almuerzos* and à la carte meals. The restaurant is open from noon until 9:30 pm daily.

■ Nightlife

 Wara Karaoke and **The Flamingo**, *across the street, Calle 10 de Noviembre #420,* are rocking places but if you want to hang out with young locals try the **Bar 77** on Avenida Sucre #460. It has pool tables, lots of loud music and a small restaurant where you can line your stomach before competing in a drinkfest with the Oreños.

■ Shopping

This is the place to purchase Carnival-related objects like masks or glittery hats and dresses. Places to buy masks are **El Kerquinacho**, Calle German Floriz #5379, and **Arco Irio** and **Ancestral Bordados** off Calle La Paz. Masks and costumes can cost anywhere from a few dollars up to hundreds.

Potosi

Altitude: 13,454 ft / 4,090 m,
making Potosi the highest capital city in the world
Population: 125,000

Potosi is high. Your breathing and heart rate will be up and your energy down until you acclimatize. However, once you are comfortable in Potosi, you will be comfortable anywhere in Bolivia. Although it is not attractive, moving farther into the heart of the city reveals many treasures. And, if you are into history, Potosi is Bolivia.

The center of town has been spruced up so that there are pedestrian *pradas* lined with international restaurants and bars. But the old does not leave and some of the streets tell their own story in their names – Hanged Man's Corner and Seven Corner Street.

The National Mint, once the only place in the western hemisphere making coins, should not be missed, especially if you've done a visit to the mine. And a city tour that informs visitors about the history of different buildings is a top priority, as are some of the close-by hiking spots. During the summer months (October to March) the weather is rainy but warmer than in winter, when temperatures can drop well below freezing. One of the secrets of enjoying Potosi is getting a warm and comfortable place to stay.

■ Getting Here & Around

If coming by bus, you will have a long walk up a steep hill to reach the main part of town. Taxis go into town and they are worth far more than their cost of 45¢ per person. The bus station is at Avenida Universitario. Some buses don't stop at the terminal but along the street close to the terminal. There is a 25¢ tax charged for using buses from the terminal.

Buses to Cochabamba leave at 6:30 pm, 7 pm and 7:30 pm daily.

Buses to La Paz leave at 6:30, 7 and 8 pm daily. **Copacabana Bus Company** offers a bus-cama to La Paz three times a week for $8 per person

This bus has a foot section that folds down and seats that fold back to make a sort of bed. The bus is very quiet; even children know not to cry while on this bus. They do not pick up passengers once all seats are filled. I can't usually sleep on night buses, but did on this one.

Buses to Oruro leave at 7 am and 7 pm. Those to Tarija go at 4 am and 4 pm and those for Tupiza/Villazon leave at 7:30 am, 6 pm, 7 pm and 7:30 pm. Buses to Uyuni leave at 11 am and 6 pm daily. Buses to Sucre leave at 7 am, 1 pm, and 5 pm daily.

The **Colonial Plus Car Company**, Calle Otero #121, ☎ 642-5101, has *collectivos* going to Sucre. It takes four hours and costs $3.50 per person.

To rent a car and driver for a private run, call **Silvero Mamani**, ☎ 718-16967 (cell). He is a fast driver, but quite safe.

There is an airport in Potosi but no planes fly there yet and the empty landing strip is a bit of a joke among the people of Potosi.

■ History

 The history of Potosi starts before the arrival of the Spanish. The city's early history is interesting and the later history is depressing. The depressing part starts with the Spanish exploitation of Cerro Rico, the rich hill.

Although there are many variations of this story, the most popular one about the birth of Potosi involves a stubborn llama that traveled with his owner, Diego Huallpa, from the ocean back to his mountain village. Along the way, Diego's animal became tired and lay down in typical llama fashion, refusing to move. Knowing it was hopeless to plead, the herder made camp, had supper and slept. In the morning he found that his pot was welded to a hard substance that had accumulated in his fire pit. The hard substance was silver. (The one flaw in this story is the fact that silver has a much higher melting point – 700-900°F – than anything a campfire can produce; maybe the mountain god did it because it seems the gods had big plans for Potosi.) Word spread of the find and an Inca chieftain from Quito, Ecuador came to visit. He was so impressed with the quality of the silver that he decided to mine the mountain and have jewels made for his court. Just as his workers began mining, a Quechua god was heard thundering, "Do not dig, the silver is not meant for you; God has saved it for others." The Chieftain listened to the god and left the mountain.

On April 10, 1545 the Spanish moved into Potosi to mine the silver. They called the city **Villa Imperial de Carlos V** after the Spanish king and they named the first mine La Descubridora. Within two years, the population of the city grew from a mere 170 Spaniards and 3,000 Indians to 14,000 people. By 1630 the town had swollen to 160,000 people, making it the largest city in the Western Hemisphere. The mountain, **Cerro Rico**, turned out to be the richest silver-bearing mountain in the world.

WORTH A POTOSI

The saying "vale un potosi" (it's worth a Potosi) became popular during the prosperous years of the city. Throughout the Spanish world and even beyond, "Potosi" meant that something was worth a fortune.

Local Indians were forced to labor in the mines under horrid conditions. The harsh treatment soon killed many. As the Indian population dropped, the Spanish imported African slaves who also died in vast numbers. This cruel treatment was justified because the Spanish believed that the Africans and Indians were not human but rather little horses. It is interesting that the Christians tried to convert the "non-human" Indians to Christianity, but they never bothered with the horses.

As the labor population continued to drop, Viceroy Toledo brought in the ancient Inca taxation system of forcing the local men to work for the state one year out of every six. Men had to work 12 hours a day, staying underground for four months at a time. Called *mitayos* or *mitas*, few of these men lived long enough to finish their year of taxation.

From the start of the silver mining in 1545 until Independence in 1825, it is believed that over eight million men died. If that figure is correct, it is an average of 28,571 men a year or 78 men a day who died in the mines. As the silver depleted, so did the population of Potosi, dropping to about 10,000 people by the mid-19th century.

ACTIONS SPEAK LOUDER THAN WORDS

A Potosi priest saw mine workers coming to town at the end of a working period, their eyes like those of ghosts, their backs scarred by the lash. "I don't want to see this portrait of hell," said the priest. "Close your eyes then," someone suggested. "With my eyes shut, I see more," he answered. But he did nothing to stop the oppression.

Locals say that there was enough silver taken out of the mine to pave a road from Potosi to Spain. Today, over 5,000 tunnels in the mountain form such a labyrinth that visitors must have a knowledgeable guide to take them through without the danger of becoming lost. The mine that has been in operation the longest is Pilaviri and it dates from 1545.

However, not all was evil during the growth of Potosi. The Spanish built a mint in 1672 to coin the silver. Today, the mint is a splendid museum, a must for the visitor. Eighty-six churches were built, some of which are

Altiplano

still standing, their architecture a sampling of the artistic richness of the times. A water reservoir constructed during this time is still in use today.

Because of the colonial architecture and the unique history of the area, the city was declared a World Heritage Site by UNESCO in 1987.

■ Services

 The **telephone office** is on the corner of Calle Bolívar and Avenida Camacho and the **post office** is on Chiquisaca, one block down from the plaza.

The **police station** is on the central plaza.

ATMs and money exchange offices are set along the *prada* (el Bolívard), on Calle Tarija, and Avenida Comanche. **Banco Mercantil**, on Avenida Padilla and Moyos, changes traveler's checks but charges a commission. Should you need money wired to you, Western Union offices are found throughout Bolivia. ☎ 800-10-5057.

■ Festivals

 Besides the usual festivals like Christmas, Easter, Carnival and Todos Santos, Potosi has a couple of special ones.

Corpus Christi commemorates the institution of the Holy Eucharist and it is celebrated in a special way on the Thursday after Whit Sunday. (Whit Sunday occurs 50 days after Easter.) There's a street procession and women sell special sweets and pastries typical of the region. The sweets are taken home by locals and eaten with hot chocolate.

The **Feast of St. Bartholomew** is celebrated August 24-26. The first day, called Chutillo, is when the people go to La Puerta, 3.7 miles/six km from the center, and raise a cross with great ceremony. The second day, Majtillo, brings a street parade with traditional music and dancing. On the third day, Tapuqullu, everyone joins the festivities and often visitors from around the world come especially to partake in the celebrations.

November 10, 1545, is the year that Potosi became a city. On that date, there are parades and, in the evenings, feasting.

■ Sightseeing

In the City

I highly recommend a **city tour** so that you will learn details about the city that I cannot possibly put into this book. A tour of the Church of the Merced gives information on its reconstruc-

N

to Bus Station

NOT TO SCALE

© 2004 HUNTER PUBLISHING, INC

Altiplano

Potosi

SIGHTS
1. San Marcos Café & Museum
2. Casa de Las Tres Portadas
3. Portada de Piedra Labrada
4. Compañion de Jesus
5. Casa de la Moneda
6. Arca de Cobija
7. La Casa (haunted)
8. Teatro IV Centenario
9. Plaza 10 de Noviembre

PLACES TO STAY
10. Hotel Central
11. Residencial Sumaj
12. Compañion de Jesus
13. Residencial Tarija, Res. 10 de Noviembre, Res. Copacabana, Santa Maria, Emperador Hotel
14. Hotel San Carlos V
15. Hotel Felimar
16. Hotel Cima Argentum
17. Santa Clara Hostal & Restaurant, La Bodequita
18. Hostal Jerusalem

PLACES TO EAT
19. Manzana Magica
20. Café Potacchi, Restaurant Kaypichu
21. Pollo Super Crock
22. Skyroom Restaurant
23. Restaurant La Boulivard, La Bode Guita
24. Picanteria el Dulce, Pub Café Kuramy, Capricornio
25. Restaurant Doña Maria & Chaplin's
26. Sumaj Orcko
27. La Teberna del Tio Anton
28. El Fogan Restaurant/Pub
29. Eli's Café
30. Candelaria Interet Café

NIGHTLIFE
31. Nico's Karaoke

tion; a visit to the Plaza de Carbon explains how extreme the discrimination between the classes was; and the buildings around the central plaza have enormous history (and many anecdotes) attached to them. Many companies run city tours. I went with Aleida Fejardo Saavedra of Victoria Tours and was very pleased.

MORE MONEY THAN SENSE

In 1639 a wealthy businessman lay dying. He called his lawyer so he could dictate his last will. He demanded that one fourth of his silver be used to build a latrine in the center of town, to be used by nobles and plebeians alike. Another fourth was to be buried in his yard and protected by four fierce dogs who were to be fed using money from his estate to buy the food. The third quarter was to be used to prepare a feast which would be left in the ditches so the worms could eat it. The final amount was to be used to adorn the asses of the town with jewels and gold vestments and then to have the adorned donkeys accompany his body to the grave.

The Mint, or Casa de la Moneda, is just off Plaza 10 de Noviembre on Calle Ayacucho. It is open Tuesday to Friday, 9 am to noon and 2 to 6:30 pm, and on weekends from 9 am to 1 pm for guided tours only. Even if you do not go to the mine, visit the mint and take the three-hour tour with an English-, Spanish- or German-speaking guide. The museum is considered one of the best in South America.

Because of the growth in commerce due to the immense extraction of silver from Cerro Rico, it became obvious that a local mint was needed. In 1572 under the leadership of Viceroy Toledo of Peru (of which Bolivia was a part) and the expertise of builder Jeronimo de Leto, the first mint was built within three years. It was used for 200 years, by which time it became to small.

Debt due to wars in Europe led Spain to another excessive round of exploitation at Potosi. Silver production increased and a second mint was built under the design of architect Salvador de Villa. Construction lasted from 1759 to 1773. Unfortunately, de Villa never lived to see the completion of the building. He was succeeded by his pupil Luis Cabello who, in turn, gave the responsibility of constructing the building to Jaime San Just. It was the largest Spanish building in the Americas.

The second mint had machinery to make uniformly perfect coins. Assurance of the perfection and quality of the coins was left to the assayer who, after inspection and approval, had to initial every coin minted.

AUTHOR NOTE: Ironically, the five boliviano coin now in circulation is minted in Canada. It is a miniature version of the Canadian "Toonie."

The 200-room building, complete with courtyards and baroque decorations, is massive. It is constructed of carved stone, cedar wood, brick and domed roofs covered in tiles. The outside walls are three feet thick and the houses inside became residences of the early directors.

At the first courtyard near the entrance is a fountain with a stone mask hanging above. Who the mask depicts is subject to great speculation. Some think it is Bacchus, the Roman god of wine. The face looks like a model who had too many drinks before sitting for the carving. Some claim that the mask is a cartoon of President Manuel Isidoro Belzu who ruled at the time of Independence. Still others think it is a representation of one of the mint's directors, E.M. Moulon (the French artist who designed the piece disliked Moulon). There are some who believe the mask is a mocking reaction towards Spain's greed. Today, the face has become the town's icon. In the second courtyard is an upright sundial. Check your watch against it.

After Independence, Spanish coins were replaced by those of the republic. In 1869 the mint received steam equipment from the United States. This helped production until 1909, when the mint was again updated and supplied with electrical equipment. Finally, in 1953, the mint was closed and the building transformed into an archive, a museum and an art gallery. The gallery houses over 700 paintings and the archives have over 80,000 documents about life in Potosi.

In the Colonial Hall Gallery, along with pictures of people important to Bolivia's history, is the oil on canvas of La Virgen del Cerro painted in the 18th century by an unknown artist. It is believed to have been done by someone of Indian background because of the triangular shape of the virgin's robes (the pre-Hispanic deity Pachamama was triangular in shape). The Virgin's robe in the painting could also be compared to Cerro Rico. In the painting, the Virgin is being crowned by the Holy Trinity. However, the crowning is also being observed by Inti, the sun god, and Quilla, the moon goddess of the Inca. The gown of the virgin holds images of the history of Potosi.

Other areas in the mint contain domestic and personal items that were crafted from Potosi silver and used during Potosi's height. There are numerous coins from every era (1575-1953) and some interesting security boxes or safes. Early coins were 90% silver, 10% copper and are odd shapes. Coins produced later were stamped perfectly round and contained 80% silver and 20% copper.

The most interesting items from the past are the pressing machines, with a series of wooden gears and axles that rotate with precision. The entire set of wheels and gears is far too complicated to describe, but the source of power was simple: four mules, attached to a drive shaft, going round and round on the level below.

Altiplano

The museum also has artifacts dating between 1,000 and 2,000 years ago. They are from the indigenous cultures that lived around Potosi.

A bookstore offers some English-language books. Pick up the *Museum Guide of the Mint of Potosi*, an inexpensive publication with a lot of information. The translation from Spanish to English is excellent.

The **Museum of Santa Teresa**, open every day from 9 am to 12:30 pm and 3 to 6:30 pm, costs $3 per person for a guided tour. Each tour takes a minimum of two hours. Santa Teresa, originally a convent, was built in 1685. The outside of the building is adorned with three coats of arms, the center one being that of the Order of the Carmelites and the other two belonged to the building's founders. The woman responsible for the convent being established was Santa Maria de Jose para Jesus. She was from Paraguay. Her body is lying in a coffin at the monastery and is totally intact. This, people believe, is a miracle since no preservatives or embalming fluids were used. I didn't check to see if Maria really was all there.

There were never more than 21 nuns present at one time in the monastery and only when one died was a new nun brought in. The girls who were permitted to enter the order (Carmelite) were the second daughters of aristocrats. The entering nun had to have a dowry (some dowry items are displayed in the museum) equal to 2,000 pieces of gold, exclusive of the dress. The dress had to be very expensive and was given to the mother superior who did God knows what with it.

The girls entered at around age 15 and once they passed through the heavy wooden doors of the convent, they never saw or touched their families again. They were allowed one visitor a month for one hour. During visits, the girls sat behind a screen and spoke to their visitor (they were allowed to speak only two hours a day). The rest of the time they embroidered and thought about God. There was also the practice of flagellation – some used iron whips on themselves for penitence – it must have been the most exciting thing that could happen in their lives. The whips can be seen in the museum. Frankly, while on this tour I started to imagine some wild scenarios that would be caused by sexual repression among 21 women living with a dead body and a huge pile of expensive dresses. It was an example to me of the weird forms that religious enthusiasm can take. These girls were sold into slavery by their families in exchange for credit in heaven.

The ornate church altar is covered in gold leaf. Some of the Christ statues are a bit gory but some of the paintings done by indigenous artists are interesting.

La Portada Torre de la Nave de la Comapñion de Jesus is the high Mogul-styled tower visible from around town. It was built between 1700 and 1707. The architect was Sebastian de la Cruz and he combined baroque with indigenous art but used the main design of the Arcs de

Triomphe du Carrousel, a copy of the Arch of Severus in Rome. The sad history of this building is that some city councilors could not see its historical or cultural value and wanted it torn down and replaced with a modern one. A huge civic struggle arose and a compromise was reached. They tore down the church, leaving the front façade with modern offices behind it. On the front portal of the arch are the words ALABA DOSEA. "Alaba" means in praise of, but the meaning of "dosea" has been lost. The towers' bells rang all day long on the day of Independence. You can enter the tower on weekdays between 8 am and noon, and 2 to 6 pm. The cost is $1.50.

The **Arch Cobija**, on Avenida Cobija just past Calle Oruro, is a stone arch built during the peak of the silver mining period to draw a definite line between the Spanish and Indian sections of town. The Spanish, of course, lived on the upper levels. The silver, loaded on donkeys, passed through the arch and down the valley all the way to the Pacific. Just beyond the arch on the Indian side is a wall made from mixing calicanta, iron, chalk and egg white – it shows no sign of disintegration.

Mirador Pari Orko is the green monstrosity that can be seen from anywhere in town. Walk over and take an elevator to the restaurant at top. The views make it worth the effort. The mirador was not open when I was last in Potosi, but was rumored to be opening soon.

The **post office**, set in a colonial building on Calle Lanza #3, is worth poking into. It has stamps, post restante, collectors' stamps and a fax and phone service. The building has been restored to a functional level. It is open Monday to Friday, 8 am to 8 pm and on weekends until 6 pm.

Tres Puertales, Calle Bolívar #1052-60, has three decorated doorways from the colonial period. The center one has an overhanging balcony like those seen along Avenida Ayacucho and Cochabamba. The balconies were built in such a way that people could see up and down the street and the houses built on corners also had two doors, one facing each street, giving people easy access. All houses on Avenida Ayacucho have green doors in order to keep out evil spirits. They were built in the 1600s and today have been painted only in colors obtained from Cerro Rico. This project was started in 1992 and since then the entire city has followed suit.

During the days of the Spanish, the streets of Potosi were safe only in the day. At night they became treacherous. The Creoles (those of Spanish descent but born in America) and the Spaniards (mostly officials and soldiers sent from Spain) often had sword fights. This hatred for each other eventually culminated in 1612 when the Spanish and the Creoles went to war. It ended in a bloody mess with the Spanish still in control.

San Marcos Café, Restaurant and Museum on Calle La Paz and Betanzos, ☎ 622-2366, is open every day from 8 am to midnight. However, the Textile Exposition is open only Monday to Saturday, 11 am to 3:30 pm and again from 6 to 7:30 pm.

San Marcos Mill was built at the end of the 1800s at a time when the silver was no longer pure enough to extract without using tons of mercury. To do this, the ore had to be ground. The first machines used for grinding are now inside the café/museum, along with other equipment used in silver extraction. The machines were run on water power that came from the lagoons above Potosi. Waterwheels moved huge mallets that pounded the rock. Fairly simple technology by today's standards.

La Casa, with its half-balcony, is in the indigenous area of town below Arch Cobija. It can be recognized by the constant For Sale sign painted on the walls. Legend has it that a beautiful woman fell in love with a young man, but they were not permitted to marry. He often stood on the street and sang to the woman who stood on the cement balcony. Eventually, the brothers of the woman killed the young lover and while the body was in the church waiting for burial she went home and took some poison. It's a Romeo and Juliet story. The ghost of the woman still haunts the house, keeping anyone who buys it awake until the For Sale sign goes up again.

Churches

Potosi has 34 churches. Originally nine were for the Spanish and 25 for the indigenous people.

The **cathedral** on Plaza de 10 de Noviembre was first built in 1564 but, after the center aisle collapsed, had to be totally reconstructed at the beginning of the 1800s. It took 28 years to complete. The final architect of the building was Fray Manuel Sanahuja. Inside, sculptures are by Gaspar de la Cueva and the gold moldings on the white background are all reminiscent of the Jesuit Missions out of Santa Cruz. The mausoleum is also worth checking out. Half-hour tours are offered every day except Sunday and at $1 are well worth taking.

The **Church of San Lorenzo** is behind the market on Calle Heros del Chaco and Bustillos and has the finest mestizo-baroque carvings in Potosi. They depict both Indian and Spanish culture. The floor inside is original and there is one nave. San Lorenzo was reconstructed in the 18th century, when the present façade was carved and the original chapel was removed. Inside are paintings by Melchor Perezde Holguin, one of Bolivia's more celebrated artists. This is probably the most photographed church in all of Bolivia.

The **Museum and Convent of San Francisco**, on Tarija and Nogales, was founded by Friar Gaspar de Valverde and built in 1547, making it the oldest convent in Bolivia. It was rebuilt, bigger, in 1707. The nuns will take you on a tour of the museum that houses religious pieces such as medallions of St. Francis, a sacred heart and 25 oil paintings by Gregorio

Gamarro on the life of St. Francis of Assis. Just outside the vestry there are paintings such as the Flagellation (yuck) and the Holy Virgin. A wood carving between the two paintings represents Prayer in the Garden. Inside the vestry is a painting by Melchor Perez de Holguin. The outside entrance to the church was carved by Sebastion de la Cruz.

San Martin on Calle Moyos and Pizarro was originally one of the churches built for Indians who were forced here to work in the mines. It belonged to the Order of the Merced and was constructed in 1592. One wall on the inside is still of mud brick. The church of the mestizo-baroque design. Take note of the two door knockers, one set higher than the other. The lower ones were for people on foot and the upper ones were for people on horses.

The **Church of Bethlehem**, now used as the Omiste Theater, is on Moyos, just off the central plaza. It was originally established to take care of hospitals in Potosi and the Real de la Vera Cruz was run by them. Because of the work of the church, the Order of Our Lord of Bethlehem of Potosi was formed. In 1725 the building disintegrated under heavy rains, so Bernardo Rojas Luna and Saldana worked together to create the new one. Completed in 1753, the new building was used for the Faculty of Arts and Sciences for the University of Potosi and finally in 1862, it was made into the public theater. Its latest facelift won two prominent awards for architecture.

The **Church of Copacabana** on Calle Fanola and J. Matins, was built in 1589 and is another exceptional building similar to San Lorenzo. It was built in Mudejar style, a melding of Spanish and Arabic influences. Its chapel is built, in part, of orange wood, and the main altar is of carved stone. At one time this church was considered the most beautiful in America.

San Benito on Plaza Diego Huallpa on the east end of town was built in 1587 in the traditional shape of the Roman cross. Another Mudejar style building, it has Byzantine domes and mestizo carvings on the doorway.

Companion de Jesus is across from the mint and was built between 1580 and 1590. The walls, three ft/one m thick, are original. The roof is cane lashed together with llama hide and the stairway has part of an original mural. With financial help from Spain, the building is being restored. The closed arches between each room were originally open so nuns could speak to each other. The building is now being used for a school.

Out of Town

Hacienda Cayara is a resort and museum 15 miles/24 km from Potosi on the road to Oruro. To get here, take the bus from the market area near the bus station to the village of Cayara. The bus will turn onto a side road nine miles/15 km west of Potosi and go for 5.5 miles/nine km uphill to the village of Cayara. I have no phone number for the resort and I did not visit, but when I contacted them to ask specific questions, I was sent a price list. The old house has four rooms available – two have two beds, one has a king-sized bed and one has four beds. All have a private bathroom. Rates are $25 per person, breakfast included. Lunch is $5 and dinner is $4.

Constructed in 1557, Cayara is considered one of the best-preserved haciendas in the country. It still has some of its original tiles. Crystal chandeliers and oil paintings decorate the ceilings, and period furnishings are found throughout the building. Since the hacienda is still a working dairy farm, fresh products are available at the on-site restaurant. You can visit and tour the building, enjoy the furnishings and paintings and then stay for the night or just for a meal. Visiting the hacienda will help you to see why the 1952 revolution/land reforms took place. The landowners were living pretty luxurious lives on the backs of their Indian serfs.

■ Adventures on Foot

 Cerro Rico stands at 17,049 ft/5,183 m and has a circumference of one league (over 18,000 ft). Called Sumaj Orko in Quechua, it is an impressive hill and I recommend a visit to its mine.

LUCKY GIFTS
It is customary to purchase gifts like coca leaves, fuel, boots, clothing or anything you feel you can afford to give to the miners. Your guide will assist you in this. The gift giving is thought to bring luck to the miners.

Run mostly now as a cooperative, the mine, even with all its improvements, doesn't look to me like an attractive place to work. The major difference from early days is that miners are looking for silver, lead and zinc instead of just silver. Apprentice miners must be 12 years old before they can start work here, and they must work three years hauling ore in backpacks to the pulley shafts where the ore is then hauled to the surface, before prospecting on their own. Apprentices earn between $4 and $8 a day, depending on the quantity and quality of the ore.

Prospecting in Potosi is no different than anywhere in the world; the lure of glitter keeps a man going under horrific conditions. In Cerro Rico, if a man finds a vein of silver he will become rich overnight. Our guide had a friend who found a vein. This man purchased a house for himself and his mother and a car and still had enough left over to never work again.

Some miners are independents, rather than part of the cooperative. However, to be independent, you must be able to purchase a jackhammer and drill which will cost anywhere from $1,000 to $4,000. Any sophisticated mining machinery will cost up to $20,000. That kind of money is out of reach for most Bolivians; 70% of the work here is done by the traditional manual method.

Some mines, like Rosario Bajo and Candalaria, are built on five levels and run only 658 ft/200 m deep, while others go 1,579 ft/480 m deep, passing through 17 levels on the way. The men work 12 hours a day and in an emergency are known to work around the clock. Presently, the 500 miners at Potosi supply 46 private processing plants owned by international corporations.

Health problems are rampant. Silicosis is common, as are stomach ailments. Arthritis of the neck and feet, felt by most working underground, is caused from the wet and cold conditions. Tuberculosis is also common. Because zinc and lead release a lethal gas under certain conditions, the men face the danger of inhaling the gas and dying within 15 seconds. The odor can be detected, but most often there is not enough time to escape the fumes.

PRAY TO THE VIRGIN, THE GODS

As you enter the shaft you will see blood stains on a stone at the side of the entrance. This is where, twice a year, up to 40 llamas are sacrificed for the protection of the men working underground. There is also a statue of the Virgin, where miners share something that they have with her in return for her protection.

After climbing down ladders and squeezing through tunnels, you will come to the sacred spirit of Tio, or uncle. Tio, a straw and cloth deity, is covered in ribbons and has many candles lighting his place of residence. The miners offer him coca leaves, llamas, alcohol, cigarettes or anything else that may appease him. Every Friday, the miners ask Tio for guidance. After accepting the gifts, Tio keeps the miners safe while they are underground. Some of your gifts, especially cigarettes and alcohol, will be enjoyed by Tio.

The second deity you could meet is Diable, or the devil, recognized by his goat's beard, horns and red skin. He is everything I imagined the devil to be. Diable is bad luck, as are women, who are never permitted to work underground. This is one of the rare instances when I approve of sexism.

Altiplano

If you want to learn more about this way of life, join the miners to drink alcohol on the last Friday of every month at any of the bars near the market area in town. This may be a good time to share some of your treasures (extra beers) with them for stories.

■ Potosi Miner's Profile

Salary: $40 to $135 a week

Age: 23½ years

Married: 50%

Push railway cars by hand (they weigh one-two tons each): 30%

Make dynamite holes ready for blasting: 66%

Work on the pulley system: 16%

Manual laborers: 40%

Miners receive 10% of money earned from mine tours.

Lagunas de Kari Kari is a hike that can be as long or short as you wish, ranging from a few hours to an overnighter. Most people walk a circle up to the lakes and then around Cerro Masoni. Walking up to San Sebastian Lake takes just over an hour and is recommended for birders even if you do not go past the rest of the lakes. If you do continue, take warm gear as rain/hail/sleet can fall at any time. Kari Kari itself is glacier-fed and it flows into Lake San Ildefonso, Lake Ray, Lake Reina and Lake Challviri. Twenty-two lakes were created to hold the water needed by the silver refineries; the lakes mentioned above are some of them. In 1626 Lake Kari Kari broke the dam and flooded the city of Potosi, killing thousands (so many, in fact, that Spaniard, Creole, Mestizo and Indian were placed together in a common grave). The floods did not stop, so legend goes, until the priests paraded through the streets carrying their carved rendition of Christ on the cross.

To get to the trail, go east from the main plaza to Plaza Sucre. Continue up toward the fields until you can see the lake and a white plastered church. The trail becomes clear from there. Continue above the river on the east side. You will pass a small farming community with stone huts. Just beyond are some pleasant caves in which to eat lunch. Before you turn west to start your circumnavigation of the mountain, the valley narrows. Although long (12 miles/20 km), this is an excellent day hike.

FROM BOY TO MAN, A LESSON IN LISTENING

Quechua boys, during the rite-of-passage when they reach the age of five, are presented with a special cap made from llama wool. This cap is worn while the boy learns to listen to the earth and sun, walk with the spirits and animals, and talk to the rocks and wind. The young boys also learn how to collect birds, mushrooms and snails, all lessons essential to survival in the Altiplano. When the learning is complete, the boy becomes a man.

La Puerta is 3.7 miles/six km from town along the road to Oruro. Follow Calle Antofagasta across the tracks and keep going. Along the road you will pass the Devil's Cave, made obvious by the red soil and rocks. The Puerta also has the chapel of St. Bartholomew that was built in 1598. Although buses travel here, it is best to walk at least one way. The walk allows you to watch local activities in a non-obtrusive manner.

■ Adventures on Water

Tarapaya Lake & Hot Springs was revered by the Inca for its healing powers. Today, there are signs around the green-watered pool that warn swimmers not to enter due to dangerous currents. This volcanic hole is a perfect circle about 330 ft/100 m across that emits hot water, rather than lava. The walk to the public hot springs about a kilometer beyond the lake is spectacular. The mineral-laden mountains are a bright contrast to the sludge-filled river below and the lake that is the source of the public hot springs farther along.

To get here, take a bus from Potosi market to Tarapaya and ask the driver to let you off at the trail going up the mountain to the lake. From there, walk along the upper ridge for as long as possible before going down again to follow the road to the pools. The last bus returns to Potosi at five in the afternoon. The driver, if he knows that you are on the mountain or at the public pools, will honk for you.

Miraflores Watering Place is 1.2 miles/two km from Tarapaya and just beyond the public swimming area. Although not as popular as Tarapaya, it too can be visited for a long soak. Small restaurants offer meals.

There are changing rooms, a snack bar and three pools, each with water at a different temperature. One pool is Olympic-sized. On the far side of the river are some resorts where you can rest for a few days near the hot springs.

■ Tour Agencies

Jorge Gutierrez & Liliana Montes, Calle Cobija #90, ☎ 624-2377, take groups or individuals down into the mines. Jorge and Liliana work in their spare time at improving conditions for miners. Jorge's English is excellent and he is able to answer any questions you may have.

Koala Tours, Calle Ayacucho #5, ☎ 622-4708, www.koalatourbolivia.com, offers the mine tour for $10 per person with a maximum of eight people. Fifteen percent of the tour fee goes toward the well-being of the miners. This company goes into the Candelaria Mine, one of the earlier mines dug hundreds of years ago. This is a five-hour activity. Rubber boots, jacket and helmet are provided at no extra cost. The headlamps are electric rather than calcium flame. Excursions to Uyuni Salar cost $50 per person with six people or more (a private tour costs $300).

Koala also takes visitors to a Tinku Festival, where rival villages engage in hand-to-hand combat that occasionally ends in death. The death ensures better crops for the coming year. I never did learn for which village, the winning one or the losing one. The prerequisite to the festival seems to be total oblivion from home-made hooch.

Silver Tours, Calle Quijarro #12, ☎ 622-3600 or 622-8202, offers mine tours, guided treks to Kari Kari and a tour to Tarapaya. Two-hour city tours cost $7 per person, with a minimum of two people.

Andes Salt Expeditions, Plaza Alfonso de Ibanex #3, ☎ 622-5175, tourismo_potosi@hotmail.com, also has an office in Uyuni. They specialize in the Salar tours either from Potosi or Uyuni, and also run a mine tour, a trip to Tarapaya, a hike to Kari Kari and a city tour that includes a trip to the Casa de Moneda. The Salar trip can be done in two days, three days or four days and price depends on time. However, it is only the four-day tour that goes down to Laguna Colorado and Laguna Verde.

Victoria Tours, Chuquisaca #148, ☎ 622-2144, has the best city tour of all the companies in Potosi. The tour guides working for this company have a specialty where they learn everything available about their topic. Aleida Fejardo Saavedra is the guide that should be requested for a city tour. Her Spanish was such that even those without much Spanish could understand her and her English was excellent for those with no Spanish. She was humorous and knew her topics well. The cost for a tour with Victoria is less than any other company in town and the time spent is much longer. Although I did not go with this company on other excursions, they were so good with the city tour, I assume the rest of the trips would be equally good.

Sumaj Tours, Calle Oruro #143 (at Hostal Jerusalem), ☎ 622-4633, has English-speaking guides who specialize in trips to the mines. If mines are what interest you, use Sumaj.

■ Places to Stay

HOTEL PRICES (US $)

Per person, per day, unless noted otherwise.

$...............................	$2-$5
$$..............................	$5-$10
$$$.............................	$11-$17
$$$$............................	$18-$25
$$$$$...........................	Over $25

Huespedes Maria Victoria, *Chuquisaca #148, no phone, $*, has a large colonial mansion with bright comfortable rooms set around a central courtyard. There are rooms with or without private bath. Antiques decorate the courtyard. A new section is being built and, during the early stages of construction, an old passageway to the streets was found. It is now being restored. Breakfast is available in a heated dining room off the courtyard for an extra $1.50 for an Americano. The hotel was always more than 50% occupied when I was there.

Hotel Central, *Calle Linares and Oruro, no phone, $*, is basic and dreary, cold and drafty. Rooms are set around a common and untended courtyard. Hot water is available but must be asked for in advance. This is a backpacker's favorite.

Residencial Sumaj, *Calle F. Gumiel #12*, ☎ 622-3336, *$*, is very basic with dark rooms and only communal baths. Kitchen facilities are available, or you can order breakfast for a small fee. There is a TV room and Internet access on site. This is a backpacker's favorite.

Compañion de Jesus, *Calle Chiquisaca (no phone), $$*, has dull rooms; those at the back of the building are not worth the cost. This hotel seems to be in a constant state of construction. However, the showers are hot. Breakfast is included although it would be better to negotiate a lower cost for the room and skip the breakfast.

Residencial Tarija, *Avenida Serrudo #252*, ☎ 622-2711, *$$*, has plain rooms with private bathrooms that are tiled and clean. The building is off the road so it has a better chance of being quiet. There is also a car park. Across the street are Residencial 10 de Noviembre and Copacabana, both basic and inexpensive.

Altiplano

Hostal Carlos V, *Linares #42, no phone, $$,* is a well-kept colonial house with rooms around a central courtyard. It is a step up from many hotels in town, although the rooms are a bit small.

The **Santa Maria**, *Calle Serrudo #244, no phone, $$,* is a dark and dreary three-star property. How Bolivians earn their stars is beyond me. I'd avoid this place unless really desperate.

Hostal Jerusalem, *on Oruro 143,* ☎ *622-4633, $$,* is a member of the International Hostelling Association. Set in a clean old colonial building, it offers large rooms, private bathrooms and hot water. The courtyard, dotted with flowering plants, is a good spot to sit on a warm day. Amenities include laundry service, TV, telephone, safe and luggage storage. The owners are helpful.

Hostal Felimar, *Avenida Junin #14 and Calle Bolívar,* ☎ *622-4357, $$,* is just off the *prada*. It has rooms with or without bath. Each room has a color TV and a fridge/mini-bar. The Felimar looks clean and comfortable, but the staff is not much interested in foreigners.

Santa Clara Hostal, *Calle Ayacucho #43,* ☎ *623-0092, $$$,* has clean and cosy rooms, all with private bath, closet, heater, large windows and cable TV (50 channels, some of which are in English). The Rosicler restaurant downstairs is convenient, as are the car park and laundry service.

The Emperador Hotel, *Avenida Serrudo #167,* ☎ *622-3756 or 622-4700, emperador@cedro.pts.entelnet.bo, $$$$,* has small rooms that are very pink. There is a sitting area on each floor and the staff is friendly. Continental breakfast is available for $1 per person. There are better deals in town.

Hotel Nuevo Milenio, *Avenida Universitario #450,* ☎ *624-3865, $$$$,* has single and double rooms. The hotel is done in oriental motif with four floors around a central patio that holds a restaurant. The place is clean and bright, but there is no elevator and four flights up in Potosi can be a challenge. Each room is carpeted and has color, cable TV and a phone. I found the staff near comatose.

Hotel Cima Argentum, *Avenida Villazon #239, four blocks up from the train station,* ☎ *622-3865, info@hca-potosi.com, $$$$$,* is a classy new hotel considered one of the best in the city. It has nine rooms – some hold up to four people, while others are suites complete with kitchen area and sitting room. The standard rooms have carpets, tile in the private bathrooms, hot water from a central tank, 50 channels on the television, telephones for national or international calls and heaters. Rates include breakfast and there is a discount offered for stays of longer than a week. An on-site restaurant is open from 7 am to 11 pm daily. This hotel also has nice cabins at Tarapaya and can arrange stays at them. They work with Andes Salt Expeditions so you can visit the salt lakes (or do any other tour) at your convenience with all arrangements made from the hotel. Rates: $33 single; $46 double, $52 apartment for two people; $60 apartment for three. An apartment has two rooms and one bathroom.

■ Places to Eat

 Potosi's *prada* is where most trendy restaurants and shops are located. No vehicles pass along the walkway, but the number of locals checking things out is amazing. The street is called, simply, **el Bolívard**.

Manzana Magica, *Calle Ayacucho and Avenida Bustilla*, is a vegetarian restaurant with food made from organically grown veggies. The coffee, although *distilado*, is the best in town. Try to miss rush hours like *almuerzo* when the locals rush there to eat meals. Open 8 am to 10 pm, Monday to Saturday.

Café Potacchi, *Calle Millares #13*, ☎ *622-2759,* offers live music on Wednesday and Friday nights. It serves local dishes like llama steak and *quinoa* soup that is really good. You must order every item as a separate dish – steak does not automatically come with potatoes or rice. I recommend their *reichti*, a spiced potato done up Swiss-style. Most meat dishes are $2 and soup is $1. The convivial owner speaks English. A propane heater is kept going, so you can eat without chattering teeth.

Restaurant Kaypichu, *Calle Millares #16*, ☎ *622-6129,* is across the street from the Potacchi and is open Tuesday to Sunday, 7 am-1 pm and 4-9 pm. It has a pleasant atmosphere, is totally vegetarian and has good prices. Breakfast includes natural fruit juice, muesli, granola, yogurt or oatmeal. The café is operated by the same people who own the one in Sucre and it's every bit as clean and efficient.

Pollo Super Crock, *Calle Padilla #6*, ☎ *622-6938,* offers good and inexpensive chicken and chips. Even though I had already had enough chicken and stopped eating it weeks before, I did like this place and the quality of food. The staff is friendly and the building is warm.

Skyroom Restaurant, *Edificio Matilde, Calle Bolívar #701*, ☎ *622-0138,* is on the third floor (yes, you must climb the stairs) and offers the best *almuerzo* in Potosi for $2. Not only is the food good (indicated by the number of patrons), but the views are excellent. Cerro Rico stands as a backdrop for the red-tiled roofs of the village. Some English is spoken and there's an English-language menu.

Candelaria Internet Café, *Calle Ayacucho #5*, ☎ *622-8050,* is a groovy spot that offers traditional dishes, hamburgers and pizza, plus vegetarian meals for $1.50-$2. The Internet room on the third floor is very good, but the cappuccinos are not and I suspect they may be made from a mix. A craft shop sells weavings and Potosi silver. Their prices are average.

Santa Clara Restaurant, *el Bolívard #33,* ☎ *622-3746,* is open Tuesday to Saturday, 8:30 am-1 pm and 3-10:30 pm (on Sundays they open at 10:30 am, after church services). This restaurant is a chain. There is a second one on the Plaza (☎ 622-6547) and another inside the Casa de Moneda Museum. The pastries and ice cream are an excellent way to finish off any meal obtained elsewhere. It is a popular restaurant with locals.

Rosicler Restaurant, *Santa Clara Hostal, Calle Ayacucho #43,* ☎ *622-5270,* offers excellent service, international food, pleasant ambiance and a welcoming staff. This is a recommended place to eat, although the food is not cheap (but then neither is anything else about the Rosicler). During high season, a reservation is recommended.

Restaurant La Boulívard, *#852, no phone, in the back of the courtyard,* has a menu that is not for vegetarians. Their house special, called Plata de la Casa, includes beef, chicken, pork, llama and sausage. Prices are not listed; this a "treat-only" place that needs budgeting for. The ambiance is French and the food is of the same high quality found in good restaurants in France.

Picanteria el Dulce, *Calle La Paz #1133,* has ambiance, a heater and good food. The heater is essential.

La Bode Guita, *el Bolívard, (no phone),* has a great *almuerzo* (some say it is the best in town) for $1.75. Offerings change daily. Locals patronize this place so getting here early is essential.

Pub Café Kuramy, *corner of Calle Chiquisaca and el Bolívard,* can be spotted by the bright blue door and an icon above of the five boliviano coin (the bi-metallic one minted in Canada) now in circulation. It's a great hang-out for *gringos* to drink beer, eat hamburgers and stay warm. Some locals come here, too.

Restaurant Doña Maria, *Calle Mateos #81,* is upstairs and has an intimidating entrance. This is a local restaurant, serving only local foods at local prices. The food is delicious and, if you are sitting by the window, the view is also good.

Restaurant Capricornio, *el Bolívard #1,* is *gringo*-land, serving pizza, spaghetti, apple pie and other such things. They get the *gringos* because they know how to serve just a bit of what you left at home.

Eli's Café, *Linares #26,* ☎ *622-8609*, is open every day, even through siesta. It's set on the upper part of the plaza. The pastries are okay, but the coffee is not good. Have a beer instead.

Sumaj Orcko, *Calle Quijarro #46,* is an excellent restaurant serving both *almuerzo* and à la carte meals. A dish of *pique de la macho* (a spicy stew cooked with special sausage and served over French fries) is huge and delicious and costs less than $2. Unless you are ravenous, I'd suggest ordering the half-portion. Because of its popularity, Sumaj Orcko gets busy so try to eat here between rush times when you will get better service.

Chaplin's, *Calle Mateos,* serves many vegetarian dishes and a lot of snacks to go with the beer. It's closed on Sundays and all holidays.

■ Shopping

 Artesenia El Chasqui, Calle La Paz #1649, ☎ 718-36701 (cell), is a non-profit organization run by Rosario Angulo Martinez, a social worker with energy to spare. She has been recognized by numerous government officials and other organizations (far too many to list) for her endless efforts in promoting artistic works from the villages around Potosi. Some who have recognized her abilities are: Comite Impulsor de la Ruta Diagonal Jaime Mendoza (this document was approved and endorsed by 19 other civic communities), Feria International de Zagreb in Croacia, Ecargada de Ferias Internationales in Bolivia, Ministerio de Educacion, and Cultura y Deportes in Potosi.

Rosario gathers and sells artists' work, ensuring that they get some money. She herself makes *chascasitos*, little dolls that sell for 75¢ each. The money goes to help the poor in the area. Chascasitos, during the Inca days, delivered the mail. They carried a pouch and ran from station to station, passing the bag to the next runner. After resting, they would run back to their own village, carrying the mail in that direction. It took 15 days to get a letter from La Paz to Potosi.

I encourage all travelers to purchase something from this store, no matter how small. Every penny goes toward helping struggling artists.

The **Handicraft Market** is at Plaza Saavedra on Calle Sucre and Omiste, where numerous shops are located. Silver and Potosi weavings, called *bayetas*, are the desired products from Potosi. Prices are comparable to anywhere in Bolivia, although slight bartering is required (Bolivians do not like to barter much). If you are into silver, there are many items available. Besides jewelry, there are cake knives and lifters, letter openers, spoons and ornaments.

■ Nightlife

El Fogan Restaurant/Pub, Calle Oruro and Frias, ☎ 622-4969, is open from 11 am until midnight. It is a good place to hang out in a relaxed atmosphere and many locals come here.

Nico's Club Karaoke, el Bolívard #789, is a swinging place for the young and rowdy.

La Taberna del Tio Anton, Calle Simon Cachon #19, opens at 5 pm daily. It is situated in an old building, has great atmosphere and is popular with the quiet crowd.

La Bodequita is next to the Santa Clara Restaurant on El Bolívard. You must go to the back of the hall and then down stairs. It's an artsy place and has a good atmosphere – a great place for drinking hot rums.

Uyuni/Eduardo Avaroa National Andean Wildlife Reserve

Altitude: 12,069 ft / 3,669.26 m
Population: 10,500

The main reason anyone comes to the desolate town of Uyuni is to travel to the Salar (salt flats) and lakes. Some use this route to get into Chile. The salt flats are the largest on the planet and are a unique landscape. They are located in a park – **Eduardo Avaroa National Andean Wildlife Reserve** – which welcomes 24,000 visitors a year to its 1.5 million acres/820,000 hectares of land.

The town of Uyuni has few things of interest for the traveler, but there are nice places to stay. Tourists, especially packer types, love to hang out on the main drag up from the railway station. It is a street that has been turned into a kind of plaza, lined with bars, cafés, pizza parlors and tour companies. There are plenty of benches and raised flower beds, and tables and chairs from the cafés spill out onto the streets.

> **LOCAL LINGO:** Uyuni comes from the Aymara word uyu that means barnyard. When you go to the outskirts of the town and see the *cementerio de las bolsas* you will see why the name is appropriate, although an Aymara word meaning "landfill" would be better.

■ Getting Here & Away

Trains continue south from Uyuni toward the border or north to Oruro. The Express goes north Monday and Thursday at 10:15 pm and the Wara Wara, the slow train, goes Sunday and Wednesday at 2:30 am. It takes about seven hours to get to Oruro from Uyuni on the fast train and nine on the slow one. Dozens of hawkers meet the train offering tours and hotels.

Uyuni & Vicinity

N

Huachalla
Escara
Andamarca
Orinoca
Lake Poopo
Challapata
Santiago de Huari
Ventilla
Sabaya
Laguna Coipasa
Concepcion
Quillacas
Thola Palca
SALAR DE COIPASA
Salinas de Garci-Mendoza
Rio Mulato
Yocalla
Potosi
Volcan Tunupa
Atulcha Archeolﾗgcial Site
Colcha
Chaquilla
Kuchu Ingenio
Llica
Canquella
SALAR DE UYUNI
Isla de Pescado
Tomave
Yura
Ticatica
Sinalaco
Villa Martín Colcha
Colchani
Uyuni
Pulacayo
Ubina
Tumulsa
San Pedro de Quémez
Rio Grande
Tolapampa
Cerdas
Atocha
Quechisia
Santiago de Cotagaita
Estación Avaroa
Chiguana
San Juan
San Vincente
El Puente
Hornillos
Tupiza
Suipacha
Galera
Soniquera
San Pablo de Lípez
Yunchara
Mojo
Arboles de Piedra
Laguna Colorada
San Antonio de Lípez
San Antonio de Esmoruco
CHILE
Tocone
Piedras Blancas
La Quiaca
Caspana
Hot Springs
Laguna Polques
Salar de Chalviri
Laguna Salada
Colipa Laguna
El Valle de Dalí
Sol de Mañana
EDUARDO AVAROA NATIONAL ANDEAN WILDLIFE PRESERVE
Volcan Licancahur
San Pedro de Atacama
Laguna Verde
ARGENTINA

······· Railroad

60 KM
40 MILES

Altiplano

© 2004 HUNTER PUBLISHING, INC

Buses to Potosi take seven to nine hours and leave at 10 am, 10:30 am and 7 pm daily. The road is not bad.

Buses to Oruro also leave daily but go in the evenings, at 7 and 8 pm. It takes four hours and all buses going to La Paz must pass through Oruro. Most people use the train for this section of their journey as it is more comfortable and interesting. Buses going direct to La Paz leave Sunday and Wednesday at 6 pm for the eight-hour journey.

The route to Tupiza is serviced by 11 de Julio and they go Sunday and Wednesdays. It takes seven hours and costs $4. The road is not good. A jeep to Tupiza costs $7 and takes five hours. Belgrando and Bus Quechisla have jeeps going every day. The price and time is the same with all companies. The jeep leaves at 7:30 am and makes one stop in Atocha for lunch and vehicle change. You should purchase your ticket at least one day ahead as there is room for only 10 people. Regardless of what seat you get on the first leg of the journey (and what the company tells you), you will not get the same seat on the second leg, out of Atocha, unless you are very assertive. Once in Atocha, where you have an hour stopover, insist on choosing the seat you want for the next vehicle. Do this before you do anything else. There is nothing that makes a Bolivian happier than to see a bunch of *gringos* crammed into the very back of a jeep with their chins resting on their ankles as they bump along through the rough roads. Should this happen, plan a mutiny. There is a second break about an hour before Tupiza where grilled llama steak is served for $1.25 by the driver's sister/wife/cousin.

Atocha is also where you turn south to go to San Vicente should you wish to follow the Butch Cassidy and Sundance route. There are places to stay in Atocha if you have missed a vehicle heading south.

Chile is along the asphalt highway that goes to Iquique, Calama or San Pedro de Atacama. The border crossing is at Laguna Verde (Hito Cajon).

■ History

 Before tourists started to visit the reserve and salt flats, Uyuni was barely a hamlet. The National Reserve of Eduardo Avaron was established in 1973 to protect the three types of flamingos, the queñua forests and the area's archeological sites. It eventually included the area down to Laguna Colorada. The park has six levels of protection, ranging from areas to be used only for scientific study to areas that are open for tourism.

■ Services

The **telephone office** is on Avenida Potosi just up from the clock tower.

The **post office** is on Avenida Cabrera, a block before the bus stop area.

The **police** are on Avenida Ferroviaria, across from the train station.

Banks are on Avenida Potosi, but they do not change traveler's checks nor is there an ATM in town. Bring American cash.

The **tourist office** is on Avenida Potosi, but it is useless. The staff were not even able to tell me if there was a nearby town called Pulacayo (it's down the road). For information, it is better to go to the park office under the clock tower.

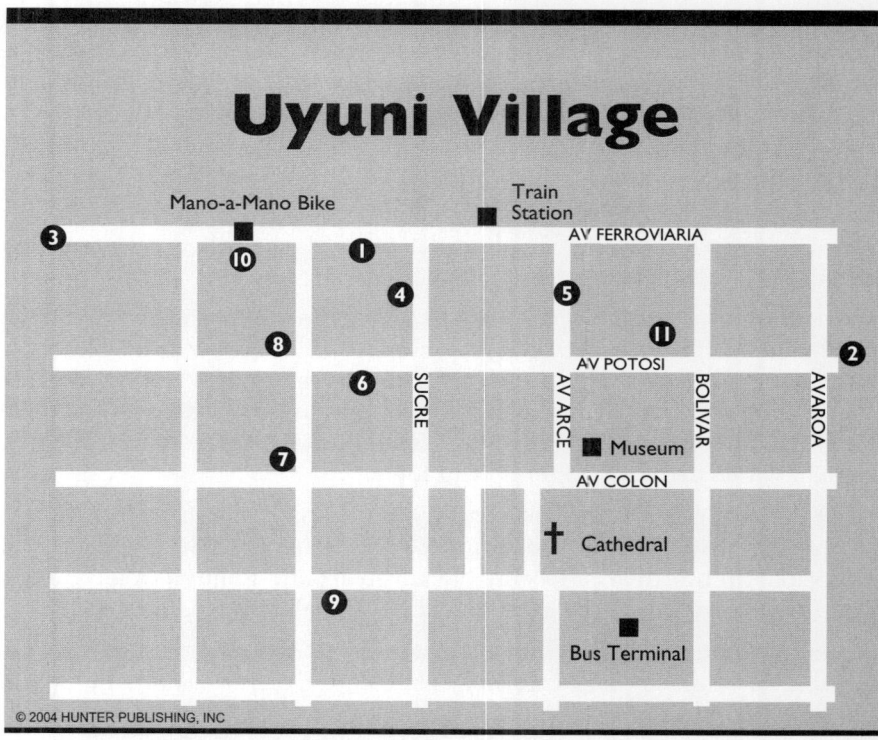

Uyuni Village

© 2004 HUNTER PUBLISHING, INC

PLACES TO STAY & EAT
1. Hotel Avenida Uyuni
2. Hotel Marith
3. Hotel Samaj
4. Resdencial Sucre
5. El Salvador Hospadaje, Palace Hotel, Rest.16 de Julio,
   Pizzeria Arco Iris, Raso Dorado, No Name Rest., Paladium Pitzzeria
6. Hostelling International
7. Hostal La Magia de Uyuni
8. Kory Wasy Hotel
9. Hotel Joya Andina
10. Toñito Hotel
11. Don Oscar, Kaktus, French Rest.

Altiplano

The **park office**, Avenida Potosi #23, ☎ 693-2400, below the clock tower, sells a couple of English-language books about the area. A bird book I saw included descriptions of the reserve and its animals, plants, insects and special features. It sells for $5. Another good one is the *Travel Guide to Eduardo Avaroa National Andean Wildlife Reserve* by the Bolivian Conservation Association, for $6.

■ The Land & Its Inhabitants

 The reserve is 13,000-16,500 ft (4,000-5,000 m) above sea level and is characterized by volcanic activity and landscapes formed by glaciation or wind and water erosion. Some of the rock formations, vents and fumaroles, can be seen on a three- or four-day tour. The hot springs at Laguna Polques are always a popular attraction.

The salt flats cover an area of over 4,633 square miles/12,000 square km and are the largest in the world. They have an unusual amount of ulexite, a mineral used in the manufacture of borax, fertilizers and enamels for ceramics and glass. Kollpa Laguna has a substance called kollpa, which is used by locals as a detergent.

These flats were originally part of Lake Minchin, an inland sea that once covered most of southwest Bolivia, including what is now Lake Titikaka. After Lake Minchin dried, the Uyuni and Coipasa flats were left dry, but Lake Poopo and Uru Uru were left with a thin layer of water. In the middle of the flats is Isla del Pescado, Fish Island. It is covered with cacti, some of which are over 26 ft/eight m high.

Along the Chilean border is a spine of mountains that range from Mount Linzor at 16,740 ft/5,089 m to Mount Uturunku at 19,763 ft/6,008 m. The two peaks that form an imposing backdrop around Laguna Colorada are Mount Chijlla at 18,780 ft/5,709 m and Mt. Pabellon at 18,085 ft/5,498 m.

Although there are a lot of lakes in the reserve, not much of the water is suitable for human consumption. The only river without salt is the Quetena. Most of the lake water has a high mineral content and toxic elements like arsenic. Laguna Verde is the lake with the highest arsenic content, while Laguna Colorada, with a depth of about 14 inches/35 cm, has a high salt content. Laguna Colorada also has the red algae called *Dunaliella salina* that gives the lake its red color, usually between the hours of 11 am and 4 pm when the winds increase and stir up the waters. This algae also gives the flamingos their pink plumage and the flamingo egg shells their orange hue.

There are often as many as 25,000 flamingos in the reserve and they create up to 5,000 nests every year. There are three flamingo species here. The **Chilean flamingo** is salmon-colored with reddish feathers on the upper wing. Its beak is whitish-pink with a black tip and its legs are blue-grey in color. The smaller **Andean flamingo** has a purple patch on its upper breast. It has a black beak with a yellow base and its legs are yellow with orange knees and toes. The **James flamingo** is smaller than the other two and the lower part of its body is black. It has a few pink feathers on the chest and its beak is yellow with a black tip.

Of the 190 different plants in the reserve, the most interesting is the **yareta** that grows about half an inch/one cm a year, making some of the bigger plants around 2,500 years old. The yareta looks solid and dense, bright green in color and firm to touch. The **queñua** tree, also interesting, grows at elevations from about 13,000 ft/4,000 m, all the way up to the snow line. This shrub has a red bark that peels and flakes. The ubiquitous grass seen on the Altiplano is called **ichu** and is spiky to the touch. It is often burned as a fertilizer. The **thola** plant seen dotting the landscape comes in six or seven varieties and is used by locals for fuel. Aside from these four there are the medicinal plants used by locals for curing everything from stomach ache to cancer. Those would have to be pointed out and described by your guide when on tour.

Of the wildlife species, the most common are the **vicuña**, the **vizcacha** (a high-jumping rabbit) and the **Andean fox**, which actually looks like a coyote.

There are some archeological remains, but they are of interest only to dedicated archeology buffs. There are *jaranas*, stone huts used by travelers to sleep in, *tambos* (trail markers), some rock paintings near the community of Quetena Chico and a ceremonial site lying in a depression between two volcanoes.

MOST INTERESTING SITES

Arboles de Piedra (trees of stone) is in the Pampa Siloli Desert. This collection of rock formations is interesting to explore and photograph.

Laguna Colorada is 37 miles/60 km long and turns a bright red after the wind comes up during the day. The red is caused from the algae growing on the bottom. The lake is home to many flamingos.

Sol de Mañana is the geothermic area where, if you visit early in the morning, you can see the boiling rock on the earth's surface.

Laguna Polques in Salar de Chalviri has hot springs. This salar also has mounds of white minerals that are different from anything found at Salar de Uyuni.

El Valle de Dali has a landscape that shows all the colors of the rainbow. It's an excellent spot for photographers and wildlife enthusiasts.

Laguna Verde turns a bright green after the winds start the waters moving. Here, the color change is due to arsenic content.

Altiplano

MOST INTERESTING SITES

Volcan Licancahur and **Volcan Uturuncu** can be climbed if you choose the right tour company. This high-altitude experience will take you over 20,000 ft/ 6,000 m.

Atulcha, also called Chullpares, is an archeological site in a cave on Tunupa Volcano. It is interesting, but you must be acclimatized for the hike up the mountain.

■ Sightseeing

 For a good introduction to the area, head to the **Uyuni Museum** on Avenida Arce. The greatest treasures here are four weavings (*chelapas*) from the Nor-Lipez culture (1200-1500). There are also skulls and pottery. At present, it takes less than a half-hour to go through the museum, but still it provides interesting information about a spectacular area.

■ Adventures on Wheels

 When choosing a tour company (there are 20 in Uyuni), you must first decide what you want to see and how long you want to stay away. Second, decide if you need the driver/guide to speak English. The other aspects of these tours are the same for everyone. Accommodations en route are usually basic, but adequate. Meals excellent; usually a cook accompanies you with bags of food, utensils, a propane burner and a tank. Beer or wine should be brought along in your baggage. A sleeping bag is also recommended, although most places will supply warm blankets.

- One-day tours will take you to the salt flats, Fish Island and back to Uyuni.
- Two-day tours will include everything the one-day tour offers plus the salt hotel, the salt mounds, and Tunupa Volcano. The volcano is exceptional in itself and there are some archeological areas nearby that could be of interest.
- Three-day tours include everything on the two-day tour plus San Juan, Laguna Colorada, the geisers, Laguna Verde and the chance to cross at the Chilean border to San Pedro de Atacama.
- Four-day excursions add a visit the Siloli Desert and the stone trees. You get more time at the geothermic areas, a dip in the hot springs, and a visit to the train cemetery.

- Six-day tour includes a night at Tunupa Volcano, the cave of the devil, Laguna Blanca and the opportunity to climb Mount Licancabur at 19,473 ft/5,920 m.

Tours runs anywhere from $70 to $150, depending on how long you stay and what you visit. Be aware that the competition is great and the tour operators are desperate. They will often promise you a side trip to the moon to get your money. When first in Uyuni, talk to other travelers and see who is good and who isn't. This information changes often. Companies will occasionally combine groups so that you get to travel with others who have the same interests as you do.

If you get a good tour, the trip will be both a unique and memorable experience.

■ Tour Operators

Although some guides are considered English speaking, many are not. It seems that if the guides can say hello, goodbye and thank you they are considered fluent. When going on a tour try to include in your group someone who has at least a smattering of Spanish and is willing to interpret.

> **AUTHOR NOTE:** Tour companies do not include park fees in their prices. To enter the park costs $4 for foreigners, including entry to Fish Island, and it's $1 if going only to Fish Island.

Besides the 20 companies in Uyuni that offer tours, there are also a number from La Paz, Potosi and Tupiza. The following are the ones with whom I spoke while in Uyuni.

Pucara Tours, Avenida Potosi and Calle Sucre, ☎ 693-2055, is owned and operated by the same people who run the International Hostel. I went on a four-day tour with Pucara and was pleased. The services they promised were actually given, the food was cooked fresh every day, the driver stopped whenever we wanted to take a photo and the guide was knowledgeable about the region.

Somja Jallpha Tours, Avenida Ferroviaria, ☎ 693-2410. These people speak English well. A one-day tour ($25) goes across the Salar to Fish Island and includes a hike to a lake partway up Tuñupa Volcano, the iron-laced volcano not far from Uyuni. From there, you can see the entire Salar. A two-day tour ($35) includes a night in a hostel near the volcano. Three days costs $65 and you see two islands – Fish Island and Bell Island, made of coral. Going for three days allows a trip to Atulcha, the archeological site that has mummies inside a cave. All tours include a visit to Yodadora Salt Plant. In the village you can watch people working with llamas, sheep, and quinoa. This company will take six people plus a driver and cook on each tour. Four-day tour prices are discounted during low season. The agency also give a complimentary t-shirt with a photo of the salar in front and their company name on the back.

Olivos Tours, Avenida Ferroviaria #23, ☎ 693-2173, olivostours@ hotmail.com, also books out of Marith Hostal on Avenida Potosi #61. This agency offers many combinations. A one-day tour includes a visit to Colchani, salt plant tour, Salar de Uyuni, Isla del Pescado and Cementario de Trains. Two-day trips add Conquesa, Chulparis and Tuñupa Volcano. On a three-day trip you also visit Laguna Atulcha, Cañapa, Laguna Hedeonda, Arbol de Piedra, Laguno Colorada, geysers, hot springs, El Valle de Dali (Altiplano landscape) and Laguna Verde. Four days, in addition to the above sites, will net you San Cristobal and a colonial church for $75 in low season and $95 in high.

Esmeralda Tours, Ferroviaria and Avenida Arce, ☎ 693-2130, charges $65 for four days in low season and $80 during high. I wasn't impressed with the workers, who were not enthusiastic to sell me a trip and couldn't convince me they were the best. Esmeralda offers anything from one-day to five-day tours to all the above mentioned places.

Turismo El Desierto, Avenida Arce and Potosi, ☎ 693-3087 or 693-2953. This company is interested in pleasing the public and offers up to four days through and around the park. El Desierto also runs a trip up Mt. Lincancabur and will go to Tupiza to cover the Butch Cassidy route.

Jhovovana Tours, Avenida Arce, ☎ 693-3078 or 693-2477, jhovero@ hotmail.com, seems to prefer hiking volcanos rather than sitting in a jeep and traveling around. Discuss with them what you would like and for how long.

Expeditions RELI, Avenida Arce #335, ☎ 693-3209, offers the four-day classic tour to the Salar, Tuñupa Volcano, Fish Island, the Arbol de Piedra and Lagunas Verde, Blanca and Colorada.

Manacar Tours, Avenida Arce between Potosi and Colon, ☎ 693-3093, offers one unique destination – Ollague Volcano. They will also drop you off at the border so you can go to San Pedro de Atacama.

Turismo Tierra Hermosa, Calle Sucre, between Avenida Ferroviaria and Potosi, ☎ 693-3110, goes to Laguna Celeste and Los Pipez in the park. They also go to Tupiza and tour the Butch Cassidy route.

Toñito Tours, Avenida Ferroviaria #152 between La Paz and Sagarnaga, ☎ 189, 233-6250 (in La Paz), www.bolivianexpeditions.com, has been in business for eight years. They are proud to keep their drivers employed year-round instead of contracting them for just one trip. Vegetarian meals are available. This tour can be booked in La Paz, but it makes the trip expensive. Better to book in Uyuni.

Toñito has one hotel in town and a second opening at Bella Vista on the other side of the Salar. The upscale Bella Vista location has an old burial tower and some groomed hiking trails for visitors to use while exploring, birding or photographing. Chris Sarage, one of the owners, also hopes to have mountain bikes for hire and to offer Salar treks with llamas.

Playa Blanca Tours, Ferroviara #304, ☎ 693-2772, playablancatours@ hotmail.com, offers anything from one- to four-day tours. The staff was friendly and helpful. I spoke with one person who went with this company and he was especially happy with the meals.

Oasis Odessey Tours, Avenida Ferroviaria, ☎ 693-2308, has a flashy brochure and good-quality vehicles. The English spoken in the office was quite understandable and they were interested in trying to offer me what I wanted.

Tunupa Tours, Avenida Arce, ☎ 693-2823, does the usual trips and will take traveler's checks in payment – a bonus, since changing money in Uyuni is difficult.

■ Places to Stay

HOTEL PRICES (US $)

Per person, per day, unless noted otherwise.

$.	$2-$5
$$.	$5-$10
$$$.	$11-$17
$$$$.	$18-$25
$$$$$.	Over $25

Z^{ZZZ} **Hotel Avenida Uyuni**, *Avenida Ferroviaria #11*, ☎ *693-207,8 $*, is across from the train station and was the first hotel in town. The owner opened 30 years ago with 24 beds and, due to the increase in tourism, now has 70 beds. Twenty-three rooms have private baths. The two floors of rooms are set around a central courtyard. There is a constant hum of activity at this exceptionally clean property: someone washing linen, repairing cement, painting walls, cleaning windows. The only negative thing I could find is that sounds echo, but everything was certainly quiet by 9 pm. Rooms have tables and chairs and the walls are painted with an oil-base paint. The floors are all matching tile. There is a closed-in sitting area in the courtyard where guests can eat. The main entrance has two tables made out of salt blocks and lots of posters describing the area. Laundry costs 75¢ per kilo. This is a top-notch establishment. There is secure parking and hot water is available in the communal showers from 7 am to 7 pm.

Altiplano

Hotel Marith, *Avenida Potosi, #61,* ☎ *693-2174, $,* is a short walk from the center (three blocks) and has 24 clean rooms around a central courtyard. This is a comfy place to stay, quiet and clean. Rooms have wood floors and painted walls. There are no toilet seats, but the shower water is hot. Laundry is 15¢ per item (two socks are considered one item).

Hotel Samaj, *Avenida Ferroviaria #96, corner of Calle Sucre,* ☎ *693-3099, $,* was previously called Hotel Europa but management has changed hands and reputation. The new owner, Freddie Olvino Gomez goes out of his way to give guests all the comfort they need. There are 14 rooms, two with private baths. Rooms are plain, with wood floors, and the soft beds have 12-inch-thick mattresses and three heavy wool blankets for cover. There is a tiny kitchen that guests can use and a stove to boil water. A fireplace in the kitchen can be used on really cold days. There is a luggage deposit. People passing through Uyuni, who are not taking a room, can have a shower for 75¢. The water is heated by a gas water tank.

Residencial Sucre, *Calle Sucre #132,* ☎ *693-2047, $,* has six rooms that hold 20 beds. The rooms are large and basic and the carpet is dirty. This is not my first choice. The showers are communal.

El Salvador Hospadaje, *Avenida Arce #346, between Cabrera and Peru, just up from the bus terminal,* ☎ *693-2407, $,* has private rooms as well as dorms. The small rooms have wood floors and a tiled bath, but are a bit drab.

Palace Hotel, *Avenida Arce #7,* ☎ *693-2259, $$,* has cool and quiet rooms with carpets and private baths for $6 per person or $2.50 for a room without bath. The price includes breakfast. The place is clean, English is spoken, and there is a rooftop salon for those wanting to get a good view. If you arrive late at night, ring the bell. There is someone available at all times.

Hostelling International, *Avenida Potosi and Calle Sucre,* ☎ *693-2228, www.hostellingbolivia.org, pucara_tours@yahoo.com, $$,* is run by a native Uyunian, Vincente Ivor Nina Gallado (Ivor, for short). There are 13 rooms, eight with bathrooms attached. The beds have thick mattresses and the showers are always hot. Because Uyuni often has a water problem, Ivor installed a storage tank so the hostel never runs out. Each room has a cupboard where backpacks can be locked up. The hostel is bright and clean and your room rate includes breakfast. Parts of the hotel – like the TV sitting room and the reception area – are made of salt blocks. Hand-painted murals adorn the walls and the sitting rooms are tastefully decorated with a warm feel to them. There is also Internet access available and a kitchen that has everything, including a fridge and microwave. The dining room is separate from the kitchen. English is spoken. The hostel has been open since September, 2002. Once people know about it, rooms will be hard to get. The same man owns Pucara Tours, next door, and I know from experience that they run a good tour.

Hostal La Magia de Uyuni, *Calle Colon #432,* ☎ *693-2541, magrano_uyuni@yahoo.es, $$$,* is a rustic, well-kept building with rooms around a grassy courtyard where a stuffed armadillo stands guard. The small rooms have carpets and private bathrooms. Three water tanks supply the showers for guests. Breakfast is included in the room rate. There is also a garage, laundry service, and Internet access on site.

Kory Wasy Hotel, *Avenida Potosi #304,* ☎ *693-2670, kory_wasy@ hotmail.com, $$$,* is run by Lucy Depares, a motherly figure who wants your every need met. All her rooms are carpeted and have small private baths with hot water that is available all day. The $10 per-person rate includes a buffet breakfast. The biggie is that Lucy provides hot water bottles for guests during cold weather. Plus, a doctor is on call. The hotel is built with cactus doors; according to local legend, anyone passing the night protected by these plants will have good luck. The stairs going to the upper level are steep, so hold the handrail. Lucy has a 4x4 available for four-day tours at $600. This price is for up to six people and includes a driver, a cook and all food. The hot water bottles go on the tour too.

Hotel Joya Andina, *Calle Cabrera #473, between Sucre and Comacho,* ☎ *693-2067, reservasjoyaandina@hotmail.com, $$$,* just up from the bus area, is brand new. It has 10 bright, tastefully decorated rooms, with matching bedspreads and curtains. Each room has a stereo system and TV, as well as a private bath. The showers are separated from the bathroom area and the hot water comes from a water tank. There are lights over the beds, clean scatter rugs, mirrors and a garage. Rates include a buffet breakfast. This is definitely a shining light in Uyuni.

Toñito Hotel, *Avenida Ferroviaria #60,* ☎ *693-3186, $$$$,* has 19 spacious rooms with private baths and queen-sized beds. They offer luggage storage and have the best book exchange in Uyuni. Rooms are comfortable, there's hot water all day, and the price includes breakfast. A Minuteman Pizza parlor is on-site and the bar is active in the evenings. They are opening a second hotel at Bella Vista on the other side of the Salar. It is a slightly upscale version of this, but will also have the famous Minuteman Pizza. Expedition supplies like granola and peanut butter will be available. The site at Bella Vista has an old burial tower and some groomed hiking trails for visitors to explore. Chris Sarage, one of the owners, also hopes to have mountain bikes for hire and to offer Salar treks with llamas.

■ Places to Eat

Pizzeria Arco Iris, *Avenida Arce #27,* ☎ *693-2517,* is popular with tourists. Pizza is the big draw, but they also have cold Potosiña beer in a one-liter bottle for $1.75. Country and

Western music plays (it's sometimes more welcome than pan flutes) and the service is good.

Don Oscar, *Avenida Potosi,* offers a tortilla (actually an omelet) stuffed with tons of veggies for $1.25. Their fruit juices are thick. Don Oscar's is clean with no music blaring.

Kaktus, *Avenida Potosi, next to Don Oscar,* also has good omelets, called "omletts" on the menu. Kaktus is often full of tourists (an empty café is a bad sign), but they do play their music loud. Their fruit juices are also a bit thinner than those at Don Oscar's.

Restorante, *Avenida Arce, next to Residencial San Cayetano,* is clean enough, but the meals are small for the price. I got half a cucumber, a tomato, a bit of cabbage and half an avocado for $1.75. The restaurant across the street serves twice as much for half the price.

Restaurant Uyuni, *Avenida Potosi, next to Samaj,* has friendly staff, good food and clean tables, but don't look at the ceiling. A burger with fries is $1.60, one with egg and cheese is $1.15 and a pancake with chocolate is $1.25. This restaurant is far better than Raso Dorado on the square.

French Restaurant, *Aveninda Potosi,* is just one block from the square and has by far the best food in town. Thanks to Adriana Boon for trying this place first. The prices here are also exceptionally good. Everyone in town was talking about it.

Restaurant 16 de Julio, *Avenida Arce,* serves huge meals that have a lot of flavor. I recommend *silpancho*, a local dish that consists of a layer of rice with boiled potatoes covered with spicy fried meat. The meat is covered with an egg and the egg is covered with chopped onion and tomato. It was more than I could eat.

Raso Dorado on the square has had too many tourists. I ordered a burger that was served on an Inca bun (made of stone). When I brought this to the attention of the staff she at first argued with me saying that it was not stale. When I kept banging the table top with the bun, I think she decided to give me a new one for fear that I would chip the table. When she brought the second bun, she threw it on the table and said I could do what I wanted with it.

The No Name Restaurant, *Avenida Arce and Potosi,* ☎ *693-2670,* has great fries and thick fruit juices. The staff is friendly too. They have dried cactus on the doors for good luck. They will get it.

Restaurant Paladium Pitzzeria (spelled this way), *Avenida Arce and Potosi*, is another pizza parlor and the food is fairly good.

■ Nightlife

The **Mano-a-Mano Bike Tournament** is held every Saturday at the Tuñito Hotel. The contestants choose a name for themselves, write it on a piece of paper and place it in a hat. There is a prize for the grooviest name. The names are drawn and two contestants enter the ring facing each other, each on a bike. The object is to make the opponent touch the ground with hands, feet or body while cycling past each other. The first one to touch the ground loses the match. Process of elimination is how the tournament proceeds. Gear is provided, including the Kona Mountain bikes. The cost is $4 per person. First prize is bragging rights in all of Bolivia, a Llama Mama t-shirt and a Minuteman Pizza.

The **bars** along Avenida Arce are where everyone coming back from a tour heads. Which bar? It matters not, as long as there is food, booze and service. The high after the trip is burned off before travelers head out of town.

Pulacayo

Altitude: 12,203 ft / 3,710 m
Population: 700

Pulacayo is an almost abandoned mining village that at one time was the largest and most prosperous mining town in the country. Today, barely 700 people live here; in the 1950s, over 30,000 called Pulacayo home. However, the mine is still operating.

If you have time to explore the Uyuni region and/or are interested in old mining sites, Pulacayo is intriguing. Besides being a mining community, the town also possesses a train that Butch Cassidy shot up. Rumors say that the bullet holes in the side of the coach were actually meant for him, while others indicate that he put them there. This is worth seeing and speculating upon. Pulacayo also has Bolivia's smallest train.

■ Getting Here & Around

Pulacayo is 12 miles/20 km north of Uyuni on the road to Potosi. Most tour companies will take you there for $25 per person. If a group of six or seven wants to go, the per-person price goes down.

A **bus** to Pulacayo leaves every day at 12:20 pm from the bus station in Uyuni. It returns the following morning at 8:30 am. For $1.25 you can also take the Trans Emperador bus that is going to Potosi and get off at Pulacayo. This price ensures a seat. Returning to Uyuni the same day is bit more difficult because the buses and trucks are often full. The cost back is 75¢. That does not give you a seat, but it is a short ride (under an hour) back to Uyuni. Four Trans Emperador buses return every day, the first at 10 am. But there are also places to stay if you wish to overnight and return the following morning on the local bus.

■ History

 The mountains were being mined for silver at Pulacayo before the War of Independence. However, due to political problems, they were closed for a period and then re-opened by Huanchaca of Bolivia mining company in the late 1800s. The company also opened mine sites at Mesa de Plata and Porco. These mines, located in the cone of a volcano, continued to produce silver until 1959. At that time, the company employed between 20,000 and 30,000 people.

Pulacayo was also a political hot bed. During the height of the mining era, the first railway was built connecting the area to Chile. From 1946 until the mid-1950s, miners worked toward forming a "people's" political group that would help them get better working conditions. The Thesis of Pulacayo was drawn up, which resulted in Bolivia's first communist party being formed. However, the party was unable to stop the decline in world markets and the mines closed in 1959.

■ Services

 There are no services in this town. If you need the phone, you must go to one of the two hotels. There is no tourist office, no police and no medical service.

■ Adventures on Foot

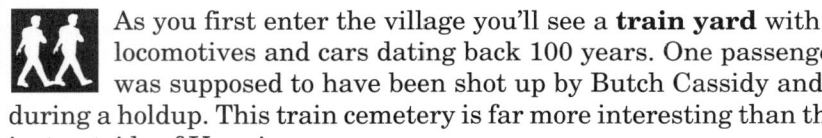 As you first enter the village you'll see a **train yard** with some locomotives and cars dating back 100 years. One passenger car was supposed to have been shot up by Butch Cassidy and gang during a holdup. This train cemetery is far more interesting than the one just outside of Uyuni.

Beyond the train yard is a **church** and a fascinating **kids park** built in 1954 with long-lasting equipment. I played on the swing for over half an hour. There is also a **mansion** built in 1878 by one of Bolivia's earlier presidents, Aniceto Arce. The lower level is now being used as offices for mine administrators. The upper level of this lovely wooden building was not open when I was there, but is supposed to contain the ex-president's belongings as they were when he left. Bolivia's first locomotive (a small one for the mine tunnels) is parked in front of the mansion.

The **cemetery** at the top of the hill has graves dating back to the early 1900s and it's fun to walk through. The dead are in mausoleums or above-ground crypts made of mud brick or cement and sometimes marble. At burials, the coffins were shoved into these and the entrances bricked up. A lot of entrances have since been removed so you can see the coffins and some dehydrated body parts inside. My favorite was a Brit by the name of Bill Bailey (he won't be coming home), who died in 1910. He is spending eternity with a Chilean who died the same year. You can see their bodies where part of the coffin lid has been removed.

BILL BAILEY SINGS
(taken from a Spanish songbook)

Lonesome I am for thee
Country that suckled me
If luckless I should die
In the mountains bury me high
So that my body in the grave
Won't miss the land I crave
Bury me high as you can bear
To see if I can see from there
The land for which I shed a tear.

A Pulacayo man told me that the Europeans buried in the cemetery were usually engineers hired to supervise the work and building of the mine. Many of them died in accidents.

Walking to the cemetery and back requires that you pass through some of the laborers' quarters. Note the fences around gardens and back yards, made of leftover tin, containers and parts of mine machinery. The mostly abandoned streets, named after places like Chicago and London, are lined with mud brick row houses, each with a tiny back yard. Mine laborers were given a house and, in turn, sold their souls to the company. Kind of depressing.

You can also go on a guided tour of underground mine tunnels. There are two guides in town – Antonio Rafuente and Angel Zibera. They charge $3 for a 1½-hour tour and speak only Spanish. To find these men, go to either hotel and ask. Or just ask anyone walking around the village; there's a good chance that one of the guides will be the person you approach.

You can also walk to **Huanchaca**, a village three miles/five km from Pulacayo where both tin and silver were once mined. It is an old place with interesting rockwork. If staying in Pulacayo for the night, this is a good walk. If going back to Uyuni on the same day, you would not have enough time to do it and see the town of Pulacayo.

Along the same route is a **lake** seven miles/12 km from town. Locals say it is a two-hour walk, but at this elevation, I suspect it is a tad longer.

Altiplano

■ Places to Stay

There are two hotels in town, but I went only to **Rancho One**, which has 24 rooms for $1.25 per person. It has very basic quarters and a communal bathroom. The building is fairly old, with wood floors, ancient furnishings and, for contrast, a computer in the back room. The entire place is clean and warm. The building seems to be much as it was when the town was abandoned, only what was modern at that time has now become antique (the phone for example).

The second hotel is on the same standard as the first. It is just above the hill from Rancho One and is called **Rancho Two**. Meals can be prepared at the hotel so long as the lady knows a few hours ahead of time.

The Yungas

The Yungas (the part around Cochabamba is also known as the Chapare) is located on the eastern foothills of the Andes, usually between 4,000 and 9,000 ft/1,250-2,700 m. It is primarily steep jungle-covered mountains that eventually meet with tropical lowlands.

The upper transitional forests are often called the eyebrow of the jungle in Bolivia. As you drop, the vegetation becomes thick and difficult to pass through unless there is a road. It is the wet climate of the Yungas (they get about 40 inches/100 cm of rain annually) that produces the heavy vegetation. Canopied areas with lush, fast-growing grasses for undergrowth are common. As you get lower, large ferns are replaced with mosses, bromeliads and orchids.

The cultivated fields produce fruits and vegetables for highland residents. Another region grows coca plants, legally. Throughout the Yungas, at all times of the year, birds and interesting insects are abundant.

The above information about the Yungas was provided by Tim Miller of Explore Bolivia.

BOLIVIA IN NO TIME

There is a great route that can be done for those in Bolivia for a short time but wanting to see many different landscapes. From La Paz in the Altiplano you can cycle to Coroico in the rainforest, bus to Caranavi, where coffee and coca are grown, and then go on to Rurrenabaque, on the Beni River in the Amazon Basin. From Rurrenabaque you can either continue through the jungle to the border with Brazil or return by plane to La Paz.

Sorata

Altitude: 8,809 ft / 2,678 m
Population: 5,000

This town, tucked into the hills of the Andes, is only four hours from La Paz by jeep and is one of the most popular destinations for the hiking and climbing crowd. They call it the Banff of Bolivia. The trails near town go to the impressive mountains of Illampu and Jacuma dotted with alpine lakes and hanging glaciers. Available accommodations are comfortable, the guiding services are excellent and the food is good, especially if you are into pizza.

I have given the details of a few hikes and climbs in the area, but this is only a teaser. Once you are in Sorata, speak with other travelers and those living in the area to learn of the latest climbing/hiking hot spot.

■ Getting Here & Around

The road here is gravel and rock and narrow and winding. There is one high pass to be crossed between Achacachi and Sorata.

To hire a jeep from La Paz, work with a travel agent of your choice. Prices vary between $50 and $100 for the one-way trip into Sorata that takes four hours. A jeep leaving Sorata costs $30 to Achacachi and $50 or $60 to La Paz.

Buses leave La Paz every other hour. The two companies servicing Sorata are Transportes Larecaja and Flota Unificado Sorata.

You can also hop over to Sorata by *trufi* or taxi starting at the Peruvian border or at La Paz. From the border, the change places are Copacabana, Huarina, Achacachi and finally Sorata. Although this takes time, the vehicles are usually much smaller, making the passage safer than a bus ride.

A new adventure is to cycle to Sorata (my first choice). See *New Milenium Tour Company* in La Paz, page 127, for information on this option.

Once in Sorata, hire a guide with a mule for longer trips as most food must be taken with you. There is a guide service in the village.

■ History

The Sorata area has been settled for centuries. The climate is perfect and the hills surrounding the town are excellent for growing food crops. Those living here are also away from the malaria and bug-riddled lowlands of the Amazon just a bit farther down the mountains. The early civilizations used the lakes above town for ceremonial purposes. There are rumors that Lake Chillata holds treasures of gold thrown in by locals to hide it from the Spanish.

The Spanish gold seekers were the first Europeans to come into the area and use it as a starting/stopping off point for access to the Amazon Basin and its gold-rich creeks and rivers. But work in the jungle resulted in many deaths due to malaria. Quinine, available in the bush above the basin, held the cure.

By the mid-1800s the trail from Sorata to Mapiri was used by slaves to carry quinine to the highlands. However, when a synthetic counterpart was developed the quinine market declined and the area was forgotten by the Western world. Rubber was the next hot commodity and the same trail was used again by slaves to carry latex into the hands of the Spanish.

In the early 1900s, Colonel Percy Harrison Fawcett worked from Sorata when he charted the border between Bolivia and Brazil. His writings about the area attracted others. Soon, a town developed and hotels and merchant houses were built. Then came the tourists. The town has boomed ever since.

Sorata's cemetery rises high.

■ Services

The **telephone office** is on the square in front of Hotel Panchita.

The **police station** is opposite the telephone office, next to Residencial Sorata.

The **hospital** is up the hill from the square (take either set of steps) toward the right and along the main highway going to La Paz.

There is no **tourist office** in Sorata. The best information comes from **Louis** in Residencial Sorata on the square or at the **Associacion de Guias Turistica**, Calle Sucre #302 and just across from the Residencial Sorata.

■ Festival

The **Homecoming Festival** on September 14 is a religious ceremony celebrating the Exaltacion de la Santa Cruz (Cheers to the Holy Cross). People dance in colorful costumes, accompanied by brass bands, and all day there are parades with music, dancing and singing. Traditional foods and beverages are served and everyone joins the festivities. The festival is culminated with a holy mass held in the main church.

■ Adventures on Foot

Hiking

SAN PEDRO CAVE: The cave takes about three hours to reach walking at a leisurely pace. It is a 13-mile/22-km trip with a 987 ft/300 m change in elevation with the upward slope on the return. The cave is open from 8 am to 7 pm and there is a 50¢ charge to enter. You should have water, a flashlight and good walking shoes (boots are not necessary). There are lights in the cave, but the electricity can be a problem so it is best if you take a flashlight.

To reach the cave, follow the road past Altai Oasis toward the village of San Pedro. You will pass steep cliffs and red clay gorges. Walk on the trail above the river; the one beside the river disappears into nothingness. As you walk you will see the village of Pocabaya on the opposite side of the river before reaching the village of San Pedro, where a sign directs you to the cave. The cave is at the bottom of a 148-ft/45-m marble cliff.

A karst cave with marble streaking, San Pedro goes in about 2,138 ft/ 650 m, at the end of which is a lake that is believed to have hidden treasures at the bottom. Legend has it that pieces of stolen gold were hidden here by the Spanish. They were going to come back and retrieve their loot, but never did.

Before reaching the lake, you must crawl through a narrow opening that leads to a large room, at the back of which is the lake.

This is an excellent day hike and can be done without a guide.

CHILLATA LAKE: Also called Khotapata, this lake sits at 13,901 ft/ 4226 m above sea level and is at least an eight-hour hike from Sorata if you are carrying gear. That means you must spend a night at the lake. Or you could spend two nights at the lake and do a day hike up to **Glacial Lake** (16,530 ft/5,025 m), on the col between Illampu and Ancohuma mountains. It is believed that the glacier on the col once flowed down to Chillata Lake (see below for details on that hike).

Chillata is a sacred body of water where visitors are not welcome during a new moon because the Kallawaya hold secret religious ceremonies at that time. Up until 1995, no tourist had visited here.

GOLDEN LEGEND

Legend says the lake is full of gold. The Inca built a fortress on the hill overlooking the water and when the Spanish approached, the Inca threw their gold into the lake. When the Spanish attacked, the Inca were able to turn them away. Scuba divers in the late 1990s decided to head for the bottom and find some gold. However, they were turned away by the Kallawaya.

Because of the maze of trails leading from Sorata to the mountain villages, it is highly recommended that you hire at least one guide and, if you want luxury, hire a porter with a mule too. However, if you strike out on your own and ask villagers along the way, you may be lucky and get to the lake without problems. Boots, rain gear, a tent, a warm sleeping bag, food for two or three days, and a sun hat are essential for this hike.

Leave the village of Sorata and head up toward the hospital, taking the stairs outside the hospital gates. Continue along that road. At the fork, take the trail to the right (a left will take you above a water cistern and to another trail, although eventually the two trails come together). A small footbridge leads onto a ridge. Veer to the right once you are over the bridge. Note that there is no vehicular traffic on this road due to landslides and washouts. Switchback up the ridge and then cross it. Follow the road past a sign saying "Beinvenidos, Unidad Educativo Jumoco." The road has been washed out about 1.8 miles/three km farther along, so it is better to follow a trail where locals go down to the River Lakataya and over this second bridge. If you continue along the main road toward

Quilambaya and try to cross the river at the washout, you will not be able to unless water levels are low.

Work your way up the hill to the village of Colani (10,339 ft/3,143 m). Unless you are acclimatized, you will breath twice for every step you take here. Eggs and Coca-Cola (an interesting mix) are offered for sale in the village, but anything more should be brought with you.

Continue along the main road that goes east and parallel to Rio Tusca Jahuira. If you become uncertain about the way, you can either hire a guide (be prepared to feed and probably partially clothe him) or ask people along the way. This is not an isolated trail.

After 4½ to six hours and a 3,550-ft/1,000-m elevation gain, you will come to a bowl with the lake tucked inside. The mountains around are fairly steep and dotted with alpine grasses. You may spot tiny black patches that are the remains of ceremonies. The lake is deep and steep near the shore. Illampu can be seen in the background.

There are some ruins on the hill at the far side of the lake. There is not much to see other than the outline of a residence. To visit the ruins and enjoy the scenery, give yourself about two hours.

GLACIAL LAKE: Laguna Glacial, also called Lichikhota, sits 17,000 ft/ 5,130 m above sea level in the col between Illampu and Ancohuma mountains. It is often used as a high camp for climbers. From Chillata, continue south and hook up with a small road that leads to Titisani Mine site (often the base camp for climbers going onto Illampu). From there, the terrain becomes more rugged with jagged outcroppings and talus slopes. The lake is in the saddle between the two peaks. The closer to the lake you get, the windier and less-vegetated the environment becomes. Soon, lichen takes the place of grasses and Lake Titikaka becomes visible in the distance. The glacier pours itself into Laguna Glacial. In the other direction you can see the clouds of the Yungas as the heat meets cold mountain air.

> **AUTHOR NOTE:** Going to Laguna Glacial should be attempted only in good weather. If it is foggy, raining or snowing, the trail becomes slippery and dangerous and the way becomes difficult to find. Besides, why go to so much work when all you will see is a white blur?

Birds are one reason people come to Bolivia and a good bird book should be carried if you have even the remotest interest in birding. In this area, you may see a condor or giant hummingbird, a tanager or mountain caracara (these I am told are quite rare).

ILLAMPU CIRCUIT: This route takes at least a week and is one of the most spectacular hikes in Bolivia. But I am a poor judge as I say this

Above: Twin Volcanoes from afar, Sajama.

Below: Musicians in the making, La Paz.

Ornate façade, Concepcíon, Santa Cruz.

The path of the Zongo River, Fotosi.

Above: Geysers, Sajama.
Opposite: Tartara market wares.
Below: Kids from Hotel Geysers, Sajama.

Miner's Monument, Oruro.

Hike to Cave, Sorata.

Above: Salt Lakes, Uyuni.
Opposite: Tio Diablo in mine, Potosi.
Below: Diezel Bar, La Paz.

Above: Station of the Cross, Copacabana.
Opposite: Copacabana Cathedral.
Below: Lago Verde.

Above: Colorful fruit at Oruro market.
Opposite: San Ignacio Church, Santa Cruz.
Below: Taxi Stand, Copacabana

SAN MARCOS

Traditional weaver, Sucre.

Canyon del Dueño, Tupiza.

Above: Siquani, Lake Titikaka.

Below: Weavings for sale, Tarabuco.

about every hike. You should take a guide or, at the very least, purchase *Trekking in Bolivia* by Yossi Brain, Andrew North and Isobel Stoddart and published by the Mountaineers. The hike goes over three passes that are higher than 13,000 ft/4,000 m and one of those is over 16,500 ft/5,000 m. The total ascents and descents on this trip come to about 15,000 ft/4,500 m, so it can be classified as a grueling hike.

You must carry all your food, have good rain gear, heavy hiking boots, warm (winter) clothing, sunglasses, tent and a sleeping bag rated to at least -10°C.

To begin the trail, follow the road past the hospital, up the steps and around the hill going toward Quilambaya. Stay on the road and continue up the valley until you can see the bridge over Lakataya River. Cross the bridge and stay on the right, heading upward (is there any other direction?) until you reach the village of Lakataya at 13,000 ft/4,000 m. There are some stone houses, but not much else here.

From Lakataya, head for the Abra Illampu pass at 4,750 ft/14,500 m. The pass is where the dark red rocks high above can be seen. The way is marked by some cairns and the pass has a memorial with the remains of booze containers. It may look distasteful to us, but the local people often offer Pacha Mama alcohol in exchange for a safe journey.

From the pass, it is possible to reach the road in about an hour. Turn right and head toward Anacoma, where you can camp and stock up on basic supplies like beer. From there, follow the road over the pass of Kalamuntani at a mere 14,500 ft/4,350 m and take the long drop down into Cocoyo, where more basics can be purchased. Cross the bridge and continue through the village. There is camping about half an hour out of Cocoyo along the river flood plain. From Cocoyo, take the trail up the valley toward Calzada Pass (16,500 ft/5,000 m) between the Calzada and Kasiri peaks. This is a difficult climb, and if you can't make it stop to camp halfway. More camping is available on the far side of the pass. On the way down, you pass the Chajolpaya River and some alpine lakes before reaching Laguna San Francisco, where camping is again possible.

After San Francisco, the walk to Sorata is down and far but not difficult. There are numerous options on this hike and it is highly recommended either to take a guide, join a tour or at least purchase the hiking guide and ask at the Tourist Guide's Association about the walk. Rivers often change the trails and the receding of the glaciers makes things a lot different each year.

MAPIRI TRAIL: This trek takes seven days through jungle mud and vegetation along a trail laden with horrid mosquitoes and sand fleas. But before the jungle, the trail follows a river and then goes up a ridge at about 13,000 ft/4,000 m. You undulate through the mountains with the big peaks always in view (if the weather is good) and then go up even far-

The Yungas

ther to the Paso Apacheta National Park. The trail falls into the Mamarani River and then heads uphill again to Abra Nasacara Pass. The ridge above two river valleys, the Chiñijo and the Corijahuira, is the one to follow into the jungle. Once you arrive at the end of the trail, head to Guanay, where there are showers, beer, soft beds, beer, insect bite medicines and more beer. Or you can join a group going down the river to Rurre for more jungle excitement. See Guanay section, page 293.

According to Louis Demers of Sorata, the Mapiri Trail, which was completed in 1879, was originally created so quinine could be carried out of the jungle. However, as soon as the trail was completed the need for Bolivian quinine declined because it was being commercially produced in more accessible places. Rubber became the next product transported along this route and slaves were forced to carry the goods up the trail from the Amazon. (Africans slaves were preferred because of their resistance to malaria.) The export of rubber lasted until the mid-1950s. Because of disuse, the trail disappeared until 1989 when men searching for gold reopened it.

FAWCETT'S FATE

In 1906 Colonel Percy Harrison Fawcett, a Brit working for the Royal Geographic Society, took a commissioned position to find a logical border between Brazil and Bolivia. Apparently, the two countries could not reach agreement on the topic and the Society was asked to intervene.

Fawcett had become a colonel by the age of 19 and worked in Hong Kong and then Ceylon, where he met and married his wife. But ordinary military life for Fawcett was boring so he worked for the secret service in North Africa. In 1906 he negotiated with the Royal Geographic Society to go to Bolivia.

Fawcett wrote that the trail to the jungle first went over a 16,500-ft/5,000-m pass. It took two hours to go four miles and the pack animals managed to go only 33 ft/10 m before having to stop and rest. When he finally arrived in Cojiba, after following the Mapiri Trail that was riddled with mud, bugs, bats, Apazauca spiders and unfriendly natives, he found the natives in the jungle village were unfriendly and often drunk. The death rate among the natives (according to Fawcett) was 50% per year.

While on his first trip mapping the border, he heard about a mythical city of temples filled with gold and white-haired rulers tucked somewhere in the jungle. His reports to the Society and his stories that appeared in newspapers inspired Conan Doyle to write *Lost World*. After finishing his assignment, he returned to England, left the military, and came back to the Amazon six more times.

On his final journey in 1925, Fawcett took his son with him. After sending his wife a message saying everything looked normal and inviting, he sailed down the Rio Verde into the Amazon never to be seen again.

In 1996 a group of adventurers decided to follow the footsteps of Fawcett, but when they got deep into the Amazon, they were met by a group of natives who took them hostage. After many days, the natives agreed to set them free in exchange for the $30,000 worth of technological equipment the group was carrying. The moral of that tale is that if you hike this trail, stay on the path, rather than exploring the bush.

You will need good boots, a warm sleeping bag, a tent, water bottles, insect repellent, eye protection, water purification tablets and a guide. It is most advisable to hire someone to help you or at least purchase the hiking guide to Bolivia so you have in-depth descriptions of the trails. Even then, expect to get lost often. The distances are deceiving, the trails and tracks numerous, and the language confusing.

CAMINO DE ORO: This six- or seven-day trip runs along a thousand-year-old road in a dramatic landscape with lush vegetation. You'll also see modern-day devastation from today's gold diggers. If starting in Ancoma, three hours by jeep from Sorata, the trail follows mostly along a river where you will either be near the water or on the ridge above the water, but never in the rugged mountains that are so intriguing. It is not possible to take a jeep beyond Ancoma because the road stops (the contractor who started the work never got paid). However, in Ancoma you can hire mules to help carry your gear down to Guanay. For information on Guanay, see the Yungas section, page 293. For the latest trail information in the Sorata area, visit **Luis Demers** at the Residencial Sorata or stop in at the Guides Association (Calle Sucre #302, ☎ 213-6698).

Climbing

The best months to climb are June, July and August.

Ancohuma (21,141 ft/6,427 m) and **Illampu** (20,947 ft/6,368 m) form a massif with about 30 peaks over 16,500 ft/5,000 m high. This is an impressive landscape for any climber. Most people make base camp at the Titisane Mine site or Aguas Caliente and climb from there when weather permits. You will need at least one guide and porters with mules are highly recommended. There are outfitters who arrange everything before you arrive in Bolivia and then there are the guides who can be hired in Sorata or La Paz. The more locals involved in the expedition, the better it is for Bolivia. However, not all guides are experienced in climbing. Be certain yours is equipped with boots suitable to take crampons, and they at least know how to do an efficient self-arrest.

Some of the peaks, like Pico Schultze, have amphitheaters with 200-ft/60-m walls to climb and the pitch on Huayna Illampu is 70°. Reaching the summit and getting back down will take skilled climbers up to 10 hours for some routes. For in-depth descriptions, see Yossi Brain's book, *Bolivia, a Climbing Guide.*

To reach base camp at Aguas Caliente, hire a jeep, porters, mules and guides in Sorata. The jeep will take you to the village of Ancoma. From there it is a three-hour walk to Aguas Caliente (15,000 ft/4,600 m). The name of the site is not quite accurate as the water is anything but hot.

If making Titisani or Laguna Glacial the base camp, you must hike most of the way, which takes days. See directions for hiking to Laguna Glacial, above. This is considered by the guides in Sorata to be the best way to access Illampu.

■ Tour Operators

Associacion de Guias Turistica (Association of Tourist Guides), Calle Sucre #302, ☎ 213-6698, guiasorata@hotmail.com, is an organization that hires qualified guides, rents equipment and arranges everything needed for trekking in the area. The administrator, Eduardo Chura, can speak some English and will help with arrangements. The association has 18 qualified guides and 25 porters. The work these men manage to get through the Association supports over 50 local families, about 250 people. The cost to hire one of these men is $15 per day, a two-person tent costs $4 per day, and a sleeping bag runs $2.50. The association also has cooking equipment and utensils for rent. Although most of the guides are good, the one who was especially recommended to me was Toribio Quispi.

Trekking Guides, Calle Villavicencio #116, ☎ 213-5044, guiasorata@hotmail.com, also offers guided trips into the mountains. If the Association of Tourist guides is not able to meet your needs, try these people. They hire only local guides.

Kon-Tiki Tours, ☎ 719-38889 (cell), kontikisorata@yahoo.com, owned by Ermanno and Silvi Antonini, take people hiking and climbing.

Adventure Climbing and Trekking Co., PO Box 100, Saida, CO 81201, ☎ 719-530-9053, info@adventureco.com, specializes in climbing, although they do take trekkers for adventures too.

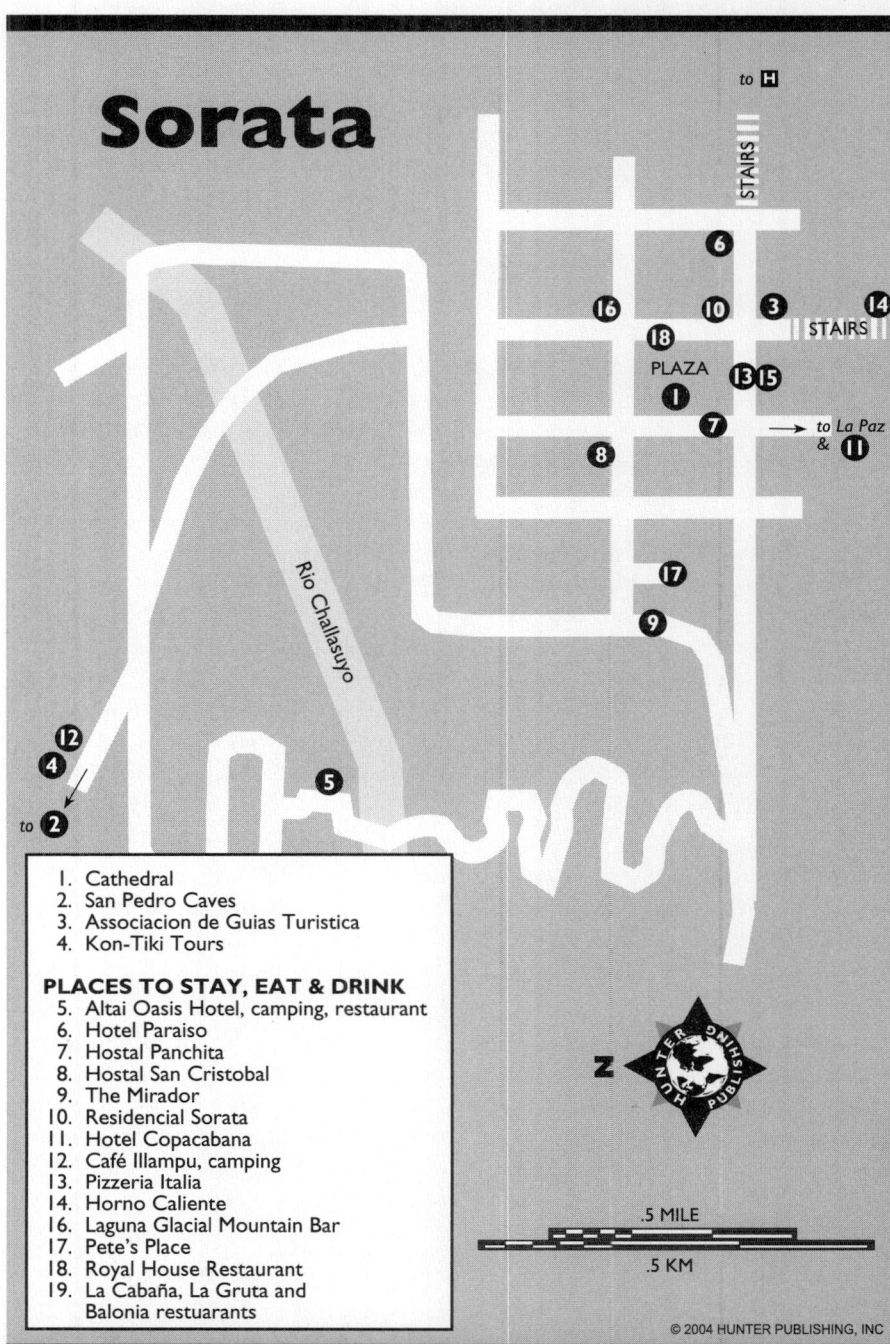

Sorata

1. Cathedral
2. San Pedro Caves
3. Associacion de Guias Turistica
4. Kon-Tiki Tours

PLACES TO STAY, EAT & DRINK
5. Altai Oasis Hotel, camping, restaurant
6. Hotel Paraiso
7. Hostal Panchita
8. Hostal San Cristobal
9. The Mirador
10. Residencial Sorata
11. Hotel Copacabana
12. Café Illampu, camping
13. Pizzeria Italia
14. Horno Caliente
16. Laguna Glacial Mountain Bar
17. Pete's Place
18. Royal House Restaurant
19. La Cabaña, La Gruta and
    Balonia restuarants

.5 MILE

.5 KM

The Yungas

■ Places to Stay

HOTEL PRICES (US $)

Per person, per day, unless noted otherwise.

$. . . . . $2-$5
$$. . . . . $5-$10
$$$. . . . . $11-$17
$$$$. . . . . $18-$25
$$$$$. . . . . Over $25

Altai Oasis, ☎ *715-19856 (cell)*, *$*, has a variety of accommodations including camping on their five acres of rainforest on the banks of Rio Challasuya. Two buildings suitable for families or larger groups have kitchens, bathrooms, patios and lofts for bedrooms. One cottage has three bedrooms. Other buildings have either two or three bedrooms with shared bath. Standard rooms cost $3 per person and the cabins run $5. Campers ($1) have a covered cooking area and a private shower spot right on the river. The on-site restaurant is good. The well-tended grounds at Altai Oasis contain a menagerie of animals that were mistreated or abandoned and then rescued by Roxana and Johnny Resnikowski. They have dogs, cats, monkeys, toucans, a macaw and other colorful birds. The only drawback to staying here is the healthy walk back uphill from the river when going into town. When I was there the showers ran on water piped down from Sorata, which wasn't dependable. The Resnikowskis were digging a well. Johnny speaks German and English.

Hotel Paraiso, *Calle Arce just up from Residencial Sorata*, ☎ *213-6671*, *$*, has clean carpeted rooms with closets, big windows and fairly soft beds. The private bathrooms are tiled to the ceiling and some have huge tubs. You can order breakfast at the hotel; a continental is $1.50 and an American is $1.75.

Hostal Panchita *$*, *on the plaza next to the church*. To enter the hostel either go through the Entel office to the back or go to the side of the building and in the first door. There are 11 basic but clean rooms, all with shared bath. There are two floors, each with a bathroom. Rooms are set around a central patio that has a small garden. The owner is friendly and helpful. There is also a luggage storage facility, hot water all day and laundry service.

Hostal San Cristobal *$*, in the market area down from the plaza, has very basic rooms.

The Mirador, *Calle Munecas #400*, ☎ *289-5008*, *$*, has the best view in town from the patio, which looks toward San Pedro Cave. Rooms are large and clean with windows that overlook the valley. The owners are friendly and breakfast is available. This is a good deal.

Residencial Sorata, *on the plaza*, ☎ *213-6672, resorata@ceibo.entelnet. bo, $$,* is an old trading house once called Casa Gunter. It was built by the Richter family in the 1830s. At that time, it had everything for sale from socks to salt to pianos to whiskey. It was located on the main quinine, gold and rubber trade route from the Amazon jungle to the Altiplano. After World War II, the rubber trade flopped and, because the building was owned by Germans (even though they had lived in Bolivia for generations), the place became blacklisted. The land reforms in 1952 saw more hardship for the house. Eventually, someone saw the value of a hotel in Sorata and the latest transformation occurred. In the late 1980s, Louis Demers from Québec, Canada became the manager. He had toilets installed, floors painted, furniture rearranged and everything cleaned to a whistle. Gardeners rejuvenated the plants and Louis built a gazebo. Today, there are 11 huge rooms with high ceilings, antique furniture and private baths that cost $6 per person. Sixteen smaller rooms around the building have shared baths. The rooms rent for $4 per person. The best antique is a round, sunken, porcelain tub found in the bathroom off the garden. The water comes from a wood-heated tank that sits beside the tub. In addition to a garden restaurant and a formal dining room, there is a reading room and a TV room with a fireplace. One room is decorated with three faces of German Kaisers carved in wood. There is a fourth one of a little guy with a mustache; it was removed in 1939. Staying here is comfortable. It is also interesting for history buffs and antique lovers.

Hotel Copacabana, *$$$, on the way into town.* This is the best place to go if you are in search of entertainment and a good bar.

Kon-Tiki Tours, ☎ *719-38889 (cell), kontikisorata@yahoo.com*, is owned by Ermanno and Silvi Antonini. They have a house along the road to the cave with five rooms overlooking the Sorata Valley. It is peaceful, but a little way from town. There is also a small restaurant at their place. They are not open during low season.

Camping at **Café Illampu** is possible for $1 per person. To get there, take a taxi (truck) or walk toward San Pedro Cave. It's about a 45-minute walk from the center of town. Staying here would assure you first choice of the baked goods hot from the oven. I have no contact numbers for this place.

■ Places to Eat

 Pizzeria Italia, *Plaza Enrique Peñaranda #143*, has branches in Copacabana and Rurrenabaque. They are open from 7 am until 9 pm daily. Besides the thin-crusted pizza with thick toppings, they serve spaghetti, lasagna, tortellini and ravioli of very high quality. As a bonus, for dessert they serve real Italian ice cream.

CHEFS STEP OUT ON THE PLAZA

At one time there was a prosperous restaurant in the Residencial Sorata but hard times fell and all the highly skilled chefs had to move on. Most just went around the corner to the plaza and opened their own places. Pizzeria Italia is one such place.

Restaurant Altai Oasis is on the porch of the main house and they serve excellent goulash for a mere $3.50 per serving. The steak, on the other hand, was tough. Breakfast and coffee were great. To get to Altai Oasis, walk from town to Rio Challasuyo on the way to San Pedro Cave. The food and hospitality of the owners will make the walk worth the effort.

Horno Caliente is where you can pick up hot bread every morning. It is half a block up from the plaza. Take the stairs from the street that passes in front of the cathedral. There is a tiny sign over the door and, as you walk into the courtyard, you will see piles of wood and smell fresh bread. The cost is pennies per hot crusty roll.

Café Illampu is along the road that goes to San Pedro Cave and about half an hour past Altai Oasis on the cave side of the valley. They specialize in German pastries, whole-grain bread and great coffee. After a walk to the cave, this is a good place to recharge your energy for the return to town. Or just drop in and play a game of chess while enjoying a beer and cake and forget the hike. They also have a book exchange. The café is closed on Tuesdays. I have no contact numbers.

Laguna Glacial Mountain Bar on the plaza has happy hour every day between 6 and 8 pm. They make excellent cappuccinos and pastas, but it's the vegetarian meals that are a feature. The owner is one of the skilled chefs who worked at the Residencial Sorata before opening his own business.

Pete's Place, *Plaza Enrique Peñaranda #13*, ☎ *289-5005*, is famous for curried dishes made with spices imported from England and mixed with skill by the cook. At least one stop here is necessary. Pete's is open daily from 8:30 am to 10 pm. While enjoying curried chicken (highly recommended) you can scan maps and books for trails you may want to hike.

Royal House Restaurant, across from the market on the dead-end side street, serves a good *almuerzo* for less than $2 per person.

La Cabaña, **La Gruta** and **Balonia** are all located around the square and make up the rest of the relocated chefs from Residencial Sorata. All are good and, during peak season, usually full.

■ Shopping

 Artesania Sorata, Plaza Enrique Peñaranda, ☎ 811-5061, cnsorata@ceibo.entelnet.bo, has a wide assortment of handmade dolls, wall hangings and hand-knitted sweaters for children and adults. They also have a large supply of postcards. The company has a second shop on Calle Sagarnaga in La Paz. The English spoken here is excellent.

Coroico

Altitude: 5,757 ft / 1,750 m
Population: 3,500

Coroico is tucked into a hill in the rainforest that is lush with vegetation and teeming with birds at all times of year. The town is small, quiet and a good place to rest (after coming down the Road of Death). There are some short hikes, a few interesting villages in the vicinity and some exciting whitewater rafting. Coroico and the surrounding villages make up one of the few places in Bolivia where you will see an African influence. Africans who were brought as slaves to work in the Potosi mines and survived the ordeal came down to transport rubber and quinine in the Yungas. It is odd to see people with African features robed in Aymara clothing, but this is common in the area, especially in Tocaña. It is also interesting to see the integration of the two cultures.

■ Getting Here & Around

The best way to get to Coroico, 59 miles/96 km from La Paz, down the Road of Death is to take a **bicycle** from La Paz. Once in Yolosa at the bottom of the hill, five miles/eight km from Coroico, your support vehicle will drive you to your destination. It takes seven

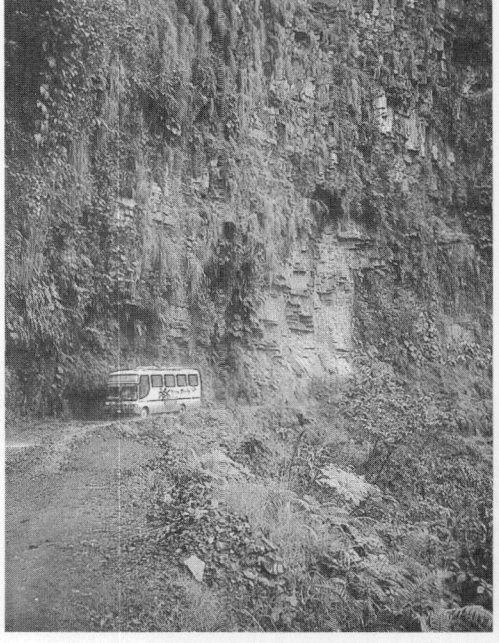
The Road of Death.

The Yungas

hours to cycle from El Cumbre, just 16 miles/26 km from La Paz.

If cycling is not your thing, the next best way to get here is to **walk** along the Takesi or Choro trails, on an ancient paved road that is steep enough to cause knee damage and require that you rest in Coroico. It takes three or four days to walk to Coroico from La Paz.

Trufis and **taxis** leave El Cementario in La Paz about once every hour for Yolosa. From there you must catch a bus, *trufi*, taxi or truck, or you must walk the last three miles/five km up the hill to Coroico. If you arrive in Yolosa late and can't get to Coroico, there are some basic *alojamientos* in town, but nothing I'd really want to stay in. You should book hotels ahead during peak season.

Totai Tour, ☎ 221-2391; Palmeras, ☎ 221-9442; Yungeña, ☎ 221-3513, run scheduled trips all the way to Coroico (rather than stopping in Yolosa) and back. It takes three to four hours by bus and costs $2.

If you take a **bus** from La Paz, the vehicles coming downhill must ride on the outside of the road so that the driver can see how close the tires are to the cliff edge. Quite often, drivers misjudge exactly how close they are. Taking a bus or truck uphill is much safer as those vehicles must drive on the inside, close to the cliff wall. I would ride a *trufi* rather than a bus, and a taxi rather than a *trufi*. The smaller the vehicle the better, it seems.

A bus from Yolosa takes 15 to 16 hours to reach Rurrenabaque and costs $10. It leaves Yolosa around 3 pm. The road between Yolosa and Caranavi is another road of death that has many accidents every year. Washouts are common in rainy season.

Caranavi is three to four hours from Coroico and Yucumo is five or six hours from Caranavi. Small trucks go every day from Yolosa to Caranavi and they leave around 11 am.

■ History

 Coroico was first located on the Coriguayco River where gold-seekers settled. But local natives didn't like foreigners and they often attacked the miners, who sought refuge farther into the jungle. While searching for a spot, a storm arose and the men were forced into a cave for protection. The cave was just below the spot where the present church is located. The men lived in relative peace until the War of Independence. At that time 5,000 Aymara attacked the 500 residents of Coroico. However, the village's location atop a hill gave its residents enough of an advantage that they forced the Aymara to withdraw.

As Bolivia grew, districts were formed and Coroico became the capital of North Yungas in 1899. At that time fruit, coca and wood were grown on large land holdings and the produce was exported to La Paz. Then, in the early 1950s, a revolution occurred and land reforms forced a redistribution of the land. Today, Coroico still produces coca, fruit and wood for those in La Paz. It is a relatively prosperous area because it is so close to a major city.

■ Services

 The **telephone office** is on the plaza on Avenida Guachalla. There is a second office on Calle Heroes del Chaco.

The **post office** is across from the Bank of Bolivia, just a few feet from the plaza on Calle Heroes del Chaco.

There is a **bank** on Calle Julio Zuazo Cuenca, on the plaza and across from the post office.

The **hospital** is on the upper road going to Sol y Luna. From the plaza, follow Linilla Rafae Miranda all the way out.

The **tourist office** is on the square, but I found the young woman quite surly and uninformed. For accurate information, go to the office of Inca Land Tours, also on the square, opposite the cathedral. That gal will open the office even during siesta if she knows you want something.

■ Festivals

October 20th is the day when Coroico became a village. This is the biggest celebration the town has, with everything from music to dancing to parades to *chicha* (corn beer) and more *chicha*.

The **Coroico Coffee Festival** in mid-June has been a celebration since 1998 and all the coffee-growing communities in the area participate.

BOLIVIAN BREWS

Bolivian coffee grown in Coroico is the best in the country and is served at Alexander Coffee shops, where it is sold by the bag under the name Alexander Coffee. Royal Bolivian Coffee, available in the Tarija area, is also good. The best thing about Bolivian coffee is that all the caffeine isn't roasted out of it. The lighter the roast, the higher the caffeine content. Be aware that Haiti Coffee, sold in La Paz, is a heavy roast; I don't recommended it.

■ Adventures on Foot

 TOCANA: The village of **Tocaña** is 14 miles/23 km from Coroico. You can walk here along a dirt road in the heat, but I suggest taking either a taxi or a truck at least one way. If you go to the village, poke around for a few hours and walk back, it will take you all day. Be certain to have sunscreen, a hat, water and good shoes.

Tocaña is an Afro-Bolivian settlement of about 50 families. The village is surrounded by rocky terrain. There is a school and the Audubon Society has posted teachers here under the sponsorship of the School Yard Ecology Education Initiate, whereby children learn about the natural environment. This is important around Tocaña. Of the 1,375 species of birds found in Bolivia, about one third can be found in this area. Tocaña is also one of the villages where it is legal to grow coca. A potato grown exclusively in this area carries the same name as the village.

The village is friendly and does not see many foreigners.One man I spoke with arrived here when a funeral was taking place and he was expected to join in. If you are lucky, you will be here during a festival. The locals use an instrument called a *reque-reque* that accompanies a *bombo* (drum) as they dance the Saya, a fast rhythmic dance accompanied by clapping hands of those watching. The Saya is led by a *Caporales*, a dancer dressed in a blouse with billowing sleeves, a pair of trousers and boots that come to the knee. He carries a whip that is symbolic of his position. The dance symbolizes days of oppression and punishments when the *Caporales* enforced discipline for the landowners. The *Caporales* has bells on his ankles that jingle when he dances as he guides the rest of the troupe. This presentation of dance requires some skill and lots of stamina.

THREE WATERFALLS: Tres Cascadas is a 4.3-mile/seven-km, half-day walk (don't believe the official tourist sheet that states you can walk to and from Tocaña in three hours). To get to the waterfalls, follow the road up toward Hotel Esmeralda and El Relincho, where horses can be hired. At the sign pointing toward the horse coral, go straight up the hill to Hermita Calvario, a small chapel, and the aqueduct. Follow the trail down to the waterfall that cascades through the jungle, dropping about 49 ft/15 m into a pool where you can dip. This is a popular hike. Birds, again, are a big draw.

CERRO UCHUMACHI: The summit of Cerro Uchumachi is a popular place to go on June 21st for the winter solstice. People go up on the 20th and camp overnight so that they can see the sun rise. As a day hike, it takes four to six hours round-trip, depending on your speed. Follow the same trail as you do for Tres Cascadas, except, at the chapel, go to the right. Behind the chapel is an easy-to-find trail through dense vegetation to the top of the hill, where there are three crosses. You can see for miles across the valley. Note the road across the valley that never has traffic on it. It was built to replace the Road of Death, but there was not enough money for a tunnel. Until the tunnel is completed, the road accesses only a few farms and villages.

MURURATA BRIDGE: Puente Mururata can be reached by following Avenida Ayacucho out of town past the Cerro Verde hotel until you come to a trail that goes off the road and down the hill. Follow it to the river. The bridge is just off the trail. Go upstream if you want a dip in the pools. The downside of this hike is that you must climb back up the trail to return to the village.

■ Adventures on Water

Rio Coroico has two possible runs, one for average rafters and kayakers and the other for the more skilled thrill-seeker. The first run passes through Class III rapids and is a six-hour paddling session There are only a few challenging spots and the drops and rapids are minimal. However, the lush jungle is a draw for birders as they can concentrate on the wildlife rather than running the boat. One friend of mine went on this run with the idea that a Class III run was easy. He ended in the drink. Luckily, he had a life jacket on. The trip starts at Puerte Carmas and goes to Puerto Chaña. On the way it passes the impressive waterfall of Puerto Leon. The cost is $65 for a six-hour day.

The second trip has some Class IV rapids and, during high water, Class V. This stretch has many areas where rapids come close to rock-garden status and the shoots are narrow and swift. There are pools and holes, drops and surfing waves (for kayaks) with a few easy eddies to pull into when the rush gets a bit much.

Rio Unduavi is another possible run, but is farther and harder to reach from Coroico. I'd rather paddle than drive. The lower section of the river has everything up to Class IV water. The advantage of going to this river is that it is a bit more isolated than the Coroico.

■ Adventures on Horseback

El Relincho, ☎ 719-23814 or 719-59072 (cell) can be found on the road between the Esmeralda Hotel and Sol y Luna. Renoldo, a gentle man, and his unassuming wife Gladys, operate this family business. Gladys is the cook and I can attest to the quality of her food. This company comes highly recommended. There are 10 horses in all that cost $6 per hour for guided rides in the area. They require two days notice for overnight trips. Their prices are reasonable and the family tries hard to please.

You can circumnavigate Uchumachi Mountain on horseback. This is a two-day trip that passes small villages such as Chocayo, Arapata and Chuso. The first night is spent at Chuso. The second day you ride on to Santa Barbara and back to Coroico via Cruz Loma. The cost is $70 per person with a minimum of four people and a maximum of eight. Food is supplied but you must have a tent. If you don't have one, Renoldo can put up a tarp but the mosquitoes are ubiquitous and a tarp doesn't keep them off. Another trip Renoldo offers is a three-day ride to La Paz along the Chustipata Trail. The cost is $100 per person, with a minimum of four people.

■ Adventures in Nature

 Cotapata National Park and the **Tunquini Biological Station** are both a draw for the birder. To get to the park, take the bus going toward La Paz and get off at the Cotapata Service Station between Undavi (29 miles/48 km from La Paz) and Chuspipata just before the pavement starts. This road has lots of traffic from early morning until around seven at night, so catching a ride to La Paz from here should be no trouble. Going back to Coroico would be difficult. If staying in Coroico, hire a jeep for the day and take in more than one place. From the service station, take the track across the road that leads up the hill and down the other side. There is 154 square miles/400 square km of park that sits at about 3,500 feet above sea level. The Choro Inca trail passes through this area.

Cotapata is where the *Diademed tapaculo* was found in 1992. The bird species had never been recorded as seen before and the park is inundated with them. Another rare attraction is the sickle-winged guan that is found only here and in the Zongo Valley. There are also condors and eagles, as well as the speckled bear. There have been numerous studies of the bear, but I couldn't get a number on the sightings.

The book to use as a guide is ***Birdfinding in Bolivia*** by Lawrence Rubey and Bennett Hennessey. It was not available at time of writing, but when it does come out, it will reveal many excellent spots like Cotapata Park for birders to use.

Tunquini Biological Station is closer to Coroico and a jeep is needed to reach it. Once there, you can camp as long as you are totally independent. To get there, take the road off the Coroico-La Paz road that leads to the Rio Silva Resort, 6.7 miles/11 km in, and the village of Chairo a few km past that. In Chairo, cross the river and turn left. Follow that trail for three miles/five km and you will be at the station.

Trails here offer such birding prizes as the scimitar-winged piha, the Bolivian spine tail, the great-billed hermit, the sickle-winged guan and the white-crowned tapaculo. If you have a tent and can stay awhile, your possibilities are unlimited.

For more information about birding in Bolivia, go to www.birdlife.net/worldwide/national/bolivia/index.html.

Coroico

Three Waterfalls

tc Cerro Uchumachi

CAMINO A CORIPATA

CAMINO A CARAVANI

El Ranchero

PINILLA RAFAEL MIRANDA

ANTEZANA

PANDO

JULIO ZUAZO CUENCA

ITURRALDE

PACHECO

SAGARNAGA

TOMAS MANNING

ORTIZ

Post Office

HEROES DEL CHACO

Bus Terminal
Inca Land Tours

← Market area

CIRCUNVALACION

AYACUCHO   GUACHALLA

to Puente Mururata
& Tocaña

N

HUNTER PUBLISHING

·········· Trails

© 2004 HUNTER PUBLISHING, INC

NOT TO SCALE

PLACES TO STAY
1. Hotel El Viejo Molino
2. Hotel Don Quijote
3. Hotel Esmerelda
4. Hostal Sol y Luna
5. Hostal El Cafetal
6. Jazmines Hotel
7. Hotel Bella Vista
8. Hotel Cerro Verde
9. Hotel Moderno
10. Hostal La Casa
11. Hotel Kory
12. Hotel Gloria
PLACES TO EAT
13. Diegu's Snack Bar
14. Bamboos Café & Bar
NIGHTLIFE
15. Disco/Karaoke

The Yungas

■ Adventures of the Brain

 Spanish lessons in Coroico are near total immersion as there is little chance to use English (not that there is much English anywhere in Bolivia). Courses are offered by **Dula and Jose Parija**, Calle Panckeko, ☎ 243-2067.

■ Tour Operators

 South America Rafting, ☎ 715-00556, southamericanrafting @hotmail.com, is in Coroico just one block from the plaza. If you make up your mind at the last minute to raft or kayak, you can book with them. They offer trips down the Zongo River (which they classify as difficult) and down the Tuichi River (intermediate).

El Relincho, ☎ 719 23814 or 719 59072 (cell), has horses for hire and can be found on the road between the Esmeralda Hotel and Sol y Luna. See *Adventures on Horseback* for a description of their most popular rides.

Inca Land Tours, on the square, ☎ 719-81990, has jeeps that can go to Uagante for $24 per person, to Tocaña for $25 per person, and to Rurrenabaque for $30 per person, with a minimum of four people. All fees include a guide. The Rurrenabaque excursion takes 11-12 hours and is much safer in a jeep than in a bus. This will change as road conditions improve. A jeep can take four to seven people.

Tours Palmeras, just off the square near the market (no phone), has an impressive timetable but buses go only when full. My experience with this company was that the driver was competent and careful, important factors when traveling the Road of Death. Our driver got us up the road through horrid weather and never once lit a cigarette until we were on the paved section of the highway, safe from landslides or bus slides. I could tell he needed a cigarette. I was tempted to take up the habit.

■ Places to Stay

 There are many places to stay in Coroico that are not mentioned here. I have taken the better of the mid-range places and named a few high-priced ones, but there are numerous budget digs around the market that seemed safe and clean enough.

La Casa, *Alidad Linares #3511*, ☎ *022-1360, lacasa@ceibo.entelnet.bo, $*, has very basic cement-floor rooms with or without private baths. The place is pleasant and overlooks the valley. If there are more than one of you, try to get the double room overlooking the Yungas – the view worth staying for.

HOTEL PRICES (US $)

Per person, per day, unless noted otherwise.

$......................................$2-$5
$$......................................$5-$10
$$$......................................$11-$17
$$$$......................................$18-$25
$$$$$..............................Over $25

The Roman Palace, *Calle Santa Cruz, 266A,* ☎ *757-2102, romano440@ latinmail.com, $$.* All rooms are large with private baths and hot water and many overlook the valley. There is a pool in progress, and a restaurant that wasn't open when I was there. Other than barking street dogs, the place is quiet and away from the square.

Hotel Kory, *Calle Casella #6020,* ☎ *243-1311, koryhostalcelia@hotmail. com, $$.* Rooms at the Kory are big and clean with tiled floors, closets, and tables and chairs. If staying longer than three days, the hotel offers a discount. There is a swimming pool and a nice patio with flowers. The owner changes traveler's checks without charging a commission and laundry service is available. Bicycles are available for rent at $7 per day, but I did not see them so I have no idea how good they are. The owner has a wealth of knowledge about the area, but he speaks only Spanish. The restaurant makes excellent banana shakes and serves vegetarian and international foods.

Sol y Luna, ☎ *236-2099, www.solyluna-bolivia.com, $$.* Prices vary depending on the accommodation you choose, a basic room, a cabin or a luxury cabin. There are five rooms in the main building, six cabins for rent and camping in the garden for $2 per person. Firewood is 75¢ per bundle. It is a 30-minute walk uphill from the plaza to the hotel. This is a holistic place offering tarot card readings and lessons as well as massage therapy. It has a meditation room devoid of distracting furniture. There is also a pool and hot tub ($6 per hour) that holds up to three people. The on-site restaurant serves mainly vegetarian dishes. As a sideline, the hotel also sells ceramic jewelry that is made locally ($6 for a plain necklace).

The Moderno Hotel, *Guachalla #32,* ☎ *715-20411, $$,* is a well-kept building just off the square. It has 21 rooms and is run by a jovial chap who tries hard to please his guests. The rooms are clean and pleasant, the shower water comes from a tank and the floors are tile. There is a pool and parking.

Buena Vista, ☎ *715-69237, $$,* is just 329 ft/100 m off the square and overlooking the valley to the east. The mountains can be seen through the huge windows opposite the beds. This is a hacienda-style building, bright and well decorated with 11 rooms that can hold 21 people. The clean rooms have soft beds and ceramic tile floors. There are gold taps in

The Yungas

bathrooms and hot water is supplied from a tank. A sitting area is located on each floor, and there's also a racquetball court and a restaurant on site. This is a good deal.

Hotel Cerro Verde, *Avenida Ayacucho #5037,* ☎ *719-57592, cerrove@ hotmail.com, $$,* is a new place built in colonial style. It has fairly large, clean rooms with private baths and is quiet. There's a refreshing pool, a well-tended garden, and a view that is worth every penny you pay for the room. The people are friendly. This is a good place to stay close to town.

Hotel Don Quijote, ☎ *236-0007, $$,* is about a half-mile/one km down the road to Coripata. (Just after the fork between the road to Caranavi and Coripata is the Bambus Restaurant; three blocks beyond that is the hotel.) The Don Quixote is clean as a whistle and a good deal. Being slightly out of town, you get the sounds of the jungle at night while still having luxury surroundings. There is also a good restaurant on-site, though the one in town (called the Bamboo Bar and owned by the same people) is strong competition.

Esmeralda Hotel, ☎ *213-6017, reservas@hotelesmeralda.com, $$$,* is the most popular place to stay in Coroico. The 31-room hotel has large rooms with foyers and balconies, tiled bathrooms, soap, towels, toilet paper, closets and seven TV channels. The hot water is supplied from a water tank rather than an electrical shower heater. The owner will either pick you up in town or pay for a taxi if you stay at the hotel. This is a bonus because the walk up the hill is at least half an hour and, with luggage, could be longer. Laundry service is available for $1 a kilo. But it is the grounds at this hotel that are exceptional. Bananas grow beside yellow copa de oro flowers, Tai plants, rubber plants and more. High flower season is April, May and June, but even in low season this garden is lush. Interspersed among the vegetation are board games, videos, fooze ball tables, pool tables and a great butterfly collection. There is a large pool with a sauna nearby. Food in the restaurant is served buffet style and is in the top 10 for quality. An all-you-can-eat breakfast costs $2, lunch is $2.50 and supper is $3. The owner speaks English, German and Spanish and is knowledgeable about the area.

Hotel Gloria, ☎ *240-7070, www.hotelgloriabolivia.com, $$$,* has seen better days. At one time this hotel was a classic, with high ceilings, heavy chandeliers, dark wood cupboards and four-piece baths. Then it went into a period of decline. However, the management is now remodeling and Hotel Gloria should, in the near future, be a good place to stay once again. Since Gloria is a chain in Bolivia, there are special rates for those booking at three hotels in different locations. The gardens at this hotel are an attraction. The bougainvillea is as old as the corner stones and seems to dominate the center of the front yard. The hotel is at the bottom of the hill (follow the stairs down from the plaza) below the soccer field. The on-site restaurant serves okay food in a colonial dining room.

Hotel Viejo Molino, *.6 miles / one km along the road to Santa Barbara,* ☎ *220-1519, viejomolino@vaimatours.com, $$$$,* is a five-star hotel with everything in the rooms to make you comfortable, including TV, private bath and matching décor. Your breakfast is included in the price. There is a sauna and restaurant on site.

Jazmines Hotel, ☎ *222-9967, $$$$, on the road between Yolosa and Coroico and just .6 miles / one km from the center of Coroico,* is a four-star, two-storey building surrounding a pool. The hotel is clean and luxurious and has a restaurant, racquetball court, tennis court, beach volleyball and three pools.

■ Places to Eat

In addition to the hotel restaurants, there are numerous places to enjoy a meal.

Diegu's Snack Bar *(no phone), on the square,* offers an egg sandwich with a banana milkshake for less than $1.50. They are open fairly early, around 7:30 am, and stay open at night until around 9 pm, depending on the amount of people in the restaurant. The food is good, the place is clean, the kids are cute.

El Cafetal *(no phone), up the hill beside the hospital*, is run by a flamboyant Frenchman who, true to his culture, serves the best meals in town. You can also stay on the premises for $3.50 per person without private bath if you can't make it home after your meal. The restaurant overlooks the valley and this is good because it takes time to eat with the French. While the owner prepares your meal, you need to sip on wine and gaze at the landscape. A hamburger with fries costs $1.50, spaghetti, lasagne and soufflés cost $3.50-$4. A bottle of Bolivian wine is around $7. They also carry things like Johnny Walker whiskey that sells for $3.50 a shot. Better to stick with the wine. Make an effort to have at least one night of true entertainment at this restaurant before leaving town.

Bamboo Bar, Calle Iteralde, just two blocks from the square, is a great place for a Mexican dinner. The food is good, the service cheerful and quick. They serve, among other dishes, vegetarian burritos and tacos and they have a happy hour every day from 6 to 7 pm. This is one of the better places to eat in Coroico. There is live music on the weekends. The restaurant is part of the same business as the Don Quixote Hotel.

■ Shopping

Artesanias Arco Iris on the square has good quality jewelry, some made with lapis lazuli, others made with silver from Potosi. It is all unique. They also sell local coffee beans and a few

The Yungas

small woven purses. Coffee from Caranavi, just a few miles away, is used by the best coffee shops in Bolivia.

■ Nightlife

 There are two discos in town, both close to the entrance of the village on the road to La Paz. The name of the road is Tomas Manning and the name of the most popular disco with the Bolivians is La Tropicana (the other disco is referred to as "the disco"). But just hanging out in the plaza with a beer attracts attention in Coroico. Most foreigners go to the restaurants and poolside bars when in need of entertainment.

Caranavi

Altitude: 1,993 ft / 606 m
Population: 1,000

Caranavi is a market village along the Road of Death that continues past Yolosa and the Coroico turnoff. This road follows the Coroico River, which has formed an impressive gorge that you will pass. The fields in the valley are full of coca plants, coffee and citrus fruits. The price you pay for this splendor is the heart attack you will have while teetering on the edge of a cliff as a truck tries to pass your bus. While I was there one bus went over the edge, killing 12 and injuring 45, some seriously. This trip lasts only four hours past Yolosa.

The reason to visit Caranavi is to continue through the Amazon to Trinidad or Rurrenabaque and its jungle river trips. If you have been in Coroico, getting a seat for a trip on a bus going into the Amazon is often difficult, so you must go to Caranavi to get one.

The road forks at Caranavi, with one branch going to Guayay where you have access to the Caca River, a tributary of the Beni.

■ Getting Here & Around

 Buses leave La Paz every hour or so and they pass Yolosa on the way to Caranavi. There are also buses going to Rurrenabaque and Trinidad from the main terminal in Caranavi. Travelers going to Guanay (if doing the gold circuit) can find micros (vans) in the market. Six buses go to and from Guanay every day, with the first one at 6 am.

A **jeep** is recommended for the road from Caranavi, from Coroico, or La Paz. One can be hired, with a driver, at Inca Land Tours in Coroico, or you can get one in La Paz to go all the way to Caranavi. The cost from Coroico is about $75 for the four-hour trip. Besides safety, the second advantage in taking a jeep is that the driver will stop often so you can do a bit of whatever interests you the most, whether it be birding, photography or wildlife/plant viewing.

■ Adventures on Foot

Caranavi is a **coffee**-producing region that has recently gone organic. There are 41 coffee producers in the area on farms that run from three to 11 acres each. It was the second land reform that took place in Bolivia in 1991 that gave a lot of the land to the indigenous people of the area. They are the ones running the farms at present.

The coffee here is picked three times a year, during March/April, May/June and August/September. Actual picking dates change according to weather and growing conditions. All beans are hand-picked. The coffee is slightly spicy and full- to heavy-bodied.

If you stay in Caranavi, it is possible to walk to the outskirts of town and visit some coffee plantations. If you are addicted to the product, this is highly recommended. You will be welcome by the local farmers.

■ Adventures on Water

There is a five-day trip that is an opportunity more than a tour. It includes a six- or seven-hour motorboat trip down the Caca River from Caranavi to the village of Luquimuni. The night is spent at the house of Don Pedro. On the way you pass miners panning for gold and will be given the opportunity to try your own luck. The second point of interest for the day is a parrot haven where thousands of birds can be seen nesting on the cliffs along the river. The second day you will travel to Torewa, stopping at villages along the way. After dinner you will do a night walk looking for nocturnal creatures. The next day is spent learning about medicinal plants, going on a hike/ safari and learning about jungle survival. From Torewa, you float down the river through some scenic canyons to Rurrenabaque. See Kon-Tiki Tours or Sky Bolivia Tours in La Paz for information (read their reviews on pages 80 and 81).

■ Tour Operators

Floating Bolivia Tours, Calle Cobija #13, ☎ 823-2396 or 715-19427 (cell), floatingbolivia@hotmail.com, offers the boat trip down the Guanay River to Rurrenabaque. They also have an overnight camping trip into the Taipiplaya jungle close to Caranavi.

WHEN YOU WISH UPON A... GRAPE

During the New Year in the Caranavi area it is customary to fill a glass with champagne and add 12 grapes. At the stroke of midnight, you drink the wine and eat the grapes, making a wish for each month of the year as you chew each grape.

Sky Bolivia Tours and Travel, Calle Sagarnaga 367 in La Paz, www.skybolivia.com, offers a tour you can join in Guanay or La Paz. It follows the Rio Caca to the Beni and then goes down to Rurrenabaque. Their trip is good if you want to learn about medicinal plants and have a general lesson in jungle survival. The cost is $35 a day for the five-day trip. Sky Bolivia provides everything except your clothes and sleeping bag, booze and tips.

It is recommended that you have good shoes, long-sleeved shirts and long pants, sun block, sunglasses, sleeping bag, sun hat and mosquito repellent for this trip. I suggest you have lots and lots of film as the wild life is abundant. If you can also carry a zoom lens, do so. Since you are in a boat, any additional weight isn't too much of a bother. Just be careful not to get it wet.

■ Places to Stay

There are a number of small and basic places to stay around the Caranavi market and near the square. For something a bit more upscale, try the **Canturra Inn**, ☎ *823-2209, $$$*, which has thatch-roofed cabins with bamboo walls (on the outside). Each room is clean and has tile floors, private bathrooms and extras like bed lamps and fans. The cost is $15 for a single and $20 for a double. There is a well-kept garden and a pool in which to cool off after your walk to the coffee plantation. The price includes breakfast. There is also a restaurant and bar on the premises.

The inn has guide service and will take you for a canoe paddle to some Amazonian villages or in a 4x4 to a banana plantation.

■ Places to Eat

Unless eating in the Canturra Inn, you will have to make your way around the eateries close to the square or market. There are not many choices and the food is mostly chicken.

■ Shopping

 Antogagasta Market in Caranavi sells organically grown coffee. This should be purchased while in Bolivia. I can personally attest to its flavor. At one time I was sold on Guatemalan coffee, but nothing beats a cup of coffee made with beans from Caranavi.

Guanay

Altitude: 1,500 ft / 500 m.
Population: 500

Guanay is a gold-mining town tucked onto the shores of the Caca River with high hills covered in rainforest above the village and cultivated farms along the flatlands. It is down these hills that the gold is flushed from the high Andes during rainy season, often along with a landslide. As can be expected, the lure of gold attracts the miner, usually a rough and tough, hard-working dude who cares more for the glitter than the landscape.

■ Getting Here & Around

Guanay is usually reached by foreigners who walk the Gold Trail from Sorata (page 273) or those who walk the Mapiri Trail (page 271) and then take a boat to Guanay. The next leg of these journeys is usually a bus to either Caranavi or Rurrenabaque. Those wanting to go up the Mapiri River can catch a boat at the town dock every morning. The five-hour trip may need to be done in a jeep during the peak of dry season.

Bus tickets can be purchased from the companies who have offices around the plaza. Most buses leave between 6 and 8 am for the morning run, while others leave after 5 pm for the night run. There are six buses every day to Caranavi. It takes four hours to get there, and around 12 hours to reach La Paz.

■ Adventures on Water

 A boat trip, whether it be a motorized river boat, canoe, kayak or raft, starts in Guanay and goes down the Caca River to its confluence with the Quendeque River before it reaches the Beni. From there it is a quiet float down the Beni to a scenic canyon called Angosto del Bala. The trip through the canyon can be a bit difficult. The river goes on to Rurrenabaque.

Once past the Quendeque, the only villages you'll see before Rurre are San Miguel and Susi, isolated communities that are interesting to visit. However, barges carrying bananas, citrus, coffee, gasoline, tinned foods, radios and all other imaginable goods are seen going up and down the river on a regular basis.

This five-day trip includes camping in the jungle, some of it in Madidi National Park. Because not many people do this trip, the wildlife viewing is incredible.

A TAIL TELLS A TALE

The common squirrel monkey usually travels in groups of 20 to 100 animals. Their tails are called prehensile because they use them to grip, as a kind of fifth hand, to help when hanging from a limb or swinging to another branch. Monkeys with prehensile tails are called New World monkeys, while those without, like the African or Asian monkeys, are called Old World monkeys.

■ Places to Stay

There are numerous places to stay in the village, all basic and catering to the gold miner. However, **Residencial Zuñjga** is a little upscale and is where NGOs stay when they are passing through. I have no phone number for this place, but Guanay is not a metropolis and the hotel is easy to find.

Mapiri, usually reached by walking the Mapiri-Colonel Fawcett Trail, has basic places to stay and eat. Boats go daily up and down the river between Guanay and Mapiri.

Chulumani

Altitude: 5,395 ft / 1,640 m
Population: less than 2,000

Chulumani is in the South Yungas, off the main highway that runs between La Paz and Coroico. Shortly after Unduavi a side road turns south and then plunges down the mountains toward this village. Although perched on the side of a steep hill, surrounded by lush jungle and thick with wildlife, Chulumani is not often frequented by foreigners except birders, who flock there. Regardless of how or why you arrive, be certain to watch for the **Bridal Veil Waterfalls** on the way to Chulumani. They are after Unduavi but before Chulumani.

In the town you'll see Aymara people living next to Afro-Bolivians who wear the clothing of the Aymara but practice their own dancing and music. For more information on this culture, see the section on Tocaña, page 281.

■ Getting Here & Around

 Those **walking** the Yungas Cruz trek finish in Chulumani and those walking the Taquesi hike without a tour group often make the effort to get a truck into Chulumani.

Buses leave from Villa Fatima bus area in La Paz four times a day for the four-plus-hour ride to Chulumani ($2.50). The first bus leaves at 6 am and the last at 2 pm. The ride down to Chulumani is not as scary as the one to Coroico.

All *trufis* and **micros** leave Chulumani from Plaza Libertad starting shortly after dawn. Those wanting to go from Chulumani to Coroico should take a bus to Unduavi and catch a bus going down to Coroico.

■ Adventures in Nature

Apa-Apa Ecological Forest Reserve is north of Chulumani and is the best place in the Yungas for spotting birds that like the middle montane Yungas environment. The elevation is about 7,566 ft/2,300 m with subtropical and lower temperate forests. Apa-Apa is owned by the Bolivian/American couple, Ramiro and Matilda Portugal. They have done an exemplary job of preserving the environment around their five-acre parcel of land that is accessed by numerous trails. Guided tours through Apa-Apa Reserve, in English, make many stops where your guide talks about the environment. There are also numerous trails that wind in and out of the five-acre parcel. Tours take three to four hours and cost $5 per person, with a minimum of five people.

Visitors can stay at the 160-year-old hacienda in the reserve for a reasonable price (see below). The surrounding landscape is farmland and scrub that is not so hot for birding. Better sighting possibilities are close by, along the river. The best birding can be found up the hill behind the hacienda. The rare scimitar-winged piha is reported to hang around here. If you are not lucky in seeing one, you will still see hummingbirds, short-tailed hawks, turkey vultures, Andean guan and wood quail, among hundreds of others. Walking for about an hour will put you into the cloud forest, where fig trees covered in bromeliads, interspersed with bamboo, line the slopes. It is not uncommon to see well over 100 birds within a few days.

The Yungas

To stay at the hacienda or take a bird tour, call Ramiro or Matilda Portugal, ☎ 2213-6106 (cell) in Chulumani, or 233-4495 in La Paz. To get here you will need a ride as there is no public transportation to the site. The reserve is 5.5 miles/nine km before Chulumani along the main road and then another 1.2 miles/two km uphill on a tertiary road.

■ Places to Stay

HOTEL PRICES (US $)

Per person, per day, unless noted otherwise.

$	$2-$5
$$	$5-$10
$$$	$11-$17
$$$$	$18-$25
$$$$$	Over $25

Panorama, *Calle Murillo*, ☎ *811-6109, $$$*, is the best that is available in Chulumani. It has clean rooms, a relaxing garden and a pool.

The more basic and less expensive places are **Boliviar**, *Calle Bolívar #26 (no phone)*, and **Dion**, *Calle Alianza #16 (no phone)*. Dion has two levels of rooms with the upper ones being a bit more expensive. **Garcia**, *Plaza Libertad #20*, and **Manarca**, *Calle Circuvalacion #17*, ☎ *811-6121*, are okay too. **Huayrani**, *Calle Junin*, ☎ *811-3117*, has spacious apartments that hold up to four people ($10 per person). They have a fully equipped kitchen, two bedrooms and a sitting room as well as a tiny pool in the garden.

Apa-Apa Reserve Hacienda, ☎ 2213-6106, apapyungas@hotmail.com, has rooms with private bathrooms for $6 per person. This is a real deal. Not only do you get the room, but you can purchase homemade ice cream, milkshakes and other homemade meals from their milk bar. The cost of a meal is between $1 and $3. If you wish to camp, you pay a $10 overall fee that is good for the year, plus a dollar a night. There are barbecue pits, bathrooms with showers, a pool and tenting spots shaded by jungle trees.

El Castillo, ☎ *235-9881 $$$*, is 12 miles/20 km from Unduavi on the road toward Chulumani. This three-star hotel includes breakfast in the room rate. Clean and comfortable, its distinct castle design makes it impossible to miss. It was once called the Castillo del Chaco. There is a pool. All around is thick jungle dotted with a few waterfalls.

Tamampaya is on the road between Chulumani and on the La Paz side of the hamlet Puente Villa, ☎ *279-6069, $$$$*. This four-star hotel perched on the mountain surrounded by rainforest that is seething with birds and other critters like bugs and butterflies. A campsite here has a shower hut and cooking facilities. The 2.4-mile/four-km hike just above the hotel, where cock-of-the-rock birds have been sighted, is recommended. The setting of this hotel is conducive to seeing lots of birds commonly found at 5,000 feet/1,500 m.

Motel San Bartoleme, *Avenida Arce #2177,* ☎ *811-6114, $$$$$*, is a five-star hotel with everything you might find in a Radisson Hotel. Each room has a safe along with a well-stocked mini bar. The hotel has a Jacuzzi, massage parlor, sauna, pool, restaurant, bar and a coffee shop. And, new for Bolivia, it even has wheelchair access. Rates: $173 to $216 double, depending on the room.

Las Colinas

Sucre

Altitude: 7,829 ft / 2,380 m
Population: 210,000

Sucre is often called the white city because of its colonial buildings that, due to a municipal ordinance, must all be white. Considered the official capital of the country, it is actually the judicial center, while La Paz is the seat of government. But Sucre is more than a government town, it is a university town with 60% of the population under the age of 23. With the high student population, Sucre is often referred to as the international center of Bolivia.

Sucre is a town that sparkles like a diamond in the dry brown mountains surrounding it. There are many cycle and horse trips that can be enjoyed in the area, plus an exciting bus/truck/hike into the ancient crater of a long-blown volcano. People come to check out the famous dino tracks right on the edge of town. Finally, Sucre is a good place to find textiles.

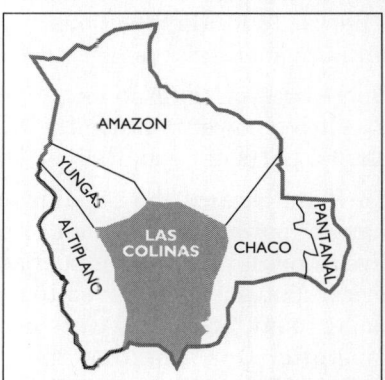

■ Getting Here & Around

  Buses to Potosi leave at 7 am, 1 pm and 5 pm. To Uyuni, they leave at 7 am and 1 pm. Those to Villazon and Tupiza leave at 1 pm, La Paz at 5:30 pm, Cochabamba at 6:30 pm and Santa Cruz at 5 pm. Tickets for the Sunday market in Tarabuco can be purchased in town or at the bus station. Bus tickets can be purchased in the center of town (Calle Arce #95 on the corner of San Alberto, Real Audiencia, Office #4, ☎ 644-3119) for the same price as those at the bus station.

Daily flights with all the major airlines run between Sucre and La Paz, Cochabamba, Santa Cruz and Yacuiba. Those to and from Cobija and Trinidad go only once a week. See page 87 for airline contact information.

A **taxi** from the airport to the center of town is about $2 for up to four people. Colonial Plus Taxi Service, Avenida Ostria Gutierrez, ☎ 642-9750, has vehicles for hire. They also run a *trufi* to Potosi. The cost of a private taxi is $30 a day for travel on the main roads. If you need a taxi to go to Potolo during the rainy season, the fare may be a bit higher ($130).

A fast driver is **Silverio Mamani**, ☎ 7181-6967 (cell). He is also fairly safe. However, I did have to talk to him to keep him awake when the heat got high at siesta time. Another good honest driver is Martin Espendola. He charges about $15 for a full day on paved roads. For a day on the road to Potolo he charges closer to $60 or $70 during dry season. Call ☎ 42000 and ask for number 21.

■ History

 Sucre was established in 1540 in the Indian territory of Choke-Chaca by Pedro de Anzures. Through the years, it has gone by numerous names, many of which are still referred to today, such as Chiquisaca (a bastardized version of the Indian name), La Plata, Charcas (a local indigenous group), Ciudad Blanca (because of its white buildings) and Sucre.

Sucre became the Audiencia de Charcas, the official judicial center with executive powers, under the Spanish king. The territory it covered included parts of Peru, Bolivia, Paraguay, Chili and Argentina.

La Plata became the popular name for the city when Potosi was the financial powerhouse of South America and middle class people wanted to live in mansions and conduct administrative duties away from the high-priced Potosi. They moved to Sucre and built the mansions that we still enjoy today. Still, they were making their money from the mines. It was long after this time that the miniature Eiffel Tower (the original was built in 1889 in Paris) was built and when some of the victory arches were erected.

The name Sucre was given to the city in honor of the first president, Antonio José de Sucre, and after the country gained independence from Spain in 1825. Liberty House, on the plaza, is where the Declaration of Independence was signed.

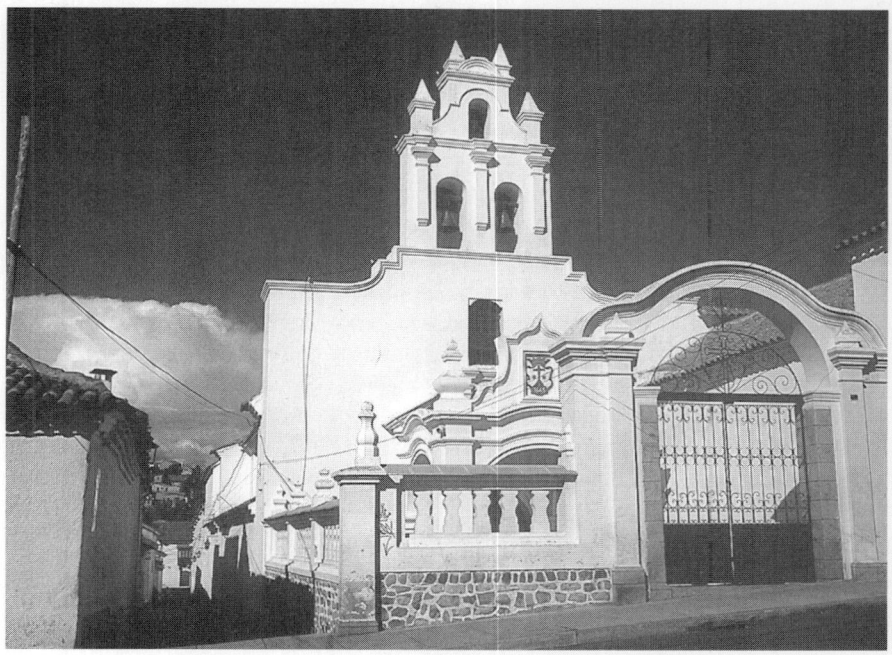

Cathedral, Sucre.

While Sucre was in power he reformed the tax structure to help finance public expenditures. He used some of the money to revitalize silver mining in Potosi. He also confiscated church money and closed many monasteries, thus stripping the Catholic Church of a tremendous amount of its power. But his methods of reform resulted in an economic success only in part. As opposition built, a new leader was found and a battle ensued. Sucre won the battle but lost the presidency to **Santa Cruz**, who brought about a stable economy and political peace (for a while).

The first Bishop in Upper Peru was established in Sucre in 1609 and because of that the first university (third in the Americas), the University of San Xavier, was opened in 1624. Its purpose was to train the religious leaders of the area. The university town was born.

In 1991 UNESCO declared Sucre a World Heritage Site because of its history and, even more so, because of the colonial architecture.

■ Services

The **telephone office** is on the Plaza 25 de Mayo along Avenida Ayacucho.

The **police station** is on Plaza Zundonez along Avenida Olañeta between Junin and Bustillo.

There is a **tourist office** on Calle Argentina and Olañeta. The official office is in the Casa de Cultura on Calle Argentina. It is useless.

Laundry, Calle Loa #407 and Avenida Siles, close to the central market, ☎ 642-4066, is open daily, including holidays. They can have your clothes ready within two hours if needed.

■ Sightseeing

 Casa de la Libertad is on the main plaza and is where the declaration of independence was signed on August 6, 1825. Inside the building are portraits of past presidents, military decorations and documents (one of which was signed by Simon Bolívar). You can also tour the Senate room where the legislative assembly convened for over 50 years. The original carved chairs and tables are still in place. Today, the University of St. Francisco Xavier uses the room for its senate meetings.

Glorieta Castle was built by the Prince and Princess of Glorieta, a name endowed to Francisco Argadoña and Clotilde Urioste by Pope Leon XIII for their charitable work in Bolivia. Most of the family fortune came from the profits of the Huanchaca mine, close to Uyuni. They built the castle between 1893 and 1897 using European styles, so you can see hints of gothic in their clock tower, renaissance in their furniture, baroque dotted throughout and neoclassic designs in the imported pink marble and wood. The building was used as a military base from the 1950s until recently, but restoration is in progress and the results are good. The grounds come complete with a man-made lake, a miniature railroad, fountains and gazebos surrounded by marble statues. There is even an outdoor dining room. This is not the way I would design my house if great wealth came from the royalties of this book, but visiting the house makes for a fun day.

To get here, take minibus #4 from Calle Ravelo and Arce. It's a half-hour ride. You can also walk the 3.7 miles/six km along Avenida Argentina (it changes names) to Destacamento Chuquisaca (passing Otto-Chiquisaca on the way) or rent a bike from Joy Ride Tours (Calle Oritz #14, ☎ 642-5544, www.joyridebol.com). The house is open daily, 8:30 am-noon and 2-6 pm, and costs $1 to enter.

■ Adventures in Culture

 Festival de la Cultura, FSCC@pelicano.cnb.net, holds an annual two-week arts festival at the beginning of September. It involves classical, jazz and rock music events. Theater, drama, opera and ballet are performed. There are showings of contemporary paintings and plastic art, as well as a cinema to watch and literature to

Sucre
Sights

to Buses &
Dino Tracks

CALLE A O GUTIERREZ

GERMAIN MENDOZA

JAMIE MENDOZA

LEMOINE

MAESTRO
VON BRAUN
MENDOZA

MOLINA

VENEZUELA

Parque
Simon
Bolivar

SILES

LOA

RAVELO

JUNIN

ARENALES

AYACUCHO

TARAPACA

MORENO

OLANETA

DESTACAMENTO 111

PASTOR SAINZ

URRIOLAGOITIA

CALAMA

JAPON

CORDOVA

COLON

LA PAZ

LOA

JUNIN

ANICETO ARCE

ESPANA

SAN ALBERTO

SAN BOLIVAR

CAMARGO

CAMARGO

AVAROA

POTOSI

CALVO

ORURO

PADILLA

SUPACHA

GRAU

ARGENTINA

DALENCE

AZURDUY

RAFAEL BUSTILLO

J J PEREZ

ECHEVERRIA

to Cemetery

■ Post
Office

© 2004 HUNTER PUBLISHING, INC

NOT TO SCALE

SIGHTS & ATTRACTIONS
1. Plaza 25 de Mayo
2. Casa de la Libertad
3. Cathedral of Guadelupe, Government Building
4. Gutierrez Valenzuela Museum
5. Casa de la Cultura
6. Gran Mariscal dey Ayacucho Theater
7. Supreme Court
8. Recoleta, Tanga Tanga Children's Museum
9. Santa Teresa Convent
10. Casa Capellanica
11. Santa Clara Convent
12. Indigenous Art Museum
13. University Museum (Charcas, Anthropological, Contemporary Art)

listen to. Some of the events are in the theater while other events are per-formed on the streets or in the plazas. One year the festival had the phil-harmonic orchestra playing on the Uyuni Salt Flats. The festival is an exceptional event and, if in Bolivia during this time, you should attend.

Masis Cultural Center, Calle Bolívar #561, ☎ 645-3403, losmasis@ pelicano.cnb.net, is a fascinating center where kids come to learn tradi-tional music from a master of the art, Roberto Masis. It is a delight to watch them perform. The center is open daily at 6 pm. There is no charge, but a donation is appreciated. The money goes directly to the kids – often for snacks or refreshments, and sometimes toward the purchase of in-struments.

If you wish to purchase a pan flute or churango, the ones for sale in the shop are of excellent quality – all are handmade under they eye of the master, Roberto. He and his group of musicians have over 20 recordings, all of which can be purchased at the shop. Ceramics are also for sale.

Music lessons can be had at the reasonable cost of $20 per month for three lessons a week. The teacher will be either Roberto himself or his son Roberto. This would be a group lesson.

AUTHOR NOTE: CDs purchased on the street usually will not work on your players at home. They are good only for the computers on which they were made.

The **Museum of Natural History**, on Plaza 25 de Mayo, is on the main floor of the building. The entrance fee is $1.25; open hours are Monday to Friday, 8 am-noon and 2:30-6 pm, Saturday, 9 am-noon and 3-6 pm. The museum has stuffed animals and birds interspersed among trees, shrubs and rocks. The condor is in better shape than the one in Sajama, but also much smaller. A good rock and gem collection illustrates the geology of the area.

Upstairs is the **Dr. Alfredo Gutierrez Valenzuela Museum**, which features a collection of Louis XV and Louis XVI furniture, some of which belonged in the Castle of La Glorieta (see above). There is also a collection of gold-trimmed/painted vases, crystal, marble carvings and porcelain pieces. This is a lovely museum with many pieces collected by Dr. Gutierrez. It takes a couple of hours to visit. Open Monday to Friday, 8:30 am-noon and 2:30-6 pm; Saturday, 8:30 am-noon and 3-6 pm.

The **Anthropological Museum**, Calle Bolívar #698, ☎ 645-3285, has three sections: colonial art, archeological artifacts and contemporary art. The contemporary art area has some fine works like those by Jorge Imana Garron, wood carvings and paintings from 1916, 1925 and the 1930s. One room is dedicated to portraits of the longer-lasting Bolivian leaders like Bolívar and Sucre. Even if you do not know the history of

Bolivia, you will recognize many of these names because they are often used as street names. The colonial art section includes nicely framed images of inspiring things like St. Simon being cut in half with a saw and some other hero being clubbed to death. Interesting old furniture that has not been restored is dotted around the rooms. I'm glad I didn't have to sit on some of those couches wearing a corset – St. Simon would have had it easier. The archeological area has numerous skulls, some normal and some deformed. They are labeled male and female (how they figured this out is beyond me). There are also some mummies on display. The doll collection shows changes in styles over the years. In the 20 years that I have been visiting the area, I can already see a difference in the design of the dolls. Centuries would make a big difference.

The museum is not cluttered and it takes about two hours to see everything. It's open Monday to Friday, 8:30 am-noon and 2:30-6 pm, and Saturday 8:30 am-noon. The cost is $1.50.

The **Ecclesiastical Museum**, Calle N. Oritz #61, ☎ 645-2257, is open Monday to Friday, 10 am-noon and 3-5 pm, and on Saturday until noon only. It's housed in a cathedral that was built in 1559. I found the outside of the church area far more pleasing than the inside. This museum is one of the richest in Bolivia with every type of jewel possible, many of them stuck to garments of long-gone priests. There is one diamond, displayed in a case of its own, that is worth more than the Hope diamond. The Chapel of the Virgin of Guadalupe has a statue of the Virgin covered in a robe of pearls, diamonds, rubies, emeralds and gold – it looks pretty heavy to me. One room has nothing but robes on display. The art gallery has oils from some of the European masters like Van Dyck and Forchaudt. It takes about two hours to visit this museum without rushing.

The Recoleta and the **Tanga Tanga Child's Museum** is on Calle Polanco #162, ☎ 645-1987. It is open from Monday to Friday, 9 am-noon and 2:30-4:30 pm. The cost is 75¢. The walk up Churuquella hill and the Stations of the Cross can be combined with a visit here.

Founded in 1600 by Francisco de Morales, the courtyard of the convent has a cedar tree that is said to be 1,000 years old and that was declared a historical monument in 1956. The church beside the convent was built a hundred years or so after the convent and its choir loft is designed in 17th-century baroque style, with carved chairs and backboards. The walls behind the chairs are carved to match. The heavy rich wood is local cedar. The courtyard has an area of archways that overlook the city and make for a wonderful view, especially when the sun is setting. Below the arches is the Ananday gift shop, selling upscale items at upscale prices, and the Gourmet Café where you can get excellent cappuccinos. The prices are high, but sitting in the garden overlooking the city is worth the rent. La Recoleta Restaurant next to the church is under new management and now has an excellent reputation for gourmet meals.

The Tanga Tanga museum is up the side stairs from the central courtyard and is made with every child in mind, regardless of age. I had fun there. It's open Tuesday to Sunday, from 10:30 am to 6:30 pm and costs just over a dollar to enter. The museum's four floors symbolize the four areas of Bolivia; the Altiplano, the valleys, the Chaco and the Amazon. The connecting hallways have touch science projects on display and a puppet theater. A section for youngsters allows them to play roles like market mummy or wheat field daddy. A library and reading room are on site. There is also an outdoor cafeteria, theater and park.

Santa Clara Convent, Calle Calvo #212, ☎ 645-2295, is open Monday to Friday, 9 am-noon and 2-6 pm. It was built by the Franciscan Fathers in 1636 and is now filled with religious art. The big draw is the pipe organ, built in 1792 and reported to have the best sound of all organs in the country. The pipes are encased in an ornate brass holding.

The Indigenous Art Museum, Avenida San Alberto #413, ☎ 645-3841, is open Monday to Friday, 8:30 am-noon and 2:30-6 pm. On Saturday it is open only until noon. Entrance fee, $2.50. If you are not on a tour, they will give you a pamphlet written in English describing the museum. You may not take your pack into the museum. Instead, you hand it to a staff member who will throw it on a pile with everyone else's. When you leave, you are asked to pick one from the pile. Although they give you a tag, they didn't check mine when I retrieved my pack. If you're not on a tour, avoid going through when there is a group, as it can be distracting.

There are 12 rooms in the museum that feature Tarabuco and Jalq'a weavings. The first room has general information about weaving, illustrated with original objects plus some photos. The next few rooms have natural dyed weavings, woven sling shots called *hondas*, coca bags called *chupas*, ponchos called *unku* and tapestries. The dolls woven into the *machas* (the weavings worn around the waist when not needed as a cape) hang like tassels and are from the Potolo region. Some of these pieces are around 2,500 years old. Jalq'a weaving is one of the superior styles in the world.

The rooms move on to examples of weavings used for religious ceremonies and then weavings from specific areas/villages. A room downstairs demonstrates what archeologists believe the people were like before recorded time. The hair braids are especially interesting. One section has instruments, bows and arrows, jewelry and baskets. Weavers, dressed in traditional clothes, demonstrate style and technique and are there to be photographed.

Jalq'a weavings are usually red/orange on black, with every style of animal or human image possible woven into the garment in a double weave so both sides of the garment are the same. Only the colors are different. The characters are called *khurus*, which means wild and incapable of being domesticated.

Tarabuco weavings are symmetrical and have recognizable figures worked in. These are usually of wool woven into a cotton background. The best feature of the weaving is the subtle way color is blended so that it accents the figures in the textile.

Although there are some irritating things about the administration of this museum, if you are at all interested in this craft, you should come here. The ASUR Indigenous Art Association is an organization that has managed to revitalize the art of weaving in Bolivia and their attempt has resulted in many of the people getting a fair price for their product.

Weaver, Sucre.

Museo Sacro Jerusalen, Avenida Camacho and Avenida del Maestro, is open 9 am-noon and 3-6 pm on Monday, 4-8 pm, Tuesday to Friday, and 8 am-noon on Saturday. Entry costs $1. The church was built in honor of the Virgin of Candelaria in the early 1600s. Evidently, the most interesting items are the religious oil paintings, some done by leading European painters of the day. One, an example of Virreinal Art, is a mural that covers most of one wall. (Virreinal Art is a Colonial art style that encompasses history and iconology. One of the leading professors of the art is Ramon Meyica of the University Mayor de San Marcos in Peru.) I did not go into this museum as they were always closed when I was there.

LEND A HAND

Nanta Educational Center, Plazuela Cochabamba #315, ☎ 645-2523, is a non-profit organization that works with under privileged kids. They depend solely on donations and volunteers. Their brochure says they will take volunteers for one week or one year, whatever suits the person. If you have skills in teaching especially in the elementary areas, photography, with video equipment, music, organizational skills for expositions, fund raising, advertising or anything similar, they can use you.

Festivals

Yotala is a colonial village just nine miles/15 km from Sucre. Its biggest attraction is a **religious festival** in honor of Santa Rosa. The locals eat roasted pork, drink *chicha* and have fun. The name of the town means "the place where three rivers meet" in the local language. At 8,000 ft/ 2,450 m above sea level, the climate here is warmer than that of Sucre.

The one thing that can be done from Yotala is to hike across the tracks following the trail that goes up and over the ridge, then down to the Cachi Mayu River. Since this village is just past La Glorieta, it is a nice trip to do by bicycle. Cycle to Glorieta Mansion, take a tour, ride to Yolata and have lunch before cycling back (see *Joy Ride*, below). This route can also be done using local transportation.

Tarabuco is a village just 37 miles/60 km from Sucre and its Sunday market is a must. The villagers come from miles around to trade, eat and gossip while tourists come to shop, photograph and gawk. Although there are places to stay in the village, there is nothing going on except for the Sunday market so it is best to take the tourist bus from Sucre out in the morning and return at midday.

There are many fine weavings for sale in Tarabuco, but the variety and prices are no different than in Sucre. The most interesting thing is watching the locals in their colorful dress, leather or sequined hats, trading with each other or trying to get the tourists to pay for a photo. Of interest also is that the village was originally built to block the passage of the Chiriguano and Inca during territorial battles. If you look at the approach to the village, you will see some of its strategic advantages. Sneaking up would be hard with the gullies that surround the area.

On the second Sunday of March each year there is the **Phujllay** (POOK-yea) celebration when locals dress in their finest clothes and come to town to play ancient instruments, perform dances and sing songs about the legends. The dances are performed only by the men. The common belief is that this celebration is in memory of the Battle of Jumbate in 1816 when the people of the area killed a battalion of Spanish troops, leaving only their young drummer boy alive. After the battle, the men ate the hearts of the dead Spaniards in revenge for past abuses. However, this celebration was going on long before the Spanish came. The second legend has Tata Phujllay, a good devil, arriving in town on his horse and scaring the people because they did not know he was good. To make up for the fright, Phujllay left music and weavings. Also, he fertilized the land.

During this event, there is also a ceremony to honor the dead. Local decorators, called *damachis*, adorn two logs with flowers, fruits and local foods. The man in charge, the *Pasantes*, passes the abundance of goods on to the next leader, the *Pucara*. In acceptance of the leadership, this person must sow extra wheat, potatoes and barley in the fields.

This is one of the most colorful celebrations in Bolivia (next to Oruro Carnival).

Getting there and back is easiest by tourist bus. Tickets ($1.50) can be purchased at almost all hotels and at the office on Calle Arce #95 at the corner of San Alberto, Real Audiencia, Office #4, ☎ 644-3119.

■ Adventures on Foot

The **Cal Orck'o dinosaur tracks** are just 3.7 miles/six km from the center of town, in a quarry that is still being mined. Even though the workers looking after the tracks just found the first dinosaur bone the day I was there, they can't convince the local company or the government to leave the world's largest paleontological site in the world to paleontologists.

Cal Orck'o means Lime Hill in Quechua. The tracks come from now-extinct animals walking across a mud field. Because of tectonic movement, the once flat land has been pushed up so that it looks like a wall. On this wall are over 5,000 dinosaur impressions and fossils belonging to 290 animals dating back some 68 million years. Slabs of old lake bed sometimes slide off the wall, revealing even older tracks.

Take a ride in the Dino Truck.

The site was discovered in 1994. Dr. Christian Meyer from the University of Basel, Dr. Martin Lockley from the University of Colorado and Dr. Giusepi Leonardi from the University Della Sapienza in Rome investigated the site four years later. They found that the tracks of the titanosaurus indicate that these animals were up to 82 ft/25 m in height, much larger than was previously believed. There is another spot where one set of tracks covers a distance of 1,151 ft/350 m, the longest continuous dinosaur track in the world.

The Dino Truck, operated by **Abbey Path Tour Operators**, ☎ 645-1863, leaves the plaza in front of the cathedral every day at 9:30 am, noon and 2:30 pm. The cost for the ride out and back is $1.50 and the cost to enter the site is $3 per person. If you wish to walk one way and take the truck the other, you will be charged for a two-way ticket. During Carnival, the truck is a prime target for *globos*. At the site a hard hat is supplied and must be worn and you must travel with a guide. Guides speak English well and were as entertaining as the tracks themselves.

If you wish to walk to the tracks, follow Avenida Ostria Gutierrez past the bus station and the intersection for the road to Tarabuco. Continue along that road for about an hour or so and you will see the quarry on the hill alongside a huge slab of rock that leans on an upward slant. It is an interesting walk through residential and light industrial areas.

Two other sites have tracks nearby. One is at **Calancha**, just 4.3 miles/ seven km from town, and the other at Nucchu, 14 miles/23 km from town. Calancha has about 80 prints dating back 65 million years. However, the best ones are at Cal'Orcko.

Hiking

CEMETERY: The cemetery on Calle Linares and Bustillos is considered the most beautiful in the country. Everyone in Sucre will tell you not to miss the cemetery. Gardens separate the tombs of ex-presidents and people like the Prince and Princess of La Glorieta, and there are marble mausoleums and headstones that are worth a look. I agree with the locals that this is one of the prettiest cemeteries in the country. At the entrance is the inscription, "Hodie Mihi Cras Tibi," which means "today for me, tomorrow for you." My translation is, "You'll be joining me here soon, buddy."

CHURUQUELLA & SICA SICA: These two hills flank the southern border of the town. Legend has it that during the time of the Potosi mining boom, two men hid some treasure in the hills. The treasure has never been found, but maybe on the walk up you'll notice it. One hill features the Stations of the Cross. These are not spectacular stations; they are stone stands with a few ceramic pieces depicting what stage Christ was in while carrying his cross to Calvary. Some of the large cactus on the hill are worth noting. The second hill has nothing on it but shade and a few trails. There are no services on the hills, so take water.

OBISPO MOUNTAIN: At 11,350 ft/3,450 m, this is the highest in the Sucre area. Although not snow-covered, it is a challenge to hike on an overnight trip. If you do not have your own camping gear, do a day hike and have someone drop you at a start point so that you hike only 12 miles/ 20 km of the trail. Sur Andes (☎ 645-2632) in Sucre offers this hike on a regular basis. You can also hire a guide in town to take you on the trail.

The start of the trail is at Yolata where you cross the tracks and follow the trail (road) up over the ridge and down to Rio Cachi Mayu. From there you must cross the river to San Antonio and continue along the trail to Obispo Pass. Then it is downhill to Quila Quila, 16 miles/26 km from Sucre. Near the village are the Marka Rumy petroglyphs. From Quila Quila you will start to head back toward San Juan. This is a long hike, made interesting by the desert-like landscape.

MARAGUA CRATER: The crater is a giant hole covering about six square miles/15 square km. Geologists believe it was made by a meteorite thousands of years ago. In or near the crater are a number of villages, each with something of interest. There are also the rock paintings that should be visited. Potolo, perched on the edge of the crater, is where the most-difficult-to-design weavings originated. Maragua is the only village that has some basic services. The town is inside the crater. There's a beautiful hacienda in Chaunaca that can be used as a central base for exploring (a stayover is better than day-tripping from Sucre). If you do return, the last bus leaves Potolo about 3 pm daily in dry season.

INCAMACHAY & PUMAMACHAY: These rock paintings are 18 miles/30 km from Sucre and a two- to three-hour hike (about six miles/10 km) from Chataquila (see below). They come from the Huruquillo culture and depict animals, plants and abstract designs. The paintings from Incamachay are about 1,500 years old and are mostly red and white, while those at Pumamachay are about 2,000 years old and done in black. The paintings have suffered from vandalism and modern graffiti. One character (I don't know if he is old or new) looks like a school kid jumping up and pulling his hair out.

The walk is better than the paintings. It takes about three hours for the return trip. To get here you can take a long hike from Chaunaca (see below) or take a bus to Chataquila, walk to the paintings and then return to Sucre on the same day. The last bus leaves Potolo at 3 pm and would pass Chataquila about an hour later. You can also join a tour.

CHATAQUILA TO CHAUNACA: This is a three-mile/five-km hike along a pre-Inca trail. If staying at the hacienda in Chaunaca, you can also take in the rock paintings at Incamachay and Pumamachay.

To get to the start of the hike at Chataquila, where the pre-Inca path and the road to the paintings are, you must take a truck heading to Potolo. You ride in the back of a truck shared with a hundred locals, their children, chickens, goats and sacks of corn. The ride to Potolo is possible only during dry season. Three sprinkles of water make the road too slick. With four sprinkles, the sides of the mountains start to slide. The last bus coming back leaves Potolo at 3 pm and passes Chataquila about an hour later.

At Chataquila, less than two hours from Sucre, you jump off the truck and start the hike. The one along the pre-Hispanic road is steep in places and occasionally without pavement. It is less than six miles/10 km to the end of the road and the bottom of the hill where the village of Chaunaca is located. Along the trail are some old retaining walls and drainage systems.

In Chaunaca you can stop and have something to drink, but there is no place to stay except the school (reported to be uncomfortable) or the restored hacienda, Samay Huasi, where you can enjoy the area in style.

Samay Huasi, ☎ *645-4129, samay_huasi@latinmail.com, $$$$,* is a colonial resting house at 9,375 ft/2,850 m above sea level. It is perfect to use as a home base for other activities like seeing the rock paintings, visiting the dinosaur tracks nearby and hiking the pre-Hispanic trail again. The hacienda is on the confluence of the Potolo and Ravelo rivers just 24 miles/40 km from Sucre and shadowed by three high Andean peaks that are challenging to hike even though they are not high enough to be snow-tipped. It is possible to spend a month in this place and never become bored. Mules and bicycles can be rented from the hotel owners. The rooms at Samay Huasi are clean, with white plaster walls and windows overlooking a courtyard. Each has a private bath and hot-water showers. There is no electricity in the area, so night light is either by candle or propane lamp. There is a restaurant on site and you can opt for an all-inclusive package. The cost for all-inclusive is $25 per person in low season and $30 in high. This is a bargain.

CRATER HIKE: The hike to the edge of the crater from Chaunaca takes another two hours, minimum. From Chaunaca take the trail going south through the fields rather than along the road. Once at the crater's edge, use binoculars to pick out the obsidian deposits that are always on the surface and sparkle in the sun like black glass. This rare rock was usually chipped into knife blades and was highly prized by indigenous people from Alaska to Tierra del Fuego. Other things of interest in the crater are stalagmites and stalactites that indicate there was once a cave here. Without binoculars you can see the green and red hills that blend together to form an arch called the **Serranias de Maragua**. The green is from copper deposits and the red is from iron. Any of the other colors are from rarer mineral deposits and plants. The occasional dots that move along the landscape are people dressed in the best of weavings. If not staying in Chaunaca, continue down to Maragua where there are basic places to stay.

POTOLO HIKE: Potolo is a tiny village where the people live in stone houses with stone fences separating properties. The women wear black dresses that have a full skirt and embroidery along the hem. At the waist they wear a woven band that is usually red, pink or orange on black with mythological figures woven into the pattern. This is the Jalq'a style of weaving and is one of the most complicated styles in the world.

To get there you can continue on the truck that stops at Chataquila or you can join a tour. If walking from Maragua, take the trail going to Lajalaja and, once over the lip of the crater, continue to your left (south) along the road to Potolo. The walk is spectacular and the arrival in Potolo is reminiscent to visiting highland villages in remote areas like Tibet or Guatemala. This is a true adventure. To return to Sucre, you must go the same way you came, either by truck or walking.

■ Adventures on Wheels

 There are a few places recommended for riding a bicycle from Sucre. These routes take between three and seven hours and, because of elevation, are not easy unless you are fully acclimatized. If going with Joy Ride (see *Tour Operators,* below), they can take you to the top of a hill in a truck so that you aren't exhausted before you start. Or you can rent a bike, get trail descriptions and head out on your own.

K'atalla, or the **Seven Waterfalls**, is five miles/eight km north of Sucre on the Quirpinchaca River. The ride is mostly downhill going there, but 70% uphill coming back. This is an easy route and no guide is needed. The owners of Joy Ride will provide a map when you rent your bike.

Share a van ride to the hilltop, then cruise downhill.

The waterfalls themselves are really not seven falls. They are more like two, but the area is pretty, standing at 9,046 ft/2,750 m and overlooking the valley. Here it is quiet and the water is green. Birders should flock to the area to spot some of the dry-land birds. There is a campsite near the falls.

The **Loyola to San Juan to Aranjuez** trip is an all-day ride that covers about 18 miles/30 km. It is 100% downhill if you go on a tour. The driver will take you to the top of the hill across the valley from Cerro Obispo and overlooking the Chullchuta River. The cycle down to the river is easy. It is not too steep and the scenery is excellent. It takes a couple of hours for those who want to admire the scenery and less than an hour for those racing. At the bottom of the hill is a spot where you can have a snack, load the bikes and go to the next hilltop. From there you can cycle back to Sucre with just 5% of the ride being uphill.

You can eliminate the second hill run if you're short on time. See Joy Ride for information and recommendations that will suit your skill level.

■ Adventures of the Brain

 Academia Latin America, Calle Dalence #109, ☎ 646-0537, www.latinoschools.com, is run by Sandra del Corral de Maldonado. This language school has been in South America for about 14 years and the one in Bolivia has been around for five. They give a placement test before setting you up with a group. Usually, students take one month of lessons, studying four hours per day, five days a week. They also live with a family. The cost is between $5 and $7 per hour for lessons and $12 per day for room and board. This is a high cost of living. The school uses tapes and videos to supplement the teaching. Homework is given and your assignments increase in difficulty with your skill level. They also encourage extracurricular activities like dance, cooking, sports or films. The school is accredited with 18 American universities.

The recommended time for survival Spanish is two to three weeks for upper level students and three to four weeks for medium level. If you want proficiency you need eight to 12 weeks. New classes start every Monday and cost $100 for 20 hours of group study. The teachers are professionals who have been lawyers, engineers, and so on. You are encouraged to volunteer for some work in your own area of expertise.

> **AUTHOR NOTE:** You may want to pay by the week rather than for an entire month, just in case you are not happy. Also, I suggest you find your own home to live in, rather than booking through the school. That way, the family gets a better cut.

Fox Language Academy, Calle San Alberto #30, ☎ 644-0688, offers conversational Spanish for beginners. They have a home-stay program and run cultural excursions so that the student will be able to practice while a teacher is around to help with grammar. The cost is just over $5 an hour. This is a small school, but certainly not inferior to others in town. Fox also teaches classes in Quechua.

Cultural Institute of Bolivia, Calle Avaroa #326, ☎ 645-2091, www. icba-sucre.edu.bo, is affiliated with the Goethe Institute of Germany. They offer 45-minute classes and as many as eight a day can be attended. The staff speaks English, German or French in addition to their own language. The cost is $6 per lesson for individual classes, $4 if there are two students and $2.50 per person if there are three to five in the class. You get one free lesson for every 16 you take. They have a minimum of 12 lessons per course, but this could be completed in a very few days if only survival Spanish is wanted.

For those staying longer, home-stay programs can be arranged. There is also a good library for students, with books, tapes, magazines and newspapers in Spanish, German and English.

■ Tour Operators

Joy Ride Motor Bike Tours, Calle Oritz #14, ☎ 642-5544, www.joyridebol.com, use Honda XR 400s for their tours. To go on this tour you must have a motorbike license and be serious about riding. If you do not have a valid license you can ride but you must leave a $1,000 deposit to cover costs if there should be an accident. The bikes are not automatic; they have a clutch. A two-day trip to the Altiplano is an extreme-type trip. You can start riding in the morning when the temperature is 19°F/-7°C. This is cold. Insurance is included in the price.

Joy Ride also has bicycles, Raleighs and Konas (16 gears) with front-end suspension. You can rent bikes and go on your own for $2.50 an hour or you can join one of their guided and already scouted-out routes that cost anywhere from $12 to $39. These trips last three to seven hours. To cycle up hills, you should first be acclimatized. This is an excellent way to enjoy the area. There are waterfalls and small villages to visit. Some tours include a motorized lift to the top of a hill.

Candelaria Tours, Calle Estudiantes and Oritz, ☎ 648-1601, www. candelariatours.com, 8:30 am-12:30 pm and 2:30-6:30 pm daily, opened in 1975. Candelaria offers specialized tours such as to weaving centers or archeology sites. They also run Hacienda Candelabra, 13 miles/22 km from Tarabuco. You can stay at the hacienda and be introduced to skills like baking in a clay oven or weaving. Ecla Canyon is nine miles/15 km from the hacienda; if you wish to visit the canyon, you must stay at the hacienda overnight, spend the next day hiking and return to Sucre the following day. The historical tour that goes with the hacienda stay includes a lecture on topics like the granaries, the chapel and events that occurred during the land reforms of 1952. Returning from the hacienda, you will stop at the Sunday market in Tarabuco. English, German and Italian are spoken by the guides.

Eclipse Travel, Calle Avaroa #310, ☎ 644-3960, offers hiking tours around Sucre from three hours to four days. The most interesting and difficult sites to reach are the Maragua crater and Potolo. Due to the variety of things to see in the Maragua crater area, there are numerous hikes from which to choose.

Tourismo Sucre, Calle Bustillos #117, ☎ 645-2936 or 646-0349, offers tours to Maragua crater, Chataquila, Potolo and the Chaunaca pre-Inca trail. The cost is $10 for half a day and $18 for a full day. These tours do not operate during rainy season. This company also has a half- or full-day city tour. In a city as interesting as Sucre, a tour is a great opportunity to learn about things not covered in guidebooks.

Sur Andes, Calle Nicolas Oritz #6, ☎ 645-2632, offers half- and one-day horseback riding trips into the mountains. Their half-day trips require very little riding experience. The full-day option, which includes a dip in the Cachi Mayu River, requires some experience with horses. The route has some steep descents and covers about 10 miles/16 km. Rates are a mystery. I tried to get information from the company, but was unable to do so. The girl at the desk refused to tell me. However, if a horse trip is what you want, you may have to deal with them.

Marco Polo Tours, Calle Quijarros and Matos, ☎ 622-6143, also offers tours to the outlying villages of Potolo and Maragua. One of the advantages of going by tour rather than independently is that the villagers expect you and are prepared (because they are paid) to tell stories and legends. The tours cost about $30 a day.

Altamira Tours, Avenida del Maestro #50, ☎ 645-3525, offers three-to-five-day tours in vehicles, or a three-day walking trip into the Potolo and Maragua crater area. Custom hiking trips are also offered and their prices are comparable to everyone else's (between $25 and $50 a day).

▪ Places to Stay

Katalla Camping, ☎ 771-28627 *(cell)*, *$*, is five miles/eight km north of Sucre near the Seven Waterfalls. It's a rustic place tucked into the vegetation where camping costs $2 per person and a basic cabin costs $3.50. There is a fully supplied kitchen and a bench-style dining suite. Hammocks hang around the porch and a comfortable games room offers dominos, ping pong and cards.

Las Colinas

Sucre
Hotels &
Restaurants

Bus Station

CALLE LOAYZO

CALLE A O GUTTEREZ

GERMAIN MENDOZA

JAMIE MENDOZA

to 26

LEMOINE

MAESTRO VON BRAUN MENDOZA

MOLINA

VENEZUELA

Parque Simon Bolivar

URRIOLAGOITIA

PASTOR SAINZ

MORENO

OLANETA

TARAPACA DESTACAMENTO 111

COLON

CORDOVA

LA PAZ

LOA

JUNIN

SILES

LOA

RAVELO

ARENALES

AYACUCHO

ANICETO ARCE

JUNIN

ESPANA

BOLIVAR

CAMARGO

SAN ALBERTO

AVAROA

GRAU

ARGENTINA

AZURDUY

RAFAEL BUSTILLO

J J PEREZ

DALENCE

POTOSI

CALVO

ORURO

PADILLA

SUIPACHA

PLACES TO STAY
1. International Hostal
2. Residencial Gloria, Hostal Austria
3. Huespede San Marcos
4. Villa de la Playa
5. Hostal Charcas
6. Residencial Bolivia
7. Hotel Real Audiencia
8. Capital Plaza Hotel
9. Grand Hotel
10. Hotel España
11. Hostal Indepencia
12. El Hotal de su Merced
13. Premier Hotel
14. Del Rosario Hostal
15. Hostal Paulista

PLACES TO EAT
16. Chifa Restaurant Hong Kong
17. Joy Rider Bolivia
18. Restaurant Suizo
19. La Repizza
20. Café Travieso
21. La Choza Restaurant
22. Café Gourmet Mirador
23. Kaktus Restaurant
24. Kaypichu Vegetarian Restaurant
25. El Germen
26. El Huerto Restaurant
27. Café Tertulias
28. Café Berlin
29. Gnadenlos Café
30. Café Capota, Snack Pascana
31. La Taverne
32. El Virgelito Restaurant
33. Salamandra Café & Bar
34. La Milaneza
35. El Solar
36. Pata Ti Chocolate

NOT TO SCALE

HUNTER PUBLISHING

HOTEL PRICES (US $)

Per person, per day, unless noted otherwise.

$....................................	$2-$5
$$...................................	$5-$10
$$$..................................	$11-$17
$$$$.................................	$18-$25
$$$$$................................	Over $25

The **Hostel**, *part of the Hostelling Association of Sucre, Calle Guillermo Loayzo #119,* ☎ *644-0471, $,* is one block from the bus station and, like the hostel in Uyuni, is a fine place. In addition to regular rooms, they offer a colonial bedroom for two for $20. It has a larger-than-average bathroom with a Jacuzzi tub. Everything here is colonial. The colonial furniture throughout is glittering white and interspersed around the colonial building are balconies overlooking a flower garden. There are ceramic tiles on the floors and the cheaper rooms without bath have lockers. The bathrooms and the kitchen are spotless. The dining room is huge and there is laundry service. The only drawback is the location, about a 20-minute walk down to the plaza.

Residencial Gloria, *Avenida Augusto Gutierrez #438, across from the bus station,* ☎ *645-2847, $,* has 15 rooms and rates include breakfast. It is bright and clean, with wood floors, large windows, a patio and clean communal bathrooms.

Huespede San Marcos, *Calle Arce #233,* ☎ *606-2087, $,* is just three blocks from the plaza, tucked back off the street where it is quiet. The 14 rooms (with and without a private bath) are set around a flower garden. They are large and nondescript, with wood floors and tiled bathrooms. Best of all is the fully equipped kitchen that is as clean as the rest of the place, plus a porch where one can relax. This is a real deal.

Residencial Los Angeles, *Avenida Jaime Mendoza #1802,* ☎ *746-2516, $,* has rooms with or without a private bath. This is not an inviting place.

The new **Villa de la Playa**, *Calle Arce #369,* ☎ *642-2577, Iisis208@yahoo.com, $$,* is run by Ruth Cabrera. It can accommodate 12 people in all. There are two, two-bedroom suites that have a kitchen, living room and bathroom. Ruth also has two tiny rooms on the patio that can be rented by students for long-term stays. Upon arrival, you must ring the doorbell as the house is kept locked. The place is spotless. Ruth is friendly and helpful and guests (including me) do not like to leave. The patio has a sitting area and a hammock. This is a real deal and highly recommended. I suggest you e-mail to make reservations.

Hostal Charcas, *Calle Ravelo #62,* ☎ *645-3972, $$,* has three floors of rooms set around a central courtyard. Rooms are of average size, clean and fresh. The water is so hot that cold needs to be added when shower-ing. If you need a guide or information on schools, ask to see Elva Ines de Bueno, ☎ 644-1892. She is knowledgeable and helpful and, if not working at the hotel, may be your guide on a tour to Potolo. She knows the area well.

Residencial Bolivia, *Calle San Alberto #42,* ☎ *645-4346, $$,* has rooms with or without private bathrooms. The rooms are large, clean and have wood floors. This is a good deal.

Hostal Austria, *Avenida Ostria Gutierrez #506,* ☎ *645-4202, $$,* has large, bright rooms with nice curtains. The hotel is really homey.

Hostal Paulista, *Avenida Jaimi Mendoza #1844,* ☎ *644-1769, $$,* has 41 clean rooms of moderate size with no outside windows. Discount are of-fered for longer stays. To get to the front desk you must walk along a hall-way that has the display windows from a paint store. The Paulista is a 15-minute walk from the main plaza.

Del Rosario Hostal, *Calle Azurduy #151,* ☎ *644-0464, $$$,* has rooms around a central courtyard. Though small, they do have cable TV, tele-phones and private bathrooms. The hostel is near the cemetery.

Hotel España, *Calle España #138,* ☎ *644-0850 or 646-0295, hoespana@ cotes.net.bo, $$$,* offers rooms with private bathrooms and breakfast in-cluded in the rate. Located around a covered central courtyard, the rooms are large and clean, with wood floors and matching décor. They also con-tain writing desks and VCRs.

Grand Hotel, *Calle A. Arce #61,* ☎ *645-1704 or 645-2461, $$$,* has been in Sucre since 1960. It is a grand old place, modeled after the one in Paris. All rooms have private bathrooms and cable TV. The restaurant is always busy for lunch with the business crowd and the staff is friendly and atten-tive.

Hostal Indepencia, *Calle Calvo #31,* ☎ *644-2256, $$$$,* has singles, doubles, triples and suites. The price includes a buffet breakfast. This is a lovely place with large bright rooms, great colonial architecture, color TVs, mini-bars, Internet service and a restaurant. There is a flower gar-den in the patio and ceramic tiles in the halls.

Premier Hotel, *Calle San Alberto #43,* ☎ *645-2097 or 645-1644, $$$$,* is a four-star hotel that includes a buffet breakfast in its rates. Spacious rooms are set around a bright and cheery courtyard. They have a king-sized bed, double dresser with mirror, tiled bathroom and plush carpet, as well as a stocked bar and cable TV. The hotel is clean. The restaurant, La Candela, has formal décor and is open to the public. There is safe parking inside the premises and laundry service is available.

El Hotal de Su Merced, *Calle Azurduy #16,* ☎ *644-2706 or 644-5150, $$$$,* is an immaculately restored colonial house. Tastefully decorated rooms are set around a central garden and all have private bathrooms. Some include a small sitting area. There is laundry service available and a restaurant where the complimentary breakfast is served. Special diets will be catered to. This is an attractive place that has accommodated some of the leaders of South America.

Paola Hostal, *Calle Colon #138,* ☎ *644-1419, $$$$*, is another finely restored colonial mansion that has plants and pottery around its lush garden. The inside courtyard is tiled and sparkles. Rooms are large and comfortable, with cable TV, sitting areas, stocked fridges and Jacuzzi tubs in the tiled bathrooms. Breakfast is included and special diets can be accommodated.

Capital Plaza Hotel, *Plaza 25 de Mayo #28,* ☎ *642-2999 or 645-3242, www.capitalplazahotel.com, $$$$$.* This old hotel was built in 1917 and has been continually restored and remodeled so it can offer modern luxury. Moderately sized rooms are carpeted and have comfortable beds and night tables. The bathrooms are tiled. There is a central courtyard, a formal restaurant and piano bar on site, plus a pool and business center with free Internet access. You can change traveler's checks here and the staff can arrange car rentals. Rates: $45 single; $55 double; $70 triple; $80 suite.

Hotel Real Audiencia, *Calle Potosi #142,* ☎ *646-0823, real_aud@mara. scr.entelnet.bo ,$$$$$*, has rooms and suites. Room rates include a buffet breakfast and the hotel offers a small discount if you stay longer than one night. This is the classiest hotel in Sucre and it offers a pool, saunas (both dry and wet), and a terrace with a view of the entire city. Free transportation to and from the airport is available. The foyer of the hotel is a classic lounge area decorated with plush antique-styled furniture. The halls are wide and interspersed with couches and chairs. A well-kept flower garden is a good spot to sit and relax, too. The huge rooms have a sitting area, TV, private bath and a fully-stocked fridge that even includes some Para Ti chocolate. Bedroom furniture is made of cherry wood and the bathroom has everything, including a hair dryer. The hotel is close to the Indigenous Art Museum. Rates: $40 single; $50 double; $60 suite for two.

■ Places to Eat

Joy Ride Bolivia, *Calle Nicolas Oritz #14 at Sucre,* ☎ *464-5455 or 462-5544*, has a groovy restaurant that serves espresso coffee (from a machine). They also offer fruit with yogurt and granola for breakfast. Their pancakes served with cane syrup can't be beat. The restaurant opens at 8 am so they are one of the few places that provide gringos with breakfast at a time when they want to eat it. Joy Ride also stays open at night until the last partier staggers down the street. There is an outdoor patio that has overhead heaters that are turned on during the cold weather. There's live entertainment on weekends. There is a useful travelers' bulletin board in the main restaurant area.

Chifa Restaurant Hong Kong, *on the plaza on Avenida Emilio Mendizabal #754,* ☎ *644-3962, and at Plaza 25 de Mayo #46,* ☎ *644-3272.* They have real Chinese food at both locations. The stir-fried veggies are a treat and the sweet and sour dishes are also well done in a Hong Kong style, rather than the bastardized American style. The portions are good and the prices are reasonable, $2-$2.50 a meal.

La Concepcion Bodega, *Calle Camargo #461,* ☎ *644-2876,* sells the best of the Concepcion wines. The owners are helpful in choosing a bottle to suit your occasion.

La Repizza, *Calle Nicolas Oritz #78,* ☎ *645-1506,* is popular with locals for lunch, but skip their pizza – it is all crust and not that good a crust either. Their lunches offer three good salad choices, as well as vegetarian lasagna, chili and spaghetti. Crêpes are on the breakfast menu.

Café Gourmet Mirador, *Calle Iturricha #281, at the Museo de los Niños, Tanga Tanga,* ☎ *644-0299,* has a new cook and menu. It is a highly recommended place to have a snack after or between museum visits. The cold cappuccino lathered in thick sweet cream will make you want to climb the hill just beyond the café.

Restaurant Suizo, *Calle Nicolas Oritz #42,* ☎ *642-3985,* is a clean little place that offers both Swiss and Bolivian foods. I had their curried chicken that was well presented and tasted just as good as it looked. The gypsy kabob was tasty too, but the Greek salad was nondescript. Both meals cost $3 and the salad was just under $2. Portions are adequate, but not large. They have live music on Saturday nights.

Café Travieso, *Calle Arce #237,* ☎ *644-7979,* has metal folding chairs and tables with tablecloths. Although the décor isn't the Hyatt, the food and prices are. They serve lasagna for $1.75, ravioli for less and tortellini for $1.50. They also have goulash or schnitzel and if you order in the morning you can have fondue. All the food I had here was excellent. This is a real find.

La Choza Restaurant, *Avenida O. Gutierrez #119,* is open at 8:30 am and does not close in the afternoon. It has a bamboo theme and each table is in a separate little cubicle. Their soups are less than a dollar and meat cooked on the grill runs from $1 to $1.50 per meal. On weekends they offer a special *chicharron* (sausage) in two portion sizes for $1 or $2. The place is spotless and the meals are tasty.

El Huerto Restaurant, *Calle Ladislao Cabrera #86,* ☎ *645-1538 or 642-9579.* To get here you will need to take a taxi, but your meal will make the fare worthwhile. El Huerto's is noted mostly for meat dishes like steak done on the barbecue. Although I never ate here, every taxi driver in the city recommends it.

Kactus Restaurant, *Calle España #176*, ☎ *644-7376*, opens every day at 7 pm. It's a small place that will soon have to be expanded because of its popularity. There is an extensive menu and I never heard "no hay" to any request. The meals are huge. Try the sweet and sour barbecue ribs for less than $4 – they are exceptional in flavor and size.

El Virgelito Restaurant, *Calle Cruz Verde #51 off Arce*, is not fancy but its Italian dishes are. This is off the main routes and usually patronized by upper class locals (and me).

Kaypichu Vegetarian Restaurant, Calle San Alberto #168, ☎ 644-3954, serves *almuerzo* Tuesday through Saturday in a tastefully decorated room (sadly, the seats are backless stools). The food is excellent and comes from a spotless kitchen. Breakfast here is the best in town, but the coffee at Joy Ride was better. The staff is friendly and useful; some speak English. There are piles of *Time* magazines (in English) around for the homesick. Open Tuesday to Sunday, 7:30 am-2 pm and 5-9 pm.

Café Capital and **Snack Pascana**, *Calle Anicito Arce, just below the square,* are good for simple and quick breakfasts. However, they don't open before 8:30 am.

El Germen, *Calle San Alberto #231*, ☎ *7713-1940 (cell)*, claims to be open from 8 am to 10 pm, but I often found it closed during those hours. It serves all vegetarian foods and excellent pastries. Along with a coffee, nothing could be better. There is also a book exchange.

Café Tertulias, *Plaza 25 de Mayo #59*, ☎ *642-0390*, is popular with travelers who come for a late-afternoon beer. The restaurant opens from 9 am to noon and then again from 4 pm to midnight. The food is more sandwiches and salads than full meals, although they do serve pasta and meat dishes.

Salamandra Café and Bar, *Calle Avaroa #510*, ☎ *691-3433*, was recommended but I didn't try it. This is not the place for a quick bite. You come here to dine.

Plaza Restaurant, *Plaza 25 de Mayo, up from Tertulias*, is a nice place to sit on the balcony overlooking the plaza. The food is not exceptional, but the waiters were pleasant.

La Milaneza, *Calle Argentina #49*, ☎ *642-2775*, specializes in fast food *Milaneza*. *Milaneza* is a meat that is pounded thin, breaded and fried. It is just as quick to cook as hamburger.

El Solar, *Calle Bolívar #800*, ☎ *645-4341*, serves local and international cuisine. Open since 1977, it has a reputation of serving the best *pique de la macho* in town ($4).

La Posada Café Restaurant, *Calle Audiencia #92*, ☎ *646-0101*, has an inside dining room and an outside patio. They have a different *almuerzo* every day. They are open Monday to Saturday, 10 am-10:30 pm, and Sunday, 11 am-3 pm.

Café Berlin, *Calle Avaroa #326,* is a good place to have your early evening beer and snack. Recommended are the Swiss-styled potatoes (*rellenas*) that are spiced and fried. However, it is the pastry that I really liked.

Gnadenlos Café, *Calle Bustillas #121,* ☎ *644-8258,* is open for breakfast around 8:30 am and serves granola with fruit and yogurt. This is always a draw in hot weather. They have a lot of vegetarian choices too. The owners also exchange books, arrange tours and know where there is a good Spanish teacher.

La Taverne, *Calle A. Arce #35,* ☎ *645-3599,* is both a restaurant and a cultural center where the French language is taught to local children. The restaurant is open daily from 8 am to noon and 6 pm until 11 pm. They specialize in French dishes and you have the choice of sitting inside under subdued light or out on the patio in the sun. Videos in French can be viewed on Wednesday, Friday and Saturday evenings at 7 pm for 50¢. There is often live music in the patio during the day.

■ Nightlife

Alaska Disco, Arce #4325, is fairly new, clean and not too loud. Since it is just up from the plaza, you get the quieter crowd (older than 20) patronizing the place.

Joy Ride Bolivia, Calle Nicolas Oritz #14 at Sucre, ☎ 464-5455 or 462-5544, is the *in* place to meet other *gringos*, drink beer and talk about things like travel, bikes and entertainment preferences, or just tell jokes. The bar sponsors a lot of specialty nights, like "Hawaii Night." They also bring in live entertainment on the weekends. For an idea about some of their crazy nights, go in and have a look at the photos on the walls. They are a fun bunch.

■ Shopping

Ajllay Wasi Arts and Craft Shop, Calle Audiencia #17, opens daily from 9 am-12:30 pm and 3-7:30 pm. It is just around the corner from Joy Ride and sells high-quality weavings for groups of women not involved with the co-op at the Indigenous Art Museum. Some smaller *chulpas* sell for $30-$40, a good price for good work. On the street, a slightly larger *chulpa* will cost $20 to $25, but the quality may be lower. This shop sells only the best quality Jalq'a weavings. Look to pay around $100 for a large wall hanging. I got a belt with weaving so tight it looks like the designs were painted on.

Para Ti Chocolate, Calle Arenales #7, ☎ 645-5689, www.chocolates-para-ti.com. If you come to Sucre and fail to taste the chocolate you are missing a main feature of the city. Visiting Bolivians take these chocolates home as gifts. The main shop is less than 100 ft/30 m off the square. Para Ti put out its first chocolates 50 years ago from a factory that had three machines. A few years later, it had 20 machines that produced chocolates using cacao from the Beni region of the Amazon. The company was bought out by Gaston Solares in 1990 (Solares decided on a career change, from brewing beer to making prize-winning chocolates). Some Para-Ti chocolates are made with a variety of grains melted into the chocolate for flavor and nutrition. Grains used include amaranto, one of the original cereal grains of the Inca, and quinoa, a grain grown in the Altiplano. However, in the shop, I did find the clerks rather dour.

BANG FOR YOUR BUCK

Quinoa can be puffed like popcorn, ground into flour, made into a paste or used as a cereal like couscous and is the only vegetable that has all eight of the essential amino acids.

The shop at the **Indigenous Art Museum**, San Alberto #413, ☎ 645-3841, does not allow you to take your pack into the store. They sell Jalq'a waistbands for $18 and good-quality *chulpas* for $30. Their selection is large and they often have numerous pieces of the same design. They are an Inca Pallay Co-op and purchase only from members.

Inca Pallay Co-op, Calle Bolívar #682B, ☎ 646-1936, is an association with locations in Sucre and La Paz. It helps weavers and artists from the Tarabuco and Jalq'a areas by putting their products on the world market for a fair price. They also give workshops and help administer them for local artists. The association manages the Indigenous Art Museum in Sucre (see above). On Sundays in Tarabuco, they occasionally sponsor traditional dancing demonstrations. They carry the works of many weavers who are not part of the Azule Co-op. The price of an average-sized *chulpa* runs $30-$40 for those from the Tarabuco area. You'll also find some wood carvings and silver products.

Campesino Mercado, is on Calle Arce just below Mendoza and covers several blocks. It doesn't have many souvenir-type crafts but is full of things locals need. I purchased a finely designed dress like those worn by the women from Potolo and I paid the same price *campesinos* would pay. They were happy to get my business and I was pleased with what I got. There are also hand-carved wooden spoons that I have found excellent in the kitchen. I have yet to figure out what makes them so comfortable to use.

Artesenias, Calle San Alberto #50, is open daily from 9 am to around 8 pm. The shop has one of the largest selections in the city. The lady in charge was suspicious when I spoke with her so a name and telephone number were not forthcoming. However, she is not pushy when you go inside to have a look. Her dolls are especially abundant and varied.

Ananay Craft Store, Plaza de la Recoleta, ☎ 644-0299, www. artesaniasdebolivia.com, carries, among other things, unique and creative ceramic pieces. I found a woven vest that was of better quality than some I saw in specialty shops in La Paz. The price was also higher. If looking for something different, stop in.

A TASTY OFFERING

Ch'alla is a wine made specifically as an offering made to Pacha Mama, Mother Earth. It is sold in markets. During a festival, locals sprinkle ch'alla on a floor or field in Pacha Mama's honor.

Supermercado SAS, Calle Bustillos #131, ☎ 646-2443, is for those products you don't want to buy in the market, like shampoo, razors or batteries. They are open daily from 8 am to 10 pm.

Tupiza

Altitude: 9,704 ft / 2,950 m
Population: 30,000

If you travel between Tupiza and Uyuni (the most common route used by travelers), the dry landscape goes from bleak desert dotted with plastic bags to hills that are carved by the wind, the debris creating sand dunes. A true desert is in the making. Once past Atocha the landscape becomes Grand Canyon-like, except the rock is loose conglomerate that is easily eroded by wind and rain. A few miles farther, the earth and sandstone turns red and the landscape is rugged and dry. The scenery grows more and more dramatic the closer one gets to Tupiza. If coming from Tarija, the route is on another of Bolivia's death roads. But the landscape is stunning and, as you cross the two high passes, you should see lots of wildlife.

Once in Tupiza, pull out your hiking boots as you will not be able to resist entering the canyons and ravines that are gates to the devil's home and places where ghosts and goblins hide. If you are not a hiker, try riding a horse the way Butch Cassidy and the Sundance Kid did. They are legendary around the area and it is fun to follow their trail. You can get in the mood by watching the movie, available at most hotels. If none of those activities are interesting, try visiting the Kallawaya naturopath living in town, ready to help with some of your ailments or just to give advice on how to live.

The longer people stay in Tupiza, the better they like it. The climate is dry and warm, the people are relaxed and happy.

■ Getting Here & Around

Most people come to Tupiza by bus or jeep. The mountain road into Tupiza from Uyuni is rough, but not the worst in the country.

There are daily buses to Potosi that leave at 7 pm and cost $4 for the seven-hour ride. There is one bus a day going to La Paz that leaves around 7 pm (but check because times change). The trip is 14 hours and costs $8 per person.

Numerous buses leave daily for Tarija, but if you want a day-time bus, you must wait until one of the companies has enough passengers to warrant the trip. Crystal frequently offers day-time trips at $7 for the nine-hour ride. The distance is 133 miles/218 km along another "Road of Death." Wise travelers will consider hiring a jeep, available through one of the tour offices. If going into the Chaco, to Argentina or Santa Cruz, you must get to Tarija to make connections.

■ History

The indigenous history of Tupiza is sparse due to the fact that most of the architectural and cultural remains disappeared even before the arrival of the Spanish. The **Chicha Indians** dwelled in the area but were absorbed by the **Inca** when they moved through on their way to places like Chile and El Fuerte in Samaipata. The Chicha called the area Tupesa, a word that is believed to mean red rock.

The **Spanish** arrived on the heels of the Inca but found little reason to stay and so moved on to Chile. In 1574 **Captain Luis de Fuentes** officially founded Tupiza while on his way to Tarija, the wine capital of Bolivia. He left behind a few Spaniards who established some fairly large ranches. As the struggles for independence heightened in the early 1800s, the indigenous groups became more militant and small battles in this region helped in the overall outcome.

After independence, mining companies moved in and developed silver, tin, antimony and lead mines. During the late 1800s, the Concordia Tin Mine, the Compaño de Aramayo, and the Chocaya Mining Company became exceptionally big and then Tupiza got its best break. Butch Cassidy and the Sundance Kid decided to make off with some of the mine's payroll. Little did the locals know the benefits in tourism that would result.

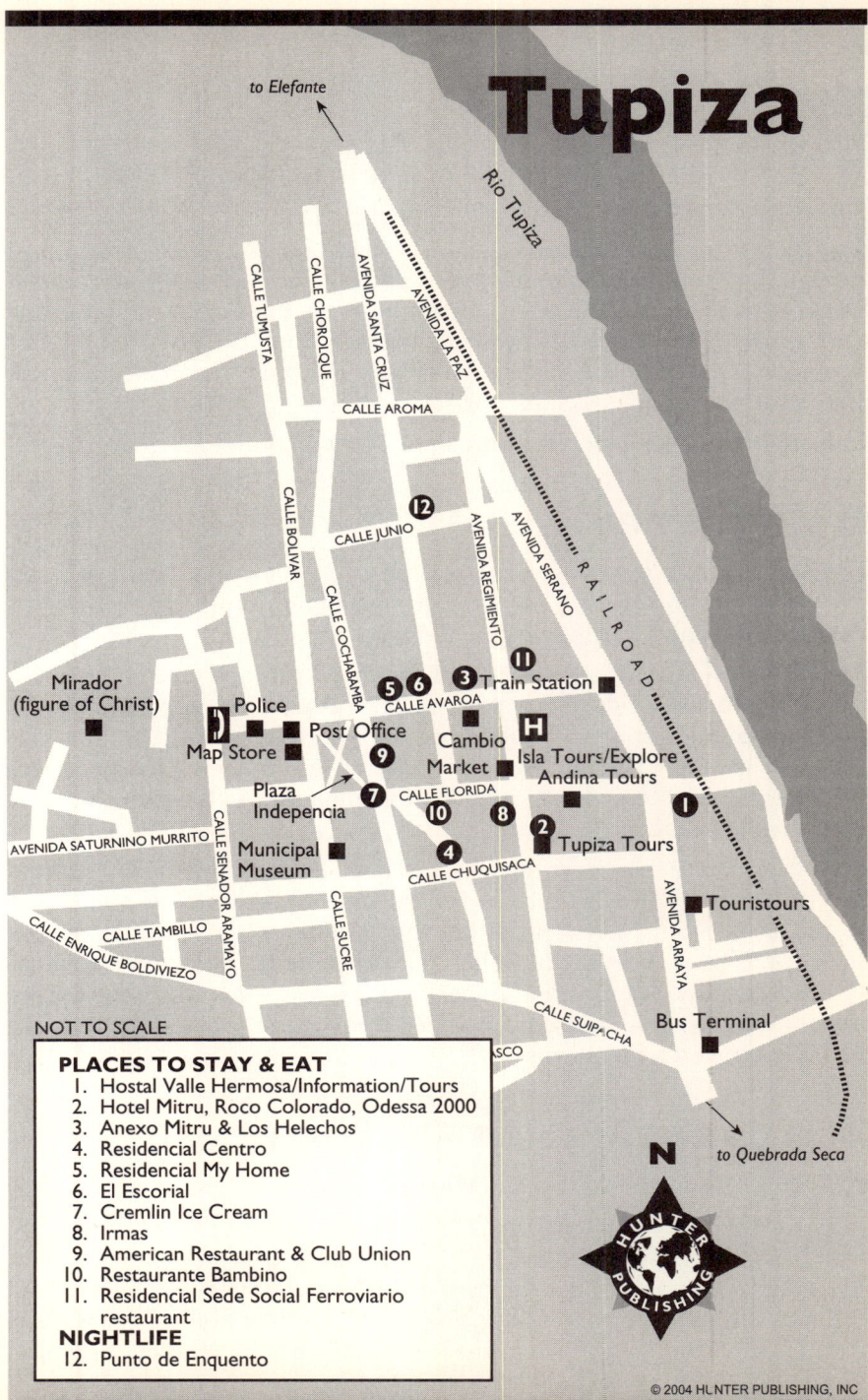

to Elefante

Tupiza

Rio Tupiza

CALLE TUMUSTA
CALLE CHOROLOQUE
AVENIDA SANTA CRUZ
AVENIDA LA PAZ

CALLE AROMA

RAILROAD

AVENIDA SERRANO
AVENIDA REGIMIENTO

12

CALLE JUNIO

CALLE BOLIVAR

CALLE COCHABAMBA

Mirador
(figure of Christ)

Police

Post Office

Map Store

5 6 3 Train Station
CALLE AVAROA

11

H
Cambio
Market
Isla Tours/Explore
Andina Tours

9

Plaza
Indepencia

7 CALLE FLORIDA

AVENIDA SATURNINO MURRITO

10 8 1

Municipal
Museum

2 Tupiza Tours

4
CALLE CHUQUISACA

CALLE SENADOR ARAMAYO

CALLE TAMBILLO

CALLE ENRIQUE BOLDIVIEZO

CALLE SUCRE

AVENIDA ARRAYA

Touristours

CALLE SUIPACHA

Bus Terminal

ASCO

NOT TO SCALE

N

to Quebrada Seca

HUNTER PUBLISHING

PLACES TO STAY & EAT
1. Hostal Valle Hermosa/Information/Tours
2. Hotel Mitru, Roco Colorado, Odessa 2000
3. Anexo Mitru & Los Helechos
4. Residencial Centro
5. Residencial My Home
6. El Escorial
7. Cremlin Ice Cream
8. Irmas
9. American Restaurant & Club Union
10. Restaurante Bambino
11. Residencial Sede Social Ferroviario
   restaurant
NIGHTLIFE
12. Punto de Enquento

■ Services

The **telephone office** is on Calle Senador Aramayo and Calle Avaroa.

The **post office** is on Plaza Indepencia on Calle Sucre.

The **police** station is on Plaza Indepencia.

A **money changer**, Cambio Latin America, Calle Avaroa, #154, ☎ 694-2985, charges 4% off the official rate on travelers' checks. She changes euros, Argentinean, Chilean, English and Peruvian money. She does not change Canadian currency. If you change more than US $100, she offers a discount on the commission. She is fast and efficient. The money changer across the street charges a higher commission.

The **hospital** is on Chichas between Calle Avaroa and Florida.

■ Sightseeing

Casa de Aramayo is an old estate that is going to ruin but still offers interesting exploration and photographic opportunities, especially in the soft sun of dusk.

Carlos Victor Aramayo, grandson of Avalino Aramayo (1809-1882), the man whose bust stands in the main plaza, was a tin and silver baron who owned the richest mine in the area before the revolution in 1952. It is also the company that Butch and Sundance robbed in their last job before meeting their deaths. It is a splendid hacienda and well worth the short walk over to see it.

To get there, cross the river at the south end of the city by the bus station and walk north until you are at the unfinished bridge that has no entrance or exit (only a center). From there, walk east toward the mountains. Once past the football field, you will come to the Aramayo estate with the remains of many buildings. Their roofs are gone so, unless some conservation is done, the mud brick will continue to deteriorate in the rain until the mansion is gone.

■ Adventures in Culture

Kallawaya Medicine Man is on the north side of the river across from the incomplete bridge (there is a center, but no on or off ramp).

Silvino Paredes Ricana comes from a Kallawaya family in the north of Bolivia. As a younger person, he grew up learning the Kallawaya ways of healing. He later studied naturopathic medicine from a school in Miami and a second school in La Paz. He has been practicing naturopathology since 1970.

Silvino has three beds and a special bath that he uses for his patients. For some conditions, he takes patients to the Salar de Uyuni where he uses special mud packs. This treatment is usually for digestive disorders, but his specialty is blood pressure disorders. He is an interesting man. However, you must know a fair amount of Spanish to understand what he is saying. If you need help and prefer alternative medicines, drop in for a visit.

The **Museum** on Calle Sucre is upstairs and next door to the military map office. It is they who have the key to the museum, which is open from 8 am to 6 pm. There is no charge to enter. The museum has one room packed with artifacts from the area. There are postcards from the Chaco war and a Paraguayan mauser, typewriters and typesetters from mine offices, ancient sewing machines, horse whips, stirrups and saddles, and news photos of Sundance and Butch Cassidy.

■ Adventures on Foot

There are many trails from Tupiza. The few described here are the easiest to access. However, once you become familiar with the area, ask around about other trails.

> **AUTHOR NOTE:** All these hikes require proper boots and you should carry at least two liters of water. Wear sunscreen and a peaked hat to shade your eyes and cover your head. Some snacks are a good idea.

ELEPHANT HILL: You'll see why Cerro El Elefante got its name as you walk this route. Going into the valley from the south end of town allows you to return by the same route if you have limited time. To get there, cross the river at the south end of town just past the bus station and walk north, or cross on the pedestrian bridge that is at the north end of the market and walk northeast. There is a good view of the elephant-shaped terrain from the pedestrian bridge. The cross on the top of Cerro La Cruz can also be seen. Go through a gap in the hills to the right of La Cruz. The hill always looks a bit like an elephant, but the view from the pedestrian bridge is the most convincing. Once through the gap, there is a wide valley or washout, populated by goats mostly. There are two or three haciendas in this unlikely place.

Head for the elephant's trunk. About halfway into the valley and to the left are some hobbit-like formations made from rock and red clay. One is a gigantic doorway where you can start making your way over the hills to another washout with a road running through it. There is no clear route from the stone doorway straight over the hill to the road on the other side. We went through and followed a dry creek-bed up and to the right. In the heat of the day, it was a grunt to get over the top. Staying in the channel generally keeps you out of the hawthorn bushes, but means you have to do some rock clambering and climbing. Once you are on the road, head left and pass through a smaller gap onto another road. Continue to the left on that road, through a highway checkpoint, down to Tupiza.

Should you continue farther up the valley in front of the elephant (rather than going through the hobbit-like doorway), you end up in an amphitheater surrounded by a high ridge. We could find no easy way through this hill to the road.

Approaching the trail from the opposite direction is easier for a circular route. To do this, walk out of town through the market, following the railway tracks. Follow the road that goes to Potosi, past the highway roadblock, past Escuela Genolieva and Bar and Pension Dos Hermanos. The road splits. Stay right, past another bar/pension and the highway checkpoint. A large washout will come from the right. Follow this into the hills. Four by fours have gone here. A second washout will flow into the first after about 15 minutes. Follow it to the top of the hill. You must go up into the hills before you come to the front of the elephant's snout. We were here in November, rainy season, and there was no water in the area.

Once at the top of the hill, pick your way down, veering toward hobbit land. You must go to the bottom on the far side of the doorway. You can return to town by walking down the gravel to the gap in the hills. This should take about three hours, depending on how much time you spend doing other things besides walking. Back in the village, walk to the south end and across the large bridge, beside the bus station. But first stop at the naturopath and Casa de Aramayo. Another option for returning to town is to work your way over to the walking bridge from the entrance/exit to the trail. This gets you to a soft drink much quicker.

When in the valley, regardless from which direction you enter, you can follow a trail up to the elephant on the far side of the valley. There is a waterfall up there during wet season. This is a nice four- to five-hour exploration.

GOBLIN CANYON: Cañon del Duende is at the beginning of this trail, but a little farther is the Valle de los Machos and beyond that the Cañon del Inca. Go in as far as you like and return by the same trails.

To reach the trailhead, walk south of town past the bus station. When the road turns east at the tracks, you turn south. Don't cross the tracks and don't cross the bridge going over Rio Tupiza. Continue south. This route runs beside the railway tracks and will eventually hook up with a road. Walk along the road for about an hour, past a swimming pool (it's clean and costs only 50¢ for the day – there is a smaller pool beside the main one for children). Continuing along the road, walk up the hill and, when you see a trail down below on your right, cut across land to meet it. Follow it back in the direction of town. You will find yourself in a gravel wash that has been used as a landfill. It is disgusting, but walk through a gate of high conglomerate pillars and you are in the canyon. The rocks on the wash where you are walking get bigger the farther in you go and the red fins of the mountains close in. This is a spectacular spot.

After walking for about a half-hour you will encounter a rock on the passage blocking the way. During high water this would be a waterfall. Although you can free climb past

Hiking Goblin Canyon.

the obstruction, I don't recommend it. An accident out here could turn ugly. We swung left (at the tree) and up a gully, hoping to get high enough to see Tupiza. We did, but we had to go back by the same way we came and then walk the road back to town. This is a spectacular all-day excursion.

DEVIL'S DOOR: Puerto del Diablo is close to town and popular for a day hike/photo session/horse trip. Walking in this dry landscape seems to leach the water out of your cells, so keep drinking. You should drink at least two liters every four hours.

To hike, cut across town toward the Mirador. Once on the street called Sanado Aramayo, turn south. You will pass a small park. Continue weaving your way through the streets past a children's park and then to the military practice grounds. Stay on the same path until you reach the garbage dump. Turn just before the dump and follow that trail into the hills, canyons and conglomerate fins. It's about three hours before you come to a waterfall. But going beyond the fall is also recommended. As you get to the Valley de los Machos you may (with the help of a guide) be able to find some Chichas Indian rock paintings. I did not do this hike beyond the Puerto del Diablo. The rock formations in this area are like nowhere else in South America. The most popular way to see this trail is on horseback.

Tupiza & Vicinity

to Uyuni   to Potosi

Flores Palca

Oploca

San Miguel

San Vincente – Butch Cassidy
& the Sundance Kid Route
(120 km)

Charahota

Magic Canyon

foot
bridge

Chilcobija

Palala

Cerro de
la Cruz

Elephant Hill
(3 km)

El Sillar

El Cañon (8 km)

Casa de Aramayo

incomplete
bridge

RAILROAD

TUPIZA

········· Trail

N

Puerto del Diablo (5 km)
Valle de los Machos

Garbage
dump

Swimming
Pool

Inca Canyon

Goblin Canyon (12 km)

El Angosto

Quebrada Seca

Rock Blocking
Pass

Palquiza

Toroyoj

La Torre

Chacopampa

Quebrada Yumia

Monte

Quiriza

Viscachani

to Talina

to Villazon

© 2004 HUNTER PUBLISHING, INC

NOT TO SCALE

EL CANON: El Cañon is reached by following Calle Chiquisaca until opposite the Mirador (with the huge Christ figure). Turn left along a washout that soon closes in. This area is especially known for its splendid cactus that blooms in a flaming red or creamy white around mid-December.

■ Adventures on Water

The pool next to the bus station is popular with local kids. They charge 50¢ for half a day. Another pool is on the road to Cañon del Duende (see above). The second pool has a large deck, clean water and charges 50¢ for the day. It is the one I would choose if I needed a swim.

■ Adventures on Horseback

Taking a horse on the trail of Butch Cassidy and the Sundance Kid from Tupiza, where the two planned their first Bolivian robbery, to San Vincente, where the two died, is an adventure. See *Tour Operators*, below, for a list of outfitters who can saddle you up.

Before going on the horse trip, be certain to watch the 1969 movie starring Robert Redford and Paul Newman portraying the life, Hollywood-style, of the two men. Also read Bruce Chatwin's book, *Patagonia*. He tells the story well. Villa Hermosa Tours offers this trip, as do other tour companies in town. However, it is from Jerome Luis and his wife Lilian of Villa Hermosa that I got the history of these two characters.

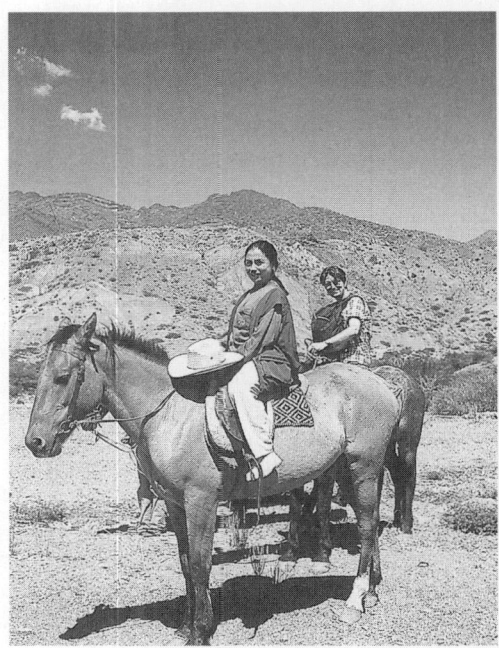

On the trail.

TRAIL OF BUTCH CASSIDY

Butch Cassidy was born in Utah as Robert LeRoy Parker on April 13, 1866. His grandfather was a Mormon who walked partway across the US 10 years before the birth of Robert, leading other faithful followers to Salt Lake City. On the way, Robert's father Max, who was 12 years old at the time, helped his mother bury her husband, Robert's grandfather, because he froze to death during the night in his sleeping bag. Once in Salt Lake City, Max married and started a family.

Butch Cassidy had worked in a butcher shop as a young man and, when a nickname was wanted (nicknames were popular in those days), he chose Butch. I am uncertain where the name Cassidy came from. His buddy, the Sundance Kid, got his name from the place where he spent his first and only jail sentence, in Sundance, Wyoming.

By the mid-1880s Butch was a handsome young dude wanting to experience the thrill of a wild ride and a few wild women, so he headed west with Sundance. However, he needed money to pay for the whiskey and the women, so the two, along with Tom McCarty, Matt Warmer and Bart Madden, pulled a job at the bank in Telluride, CO and netted $10,000. It was 1889. Butch was 23 years old and the occupation he took for the next 19 years of his life was decided upon.

After he served a few months in prison for possession of a stolen herd of horses, Butch teamed up with Kid Curry and formed a gang with the romantic name of the Wild Bunch. The gang was a motley crew that included 20 people. Some were card sharks, others were fast with a gun and three were women who worked in sporting houses. It was 1896 and the west was still wild and dangerous.

By 1897 the group was being hunted by the Pinkertons, the best bounty hunters in the Americas. The Wild Bunch broke up. Butch and Sundance, now with $4,000 on their heads, rode down to Mexico. But they were being pursued and so continued south by boat and eventually settled in Argentina. There, they purchased a ranch and tried to lead a crime-free life. But that soon got boring so they pulled a trick or two before heading into Bolivia. They crossed the border in 1906.

In the movie, this is where Butch says to Sundance, "So, when I say Bolivia, you just think California. You wouldn't believe what they're finding in the ground down there. They're just fallin' into it. Silver mines, gold mines, tin mines, payrolls so heavy we'd strain ourselves stealin' 'em."

The two started out by robbing a bank in Eucalyptus, not far over the border. Then they hit a train near the same village. With their pockets lined, they started working for the Concordia Tin Mines near Tupiza. They still had Etta with them, one of the original Wild Bunch members (she's the school teacher in the movie), but at this point she left and went back to the States for surgery and the boys became part of the social life of the community.

Butch liked his booze and his tongue was always loosened after a few drinks. He often bragged about one or two of the jobs he'd pulled. A few robberies occurred that were unaccounted for and although locals became suspicious, they did nothing.

Working for the mining company gave Butch and Sundance inside information as to when and where the payrolls would be passing. It was in the square of Tupiza that they made their plans to rob the payroll belonging to the Chocaya Tin and Silver Mine. As the heavily laden mules were passing over the mountains going toward San Vicente, Butch and Sundance struck.

Shortly after that heist, they went to visit a Scottish engineer who lived in Verdugo about 12 miles/20 km south of Tupiza. The two bandits planned on robbing the Tupiza bank but, just before the heist, they learned that it was heavily guarded by the Bolivian army. Because they had been successful in robbing the payroll of the Chocaya mines, they decided to do the same when the mules carrying money for the Aramayo mining company were heading to Quechisla.

On November 3rd, 1908 Butch and Sundance followed the payroll caravan from the Ayamaro Hacienda in the village of Salo as it snaked its way up Vaca Huañusca Pass. They rode up, took the money with no trouble and rode off with no adieu.

But miners are not men to be bargained with. They were angry that their payrolls had disappeared so they formed a posse, informed border guards by telegraph to watch for the *gringos*, and joined the army that was already on the trail of the two bandits.

Butch and Sundance learned of the chase from their Scottish friend who, after some questioning, got a confession out of the two as to who they were. Butch and Sundance headed into the mountains towards Uyuni crossing the pass near San Vicente. They stopped in the village to feed themselves and their horses. There was no hotel in San Vicente so the two got food from a local (Bolivians will help anyone). But when they paid in cash, acted nervous, and asked many questions, including border crossing particulars, the Bolivian became suspicious. He said he was getting some beer, but instead left and informed the army.

When the army approached the house, Butch saw them and started shooting. He killed one soldier and the gunfight began in earnest. When darkness came, all went quiet. The next morning, the army officer went to the door of the cabin but there was no response to any questions. Inside, the officer found that Sundance had been shot numerous times with the final bullet, probably delivered by Butch, in his (Sundance's) head. It also looked like Butch had shot himself. And so, the manhunt was over. The two were dead and shortly after buried in Bolivia.

It is not confirmed that the bodies in the San Vicente cemetery, in the grave with the crude wooden cross that simply says "fallecer" (to pass away or to die) on it, are those of Butch and Sundance.

■ Tour Operators

The advantage of taking the tour from Tupiza is that, as a home base, Tupiza is a nicer place to stay than Uyuni.

Valle Hermoso Tours, Avenida Pedro Arraya #478, ☎ 694-2370, in the hotel of the same name, offers numerous tours, including a four-day excursion around the Salar de Uyuni by jeep. This company is best known for its horseback trips that go from half a day up to four days. The horses are gentle (even I could manage them), the saddles are padded with sheepskins, and the guides know how to handle and care for animals. The horses I saw had no sores, were not skinny, and were shoed. A horse with a split hoof is not a happy animal. If your horse throws his neck around, it means that something is wrong, he hurts somewhere. Be aware of this. The English spoken at Valle Hermoso is excellent. Horses rent for $2.50 an hour. Hermosa offers tours to Puerto del Diablo, the Valle de los Machos, and across the Bolívar Valley to Angosto, where you will pass through two natural tunnels, one for vehicles and the other for trains. This is also where the legendary Devil's Drum is located (see below). The ride ends at La Torre, a rock tower where you can have a swim before returning. The classic four-day trip covers the route of Butch Cassidy and the Sundance Kid. If you have time, this excursion, like Uyuni Salt Lake, is a must.

MAYHUATO RUNS WHEN THE DEVIL DRUMS

In the mountains near the natural tunnels of El Angosto are many caves where creatures can hide. There is also a stone shaped like a drum. Some nights, the sound of a drum can be heard through the mountains. The locals believe the devil plays the drum to scare away Mayhuato (my-WAT-o), a hairy creature much like the Yeti of Tibet or the Sasquach of Canada, who lives in the caves.

This story was told to me by Jeronimo Luis.

Tupiza Tours, Avenida Chichas #187, ☎ 694-3001, www.tupizatours.com, is in the lobby of the Mitru Hotel. They offer anything from a half-day tour by jeep or/and horse to a four- or five-day trip ending in Uyuni. A half-day jeep trip with a full group of six people can cost as little as $7 per person. Horse trips can last three, five or seven hours or take up to two days. Rates are $20 per day, including food. One of their trips includes a visit to Talena, the oldest village in Bolivia, while the two-day Butch Cassidy tour includes watching the video. The final draw to Tupiza Tours is that if you are there on your birthday, you will receive a reduction in price on one of the services you use that day, plus a little gift.

Isla Tours, Calle Florida (Avenida Ferrovairio and Uyuni), ☎ 7183-2712 (cell), has offices in Tupiza and Uyuni. They offer the same tours as everyone else in Tupiza, but they try to compete by cutting their prices and, of course, their meager profit margin. This is one of only two agencies in town that is not attached to a hotel.

Explore Andina Tours, Avenida Chichas #220, ☎ 694-2633, is on the main floor of Roca Colorada Hotel. They offer a number of tours, including a city tour, a tour to Uyuni, a two-day Butch Cassidy tour, and up to three days on a horse. Andina also has a number of different vehicles for rent. A Land Cruiser costs $70 a day with a 60-mile/100-km limit, $600 per week with a 600-mile/1,000-km limit, and $2,400 a month with unlimited mileage. A car with the same mileage limit costs $40 per day, $250 a week and $1,000 a month. Using a vehicle in this area seems fairly safe to me and this is one place in Bolivia where driving would have advantages.

Touristours, Avenida Pedro Arraya, ☎ 694-4534, tourslossalares@hotmail.com, offers all the usual tours plus an exceptional trip to the village of San Pablo de Lipez, in the municipality of Portulos, near the Argentinean border. The tour can be as short as four days or as long as 12, and part of it may be done as a llama caravan. You will be involved with Los Ripes indigenous group. San Pedro village (16,500 ft/5,000 m) has mud brick structures with thatched roofs. For this trip one must be prepared for full cultural immersion.

WAKI

Touristours assisted Margaret E. Bolton in an anthropological study in San Pablo de Lipez where she recorded the events around the exchange ceremony called "waki" that takes place between the living and the dead. In that exchange the living ask for things like fertility and rain as they offer liquid and food to the spirits of the dead.

The people running this office are sincere and interested in promoting their cultural background. If you have even an inkling of interest in these types of trips, talk to them. Their prices are comparable to everyone else in town.

■ Places to Stay

HOTEL PRICES (US $)

Per person, per day, unless noted otherwise.

$	$2-$5
$$	$5-$10
$$$	$11-$17
$$$$	$18-$25
$$$$$	Over $25

Hostal Valle Hermoso, *Avenida Pedro Arraya, #478,* ☎ *694-2370, $,* is a five-minute walk from the bus station. Its rooms are clean with tile floors and windows overlooking a small courtyard. There is a rooftop patio and a dining room where, if you order ahead, breakfast can be served. A TV and VCR allow you to watch *Butch Cassidy and the Sundance Kid*. Luggage storage and laundry service are also available. Should you want or need anything, the lady in charge can and will produce. She runs the show. However, I had to insist that they clean the room after I'd been there for a few days.

Residencial Centro, *Avenida Santa Cruz #287,* ☎ *694-2705, $,* has basic rooms and good rates. The place is clean, the walls are painted and bougainvillea decorates the courtyard. Parking is available and there's a guest kitchen area.

Residencial My Home, *Avenida Avaroa #288,* ☎ *694-2947 $,* has basic rooms. I found the owner friendly.

Anexo Mitru, *Calle Avaroa,* ☎ *694-3002, $$,* next to Los Helechos, has a plethora of rooms with various prices and options – with or without private bath, with or without TV, etc. This hotel is part of the Mitru Hotel (below) and if you stay in the annex you get to use the pool (in the Mitru itself) for $1.25 per day (non-guests pay $2). However, the annex is in an older building and it is showing some wear. Laundry costs $1.15 per kilo and ping pong will set you back 75¢ for half an hour. Baggage storage is available.

Roco Colorado, *Avenida Chichas and Chuquisaca, just up from Mitru,* ☎ *694-3016, $$,* has spacious rooms with large windows and nice-sized bathrooms. There is even a curtain around the shower stall. Cable TV is usually included. The place is clean. Breakfast is offered in the dining room downstairs (all rooms are on the second floor). It costs $1 for a continental and an Americano that includes scrambled eggs runs $1.25.

Hotel Mitru, *Avenida Chichas #187,* ☎ *694-3001. www.tupizatours.com, $$$$,* has a lovely flowered patio and a pool. A two-room suite is $20 for one and $35 for two. This includes a large bedroom with tile floor and cactus wood furniture. The curtains all match, the bathroom is large and has a separate shower stall, and cable TV is in the sitting room just off the bedroom. The sitting room has a couch, chair and coffee tables. These suites are a luxury for Bolivia. Towels, shampoo and breakfast are all included in the price. The hotel has rooms with private bath that cost $5.50 per person, and simple rooms without baths go for $2.50 per person. However, there is a 75¢ per-day fee to use the pool. Other amenities include laundry service ($1 a kilo), luggage storage, a book exchange and a safe car park. There are presently 110 beds available and a new addition will be completed soon.

The Mitui family opened this establishment 50 years ago. They come from a Greek background and have been in the hotel business for over 100 years. Their experience shows in the services they offer. At the hotel, there are people who can speak some English, French, and Italian.

Residencial Tupiza has been closed since 2001 even though the sign is still up.

■ Places to Eat

Los Helechos, *Avenida Avaroa,* ☎ *694-3002,* can have sullen waitresses, but the food is good and the restaurant is clean. An egg sandwich is 50¢ and a banana milkshake is 60¢. The shakes are strong on banana and the sandwiches have lots of onion. The continental breakfast comes with the usual bad bread often seen in Bolivian restaurants.

El Escorial, *Avenida Avaroa and Santa Cruz,* has their menu on a sandwich board on the street. The portions are not large (I had to order two pieces of chicken) but the flavor was good. The service is quick. This place draws many upper crust Tupizians.

Cremlin Ice Cream, *Avenida Cochabamba and Calle Florida, on the square,* is the most popular parlor in town. The best dish to try is the papaya split. The prices are low.

Residencial Sede Social Ferroviario, *Avenida Avaroa just up from Anex Mitru,* is the railroad workers' place located in a large hall with cement floors and high ceilings. They serve only traditional foods. *Almuerzo* is $1.15. The meal changes daily, but the place is closed on Sundays and holidays.

ORDER A TUPIZA SPECIAL

Tupiza has some unique dishes to try. *Tomales* are made with spiced llama meat. *Humintas* is a sweet corn dish that has ground and cooked corn mixed with a spiced cheese. The mixture is wrapped in leaves and cooked in an oven. *Pelado* is a large-kernel corn cooked with peppers, onion, a little beef, garlic, chili and rice.

Irmas, *Calle Florida,* has a sign in English painted on the wall, below the red and white sign that says "Agency Cascada." The sign advertises home-cooked meals. Irma is always in the *tienda* "Frial Castro" that is located just below the sign saying "Agency Cascada". You must order your meals two hours ahead of time. A full supper includes everything that an *almuerzo* would include and costs $2.50. Breakfast is $1.25. You get to eat in her dining room, and talk to her two kids or to her. This should give you a sense of Bolivian home life. The big payoff is the excellent food (including vegetarian). At least one meal should be enjoyed with Irma while in Tupiza.

The Odessa 2000, *Avenida Chichas, across from the Mitru Hotel,* is a small pleasant shop where you can stop for a beer or pop. The music is played at a reasonable level and the shop is set off the street.

American Restaurant, *on the plaza,* is named after its clientele. It serves a small pizza for 75¢ and a large for $1.25. The place is always full of tourists looking for the usual North American foods. I was not all that impressed with the food or the portion size.

■ Nightlife

 Punto de Enquento, Avenida Santa Cruz & Calle Arandia, is the karaoke bar where the young crowd goes on Saturday nights. The other popular, but nameless, place is at the bottom of the stairs that lead to the mirador on the hill where the Christ figure, which can be seen from anywhere in town, is located. These dance bars open at 8 pm, but nothing really starts happening until after 9 or 10 pm. The cover charge is under 50¢ and traditional music is played.

Line dancing is the most popular dance at the moment in Tupiza. The open-air sports center in town across from the train station often has dance competitions on Saturday nights. Check with your hotel owner for information.

Villazon

Altitude: 11,332 ft / 3,445 m
Population: less than 2000

The border town of Villazon is a grubby place that at one time was filled with Bolivian migrants heading for Argentina, with its better standard of living. Today, the floods have reversed and the Bolivian expatriates are returning home.

Villazon can be reached by rail or by bus. It has a few places to stay and eat, and some money changers. The exchange rate is better in Bolivia than Argentina. However, this could change as the economies change.

The border crossing is easy. Walk from the plaza to the frontier, get your exit stamp, go a few more feet, and get your entry stamp to Argentina.

■ Getting Here & Away

Buses to or from Tarija take eight hours. There is one bus in the morning and the rest go at night so you can't see the steep cliffs you must pass to get into the valley. There are many buses to Tupiza, three hours away. This is probably the best destination from the border.

The **trains** run between Villazon and Tupiza three times a week and take the same time as the bus. This service is threatened by privatization of the rail service.

■ Places to Stay & Eat

I suggest you stay at the **Hotel Plaza** *on the square,* ☎ 596-3535, $$. It has clean rooms with bath and color TV. If this is not an option, there are cheaper and more basic places to stay near the bus terminal.

Residencial Bolivia, *Calle Deheza #55,* ☎ 596-3504, $$, has been recommended as a good option. They have rooms with bath and the place is reported to be clean.

For food, try the **Chinese Restaurant** opposite the bus terminal. If they have nothing else but a good soup or a stir fry, you can rest assured it will be palatable. The other place to eat is at Hotel Plaza.

Tojo & Iscayachi

These two villages are located on the road between Tupiza and Tarija. They have places to stay and places to eat, but nothing else for the tourist. The information is included in the event of an emergency or if the very adventuresome would like to experience Bolivian life at its most conventional.

Hotel Torino charges 35¢ for a bowl of soup. Across the street, a whole meal is 75¢. There is a second place in Tojo, **Hotel Aleman**, which offers drinks and snacks. I never checked these places out for rooms, but looking at the town in general I'd say you'd stay here only if you had no choice. The hotels would charge *gringos* a lot for a bed.

Once past Tojo, going to Tarija, the road ascends to the Altiplano and crosses about 60 miles/100 km through the Cordillera de Sama Biological Reserve. The reserve was created in 1991. However, it wasn't until 1996 that research projects, water resource management, and other social programs were put into effect. See *Tarija*, page 354, for details.

Iscayachi is at the top of the hill before the dramatic descent into Tarija and it is where you can jump ship before winding down the mountain for the last 36 miles/60 km in a bus that may or may not make it. Your options are walking, or taking a minibus or even a truck. After surviving the earlier part of the road, you may want to do this. I came down by bus but by then it was dark and I couldn't see how far I'd drop if the bus did go over. Iscayachi has some food stalls, plus one hotel that is better than basic if you should want to be close to the reserve.

Tarija

Altitude: 9,099 ft / 1,854 m
Population: 120,000

Tarija has many plazas that are clean and vegetated due to the almost tropical climate. A wide boulevard runs along the river and, in general, the area looks prosperous. This is due to the numerous successful vineyards and wineries in the area, plus the fact that in the past, when the Argentinean economy was better, many people from Tarija worked there for high wages. People of Tarija are known for their songs and dances accompanied by the many varieties of drums.

Tarija has a lot of beggars, which is surprising as the city looks better off than most Bolivian cities. Many of the beggars are refugees from the recent economic crash in Argentina.

Tarija is a great place to hang out and rest after some tough travel. It sees few tourists and has yet to be discovered. However, the hotels are good and the restaurants numerous.

∎ Getting Here & Around

Most **buses** between Tarija and Tupiza travel at night but occasionally, when the volume of passengers allows it, Chrystal Bus Company offers a day trip. You must go to the bus station in Tupiza and see if there are enough people going. Bolivia has many roads of death, and the one between Tupiza and Tarija ranks up there with the most deadly. The cost for the trip by bus is $7 per person. Although it's just 134 miles/218 km, the journey takes anywhere from seven to 10 hours, usually with a couple of half-hour breaks to fix the bus or have dinner in Tojo. The road is narrow, gravel and dotted with memorials to the dead. I saw a bus that had gone over a week or so earlier. Six people had died. Although the bus companies like to blame accidents on their drivers (usually they are said to have been drunk) I think it is mechanical failure that causes them. My bus had two flats while traveling this road. Fortunately, they happened on stretches that were level, rather than on 20% grade with hairpin curves. On Bolivian buses, tires are always bald, steering always loose. My impression of the drivers is good – they are incredibly skilled, both as drivers and mechanics. I'd eagerly pay double for a well-maintained bus, but that is not the way things are done in Bolivia. On the other hand, when I could open my eyes, I found the mountains and valleys that we passed on the trip were among the prettiest I've ever seen.

Buses to Potosi via Uyuni take about 20 hours. Buses direct to Potosi take 14 hours and cost $10 per person. They have only night buses, the earliest leaving at 5 pm. Camargo, 111 miles/182 km north of Tarija on the road to Potosi, can be reached by taking a bus to Potosi. You will have to pay for the entire way even though you are getting off at the halfway point. The trip is long and through the mountains. It is best to go by jeep.

Buses to Villamontes ($7) take 12 hours to go 158 miles/258 km. The slow time indicates that it is another treacherous road. A hired taxi takes 10 hours and costs $130 for up to four people (see Suzie at Dinar Travel, ☎ 664-8000, if you wish to do this). You can find a taxi to do the run for a lot less; ask around.

Trains leave Wednesday and Saturday for Santa Cruz.

Planes fly to and from Villamontes on Friday and Saturday. Planes to or from Santa Cruz go every day during the week and cost $75 per person. Planes do not fly if it is raining.

Taxis in Tarija cost 45¢ per person, anywhere within city limits. Tarija has all one-way streets, and every corner has a huge sign indicating the name of the street and numbers in that block. This makes getting around easy and safe.

■ History

 Tarija was founded on July 4th, 1574 by **Captain Luis de Fuentes y Vargas**. He had been in Tupiza on the other side of the mountains prior to stopping here. He called the new village on the banks of the Guadalquivir River, Villa de San Bernardo de la Frontera. The river was named after one near Seville in Spain, as the two valleys appeared similar to Fuentes.

In 1810 Tarija declared its independence from Spanish rule, though Spain ignored the declaration. On April 15th, seven years later, the citizens of Tarija, under the leadership of **Moto Mendez**, won the **Battle de la Tablada**. However, it didn't win them independence. It was at this time that the village was renamed for Francisco de Tarija, who was the first Spaniard to enter the valley.

Shortly after independence, Argentina realized the value of the fertile lands around Tarija so the governors asked the people of Tarija to unite with Argentina, but the people opted to stay with Bolivia. Every person in Tarija seems proud of this, though considering Argentina's overall greater prosperity and stability, one has to wonder. Finally, in 1825 Bolivia won independence from Spain and Tarija, in turn, concentrated on being Bolivian.

■ Services

 The **telephone office** is on Calle Virginio Lema and Daniel Campos, just one block up from Plaza Sucre.

The **post office** is next door to the telephone office on Calle Virginio Lema.

Internet access is everywhere, but the office on Plaza Sucre at Calle Bolívar is about the fastest. Many machines have curtains around them so no one can see what the operator is looking at.

The **police** station is on Avenida las Americas, between Calle Ballivan and Juan Misae.

The **hospital** is on Calle Cochabamba and Avenida Santa Cruz. **Medical Clinic** - Infirmary Varas Castrillo, Calle Alejandro Corrado #176, ☎ 664-2051, cell 7186-0163, has a diagnostic lab and blood bank. They can do electro-cardiograms and general practice. The clinic is open 24 hours a day. A general examination costs $7. If treatment is needed you will be given a sheet to take to the pharmacy. There you must purchase all your medicine, needles, IV solutions and tubes, tape, bandages etc. The only thing you get at the clinic for nothing is a smile from the nurse as she takes your payment. The one thing I can say about this clinic is that they did not scalp me because I was a *gringo*.

There's a **tourist office** on Plaza Luis de Fuentes, at the corner of 15th de Abril.

La Esmeralda Limpieza, Calle La Madrid #157, ☎ 664-2043, does **laundry** for $1 a kilo. The wash is done by machine and can be ironed if you wish. They also offer dry cleaning.

■ Festivals

 Besides the usual festivals like Carnival and Christmas, there are numerous events that mostly celebrate the production of wine. Viva Tours, ☎ 663-8325, offers four-day tours for most of these festivals.

The **Festival of the Grapes** takes place in February/March in Concepcion Valley, a colonial town that has grown to be the center of Bolivia's grape-growing region. The date changes every year and is dependent on the growing season. During the festival, each small producer, in a ritualistic way, presents a sample of his wine to the main wineries so they can see the quality of the product. Music is played, food is served and dances that are indigenous to the region take place. Of course, there is lots of wine flowing. The queen of the grape is crowned during this festival.

Carnival, in Tarija, starts two Thursdays before Carnival proper. The first Thursday is the celebration of the *compadres* (men) and the second is the celebration of the *comadres* (women). The *comadres* day is most important. This is when the ladies of the city parade through the streets with special cakes that sit in baskets decorated with fruits, flowers, cheese or other sweets. Often, the procession includes a live lamb with flowers around its neck. Once at the main plaza, the women dance around and out of the square with their cakes on their heads. As the drinks go down, so do some of the cakes. A spiritual relative (someone who has died) is then elected and celebrated. A week later Carnival starts with the devil being brought to the main square in a cage. Once he is liberated, the festival can begin. The final day is celebrated with the funeral of the *Momo* (monkey) King, who is recreated as a puppet. He is taken to

Villa Abaroa, placed in a cardboard carton and drowned in lots of *chicha* and wine before being burned.

April 15th and 16th is **Efemerides de Tarija**. It celebrates the Battle of La Tablada, when, in 1817, citizens of the area won a battle against the Spanish. They were fighting for independence. The celebration includes a rodeo in memory of the city's *gaucho* connections. There is also the **Fair of Southern Bolivia**, which features a huge display of items produced or hand-made in the area. The event is patronized by people from all of South America and is one of the biggest in the country.

The end of March or the beginning of April is the Pascua Florida, or **Easter**, celebration. In Tarija, things are done just a bit differently than in other areas. On Good Friday the women of the villages of San Lorenzo and Padcaya and those living in the suburb of La Pampa don white dresses and parade to the cathedral while chanting a mournful sound commemorating the death of Christ. They are called *Los Piadosas*, The Chanters. On Sunday, the cathedral is decorated with roses and other flowers, and rose petals are strewn on the ground. The Procession of the Resurrection occurs when the people parade to the church carrying a statue of Christ that symbolizes his rising from the dead. They are accompanied by music from violins and instruments unique to this area. The celebration is reminiscent of the one in Antigua, Guatemala.

Fiesta of the Virgin of Chaguaya is a long celebration that occurs between August 15th and September 10th. This religious festival takes place in the village of Chaguaya, 37 miles/60 km from Tarija. Many pilgrims come walking to the site where the virgin was supposed to have been seen. They pray for special things and it is considered a great honor to be able to attend this particular pilgrimage. The dishes served after the pilgrimage are traditional foods of *Criollos*, pure Spanish whites born in Latin America.

Fiesta de San Roque is between August 15th and September 12th, with the main feast day being August 16th. San Roque is the patron saint of Tarija. Although there are parades every Sunday for the entire month, the main celebration (different than feast day) occurs on the first Sunday in September when the people of the city carry a statue of the saint through the streets in a dramatic procession to the cathedral. The statue is dressed in rich robes. Onlookers shout with joy and throw flowers. Since San Roque was the saint of dogs, the people of Tarija adorn their dogs with colored ribbons. Dancers dress in Amazonian attire and gyrate in traditional fashion to the beat of drums and other instruments. This is the biggest festival in Tarija and is often compared to the extravagance of Carnival.

SAN ROQUE'S STORY

San Roque was born in Montpellier, France in 1295 and died in 1327. After the death of his parents, San Roque gave his inheritance to the poor of the city and left for Rome. As he traveled, he came across people suffering from the plague and saw that those blessed with the cross were spared death. However, San Roque himself contracted the disease and was sent to rest in a hut in Monte Sornato. A dog was said to have produced bread and water for the saint and this eventually cured him. Shortly after his recovery, the saint lost favor with the leaders of the city so he was placed in prison, where he died five years later. However, while in prison, he wrote about the miracles he had seen during his life. After his death, the document was put away for safe keeping and nothing more was said of San Roque.

In 1414 Montpellier suffered another attack of the plague. In the hope of a miracle, city leaders held processions in honor of San Roque. The plague miraculously disappeared. Given credit for the job well done, San Roque was declared a saint.

During this fiesta the devotees of San Roque, called *Chunchos*, bring out a unique instrument not found elsewhere in Bolivia. It is an *erkeycaña*, a long bamboo stem with a cow horn at one end. The people parade through the streets playing the horn, dressed in brightly colored feather hats that have veils hanging over the face. They also wear ponchos of silk. It is believed that this dance originated when the people wearing these items and honoring San Roque were spared the plague.

You will notice that the dogs of Tarija are well taken care of and many have ribbons around their necks. This is an indication that the dogs have had all their shots (in honor of San Roque).

The **Fiesta of the Virgin of Guadalupe** occurs on the first Sunday of October when the Virgin is paraded through city streets to a field on a small hill near the town. She is placed on a makeshift altar to watch the re-enactment of a battle that took place on May 17th, 1735. It was then that groups of men made up of the Matacos, Cuñas and Chiriguano (indigenous groups) fought over the possession of the Virgin. The losing side, of course, does not represent the Christians. This is a dramatic event where the actors (and the horses too) are dressed in traditional garb. The winners and those not symbolically killed in battle finally go to the Virgin and receive her blessing. She is then returned to her place at the Cathedral. The following day is celebrated with a small rodeo, numerous games and races, and a cock fight. All this is accompanied by lots of food and drink, music and dancing.

The information about the festivals of Tarija was given to me by Viva Tours in Tarija.

■ Sightseeing

In Town

 Zoological Park, Avenida Las Americas, charges 15¢ to enter. It has a small pond and a large children's playground. There is little to attract tourists except quiet benches in the shade.

Miradora de la Loma is on the hill at the west end of Avenida Domingo Paz and Corrage. Stairs lead to the park and viewpoint on top. The views of the city are good – ignore the numerous lovers. Below the hill you can see the Capilla de San Juan de la Loma, a historical church that has been well maintained and glitters in the sunlight.

Casa Dorada, Avenida Ingavi and Calle Gran Trigo, is a museum and a cultural center. Built at the end of the 1800s for Moises Navajas, the building was declared a museum in 1903. It is common for walls to be built around places in Latin American countries, but this is one place that shares its beauty with everyone on the street. The architecture, and the building's statue of liberty standing over the main entrance and flanked by statues of Victorian women, make Casa Dorada exceptional. Inside are Persian carpets, crystal chandeliers and mirrors framed in gold leaf. It is worth a walk through. Open Monday to Friday, 8 am to noon and 3 to 6 pm. The entry free is $1 per person.

The **Archeological Museum**, Calle General Trigo #0402, ☎ 663-6680, is part of the university and has archeological, paleontological and historical sections. Among the 500 fossils are the bones of the only Andean elephant ever found in South America. The archeological section has over 5,000 pieces that include jars, pots, arrowheads and spears. Admission, 25¢. The museum is open Monday to Friday, 8 am to noon and 3 to 6 pm. On weekends, it opens at 9 am.

The **Blue Castle** on Calle Bolívar was built by Moises Navaja, the same man who built the Casa Dorada. Ostentatious and beautiful at the same time, this castle, done mostly in blue tiles and white trim, can be enjoyed from the street. It gets its name from the color of the exterior. Because it is still occupied, entry is not possible.

Churches

The **cathedral**, Calle Madrid and Avenida Campero, was constructed in 1810 by the Jesuits and was declared a cathedral in 1925. The interior features oil paintings and silver and gold chalices, many inlaid with precious stones. The glass windows in this cathedral depict local peasants working in the fields.

San Juan de la Loma on San Juan Hill is a lovely white plaster church that is an historical relic. This is where the Spaniards signed a treaty of

Tarija

WHERE TO STAY & EAT

1. Baghdad Café, El Solar, Chingo's
2. Residencial Rosario, Hostal Carmen
3. Hostal Hogar
4. Res. Gualquiver, Don Galo, Tarija Valle, Andalez & Sigovia
5. Hotel Gran Buenos Aires
6. Hostería España
7. Hostal Miraflores, Luz Palace, Gran Hotel Tarija & Res. Zeballos
8. Hostal Bolivar
9. Hostal 15 de Abril
10. Hotel Londres
11. Hostal Mi Casa
12. Hostal Martinez
13. Hostal Loma de San Juan
14. Los Ceibos Hotel
15. Viña del Sur Hotel
16. Hostal Postanera
17. Restaurant Chino Hong Kong
18. La Cabaña
19. Mateos Restaurant
20. El Torpero Churrasqueria
21. El Solar Vegetarian Restaurant
22. Churrasqueria El Amigos
23. Taberna El Gattopardo
24. Konganas Restaurant
25. Don Pepe
26. Los Helechos, Karaoke Champayne
27. Nuevo Siglo Churrasqueria

NOT TO SCALE

© 2004 HUNTER PUBLISHING, INC

surrender on April 15th, 1817 after the Battle of Tablada, a field just outside the city. The battle was led by Moto Mendez. You can visit his house, which is now a museum, in San Lorenzo (page 352). To get to San Juan de la Loma, walk along Avenida Domingo Paz to the church. Behind the church is the Mirador de la Loma, an excellent viewpoint and lovers' stop.

Iglesia San Francisco, Avenida Madrid and Calle Daniel Campos, was built in 1606 and is considered the oldest church in Tarija. The library and archives, housed in the college next door, hold over 15,000 books. The church itself has some of the city's best oil paintings.

■ Adventures in Culture

 There are about 120 sites featuring rock paintings in this area, some with as many as 200 individual paintings. Some of these works are about 500 years old, while others are suspected to be up to 3,500 years of age.

The Methfessels (father and daughter), unofficial specialists in the rock paintings of Bolivia, became interested in the paintings many years ago. Lilo, the daughter, took photographs and made cards from the images that she in turn sold in her Tarija shop. As the father and daughter continued research, they realized that they had found some important archaeological treasures that were unknown to Bolivian scientists. The Methfessels registered their finds with the Archeological Department in La Paz. They also participated in the International Rock Art Symposium that took place in Tarija. This father and daughter team has been instrumental in getting these anthropological treasures brought to international attention.

The Methfessels continued researching. What they learned is that some of the paintings were set along the old salt trade routes of the llama caravans. So far, no studies have been made of the paintings and engravings, but some of the paintings show llamas strung together by ropes. It is known that llamas have been domesticated for about 3,500 years, so these paintings may have been done before domestication of the animal. Domesticated llamas are not strung together.

The Methfessels will take you to some of the paintings, but they have strict rules. You can photograph the paintings, but you may not touch them, sprinkle water on them to make them brighter or walk on them. The closest paintings are at Orozas and feature humans, monkeys, birds and other animals. Call them at ☎ 634-2062 and see my review of their services under *Tour Operators*, below.

■ Adventures on Foot

INCA TRAIL: The Inca Trail in the Cordillera Sama Biological Reserve (see below) was used long before the Inca arrived, but it has not been studied and its age is not known. Some believe it was built during pre-Inca times and that the Inca, when they arrived, repaired it in a shoddy manner. This paved trail is steep and often used by locals to get from the highlands down into the valleys. It can be walked in eight hours, but this leaves little time for exploration. It is best to spend at least one night in the reserve. While walking you will see archeological remains such as drainage troughs, platforms, an old bridge and structural walls made from huge slabs of rock. Rock paintings can be seen in six different locations and to find them you will need a guide. They are well preserved and depict llamas and birds.

The trail starts at Tajzara, where you can enjoy the wildlife that lives near the Great Lake before taking a step along the trail. The lake is surrounded by sand dunes that are spectacular in such a bleak environment. Across the main highway from the lake is Copper Hill, where queñua trees manage to survive at an elevation of 16,000 ft/5,000 m. These trees grow to a height of 10 ft/three m and have twisted trunks that seem to peel from the sun. Another forest of this kind is at Sajama. As you start to cross the Sama range, you will pass waterfalls and mountain streams on rugged terrain that is dotted with jagged rocks and sharp boulders. Above, you may see the occasional condor checking you out. The trail descends to the village of Calderillas. From there it goes to the Calderilla River ravine and down into the village of Pinos along the road to Tarija.

A private vehicle must be taken to the trailhead and another must be arranged for pickup at the end. The best time to hike is between April and September, when the trail is driest. There is camping at the lakes near the main road. You must have your own equipment for this. The village of Iscayachi, at the point in the road just before it drops into the Tarija Valley, has a fairly decent hotel. You could start from there in the morning and hire a taxi to take you to the trailhead. There is a campsite in Calderillas and Pinos has a restaurant.

FOSSIL WALK: The hills and fields around Tarija, especially along the way to the airport, are riddled with fossils from the Pleistocene era. It is illegal to take any of these fossils out of the country, but it is fun to hunt for them. Because of the sedimentary and conglomerate rock and clay, the fossils are not hard to find. It was in this environment that the huge elephant bones now in the Archeological Museum in town were found. Take water and a sun hat as the area is excruciatingly hot.

To get here, take a bus going to the airport and get off when you can see the cliffs, gulches and open fields just above the town. From there, you can follow the pipeline or just roam.

■ Adventures on Water

 Man-made **Lake San Jacinto** is six miles/10 km out of Tarija (buses leave from the Palace of Justice every half-hour or so and cost 20¢). Get off the bus at San Jacinto and walk across the bridge that spans the dam. It is an impressive site. At the 2.7-acre/1.5-hectare lake you can join the locals who hire rowboats for a trip across the water and back. Numerous food stalls line the road to the top of the hill. It is a pleasant walk and the dam, with the huge gorge behind, is interesting to see. This is a half-day trip. Many locals love to swim in the brown silty water of the lake. The bicycle path you see along one side of the lake goes back toward Tarija.

■ Adventures on Wheels

Tarija is surrounded by interesting villages that are worth a ride to visit.

Tomatita village has a park on the banks of the Guadalquivir and Erquis rivers. The area is shaded with eucalyptus trees and the river is dotted with swimming holes. There is a sign over the walking bridge (it has almost all the decking missing) that says you can't wash clothes in the river, but the bridge was being used as a clothesline on my visit. There are restaurants and *tiendas* on the main road and on the street by the river. A private pool on the opposite side of the highway is far cleaner than the river – you can play in the pool all day for just 75¢. The park has covered huts for picnics. It is best to visit this place at the end of rainy season, rather than when it has only a trickle of water during the dry season. To get here, catch a bus (20¢) marked A or B along Avenida Domingo La Paz. Both buses also have Tomatita on their list of destinations.

Along the road to San Lorenzo, near Tomatita, are numerous restaurants offering local dishes. During festivals and at peak season, these places are filled with revelers.

San Lorenzo is an interesting colonial village beyond Tomatita. Wave down a bus marked San Lorenzo in Tomatita or catch it along Avenida Domingo La Paz in Tarija. The fare is 25¢ from Tomatita and 30¢ from Tarija. The ride to San Lorenzo passes some badlands and haciendas belonging to the upper crust. The ride is pleasant.

There is no place to stay here, but there are a couple of eateries on the square. The **Museum of Jose Eustaqueo Moto Mendez** (hero of the war for independence), costs 25¢ to enter. This colonial house is almost as it was when Mendez lived there. Stairs leading up to the bedrooms and balcony are made of red brick boxed in wood and the doorway to the bedroom is low. The bedroom furniture remains, but no linen has been kept. On the main floor is a collection of swords and wooden stirrups, as well as some written materials praising Mendez. The next room (back shed) has a wooden bathtub that would make me want to stay dirty, especially when it's cold out. Two *erkeycañas* sit in the corner. These are musical instruments made of bamboo stems that have one end plugged with the horn of a cow (usually). This wind instrument is used during festivals and is found only in the Tarija district. The courtyard has many Lion's Club and Radio Club awards nailed to the stable walls. The museum takes about a half-hour to visit.

From the museum in San Lorenzo, walk to the river, past the Entel office, which is housed in a well-maintained colonial building. Follow the path along the river and make a circle back to town. On the way you will pass a children's park with a cement and steel dinosaur slide that illustrates the creative ability of the locals. If I were a kid, I'd come all the way from Tarija just for this! Small children can slide out of the dinosaur's mouth and onto the ground while bigger kids climb onto its back and have a longer slide.

Following the road two miles in the opposite direction from the children's park will take you to the village of **El Picacho**. It is a lovely walk through farmland along a shaded road. The area is clean and green. Some rich people from Tarija have built summer homes in this area. El Picacho is on the river and there are small pools in which to wade and one large rock in the middle of the river that is the pride of the locals. From El Picacho you can take a minibus to **Corana**, where there are more swimming holes (these are nicer than those at El Picacho). Or you can return to Tarija.

There are no places to stay in these villages, but there are places to eat and drink. Minibuses and collectivo taxis return from the square in San Lorenzo back to Tarija. Or you may take a minibus along the main highway from Corana back to Tarija.

Santa Ana is five miles/eight km east of Tarija in a beautiful, wine-producing valley. Its **Astronomical Observatory** has two powerful telescopes targeting the southern hemisphere. It was the first observatory in the country. Both telescopes are Russian made. The atomic clock here tells the official time of Bolivia. While in the village you can also visit the Santa Ana winery (see *Adventures of the Vine*, below). To get here, take a bus from Plaza Sucre.

Camargo is another colonial village 110 miles/180 km north of Tarija on the road toward Potosi. It takes about seven hours to reach by bus (there are two a day). Camargo has two hotels of good quality and three *alojamientos* that are basic but clean. There are a few places to eat around the plaza and at the two hotels. This is another wine-producing area that specializes in Singani (see below, page 355).

I have not been to Camargo and a visit should be mainly for the adventuresome. There are petroglyphs to see at the winery of San Pedro just two miles/three km from the center of town and rock paintings at Cañon de Cinti near the village. Towering over the village is the Vado del Perro, which features El Molino rock structures, a special rock formation from the cretaceous period that you will recognize from its white carbonates. In Camargo, the white is streaked with red sandstone. Geologists and geographers would be interested in this mountain as the formations are quite special. There is also a museum and an old church in the village that is worth visiting.

■ Adventures in Nature

Cordillera de Sama Biological Reserve (35 miles/60 km from Tarija on the road to Tupiza) has two regions, the Altiplano or puna grassland and the inter-Andean valleys. It covers a total of 270,000 acres/108,500 hectares. One of the main purposes of controlling this area is the provision of unpolluted water to Tarija and surrounding villages. The rivers delivering this water are the Tolomosa, Camacho and Guadalquivir.

The puna grasslands are in the higher and drier part of the reserve and are characterized by sparse vegetation and dominated by spiky grasses. There is often a frost at night in this environment, even during the warm periods of the year. Acidic bogs are common and attract many birds like plovers and snipes. The wetlands include four permanent lakes that account for 3,200 acres/1,300 hectares of land. They are home to 41 bird species, three of which are threatened flamingos. Also, 80 migratory bird species pass through every year. Plant life in the area is delicate and includes such species as the yareta (looks like a bright green clump of moss) that grows about half an inch/one cm a year.

Archeological sites in the reserve include remains of forts and rock paintings. See Carlos and Lilo Methfessel in Tarija for tours, ☎ 664-2062.

The reserve has problems with vandalism and looting of the archeological sites, illegal poaching of animals, extraction of gravel from the riverbeds, and wildfires that destroy vegetation and wildlife. The need to educate the reserve's 4,000 residents is most important. If they can see the benefits from tourism, it will encourage them to conserve what they have.

You can walk the Inca Trail within the reserve. See *Adventures on Foot*, above.

Tariquia Biological Reserve is about 125 miles/210 km from Tarija on the Bermejo River where it meets the Rio Grande de Tarija. Access is through the village of Bermejo, on the river of the same name. The reserve butts up against Baritu Park in Argentina.

Tariquia was established in 1989 to stop logging and fishing practices that threatened the health of the entire area. It covers 618,000 acres/ 250,000 hectares of land and is the biggest area in Bolivia of protected cloud forest. It is the source of water for many communities in the region. The steep cliffs and high elevations are subject to erosion which, in turn, will pollute the waters if logging practices are not curbed.

The most common wildlife species protected in the reserve are the Amazon River turtle, the Jucumari bear, the jaguar, the carpincho (caiman) and the giant anteater. The reserve is in a mountainous area with steep cliffs along the Bermejo River system. Threats to the reserve are farming, cattle grazing, logging and searching for oil.

The above two reserves are managed by **PROMETA**, Calle Alejandro del Carpio in Tarija, ☎ 664-5865, in conjunction with the National Protected Areas Service (**SERNAP**). For more information about these areas, contact PROMETA.

Bernejo has a resort-like atmosphere where you can get a place to stay or a place to eat. However, 11 miles/18 km from Bernejo is the Valle del Medio resort called **El Paraiso del Tordo** (Blackbird's Paradise), ☎ 664-5595. Either call ahead or contact Viva Tours (☎ 663-8325, visatour@ cosett.com.bo) in Tarija for booking arrangements. At Valle del Medio you can also climb the Pie de la Cuesta, a thickly vegetated hill where birding is excellent.

To get here, take a bus from the Parada del Chaco in the center of town. It costs $4 per person to get to the Valle del Medio or Bernejo.

■ Adventures of the Vine

Tarija is the wine center of Bolivia and the vines grow at the highest elevations in the world. There are a total of 5,700 acres/ 2,300 hectares of vines planted in the Tarija Valley. Because the grapes get more ultraviolet light at that elevation (8,000 ft/1,500 m), the flavor is more aromatic. A visit to at least one winery is a must.

Wine making in Bolivia was started between 1550 and 1570 by the Augustinian missionaries, who needed wine for religious purposes. Later, the mining industry of Potosi desired a stronger liquor than wine to stave off the cold and misery of their environment. The people of Singani village started distilling the wine and made a liquor that was about 40 proof. Singani, indigenous to Bolivia, is still being produced and is the alcohol used in a cocktail called a chufley. Singani can also be enjoyed straight. The grapes they used then and still use today are a muscatel variety. Singani was declared an appellation of origin on May 4th, 1992 and is considered an exclusive product of Bolivia.

Although the wines have not reached the level of quality that the French or even some of the Argentinean and Chilean wines have, a wine-tasting tour is fun. Concepcion and Kolberg are the most popular brands of wine in the country, but that does not mean that they are the best. Try many – they are inexpensive – and decide for yourself. A bottle of white Chardonnay costs $5 and a Cabernet Sauvignon costs just under $5. The Barbera is $4.25 and the Pinot Noir is $3.50. That is of the better qualities. There are cheaper wines. For a tour of the wineries, contact Viva Tours (☎ 663-8325, visatour@cosett.com.bo).

Casa Real, Calle 15 de Abril N, ☎ 259-664-5498, casareal@olivo.tja. entelnet.co, has their *bodega* in the Santa Ana Valley just 11 miles/18 km from Tarija. Casa Real's history goes back a ways. In 1925 Don Julio Ortiz Linares started in the wine business in the Cinty Valley, near Tarija. He specialized in Singani. Later, his grandson, Don Luis Granier Ballivian started a vineyard in the Santa Ana Valley under the tutelage of his grandfather. This became Casa Real. As their businesses grew, they retained the reputation of having the best Singani in the country. Casa Real has one of the most modern operations in the area. They use electronic monitors to watch the progress of the plants so that picking can be done when the grapes will give optimum flavor. Huge stainless steel tanks imported from France are part of their distillation process.

San Vincente, whose office is on Victor Paz and Avenida Padilla, ☎ 664-8100, maintains a vineyard and *bodega* in Juntas del Rosario in Aviles county. The vineyard is beside the Camacho and Alisos rivers. This is also the spot where in 1572 the Jesuits built churches and, of course, planted the first vines in Bolivia to produce wine for communion services. In 1996 the Chamas-Lopez family took over the business and just three years later they won first prize for quality in an international competition.

La Canaña at Santa Ana la Vieja, is nine miles/15 km from Tarija and sits at 6,414 ft/1,950 m. This company belongs to the Kohlberg family of wineries, famous throughout the country. Their vines were first planted in 1963 when Don Julio Kohlberg Chavarria bought the property. At the time he produced 15,000 bottles of wine a year. His first claim to fame was when Father Pedro Pacciardi of the San Francisco Convent started ordering wines from him. He also expounded on the excellence of the wine to others not in the church, which soon brought less religious customers to La Canaña. Because the winery did so well, Kohlberg's sons decided to study both business and agriculture in Argentina and in the United States. The skills they acquired have helped in making this one of the most efficient and successful wineries in the country. Now, after almost 40 years of production, the 284 acres/115 hectares of vineyards are producing enough so that some can be exported.

Concepcion Wines, ☎ 613-2008, owned by Serjio Prudencio, is 22 miles/36 km from Tarija. The Concepcion Valley is an area of rolling hills dedicated solely to the growing of grapes. Just 1.2 miles/two km from the colonial town of Concepcion is the winery of the same name. It has over 247 acres/100 hectares and a new machine capable of crushing 20 tons of fruit in an hour. For white wines, this includes removing the stems and skins. Red wines keep the skins during fermentation to enhance the flavor. This winery produces 920,000 gallons/350,000 liters a year. Serjio Prudencio learned early in his career that he couldn't compete with the cheap wine makers, so he looked toward the fine-wine market. In order to attain this level of perfection, Prudencio consulted with American wine companies and had his vintners trained in the States. It paid off. Concepcion won a gold medal in an international competition for its Cabernet Sauvignon in 1994; a silver medal for the same wine in 1997; and, during the 2000 competitions, was one of five finalists. Concepcion is getting recognition throughout the wine-drinking world and is now exporting its products to Germany, England, Spain, the States, Peru, Switzerland, Denmark and Japan.

Milcast Corp., Avenida Dr. Angel Baldiviezo #1976, Barrio Aranjuez, milcast@olivo.tja.entelnet.bo, was founded in 1976 by Milton Castillanos and his wife. They are in the central valley of Tarija growing grapes at 6,414 ft/1,950 m above sea level. They have 64 acres/26 hectares planted in red grapes and a bit less in white. The winery is capable of producing 1.2 million bottles a year.

Kuhlmann, kuhlmann@cosett.com.bo, is situated in the San Luis area 2.7 miles/4.5 km from Tarija (an easy day-hike). In 1930, when Kuhlmann planted grapes, he was the first in the valley after the Augustinians to do so. However, their Singani distillery was moved to the Cinti de Camargo Valley in 1973 and later to the central valley of Tarija.

Campos de Solana, at Km 10 on the highway to Bermejo, ☎ 663-0819, is the biggest competition for Concepcion and Kholberg wines. In my opinion, their wines are the best. The winery has the latest stainless steel equipment, imported from France. The plant is fairly new, but the family comes with 70 years of experience in the business. The vines at this location are planted on only 7.5 acres/three hectares of land. Some scientists from the University of Montfort have studied the enzyme CYIBI that is present in the type of grapes used at Campos and believe consumption of the enzyme is a protection against cancer. The owners welcome tourists to visit, sample and, of course, purchase.

■ Tour Operators

Dinar Travel 2000, Avenida Gral Trigo #579 on Plaza Luis de Fuentes, ☎ 664-8000, susyqui@olivo.tja.entelnet.bo. This company's owner, Susi Ouiroga, speaks excellent English and can help with just about any travel problem. If you have questions about travel in Bolivia before you arrive, e-mail her. She will help. She always advises people not to purchase in-country air tickets before arriving in Bolivia because they are much cheaper when purchased once you get here. Susi can also help you hire a private taxi or arrange a tour in the area.

This company is honest. They accidentally overcharged us for our tickets and we didn't notice. When we returned to pick up our tickets, Susi brought the error to our attention and returned our money.

Carlos and Lilo Methfessel, Calle Sucre #665, ☎ 664-2062, methfess@ olivo.tja.entelnet.bo, are probably the most knowledgeable people in Bolivia in regards to rock paintings and engravings. Their place is under the sign marked Consolado de Alemania (German Consulate). They offer half- and full-day tours to the rock painting sites for $25 a half-day, $50 for a full day, with a maximum of 10 people. A full-day tour will take you to three sites. On both tours you must have good walking shoes and be able to walk for about an hour. All garbage must be carried out.

The company offers longer tours, too. For a two- or three-day tour you must book at least two days in advance. The three-day tour costs $200 per person and includes all meals and accommodations.

Another excursion run by the Methfessels is an eight-hour hike along the Inca Trail ($200 for four people), described above. To do this hike you leave at four or five in the morning and drive two hours to the trailhead. The walk is entirely downhill along the stone path. You will be picked up at trail's end and returned to Tarija at about 6 pm. Rodolfo Raffino wrote a story about this hike for *La Nacion* in Argentina.

Viva Tours, Calle Sucre #615, ☎ 663-8325, visatour@cosett.com.bo, does a combination wine and archaeological tour that includes seeing some rock art. However, their big draw is a combination river/hiking trip on waterways in the El Chaco area in southern Bolivia that takes from four to 12 days. These trips include going into the Tariquia Biological Reserve along the Rio Grande or to Aguarague National Park. They visit cultural groups such as the Guaranies and Weenhayek, who still live in a traditional manner.

The company also offers guides specialized in particular areas. Should you be interested in birding, for example, they will send a good bird guide with you. Should you be interested in rock paintings, the guide will be knowledgeable about them. This company is professional and offers the largest variety of cultural and ecological choices for travel in the Tarija region. Contact Miriam de Abajo for full details. At time of writing, Viva didn't have a set price schedule.

▪ Places to Stay

HOTEL PRICES (US $)

Per person, per day, unless noted otherwise.

$. . . . . $2-$5

$$. . . . . $5-$10

$$$. . . . . $11-$17

$$$$. . . . . $18-$25

$$$$$. . . . . Over $25

Residencial Rosario, *Calle Ingavi #777 and Avenida Ramon Rojas, residen_rosario@latinmail.com,* ☎ *664-2042 or 663-6710, $,* would be my first choice for an economical place to stay. It is squeaky clean with rooms around a central courtyard that has a well-tended garden. The 17 rooms have large windows, tiled floors, bed lamps and clothes racks. Those with bath also have TVs. There is hot water all day, luggage storage, safe deposit and laundry service. In the lobby is a pop and water dispenser. This is a family-run hotel that has been in business for 15 years. The owners are friendly and helpful.

Hostal Hogar, *Calle Victor Paz Estenssoro, across from the bus station* ☎ *664-3964, $,* has excellent rooms with or without private bath. This family-run establishment is whistle clean.

Residencials Gualquiver, **Don Galo**, **Tarija Valle**, **Andalez** and **Sigovia** are all around the bus terminal, all basic, all about the same price ($3 per person) and not really where you'd want to stay. Across the main street is the much better **Hostal Hogar** or, still better, **Hostal Martinez** just up Avenida La Paz.

Hostal Club Social, *Calle 15 de Abril #271,* ☎ *664-2107, $$,* is close to Plaza Sucre in a rambling old building that has seen some classy days long ago. Rooms are large and have a foyer separate from the main bedroom. Each has cable TV and a telephone, large windows and storage closet, but rather narrow beds. All the bathrooms in the building have recently been remodeled and tiled. Rates include breakfast. The hotel has an interesting display of masks. There is also a games room, a restaurant and a bar. It is clean.

Hotel Gran Buenos Aires, *Calle Daniel Campos #448, near Avenida 15 de Abril,* ☎ *663-6802, hotelgranba@hotmail.com, $$,* offers single, double and triple rooms, all carpeted and all with baths. Rates include breakfast, cable TV, fan, fridge and a large closet (with hangers). The bathrooms are tiled and a gas water heater supplies the showers; towels are provided. The windows are small but adequate. The hotel offers room service, and has an Internet café, a pizzeria and a beauty parlor. This is a good spot, but it has seen better days.

Hosteria España, *Calle Alejandro Corrado #546,* ☎ *664-3304, $$,* has accommodations with and without private baths. The rooms are cleaned regularly and well laid out, with large bathrooms, cable TV, desks, closets and fresh towels. Occasionally, there is a problem with the water, but it is usually resolved promptly. The hotel has a nice courtyard, but you must ring the bell to get the door unlocked. There is some carry-over noise from the family in the house next door. The owners keep their distance, but are helpful.

Hostal Miraflorez, *Calle Sucre #920,* ☎ *664-3355, $$,* has basic rooms and those with a bath have cable TV. There is a central patio and the staff is friendly, although a bit shy.

Residencial Zeballos, *Calle Sucre #966,* ☎ *664-2068, buenaireahoteles. tarija.com, $$,* is a family-run establishment. Its flowered patio has an 80 year-old grape vine acting as the roof. The grapes, when ripe, are there for guests to enjoy. Rooms have large windows, tile floors, head lamps over the beds and telephones. Those with private baths have a TV also. Rates include breakfast. This is a good choice and the owners are friendly.

Hostal Bolívar, *Calle Bolívar #256,* ☎ *664-2741, $$,* has large rooms with baths around a central courtyard. You'll notice that it's cheaper to get two single rooms than one double. Go figure. The floors are tiled and there is cable TV and a phone in all the rooms. The hotel is clean and well maintained.

Hostal 15 de Abril, *Calle Daniel Compos #1079 on the corner of Cochabamba,* ☎ *664-5126 or 664-2459, $$,* has rooms on three floors set around an unwelcoming patio. The rooms are large, with tiled floors, wooden clothes racks, TVs and small bathrooms. You can find better deals in town.

Hotel Londres (London), *Calle Daniel Campos #1072,* ☎ *664-2369 or 664-2033, $$,* has large, clean and pleasant rooms with tiled floors and TVs. Pictures hang on the walls and some rooms have balconies. The shower water is supplied from a tank. Breakfast is included in the price. There is a sitting area on each floor and a roof-top terrace on the 7th floor, but no elevator.

Hostal Carmen, *Calle Ingavi #784,* ☎ *664-3372, vtb@olivo.tja.entelnet. bo, $$,* is across from the Rosario. It has 48 rooms, all with private bath. The owner was in the middle of an important card game when I was there and wouldn't show me a room. In this price range, I'd go to the Rosario or the Martinez instead.

Hostal Mi Casa, *Calle O'Connor #138,* ☎ *664-5267 or 663-6020, $$,* is comfortable and well decorated with tiles and rich, dark wood. The large rooms have closets and cupboards, lights over the beds and telephones. Breakfast is included in the room rate. The bathrooms are big and showers are separated from the rest of the bathroom. The water comes from a gas-heated water tank. There are 11 rooms in this Spanish hacienda-styled building. The travel-tour service can arrange jeep and micro bus tours. The staff is exceptionally helpful and pleasant. Mi Casa is fairly close to the bus terminal.

Hostal Martinez, *Avenida La Paz #251 and Avaroa*, ☎ *664-0222 or 663-6518, hos_mart@oliva.tja.entelnet.bo, $$*, is the best bet in the mid-range. Rooms are large, tastefully decorated with matching accessories (even a bed skirt), tile floors, quality furniture and soft beds. The rooms with triple occupancy are actually two rooms with a bath in-between. Breakfast is included in the room rate. The staff is friendly and helpful. This is a good deal.

Hostal Loma de San Juan, *Calle Bolívar, in front of the San Juan Church*, ☎ *664-4522 or 663-6101, $$$*, is the hidden gem of the city. Enclosed by a high wall covered in creeping vines, this tiny hotel offers rooms that look out on the old church or into the gardens. Rooms are large, with soft and clean carpets, rich wood cupboards, tables and chairs, color TVs and large soft beds with bed lamps. There is both a bath and shower in the tiled bathroom that has huge mirrors, and shampoo and soap provided. A buffet-style breakfast is included in your rate. A flower garden surrounds a clean pool and lawn chairs are lined up on the deck. A covered patio is at one end of the pool. Bottled water and fruit is supplied daily. If you like small, elegant and quiet, this is the place.

Hotel Los Ceibos, *Calle Victor Paz Estensoro and La Madrid*, ☎ *663-4430, ceibohot@cosett.com.bo, $$$$*, is, for me, the swankiest place in town. A large and inviting foyer is filled with chairs, couches and desks and the staff is friendly and cooperative. The pool is large and clean and surrounded by a flower garden. There is a bar and restaurant, laundry service and a safe for valuables. Each big room is clean, with tiled bathrooms, comfy beds and tasteful décor. For the price, this is a good deal. Large suites consist of two rooms with an en suite bathroom, a large living room and a fully supplied kitchen. This goes for $70 and will hold up to four people.

The Luz Palace Hotel, *Calle Sucre #921*, ☎ *663-5700 or 663-5701, luzpalac@olivo.tja.entelnet.bo, $$$$*, was the second place in Tarija that refused to show me a room. However, the foyer was clean and attractive and the man I spoke with wasn't rude, just uncooperative. The brochure says there are private bathrooms, cable TVs, fridges, mini-bars, Internet access and laundry service.

Gran Hotel Tarija, *Calle Sucre #770*, ☎ *664-2893 or 664-2684, $$$$*. When I arrived here the receptionist was having an interesting telephone conversation and refused to show me a room. However, I learned that the rooms have private baths, telephones, air conditioning and color TVs. There is a sauna in the hotel and a restaurant on the terrace.

Viña del Sur, *Zona Miraflores,* ☎ *663-2425 or 664-9041, vinasur@olivo. tja.entelnet.bo, $$$$$,* is the pride of Tarija. The hotel, built in 2000, sits on a hill overlooking the river. It has rooms and suites, a small shop, restaurant, pool, gym and sauna. Rooms have wide windows, a modern heater/cool air fan, cable TV, fridge, mirror and double closets. The bath is fully tiled and the place is very clean. The staff is helpful and pleasant. Buffet breakfast is included. Rates: $28 single; $43 double; $67 suite.

Hostal Postanera, *Avenida Los Americas, corner of J.M. Saracho,* ☎ *664-2851, www.hostal-postanera.com, $$$$$,* is an upscale hacienda built in an exquisite architectural design. The rooms are large, everything matches in the décor, and plants dot the halls. Each room has cable TV, closets, cupboards, and tables and chairs. Rates include a buffet breakfast (and they cater to vegetarians). Rates: $25 single; $35 double; $45 triple.

▪ Places to Eat

Restaurant Chino Hong Kong, *Calle Sucre #235,* ☎ *663-7076,* is behind the Bazar Chino and offers Chinese foods that are okay if you need a change, but they are not Hong Kong quality. The service is good, the meals substantial, and the prices low. Sweet and sour chicken with stir-fried rice and a salad was less than $3.50. The shop in front sells many items from China, like ornate knives and glass Buddhas. This restaurant and shop are owned by the same people who own the Club Social Tarija (see under *Places to Stay*).

La Cabana, *Calle Gran Trigo #435, (no phone),* is a well-kept property with a thatched roof. The tables are covered with linen tablecloths. The restaurant offers a smorgasbord of good food and you pay by the kilo.

Mateos Restaurant, *Calle Trigo and La Madrid, just off the main plaza (de Fuentes),* has fine décor complete with an indoor fountain. Mateo's salad bar (part of the *almuerzo*) offers three or four varieties of salads that you can have before soup. There is usually a choice of main course foods that include chicken Milanesa or lasagna. They make real mashed potatoes (not instant) and include cooked veggies with the main course. The flan I had for dessert was excellent. The *almuerzo* cost $2.50 and the pop was $1 extra.

Baghdad Café on Plaza Sucre is a noisy, dingy bar and not a place to patronize.

The spartan **El Solar**, also on Plaza Sucre, has low-backed booths and serves delectable veggie foods.

El Torpero Churrasqueria, *Calle V. Lima #226 and Daniel Campos, across from the Entel office*, is a popular place for *pique de la macho*, a meat stew loaded with spiced sausages. Locals often bring their instruments and play at this restaurant, rather than listening to the ubiquitous radio/cd player. El Torpero is set in a flowered courtyard away from the street.

El Solar Vegetarian Restaurant, *Calle V. Lima and Campero*, tries to look new wave with bold colors and oddly shaped furniture. In Bolivia, the vegetarian trend hasn't caught on yet and the beef-eating locals often poke fun at those patronizing vegan eateries. El Solar has a limited menu, but the food is supposed to be good. I did not try it.

Cafe Mokka, *Calle15 de Abril on Plaza Sucre*, is popular. Although their bread can be a bit stale, it is of better quality than breads offered at many other places. The food is good and moderate in quantity. The sandwich with fries that I had cost $1.75 and was stuffed with cheese, tomato, lettuce, onion and meat.

Churrasqueria El Amigos, *Calle V. Lima and Ballivan*, ☎ *664-6929*, has linen on the tables and wooden chairs, rather than the more common plastic ones. They serve tasty traditional dishes – try the *ranga-ranga* (roast pork). On weekends, they often have local musicians playing during or after dinner. The standard meal is about $3 per plate.

Taberna El Gattopardo, *Calle La Madrid #318*, ☎ *663-0656, on Plaza Luis de Fuentes*, has tourism figured out. It is open from 8 am until midnight every day, including holidays. You can sit on the street or inside at the open windows or deep inside where the décor is pleasing and the beggars can't get at you. The restaurant has an à la carte menu and offers dishes like omelets and spaghetti. Prices are higher here than at places patronized mostly by locals. This is a popular restaurant with the over-21 crowd, both local and tourist. The food is good and the portions almost adequate.

Konganas Restaurant, *Calle Virginia Lima and Avenida Suipacha #786*, ☎ *611-2452*, offers set meals like spaghetti or goulash for about $2 per plate. The inside of the restaurant is dimly lit and nicely decorated. There is also an outdoor patio and tables on the street so you can watch the action on Plaza Sucre. The food is good, but the portions are small.

Don Pepe, *Calle David Campos #138*, ☎ *664-2426*, is a classy place. Waiters are dressed in black and white, drinks are watered down and meals are excellent. Steaks are smothered in salty mushroom gravy, cooked as requested. The service was excellent, the music classical and everything was clean. Don Pepe's is occasionally rented for private parties, but never do they bring in local bands for entertainment.

Chingo's, *Plaza Sucre*, ☎ *664-4864*, is where young locals come to drink and party. They celebrate football game losses and wins, graduations, weddings and christenings, or anything else they can think of. Occasionally, they even eat. The steak specialty at $3.50 is good, but the atmosphere is too intrusive for an intimate dinner. Go here if you want to hang with the local younger crowd. I partied with a soccer team who were drowning their losses in beer. I had a blast.

Nuevo Siglo Churrasqueria, *Avenida Los Americas #888*, ☎ *664-6488*, has good meat. The steak is recommended, but the best dish is *piquante de gallina* (chicken).

Los Helechos, *Avenida Avaroa, half a block up from the train station*, offers breakfast of meusli, yogurt and fruit. This is fairly uncommon in Bolivia. They also have pizza and hamburgers, chicken and omelets, desserts and beer. The prices are good and so are the meals – especially breakfast.

■ Nightlife

 Karaoke Champayne, 15 de Abril #274 and Calle Sucre, is a dark and dingy place where all sorts of sins can be indulged, especially being inebriated. The place is popular with locals.

■ Shopping

 Supermercado Urkupeña, Calle Sucre and Avenida Avaroa, has a large selection of goods like wines, shampoo, dishes and junk food. The value of a market like this is to check the price of things before bargaining and making a purchase in the open market.

Foto Sistema Laboratorio Color, La Madrid #125, ☎ 664-8676, sells film and develops color prints. The technician here can repair minor camera problems, and some major ones too. I had a problem with my Nikon SLR and he had it running within a day (although the problem returned the following day). His price is not low – he charged double the quoted price. Establish the price in writing before leaving the shop.

Artesanias 15 de Abril, Calle 15 de Abril #161, between Calle Campos and Avenida Colon, ☎ 664-0813, offers products locally made from silver, wood, ceramic, wool, copper, stone and palm. Be careful when dealing with the owner. She tried to sell me an advertising brochure for 25¢. She may charge for the air you use while in the shop. The most interesting thing she had, although it was not for sale, was a hairless dog that had a sprinkle of hair only on its tail and head.

Artesanias Andaluz, Calle 15 de Abril, between Avenida Daniel Campos and Calle Sucre, ☎ 664-3709, offers well-crafted leather articles, straw weavings from the same type of grasses that are used to make Panama hats, and I got a butterfly collection (11 mounted) for $20. This is the best shop in Tarija for souvenirs.

Café Royal, Calle Ungavi #371 and Avenida Gran Trigo, sells local coffee beans that cost anywhere from 75¢ to $2 per kilo, depending on quality. It has a grinder, if you need it. Coffee is a good gift for friends and this is a place to replenish your own supply.

Camiri

Altitude: 8,224 ft / 2,500 m
Population: 3,000

Camiri, also known as the capital of black gold, is an oil-boom town connected to the Chaco, though it is really tucked into the foothills almost 6,000 ft/2,000 m above Villamontes. The greater height makes the climate pleasant. Just south of town along the highway is the huge rock known as the Devil's Tooth. It's a great place to walk. The area is rocky with lush jungle vegetation hanging onto every molecule of earth. The only other activity in Camiri is to hang out. The people are friendly and often take the time to chat.

I liked Camiri much more than Villamontes. Also, Che Guevera stayed here in Alojamiento Londres (see below).

■ Getting Here & Away

Buses coming in from the south start at Yacuiba, at the southern border. One leaves in the morning and then a number of buses leave at night. You can catch this bus either at the border or in Villamontes.

There are shared taxis between Villamontes and Camiri. The last one leaves around noon going in either direction (see *Villamontes*).

Numerous buses go to Santa Cruz from Camiri, but only one leaves during the day (8 am). There is no bus terminal in town. The bus companies are all on Calle Bolívar and Cochabamba. Most buses leave for Santa Cruz around 7 pm and the cost is $7 per person. The company with the most comfortable buses is Guzman and their buses (two of them) leave at 7 pm.

■ Places to Stay

Hotel Oriente, *Calle Comercio #78,* ☎ *952-2564, $,* has 22 rooms plus a garden and sitting area. The reception and patio are decorated with old instruments and Bolivian hats. The rooms are clean and the owner is friendly. Consequently, they have many return guests. There is also a car park. The hotel was the first in the town and is about 50 years old, but the present owner has had it for about 10 years. There are connections to Che Guevera: Che stayed in the owner's uncle's place and the uncle remembers him.

Hotel Sun, *Avenida Busch #39,* ☎ *952-4444, $,* has 30 beds in clean rooms. Breakfast is included in the price. The owners are helpful and pleasant. The first tourists they ever had were two Canadian cyclists with whom they still communicate.

Alojamiento Londres, *Avenida Busch #154,* ☎ *952-2726, $,* is basic and the communal bathrooms fall under the primitive category. This is more a Bolivian guy's place. However, Che Guevera stayed in room #4 during his run through to Valle Grande. There are elders of the village who remember Che's visit. Probably, some are glad they decided not to join him.

Residencial Primer, *Avenida Busch #60,* ☎ *952-2204, $$,* is a nice place and the owner is friendly and helpful. All rooms have large windows, towels, toilet paper, a large closet, balcony and remote control for the cable TV. Those with air conditioning and TV cost a little extra. There is a lounge area.

J. R. Hotel, *Avenida Sanchez #247,* ☎ *952-2200, $$,* has 17 large rooms and a pleasant sitting area on every floor. Each room has air conditioning, cable TV, private bath, gas-heated hot water, big windows, telephones, tile floors, towels and curtains that match the bedspreads. The price includes breakfast. There is also a restaurant, bar and car park on site.

Charagua

Between Camiri and Santa Cruz is the village of Charagua. Most people who stop here stay at the Hombre y Naturaleza station and visit the **Kaa Iya Gran Chaco National Park**. The station is in a colonial mansion just outside of Charagua. To make arrangements for a stay, contact Hombre y Naturaleza in Santa Cruz, ☎ 923-2239, hynb@bibosi.sca. entelnet.bo or prowames@cotas.com.bo. Their English is perfect, their Spanish is even better and they will be able to tell you how to get from place to place or recommend the best place for you to go (it may not be Charagua) considering your interests and time.

Tucked in a seldom-visited area 46 miles/75 km from the Paraguayan border, Charagua is a special place with an incredible landscape. Here, Hombre y Naturaleza is trying to protect lands around the new highway construction, attempting to keep pollution out and damage to the vegetation minimal. The group wants to educate local residents so they will be part of the protection process.

This area also contains Kaa Iya Gran Chaco National Park, which covers 8.4 million acres/3.4 million hectares of forest being managed as much as possible by the Izoceño-Guanari peoples who have lived there since before the Spanish arrived. Through the park runs the Parateti River, an inland delta that ends in a tectonic depression. The delta is referred to as the *cañadas*. The river delta is comparable in vastness to the McKenzie delta in northern Canada and the wildlife and bird life are varied and abundant. For further information about the park or a place to stay, contact Hombre y Naturaleza in Santa Cruz, ☎ 923-2239, hynb@bibosi.sca. entelnet.bo or prowames@cotas.com.bo.

The forest around Charagua and Kaa Iya Gran Chaco National Park is considered dry, even though it receives between 15 and 39 inches (400-1,000 mm) of rain every year, most of which falls in January and February. The forest houses animals such as the armadillo, panther, peccary and tapir. It is an important genetic corridor for animals between the Chaco and the Amazon Basin.

■ Getting Here & Around

 A **bus** leaves Santa Cruz every day at 1 pm and arrives in Charagua at 8 pm. During rainy season, it is an adventure getting here. Buses return to Santa Cruz every day at 8 pm (if running on schedule). If, due to problems on the road, the bus is late arriving, it will also be late returning.

A **train** leaves Santa Cruz every day between 3 and 6 pm. It arrives in Charagua just after midnight. Passengers must watch for the stop as there is no announcement. If you miss it, the next stop is in Camiri. To return by train is not so hot. The train will stop in Charagua any time between midnight and 6 am. That means waiting in the station for hours. The best plan is to take the train down and the bus back.

There are taxis at the bus station and the train station and it takes only a few minutes to arrive in town where there are basic places to stay. However, I suggest staying at the Hombre y Naturaleza station. The staff runs trips into the park and out to the delta. To get out to the station from the center of Charagua will cost $15 for a single and $10 per person for two or more. All trips start and end at the station (Valencia House), where accommodations are available (see below).

■ Adventures on Foot

WATERFALL & ROCK PAINTINGS: This day-trip starts with a hike to the Tacuarembo View Point where you can see the Parapeti River and the vastness of the park. From the mountain, you will follow a small river through a canyon to a waterfall where you can swim. On the way back to Charagua you will stop at Guirakuputi where, after a short walk, you come to the best rock paintings in the area. There is also a spot near the Ovai mission where, due to land erosion, an ancient ceremonial and burial site has been uncovered.

■ Adventures on Wheels

A day trip in a 4X4 to the park includes passing a more traditional Mennonite community where the people do not use motorized vehicles, electricity or modern conveniences. Once near the river, you will visit traditional *Chiriguanos* whose lifestyle is reminiscent of the Arawak Indians from the Amazon Basin to the north. The immense sand dunes you cross on the way to the Bañados del Izozog are a good place to view wildlife. This is a two-day trip. If you would like to spend three days in this wonderland, you could combine this with the hike, above.

The cost for these trips varies, depending on what you would like to do and how many there are in the group. A three-hour trip to some springs for one person is $35 and for two is $18 per person. A four-hour hiking trip costs the same. A full-day trip will cost between $55 and $65 for one person and $45 to $55 each if two people go. If going for two days to the mountains and then the Paraguay border, the cost is $330 for one and $200 each for two. On the other hand, a two-day trip into the park and near the river is $170 each for two people. Contact Hombre y Naturaleza in Santa Cruz, ☎ 923-2239, hynb@bibosi.sca.entelnet.bo or prowames@cotas.com.bo. They will arrange pickup in town and will take care of other details.

■ Place to Stay

To stay in the colonial **Valencia House**, contact Hombre y Naturaleza in Santa Cruz, ☎ 923-2239, or hynb@bibosi.sca.entelnet.bo or prowames@cotas.com.bo. They will arrange pickup in town and any other arrangements that need to be made. Staying here costs $10 per person for a single room or $7 per person if sharing. This includes breakfast. Lunch and dinner cost $5 per person and the cost of a ride to the station is $15 for a single and $10 per person when two or more share the vehicle. Valencia House has comfortable rooms, a restaurant and a museum containing artifacts from the Guanari culture. All trips offered by Hombre y Naturaleza start at the station (Valencia House).

Buena Vista

Elevation: 1,000 feet / 300 meters
Population: Under 5,000

This is a little town on the new highway between Santa Cruz and Cochabamba that had big hopes for the tourist industry. However, it never really caught on, so there are empty hotels and a few tour guides left behind still waiting for the boom. The rest have gone to Santa Cruz. However, Buena Vista is a good base from which to visit Amboro National Park if the big city of Santa Cruz gets to be too much and things in Samaipata have been explored.

■ Getting Here & Around

To get to Buena Vista, take a bus from Santa Cruz that is going to Yapacani and get off at Buena Vista. The *trufi* can be caught at the *trufi* stop near the old bus station. The cost is about $3 per person. To return to Santa Cruz you can catch a *trufi* on the plaza. Departure times are on what I call the when-full schedule.

Most buses going to and from Cochabamba on the new road will let you off at Buena Vista.

■ Adventures on Foot

A "Multiple-use Zone" lies in part along Rio Surutu. Multiple-use is a fancy name for an area no different from any other slash-and-burn farming region that may also have petroleum exploration, mining and ranching. You can walk along the river and gaze at the park on the opposite side. Remember that "park" in Bolivia often means just a slash-and-burn farming area.

Amboro National Park

Amboro is accessed from the new road between Cochabamba and Santa Cruz. It is about 62 miles/102 km (three hours by car) west of Santa Cruz. You can also get to Amboro from the old road that passes through Samaipata. There are two main areas to visit, the fern grove and the higher canyon area.

Amboro is over a million acres (442,000 hectares) of wonderland park abutting the foothills of the Andes. It has many forests, including humid rainforests, higher subtropical deciduous forests, the woodlands of the Chaco and the higher temperate forests of the Andes. Cloud forests sit at 5,921-6,908 ft (1,800-2,100 m) in elevation and are dominated by trees hundreds of years old.

Four major rivers pass through the park. The **Yapacani**, a major tributary to the Amazon that can get as wide as 2,600 ft/800 m in places, serves as a park border. Another important river is the **Surutu** that passes close to Buena Vista and has hiking trails along its banks. These rivers also offer canoeing and rafting opportunities.

Macuñucu Tropical Forest is a popular destination because of its 132-ft/40-m waterfall that has a swimming pool at the bottom and a cave system nearby. Hugging this waterfall are some of the 2,961 species of plants that have been identified in the park, belonging to a total of 200 families. The most impressive are the 33-ft/10-m arboreal ferns that date back about 300 million years. They are in the rainforest. But the trees include everything from pine to palm with many serving as hosts to about 100 varieties of orchids and bromeliads.

Within the forests and along the rivers are 127 species of mammals and 815 species of birds (60% of the country's total). These include the more common rock hens, blackbirds and condors. Over 100 species of reptiles have been identified and 43 species of bats. However, these numbers change frequently as more species are added. As the interest among scientists increases, so does the interest of tourists.

Park Headquarters are just off the main plaza in Buena Vista and they can provide guides to take you into the park. The cost is about $10 per day for a group of up to four people.

La Chonta Station is a hut with bunks protected by mosquito netting. It has cooking facilities, a shower and bathroom for $4 per night, per person. There are hiking trails and swimming in the river. From the station, you can walk even farther into Amboro park (a guide is required).

To get to La Chonta, take a *trufi* to Huaytu and walk down to the river. Cross the river (during high water you will need to hire a canoe) and walk up the track for nine miles/15 km. There is a lot of wildlife to enjoy while trudging up the trail. There is another hut at Macuñucu that can be reached from Santa Rosa (still farther up the road, on the south side of the river) and one at Villa Amboro. I did not visit these places. Because of the difficulty in getting to them, I suggest you hire a tour company or at least a guide to take you in.

Also see Samaipata section, page 379, for 4x4 trips into the park.

■ Places to Stay

HOTEL PRICES (US $)	
Per person, per day, unless noted otherwise.	
$	$2-$5
$$	$5-$10
$$$	$11-$17
$$$$	$18-$25
$$$$$	Over $25

Residencial Nadia, ☎ *932-02049, $$*, is just off the square. It is basic, dingy and noisy.

Flora y Fauna Cabins, *$$$$*, are out of Buena Vista about three miles/five km, part of it uphill. To get there, take a moto-taxi from the plaza. The cabins are owned by the famous birder/naturalist Robin Clarke, who was instrumental in the formation of the park. The cabins, built on a ridge overlooking the valley, were constructed in 1997 and have large rooms with private baths and fans. There is a bird observation tower on the premises from which up to 100 species have been sighted. Meals can be included in the deal. This is the most popular place to stay in the Buena Vista area.

Cabañas Gualtu, *$$$, .3 miles/.5 km from town on the road toward Huaytu (no phone)*, has cabins that can sleep up to six people. They have private bathrooms, kitchen facilities and a sitting area. There are also camping sites available for $3. These have clean bathrooms. Beyond the cabins are the Quimori Cabins, which run about the same price. They are just a bit farther up the road.

Samaipata

Altitude: 5,000 ft / 1,520 m
Population: 20,000

Samaipata is a colonial village tucked into the hills above Santa Cruz and overlooking the sandstone mountains of Amboro National Park. To visit Samaipata, you need time. The place makes you slow down and enjoy a tea at the Vesperes Garden Café or a cake from the German bakery. The comfortable climate and spectacular surroundings bring out even the most bored person's desire to explore.

There are long and short hikes around Samaipata and there are historical horse routes that can be followed. Visits to Amboro and the ruins of El Fuerte are a must. Whether you like to use a guide or go it alone, the area is perfect for exploring. Like so many places in Bolivia, there is wildlife everywhere. Once you are in the uninhabited areas, the possibilities for adventure are endless.

Places to stay are varied, but most are upscale in comfort while moderate in price. Samaipata is also trying to compete with Santa Cruz for culinary excellence and is giving them a good run.

■ Getting Here & Around

 Micros and shared taxis go from Santa Cruz to Samaipata. A shared taxi with four passengers costs $3.50 per person and takes about three hours. Vehicles leave Santa Cruz from Calle Omar Chavez and Soliz de Hulguin, around the corner from the old bus terminal. There is a daily bus that goes to Cochabamba along the old road and passes through Samaipata. It leaves from the bi-model station at 4 pm.

From Sucre there is one bus a day and it passes through Samaipata during the night. From Cochabamba there is a bus that passes daily but, again, it is a night bus. Going to Cochabamba, you should purchase a ticket through one of the tour agents or go to Mairana, 10 miles/16 km down the road from Samaipata, and catch the bus there as it does not stop in Samaipata if it is full.

■ History

 The present Samaipata was founded in 1680. There are two theories as to the meaning of the name; one from the local culture means a "resting place," while the word from the Tihuanacan language means a "marriage place." About 20 years ago, Europeans started buying property here. It seems they now own half the town. You know what that means – hot showers, real coffee, good bread, English.

■ Sightseeing

 The Plaza in Samaipata is the most interesting in all of Bolivia. It has stone works that are reproductions of the carvings at El Fuerte. There is one walkway with a serpent, another with the puma and a third with a condor. Look at them here before you go to El Fuerte so you can recognize them more easily.

On the east side of the plaza a circular step sits in front of a sculpture. Stand at the side of the circle and say something to the statue and then stand in the center of the circle and say the same thing. You'll hear an echo when you are in the circle. The acoustics are wonderful. This phenomenon came about by accident.

Sampaita

TOUR OPERATORS
1. Don Gilberto
2. Blendinger Nature Tours
3. La Vispera - Boliviajes
4. Amboro Tours
5. Roadrunner

WHERE TO STAY & EAT
6. Achira Resort
7. Campeche
8. Finca La Vispera
9. Quinta Piray Cabanas
10. Hamburg Café, Hotel
Comer y Cuartos
11. Amboro Café
12. Land Haus Hotel, Restaurant
& Coffee Shop
13. Traudi's
14. Hotel Aran Juarez
15. German Bakery
16. Casa Blanca, Hotel Kim
17. Don Jorge Residencial

to Santa Cruz & ❻

to Amboro National Park

to Sucre, Cochabamba, Vallegrande

Taxi ⑭

H

CAMPERO

Museum

Police

Market

EL ESTUDIANTES

R TERRAZAS

Bus Station

Bus Station

SUCRE

© 2004 HUNTER PUBLISHING, INC

El Fuerte is open daily, 9 am-5 pm. It is the second-largest ruin in Bolivia and during its time must have been quite an impressive city. The first excavations started in 1951 and after the importance of the fort was realized, it was declared a national monument. More excavations didn't occur again until 1974 and then again it was left until 1992.

The site's main ceremonial center is a huge carved outcropping 658 ft long by 18 wide and 82 high (200 x 60 x 25 m) with niches that at one time held gold-plated statues. There was a virgins' quarters that held about 2,000 virgins and a grand plaza. There are signs of buildings lying under the present structures that indicate an earlier civilization having been there prior to the Tihuanacans and Inca.

The center has three creatures carved into the top of the outcropping. The first is the snake that, to the Inca and pre-Inca civilizations, represented the underworld. The canals that are part of the snake carvings are believed to have carried blood, water or *chicha* during religious ceremonies. The second animal, on the lower top surface of the rock, is a puma, which represented life on earth. A photograph taken in 1945 shows the outline in the rock of three cats, rather than just one. Because the rock is so soft, the image has been worn away by weather. The final image, near the puma, is of the condor that represented the afterlife, or life in the heavens. The seats carved into the south-central side of the rock suggest people sat there to watch ceremonies.

The niches, carved into the south side of the ceremonial rock are of three designs. One is triangular, the second is rectangular and the third is trapezoidal. The first two designs are thought to belong to a culture that was here before the Inca. The trapezoidal niches belonged to the Inca. Some of the smaller designs were also carved at different times. Of those, some are believed to have been made before Christ.

Located just south of the ceremonial area was the Five Bakers' Temple. This site is under the care of Stonewatch (an organization that monitors and protects significant stones worldwide). One of the reasons for their interest in the ruin is that the sandstone on which it sits is thought to be like a sponge. During rainy season the rock is saturated and during dry season the water seeps out of the rock onto the ground. There are only two or three places in the world where this occurs.

When the Inca first came to El Fuerte they followed their usual custom by offering peace. If the peace was accepted, the two cultures melded. This is what archeologists believe happened at El Fuerte because there are both Inca symbols and those of the previous religion carved in the rock.

War Song of the Incas
We will drink from the skull of the traitor
And from his teeth a necklace make
Of his bones we will make flutes
Of his skin a drum
Then we will dance.

During those days, if a village was attacked and refused the peace offered by the Inca, the men were killed and the village was burned. Women and children were not harmed. A new village would be built and the survivors integrated into the new group without any remnants of their past culture.

Although the site isn't breathtaking, it is impressive and should not be missed. There is an elaborate wooden infrastructure built around the rock, with viewing platforms. Take binoculars.

Much of the information I received about the ruins came from the works of Hugo Buero and Oswald Rivera Sundt and was told to me by Olaf Liebhart of Roadrunners.

To get to El Fuerte you can take any vehicle going toward Santa Cruz and get off at the road that leads uphill to the ruins. There is a sign. The walk from the road is 4.3 miles/seven km. This is a long haul with good views. Alternately, you can join a tour. The advantage of going on tour is the added information you will receive from your guide, which always makes a place that much more interesting.

Another option is to take an overnight horse trip to the ruins. This includes spending one night close to the headwaters of the Pirai River. On the second day you would arrive on Cerro del Inca and walk down to the ruins. The ride back to Samaipata is in a vehicle. The cost is $155 per person if two people go and $123 if three or more go.

■ Adventures in Culture

 If visiting the small museum in Sampaipata, your entry ticket covers both the ruins and the museum. You cannot pay for only one place. However, the museum is worth it. And to appreciate the ruins, you need information. Foreigners pay $3, while locals pay $1.75. The museum is open Monday to Saturday, 8:30 am-12:30 pm and 2:30-6:30 pm. The ruins are open daily, 9 am-5 pm.

The museum has a scaled model of El Fuerte in one room with photos of what it looked like when it was first found. The Ceramic Room has many pieces, some showing that Amazon trade goods reached this far many centuries ago. There is also one interesting wooden vase carved in relief.

Samaipata's town square.

■ Adventures on Foot

CERRO INCA: Walking to this hill is recommended because it gives a view of the entire site of El Fuerte and allows the imagination to really see what it was like hundreds of years ago. From the hill you can see the carved ceremonial outcropping, the place where the grand plaza stood and the field where the huge administrative building may have been.

From the ruins where the fence is located, follow the trail downhill and away from the parking lot. When you come to a fork, go to the left and continue down to the river. Cross the river on dry rocks; the wet ones are slippery. Go straight up from the river. At the top, the red rock walls near Amboro National Park and clouds over the rainforest can be seen. In the opposite direction the wilderness stretches ahead, rugged but green. The curious condors in this area seem to like to keep an eye on people.

Roadrunners Tour Company (see *Tour Operators*, below) in Samaipata will rent a GPS with the route of this climb mapped out. If you feel you would like to use one, see them in town. You must leave your passport as security.

TRUMPET OF DEATH

Trumpet flowers, common to the valley are white or pink in color and look like trumpets. They are beautiful to look at but deadly to eat.

CERRO DE LA PATRIA: To get here from the center of town follow the signs uphill to the Campeche Cabins. Cross the soccer field in front of Campeche and walk along the edge of the forest until you come to a road. Follow it to the end and then head up the mountain. Be aware that snakes like to curl up in the grass. On top of the hill is a wire fence. Cross it and go left. After a short distance there are some stone circles, actually Inca silos. Return by the same way. This is a two-hour walk.

CONDOR HIKE: For those with a strong leg and determined spirit, this hike will take you to where condors meet, nest and bathe in natural rock pools. However, the

Look at, but don't eat, the pretty flowers of the trumpet tree.

hike is about four hours straight up (don't forget the heat) to a ridge where these magnificent birds hang out. You may do this either as a long one-day trip or as a two-day trip with an overnight at La Pajcha Waterfall.

Pieter at La Vispera has found this spot, developed the route and knows the easiest way to get there (although no way is really easy). You must see Pieter in order to do this hike.

On the one-day trip, you leave Samaipata at 7 am, drive for two hours to trailhead, then walk for a minimum of six hours. Rest and observation time should be added on top of that. On the two-day trip, you will again leave Samaipata in the morning and drive to the trailhead, stopping on the way for coffee with locals who run a small farm. At the waterfall, you will set up camp on a tiny beach and hike in the afternoon to observe wildlife. The following morning you will head up to the condor's hideout.

The one-day trip costs $41 per person for a group of two, $31 per person for a group of three and $26 per person for a group of four. The two-day trip costs $72 per person for a group of two, $55 per person for a group of three and $45 per person for a group of four. Prices include a guide and transportation. Meals and gear are extra.

LA PAJCHA: This three-tiered waterfall drops about 11 ft/35 m and is tucked into a cathedral of vegetation. The falls end in a cool pool beside a sandy beach. The pool is just made for swimming. If you have a tent, it is possible to camp here. However, it is difficult to reach on your own as the road is bad and travel is about 10 miles an hour. It is advisable to join a tour or hire a private taxi that will take up to four people for $30.

To get there, take the road going south from Samaipata for 25 miles/ 41 km and walk about five miles along a path through the jungle. There is a sign indicating the turnoff. The walk will reveal some interesting vegetation and some birds, but nothing as compared to what is in Amboro. There is a fee of 75¢ to enter the falls area.

LAGUNA VOLCAN: This clean little lake is tucked into a flat area above the village of Bermejo. To get there, take a bus going toward Bermejo and get off .6 miles/one km before the village. A sign indicates the turnoff. Walk uphill to the north (toward the park) for two to three hours. There is a cost of 75¢ to enter the area. On the way you will see the sandstone mountains of the park, dotted with greenery. This is an excellent location for birding. There is also some hiking available by climbing the ridge above the third waterfall.

QUIRUSILLAS: This is a place to spend a laid-back weekend in a relaxed community and/or to visit the lake. Quirusillas is 18 miles/30 km from Samaipata on a secondary road going south. It sits where three valleys meet. A nine-mile/15-km circular route goes from the village to the lake and back. This lake is where the community gets its water supply.

The ridge above the lake offers views of Vallegrande Valley (southwest) 34 miles/55 km away, Mairana and Samaipata (northeast). To the southeast is Postrer Valle, where Che Guevera fought one of his less famous battles.

If you want to go farther, head from the ridge along a paved Inca road to Vallegrande. From there, you can walk to Tarabuco and, eventually, to Sucre. The full trip to Sucre takes about 10 days and a guide would be required. The trip can also be done on a horse (see La Vispera in Samaipata).

■ Adventures on Wheels

SALT ROAD TO SUCRE: This is a 4x4 trip along an old salt trade route that goes 276 miles/450 km. It takes about four days with camping along the way. It can include a side excursion to the colonial and historic town of Vallegrande. Sunday is market day in Vallegrande.

But first there is a stop at **Mataral**, where there are some 10,000-year-old rock paintings. From Vallegrande, you drive to Pucara where you can take another side-trip to La Higuera, where Guevera was killed. From there you climb out of the humid climate of the forest and get the cooler valleys of the foothills near Tarabuco and then go on to Sucre.

AMBORO NATIONAL PARK: (See Buena Vista section for general description of the park.) There are three ways to get into the park. At the western end, a 4x4 road leads from Mairana on the highway toward Cochabamba. It goes eight miles/13 km to La Yunga, from where you can walk into the forest along a track.

If you continue by jeep along the road back toward Samaipata, it goes another 11 miles/18 km to Lautas and then up to Los Alisos or back down to Samaipata. These are difficult roads and not recommended during rainy season. The walking trails that go between the curves on the road are great for seeing wildlife.

The second entry point into the park is from Achira Cabins, six miles/10 km east along the road toward Santa Cruz from Samaipata. The road into the park is a four-wheel-drive track that goes to Abra los Toros. From there you can start hiking into the fern forest. There are also the remains of an Inca fortress along the way.

The southwestern part of the park is where giant ferns, mosses and bromeliads are located. Five hundred orchid species have been found in the rainforest here, along with with numerous plants that are often used for medicine by naturopaths (like the cats claw, used to fight cancer).

MOSES CACTUS

Yucca is the tall plant that has a bunch of white flowers on top. The shape of the cluster looks like a beard, so locals call the plant the Moses cactus.

The center of the park has deep canyons formed by swift rivers. Mountains rise up above these canyons and many are dotted with bamboo groves. The lowlands of the northern area are rich in bird life. One of the rarer birds in the area is the quetzal, with its 3.5-ft/one-meter tail feathers of the kind used by the Aztecs in Mexico to make Montezuma's cape.

For a good trip, I suggest hiring a guide or a tour company. They know where to go, how to get there and what to look for. If you are interested in the fern forest, you will get rain; if you are interested in the rugged rocks and canyons, you will get heat. A tour company can help you make decisions and make certain you see most of what you would like to see.

■ Adventures on Horseback

CHE GUEVERA TRAIL TO VALLEGRANDE: Every October, Bolivians visit the school where Guevera was killed. They celebrate the anniversary of his death. Che is more of a mythological than political hero, as he is in the rest of the world. No one knows his real story or is interested in his communist ideology. He gave his life trying to fight the establishment. Plus, he was handsome. These are the important facts.

This horse trip takes anywhere from six to nine days and covers about 80 miles/130 km of trail. La Vispera (see *Tour Operators*) has horses and tents for rent; they charge $100 for the trip. The route follows a secondary road from Samaipata to San Juan del Rosario, past La Pajcha waterfall, and on down to Postrer Valle. Some of the villages en route are 600 years old and not a part of our electronic age and lifestyle.

Eventually, you must cross two passes to reach Tierras Nuevas and then cross over to Vallegrande, close to La Higuera, where Che Guevera died. From the ridge, you will be able to see the ravine where the battle took place. You can visit the school room in the village where he was shot.

In Vallegrande where Guevera's body was put in storage (and on display) is the **Che Guevera Museum**. The tomb of Tania, Guevera's friend, is in the graveyard. Guevera's grave under the tarmac is now empty because his body has been sent to Cuba. The body was kept in the laundry room in the Knights of Malta Hospital before it was buried, and that room, too, is open for view. This is also where Rodriguez (CIA agent) brought the dead body of Che out and held him up so he appeared still alive (complete with open eyes) for journalists to photograph. At this point, Rodriguez hadn't figured out his story for the Pentagon. Was it good to pretend Che was still alive, or tell the truth, that he was dead? Rodriguez later ended up being questioned because his story didn't add up. You can purchase copies of the photos taken during this event.

Hotel Ganadero, Calle Bolivar #115, ☎ 492-2176, is clean and the place to stay in town. However, there are two other choices I can recommend: **Alojamiento Teresita**, Mendosa #107, ☎ 492-2151, and **Residencial Valle Grande**, just up from Teresita (no phone). Both are good and a bit cheaper than the Ganadero. Should you be here during a festival and can't find a room, locals will offer you their home. Ask around.

From Vallegrande, there are two routes back to Samaipata. Pieter, from whom you rented the horse at La Vispera, will advise you because the conditions (and thus the route) depend on what time of year you travel.

THE LIFE & DEATH OF CHE GUEVERA

Che Guevera was born in 1928 in Argentina. He suffered from asthma and because of this was unable to participate in many children's games. Instead, he read from his father's collections of Marx, Engels and Freud. As a university student, Che became anti-Peron, although he never participated in the demonstrations that called for Peron's fall.

Guevera studied medicine and specialized in dermatology in general and leprosy in particular. But he was a restless sort with socialist ideals, so in 1949 he took his famous motorbike trip north, working along the way at everything from ditch digging to practicing as a doctor in specialized clinics for leprosy. In 1951 he arrived in the United States.

He came to Bolivia in 1952 to be part of the revolution that was occurring at the time. But he found it an opportunists' revolution (not pure enough) and refused to participate. Instead, he went to Guatemala where he earned a living writing travel articles. At that time he became an even purer socialist and rejected most forms of communism. He lived with Hilda Gadea, an Indian and Marxist who helped Che with his indoctrination. She also married him.

In 1954, Che met Raul and Fidel Castro in Mexico City and followed them to Cuba where he studied guerrilla warfare. He became ruthless in his methods of ruling, shooting, without question, those who turned against Castro or the revolution. He hated a turncoat. He also hated cowards, so he shot them too. With this type of dedication it didn't take long for Che to become Fidel's top man.

After the success in Cuba, restlessness and desire for revolution continued to drive Che. He divorced Hilda and married Olidia. Together they visited the Congo in Africa and then Che came to Bolivia believing that the country, because of its poverty, was ripe for insurrection. Also, the 12-year-long socialistic rule of the MNR was over and the generals were back in power, rolling back the clock, in Che's opinion. Bolivia also bordered five countries, so the spread of the revolution would be easy. Che entered Bolivia on November 1st, 1966. The miners were on strike but he failed to see this as the place to start. Possibly, this was his great error. Unions have leaders and Che wanted to be the leader. Instead, he formed a guerrilla training camp in Santa Cruz that attracted a few men but got no sympathy or support from the locals.

In the meantime, the US, still smarting about the Cuban Revolution and the Bay of Pigs, was tracking Che. A CIA agent by the name of Felix Rodriguez worked with the Bolivian army in the hunt. The first thing they did when they got in the vicinity of Guevera's army, in order to get support of the locals, was drop pamphlets from the air saying they would pay $4,200 for the capture of Guevera. Rodrequez then led a 650-man battalion into the area near Vallegrande.

Between March and August 1967, Che and the Bolivian military had skirmishes, but nothing serious happened until August 31, when the army killed about one third of Che's men. They also captured Che's best soldier, Paco. Che retreated and his asthma started to cause him great discomfort.

During his retreat toward the south, Che went to Alto Seco to buy food and spend the night, but he learned that one of the locals had gone to inform the military of his presence. So Che and his men went to Loma Larga, a ranch between Alto Seco and La Higuera. The peasants living there fled. Che continued on to Vallegrande, but he found that there, too, most of the villagers were absent. Shots could be heard in the distance and Che quickly surmised that they meant the Bolivian military was hot on his tail. So he and his men moved toward Valle Serrano, south of Rio Grande. He thought that if he got across the border into Paraguay he would be safe.

The group was camped on the Yuro River when an old lady passed by. Che paid her to keep quiet about their presence. However, it was an old woman who told the military that she heard voices of men on the Yuro River near San Antonio. It has never been confirmed that it was the same lady, but chances are good that it was.

The final battle started along the Yuro River. Che was shot in the leg and, as he retreated, he was hit several more times. His follower, Sarabia, picked him up and ran. Che lost his hat. Sarabia sat down in an open area and tried to defend Che. They both shot at the military but the army circled them, filling Che with bullets. He could no longer hold his gun and fire at the same time. At one point, Che shouted that he was worth more alive than dead. He surrendered. The battle ended at 3:30 pm with Che being taken prisoner. Carried on a stretcher to La Higuera, Che was placed in a school house where he lay in the dirt, arms and legs tied, hair matted, clothes torn, bullet wounds adding to his discomfort. He was also having trouble breathing. Rodriguez arrived in a helicopter. He took some photos of Che and of his diary and then, against the advice of his bosses, gave the orders to execute Guevera. Rodriguez also warned the firing squad not to shoot Guevera in the face because he wanted it to look like Guevera had been killed in battle. As Che stood facing the firing squad his last words were, "Know this now, you are killing a man."

After Che died, Rodriguez took Che's Rolex watch and later showed his souvenir to newspaper reporters. He also stored the body in the laundry room of the hospital. When journalists wanted proof that Che was still alive, the military men brought the body out and held Guevera up so he looked like he possibly could be alive. His eyes were still open. The journalists took their photos. However, when the reports went into the Pentagon, there were discrepancies. The Pentagon wanted Guevera alive and the journalists reported that he was alive. If he had died in battle as Rodriguez told the Pentagon, he should have been dead 24 hours before the time that was reported on his death certificate. Rodriguez, tried to cover his tracks. In doing this, he had Che's hands cut off to prove this was the right man. He buried the rest of Che in an unmarked grave under the tarmac of the airport at Vallegrande. As for the newspaper reports, everyone knows that journalists never get anything correct.

▪ Tour Operators

Roadrunner, ☎ 944-6193, is run by Olaf Liebhart and his partner, Frank. They are a wealth of knowledge about the area. They rent GPSs, with a number of different routes keyed in, for $10 per day. You must leave your passport as a guarantee. Roadrunner charges $10 per person for a day trip to El Fuerte (up to four people). The price drops with more people. It also runs trips into the north end of Amboro National Park for two days. These cost $50 per person, with a minimum of two people, and $30 per person if there is a group of five. This trip goes through the fern forest. The $2.50 park entry fee is not included in the price of the trip. Locals pay only $1 to enter the park.

Gilberto Aguilera, Calle Sucre #2, ☎ 944-6050, is the most respected guide in the entire village. He takes individuals or groups to Amboro National Park, Las Cuevas and La Pajcha. Gilberto is often hired by tour agencies in town and his knowledge of the area is second to none. If you book with an agency, ask if Gilberto can go along as your guide.

Michael Blendinger, Calle Bolívar, across from the museum, ☎ 944-6186, mblendinger@cotas.com.bo, offers all the usual tours and is willing to customize a trip to meet your needs. Michael is a biologist who speaks English, German and Spanish; his English is exceptional. Michael is a landscape photographer and specializes in birding tours. He offers a trip into Amboro where, during dry season, you leave your gear with donkeys that take a different route as you go through a gorge just big enough for a human to pass. Michael does a lot of photography and some photos have been on exhibition at the tourist office in Santa Cruz.

La Vispera rents horses for $3 an hour. They will also take you on a six- to nine-day trip from Samaipata to Villegrande and back to Samaipata or on to Sucre. Pieter at La Vispera runs a 4x4 trip that goes along the old salt trade route to Sucre. This is a four-day excursion (see above). Pieter will also hike from his place cross-country up to El Fuerte, arriving at the ruins from the backside. The only downside of this trip is that, after hiking all day, the final lap is an upward slog. However, what you will see is worth 10 slogs. The cost is $24 per person (minimum of two people) and the price drops to $8 per person if 15 people go.

A one-day trip into Amboro National Park for two people costs $28 per person, while an overnight trip costs $140 per person. This includes cooks, pack mules, meals and camping equipment, plus an English-speaking guide. It does not cover the $2.50 park entry fee, a sleeping bag or mat. One trip done by this company for the first time ever was a hike across the park from La Vispera, an 18-day trip. Ask about it.

Amboro Tours, Calle Bolívar #43 (across from the museum), ☎ 944-6293, is operated by the ex-director of Amboro National Park. They offer three trips into the park that take from one to three days. The first is to the volcano, the second is through the fern forest and the third is along the Rafael River to the Devil's Tooth.

■ Places to Stay

 Samaipata streets often lack names. However, the community is small enough that locating hotels and restaurants is easy. If you need direction, ask a local.

HOTEL PRICES (US $)	
Per person, per day, unless noted otherwise.	
$	$2-$5
$$	$5-$10
$$$	$11-$17
$$$$	$18-$25
$$$$$	Over $25

Mi Casa, *across from Casa Blanca, $,* has no phone and only five rooms with either private or shared baths. The rooms are basic, with bamboo and thatch roofs and brick floors.

Chilo Residencial, ☎ *944-6014, $,* is freshly painted. The central courtyard has been spruced up and everything is clean. Hot water is available all day and some rooms have TV. This is a good deal.

Alojamiento Familiar, *on the square,* ☎ *944-7001, $,* charges $2 per person for a basic room without bath.

Hotel Paola, *on the square $,* has an array of prices depending on whether you have a bath and breakfast or not.

> **AUTHOR NOTE:** I would stay at the three hotels around the square – the Paola, Familiar and the Rosario – only as a last resort.

Hostal Kim, ☎ *944-6161, $,* has basic clean rooms set around a small courtyard. They come with or without private bath. This is a small and friendly place. The entrance is inviting, decorated with plants and trees.

Don Jorge Residencial *just down from the Hamburg,* ☎ *944-6086, $,* has clean basic rooms with bath. This is a good deal.

Residencial Rosario, *on the square,* ☎ *944-6171, $$,* offers rooms with or without private bath. All guests share one kitchen. I found the Rosario hot and musty.

La Vispera, ☎ *944-6082, www.lavispera.org, $/$$,* is .5 miles/one km uphill from the center of town and is run by Dutch ex-pats, Margarita and Pieter. After traveling for 20 years, the couple came to the Samaipata Valley and stayed. They called the place La Vispera, which means "eve" – referring to the beginning of their new life.

La Vispera is highly recommended, especially for a long rest. The rooms are exceptional and the gardens could be classed as the botanical garden of Samaipata. A terraced area below the Garden Café is full of herbs and vegetables. In the garden is a huge Molle tree. Although not native to the area (it likes a much drier climate), this tree has thrived to the point of encompassing a large part of the garden. Margarita and Pieter have lived in Bolivia for 19 years. They speak Dutch, German, English and Spanish and can arrange tours, answer questions, take time to have a tea or rent you a place to stay. The food here is excellent (see *Places to Eat*).

Room rates are higher for advance reservations. The rooms are clean and comfortable with soft beds and shared bathrooms. Kitchen facilities are available and tiled porches allow you to sit and enjoy the hummingbirds buzzing around or view the distant hills dotted with white haciendas. Cabins have bedrooms, living/sitting rooms, fully supplied kitchens, private bathrooms with gas-heated water and a private porch. A **camping** area has two gas-heated showers, separate toilets in a modern tiled building, a full kitchen and a barbecue pit. If the conditions are good,

Pieter can supply wood for a campfire. Tenting costs $3 per person if you have your own tent and $4 per person if you use one of theirs.

I noticed dozens of hummingbirds and the other birds I was unable to identify were numerous. Ornithologists stay at La Vispera to work.

Pieter and Margarita will arrange your pickup from the airport in Santa Cruz for a small fee. Should you wish to spend a night in Santa Cruz and then visit a few hot spots on the way to Samaipata, that too can be arranged. This must be negotiated with Pieter or Margarita.

For those wanting to do excursions on their own, maps, information and horses are available. Pieter will go over the maps with you and help plan a route. He then introduces you to your horse. You must spend at least two days with the horse so that you are both comfortable with each other before going off on your own

HOT POTS

There are clay ovens throughout Bolivia that people still use for cooking. The one above the garden at La Vispera was built by Pieter. The ovens sit on a layer of bricks that have an eight-inch layer of salt beneath. The salt helps get and keep the temperature of the oven high by reflecting heat. To make the oven, the first layer of mud is mixed with straw and placed on a wooden frame. The mud is covered with strands of straw placed in the same direction. When this dries, a second layer of mud is laid and a second layer of straw is placed with strands going in the opposite direction to the layer below. This process is repeated until the clay/mud is nine to 12 inches thick. A fire is made inside and burned for four hours until the temperature reaches about 1,300°F/700°C. The fire is then hot enough for the oven to be used for 24 hours. To maintain a cooking temperature after that, a fire is built for one hour a day.

Land Haus Rooms, ☎ *944-6033, $$,* is up from the square three blocks and at the same place as the restaurant. Follow the signs. Rooms and cabins here hold anywhere from two to seven people. They have a private bathroom, TV, sitting area, full kitchen and a patio with a barbecue pit. Larger, more expensive cabins have fridges, two-burner stoves, double beds, separate shower stalls in the bathrooms, a dining/sitting area and fireplaces.

The yard is manicured and has old trees and flowering bushes, including a grape canopy over a large picnic table. The patios are all tile and flagstone. A swimming pool and dry sauna can be used for $20 per group for up to four hours. The sauna is large and well made and sits beside a massage mat (bring your own therapist) and a cold shower. Guests may pick fruit from the trees in the yard, which is peppered with hammocks. The two big pluses to this place are its proximity to town and the café and restaurant on the premises. This allows you to eat, drink and roll into bed all in one smooth movement.

If coming from Sucre, the bus will let you off at the bottom of the road and you need to walk only 500 ft/150 m to the hotel. German and English are spoken.

Quinta Piray, ☎ *944-6136, quinta-piray@cotas.com.bo, $$*, is another top-notch place. It's set on the hill overlooking town. The large piece of property has maintained gardens and a lawn dotted with white plaster cabins topped in red tiled roofs. The cabins hold anywhere from two to six people; the large ones have two bedrooms and two bathrooms. Some have fireplaces and all have barbecue pits. They are self contained and hospital-clean. The owners, Antje and Karl Udo-Hartwig, are enthusiastic about treating guests well so they return for a second stay. Rates vary from $20 for two, mid-week, to $130 for six during a holiday. This is a gem of a place. To get here, follow the hill to the right at the fork that leads to La Vispera and Traudi's.

Traudi's, ☎ *944-6094, $$*, is across the way from La Vispera and is run by Dr. Oscar Arce. His wife Traudi does ceramics in the shop beside the main house. Rooms come with or without bath and private cabins are available for larger groups. The semi-detached cabins (row houses) are clean and comfortable. There is a large pool for guests to use and a kitchen where breakfast can be ordered in advance. This place is peaceful, with sheep and horses mowing the lawns. If you wish to be left alone and never bothered, except for a cleaning lady wanting to fix up your mess, this is the place. The area has lots of birds and frogs to watch during the day and fireflies at night. It was here that I learned what could be done with mud bricks. Our room was mud-brick, painted in orange, brown and yellow enamel. It was beautiful.

Casa Blanca, ☎ *944-6076, $$$*, has three floors of spacious and clean rooms around a central courtyard. All the rooms have private bath and those from the second floor up are new. They have nice furniture, soft beds and tiled floors. Breakfast is included in the rate. Casa Blanca is a friendly and clean place.

Hostal Campeche, ☎ *333-6607, www.campechebolivia.com, $$$*, is a member of the International Hosteling Association. Up on the hill, the cabins are built on a slope overlooking town. Room rates range from $12.50 per person in the middle of the week to $120 for a six-person cabin during holidays. Some accommodations have only a room with a private bath, while the bigger places are two-bedroom, two-bathroom cabins with fully supplied kitchens, living and sitting rooms and a terrace with a built-in barbecue. There's a café and restaurant on site. The cabins have a lot of stonework around them and the rooms are bright.

Hotel Comer y Cuartos, *$$$*, is a new building just up from the Hamburg. The rooms are clean and moderate in size. The cost is $20 for a room with bath and $10 for a room without. This place can be a bit noisy when table tennis is being played in the main foyer.

Hotel Aran Juarez, *on the highway at the entrance to the village,* ☎ *944-6223, $$$*, is the hotel that was robbed by the followers of Che Guevera during his fatal trip into the area. From the hotel, the bandits moved to the hospital and relieved them of valuables and medical equipment (which the bandits were really going to need) before heading down to Vallegrande. For visitors today, the hotel is clean, free of militant communists and comfortable.

Achira Sierra Resort, *six miles / 10 km from Samaipata on the road to Santa Cruz,* ☎ *352-2288, $$$, www.achiraresort.com*, is the Bolivian version of Club Med, except that it caters to larger groups. The smallest cabin (except for the honeymoon suite), holds four people and the largest holds 18. Each place is self-contained and the grounds have a pool, tennis court, volleyball court, ping pong, a games room, mini golf, shuffle board, a restaurant and a bar. Rates run anywhere from $15 for a single to $95 for the largest cabin. A campsite on the 14-acre property is tucked into an orange grove and is equipped with tables and barbecue pits. The cost is $2 per person, per night.

The resort offers horses to rent and tours to Amboro and El Fuerte. Nearby are hiking trails along the Paredones River where giant ferns, wild parrots and butterflies can be seen. To get here ask the bus driver to let you off at the junction that is .6 miles/one km from the resort.

Los Volcanes Sanctuary, *near the south end of the park just outside the park boundary, no phone, $$$*, is tucked under sandstone cliffs and surrounded by jungle. It has six double rooms with private bathrooms available. It is accessible from Bermejo, 24 miles/40 km from Samaipata on the Santa Cruz road. You must cross the river and walk 2.5 miles/four km to reach the accommodations. Some of the birds seen near here are wood creepers, ant-thrushes, gnat-eaters, scarlet-breasted fruit eaters, manakins and tanagers. Howler monkeys will compete for your attention.

■ Places to Eat

Hamburg Café, ☎ *944-6153*, is decked in antiques and has a nice ambiance. It carries only Bolivian wines. The curried chicken was exceptional, but the omelet was less than ordinary. The Milanesa should have had an extra dish of vegetables with it. However, all dishes run about $3.50, a definite bargain. The Hamburg also has an Internet café with one machine. Internet access is via phone lines in Samaipata, so the service is slow. Also, it is available only from 7 pm to 7 am on weekdays and all day on weekends. The cost is about $2 an hour.

The café's book exchange has a strange policy. All books exchanged must be the same size and in the same condition as the one taken. The literary content is irrelevant.

La Vispera will give you a breakfast in their Garden Café as long as you order ahead. I had pancakes and conserves and the portion was far more than I could eat. My husband, John, went at the rhubarb jam until the jar was empty. The cost for pancakes and coffee was $1.50. They also serve muesli with fresh fruit and yogurt. Their lunchtime specialty is soup with scones and they claim it as the best in the village. I found the garden irresistible. The Garden Café is also open for theme suppers and offers traditional Dutch meals once a week. This includes *hutspot*, or red cabbage. Rhubarb pie is available almost all the time, as are herbs for tea picked fresh from the garden.

The **Amboro Café** across from Michael Blendinger has a guiding service and an Internet café. They were closed when I was there.

Land Haus Restaurant, Café and Artists' Shop, ☎ *44-6257, landhaus@cotas.com.bo*, is close to the center and is the best restaurant in the village. It serves real filtered coffee, not espresso watered down. The owner is a professional chef and his baked goods go well with the coffee. The restaurant is open Thursday to Sunday, 6 pm-midnight. There is a salad bar offered on weekends. The house specialties are German dishes. I had the stroganoff and John had the goulash; neither could be matched anywhere else in Bolivia. The food is good, the portions large and the prices reasonable ($5 each). Vegetarian fare is available. The family comes from a line of chefs so good food is a way of life.

TOCAYA!

If you meet someone with the same name as you, say "Tocaya." According to Inca custom it is a sign of good luck.

Vila's Café is open only on weekends and offers the best cheesecake in town.

The **German Bakery** carries fresh French bread, numerous kinds of cookies and chocolate brownies; it sells all the teas and conserves made by Margarita at La Vispera.

Chakana Restaurant, *on the plaza,* has a good *almuerzo* for $1.50 per person. I had spaghetti with a white sauce, salad, soup and dessert. I could not eat it all, even though it was delicious. They also make vegetarian dishes and pizzas and are open early enough to offer breakfast. This place is popular with foreigners.

Campeche Restaurant at the cabins on the hill (follow the signs) has a large restaurant that overlooks the valley. It serves both North American meals and vegetarian dishes.

■ Nightlife

 The **Mosquito Rock Café Disco and Bar** is owned by the son of the owners of Land Haus. The bar has a yellow Volkswagon on the roof and a car motif inside. Next door is the Pizzeria Las Alturas. I understand that the cost for pizza delivered to the bar is a tad high.

La Disco, in town, is open Friday, Saturday and Sunday nights and on holidays. It plays the music of "today" and is the happening-est place in town, unless you like to party at home.

■ Shopping

 La Vispera sells herbs grown in their garden. Margarita sells fresh herbs to some of the best restaurants in Santa Cruz and she dries some and sells them to the public. They are used as teas or as medicinal plants to alleviate the symptoms of diarrhea, rheumatism and circulation problems. Other herbs are mixed with oils and used for massages. The paper bags containing the herbs have windows cut in them so the product can be seen. Each class of herb is marked with an icon. Those used in the kitchen for cooking are marked with a pot and those used for medicinal purposes have a mortar and pestle. Margarita also sells mango chutney and rhubarb jam.

Pieter has **maps** of the local terrain for $6 each.

The **Land Haus Artists' Shop** sells ceramics; the paint is made and firing is done on the premises so you can watch the process. These unique designs show the blending of European with Bolivian styles. The owner also raises and sells Bolivian cactus. There is every kind ever grown in Bolivia, but they are all young rather than big.

Michael Blendinger, Calle Bolívar, sells some of his landscape photos in his tour agency/craft shop. The photos are both mounted on postcards and sold as larger images. He also has good-quality crafts and weavings done by people living in the villages around Samaipata.

Carmen Luz is a contemporary artist living in Samaipata. Some of her work is available at the Hamburg Restaurant. Her studio is near the end of the street that goes along the side of the plaza. There is a sign. She also offers Spanish lessons for $5 an hour. This is steep but the lessons are good.

Cochabamba

Altitude: 8,329 ft / 2,523 m
Population: 620,000

Cochabamba, the Garden of Bolivia, boasts the world's most comfortable climate; warm dry days with clear blue skies and cool nights. The elevation is low compared to the Altiplano, so the wind doesn't bite. But it is high compared to the Chaco and Amazon, so the breeze is fresh. Cochabamba is also a medical center and has the most advanced labs and clinics in the country. The town also claims to have the best *chicha* in Bolivia.

These are good boasts, but there is more. Cochabamba's proximity (three hours by bus) to Torotoro National Park makes the town one of the best bases for muscle-powered adventures. This is not

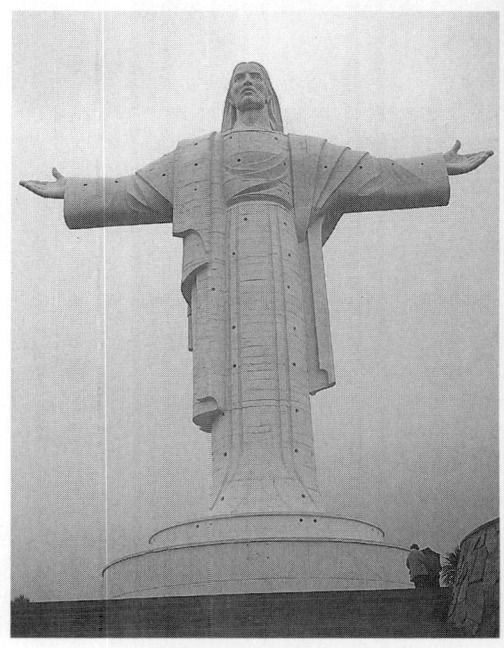

Cerro de Christo, Cochabamba.

generally known, so you will not be crowded off a river or hiking trail. Cochabamba is also within three hours by bus or three days by foot from Villa Tunari, where an animal refuge and park are located. There is a lake in the center of town where birders can add new species to their lists. And there are the caves of San Rafael to explore and Cerro Tunari, the highest peak in the district, to climb.

If you are coming from the Amazon and heading to the Andes, Cochabamba is the perfect place to acclimatize. You can hike around the colonial village of Tarata and then climb to the Heroines monument that sits on the hill of San Sebastian in town. The following day, try hiking to Cristo de Concordia, the Christ figure that sits on San Pedro Hill. The figure is the modern-day symbol of the city and is the largest figure of Christ in the Americas. After excursions like these you will be ready to rappel down a waterfall, raft on one of the whitewater rivers or spelunk into some of Torotoro's caves.

There is culture, too. One can visit some of the villages around the area for a day or longer and do things like photograph old doors or drink *chicha* in an authentic *chicharia* (a house that sells homemade *chicha*) with authentic *chichariros* (people drinking *chicha*). There are the ruins of Incallajta, with its magnificent stone walls and photogenic landscape. And there are night clubs and discos where you can rub shoulders with the local in-crowd.

In my opinion, Cochabamba has been horridly undersold. This is probably because the name comes from two Quechua words: kjocha, which means swampy, and pampa, which means plain. Cochabamba is anything but a swampy plain.

■ Getting Here & Around

LAB, ☎ 800-337-0918 (US), 800-10-3001 (Bolivia), www.labairlines.com, **TAM**, ☎ 244-3487, www.tam.com.br, and **AeroSur**, ☎ 231-3233 or 336-7400, www.aerosur.com, have daily flights to and from other major centers like La Paz and Santa Cruz. Up to six flights a day run to and from La Paz. The cost is $50 per person one way. There are also at least two or three flights a week to faraway places like Riberalta, Puerto Suarez or Cobija.

A **taxi** from the airport to town costs $3.50 for up to four people. There is a radio taxi right from the door of the airport. If you walk out to the road and hail one, it will cost about $2.

Buses to and from Cochabamba are numerous. There are eight going to Santa Cruz between 7:30 am and 9 pm daily, 10 going to La Paz between 8:30 am and 10 pm daily, two to Oruro at 9 am and 7:30 pm daily, four to Sucre between 4:30 pm and 7 pm daily and one to Potosi at 6 pm daily.

■ History

Cochabamba is situated on Rio Rocha in an agricultural valley that is about 15 miles/25 km long and six miles/10 km wide. Standing guard over the valley, at 16,563 ft/5035 m, is Mount Tunari the highest peak in the Herradura Mountains.

Quechua were living in the valley when the first group of colonists rode here in 1542. Because of the black earth and blue skies, they stayed and started farms and families. On August 2, 1571 the place was declared a city by the Viceroy of Toledo, and in 1574 Sebastian Barba de Padilla laid the foundation stone for the plaza. The city was called Villa Orapeza after the family of the ruling viceroy. But local settlers didn't use that name. Instead, they continued using Khocha-pampas and that eventually took on the slightly adjusted form of Cochabamba.

As the number of workers in Potosi rose, agriculture in the valley increased. Cochabamba earned a lot of money and the reputation of being the breakfast (bread) basket of the country. However, when the mines downsized Cochabamba lost most of its agricultural market and soon went into a depression. The city decided that it could do better on its own so, on September 14, 1810, it declared its independence from Spain. It was the first act of many to follow indicating the rebellious nature of the citizens. The next act was just two years later when the men of Cochabamba fought the Spaniard, Jose Manuel Goyeneche, and his army. When the men were no longer able to fight, the women took over and won. There is the monument to them on San Sebastian Hill overlooking the city. I don't know why the women didn't just take over permanently. When you look at them on the monument, they look as if they could have managed things better than any men.

The battles for independence continued until 1825, when it was finally won. In the 1950s the *campesinos*, along with the miners of Oruro and Potosi, fought for land reforms and won. Following that came the coca war. Although they haven't won it, the Quechua demonstrators and *cocaleros* have certainly made their point clear. This has resulted in the government allowing coca to be grown legally, in small amounts, for local consumption and religious purposes. But the *cocaleros* want more than that. They want the actual money paid out as compensation for crop eradication, or they want to be able to grow coca and sell it to anyone. Cochabamba has experienced more roadblocks and violent confrontations between *cocaleros* and the army than any other Bolivian city.

In 2000, the war of water was fought when government officials sold the water company to private enterprise. This resulted in a three-fold price hike. Huge demonstrations occurred, the roads were blocked, the military came in, lives were lost and the price of water came down.

Today, the city is peaceful, except for the occasional roadblock.

■ Services

 The **telephone office** is on Avenida Ayacucho and Calle Bolívar.

The **post office** is on Avenida Ayacucho and Avenida de los Heroinas.

The **police station** is on Avenida Ayacucho and Calle Aguirre.

Money is available through any bank machine, and there are many in town. Traveler's checks can be cashed by paying a fairly high commission (3%).

The **tourist office** is on Calle Colombia between 25 de Mayo and España. The helpful staff is aware of local events.

IAMAT Medical Center is at Edificio Servimed, 5th floor, Calle Baptista #777, ☎ 428-2192, or Clinica San Pedro, Calle Aurelio Melean #154 (no number available).

■ Sightseeing

The **Botanical Garden** is tucked below the hill holding the Christ and along the Rocha River, by Avenida del Ejercito. It is not large, just one square block, but it is well kept and some of the cactuses, when flowering, are worth photographing. There are 200 cactus species in the park and all are labeled. And there's even a Huntington cactus that can flower either a flaming red or bright orange. The park has three small ponds in which numerous ducks can be spotted.

Churches

The **cathedral** on the plaza was built by Domingo del Mazo in the 1570s, making it the oldest in the city. It has an indigenous baroque façade in a colonial structure. The columns at the entrance are the most interesting parts, with flowers, vines and cherubs. The paintings inside are colonial in style and displayed in hand-carved wood frames. The altars, of which there are three, are carved from wood and adorned with gold. The central altar is embossed with decorative silver. This church is almost always open.

San Francisco Church and Convent, on Avenida 25 de Mayo and Calle Bolívar, was built in 1581. The most interesting thing about this building is that the convent is made of wood, rather than stone (stone was the common material used at the time of building). The pulpit and main altar are original pieces of work.

Santa Clara Church and Convent, Calle de las Heroinas between 25 de Mayo and San Martin, is a little church with a Neo-Gothic façade. It was constructed in 1684 and remodeled later under the direction of architect Kanaudt.

There are numerous other churches that could be of interest. **Santo Domingo** was started in 1778, but is still incomplete, and **Santa Teresa**, built in 1760, still has its original floor.

■ Adventures in Culture

Museum Casa Santivañez, on Calle Santivañez between Avenida Ayacucho and Junin, is open Monday to Saturday, 9 am-12:30 pm and 3-6 pm. The cost to enter is 50¢. It houses the National Library of Science and Technology. Originally, the building was the home of the Santivañez family. After the family no longer wanted the

Cochabamba

SIGHTSEEING
1. Casa Santiváñez
2. Monumento a las Heroínas
3. Mercado de Ferias
4. Cristo de la Concordia
5. Archeological Museum
6. Casa de la Cultura
7. Artisans Market
8. Teleférico
9. Cathedral
10. San Francisco Convent
11. Botanical Gardens
12. Ranabol Tours
13. Fitzcarroldo Tours

PLACES TO STAY & EAT
14. El Salvador Hotel, El Dorado Hotel, Canada Hotel
15. Hostal Florida, Hostal Jordan II
16. Alojamiento Pull-man, Papichin Restaurant
17. City Hotel
18. Hotel Mary
19. Hotel Los Angeles, Hotel Los Vegas, Sucre Manta, Espresso Café
20. Regina Hotel
21. Anteus Hotel
22. Cesar's Plaza Hotel
23. Zahina Bakery
24. Los Leâs Pizza Parlor

·········· Cycling route

© 2004 HUNTER PUBLISHING, INC

AV AMERICA

MELGAREJO

AV ANICETO ARCE

TOREZ

SALINAS

SEJAS

URQUINDI

PANDO

AV UYUNI

AVENIDA RAMON RIVERO

AV DEL EJERCITO

AV PAPA PAULO III

P. BORDA

PORTALES

POTOSI

SANTA CRUZ

LA PAZ

AV SIMON BOLIVAR

AV OQUENDO

16 DE JULIO

ANTEZANA

PACCIERI

VENEZUELA

ECUADOR

25 DE MAYO

ESPANA

BAPTISTA

COLOMBIA

BOLIVAR

SUCRE

JORDAN

CALAMA

CABRERA

URUGUAY

AROMA

LANZA

SAN MARTIN

E ARZE

AGUIRRE

AV DE LAS HERONAS

14 DE SEPT

PUNATA

TARATA

AV AYACUCHO

LA PAZ

REZA

MEXICO

ROCHA

ECUADOR

COLOMBIA

JUNIN

GEN ACHA

SANTIVANEZ

CALAMA

CABRERA

HAMIRAYA

Rio Rocha

MAYOR DE SAN SIMON UNIVERSITY

URQUIDI

MENDEZ

9 DE ABRIL

Laguna Alalay

NOT TO SCALE

Bus Terminal

house, it became a Catholic University. During that time, one of the leaders of Cochabamba, Captain Manfred Kings Villa, declared the house a historical center. Today, under the administration of the Patiño Society of Geneva and the city of Cochabamba, the house is a cultural center and technical library.

There are two floors to the building, plus a great patio that is used for musical concerts. One floor has a small museum dedicated to Creole life during the 19th and 20th centuries. The paintings that line the halls are by famous Bolivian artists like Virreinal de Potosi and Cecilio Guzman de Rojas. One of the circulating exhibitions I saw was by German artist Charlotte Salomon, whose mother and grandmother died in a concentration camp when she was a child. This pain was portrayed in her work. Local artists, after being approved by a committee, may have exhibitions here.

Cultural Center and **Patiño Mansion**, Avenida Potosi #1450 and Avenida Portales, are open every day for one-hour guided tours only. The English-language tour starts at 5 pm and the Spanish one starts at 3 pm. The cost is $1.50 for foreigners and 75¢ for locals. The English tour guide is able to speak well enough, but she has some of her facts a bit twisted. She was especially good at describing the architectural styles of the mansion. After the tour you can visit the contemporary art gallery on the lower floor of the mansion.

The center is maintained by the Simon I. Patiño foundation in Geneva, Switzerland. Three of Patiño's grandchildren sit on the board. The grounds and house are obviously being kept up, unlike his home in Oruro that is in sad disrepair. Patiño was a smart man, planting his millions outside Bolivia, and setting up the foundation to plough profits back into the country under controlled circumstances so little could be siphoned off by political bureaucrats in La Paz.

As you enter the grounds (where some plants are labeled) that were designed by Japanese architectural gardeners, you see two dogs carved from marble. Patiño heard the story of a girl being lost in the Swiss Alps and rescued by dogs. I believe they are supposed to be St. Bernards, but these look like labs. Patiño loved the story so much that he had the dogs immortalized on his property. The red brick building to the left as you enter was first the stable, but is now the library. It holds about 70,000 books and/or writings. As you approach the main house you will pass a genkgo tree. This tree has never produced fruit because it is missing its necessary mate nearby. It is not known if this one is male or female. The genkgo fruit contains a chemical that assists those with memory problems.

The main house was designed by a French architect and the materials used in the construction were brought from every part of the world. The foyer has the motto, "Love to work and respect the law" inscribed over the door. Naturally, Patiño would believe in that.

The studio is on the main floor and is the only room with its original furniture, which is all made from red mahogany, as are the doors, the window casings and the wall paneling. The upper half of the walls are covered in silk damask from Asia and the desk is a copy of Napoleon's. The next room you enter is the party room, but it now serves as the meeting room for the foundation. The wall paneling in this room is made from Lebanese cedar and the upper half was also at one time covered in Asian silk damask. Marble carvings of the four muses stand over the fireplace. On the opposite wall a Bolivian flag covers a space where a French tapestry once hung. Simon's grandkids have had the tapestry removed and hung in Europe.

The upper gallery is partly open and contains bronze statues of the four seasons. At each end are mirrors that give the area a feeling of immensity. The furniture and bedrooms are carved in fine detail with gargoyles and mythical characters. Charles de Gaulle once stayed in the lady's bedroom, but became incensed when he found that he was much longer than the beds (Bolivians are generally short). The servants had to lengthen the bed for him.

The tapestry in the dining room is unique in that each color used was put into one thread, one very long thread, and woven through to make the picture. The games room is of Persian design and has passages from the Koran inscribed around the room. The carpet is from Iran. The outdoor theater was originally the public shower, built for neighbors living nearby (Patiño wanted to keep the neighborhood clean).

In the basement is the **Contemporary Art Museum**. It is well lit, uncluttered and a treat to visit. The art that I saw was varied in style and medium. Some were easy to understand while others were definitely new vogue. In 1999, there were 78 Bolivian artists displayed at the museum.

The third floor of the building is used by the grandchildren when they come to visit, which they do at least once a year. That area is closed to the public.

In 2002, the cultural center had 91 readings, 15 exhibitions of visual art, 52 musical presentations, 20 educational presentations and seven events that fell under "miscellaneous."

THE SIMON PATINO FOUNDATION

The foundation is huge in Bolivia. In memory of Simon Patiño, a native of Cochabamba who became the richest man in the world during the early part of the last century, the foundation was formed to help Bolivians. It pays for scholars to be educated in countries that are most advanced in a particular field, such as medicine or nuclear science. The payback is that the students, once they have completed their education, must give seven years of labor back to Bolivia. However, the foundation is having a hard time forcing scholars and doctors back into their own country. Less than half of the Bolivian students who became doctors on Patiño's money came back to Bolivia.

But the foundation also supports a medical clinic in Bolivia. They run an experimental farm. They help pay for public housing and they publish books. They run a research station for genetic improvement in agriculture. They also maintain one of the larger libraries in the country.

The **Archeological Museum**, on the plaza at Avenida Aguirre and Calle Jordan, is open weekdays 8:30 am-6:30 pm, and on weekends until noon. It is closed on all holidays and during Carnival. Admission is $2. Displays include about 20,000 pieces of rocks, shards, pottery, weapons, weavings, skulls, and so on, from the cultures of every group ever to live in Bolivia going back as far as 5,000 years. This includes those from the Amazon region. That makes this a huge, extremely valuable collection and it takes at least two hours to go through. The museum is part of San Simon University and a member of the Association of American Museums that help share information between professionals.

Quillacollo, nine miles/15 km from Cochabamba, is known for its festival celebrating the miracles of the **Virgin of Urkupiña**. On August 15 every year, pilgrims walk from Cochabamba to the colonial church where the Virgin is housed. Apparently, a young woman tending her flock on the hill nearby had some visions of the Virgin. She told the villagers who, when they came to investigate, also saw the Virgin. She was on the hill where the shepherdess pointed. She was yelling "orkupiña," which in Quechua means "on the hill," hence her name. When the villagers searched the area, they found the carved image of the Virgin. They carried this image to the church in Quillacollo. From there, the Virgin has continued to perform miracles. The fiesta is started with pilgrims and worshipers climbing the hill to where the Virgin was first spotted. Once they have prayed, they take a piece of rock with them to insure health and wealth in the future. Back in the village, people dance, eat and drink.

The **colonial church** on the plaza is the second attraction of the village. Inside are numerous items left in appreciation of the miracles performed by the Virgin. The Sunday market is when the artists of the area sell many of their handmade crafts.

To get to Quillacollo, catch a minibus from Avenida Ayacucho and Aromas. The half-hour journey costs 25¢ each way. Should you wish to stay in Quillacayo for the night, there are two places just 2.5 miles/four km north of town. **Eco Hostal Los Nuevos Inkas**, ☎ *446-1505,* charges $12 per person for a room with bath. **La Posada de los Cisnes** (no phone) charges $10 per person for a room with bath.

Villa Albino and the Pairumani Estate is 12 miles/20 km from Cochabamba. This is where the Patiños are buried in an ornate marble mausoleum. On the property is yet another house that Simon Patiño built, this one for his wife. The architecture and decorative interior is of French design. The gardens are really well done and have many Japanese plants. The long driveway is lined on both sides by flowering trees and at the end is a large fountain. Mansion tours are offered in English or Spanish at 2 pm daily. The cost is $1.50 for foreigners and half that for nationals.

Incallajta Ruins are 86 miles/140 km from Cochabamba and about 12 miles/20 km in from the old road to Santa Cruz. This Inca fort is interesting, although not as spectacular as El Fuerte or Tihuanaco. To get there from Cochabamba you must take a bus going to Epizana or Totora and get off at the turn-off to Collpa and Pocona. From Collpa you must walk five miles/eight km uphill to the site. The bus trip alone takes about 2½ hours. The easiest option is to take a tour or hire a jeep in Cochabamba. The last choice is to stay in Tortora and hire a vehicle or take a bus to the turn-off for the ruins.

The fort, a classical Inca building, is believed to have been constructed around 1463-1472 for Inca Tupac Yupanki. It was then expanded in 1525 by Huayna Capac, the father of the last Inca ruler, Ata Hualpa. The fort sits on 60 acres/25 hectares of land on a hill overlooking the Machacamarca River and is flanked on one side by three terraced gardens. The main building, constructed of stone with red-clay mortar, borders the main plaza. Although only the walls remain, the building measured 89 x 266 ft (27 x 81 m) and had 12 doors that opened onto the square. Cemented into the northwest and southeast walls are two huge stones believed to catch the light of the sun during the spring and fall solstices. In front of these huge stones, in the center of the plaza, was an altar. The buildings were made of stones held together by and covered with red clay. Inside the areas thought to be residences are niches in the walls that run about half as thick as the walls themselves. Niches were usually used to hold statues of gods, but it is not known if the ones here were used for statues, guns (as it was previously a fort) or dead humans (that is what the niches were used for at El Fuerte, Samaipata). The roofs were believed to have been of straw. The remains of adobe structures are found beyond the central area.

One of the main stone walls continues past the plaza to border a second square. Beyond that, locals claim there is a paved Inca road that, should you follow it for two days, will lead you to another site. I didn't look for it.

These ruins were found and mapped by Ernest Nordenskiold before World War I. It was not until 1988 that the place became a national monument and the archeological society in Cochabamba started serious work at the site.

Pocona is the village 5.5 miles/nine km south of the junction to the ruins. The village is dominated by colonial architecture with cobbled streets and old wooden doors. The center for the Assistance for Tourists is here and offers the service of guides for the ruins. There's also a small medical center and general information about Incallajta. At the center is a small archeological museum that has some pieces excavated at the ruins.

Incaraqay Ruins sit at 7,895 ft/2,400 m elevation with a 13,158-ft/4,000-m mountain guarding the rear approach. Raquay means "house without a roof" in the Quechua language. There are just a few small buildings. From the hill you can see the valley and some remains of silos built by the Inca. Apparently, this site was built during the expansionist epoch just as the Spaniards were making their way towards the empire. At this time, the Inca kingdom went all the way to El Fuerte near Samaipata. To get here you must take a bus to Sipe Sipe and walk three miles/five km uphill. The other option is to join a tour/hire a jeep in Cochabamba. However, should you want a hike in the country and need a destination, this may be a good choice.

■ Adventures on Foot

CRISTO DE LA CONCORDIA: On Avenida Rubin Dario, this statue of Christ can be seen from anywhere in the city during the day. At night, to keep the image in your mind, he is lit up bright as day. This is the symbol of Cochabamba. It is the biggest statue of Christ in South America, standing at 132 ft/40 m from feet to forehead and weighing about a million pounds/two million kilos. It is a nice climb to the top of the hill, and the view of the city spreads farther with each step. If the one-hour climb is not your thing, take the cable car up for a mere 25¢ and walk down. Inside the statue base is a restaurant patronized by everyone who has made the climb. The steps along the way have been donated by prominent residents of the area who are paving their way, little by little, to the promised land. Each year, the last Sunday of Carnival in Cochabamba is completed with an event at the top of this hill.

LAGUNA ALALAY: The lake, located along Avenida Ruben Dario and Avenida 9 de Abril, is flanked by the hill and Parque Progreso, by the Campo Ferial and by the country club. A paved walking trail and cycling road encircles the entire lake. It also goes along the second circle of the city and partially on Avenida Ruben Dario, where it turns along Avenida America for a few blocks before weaving through side streets. The trail

Cochabamba & Vicinity

Chipiriri

Villa Tunari

Cruce Paractito

Chimore

Cavernas del Repechon

to Santa Cruz (new road)

Laguna Corani

Corani

Incachaca

COCHABAMBA

to La Paz ←

Laguna Angostura

Cliza

Punata

Monte Punku

Tarata

Arani

Incallajta

Villa Rivero

Collpaciaco

Colpa

Epizana

Huayculli

Pocona

Anzaldo

Totora

to Santa Cruz (old road)

Mizque

Toro Toro

Aiquille

to Sucre

NOT TO SCALE

can be picked up or left anywhere along these streets and using it is better than walking along the road where there is traffic.

Parts of the lake are swampy and perfect for birds. The island near the path is a hot spot for some of the larger resident ones. There have been over 150 bird species seen at the lake, some examples of which are the white-tufted and silver grebe, the puna ibis, Andean gull, the grey-bellied shrike-tyrant and the yellow and blue tanager.

SAN SEBASTIAN HILL: La Coronilla is just up from the bus terminal and above Avenida Roma. San Sebastian park is across the way. The hill has stone steps up to a monument of powerful women in battle, arms raised in defiance and with children hugging their legs. This is in memory of the women who fought to defend the city after the men had been defeated during a battle against the Spanish in 1812. There is cactus around the hill and the views over the city and coliseum are good. Vendors sell soft drinks and snacks on busy days.

CERRO TUNARI: Cerro Tunari is a 17,000-ft/5,200-m cone-shaped peak in the Cordillera Oriental that can be seen from Cochabamba. Two routes ascend the mountain, one from the north and the other from the south. If going from the north, you will have to stay overnight and have camping equipment. See Ranabol Tours (☎ 458-3039 or 717-17097, ramiroc15@hotmail.com) on Avenida Ayacucho about doing this trip. They are able to show you more than just the hike up the mountain.

The climb from the south requires that you go along Avenida Ayacucho (or take bus #103) for 5.5 miles/nine km and ask to be let off the bus at the park. Follow the trail going up. In about an hour you will come to some picnic tables and more trails. Pick any one that goes up. The climb is steep. However, try to keep your wits about you. The rare wedge-tailed hillstar (bird) has been seen on this mountain. As you ascend, the vegetation becomes sparse and llamas and birds will be your only companions. The black scree makes the hillside look a bit barren. Watch also for the mountain finch, the cone bill and Torrent ducks.

If going by the northern route you will need to go to Quillacollo and then on to Chaqueri, halfway to Morochata. The best way is to take a taxi or join a tour. Taking buses will use up all your hiking time.

Chaqueri is at about 13,158 ft/4,000 m, so the change in elevation to the summit is not much. On this side, you may be lucky enough to spot condors. The hike to the summit takes five or six hours; coming back down is three or four. If doing this in one day, it will be a very long day. However, everyone who has completed this climb says the views are worth all the effort. You can see the higher peaks to the north and the city of Cochabamba to the south. The bird life is considerable.

■ Adventures in Nature

 Laguna Angostura is 10 miles/17 km from Cochabamba, situated between the old road that goes to Santa Cruz and the road that goes to Tarata. On the way to Tarata, you will pass the western and southern sides of this man-made lake. On the lake are three large hotels with restaurants and bars that overlook the water. Anglers can try their luck here. There are boats for hire. Alberto Sanjinez Santiago, a Chilean writer, once said about this lake, "To rest on the brink of madness, eating rich fish... what else can we request?" How about sex, Sanjinez?

Liruini is five miles/eight km past Quillacollo and its **hot spring** is reputed to cure kidney and liver disorders. The springs are in a bathhouse and are fairly clean. But Liruini is also for the tree specialist (I've met a few!). Located near the entrance to the river gorge is a rare species of the queñua tree not commonly found at this low elevation. For those not able to see the trees at Sajama, this is a good option.

The queñua usually grows no more than 13 ft/four m in height and belongs to the rose family. Its flower is certainly beautiful enough to be a rose. The plant was first identified in northern Chile.

Should you want to stay in Liruini, try the **Janajpacha Hotel**, ☎ 446-1234, on the road toward Quillacollo near the hot springs. It charges $9 per person for a room with private bath and all meals.

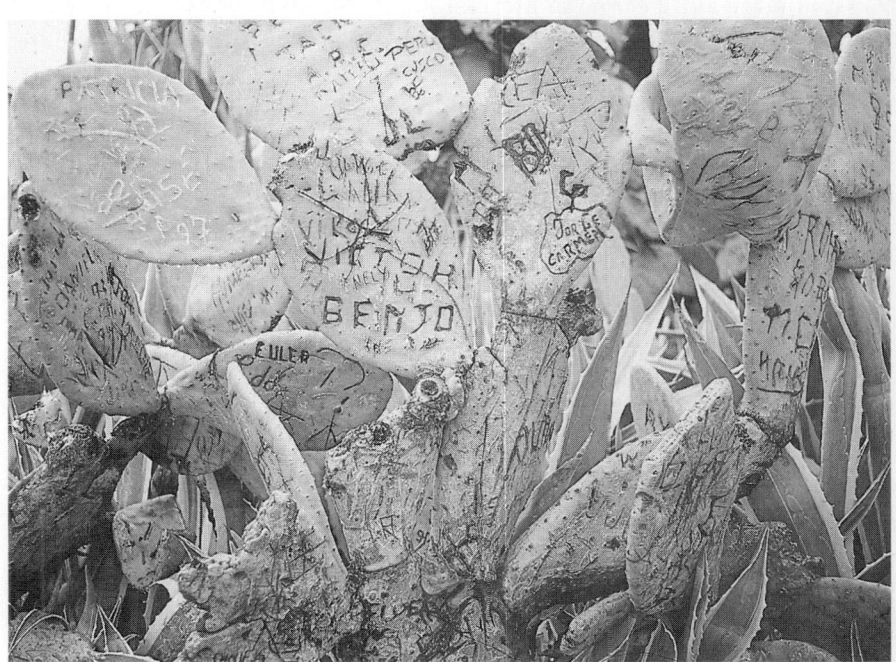

Cactus – some with graffiti – are common in the hills surrounding Cochabamba.

■ Adventures of the Brain

Escuela Runawasi, c/o Hinojosa, Casilla 4034, ☎ 424-8923, charges $1,000 for a six-week total immersion language class with a maximum of three students who are working at the same level as you. The classes can be in Spanish or Quechua, and the cost includes room and board, 20 hours of instruction per week and all materials. The school also offers advanced classes for those wanting to study literature, rather than language. Runawasi means "house of the people" in Quechua.

The school is 2.8 miles/4.5 km from the city center and most home-stay residences are in the same neighborhood. It is set in a colonial building with rooms around a central courtyard. There is also a small bar that sells beverages and snacks.

Normally, the classes are composed of three students. However, for those with no Spanish, the school may use larger groups while others may have one-to-one communication. Once some Spanish is learned, the student may be put into a group. Some prefer grammar while others prefer conversation and these distinctions are accommodated. The school uses up-to-date materials of common interest and changes teachers often so that you become accustomed to hearing different styles of speech and opinions.

Home stays can accommodate individuals or families. Some can provide private bath. If special accommodations are required, the information needs to be sent to the school prior to arrival. The host family provides all meals and non-alcoholic drinks. Laundry can be done by the student or by the host family for $1.50 for 12 pieces (a pair of socks is one piece).

Anyone arriving with children can enroll the child in a class but the school does not take kids under 15 in its adult classes. There is also a day care or kindergarten that costs $50 for a month of half-day care.

I found the owners willing to share their information, and willing to show me everything that they offered. Their gentleness seemed to reflect the Quechua hospitality so common in the country.

■ Tour Operators

Ranabol Tours, Avenida Ayacucho #112 and Heroinas, ☎ 458-3039 or 717-17097 (cell), ramiroc15@hotmail.com or ranabolraf@hotmail.com, offers the best in outdoor adventure for the area. Romero was trained in jungle survival while in the military. But he does not carry a bazooka or even a foot-long knife with a compass in the handle. In fact, he is a very soft spoken and humorous man. Romero offers a three-day bike trip to Samaipata, and a four- to seven-day canoe trip through the selva from San Francisco down to Rio Negro. His four-day hike from Cochabamba to Villa Tanuri runs through incredible landscapes and includes stops at the Repechon Cave to see bats and the guacharo, the only bird ever found in a cave occupied by bats. Romero also does three- to four-day hiking, caving and canoeing trips to places like Torotoro National Park, Carrasco National Park, Amboro National Park and Isiboro-Secure Park. In Torotoro, he will take you to the Humajalanta Cave, where stalagmites and stalactites form structures like the Sauce Tree, the Christmas Tree and the Concert Room. Geologists believe these caves were at one time under water. There is one four-day trip that includes rafting, trekking, rappelling and mountain biking.

It ends at a hotel where you can shower, eat, drink beer and massage your muscles. He also does a lot of spelunking and can arrange obstacle courses for eco-challenge types.

If paragliding is your thing, Ranabol Tours will take you where you can fly. This is the only company in Bolivia that I know of to offer such an activity to tourists. Flying over the Andes! How romantic.

Romero offers rafting, mountain biking, trekking and rapelling down waterfalls or any combination of sports for a custom trip. He has most equipment you may need and his prices are around $30 a day. Some trips have a minimum age as some of the trips can be demanding. Romero is skilled and knowledgeable, especially about Torotoro. He even knows some English. He comes highly recommended.

Fitzcarraldo Expeditions, Avenidas Aniceto & Padilla #225, at the Casa Internacional, ☎ 424-2431, tombol@hotmail.com, offer kayaking/ canoeing trips lasting four to eight days; some may include hiking. They travel on easy-to-paddle jungle rivers so you have the pleasure of enjoying the wildlife, rather than trying to stay afloat. This company is very safety conscious. You can hook up with them in Vallerroel or Santa Cruz.

Their shortest trip runs along the Ivirgarzama River near Villarroel, a village directly south of Trinidad. It costs $330 per person if three people go and drops down to $270 if five people sign up. Another excursion is for five days on the Isarzama River, not far from Cochabamba. It ends at Villarroel, where there is an eco-lodge for visitors to use. The cost of this all-inclusive trip is $390 per person if three people go and $300 if five people go. If tropical rainforest is your desire, take the trip along Snake River (named because of its curves, rather than its resident reptiles) through Bolivia's Green Hell for either five or eight days. The river passes through the most southern section of the Amazon Basin and, for part of the time, you are in the steaming jungle with a view of snow-capped mountains in the distance. This is a true adventure. The cost, depending on duration and group size, is $489-$889 per person.

Meridian Travel, Calle Arze #412 near Jordan, ☎ 450-7750, is new and very anxious to please. If anyone can get you a ticket for where and when you want to go, these guys can.

■ Places to Stay

El Salvador Hostal, *Calle Montes #E0420, on the corner of 25 de Mayo,* ☎ *422-7303, $,* has rooms with or without baths. They are large and bright. All rooms have cupboards, tables and chairs, cable TV, telephone and some have balconies. The 85-year-old widow who runs the hotel has been there for 27 years. The place is clean, the owner pleasant. This is my first choice for a room in Cochabamba.

HOTEL PRICES (US $)

Per person, per day, unless noted otherwise.

$	$2-$5
$$	$5-$10
$$$	$11-$17
$$$$	$18-$25
$$$$$	Over $25

Hostal Florida, *Calle 25 d Mayo #583*, ☎ *425-7911, floridah@elsitio. com, $*. The rooms are not big but the cable TV gets about 30 channels, including CNN in English. Those with wood floors are better than those with carpets. The big draw here is the center courtyard, but if you don't care about that, the rooms at the El Salvador are nicer.

Residencial El Dorado, *Calle 25 de Mayo #1034*, ☎ *422-1940, $,* has 25 exceptionally clean rooms around a central courtyard. The floors are tiled and each room has a small desk and chair. There is a separate TV room and a small snack place where you can get soft drinks, tea or a sandwich.

Alojamiento Pull-man, *Avenida Aroma #370*, ☎ *422-4073, $*, has two floors of rooms around a flowered courtyard. The rooms are basic, the beds are Inca (hard as stone) and the bath is communal.

Hostal Jordan II, *25 de Mayo between Uruguay and Cabrera*, ☎ *422-5010 or 422-4821, $$,* has single, double and triple rooms. All have private baths with separate shower stalls, cable TV, carpet, large windows and writing desks with chairs. Those not facing the street are a little darker.

City Hotel, *Calle Jordan #341 between 25 de Mayo and Esteban*, ☎ *422-2993 or 422-9575, $$*, is a favorite hangout for local artists and musicians, who often jam together in the bar on weekends. The uncrowded rooms have carpet, cable TV, telephones and private bathrooms that have both tubs and showers. The hotel is clean, even though there is the occasional chip here and there. Some rooms at the back of the hotel have nice views of the city. The new restaurant has more vegetarian dishes than meat choices and is open 24 hours a day.

Mary Hotel, *Calle Nataniel Aquirre #601 and Cabrera*, ☎ *425-2487 or 425-2488, $$,* has moderately sized rooms with clean carpets, tiled bathrooms, cable TV and closets. The single rooms are a good size, but some rooms have small windows so they appear a bit dark. There is an operating elevator.

Hotel Los Angeles, *Calle E. Arce #345*, ☎ *423-4523, $$*, is a good deal. The rooms are big, bright, clean and have large windows. Each has a lounge chair, a desk and a mirror. Each floor has a sitting area in the hall.

Hotel Los Vegas, *Calle E. Arze #0352*, ☎ *422-9217, $$*, is close to the square and the staff is friendly. All rooms have private tiled bathrooms with separate shower stalls. Some rooms have wood floors and the single rooms are more spacious than the doubles. The lighting is poor and some rooms have small windows, making them appear a bit drab. There is a bar and restaurant on site.

Canada Hotel, *Calle 25 de May #1000 on the corner of Montes*, ☎ *455-3315, $$$*, has 30 rooms and an elevator that works. The rooms are large and comfortable with a separate sitting area. The bathrooms are tiled and have separate shower stalls. The windows are large, the halls wide, the doors solid wood. This is a clean place. There's an on-site bar and restaurant for breakfast (included). There is enclosed parking. This is a good choice.

Regina Hotel, *Avenida Reza between España and the Prada*, ☎ *425-7382 or 422-9163, hregina@netbol.com, $$$$*, has large, bright rooms with private bathrooms, cable TV, telephones and small sitting areas. There is also laundry service, a safe for valuables, private parking and a restaurant that serves both continental and American breakfasts.

Anteus Hotel, *Avenida Potosi #1365*, ☎ *424-5067, hotelanteus@hotmail.com, $$$$*, is a small and friendly place with good monthly rates. It's across from the cultural center. Rooms here have private bath and cable TV. Purified water is supplied daily. There's a safe, private parking, laundry service, bicycle rentals and gym and the proprietors will change guest traveler's checks. There is a restaurant on the premises and an Internet café next door. This is a comfortable and clean place. During high season, make advance reservations.

Cesar's Plaza Hotel, *Calle 25 de Mayo #5210-223*, ☎ *425-0045, $$$$*, is a first-class hotel close to the central plaza. They offer a 20% discount if you stay two days or more. The rooms are spacious. There's a sauna, travel agency, beauty parlor and handicraft shop. The price includes breakfast and Internet access.

Hotel Diplomat, *Avenida Ballivian #611 near the Prada*, ☎ *425-0687, www.diplomat.com, $$$$$*, has rooms and suites. Each of the 86 rooms, on 15 floors, has a private bathroom, large bed, mini-bar, cable TV and air conditioning. They are carpeted, spacious and have small sitting areas. The hotel, situated in a middle class area just off the *prada*, offers free transportation to and from the airport. There is also a business center with Internet access. There are two restaurants and a bar on site. The one restaurant I visited had about 50 tables, but was empty. Rates: $63 single; $73 double; $83 triple.

Gran Hotel Cochabamba, *Plaza Ubaldo Anze E-0415*, ☎ *428-2551, cbbhotel@bo.net, $$$$$*, offers rooms, a suite and a presidential suite. It's an elegant old place that has been restored numerous times so the latest conveniences are offered while the charm is retained. Each tastefully decorated room has cable TV, large mirror, clean carpets and a spacious bathroom. The grounds have a swimming pool and there is a central gazebo where drinks or meals can be enjoyed. There is also a restaurant and separate bar. English, French and German are spoken by the staff. Rates: $50 single; $60 double; $120 suite; $170 presidential suite.

Portales Hotel, *Avenida Pando #1271, $$$$$,* is a first-class, five-star hotel that is part of a chain with other hotels in Santa Cruz and La Paz. It has three restaurants, a bar, two swimming pools, a dry sauna, a Turkish bath, gym, Jacuzzi, racquetball court, hair dresser, cable TV, business center and a doctor on call. The price is a mere $90 per night for two people. The big draw is the casino and disco.

■ Places to Eat

La Suisa Restaurant, *Avenida Ballivian #820,* ☎ *425-7102 or 425-7103.* This elegant restaurant has waiters in black ties ready to supply your every culinary wish. A separate bar features elevator music cranked low. Original oil paintings grace the walls and the décor features heavy wood paneling and stained glass windows. The meals keep the tone. Appetizers are free. Soup is about $1.75 and steak $5.50. A bottle of wine is $9, but the menu showed no prices for cocktails. This is probably the most elegant restaurant in Cochabamba; because of its good food and ambience, it has managed to stay in business for 15 years. Open Monday to Saturday, 11:30 am-2:30 pm and 6-11 pm (11:30 pm on Friday and Saturday).

Papichin Restaurant, *Aroma #402 and 25 de Mayo,* is a clean local eatery that serves highly recommended *chirascos*. If this doesn't suit your taste, there is also an à la carte menu. A typical *almuerzo* runs at $1.75. However, they serve only one beer per customer per meal. If you want to drink more, you must go elsewhere as this is a family restaurant.

Zahina Bakery, *Calle Arce #613,* has some excellent pastries for reasonable prices. A piece of good chocolate cake is 30¢ a slice.

Sucre Manta, *Calle Esteban Arce #356,* just behind the cathedral, serves traditional food from Sucre using grandma's secret recipes. This restaurant is a favorite with everyone. Prices are low, food is good and a pianist plays during lunchtime.

Espresso Café Bar, *Calle Arce #340,* ☎ *425-6861,* serves cappuccino and espressos. This tiny café is a favorite for those hanging around the square. The shop also has some pastries, although the coffee, with its huge glob of sweet cream, is the real draw. Open 8 am-1 pm and 3-10 pm daily.

Las Colinas

> ### ODE TO THE SPUD
>
> There are 1,290 varieties of potatoes produced in Bolivia and the country is the world's largest per capita consumer of the vegetable. One variety, called the ñojcha, is used to test the value of a new daughter-in-law. If the young lady can peel the plant's funny curves and shape without losing too much of the potato, she will make a good wife.

Burger King, *Avenida America #620,* ☎ *445-1525,* is where homesick North Americans go. The restaurant has air conditioning, clean bathrooms and the usual North American hamburger. The prices, too, are North American.

Ceviche al Paso, *Calle España #S-153,* ☎ *450-6446,* is open every day, including holidays. I did not try this place but it was recommended by a local.

Los Leñas Pizza Parlor, *Avenida San Martin #179, between Bolívar and Heroinas,* ☎ *450-0674*, is a funky two-story pizzeria that cooks excellent thin crust pizza in a traditional clay oven. The cost is between $3 for a small to $6 for a fully loaded family size. The restaurant is open for lunch and stays open until after 10 pm. This is a good spot.

Fratelo's Bar and Restaurant, *Pando #1143 and Recoleta,* ☎ *440-2050*, has good pasta and fish and is popular with the younger, rowdier crowd. Open 11 am-2 pm and 6-11 pm.

Casa Nuestra, *Calle Oruro #389 and Antezana,* ☎ *452-2038*, is classy in appearance and service. However, some of the portions are on the scanty side. Although dishes like the lasagne are laden with cheese and the size is also fairly good, the price is $5 per serving. Fettuccini is $3.50 and the portion was moderate. The pasta of the house, which I didn't try, goes at a hefty $10 per plate. Once they sort out their portion size to price, it will be a good place to eat.

■ Nightlife

 Acha Theatre on Calle España just off the plaza is the local concert venue where performing arts are presented in an elegant hall. The building was constructed in 1578 in the convent of St. Augustine and is the most famous concert hall in the country. The acoustics seem to be especially designed for the performing arts. You will need to look for posters or visit the tourist office for information about performances.

Portales Hotel, Avenida Pando #1271, has a casino where you can pull the arm, play black jack or try your luck at the roulette wheel. When you've won enough money you can go across to the disco and dance up a storm with the more affluent of Cochabamba's population.

Avalon Restaurant and open-air bar is on Avenida Potosi, next door to the Cultural Center. It is the Bolivian version of a rave club that is often manned on weekends by popular disc jockeys.

■ Shopping

 The **Cancha Market** across from the Laguna Alalay is the largest market in the area. It offers everything from local foods to modern dresses (no Christian Doir though). If you need to walk and are tired of the small market on 25 de Mayo, then have a look. The grounds are fairly new, built in the 1990s I believe.

Vicuñita Handicrafts, Avenida Rafael Pabon #777, ☎ 425-5615, near the airport, will ship goods anywhere in the world. As their name implies, they have some upscale vicuña and alpaca products. They have a similar shop in Santa Cruz.

Tarata

Altitude: 9,046 ft / 2,750 m
Population: 30,000 people in the village and surrounding countryside.

Tarata is a colonial village just 21 miles/35 km from Cochabamba, tucked into hills that are farmed to their tops. The village should be on every architectural-photographer's dream list. Some of the houses have doors that date back to the 1890s, while others are from 1907 and 1911 (signs above indicate when the door was built). The houses on which the doors hang are just as picturesque, with flowered balconies and stone façades. At one time some of these buildings were home to famous Bolivians such as Mariano Melgarejo, Esteban Arce and Rene Barrientos Ortuño (president of Bolivia from 1964-1967). Barrientos' house is just one block off the plaza.

Tarata also has some excellent weavings and is known for its fine *chicha* production. If you see a red or white flag hanging on a pole outside a house, it means there is *chicha* for sale. You can go in and purchase some or sit and enjoy a glass with the local *chichaleros*.

To get to Tarata, take a *trufi* from Calle 6 de Agosto just up from Avenida Republica in Cochabamba. Returning, the first bus leaves half a block from the square at 5 am and the last one leaves at 7 pm. It takes about 45 minutes to get to or from Cochabamba and costs 50¢.

■ Services

 The **tourist office** is on the main square. This is one of the best offices in the country. The staff was helpful and knowledgeable as to what tourists want, whether it be a place to stay, something to do or finding a phone.

■ Sightseeing

 San Pedro Church, on the main square, was built in 1605 and its organ is original. Inside is an urn with the ashes of Esteban Arce, who led a revolution in 1810 while trying to get independence for Bolivia. The church also has the skull of Mariano Melgarejo, one of Bolivia's most corrupt presidents and notorious drunks.

The **Convent and Church of Franciscan** (near the Cabañas los Piños) is also called the Temple of San Severino or the College of the Apostles of the Missions of Guarayos. It has an urn that was used by the patron saint of Tarata, San Severeno, the saint of rain. The convent's library has over 8,000 books, sermons and documents pertaining to the administration of the missions run by the Franciscan Fathers in Bolivia. The saint's day is celebrated in the village on the last Sunday of November with processions leading from the church, around the village and back again.

The **stone bridge of Melgarejo** was once over the Pilcomayo River. It now seems to be a bridge over a depression in the land. Mariano Melgarejo was president of Bolivia from 1864 to 1871. He had the military under his command, even though he was a notorious drunk who signed some of the most bizarre treaties in the country's history. He once signed a treaty with Brazil in the hope of getting water rights to the Atlantic Ocean. This resulted in Bolivia giving Brazil 39,537 square miles/ 102,400 square km of its prime land and Melgarejo getting a horse (so he could ride to the ocean). Melgarejo also sold parcels of land that didn't belong to him. He insisted that the Indians pay a large amount of money to prove ownership of their land. When they couldn't do this, the land was confiscated and sold to the Spaniards wanting to settle in the area. The logic of this alone shows the insanity of the man. The uprisings that resulted from the confiscation of land were bitter. Melgarejo was eventually overthrown and, later that same year, murdered in Lima, Peru.

Melgarejo's house is three blocks past Plaza Esteban Arce and the Church of San Francisco. When facing the church, go left and then right at the corner, so that you walk past the side of the church. Continue for three blocks and turn right again. A sign indicates the house.

On the plaza is the **Palacio Consistorial** that contains photos and paintings of important leaders from Bolivian history who were born or lived in Tarata. There are also some documents that have the signatures of Bolívar and Melgarejo. Other buildings on the plaza have the old hanging balconies and picturesque doorways.

■ Places to Stay & Eat

 Alojamiento Municipal is right by the bridge going over the Calicanto River. It is reached along the main road going to Cochabamba. The rooms are simple and the cost is $4 per person. There is no phone.

> **AUTHOR NOTE:** If you want help in finding the hotel (or a phone), go to the tourist office on the main square.

Cabañas los Pinos, ☎ 774-98853 (cell). Ask for Rene. He charges $17 for a double room with private bath and a kitchen. Camping, with access to showers and a bathroom, costs $3.50 per person. You must have your own tent. On the hotel premises is a garden with a basketball court and a swimming pool. I cannot say what the cabins are like or how many there are as the proprietor wouldn't let me see them. I'd be hesitant about staying here as the place seemed to be in disarray due to extensive renovations.

The only place to eat in the village is at the **market** near the Church of Franciscan. The *churascos* sold here are excellent – a full meal of more than I could eat was about 50¢. Other traditional dishes are *aloja*, a drink similar to *chicha* but without alcohol, and *chanca de conejo*, a soup made with rabbit, potatoes, green onion, green beans, yellow chilies and tomatoes.

■ Shopping

 Huayculli, 4.3 miles/seven km from Tarata, is the center for local ceramics. The best pieces are items used in the kitchen such as plates, pots and cups. These ceramics are among the finest quality in the country and Bolivians often travel a long way to purchase them.

The last Sunday of every month is **market** day in Tarata and villagers come from miles around to sell or trade their goods and handicrafts. I met a young artist selling his hand-painted ceramic flutes that had a design like no other that I'd seen in the area. The cost was less than a dollar per flute.

Colonial Village Circuit

These tiny colonial villages that branch off the old road between Cochabamba and Santa Cruz are culturally interesting. They are out of the way, yet not difficult to reach. However, they can be difficult to visit on a day trip from Cochabamba.

Villa Rivero, Arani and Collpaciaco are three villages just beyond Tarata along the same road. They could be visited in a day if staying in Tarata by taking a *trufi* or minibus from the square in Tarata. You can head either to Villa Rivero, then Collpaciaco and, finally, Arani, or go to Arani first and work your way back around. It is 16.5 miles/27 km from Tarata to Arani.

■ Arani

 The second to last Sunday in November is when Arani has the **bread festival**. During that time, every shape and style of bread ever made in the country is put on display and sold or entered in competitions. Colorful baskets are also available.

In town is **Saint Bartholomew Cathedral**, on the plaza. It was built in 1610 and designed by European architect Lucas Cabral. The altar inside is extremely ornate in its carvings, but the entire design is not overpowering. The statue of the virgin is called the Virgin La Bella (Beautiful Virgin). She's not bad.

■ Villa Rivero

 Villa Rivero is 12 miles/20 km from Tarata. The big draw to this village is the weaving and embroidery (the two skills are sometimes incorporated in one piece). Even if you are not shopping, it is interesting to watch the way they make the textiles. Because these villages are not visited by hundreds of tourists every day, the hospitality is excellent and the opportunity to learn something is even better.

■ Collpaciaco

 The convent at Collpaciaco, Convent of Santa Catalina, was built in 1570 by the Augustine Fathers. The central patio has stone patterns that are of interest. The Celebration of Spring takes place on May 15, when the farmers plow their fields and then party.

■ Totora

Colonial Totora was, at one time, the cultural center of the entire valley. Caravans of mules carried goods like pianos over the Andes from the Pacific Ocean for the Europeans who were coming to make the area home. The village plaza is a lovely colonial structure with archways all around. Many of the houses have the hanging balconies and old photogenic doorways.

■ Mizque

Mizque has cock fights and a watered-down version of the running of the bulls in Pamplona, Spain. This happens during the festival of **Señor de Burgos**, held on the second weekend of September each year. The week before the festival is the religious procession in honor of the Virgin of Mercy. In 1767 the town built three convents as well as the Inglesia Matriz, under the administration of the order of San Juan de Dios. They may have been hoping for a large influx of religious fervor. My theory is that so many guys got wiped out during the running of the bulls that the church had to build convents for the widows.

Mizque is four hours from Cochabamba. Buses ($2) leave from 6 de Agosto and Republica around noon and return every day at 3 pm. You also get here from Tarata or Sucre (but the bus arrives in the middle of the night and you must pay full fare between Cochabamba and Sucre).

There are five basic **hotels** in the village. All charge about $3 per person for a room without a private bath.

From the village, you can hike to **Kuri Canyon** (493 ft/150 m deep). This is where the Bridge of the Liberator, used by Simon Bolívar, spans over the canyon. Also, you can walk to **Pajcha Pata waterfall**, which drops about 411 ft/125 m, and visit the cave paintings in Aguada and Tablada. For these two trips you will need a guide. One can be hired in town for $10 to $30 per day. This is a grape-growing area, although I do not know of any wineries.

From Mizque you can travel to the K'ullai *charango* capital of Bolivia at **Aiquile**. There are basic places to stay and eat. If you are thinking of purchasing a *charango* (the ukulele-type instrument), Aiquile is where you will get the best quality with unique designs.

> **AUTHOR NOTE:** Remember that it is illegal to take any *charangos* made from armadillo shells into North American or European countries.

Torotoro National Park

Altitude: 9,211 ft / 2,800 m
Population: 500

The big draw to Cochabamba is Torotoro National Park, where there are dinosaur prints, fossils galore, a river gorge, a lake with blind fish, rock paintings, caves and insignificant ruins. Hiking can be done almost anywhere in the park's 41,000 acres/16,570 hectares, which is dotted with deep canyons, hanging valleys and waterfalls.

Due to the earthquake in 1998, when many places in the village were destroyed, there are mostly new-styled buildings in town – not very interesting, but adequate. The locals have a deal among themselves as to who will feed a *gringo*. Ask where you are staying and they will direct you to the producing eatery.

■ Getting Here & Around

Torotoro is difficult to reach. There is a bus direct from Cochabamba on Thursday and Sunday that leaves at 6 am and returns on Friday and Monday. Catch it on Avenida 6 de Agosto and Republica in Cochabamba and on the plaza in Torotoro. The trip is seven hours in all with the last 24 miles/40 km on a horrid track that occasionally, during rainy season, becomes impassable. This section takes three hours during dry season.

The surrounding mountains that have been pushed and heaved into odd positions from tectonic movements are red in color. This makes a great backdrop for any hiking. Before turning onto the Torotoro road and about three hours from Cochabamba, the main highway passes the man-made Laguna Corani, where Cochabamba gets its water supply. The road then plunges down to the rainforest. Once in the lush jungle, the turnoff to Torotoro is reached and the rough ride begins.

When you first arrive at Torotoro, you will be encouraged (forced?) to pay your $2.50 park fee. This is a one-time cost and covers all the time you are in the park. You can also hire a guide who will charge about $10 per day for up to four people.

■ Adventures on Foot

DINOSAUR TRACKS: The tracks on Cerro Huayllas are easy to find. Walk from the plaza down to the river, cross where everyone crosses and then walk upstream for less than 300 ft/90 m. Follow the track on the left that goes uphill. Nearby are three-toed dinosaur tracks stomping across the landscape. If you return to the river and go a bit farther upstream, you will find more tracks. These prints were made around 70 million years ago. Some were left by three-toed meat-eaters that grew to about 23 ft/seven m in size. Their prints are usually about 10 inches/25 cm wide. The bigger, four-toed Sauropods, vegetarians who grew to around 33 ft/10 m high, are responsible for the larger prints. Once the animals walked across the mud, leaving their prints, the mud dried, solidified and petrified. Then tectonic movement forced the land upward, thus giving the appearance that the tracks are walking up-hill. This area, along with the cement quarry in Sucre, is the Jurassic Park of Bolivia.

ROCK PAINTINGS: Batea Cocha is a spot where the rushing water during rainy season has smoothed and sculpted rock to form what looks like washbasins in the stone (thus the name). Just before the basins, on the wall to your left, are rock paintings. These are from Inca times. One image looks like it could be a snake, but the paintings are faint and some damage has been done to them. This section of the river is downstream from the dino tracks.

Just a bit farther downriver are a series of waterfalls and a canyon where the cliffs along the river's edge plunge 987 ft/300 m into the earth. The cliffs are dotted with trees and covered with bromeliads. A red chocolate river rages beneath. This is a spectacular spot. However, it is not possible to walk alongside the creek to reach it. To get to the canyon, walk along the road to Cochabamba for about 20 minutes and, at the curve, follow the trail on the left. Another 20-minute walk will bring you to a set of stone steps that lead to the river. At the bottom, continue following the river downstream. Going to the canyon is a two-hour walk, one way. Spending the entire day in the area is not unreasonable.

FOSSILS: The **Tarya site** is about an hour's walk west from the town. As you head up the trail that winds up the mountain, check the river beds for fossils of turtles, fish, seashells and algae. Scientific research has discovered bones from about 55 mammal species that lived during the middle Pleistocene period. Mammals found include llamas, rodents, deer, horses, mastodons and tapirs. Some of these fossils are believed to be 350 million years old. You may not take any of these rocks out of the country.

UMAJALLANTA CAVES: The caves are 5 miles/eight km from Torotoro, about a two-hour walk, one way. See the park office for explicit directions but, generally, you will head in a northwest direction along the road, past the turnoff to the mountain with fossils, and past some four-toed dino tracks belonging to one of the vegan dinos (these tracks seem to be less directed than the ones near the town). Shortly after, you will see the cave entrance.

The cave itself was carved by the Umajallanta River that disappears at this point and comes out again at Torotoro canyon. Inside is about three miles/five km of explored cave area with more yet to be explored. A guide may be useful and a flashlight is essential. As you enter the cave, the passage seems okay, but then it narrows and sometimes becomes only 10 feet wide. Some of the stalagmites and stalactites have been broken and taken by visitors who do not have enough weight in their backpacks. There are vampire bats, but they bite only during a full moon or when tourists threaten to break the rock formations. As you work your way into the cave you will come to a small lake. This is where the blind fish are supposed to be.

LLAMA CHAQUE RUINS: These ruins, 10 miles/16 km from Torotoro, make a good hiking destination for those with camping equipment. The ruin, not much more than an outside wall, overlooks Rio Caine. This Inca site was a strategically good spot from which to see enemies approaching. I have been told there are also some quiñua trees in the area. If you are not able to see them at Sajama, this may be a good scouting expedition. Birding too, is supposed to be excellent.

To get to the ruins you should have a guide or some Quechua language so you can ask directions. Guides can be hired at the park office in the village for $10 a day.

■ Place to Stay

The village of Torotoro has a few basic places to stay and even a nunnery that can give you a bed. The most popular hotel is the **Charcas**, ☎ 413-3927, that charges about $3 per person for a clean room with a communal bathroom and clean showers. The water supply is often sparse and always cold and the electricity is on only two hours a day.

Villa Tunari

Altitude: 1,000 ft/300 m
Population: 1,000

Villa Tunari is three hours by bus from Cochabamba to the east on the northern highway that leads to Santa Cruz. Most of the residents in the immediate area live mostly by farming. The village is on the banks of the Santo Espirito and San Mateo rivers.

At one time this was a rich cocaine center and the main street with its lush hotels and glitzy restaurants is a relic from that period. Now, the village is mainly patronized by workers from aid agencies and the animal shelter. However, it is in the Chapare region where the American drug enforcement agency is adamant on stopping the drug trade. This has resulted in hardships for the locals and, if there is an uprising in the country, you can rest assured the road between Cochabamba and Santa Cruz will be closed. It is not advisable to try to cross the roadblocks, although some people do. People have been killed by rocks thrown in anger by *cocaleros*.

JUNGLE JITTERS

In April of 2002 an American journalist was arrested by the military for no apparent reason. All his papers were in order and he was in the area for legitimate reasons. The arrest was violent and the detention was almost as bad. The military explained that it was protecting the journalist from drug traffickers. In order to ensure he stayed in protection, they had to beat him up. If in the area, stay out of the jungle.

■ Getting Here

 Buses leave from Cochabamba or Santa Cruz at 7:30 am, 9:30 am and 7 pm and 8:15 pm daily. It takes seven hours by *flota* to get to the village from Santa Cruz and three hours from Cochabamba.

■ Adventures (without cocaine)

 Inti Wara Yassi Community (Villa Tunari Animal Shelter), ☎ 04-413-6572 (ask for Nina, the administrator) on the new road to Cochabamba, www.intiwarayassi.org or www.geocities.com/refugiobolivia/, is an animal rehabilitation center that takes volunteers for a minimum of two weeks to work with rescued animals. Prospective volunteers show up, make a deposit ($70) to guarantee their stay and start working. The deposit pays for accommodations and kitchen use. Volunteers who leave before the two weeks of committed time, lose the deposit. If they stay longer, they are made even more welcome than they were when they first arrived and they pay only $2.50 instead of $5 a day for their stay.

As a fundraiser, volunteers often make a meal and sell it to the other volunteers. They give the profits to the shelter. This money is used to purchase food, new cages and equipment for the animals.

Volunteers can also work at the new station near Guarayos, on the road to Trinidad, but they must first turn up at Villa Tunari. The cost to work at the second station is a deposit of $45 for the first two weeks. Presently, Juan Carlos Antezana, president of the organization, is trying to convince local farmers that they could have a better life if they conserved the jungle and its animals for tourism rather than slash and burn for farming. This has worked in other countries, like Belize.

Non-volunteers can visit the shelter, go on a tour and make a donation toward animal upkeep. The cost of a tour is about $1 per person. You pay $2 for the privilege of using your camera and $3 if you want to use a camcorder. This money does not go toward the upkeep of the animals. Instead, it goes to the landowner.

To get to the shelter from Cochabamba, take a bus heading to Santa Cruz and ask the driver to let you off at the park, rather than the village. Enter the first building on the left. This is called the Casa. There among armadillos and toucans you will find a volunteer or two who will direct you. If coming from the village, walk along the road toward Cochabamba. Once you are over the bridge that crosses Rio Espirito Santo, turn right.

The shelter's aim is to rehabilitate animals that have spent time in captivity. They get pumas, Jeffries cats, monkeys, birds and turtles.

GATO'S GAIT

Gato is the famous puma who was taken away from a circus. The circus trainers had him jumping through a ring of fire. Because Gato was bitten and given a bad diet, he became crippled in his back legs. When the cat came to the shelter, he could not walk. A volunteer started him on a physio program. The result was that the volunteer stayed nine months and Gato can now walk. Gato has two volunteers who spend all day walking in the jungle with him. Although he can go on his own, Gato is always kept on a leash.

After a volunteer has been assigned an animal, it is that person's job to care for it, keep records, maintain a rehab routine and train a new volunteer to replace him/herself. Bolivians are usually assigned baby animals because babies must stay with their people 24 hours a day. If it is a monkey, for example, that means taking it to bed.

The program is popular and there are usually 25-50 volunteers here at any one time. Often, these people become so involved that they stay a long time, over a year. The job is seven days a week and each day includes all your waking hours.

A veterinarian working at the shelter first checks newly arrived animals. If no immediate medical attention is required, the animal is then put into quarantine for 40 days to prevent spread of disease. A rehab program is designed for each individual animal. For example, toucans living in captivity often can't walk, so they go on a program to get their feet working again. Birds like hawks can learn to fly as long as their wings have not been cauterized after clipping.

Quest Overseas has become involved in the program. In 2003 the group sent 20 people to work here and it plans to send more in the future.

The stories told by the volunteers are heart warming and sad, but always character-building. I want to thank Daniel J. A. Prior and Susanne Fritscher for the information they gave me about the shelter.

Villa Tunari Orchidarium, ☎ 413-4153, orchidarium@aol.com, has one square mile/2.5 square km of reserve on Rio Espiritu Santo dedicated mainly to the preservation and enhancement of orchids. However, frogs, amphibians, trees, bromeliads, birds and animals are also a draw. This little reserve is privately owned by two German men.

■ Places to Stay

HOTEL PRICES (US $)

Per person, per day, unless noted otherwise.

$	$2-$5
$$	$5-$10
$$$	$11-$17
$$$$	$18-$25
$$$$$	Over $25

Hotel Las Vegas, *in the village*, charges $5 per person for a room with private bath. It is very plain and simple.

Hotel San Martin, *Avenida Integration*, ☎ *411-4115*, *$$*, has plain rooms around a central garden. Each room has a private bath and a fan.

Hotel Querencia, *a block from the main road*, ☎ *411-4189*, *$$*, has basic rooms with private bath and cold water only. Rooms overlook the river.

Hotel Las Palmas, *Avenida Integration #777*, ☎ *411-4163*, *$$$*, has cabins on the San Mateo River. They charge $24 for a cabin that holds two people or $10 per person for a room with private bath. The on-site restaurant is noted for its fish dinners.

The Toucanes, *Km 162 on the highway*, ☎ *411-4108*, *$$$*, has cabins on the Chapare River. This well-kept place has palapa huts around the grounds for guest use.

El Puente Jungle Lodge, *2.4 miles/four km along the road toward Cochabamba*, ☎ *445-9392*, *$$$*, offers cabins that take two people. They are fully contained and include a private bath, fan and breakfast. There is a pool and restaurant.

The Bridge, ☎ *411-4712*, *$$$*, has cabins tucked into the forest beside the river where you can go for a refreshing dip. All have private baths and there is a restaurant on site.

Banana Tropic, *Km 157 along the highway*, ☎ *423-0386, $$$$,* is both a hotel and time-share property. But if you need luxury and to schmooze with the upper crust of Cochabamba, you may want to hang out here for a while. Spacious rooms have private bath done in tile, air conditioning, double mirrors and wide windows. There's a restaurant, bar, discotheque, pool, basketball and volleyball courts. Banana Tropic offers easy access to the Espiritu Santo River.

■ Places to Eat

 The Palmas, *Km 161 along the highway*, ☎ *411-4163*, is known for its fish dinners. **San Silvester**, .6 miles/one km farther, has excellent steak. Both restaurants are clean and the prices are reasonable.

■ Nightlife

 Jazmin Bar, Restaurant and Karaoke, *Calle Chiquisaca,* is the most active place in town. Drinking, eating and singing all in the same place is often beneficial, but sometimes the singing can put you off your food.

The Chaco

Santa Cruz

Altitude: 1,438 ft / 437 m
Population: 1,200,000

Santa Cruz is usually windy, often flooded and always hot. The streets, unless they have a boulevard, are all one-way but travel is confusing. The main thoroughfares go in circles and are called *anillos* (an-EE-yos). Between these circles, streets form a grid, sometimes pie-shaped. Since there is no other town in Bolivia that is quite as confusing to get around as Santa Cruz, a compass is essential. All the major intersections are adorned with a statue, usually of a person with historical importance. These are used as landmarks. There is also the large Christ figure on the second *anillo* at avenidas Banzer and Cristobal de Mendoza. The people of Santa Cruz are proud of their Christ.

Santa Cruz is the economic capital of Bolivia. Much of it is new. You will see, on the highway to the airport for example, the big showrooms of John Deere, Caterpillar, Volvo, Ford and so on. These are the installations of corporate giants that are supplying the agriculture and petroleum industries. Both industries are conspicuous in the surrounding countryside. For example, there are few small farms. It is agribusiness growing vast fields of soy and sunflowers for oil. The tractors and silos are huge. Some large holdings are Mennonite, and members of these groups can be seen in their straw hats and bib jeans. The women are in floor-length dresses and beanie-type hats.

There is a kind of independence movement in Santa Cruz that would like to cut La Paz off as the corrupt middleman in dealings with the corporations and banks so that Santa Cruz could get more of the benefits of capitalism.

If for no other reason, visitors should come to Santa Cruz to eat because the restaurants are second to none in all of Bolivia. These first-rate places were formed to accommodate those working in the oil and gas trades, the rich cattle ranchers and the large-scale farmers living in the area. Bolivia's first and (so far) only Yogen Früz and Subway are in Santa Cruz.

Tourists use Santa Cruz as a base from which to visit Noel Kempff National Park (see page 489) in the Amazon or to explore the Pantanal. Others head over to Samaipata and Amboro National Park, while culture seekers visit the unique Jesuit missions where wood carvings are the things to buy. Birding is big in the area. Regardless of your interests, you will find Santa Cruz rich in culture, history and art, with good food and comfortable hotels.

■ Getting Here & Around

 LAB, ☎ 800-337-0918 (US), 800-10-3001 (Bolivia), www.lab-airlines.com, and **AeroSur**, ☎ 231-3233 or 336-7400, www.aerosur.com, have daily **flights** from La Paz to Santa Cruz via Cochabamba for $60 per person. If flying during a fiesta, you will receive a small gift or card. The flight is half an hour from Cochabamba and just over an hour from La Paz. You will get a complimentary soda on this journey. There's also a direct one-hour flight from/to Tarija twice a week. It beats the dangerous bus trip across the mountains down to the flatlands. The flight over the Amazon from Santa Cruz to Trinidad goes daily in a small plane and crosses the mysterious earth mounds of the Moxos that anthropologists are now studying.

The airport in Santa Cruz is the only international airport in the country besides the one in La Paz. Should you not want to fly into La Paz because of its high elevation, coming to Santa Cruz from out of the country is an alternative. Numerous companies – like Varig, Continental and Lan Chile – fly into Santa Cruz from places like Miami, Florida, Santiago, Chile and Lima, Peru. The airport is nine miles/15 km from the center of town and a taxi ride there costs $10. Public buses go from the airport as far as the second *anillo*, a few blocks from the main plaza, and charge $2 per person.

Buses from Santa Cruz to Villamontes take anywhere from 12 to 18 hours during a good dry spell. If the roads are bad it takes longer. The daytime bus leaves at 8:30 am and costs $10 per person. Night buses leave between 5 pm and 7 pm. The road is paved as far as Abopo, after which it becomes a mud-hole. The road picks up again at Camiri which means most of the trip is through the mud hole.

Buses to Trinidad in the Amazon take 12 hours during dry season. In the height of rainy season, you must fly. These buses all travel at night, leaving Santa Cruz between 5 and 8 pm. The fare is about $10 per person.

There are two roads to Cochabamba and both are on a paved highway so travel is fairly quick. It is a 12-hour ride whether you take the old or new road. Only one bus a day takes the old road through Samaipata, while numerous buses go along the new.

Sucre is about 16 hours by bus from Santa Cruz, as is Puerto Suarez on the Brazilian border. Most people take a train to Puerto Suarez.

Many buses around Santa Cruz are a bit road worn so comfort is minimal. Bolívar Bus Line is a good company, but their windows often leak. Copacabana Bus in other parts of the country is excellent, but the scam out of Villamontes (see page 462) makes me want to avoid them. Ask other travelers or locals as to who is giving the best service. This changes all the time.

Trains go to Yacuiba on Monday, Wednesday, Friday and Saturday at 1 pm. The super Pullman costs just under $10, while the second class costs $2. Children under three do not pay and those up to age 11 pay only 50%. I'm happy to report that the cost of a ride to San Jose is much less than a ride to the border (some bus companies charge for the full distance to the end of the line, even if you get off earlier).

Trains to Quijarro on the Brazilian border leave every day except Sunday at 3:30 pm and the cost is $14 for a super Pullman or $2.50 for second class.

There is also a ferrobus night train that goes to the border and leaves Tuesday, Thursday and Sunday at 7 pm. A bed costs $35 per person all the way to the border and a semi-bed (which, in reality, is a reclining seat), costs $30. This includes air conditioning, TV, food and bathrooms.

Those people wanting to visit the missions can take a train to San Jose de Chiquitos, the first village along the circuit, and then bus it the rest of the way. If going super Pullman class, all meals and some soft drinks are included in the fare. There is toilet paper in the bathrooms (for a while anyway) and supper is served in a dining car. The trains are comfortable, though you must endure watching Spanish-language kung-fu videos.

A large train/bus station called the Terminal Ferraviaria, on the third *anillo*, is where buses, trains, tickets and schedules can be obtained. The compound is often called the "bimodal." Hawkers outside sell traditional foods. Taxis are not allowed within the gates. It is a hustle and bustle place, but fairly well run. Considering that train tickets can be purchased only on the day of travel, the lines are well managed. Note that some people make a living by standing in line and selling their places to others who arrive later. This is an accepted practice.

Transportation from the bimodal to the center of town costs 45¢ per person by taxi. Buses cost 15¢, but luggage can be a problem. Taxis in town cost 45¢ to anywhere within the first two *anillos*. It is a half-hour walk, without a pack, from the bimodal to the center of town. The climate is hot, so to walk with a pack would require a few beer stops on the way.

Taxis can be hired for the day from Rembarto Artegoa, radio mobile #99, ☎ 422-2020 or 716-196-682 (cell). He charges between $25 and $30 for a full day, gas included, and can take up to four people.

■ History

Santa Cruz de la Sierra was founded by explorer Nuño de Chavez in 1560. He was a Spaniard who named the city in honor of his own city, Extremadura in Spain. But the Bolivian version was later renamed after the third president, Andres de Santa Cruz, the man responsible trying to unite Peru and Bolivia into one country. Originally built on the plains of Grigota near the village of San Jose de Chiquita, 135 miles/220 km east of its present location, Santa Cruz was destroyed by local Indian tribes within three years. The town was moved to Rio Guopay, and by 1595 it was moved again to Rio Pirai, where it now sits. The city quickly became the center of religion for missionaries of all orders. It has been known by four different names; Santa Cruz de la Sierra, San Lorenzo de la Frontera, San Real Lorenzo and San Lorenzo of the Ravine.

Although isolated from the rest of the country, Santa Cruz supplied Bolivia with cotton, rice, sugar and fruits. These goods were transported mostly on the backs of mules up to the Altiplano. However, competition and easier transportation routes from Peru sent Santa Cruz into a slump until the middle of the last century, when gas and oil exploration required more and better roads that were soon used to transport agricultural products.

The other thing that helped the economy of the area was the coca trade. It brought both money and corruption. It was coca that first made Santa Cruz a boom town. However, the drug trade has been countered or decreased by the American war on drugs. Those who can make almost the same money working honestly usually do. Only constant road blocks between Santa Cruz and Cochabamba indicate that the struggle over coca is still on. Also, immigration of Japanese and Mennonite farmers added to the prosperity of the agricultural industry. These people are obviously prospering in the region, while the cocaine industry is slowly declining.

■ Services

 The **telephone office** is on Warnes #82, just off the plaza. Telephone booths on the streets take the shapes of various local birds. I especially like the pelican.

The **post office** is on Avenida Bolívar and 21 de Mayo.

Internet service is available at many places. Try the one at Avenida Ayacucho #208, ☎ 333-7981, upstairs. It has the fastest machines and the room is cool inside.

Money exchange is done on the plaza at the Western Union office. They charge a mere 2.5% commission for travelers' checks but give the going bank rate minus .01 peso. Bank machines charge a minimum of $2.50 per transaction so unless you can take out a large amount at one time you may still be better off with travelers' checks or cash. There is no commission charged for cash.

A **clinic** that is recommended by IAMAT is **Clinica Angel Foianini**, Avenida Irala #468, ☎ 623-2465. The director is Jorge Foianini. The main hospital in the center of Santa Cruz is on Avenida Canoto (the 1st *anillo*) between Avenida Ibanez and Rafael Peña.

■ Sightseeing

 Plaza 24 de Septiembre seems to be as busy a place as the cathedral flanking its side. I read, in numerous places, that sloths live in the trees around the plaza, but look as I did I found nothing. It seemed to me that the locals were laughing at me as I searched. There is always activity on the plaza, whether it be vendors selling, children playing, unions and groups demonstrating or locals relaxing. It is a fun place to spend time.

The **Zoological Park** on Avenida Cristo Redentor has animals like wolves, wild dogs and wild pigs tucked into jungle vegetation and is considered one of the better zoos in Bolivia. Don't believe it. The climate is not conducive to the health of all the animals (like the bear or the llamas) and because Bolivia is strapped for cash when it comes to the care of animals, they don't have adequate housing. This zoo would be a great project for the Villa Tunari group who rescue damaged or mistreated animals and put them on rehabilitation programs so the animals can become healthy. The zoo is open daily from 9 am to 8 pm and admission is $1.

Rio Pirai at the end of Avenida Roca and Coronado has a resort atmosphere, with numerous places to eat, drink beer, enjoy the sun (or get out of it) and play with locals in the 104°F/40°C temperatures. Because Santa Cruz is such a culinary hot spot, eating here could be as good a bet as going to any of the better restaurants.

A park area close to the river has dry forest, grassland and a small marsh. Birding is excellent in the mornings, although the afternoons can be a waste of time as some birds, like the locals, prefer to rest during the height of the heat. Examples of rare birds seen here are the Matto Grosso antbird, the peach-fronted parakeet, the yellow-chevroned parakeet and the antshrike.

The **Botanical Gardens** are seven miles/12 km from the center along Avenida Suarez Arana, on the road to Cotoca, east of the city. The gardens are a haven for birders. This is a fairly new park and work is ongoing. The area covers some of the most important dry forest in the country, along with grassland and a small marsh so the variety of birds is large. Most of the many plants are labeled and park benches are scattered around. This is a well-tended area and a peaceful place to visit. Vendors sell drinks just outside.

Parque Arenal and **Municipal Ethnographical Museum** is between Vaca Diez, 6 de Agosto and Caballero, four blocks north of the plaza. Walk along Calle Chiquisaca and you will come to it. The park's famous ceramic-tile mural, La Gesta del Oriente Boliviano (The face of the eastern Bolivian), was created in 1969-71 by the artist Lorgio Vaca. It shows many people as they march along waving banners.

The museum has a grand collection of musical instruments like handmade violins and drums from the missions area. Many items on display were used for agriculture, hunting and for cooking by the people living in the Amazon Basin and the Chaco. This includes items from the Chiquitanos, Ayoreos, Izoseños, Guarani and Guarayos cultures. There are traditional clothes on display – some decorated with feathers, others made of jute – and wooden masks (uncomfortable to wear) and costumes worn during religious ceremonies. The exhibits are well set up and give you a good idea of what life was like in the Amazon Basin and the Chaco.

SYMBOLIC DANCE

One of the dances indigenous to the region and often practiced on the streets of Santa Cruz has the dancers with ghost-white faces parading through traffic on stilts. This display is supposed to depict the conquering of pagan deities by Christianity.

The **Museum of Natural History**, Avenida Irala #565, ☎ 436-6574, is open 9 am to noon and 3 to 6 pm daily. Admission is $1.25. The building is well kept and the displays are worth seeing. Exhibits include rocks and gemstones found in the area as well as fossils and dead amphibians (often in jars of formaldehyde). But the big display is the insects. It features carnivorous tarantulas, some having teeth loaded with venom that paralyzes their prey, some with a leg span of eight inches. These creatures can

Santa Cruz
Sights

to ⑩

Col. La Salle

AV GEN MARTINEZ

AV LA SALLE

AV SAN MARTIN

FINOT

JAIME FREIRE

STRONGEST

AV BUSCH

VENEZUELA

AV MON RIVERO

LOS TAJIBOS

⑨ AV CRISTOBAL DE MENDOZA

MAXOS

AV TRINIDAD

AV URUGUAY

CASTEDO

IBANEZ

VACA DIEZ

to ⑪

CHIQUITOS

AV ARGOMOSA

RAFAEL PENA

⑯ CUELLAR

6 DE AGOSTO

⑮ ⑧ CABALLERO

AV SUAREZ ARANA

SEOANE

24 DE SEPTIEMBRE

⑦ CHARCAS

TENALES

AV CENTENARIO

GUENDA

CARDONNA

PALERMO

ICHILO

AV CANOTO

BUENOS AIRES

SARAH

SANTA BARBARA

ESPANA

FLORIDA

21 DE MAYO

LIBERTAD

BOLIVAR

⑥ ⑤ ⑭

④ ③

LA PAZ MURILLO

AROMA

QUIJARRO

CAMPERO

BOLIVAR

AV VIEDMA

② BALLIVIAN

AV LANDIVAR

A JORDAN

VELEZ

CORDILLERA

VALLEGRANDE

AV AYACUCHO

INGAVI ⑬

FIGUEROA

RENE MORENO

CHUQUISACA

NUFLO DE CHAVEZ

WARNES

⑫ REPUBLIQUETAS

TARIJA

to Train Station

CATOLICA

PARI

COLON

VELASCO

MERCADO

INDEPENDENCIA

SALVATIERRA

POTOSI

MOLDES

SALVATIERRA

M FLORES

M SAUCEDO

ZOZOY

PARAPETI

LEMOINE

LA RIVA

SAAVEDRA

①

AV ARGENTINA

CHARAGUA

GUARAYOS

Bus Terminal ■

MUCHIRI

AV GRIGOTA

AV IRALA

AV EJERCITO NACIONAL

AV VELARDE

MENDOZA

ANDRES MANZO

AV LAS AMERICAS

AV CAP M ARRIEN

Parque Urbano

AV TTE M CUELLAR

H

UNIVERSITY CAMPUS

© 2004 HUNTER PUBLISHING, INC

N

SIGHTSEEING
1. Museum of Natural History
2. Museum of Art
3. Cathedral
4. Casa de la Cultura
5. Plaza 24 de Septiembre
6. Chiquitas Art
7. San Andres Church
8. Arenal Park
9. El Cristo
10. Zoological Park
11. Botanical Gardens

TOUR OPERATORS
12. Bolivian Adventure Tours
13. Vicuã Tours
14. Cambaur Travel Agency
15. Forest Tour
16. Rosario Tours

HUNTER PUBLISHING

1 MILE

1 KM

The Chaco

go for 2½ years without food and up to 80 days without water during hot summer months or seven months in cooler winter months. The roach display has 3,500 species, some whose ancestors go back about 320 million years. I like the cicadas with their transparent wings. Their sound in the jungle can be heard for up to half a mile. Plan on spending a few hours in this museum.

Historical Churches

Plaza 24 de Septiembre on Calle Ayacucho and Avenida 24 de Septiembre has a brown-brick **Basilica Menor de San Lorenzo** dominating one side. It is an imposing building, the most recent in a long line of cathedrals on this spot. It is constantly hustling and bustling with people, vendors, beggars, pilgrims and priests. Built by Mercedario Fray Diego de Porres in 1605 under the directorship of the Viceroy of Teledo, the cathedral was reconstructed by Bishop Ramon de Herbosos in 1770. Finally, in 1835 Marshal Andres de Santa Cruz (third president) wanted something worthy of the city so, under the guidance of French architect Felipe Bestres, the new cathedral came to be. It is nice to see brown brick rather than stone as the architectural base.

Go inside whenever the doors are open. The altar is of worked silver originally from the Jesuit mission of San Pedro de Moxos, as are four hand-carved wooden confessionals with intricate paintings over the wood. The ornate interior of the cathedral is quite a contrast to the exterior.

The **Carlos Gericke Suarez Museum**, attached to the cathedral, is divided into four rooms, one featuring silver, one jewelry, one paintings and one woodwork. All rooms have relics from the Jesuit Missions farther east as well as gold and silver workings from the 18th century. The most beautiful piece of work is an ivory carving of Christ on the cross. It has filigree trimmings in silver. The museum was named after a university professor from the area whose silver work was used as an example of craftsmanship throughout the 17th and 18th centuries. The museum is open Tuesday, Thursday and Sunday, 10 am to noon and 6 to 8 pm.

The **Church of San Andres** on Avenida Beni and Charcas has a wooden nave (the cross-section of the church near the front) with wooden columns carved from the hard horcon wood from the Amazon area. The columns are carved in baroque style, interspersed with vines, fruits and birds from the area. The outside of the church has columns done in the Greek style.

■ Adventures in Culture

 Casa de Cultura de Raul Otero Reiche, on the plaza, is used as a cultural theater, offering plays, concerts, movies, exhibits of photography, sculpture and contemporary paintings. The theater halls are lined with old paintings and there is also a library featuring regional publications. Try to get tickets to a concert while in town. Watch for posters at the entrance.

The **Museum of Art**, Avenida Sucre and Calle Potosi, ☎ 334-0926, is in the same colonial building as the tourist office. The artwork is good, mostly contemporary sculptures. There are numerous rooms, some with works of young artists not yet famous and other rooms with works of artists like Lorgio Vaca. There is usually a new display of Bolivian work every six months or so.

Chiquitas Art at the Santa Cruz Museum of History, Avenida La Casona and Calle Junin, just in front of the post office, ☎ 332-4620, is open Monday to Friday, 9:30 am to noon and 3:30 to 7 pm. The art display has works that blend old styles with contemporary ones. This is a permanent exhibition.

Okinawa is the Japanese settlement near Santa Cruz. The first settlers came over a hundred years ago, although most arrived after World War II when Japan was in serious depression. In 1953 the Bolivian government agreed to give the immigrants land if they worked. Those leaving Japan got start-up money from the Japanese government and came to grow rice and soy and to raise chickens. The first influx numbered around 5,500 people and a second wave in 1970 doubled that number. Visit here if you are interested in Japanese culture. Take a micro from the station to Montero and a second one from there to Okinawa. Each bus costs 50¢.

■ Adventures on Foot

Hash House Harriers is a club of runners who usually have a fun run once a week in Santa Cruz. A hash run goes like this. There is a route, fixed by one of the club members, that the runners must follow. However, the runners don't know where the route goes or what the markers are. The runners start running and, as they figure out the markers and are able to follow them, they holler "on-on" in Spanish, of course, and everyone follows. This is done at a jogging pace. When the run is finally over, everyone usually congregates for a few hours of socializing. In Santa Cruz they welcome anyone, members and non-members, from the ages of zero on up. They run on Mondays at 5:30 pm and have a dinner after the run. The contact persons are Jim Bibb, ☎ 558-5003, jimbibb@its.com.bo; Susan Guillen, ☎ 355-0000, susan.guillen@bg-bolivia.com; and John Naphan, john.naphan@transredes.com.

Lomas de Arenal del Palmar is 9.8 miles/16 km east of the city along the highway to Palma Sola. This odd landscape, nestled in the tropical jungle, is a desert complete with sand dunes and a tiny lagoon that is good for swimming. Originally designed to be part of the sewage system, opposition from locals resulted in this area becoming a park instead. The sand is believed to come from erosion of surrounding rocks. Bird activity is high. There are trails and a camping facility. To get here, catch the Palmar micro from Calle Grigota and Cañoto, or take a taxi (less than $5).

Las Cuevas is a set of waterfalls between Samaipata and Santa Cruz along the old highway. To get to the falls, catch a minibus going toward Samaipata. Ask the driver to let you off for the walk to Las Cuevas. It is barely half an hour from Santa Cruz to the turnoff. The walk starts along the river that crosses the highway. Go about 650 ft/200 m upstream and follow a trail uphill on your right. At the top, face the valley and hike to your left (not right, or you will fall off the hill). Continue along the ridge until you come to a road. Follow this back down to the highway. The reason most people do this hike is to watch for birds. Bring your reference book, binoculars, some water, sun hat and bird list. The place literally twitters.

■ Adventures on Water

There are two public swimming pools in Santa Cruz and, with the heat, you may want to patronize them. The first, called **Aqualand**, ☎ 385-2500, is seven miles/12 km on the highway going north toward Trinidad (see below). The other, **Pescina de Santa Cruz**, is three miles/five km along the old highway toward Cochabamba. This one is an ordinary pool for those wanting only to swim. The entry fee is 50¢ and open hours are about 9 am to 6 pm daily.

Aqualand at Km 12 on the northern highway just past the Viru Viru Airport (not to be confused with the swimming pool, above) is 16 acres of water fun. It has a capacity to hold 5,000 people and employs up to 60 lifeguards during high season. Inside is the usual water park with slides and a wave pool that is capable of making huge waves. A sandy beach surrounds the pool. A lazy river section has gentle waves and current for those wanting to float along. A speed slide attracts high rollers, while the kiddy slide sees more sane visitors. A family raft that carries a number of people down the slide together is popular. This is the only water slide park of its kind in Bolivia. The entry fee is $10 and open hours are Friday to Sunday, 9 am to 6 pm.

Laguna Palmira is five miles/eight km from town to the south and behind the oil refinery. Locals come here to watch Jet Ski races on weekends. I've mentioned these races so you can stay away and avoid the noise pollution.

Cotoca is 12 miles/20 km east of Santa Cruz and is known for the sanctuary of the Virgin of Cotoca administered by the Dominican Fathers. For 10 days starting at the end of November, the town celebrates the Fiesta of the Immaculate Conception of Mary. At this time, no alcohol or gambling is permitted within the town. The parade starts by taking the statue of the Virgin of Cotoca from the sanctuary in the cathedral and parading her through the streets. Some of the people decorate their carts, pulled by horses, with palm leaves and colorful streamers and balloons. The women in the village sell the best of their pastries and cheese dishes, which are famous. The community is also famous for its pottery. They make unique pieces such as figures of people sleeping or working at various tasks. Other items include huge jugs and vases and many different renditions of the moon, sun and/or stars.

■ Tour Operators

Bolivian Adventure Tours, Avenida Chiquisaca #561, ☎ 336-4848. Ana Maria Garcia, who runs the company, speaks English very well. If you have questions or problems about travel, she would be able to help. The tour agency's specialty trip is a run down the Beni River on a luxury boat, *Reina de Enin*. The company flies you to the Beni in a small plane from Trinidad (you must get to Trinidad on your own). The other big offer is a trip to Noel Kempff Park for three days at a cost of $600 per person (all-inclusive) with a minimum of two people. Their final area of expertise is a trip to Amboro National Park at a cost of $70 per day, per person. Bolivian Adventures can also take you on a three-hour city tour or around the Jesuit missions for a couple of days. This company is part of a larger organization that includes Hurva Tour, based in Peru.

Hombre y Naturaleza is mentioned numerous times in regards to trips around the Pantanal both in the north and in the south. There are also stations in the mission circuit and one at Charagua, south of Santa Cruz and 46 miles/75 km from the Paraguayan border. Contact them in Santa Cruz at ☎ 923-2239, hynb@bibosi.sca.entelnet.bo or prowames@cotas. com.bo. Their English is perfect, their Spanish is even better, and they will assist in planning a trip to meet your needs. They are a NGO and their entire focus is on preserving the environment.

Vicuña Tours, Calle Independencia and Avenida Ingava, ☎ 337-2460 or 336-1982, vicunitatours@hotmail.com, were pretty disinterested in trying to sell me a tour. Their cost for four days and three nights at Flor de Oro in Noel Kempff Mercado is $1,674 per person with a minimum of two people. Vicuña can do simple things like book a direct flight to another town, but if you want anything complicated like a stopover, I'd suggest you go elsewhere.

Cambatur Travel Agency, Calle Sucre #8, just off the square, ☎ 334-9999, cambatur@cotas.com.bo, does not offer tours currently because it lacks an English-speaking guide. However, this may change. Check with them before deciding on a tour. The owner, Oscar M Pinto, speaks English and can help with other travel plans.

Neblina Forest Tour Co., Avenida Paragua #2560, in Sayubu Building, room #204, ☎ 347-1166 or 2-800-488-9401 (from anywhere in the country), www.neblinaforest.com, is run by Rosario Baldomare in Santa Cruz and is part of a larger company that has tours in Peru, Chile and Equador. They offer the best birding tours in the area that go to Noel Kempff Mercado National Park, Beni, Pantanal, Amboro National Park, or the Samiapata, Comarapa, Tambo, Siberia and Pocona areas. Other excursions go to Buena Vista, Villa Tunari and Madidi National Park. This company can arrange trips for up to 16 days. However, please check their payment and cancellation policy before booking. The refund policy and price-changing policy is fairly biased in their favor.

Forest Tour Operator, Calle 24 de Septiembre #22 at Libertad, ☎ 337-2042, offers a number of outdoor adventure opportunities. Their specialties are three days on a ranch, four days in the Pantanal along the Paraguay River and a two-day hike at Robore, just outside the mission town of San Jose de la Chiquitas. Their trip into Amboro National Park can include a horse, hike or bike trip. The company is willing to adjust itineraries to suit your needs. Because of their flexibility, the Robore hike can be included with a mission tour plus a visit to the hot springs. They also offer a hiking trip to Santiago de Chiquitos. One of their more interesting aspects is that they teach forest survival courses. You can rent a jeep for about $130 a day for up to four people. I found them helpful and cooperative, although a bit expensive.

Rosario Tours, Avenida Arenales #193, ☎ 336-9977 or 336-9656, adventura@cotas.com.bo or rosario_tours@cotas.com.bo. Rosario Baldomar is the owner of this tour agency. She offers many tour combination trips, but her best go into Amboro National Park and the Pantanal. There are also the city tours and shopping tours around Santa Cruz. The four-day trekking trip in Amboro requires a minimum of three people. It runs $245 per person, including food, transportation, accommodations and a Spanish-speaking guide (an English-speaking guide costs more). You can also go for three days and two nights at a cost of $145 per person.

The Pantanal trip runs four days and three nights. If staying in the five-star hotel, the cost is $487 per person and the tour is all-inclusive from Puerto Suarez (which can be reached by train). If staying in the hostel, the cost is $374 for one, $246 (each) for two people and $206 for three people. This trip includes a visit to the Cave of Motacusito, which has vampire bats inside, a boat trip through the Santa Tecla Forest area, a trip down Rio Paraguay to Brazil and a stop at the Laguna Caceres on the way back.

Rosario's mission tour takes four days. It's all-inclusive and costs, depending on your hotel selection, $480 per person (minimum of two people) or $280 per person (minimum of four people and a maximum of seven). English- and German-speaking guides are available. The English-speaking guide with whom I spoke had good command of the language.

Rosario also offers a tour to a Mennonite community and then on to San Javier and San Julian (missions). There is a final stop at Cotoca, the traditional pottery center, on the way back to Santa Cruz.

The city tour includes the zoo, museums, monuments, plaza and craft market. This tour is with a knowledgeable English-speaking guide.

Wildland Tours, 3516 NE, 155th Street, Seattle, WA 98155-7412, www.wildland.com, takes travelers into Noel Kempff National Park starting with a pickup in Santa Cruz. In six days they cover both areas of the park and transportation services are included. Their specialties are in guided hikes, bird watching and photography. This is a company that will do everything for you except click your shutter. See page 82, *Outfitters Who Do All the Work*, for more information on this company.

■ Places to Stay

HOTEL PRICES (US $)	
Per person, per day, unless noted otherwise.	
$	$2-$5
$$	$5-$10
$$$	$11-$17
$$$$	$18-$25
$$$$$	Over $25

Residencial Ballivian, *Calle Ballivian #71*, ☎ *332-1960, residencialballivian@yahoo.es, $,* has rooms set around a large courtyard that's well maintained and full of plants. There are lots of toilets and sinks around the building (no private bathrooms) and hot water is available all day. The kitchen can be used until 9 pm, when it is shut down so the noise won't disturb other guests. The owners are friendly and helpful.

Residencial 15 de Octubre, *Calle Avaroa, #372 between Calle Suarez Arana and Avenida Charcas,* ☎ *336-3633, $,* has rooms with private bath and, for an extra charge, air conditioning. The place is fairly basic, but for the price it's passable.

Hotel Sara, *Calle Sara #85 between Calle Ayachuco and Avenida Junin,* ☎ *332-2425 or 337-2524, $$,* has large rooms, all with private bath, TV, ceiling fans, reading lights and soft beds. The rooms are cleaned daily. The owner uses solar panels for electricity so the hot water is usually cold. A continental breakfast is included in your room rate. This is a family business and the family is friendly.

Alojamiento Oriente, *Calle Junin #362*, ☎ *332-1976, $$,* is clean enough, but the rooms (with or without bath) are dark. Rooms have TVs and fans. Breakfast is included in the price. A tiny eating area has a place where you can purchase juice, eggs, sandwiches and soft drinks.

Los Pozos Hotel, *Calle Quijarro #431 and Caballero and 6 de Agosto,* ☎ *332-1245, $$,* has a number of rooms on three levels around a central courtyard. The hotel is just one block from the Parque Arenal. The rooms are large and all have private baths. Everything here is clean.

The Tourist Inn, *Mercado #555 between Cañoto and Cordillera,* ☎ *335-4759, $$,* has rooms with private bathrooms and TVs.

Hotel Bilbosi, *Avenida Junin #218,* ☎ *334-8887, $$,* has a travel service and complimentary Internet access. Rooms have fans or air conditioning (additional cost), dressers, chairs, soft beds, tiled floors, mirrors, large bathrooms and luggage holders. This is a clean and pleasant place.

Hotel Italia, *Calle Rene Moreno #167 between Ingavi and Suarez de Figueroa,* ☎ *332-3119, $$$,* is okay in a pinch but not the best value in town. Its 20 large rooms are spaced around a central courtyard. They have big windows and tiled bathrooms.

Hotel Roma, *Calle 24 de Septiembre #530,* ☎ *332-3299, $$$,* includes a continental breakfast in its rates. The rooms have TV, a clothes cupboard, hot water, air conditioning and a fridge, but the dark carpets make them appear drab. A courtyard is dotted with plants.

Excelsior Hotel, *Calle Rene Moreno #70,* ☎ *332-5924, $$$,* is directly across from the cathedral, so it's handy to the square. Rooms have private bath, air conditioning, TV, towels and telephone and come with a continental breakfast. Each has attractive wall murals painted by local artists and some rooms have built-in desks that have been painted in modern design.

Hotel Amazonas, *Junin #214 and 21 de Mayo,* ☎ *333-4583, $$$,* would not let me see a room, so I can't give an opinion about them. Apparently, each has a private bath, color TV and telephone. The staff was not friendly.

Hotel Copacabana, *Avenida Junin #217,* ☎ *336-2770, $$$,* is a three-star property that offers rooms with air conditioning (more expensive) or a fan. They are located on three floors around a courtyard that doubles as the restaurant. Each is small and clean and features large windows, tasteful décor, mirrors, TV and soft beds. The price of a room includes breakfast. Bathrooms have a separate shower stall and towels; toilet paper and soap are supplied. The rooms with air conditioning are larger and have a fridge/mini bar.

Hotel Viru Viru, *Calle Junin #338* ☎ *333-5298, $$$,* has 44 large rooms and suites. Each has a sitting area with a couch, air conditioning, a

Santa Cruz
Hotels & Restaurants

Col. La Salle

AV GEN MARTINEZ

AV LA SALLE

JAIME FREIRE

AV SAN MARTIN

FINOT

LOS TAJIBOS

17 AV CRISTOBAL DE MENDOZA

8

STRONGEST

9

AV MON RIVERO

AV TRINIDAD

MAXOS

AV BUSCH

VENEZUELA

AV URUGUAY

19

UNIVERSITY CAMPUS

AV 26 DE FEBRERO

GUENDA

AV CENTENARIO

CUELLAR

SANTA BARBARA

CASTEDO

IBANEZ

VACA DIEZ

RAFAEL PENA

H

11 **24**

16 **14**

SEOANE CABALLERO

6 DE AGOSTO

5

AV SUAREZ ARANA

CHARCAS

3

1

TENA_ES

26

AROMA

QUIJARRO

CAMPERO

BOLIVAR

AV ARGOMOSA

CHIQUITOS

CARDONNA

PALERMO

ICHILO

AV CANOTO

ESPANA

FLORIDA

SARAH

12

23 **28**

25

22 **7** **4**

10

BOLIVAR

AV AYACUCHO

21

30

2

LA PAZ MURILLO

BALLIVIAN

NUFLO DE CHAVEZ

AV VIEDMA

BUENOS AIRES

JUNIN

AV LANDIVAR

A JORDAN

VELEZ

18

6

CORDILLERA

VALLEGRANDE

29

INGAVI

FIGUEROA

27

CHUQUISACA

WARNES

REPUBLIQUETAS

POTOSI

TARIJA

to Train
Station

M FLORES

M SAUCEDO

CATOLICA

GOZOZO

PARI

COLON

VELASCO

INDEPENDENCIA

RENE MORENO

SALVATIERRA

MOLDES

20

CHARAGUA

GUARAYOS

MUCHIRI

AV GRIGOTA

PARAPETI

MERCADO

SALVATIERRA

LEMOINE

LA RIVA

SAAVEDRA

AV LAS AMERICAS

AV ARGENTINA

Bus Terminal ■

13

AV IRALA

AV VELARDE

AV EJERCITO NACIONAL

MENDOZA

ANDRES MANZO

AV TTE M CUELLAR

AV CAP M ARRIEN

Parque
Urbano

© 2004 HUNTER PUBLISHING, INC

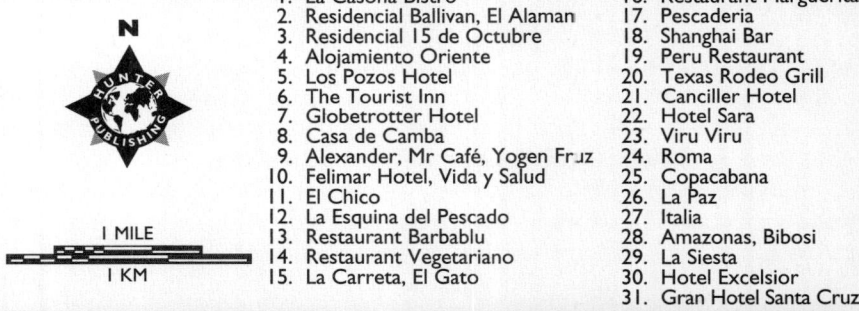

N

HUNTER PUBLISHING

I MILE

I KM

1. La Casona Bistro
2. Residencial Ballivan, El Alaman
3. Residencial 15 de Octubre
4. Alojamiento Oriente
5. Los Pozos Hotel
6. The Tourist Inn
7. Globetrotter Hotel
8. Casa de Camba
9. Alexander, Mr Café, Yogen Fruz
10. Felimar Hotel, Vida y Salud
11. El Chico
12. La Esquina del Pescado
13. Restaurant Barbablu
14. Restaurant Vegetariano
15. La Carreta, El Gato

16. Restaurant Marguerita
17. Pescaderia
18. Shanghai Bar
19. Peru Restaurant
20. Texas Rodeo Grill
21. Canciller Hotel
22. Hotel Sara
23. Viru Viru
24. Roma
25. Copacabana
26. La Paz
27. Italia
28. Amazonas, Bibosi
29. La Siesta
30. Hotel Excelsior
31. Gran Hotel Santa Cruz

The Chaco

fridge/bar, telephone, TV, closet and lights over the beds. However, the carpets were grubby. There is a small pool in the courtyard and breakfast is included in the price.

Hotel Felimar, *Calle Ayacucho #445,* ☎ *334-6677, $$$$,* has 60 rooms and breakfast is included in the rate. The rooms are large and painted in bold colors, but the carpet is tattered. There is air conditioning, cable TV, closets, dressers with mirrors, and a clean bathroom with a separate shower stall. Those facing the street have a balcony. There is an elevator, a bar and restaurant and a car park.

La Siesta, *Calle Vallegrande #17,* ☎ *334-9775, www.hotel-lasiesta.com,* *$$$$,* has 44 small bright rooms with tiled floors, cable TV, cupboards, air conditioning and a separate shower stall in the bathroom. The price includes a continental breakfast, use of the pool and Internet access. There is also a safe, garage, restaurant, money exchange and laundry service.

Hotel La Paz, *Calle La Paz #69,* ☎ *332-1728, hotellapaz@cotas.com.bo,* *$$$$,* has good rates for anyone staying a month. In this price range, the La Paz is an excellent deal. The 16 rooms are set around a well-maintained courtyard. The place is spotless and the owner is friendly. A single room is small, but the doubles are huge – some have sitting rooms. Rooms have soft beds, large closets, cable TV, telephones, air conditioning and a fridge/bar and breakfast is included. There's a travel agency on site, a safe deposit service and a car park. Many tourists stay here and repeat guests are common. Reservations are advisable during high season.

Globtrotter Hotel, *Calle Sarah #49,* ☎ *337-2754, $$$$,* is a quiet little place that includes breakfast in the rate. Rooms are large and clean, with air conditioning, cable TV and a fridge/bar. I think the price is a bit high.

Gran Hotel Santa Cruz, *Calle Rene Mareno,* ☎ *334-8811, www.gran-hotelsantacruz.com, $$$$$,* is the classiest place in eastern Bolivia. What first strikes your eye when entering the large marble foyer are the three carpets lying under leather couches. The rugs are genuine, handmade Persians. One (by the street window) is from Tabriz; the stitching (underneath) is so fine it looks more like petit point than a carpet. On the far wall of the foyer sits an oil painting of the founder Modesta A. Vivera. She opened her first hotel on the same spot in 1953. At that time the hotel had only two floors; today it has six, with 110 rooms in all.

There is a large pool at the back flanked by a bar. Above the bar is a gym and sauna, both wet and dry. The rooms are huge, with wall-to-wall windows, 80 TV channels, mini fridges, double beds, telephones in the bedrooms and bathrooms, full-length mirrors and safes in the closets. A larger, more elegant room has a sitting area with leather couches, but no Persian carpets. There are also Jacuzzis and bidets in the ballroom-sized bathrooms. The halls are thickly carpeted and interspersed with oak writing desks. The entire building has central air conditioning and/or heating, security monitors and underground parking. To date there has never been a robbery from a car in the parking area.

I was surprised at the exceptional courtesy I got from the staff. There is always an English-speaking person at the desk. Amenities include a business room, board rooms, restaurant, and bar and grill. All this costs $87 for a double or $77 for a single. An executive suite is $107 (with Jacuzzi bath). If not staying at the hotel but wanting the ambiance, have a burger and a swim in their pool for $3.50. This place comes highly recommended for a visit, even if you can't afford to stay.

Canciller Hotel, *Calle Ayacucho #220 between Colon and Velasco,* ☎ *337-2525, hotelcanciller@entelnet.com, $$$$$*, is a four-star hotel that has over 40 rooms plus a presidential suite. The rooms are spacious, use the modern magnetic strip card to open the doors, and have air conditioning, mini-bar and a sitting area. On site there is a restaurant, swimming pool, laundry service and Internet access. Rates not provided.

▪ Places to Eat

Casa del Camba, *Avenida Cristobal de Mendosa #539,* ☎ *342-7864, www.casadelcamba.com*, opened in 1986 and is the best restaurant in Bolivia. It should be experienced by everyone at least once. A taxi here will cost $1 for two people and as you pull up a waiter dressed in a straw hat, white shirt and black pants will open the car door and show you the way inside. "Inside" is outside, an open courtyard with covered areas in case of rain.

First, have a drink and read the leather-bound menu. A band or pianist will play soft, non-intrusive music. I had a *chuflay* for my pre-dinner drink. It was not watered down. My husband's beer was cold, very important in Santa Cruz. We got a dish of pickled veggies (onions, cauliflowers and carrots) on which to snack. A brazier was then placed at our table and a thick slice of pan-fried cheese was prepared and served with some hot garlic bread.

It was time for wine. The restaurant has a long list of Argentinean, Chilean and Bolivian wines. The most expensive was $14.50 per bottle. We ordered a steak with sausage and shish kabob, served with rice. However, salad was next, mixed with a mild dressing and partially prepared at the table. Then came the meat, cooked on the brazier in front of us and done to perfection. There was more than we could eat. The cost in total was $30 (price on bill was also displayed in US dollars). A taxi was called when we were ready to leave. The restaurant holds about 800 people and by 8:30 pm (on a Monday night), it was half-full. Unless you come early, as we did, you may want to make reservations. This can be done online.

The Chaco

Alexander, *Avenida Monseñor Rivero #400,* ☎ *337-8653*, is as good here as it is in La Paz. They make a cheesecake with baracuya topping that I highly recommend, while some of my friends prefer the cheesecake with strawberries. Baracuya is a fruit that has a tart, lemon-like taste. Alexander is in the center of a three-block, up-scale string of cafés and bars near the university and court house. It is a nice walk from the central plaza.

Pastic Ceria Café, Avenida Monseñor Rivero #328, ☎ 333-4410. The best pizza in town is made here. You can watch yours being made from scratch and stuck in the wood-fired oven to bake. This place has the same owners as Restaurant Barbablu, below.

Mr Café, *across the street from Alexander on Avenida Mons. Rivero #260,* gives strong competition to Alexander with excellent pastries and top-notch service. The thick sweet cream put into the coffee (if you want it) is so good I was tempted to tell them to forget the coffee and just serve the cream. They also offer some mean pasta dishes for anywhere between $3 and $7.

Don Caito, *one block from the plaza toward the north*, has good ice cream. Service is pleasant and they have a buffet for lunch that is excellent for $1.75 per person.

La Casona Bistro, *Calle Arenales #222,* ☎ *337-8495*, is a little Mexican place that serves both snacks and full international meals. The atmosphere is a big draw. Plus, it is not far from the main plaza.

El Chico, *Calle Libertad #350,* ☎ *333-0027*, is a Tex-Mex bar and restaurant chain. They have good burritos and pizza and also carry an entire line of Mexican foods. Open Monday to Thursday, 11 am-midnight and on weekends until 1 am (on Sundays they close at 3 pm).

Vida y Salud, *Calle Ayacucho #444, directly across the street from the Filmor Hotel*, serves organic veggies and is very popular both with travelers and locals.

Restaurant Ria Lia, *Calle Murilla #40,* ☎ *336-8183,* has an incredible buffet. Come hungry. When I was there they had 46 veggie dishes, both hot and cold. Those I tried were excellent. Besides that, there were five meat dishes that could be included on your plate (some locals just loaded up with meat) and three juices from which to choose. All this sells for $2 on Sundays and $1.50 the rest of the week. They are open from 11:30 am until 3 pm. A *boca libre* sign means all you can eat. Come early to eat here because Bolivians know about it too.

Salteña Caliente *on Chuquisaca, one block past Michael Angelos*, is a popular snack place and comes highly recommended.

BREAKFAST BUNS

Uñape is a small bun that has a doughy center filled with cheese. These are often sold around the bus stations during breakfast time.

El Alaman, *Calle Ballivian across from the Residencial Ballivian,* has German beer and is convenient for a nightcap if staying at the Ballivian. However, the music at the bar is always ear-piercing in volume and the owner, when he's there, likes to yell at his staff and party loudly with his friends.

Leonardo's Restaurant, *Calle Warnes #300, just down from La Vieja Café and Bar,* is situated in a huge colonial mansion. It offers one of the classiest atmospheres in Santa Cruz. Sadly, it was closed when I was there.

La Esquina del Pescado, *corner of Sarah and Florida,* looks like it takes up an entire block but, in fact, it is three places side by side. It is famous locally for its fish. To get food, you must give your order to the man at the cash box beside the barbecue. He will take your money and give you a numbered receipt. You then find a place to sit, either on the street or in one of the three restaurants. Someone will pick up your receipt and your meal will miraculously appear. The fish is good and often there are five or six choices. The cost is around $2 per meal. They start serving at 9 am and stay open till late in the evening. Saturday and Sunday are the most popular days and often the wait for a table is 15 minutes.

Burger King, *Avenida San Martin & Calle Siete,* ☎ *342-8410, or Calle Rene Moreno and Avenida Andrez Manzo,* ☎ *337-1292*, has not been run out of town by local restaurants – yet. If you want a touch of home, a sparkling clean bathroom, Arctic-quality air conditioning and a Whopper Combo for $3, then this is the place. If you're economizing, a simple burger with ketchup, mustard and one dill pickle is less than a dollar. With cheese, brings the price up to a full dollar. They also have a chef's salad for $2.25, hot apple dessert for 85¢, and two pieces of chicken for $3.25.

Restaurant Vegetariano, *24 de Septiembre #351,* ☎ *332-1794*, is open every day from noon to 3 pm and again from 6 pm to 8:30 pm. This highly recommended place offers a buffet full of organic vegetables.

La Carreta, *24 de Septiembre,* ☎ *332-1794,* has a nice ambiance with an open fireplace and an open-air patio. The food and the prices are to my liking. For example, ravioli is $1.50, sweet and sour pork is $1.75 and a filet is $1.25. The restaurant is patronized by many Bolivians.

Restaurant Barbablu, *Avenidea Ejercito Nacional #150,* ☎ *334-4037*, is known for its home-made pasta and is recommended by locals. When we were here, lots of people were eating, but many more were taking orders home. Barbablu's second place is on Avenida Monsenor Rivero #328, ☎ 333-4410. It specializes in Italian pastries. The coffee is excellent also.

Rincón Brazilero, *Calle Libertad #358,* ☎ *333-1237*, sells food by the kilo. I did not try it, but it comes highly recommended by aid workers in Bolivia.

Yogen Fruz, *Calle Cañada Strongest and Monseñor Rivero,* ☎ *337-7221*, has the entire line of frozen yogurts, plus ice cream. The shop is tiny, but the air conditioning is great. This is a real treat – far better than some of the other franchises that come out of North America.

El Gato, *24 de Septiembre #285,* ☎ *333-2040,* has a good buffet that offers ravioli, spaghetti with mushrooms, chicken, meats and salads. The cost is by weight. Half a kilo is about $1.75 with a minimum charge of $1. The buffet is available every day from noon to 3 pm, after which meals can be ordered from the menu. This is a popular place.

Restaurant Marguerita, *Calle Libertad and Junin,* ☎ *337-0285,* is open Monday to Friday, 9 am-midnight, and weekends, 4 pm-midnight. Their specialties are pizza, pastas and hamburgers along with espressos and cappuccinos, but they are expensive. A medium veggie pizza costs $5, almost twice as much as most pizza joints in town. However, the restaurant is air conditioned so it is often worth paying just for the cool atmosphere.

Pescaderia, *Avenida Cristobal de Mendosa #8 on the second anillo just half a block from the statue of Christ,* ☎ *353-7151,* serves very good fish, often along with ceviche. The prices are reasonable: a fish dish with yucca, salad and a beer is less than $4. Weekends are the best time to come for dinner as there are more varieties of fish available. During the week they serve mostly surubi, a boneless catfish. Breaded, it makes an excellent dish.

Shanghai Bar and Restaurant, *Avenida 26 de Febrero #27 (in the 2nd* anillo*),* ☎ *352-3939,* is where one should go for Chinese food. The sweet and sour ribs are excellent – similar to those I have tasted in Hong Kong. The atmosphere is classy, rather than tacky. The only drawback is the location, a little way from the center of town.

Guadalajara Restaurant, *Avenida Mons Rivero #279,* ☎ *708-59889 (cell),* is a tiny but popular Mexican restaurant that offers the usual dishes of tacos and *tejidos*. Prices are average. They often have tables on the sidewalk.

Peru Restaurant, *Avenida San Martin and 9 Oeste Equipetrol,* ☎ *336-0296*, offers the best ceviche in eastern Bolivia, as well as other dishes such as filet mignon. The portions are large and the food excellent, but prices are high, about $5 per serving. Diners are given a complimentary dish of salted corn chips before their meal. There is a rather ordinary eating area in an open patio, plus an elegant inside area that sets the tone for a romantic evening.

Chalet la Suisse, *Calle los Gomeros #98,* ☎ *343-6070,* has been recommended by many for its trout, llama, quinoa and hot peppers (among other well known Bolivian and European dishes). They also have fondue dishes with either meat or cheese. I did not try the Suisse in Santa Cruz, but the one in La Paz is excellent and has an elegant atmosphere.

Michelangelo, *Avenida Chiuisaca #502 and Sulvatierra,* ☎ *334-8403,* is open Monday to Friday for lunch and Monday to Saturday for dinner. This is considered one of the better restaurants in town, but every time I went, they were closed.

Texas Rodeo Grill, *Calle Aruma, in the Urbar Barrio, outside the second* anillo, ☎ *352-2244,* is in Hotel La Quinta and is open noon to 2:30 pm and 6-11 pm. They specialize in grilled meats and Mexican food. This is where the Hash House Harriers often go after their weekly run. I take that as a sign that the food is very good. However, I do not recommend eating breakfast here.

■ Nightlife

 La Taberna, Calle Monseñor Rivero #281, ☎ 345-3949, is a tapas bar that is popular with local yuppies. It specializes in paella made with meat, fish or vegetables.

The Irish Pub on the main plaza in the Bolivar Shopping Mall is by far the best place to fraternize with the local ex-pats, but the cost is high. A drink or a meal costs the same here as it does in North America. The pub overlooks the square and is decorated with numerous old photos of Ireland and a great poster showing famous literary characters like James Joyce and Jonathan Swift. The music is usually good but a tad loud, the lights are dim and the service is moderately quick.

■ Shopping

 R.C. Joyas, Calle Bolívar #262, ☎ 333-2725, specializes in gem cutting, mostly with amethyst, bolivianite and topaz. It offers unique designs, but is expensive. The owner speaks English and German.

Manos Indigenas Artist Shop, Calle Cuellar #16, ☎ 337-2042, has handmade works from the Guarayos, Chiquitos and Ayores indigenous groups of eastern Bolivia. There are ceramics from Cotoca and Huayculi, wood carvings and jute bags, masks and even a few instruments (although I cannot determine the quality). This is an excellent place to browse. The shop is off the main tourist areas, so you must be interested in indigenous art in order to seek it out.

Artesanias Pewter Palace, 24 de Septiembre #76, ☎ 333-8916, is filled with wooden bowls, leather items (hats especially), and pewter and silver pieces. Prices are comparable to other shops in town, but this shop has a good selection. Open 8:30 am-9 pm daily.

Vicuñita Handicrafts, Calle Indepencia and Avenida Ingavi, has a wide variety of goods and crafts such as silver jewelry, llama wool carpets and hardwood vases and boxes. Prices and quality should be compared before purchasing.

Inca Products, Avenida Cañoto and Landivar, ☎ 333-7049, incaproduct@hotmail.com, has a large selection of wood, pewter, copper, silver, alpaca wool and leather products. English is spoken and your purchases can be shipped anywhere in the world – for a price, of course. Open Monday to Saturday, 9 am-8 pm, and Sunday, 10 am-5 pm.

Joyeria Andrea, Calle Junin #177, ☎ 334-2435, is a classy shop that specializes in bolivianite, or ametrine, as it is also called. A semi-precious quartz, boliviante comes in purple or yellow and looks to me a lot like amethyst. This jewelry shop was the first to work with the stone and some of the pieces they have for sale are exquisite.

Arte Campo, Monseñor Salvatierra #407, ☎ 355-9133, is a co-op that carries the work of mission artists and distributes it around the country. Please stop into their store and maybe make a purchase. The bags for sale come from seven different groups of artists and each group has its own specific art design. The dyes are from plants and the material is from the garabata plant that women gather from the forest. The money from the sale of bags alone helps support the families of 200 women.

■ Jesuit Mission Tour

Altitude: 1,363 ft / 410 m (average)

✝ The Jesuit missions near Santa Cruz are unique and different from anything else you will see in the world. They are mostly constructed with wood beams and ceilings that have been polished and carved into different patterns using baroque designs interspersed with images of local plants and animals, such as vines, pineapples and armadillos. The plaster walls have been painted in intricate designs using natural colors of the Amazon area. The buildings have been restored.

A tour of the missions can be done with a company, by rented jeep or by public transportation. If going on your own and using public transportation, start in San Jose and end in Concepcion. This is because of the train schedules. Traveling from Santa Cruz to San Jose, the train leaves in the

Mission Tour

N

HUNTER PUBLISHING

Noel Kempff Mercado

Panorama

SAN IGNACIO
DE LOYOLA

Carmen Ruiz

SANTA ANA

SAN RAFAEL

Totaicito

SAN MIGUEL
DE VELASCO

San Juan de
Lomerio

La Manga

El Recreo

San Rafaelito

El Cerro de Concepción
Estación Quimone

SAN JOSE
DE CHIQUITOS

San Juan de Las Taperas

Robore

Aguas Calientes

to Puerto Suarez

Urubichá

Ascencion

Zuruquizo

CONCEPCION

SAN FRANCISCO XAVIER

Santa Rosa de la Mina

San Ramon

Santa Maria

San Pablo

Los Troncos

Pailón

Buena
Vista

Santa Cruz
de la Sierra

La Guardia

61 MILES

100 KM

- - - - - - Railroad

afternoon and arrives in San Jose before midnight. Going to Santa Cruz by train from San Jose means you must catch it at 2 am and arrive in Santa Cruz a bit before noon. Sitting around a train station in the middle of the night is not very appealing.

DISTANCES BETWEEN MISSIONS	
Santa Cruz to San Jose	162 miles/265 km
San Jose to San Rafael	80 miles/130 km
San Rafael to Santa Ana	15 miles/25 km
Santa Ana to San Ignacio	28 miles/45 km
San Rafael to San Miguel	24 miles/40 km
San Miguel to San Ignacio	22 miles/36 km
San Ignacio to Concepcion	111 miles/182 km
Concepcion to San Xavier	38 miles/62 km
San Xavier to San Ramon	32 miles/52 km
San Ramon to Santa Cruz	88 miles/143 km

You must carry either Bolivian or American cash as there are no bank machines or places that will accept traveler's checks on this circuit.

History

Declared a UNESCO site in 1990, the 10 missions that were built in the territory we now call Bolivia were constructed between 1692 and 1760. Others were built in Argentina, Brazil, Paraguay and Peru. There are even a couple near the north shore of Lake Titikaka and some in the Amazon area. The first Jesuit Mission was built in Juli, Peru.

When the Jesuits came, they not only brought religion but they also offered the semi-nomadic societies in the area a school, hospital and religion complete with impressive ceremonies. The Jesuits gave the people a place to express their art forms by carving and painting. But most of all, the locals were attracted to the church because of the music.

Father Martin Schmid came here in 1729. He was a dedicated musician originally from Switzerland, and he had a tremendous amount of energy. He started by designing the missions in the unique fashion, with huge halls and high ceilings, built with mud brick covered in plaster and painted. Each wood beam is made from a single tree trunk and carved by local artists of the time. Schmid also started and directed choirs, made musical instruments like flutes and violins, and copied thousands of sheets of music. Because of Schmid's influence, a new style of music developed, called missional baroque and it came to be from the blending of traditional indigenous music with classical baroque. The most famous piece to come out of this transition is called *Requiem Chiquitos* and the recording, done by present-day musicians from the area, can be purchased on a CD published by the French company K617.

Schmid was obsessed with music and even the construction of the missions is believed to symbolically represent musical keys that metaphorically allow the architecture to resonate with music. This I was told. I haven't got a clue what it means.

The villages were also built with a blend of the two cultures. Sofia Savedra Bruno, an anthropologist who studied the influence of the Jesuits on the natives, found the building style has a lot of Indian influence, while the construction techniques are European. All mission towns are formed in the shape of a cross, with the plaza being at the nave of the cross and the housing of the local people along the arms. Chiquita Indians traditionally built communal row houses with dividers for each family. The houses in the mission towns are still built in this manner. Each mission had a town hall with an administrative body that included a judicial system and an economic structure.

NOT LITTLE PEOPLE

The indigenous people were called Chiquitos, not because of their size (*chiquito* means tiny in Spanish), but because of the size of the doors to their houses. The doors were made small to keep the excruciating heat out, the cool in.

The Jesuits did not exploit the labor of the local people, although the people were expected to give of their time in the building of missions. Building the mission at San Miguel took 200 men working every day 11 years. On the other hand, the Jesuits thought the Indians were childlike and incapable of doing many things. In order to obtain more souls for the church, the priests would ring the bells about an hour before sunrise to encourage sexual activity. This shows you how much the Jesuits knew about sexual activity.

King Filipe II gave the Jesuits permission to deny entry of any white man to the churches if he felt that person might cause trouble. This excluded officials like the governor, of course. Then in 1767, King Carlos III of Spain expelled the Jesuits from Bolivia and the missions fell into disrepair. See the somewhat sanctimonious de Niro movie, *The Mission*, about his closure. During the next hundred years, they were stripped of many of their riches. The leaders of the Roman Catholic Church took a lot of these items because they felt the riches would be better appreciated by white people in big cities. However, in 1975 restoration of the missions started under the leadership of architect and priest Hans Roth, and with the help of Father Godofredo Trenker. What inspired Roth was that while he was poking around the area, he came across 5,000 pieces of hand-written music. Some of the music pieces were by Zipoli Domenico, a famous European composer who lived from 1688 to 1726. It is now believed that Father Schmid had brought this music with him, as well as pieces copied from other composers such as Vivaldi and Corelli. It was this music that was used to teach the local people how to sing and play. After Roth found the music, he spent the next and last 30 years of his life helping with the restoration of the missions. But the work was gargantuan. There were no roofs on the buildings, most of the paintings were damaged by moisture, and some of the wood had rotted. However, each community worked just as it did when the missions were first constructed in the 1600s. The results are wonderful.

Adventures in Sound

As reconstruction moved forward, the priests re-introduced music. Now, after restoration, music is back full force and if you are in the area during festival practices or performances, be certain to listen. All the missions are involved in a new music program and sponsor a bi-annual festival that is of an international standard. The event includes renowned musicians from Spain, Bolivia, Argentina, England, Italy, Germany and France playing with local symphonies. The first concert, held in 1998, was such a success that the organizers decided to have it every other year. The next festival will be in 2004. For detailed information about the festival, contact Festival International de Musica Misiones de Chiquitos, Casa Municipal de la Cultura Raul Otero Reiche, Casilla #3673, Santa Cruz, ☎ 332-2476.

As a lead-up to the festival, missions present concerts on the last Saturday of every month. In July and August, performances are Saturday at around 8 pm, with a few early morning sessions as well. The touring musicians are both Bolivian and visitors who will later participate in the festival. There is no cost for you to go and listen. Ask at the tourist office in Santa Cruz for schedules or ask at the missions as you travel the circuit. Participating missions are Santa Ana, San Ignacio, San Rafael, San Miguel, San Jose, Concepcion and San Javier. All the music is classical.

VIOLIN VILLAGE

Those very interested in music, and specifically in the violin, should visit the village of Urubicha on the road to Trinidad. Although not part of the missions, the village plays a musical role. To get there, take a bus from Santa Cruz going to Trinidad and get off at Asuncion. From there, take a micro to the village. There are basic accommodations available and places to eat.

There, under the guidance of priests, children learn to play classical music very much as their ancestors did. They memorize the notes and often play three different instruments. The priest, Father Walter Neuwirth, who has been there since the 1970s, realized that the children needed something to make them proud of their heritage. He hired Ruben Dario, a young man trained in music at the Royal Conservatory of Cordoba in Argentina. The two men formed the local music school. Now there are over 200 children who form the village choir and orchestra. The students play (practice) every day and come for lessons in-between classes at school.

The conductor of the orchestra is a young lady who plays the violin, flute and clarinet. The interesting thing is that these children, whose ancestors were first introduced to the music 300 to 400 years ago, now play the same missionic baroque music with pride. They also play their own traditional music with passion. Many of these young students take part in the biannual festival of music.

The village violin maker claims he can't make the instruments fast enough to keep pace with the demand.

Mission San Jose de Chiquitos

This is the first (or last) village on the mission circuit. The train from Santa Cruz arrives here around midnight, but the village, being in the hottest area of Bolivia, is wide awake in the cool of the night so walking to the center is not dangerous. There are also taxis available at the train station.

San Jose is a dusty, dry town that seems more like an outlaw's hideout than a religious center. Even the mission is what you would see in an old Western movie. But there are comfortable places to stay, the square is pleasant to sit in and the food is good.

The town of Santa Cruz de la Siera was first built at this location in 1592. The village was later moved to the banks of the Guopay River and then again to its present site. However, some people remained near the village of San Jose and the mission prospered.

THE MISSION: The Mission of San Jose de Chiquitos was built in 1697. It features high wooden ceilings and attractive carved wood pillars and doors. A ghoulish figure of Christ bleeding on the cross sits at one of the side altars. Some of the front façade has the original paint and is not as glittery as the rest. The ladder to the bell tower is held together by grooves and wooden pegs, rather than nails. This is how it was originally made. The beauty of this mission is the stonework and the block-long front face. It is the only mission in the country made of stone. The square

The Chaco

on which the mission sits is crowded with old toborochi trees, the ones with very fat trunks.

FESTIVALS: Festivals in this area are the usual Carnival and Samana Santa, but the unusual one is on May 3, the anniversary of the formation of the village.

Mission San Jose de Chiquitos.

ADVENTURES ON FOOT: If you have the time or desire to walk in the heat, walk to the base of Turubo Hill, the hill with some vegetation beyond the village. You will see paths going up to the top. To reach the base of the hill will take about 15 minutes from the plaza.

PLACES TO STAY & EAT: The owner of **Hotel Turubo**, *on the plaza*, ☎ 972-2037, *$*, scrutinizes her clients carefully before she rents a room. The moderate-sized accommodations have mosquito screens on the windows and the communal bathrooms and showers are clean and well kept. The Turubo offers a basic breakfast but no juice, just Nescafé coffee. However, the *salteneria* just one block north has good food. It's clean and comfortable and guests are encouraged to sip on coffee while watching the heat rise over the streets.

Victoria Hotel, *to the side of the mission (no phone), $*, can hold up to 35 people and, during festivals, you can negotiate for a hammock or even a spot for your tent. Rooms come with or without private baths, and those with private facilities can accommodate three people. The small rooms have fans and are spotlessly clean, with cement floors and small windows. There are hammocks in the patio area and a car park. The owner was friendly and went out of his way to accommodate me. Breakfast can be negotiated into the price.

HOTEL PRICES (US $)

Per person, per day, unless noted otherwise.

$	$2-$5
$$	$5-$10
$$$	$11-$17
$$$$	$18-$25
$$$$$	Over $25

Alojamiento San Jose, *Avenida Mons. Carlos Garicke*, ☎ *972-2106, $,* is under new management. It currently has 12 rooms – five with private baths – and an additional four are being built around a tended garden area. The rooms are basic and clean. The new owner is friendly and cooperative.

Hotel Denisse, *Avenida Mons. Carlos Gerike Suarez*, ☎ *972-2230, $$$,* has rooms with and without baths and air conditioning. Breakfast is included in the rate. The hotel is clean, comfortable and the beds are soft. Bolivian businessmen patronize the Denisse. The staff is impersonal.

Rafa, on the road to San Ignacio, has the best supper in town. For lunch, go to **Los Yescas** or **Casa Pyla** – both are excellent. To find them, walk along the side street by the Turubo Hotel away from the church. They are within a block of each other.

GETTING HERE & AWAY: The **bus** leaves from Calle Oriental and 24 de Septiembre daily (except Sunday) at 1 pm for San Ignacio (the second town of the circuit). The five-hour journey costs $4. The **train** for the border leaves around midnight. The train to Santa Cruz, in the opposite direction, leaves at 2 am. Plan to wait an hour beyond all scheduled departure times.

Mission San Rafael

San Rafael was founded by Father Jose de Arce, the same priest who started the mission at San Francisco Javier. This mission was started in 1693 and it was moved from its original site to the banks of the Sapoco River in 1705. It was completed in the mid-1700s and from then until the expulsion of the Jesuits it was home to over 5,000 people. Today, that number has fallen to 1,000.

THE MISSION: The church itself is one of the more ornate on the circuit, with decorative painting on the outside covering almost every inch. However, I didn't find it gauche. San Rafael is the saint whose image is inside, over the main altar. He made it big with locals because he was believed to be a symbol of one of their own gods who lived in the forests. Both the saint and this god carry fish.

PLACE TO STAY: The town itself is tiny and dusty, but there is one place to stay right on the corner of the plaza. It's basic, but if you can get no farther it is comforting to know the bench in the plaza won't be your home for the night.

GETTING HERE & AWAY: If you come by bus from San Jose de Chiquitos you will have to spend the night. Should you go on to San Ignacio you can take in this mission by returning via taxi (about $25 for two people). That way, you can also stop at Santa Ana and San Miguel. If coming the opposite way by bus, this loop in the circuit can be done either from San Ignacio or by staying at San Rafael for the night.

Mission Santa Ana

THE MISSION: Santa Ana is the smallest of the missions and the most authentic. Built in 1755 by priests who came specifically to help with a smallpox epidemic, it was administered by Jesuits for only 12 years before they left. During that time Father Julian Knogler set up a college that taught wood carving, a craft for which the area is now famous. The paintings on the walls of the buildings are of angels, flowers and musicians playing violins and singing, but the building overall is less ornate than other missions. This simplicity makes it appealing. The bell tower is a simple three-storey structure that sits on four posts and has two bells on the top storey. The bells are still rung before mass every day.

After the Jesuits left, the mission existed under the leadership of local people and so did not deteriorate like the others. However, the needed restoration was completed under the directorship of Hans Roth. In 1990 Mission Santa Ana was declared part of the group of missions considered culturally important by UNESCO.

PLACE TO STAY: Hombre y Naturaleza (based in Bolivia) and Amigos de Doñana (based in Spain) are NGO societies dedicated to the promotion and preservation of the natural world. They offer a fairly basic and comfortable place to stay next to the north side of the plaza on Calle Bolívar, ☎ 343-6968. It costs $9 per person per night for a dorm bed, $10 if breakfast is included. Private rooms with double beds cost $8 per person. Bathrooms are communal.

TOUR AGENCY: Hombre y Naturaleza offers half-day guided trips to the museum and gardens for $5-$8 per person, depending on how many are in your group. Guides offer information about museum exhibits

and the plants in the garden. The group also offers 4x4 trips to dry forests, mica mines and to Santa Teresita, the Precambrian rock that stands
1,645 ft/500 m high. Should you have a specific interest, talk to these people. They will try to help. Contact them in Santa Ana at caloping@
teleline.es or mamencill@hotmail.com; in Santa Cruz at ☎ 923-2239,
hynb@bibosi.sca.entelnet.bo or prowames@cotas.com.bo. Their English
is good and they will assist in trip planning.

GETTING HERE & AWAY: If you take the bus from San Jose de
Chiquitos, you will have to get off at San Rafael and take another bus to
Santa Ana. For exact times of buses contact Hombre y Naturaleza (see
above). You may also take the bus from San Ignacio direct to Santa Ana
(see San Ignacio section for information).

Mission San Miguel de Velasco.

Mission San Miguel de Velasco

San Miguel can be visited from San Ignacio or you can get off the bus from
San Jose and spend a night at the one basic *alojamiento* in town. San
Miguel is a small, dusty town but interesting enough. Some believe that
this mission, on the inside, is the most beautiful of them all. Plan on visiting the carving shops also. There's one at the side of the mission and another just out of town on the road to San Ignacio.

THE MISSION: To get inside, go into the yard by a side gate beside the bell tower and ring the bell of the priest's door. The current priest is from Czechoslovakia and has been in Bolivia for 12 years. He will sell you a pamphlet for $1.50 (consider this an entrance fee) before taking you on a tour of the mission.

The mission was started by Felipe Suarez and Gaspar Fernandez de Campos in 1718 and was dedicated mostly to the arts. However, in 1748 the simple adobe church was reconstructed under the direction of Martin Schmid and Father Juan Mesner and in 1765 it was finally inaugurated. At that time it was dedicated to San Miguel. It took 200 workers every day from about 1750 until 1765 to complete the construction, carvings and paintings of this building.

Inside the church, the front altar is carved wood from floor to ceiling, painted in gold glitter so that the polished wood pillars go almost unnoticed. The pulpit is the finest in all the missions. The confessionals are intricately carved and painted in gold and red. The walls too are painted with floral designs interspersed with pictures of different saints. The building's main structure is the original one.

SHOPPING: The **Artist's Workshop**, on the road going to San Ignacio and just up from the church, has carvings for sale. They are mostly reproductions of mission pieces. The prices here are about 10% more than in San Ignacio. This is because the co-op in town carries work from all the missions and the workers feel that it is better for you to purchase from the co-op and, in turn, keep more people employed. The wooden angel that is used by the missions as a logo was created by an artist from this village.

GETTING HERE & AWAY: If coming from San Jose de Chiquitos by bus, you can get off at San Miguel. To get from there to San Ignacio or San Jose de Chiquitos, you must take a taxi (there aren't many in San Miguel). The best way to visit San Miguel is via San Ignacio, where you can hire a taxi for $10 for two people, round trip.

Mission San Ignacio de Loyola

San Ignacio is a town of about 20,000 people, although I find this hard to believe as the area never seems crowded or busy. However, the action revolving around the bi-annual music festival is obvious and the tourist office strongly promotes these events. The town is one of the more lively mission towns and the places to eat are a bit more varied.

San Ignacio's biggest fiesta besides the usual religious holidays is July 31, when the town celebrates San Ignacio Day.

THE MISSION: Started in 1748 by Miguel Areijer and Diego Contreras and finished in 1761, this mission was the biggest of the group and had the largest congregation until Santa Ana and San Rafael were built. Dur-

Mission San Ignacio de Loyola

ing that time, the arts and skills of the locals were promoted and goods were exported to places as far away as Europe. The economy was healthy and the people had time to study music.

The mission was closed in 1767 when the Jesuits were expelled, but saw a brief revival in 1790 when a traveling priest came. Then the mission closed again until, in 1930, it became a college under Monseñor Bertoldo Buhel. The college served all of Bolivia. Finally, in 1984 the Jesuits returned to Bolivia and the mission started to thrive again.

When Hans Roth started photographing and recording the condition of the missions, San Ignacio's main building was in a bad state. Roth started the present restoration (there were seven restoration attempts in 250 years) on some missions, but it wasn't until 1997 that San Ignacio was worked upon. The altars, pulpits and confessionals – all from the original church – have been spruced up a bit. These pieces of carved wood have inlaid mica for decoration. However, even with restoration, the clock in the tower does not work.

This mission is one of the most active in the festival of music. Be certain to take in at least one concert.

SHOPPING: The **tourist office** on the square has a small showroom with weavings and wood carvings, some painted and some varnished.

These exceptional pieces are reproductions of original mission items. The cost for some of the moderately sized items is under $30.

San Ignacio has always been known for the family-sized **hammocks** that are made in town. The most noted family making them are the Garcias, who have passed the art down from generation to generation.

SERVICE: The **money exchange** on the plaza changes cash only.

ADVENTURES ON FOOT: Marilandia is a 5,000-acre/2,000-hectare forest on the edge of town, past Laguna de Guapoma on the road to San Miguel. It has self-guided trails, and you can also walk up the hill that has the Stations of the Cross for views of the town and surrounding area. The hill is the only one that can be seen from town.

ADVENTURE ON WATER: A reservoir at the edge of town is the local swimming hole. Walk left from the Casa Suiza hotel when going toward the plaza and follow that street to the reservoir.

Laguna de Guapoma is a clean lake that lies between San Ignacio and the village of San Miguel. This great swimming spot is used by everyone. It can be reached by taking a taxi or getting off the bus on your way into San Ignacio coming from San Miguel. In the heat, you may like a swim before getting a place to stay in San Ignacio.

PLACES TO STAY: Hotel Oriental, *24 de Septiembre and Cocha-bamba,* ☎ *962-2150, $,* is across from the San Ignacio and near the bus stop. It has a lovely garden with grapefruit and lime trees. Large rooms – with or without private bath – have big windows, fans, tables and chairs and hot water. This is a good deal.

Alojamiento El Riabe, *Calle Sucre #491,* ☎ *962-2586, $,* has large rooms with tiled floors, tables and chairs, but rough mattresses (you would need a sleeping bag). The communal bathrooms are clean.

Hotel Palace, *on the square,* ☎ *962-2073, $,* has a well-tended garden in the patio area. The small but clean rooms all have a private bath.

Hotel 31 de Julio, *on the plaza just up from the Palace (no phone), $,* is very basic. The rooms are without bath and go for $2 per person.

Alojamiento Tarija and Viajar, *$, across from the bus stop,* have basic rooms without bathrooms. Only in a strong pinch should you go there.

Hotel Plaza, *Plaza Principal,* ☎ *962-2035, $$,* is next to the mission that runs it. The 11 clean rooms have private bath with towels supplied, fan, large windows, decent-sized mirror and tiled floors. Breakfast is included. This hotel offers a lot of information about Noel Kempff park.

Casa Suiza, *a few blocks up from the bus station, $$,* is spotless. The rooms and bathrooms are large and the beds are comfortable. A good breakfast is complimentary. There is a book exchange and a garden. The guest book is full of recent information on where to go and how to get there. The hotel is quiet. To find Casa Suiza, walk from the bus station toward the plaza and turn left on Calle La Paz that passes along the south side of the plaza. Continue for four blocks. You will not see the sign painted on the side of the hotel until you are across from it. There is a dog that barks, but does not bite. Close the gate after entering and call to announce yourself.

Hotel Guapomo, *Calle Sucre,* ☎ *962-2095, $$,* is beside the cross that stands in the middle of the road. The rooms are of average size with soft beds, tiled floors, large windows and a ceiling fan. It's clean.

Hotel San Ignacio, *Calle 24 de Septiembre and Cochabamba,* ☎ *962-2157, $$$$,* has a flavor of Hawaii that is a contrast to the dryness of San Ignacio. This hotel is patronized by the upper-crust Bolivian and offers both regular rooms and larger rooms that feature a loft with extra beds. All rooms have a TV, a bar, sitting area, soft beds and tiled floors. The bathrooms each have a separate shower stall. A well-tended garden and pool are flanked by a thatch-roofed bar. Hammocks are interspersed around the courtyard. The staff is anxious to help. The place is exceptionally clean and tastefully decorated.

Hotel La Mission, *Plaza 31 de Julio, Calle Libertad,* ☎ *962-2333, $$$$$,* is actually Swiss-owned and -operated, offering rooms and more expensive suites. All rooms have air conditioning and cable TV. There is a bar and restaurant, a pool and a professionally tended garden on the premises. Breakfast is complimentary. The pillars (support beams) at the entrance to the hotel are carved wood, similar to those in the mission. Rates: $45 single; $55 double; $95 suite for two people.

PLACES TO EAT: The **Social Club** on the plaza offers a buffet lunch, including a pitcher of lemonade, for $1.50 per person. The club is popular with locals because the food is good. The buffet has at least three salads and two meat dishes and sometimes more. The large eating area is set around a huge courtyard.

Hotel La Mission, *Plaza 31 de Julio, Calle Libertad,* ☎ *962-2333,* has cold beer and excellent food in moderate-sized portions. I recommend their pasta with Alfredo sauce for less than $4. The service is good and the staff friendly but not overbearing. There were no drunks (see below) and the music was Vivaldi. The bill was even manageable. What a treat.

Restaurant Venicia, *on the corner opposite the mission*, has been recommended by many as the best place to eat. However, I found the drinking customers a bit obnoxious as they hollered comments to the women riding around the square on their motorbikes.

Renacer, on the other side of the plaza from the Venicia, is the best place to drink with locals and the clientele seemed much quieter.

GETTING HERE & AWAY: The **bus** companies by the main station near the market in San Ignacio will tell you that buses go to Concepcion or San Jose only on Monday, Wednesday and Friday. This is not true. A first-class bus leaves from a different station every evening at 7:30 pm. It takes four hours to reach Concepcion. To find that station, walk three blocks past the square along the same side as the tourist office and away from the Venicia Restaurant. Turn left one block past the hospital and walk for half a block.

Concepcion

Concepcion first became a Jesuit village in 1699 with Father Lucas Caballero as the priest/missionary. In 1722 Father Juan de Benavente moved the village to its present site. The priests knew to introduce music to the locals if they wanted to catch their attention, but they also introduced a written language with grammar and vocabulary rules.

Somewhere between 1730 and 1753 (there are conflicting dates) Martin Schmid started the construction of the mission church. It is believed that the building was completed in 1756 and within the next 10 years the village grew to 713 families with 3,276 people. At that time, eight different languages were being used. It was shortly after that the Jesuits were expelled from the country.

The Presbyterians came in the early 1800s and stayed for a few years, but it became illegal to be anything but Catholic in Bolivia so the Franciscan Fathers arrived to look after things. In 1950 the church at Concepcion was declared a national monument and in 1975 restoration began. This was completed in 1982 and nine years later the mission became a cultural site recognized by UNESCO.

THE MISSION: Because of conflicts and power struggles among the priests, the town was not established until 1719 and then its permanent location was not decided upon until 1722. The mission itself was not completed until 1756 and restoration was done in the 1970s under the directorship of Roth.

The mission has an attractive bell tower with a circular staircase that is held up by spiral support poles. The altar is partly decorated with inlaid mica to give it glitter. The most interesting part of the church is the pews. Each has a scene carved from the bible with the book it comes from recorded below. The Old Testament scenes are in the back half of the church and the New Testament scenes are in the front. The pulpit is of carved silver, as is part of the altar. A contemporary painting depicts the restoration with images of a logging truck and a guy with a chainsaw.

The **Mission Museum** on the plaza is open from 8 am to noon and 3 pm to 6 pm daily. Admission is 75¢. The house was donated to the mission by ex-president Hugo Banzer. In the central courtyard is a wooden sugarcane press. These are seen around the country and it is good to know what they are. There are three upright round logs with cut cogs at the top. Between the logs where the cane is fed are trays to catch the juice. A pole leaning out from the cogs was attached to a donkey that was made to walk in circles, thus turning the wheels that press the cane.

The museum has many original mission pieces. One set of plaster statues of Mary, San Pablo and San Ignacio are exceptional in their artistic quality (so I am told). Note the carving at the entrance to one of the rooms that has a saint with his finger up his nose. The museum is worth visiting.

ADVENTURE ON FOOT: Trek through the jungle to look for birds, amphibians and monkeys. Just five miles/eight km from Concepcion is the **Piedra de Santa Teresita**, a rock that stands 1,650 ft/500 m high. It is a Precambrian granite hill and the area is especially rich in bird life. The hike takes a minimum of three hours (some of it driving) and is considered to be of medium difficulty. It can be done either in the morning or late afternoon, depending on the heat.

Visit **Pedrito Grala**, a man who lives 37 miles/60 km from Concepcion on the banks of Rio Negro. Pedrito was a river man for 40 years before settling down. He was also in the RAF during World War II so he is proficient in English. One of the reasons to visit his establishment is to listen to his stories.

The jeep trip to Pedrito's place is along a decent road until the last nine miles/15 km. Then the road becomes an adventure. Once in the camp, you will be provided with a hammock that has protective mosquito netting. After a dinner and drinks made from the natural plants of the jungle, Pedrito takes his guests (now armed with flashlights) on a night safari looking for animals that hunt by night. Since the climate is so hot, most animals living in this area hunt at this time, including the elusive jaguar.

For this trip you will need repellent, a sun hat, lots of water and no desire for a shower until you return to Concepcion.

ADVENTURE IN NATURE: The **Pachanga** is a man-made water hole only 6.7 miles/11 km from town. It can be visited at any time of day. The area is rich in birds like the heron and the vulture, not to mention some of the smaller song birds that are ubiquitous in the long grasses.

ADVENTURE ON WATER: Zapoco Dam, 1.8 miles/three km from town, was originally built to supply electricity, but this did not happen. Instead, the reservoir is used for water activities such as swimming. The landscape has been spruced up by local authorities and now has a park. It's a pleasant place to visit, with palapas and barbecue pits for you to use. There is a chance to see capybaras at this place. The water-bird life too is abundant. During rainy season you can sit near the area where the water comes into the dam, with your back against a rock, and experience a natural Jacuzzi.

TOUR AGENCY: Hombre y Naturaleza (based in Bolivia) and Amigos de Doñana (based in Spain) are NGO societies dedicated to the promotion

The Chaco

and preservation of the natural world. They offer six different excursions that focus on science and conservation. The excursions are flexible. For example if you are interested in frogs, they will take you to an area where you may find frogs. Depending on which excursion you choose and how many people go along, the cost can be anywhere from $120 for one person for an overnight trek to Puerto Pedrito to $6 for four people on a guided hike to the Pachanga. Contact Humanos y Naturalesas, in Concepcion at ☎ 964-3074 or mabubones@yahoo.es; or in Santa Cruz at ☎ 923-2239, hynb@bibosi.sca.entelnet.bo or prowames@cotas.com.bo.

PLACES TO STAY: Hotel Grandero, *on the side street that leads to the cemetery, a half-block west of the plaza, $,* has a courtyard scattered with hammocks. The rooms are large and plain, with high ceilings, fans and private bathrooms. When we arrived at night, the place was locked up and only because the clerk heard us outside her window did she open the door. There is no bell. Once inside, the clerk had a hard time deciding where to put us as each room she opened happened to be occupied.

Colonial Hotel, *Calle Nuflo de Chavez #7,* ☎ *964-3050, $$,* has the largest armadillo hide I have ever seen. The rooms are large, with tile floors and private bathrooms, and are placed side-by-side in a row that is in traditional Chiquitos housing style. A large patio for communal use has hammocks, a clay oven and a thatch roof, also traditional. Breakfast is included.

Hombre y Naturaleza, *$$,* has 12 biological stations in Bolivia. Those in this area are at Concepcion, Santa Ana, Puerto Suarez and San Matias. To get to the station in Concepcion, walk along the north side of the plaza for two blocks. The station is an inconspicuous place with a few signs on the wall of the porch. Walk through the gates around to the back. Rooms here have basic bunk beds in a four-room cabin that costs $6 per person. It is in a quiet compound that has a fairly good reference library and a small museum with objects rescued from villages in the surrounding area. The volunteers are friendly and some speak English.

El Escondido, *Calle Pando,* ☎ *964-3110 $$,* is, as its name implies, a hideaway. This is a true little island in the jungle only six blocks from the main plaza. The hotel was recommended by many travelers as the best average-priced place on the mission circuit. It has 12 rooms around a maintained garden, all with tiled floors and private bath. They feature mission-styled trim painted on the walls. The place sparkles. The owner, a pleasant lady who is highly respected by both her fellow townspeople and foreigners, offers complimentary breakfast to her guests. She goes out of her way to make you comfortable by doing things like putting fresh flowers on the table or in your room.

Hotel Las Misiones, *on the plaza,* ☎ *964-3021, $$$,* has an attractive flowered courtyard. All rooms have bathrooms, some have beds upstairs in a loft, all have hand-quilted bedspreads and dried flowers in the bathrooms. The property is well maintained and painted with designs like those at the church. The furniture is hardwood and there is a sitting area in each room. Rooms come with or without air conditioning and breakfast is included.

Gran Hotel Concepcion, *Calle Aurelio Roca Llado,* ☎ *964-3031, $$$$,* is an elegant place that has housed important people like the presidents of Spain and Colombia (you will see pictures of them in the foyer). The hotel is built in colonial style with the rooms around a garden and attractive patio. The rooms are clean and rather plain, each with a wooden cross hanging over the bed. The elegant décor is reserved for the foyer. There is a kidney-shaped pool and French colonial furniture. Most of the furniture and books are antiques. All rooms have a fan and breakfast is included in the price.

Las Piedras, *$$$, (no phone number available) 35 minutes out of Concepcion on the road to Santa Cruz.* This hotel is on the side of a hill that is littered with rocks, some sculpted into odd formations. These interesting rocks go for a few miles to both the north and south of this small resort where there are cabins, a restaurant, a swimming pond and lots of hiking trails.

PLACES TO EAT: Restaurant Buena Gusto on the plaza is situated in a lovely flowered patio. It opens at 8 am and offers an excellent *almuerzo* with lots of salad and good soup. The lemonade was a bit too sweet and the bread was bad, as usual, but the service made up for those two faults. The restaurant gives food to some of the area's beggars.

GETTING HERE & AWAY: Buses come and go to San Ignacio every day. Buses to Santa Cruz leave at 7 am, 2 pm, 6 pm, 10 pm and 11:30 pm. A number of different bus companies are located in the same block on the same street, just up from the plaza.

Mission San Francisco Javier

This mission was built in 1691 by Jose de Arce and another Jesuit priest by the name of Antonio Rivas. San Francisco Javier is the patron saint of the Chiquitos. The mission was not built on its present site to begin with, but was moved four times before it finally found its permanent home in 1708.

This mission is between Concepcion and the mission of San Ramon on the main highway. Neither are popular stopping places and should be visited only by those really interested in missions. Since there are a number of buses going and coming from Concepcion, it is not difficult to get a ride after stopping in this village.

The Chaco

Villamontes

Altitude: 2,253 ft / 685 m
Population: 3,000

This is the hottest place in Bolivia. Not only is it hot, but it is dry and dusty. The only draw to the village is the canyon that you pass when traveling overland from Tarija and an excellent museum dedicated to the Chaco War. Although some people are friendly, Villamontes caters mostly to the young oil patch workers. If you can, spend the night in Camiri, as it is far more appealing than Villamontes. And, Che Guevera slept in Camiri.

■ Getting Here & Around

Yacuiba is 100 km/60 miles from Villamontes and has the closest airport. It is easy to catch either a bus, *trufi* or taxi up to Villamontes. Most people who fly from Santa Cruz to Yacuiba are traveling down to Argentina. **TAM** (☎ 244-3487, www.tam.com.br) and **SAVE** (☎ 212-1548) airlines fly between Yacuiba and Santa Cruz daily, usually leaving Yacuiba at 7 am. There is one on Friday that leaves at 10:30 am.

There is only one **bus** traveling from the border to Villamontes and then on to Santa Cruz each day. It leaves the border at 8 am. However, there are many *trufis* going. Once in Villamontes, you can spend the night, take a collectivo to Camiri (a much better option) or take a night bus to Santa Cruz. The duration of that trip, 294 miles/480 km, is anywhere from 12 to 16 hours on good days and a bit longer if the road is really wet.

Bolívar Bus company has nice looking buses, but the windows leak (a lot) and many of the armrests are missing. Copacabana is the only bus company that goes to Santa Cruz during the day. If you do not get on at the border town of Yacuiba (the beginning of the line), you will be charged a lot for a seat. You must pay $10.50 for the entire distance between Yacquiba and Santa Cruz. If you reserve your seat in Villamontes, you must pay an extra $8 for the girl to make the reservation. That is double the cost of a seat from Yacuiba to Villamontes. This means that if you got a ticket at the border all the way to Santa Cruz, you would pay $10.50, but if you get on at Villamontes (two hours closer to Santa Cruz) you pay $18.50 for the same seat. A night bus with a different company is another option. Night buses leave between 5 pm and 7 pm daily.

Also consider taking a shared **taxi** to Camiri. The last taxi goes around noon. The Nancahuazu Transport is a collectivo/taxi and can be found at the crossroads between Villamontes, Paraguay and Santa Cruz and just up from the bus station. From Camiri, take a day-time bus to Santa Cruz or get on a night bus with Guzmar, that charges the highest in price but is by far the most comfortable. You must book a seat early as the buses (two go every evening at 7 pm) fill quickly.

Spending the night in Camiri is a good option. It sits a bit higher than Villamontes and thus is cooler. Set in the hills, it is also aesthetically more attractive. It has great places to stay, like the bedroom that Che Guevera once slept in, and the people of Camiri are far more pleasant than those in Villamontes.

The bus from Villamontes to Tarija goes along another road of death that, in part, follows the Pilocomayo River and Canyon. The scenery is spectacular, the trip long and difficult for the drivers.

A **train** goes to Santa Cruz on Tuesday, Thursday and Saturday. It takes 12 hours minimum and the cost is about $12 per person, first class. It leaves late in the afternoon, usually around 5 pm.

■ History

 Prior to the arrival of the Spanish, the area was sparsely inhabited by **Guarani Indians**. After the Spanish arrived, it became a small army outpost, a hot and dusty place where no one wanted to be. During the Chaco War in the 1930s, General Bernardino Bilboa Rioja and Major German Busch won the territory from the Paraguayans. They also managed to secure some of the Chaco that is closer to Santa Cruz. Today, it is a hub for oil exploration and, due to this, the cost of things in Villamontes is a bit higher than it should be.

■ Festivals

 Festival dates change because they are always held on weekends. For exact dates, contact either Susi at Dinar Travel in Tarija, ☎ 664-8000, susyqui@olivo.tja.entelnet.bo, or Viva Tours, also in Tarija, ☎ 663-8325.

Villamontes Farmers' Fair, in August, has a display of all the products grown and raised in the area. The three-day fair is a tribute to the *gaucho* of the Chaco area and is honored by a rodeo. There's also music, dancing, parades and lots of food. Viva Tours (☎ 663-8325, vivatour@cosett.com.bo) in Tarija offers a five-day tour that includes some of the major events of this fair as well as birding in the area.

The **Fish Festival**, also in August, is a wild time, with dancing, plays showing historical events, storytelling and general praising of the culture that revolves around fishing in the Pilcomayo River. The fair is celebrated with lots of eating and drinking. The fishing area for the festival is up from the canyon on the river.

AUTHOR NOTE: Due to climatic changes, the Pilcomayo River is now host to the piraña, the meat-eating fish found mostly in the Amazon Basin.

■ Adventures in Culture

 The **Museum of Military Heroes of the Gran Chaco** is west of Plaza 6 de Agosto in an old colonial house complete with a wide porch where you can often see the keepers of the museum (soldiers) fast asleep. There is a 50¢ charge to enter the museum. In the yard (by far the best part of the museum) are dugouts, bunkers and the remains of bullet-riddled machinery used in the Gran Chaco War. One of the reasons the Bolivians did not win this war was because they used soldiers from the highlands of the Andes, who were not accustomed to the heat. On the other hand, the men from Paraguay had to fight at elevations they were unaccustomed to.

 A good story about the Gran Chaco war is in the book, *Fat Man from La Paz*. The story about the Chaco is called "The Well" by Agosto Cespedes and is an excellent account of thirst in the desert.

Inside the museum are photos of heroes and other characters, as well as medals and other memorabilia. The locals around Villamontes are very proud of their museum. I recommend going there if you are in town for a while. It is the highlight of Villamontes.

■ Places to Stay

HOTEL PRICES (US $)

Per person, per day, unless noted otherwise.

$	$2-$5
$$	$5-$10
$$$	$11-$17
$$$$	$18-$25
$$$$$	Over $25

 Residencial Raldes, *Calle Cap. Manchego #171,* ☎ *672-2088 or 672-2545, $,* is a fairly basic place that charges $4 per person without private bathrooms (two rooms share one bath). The rooms are cleaned daily, but the beds are the hardest I've slept in while in Bolivia and the hot water was almost too hot. In fact, to get hot water without getting a shock you must turn on the water, then turn on the electrical switch (I'm short so I stood on the toilet). When I finished, I had to get back on the toilet and turn off the switch, then turn off the water.

There is a large courtyard, swimming pool (popular with local kids) and a few rooms with private baths. The bottled water sold at the *tienda* attached to the hotel was the highest price I paid in all of Bolivia.

Hotel Avenida, *Avenida Mendejarco between Calle Ismel Montes and Avenida Ingavi,* ☎ *672-2106 or 672-2412, $$$,* is clean and friendly, but I didn't see a room because they were full of oil workers when we were there. There are private baths, air conditioning, cable TV and fridges in all the rooms.

El Rancho Hotel, *Barrio Ferravianio,* ☎ *672-2140 or 672-2059, rancho@ olivo.tja.entelnet.bo, $$$$,* is the classiest place in town. When getting off the bus, this hotel is in the opposite direction from the plaza along the main street. The newer section of the hotel has larger rooms that go for $40 each. The others cost $25 for one and $35 for two people. All have large tiled bathrooms, air conditioning, cable TV, fridges and soft beds. The place is clean. Beds have stereo sets in the headboards, so be careful when setting the volume if using the clock radio. There's a large shaded patio and a swimming pool out back that's accompanied by an open-air restaurant and bar. There is also an inside restaurant at the entrance to the yard. The hotel has been under the same management for over 25 years. This hotel is the first choice of the petroleum exploration crews, so it is often full for long periods of time.

La de Aladino. While walking along the main road toward the plaza you will notice a sign pointing to a motel. When you get to the motel, you will notice that it is securely guarded. This place rents rooms by the hour. I didn't get a price because they didn't believe that I wanted a room for 24 hours, but they did look at my husband with great respect. I should've gotten the message from the sign out front that pictures a nude couple kissing.

The four-star **Singhari** is closed and has been for some time.

▌ Places to Eat

Pizza Place on the plaza (two places side-by-side) has great pizza, is open all day and has pleasant owners.

▌ Nightlife

A *marcada* is a Chaco party to which everyone is invited. Long ago, most people arrived by horse and the party started early in the morning with a feast of meat, especially *churascos*. The

Chaco doesn't have much water, so vegetables were not grown and meat was an important part of the diet.

MUSIC OF CHACO

Long ago, musicians and singers of the Chaco were important and respected. The musicians kept the rhythm of the work going while they played. Also, the songs were a record of historical events. Over the years, the songs developed until, today, they are more satirical than historical.

Carlos Miguel Palmo, born in the Chaco in 1966, is Villamontes' musical hero. He has played in Argentina, Tarija and Santa Cruz and has two recordings with traditional music from the Chaco published by Habana Records, Calle 25 de Mayo, #1667, Barrios San Martin, Tarija. The recordings include Argentinean, Bolivian and Paraguayan music and feature Escondido, La Queca and Bolivian Zamba.

Bolivian Zamba is different than Brazil's. The music, with a good beat, is played on the guitar, a violin and drums. The drums are long and thin and beaten with two sticks. We heard some in the *collectivo* taxi out of Villamontes and weren't impressed, but our driver loved it. It sounds a bit like Country and Western to me.

Yacuiba is the border town between Bolivia and Argentina. It is hot and grubby, standing at 2,072 ft/630 m above sea level. Yacuiba was the second city ever established in the department and at one time was considered the capital of the area. However, an earthquake in 1881 destroyed all the colonial structures so Tarija became the capital. Today, Yacuiba is made up of modern places only.

The second week in September the town celebrates for three nights at one of the best folk festivals in Bolivia. Musicians come from Argentina to join the Bolivians in this event. It is excellent. Staying in Villamontes is often necessary, but getting a ride back and forth is usually not a problem unless you join in the after-singing festivities.

The Pantanal

The Pantanal covers over 81,000 square miles/210,000 square km of wilderness, an area larger than Greece. It is considered the world's largest wetland and is one of the richest wilderness areas on the planet.

The Pantanal spreads across Bolivia, Brazil and Paraguay. During the rainy season (October through March) Rio Paraguay floods the entire savannah, transforming the area into a huge swamp. Pantanal means "swamp" in Portuguese. However, during dry season the swamps disappear and the land becomes a savannah dotted with lakes and ponds. The canals formed by the river are destinations in themselves. The change in environment due to water forces the plants and animals in the region to be adaptable, to be able to live in the extreme wet and extreme dry.

The water birds seen in this reserve are countless, but there are also raptors, songbirds and dry land birds. Wild animals, such as howler and capuccine monkeys, capybaras, peccaries, tapirs, spectacled caiman, otters, marshland deer and giant anteaters are numerous and an excursion away from camp will always result in wildlife being spotted. Occasionally, jaguar are seen. Herons, storks, kingfishers, parakeets and orioles are numerous. Over 700 bird species have been recorded here and millions of migratory birds make the Pantanal their in-transit hotel during migration. Some butterflies, too, make this a migratory route. New species of fish are still being found and added to the 260 recorded species. The palms alone include the white, black, totai and the motacu.

But there are problems in such a wilderness and conservation-minded organizations are working hard to stop destruction. For example, ocelots are still being captured and sold for their skins, and the hyacinth macaw's numbers have declined to about 3,000 in the world due to the market for exotic birds. During the 1980s, over 10,000 of these birds were captured worldwide.

The World Wildlife Federation is heavily involved in preserving the Pantanal and they work in Bolivia with the National Service for Protected Areas. Their most recent project was to have a special train carrying visitors into the Pantanal (Puerto Suarez) to promote conservation. They have declared January 28 to February 2 International Wetland Week. The Federation has also opened a center in Puerto Suarez to educate visitors on the splendor and the dangers of this area. About 10,000 visitors go to the Pantanal every year. However, because Bolivia has only about 10% of the Pantanal within its borders, most of those people enter the reserve via Brazil.

This area can be explored with Hombre y Naturaleza on an exciting six-day trip that requires travel by jeep, horse and boat through Bolivia and into Paraguay and Brazil. The tour stops at the most important places in the Pantanal. The excursion starts by boat from Puerto Suarez. Once at Rio Bahia Negra you will travel for two days, crossing the immense *pampas* of the Pantanal. There will also be one day dedicated to hiking up the tupuy Sombrerito. After this you will have a restful trip back to Puerto Suarez. There is a minimum requirement of six people for this tour and the cost is $30 per person, per day. During the rainy season it is not possible to do the entire trip. I would like to thank Manuel Español for all the information he gave me about the Pantanal.

Contact Humanos y Naturalesas, in Puerto Suarez at ☎ 710-67712 or 716-28699, eltumbador@hotmail.com or eltumbador@yahoo.com; or in Santa Cruz at ☎ 923-2239, hynb@bibosi.sca.entelnet.bo or prowames@cotas.com.bo.

To reach the Pantanal you can join a tour from Santa Cruz or La Paz if you want everything taken care of for you. Otherwise, take the train to Puerto Suarez or to Quijarro and visit the preserve from there. Both villages have hotels and can offer river trips into the preserve.

For those going on to Brazil who want a travel and tour trip, Hombre y Naturaleza offers a relaxing but exciting three-day river trip down to Carumba in Brazil through the lush wetlands of the Pantanal. Along the way you will see all the wildlife the Pantanal has to offer. One of the things I found amazing in Bolivia is that when the tour operators say you will see something, you are pretty much guaranteed to see it because the areas are still so wild.

 For those interested, there is a book of collected papers (mostly scientific) about the area called ***The Pantanal of Brazil, Bolivia and Paraguay,*** edited by Frederick A. Swarts and published by Hudson Macarthur Publishers in 2002. There are 14 color photos and 46 black and whites in the book.

ROBORE

Robore is situated between San Jose de Chiquitos, on the missions circuit (see page 444), and the border town of Puerto Suarez. This is a hiker's/photographer's/birder's paradise. Besides the village, there is the mission of Santiago in the Tucavaca Valley and the hot springs at Aguas Calientes farther along the rail line. The valley has sandstone rocks dotted with caves and clear rivers. It offers an endless number of hiking possibilities. One can visit the area either on foot or by horse. There are caves with rock paintings and some spelunking can be done. Guides can be hired in the village of Robore and, because this area is still so new to the traveler, there are many spots that have yet to be explored.

Puerto Suarez

Puerto Suarez has one main street, called Bolivia, with hotels and places to eat and drink beer. Any activities like horse riding or boating up or down the Paraguay River can be arranged by the conservation group that operates El Tumbador or by the owners of Hotel Sucre.

■ Adventures on Foot

Go on a three-hour forest walk near the **Laguna Caceres**, 3.7 miles/six km from the center of town. On this route, scientists have identified four species of monkeys, numerous reptiles and amphibians, tarantulas (of which there are numerous varieties) and birds (of which there are hundreds – there are 40 to 60 species of parrots alone). Along this walk you will pass the Santa Tecla waterfalls, a refreshing stop in the steaming jungle that you share with monkeys. A hat, bottle of water and mosquito repellent are essential. This hike should be done a few times to see all the wildlife, but your first hike should be done with a guide, available at El Tumbador (see below).

■ Adventures on Water

All of these river trips offer excellent opportunities to view wildlife.

The **Paraguay River** can be visited by either going upstream to the La Gaiba Lake, the Mandiore and the Uberaba Lakes where wildlife is the main (only?) attraction. You can also go downstream, visiting villages such as Morrinho, Puerto Esperanza and Fuerte Coimbra. The canals formed by the rising and falling water levels create a constantly changing terrain. All this is part of the **Pantanal Reserve**. Those staying at El Tumbador in Puerto Suarez can take one of the tours along the river or join a river trip into Brazil. Most day trips on the river take four to six hours.

Laguna Mandiore is 122 miles/200 km upriver from Puerto Suarez and is a two-day trip. Along the way there is an area of unique sandstone rock formations that surround the lake. The wildlife is exceptional simply because the entire area is unexplored. When things get a bit ho-hum, your boatman will tell you stories and anecdotes about the area. Once at camp, there is a hammock with mosquito netting for your bed and fresh fish for your meal. All you need then is a beer (not included) in your hand. The cost for this tour is about $80 with a minimum of two people.

Bahai Negra River is a primary contributor to the Paraguay River and a trip on this gem would take four days in all. Not only would you be in the Pantanal, but you would see parts of the Chaco too. Along the way is the archeological site of Fuerte Coimbra. You will also visit the boat markets of the villages and see the way locals have traded for hundreds of years. The third day is spent on land, visiting local villages in Paraguay before returning to Puerto Suarez. This trip is an exceptional opportunity to experience cultural events and see wildlife. Should you not have four days to spend, the river can be explored for 1½ days on a tour that includes one night on the river, but this option excludes the villages in Paraguay. The cost of the tour for three days is about $80 per person with a minimum of three people.

Heading up **Rio Verde** from Bahai Negra is an exciting trip because the river is narrow and swift. One of the interesting stops is at a bunker used by the Paraguayan military during the Chaco War. It was also used as a prison because of its isolated location. This trip is not possible from February to May due to high water levels. This is a full-day excursion out of Puerto Suarez. The cost is $80 for one, or $55 each for two.

Rio Negro is well named. The water is black. On an overnight trip along this waterway, you will end at a camp on a group of islands that overlook the lights of Carumba, Brazil. From the camp you can go up a smaller river, one on which few people have traveled, and watch the abundant wildlife. This half-day trip costs $40 per person.

Coimbra Fort is a one-day tour that starts with a river trip down the Paraguay to the fort. Along the way you can expect to see toucans, many species of raptors, herons, storks, caimans, capybaras, turtles and iguanas. The fort, built by the Spanish, is on a hill overlooking the river. It was taken over by the Portuguese and then, in 1864, by the Paraguayans. Lunch will be served at the fort before the trip back upriver. This is a full-day excursion that costs $100 for one or two people. As the number of participants goes up, the per-person price comes down.

■ Adventures in Culture

 Karcha Bahlut is a tiny village along the Paraguay River where the 21st century has not yet made its presence known. There is a tiny museum in the village with tools, clothes and weapons that were used until recently. There are also sale items made from balsa wood and palm leaves. The entrance fee to the museum (25¢) is not included in the cost of the tour. This half-day tour costs $35 per person.

■ Adventures in Nature

 Ten-kilometer Lagoon is reached in a 4x4 along the road to Filidefia on Rio Negro and is a trip specifically designed for birders. Although the plant life is lush and the animals during dry season come to the lagoon to drink, it is the immense number and variety of birds that one notices. Besides aquatic species, there are jabiru storks resting here, American mycteria, birds of prey, and herons, to name just a few. This is a half-day tour ($15) that could be made into a full-day excursion. Long-sleeved shirts, long pants and mosquito repellent are needed.

Kamba'aka is another 4x4 trip to an area deep in the Chaco jungles where plant life is the big draw. There is a jungle camp where you can sleep in a tent or in a covered hammock. The guides will be able to point out different plants and some of their uses. The cost of this two-day trip is $85 – that includes everything except beer.

Cueva de Motacusito is in the forest near the town of Motacusito. A guide will be required if you want to go inside the cave. Hombre y Naturaleza offers this trip (see *Tour Operators*, below). The cave goes in a third of a mile/half a km and is rich in stalagmites and stalactites. It also has insects, fish, amphibians and vampire bats. Being in good physical condition is essential as you must squeeze through one hall that is only 27 inches/70 cm wide. However, once through, the main room is over 99 ft/30 m high and is filled with rock formations.

To get to the cave you must travel nine miles/15 km from Puerto Suarez in a 4x4 and walk half an hour or so to the cave opening. Comfortable clothes (cotton is preferable) should be worn and good boots and mosquito repellent are necessary. This trip will take about four hours and costs $35 for one person or $11 per person if four people go.

■ Places to Stay

HOTEL PRICES (US $)

Per person, per day, unless noted otherwise.

$......................................	$2-$5
$$.....................................	$5-$10
$$$....................................	$11-$17
$$$$...................................	$18-$25
$$$$$..................................	Over $25

Hotel Palace, ☎ *976-2098, $;* **Hotel Robore**, ☎ *976-2190, $;* and the **Executive Hotel**, ☎ *976-2270, $,* are all fairly simple places that cost less than $5 per person for a room with a fan and communal baths. **Bamby**, ☎ *976-2015*, charges $4 per person for simple rooms with private bath and fans in the bedrooms.

The **Beby Hotel**, ☎ *976-2290, $$,* has tiny rooms with fans for $10 per person which is high for what you get.

El Tumbador, ☎ *716-28699, eltumbador@yahoo.com, $$,* is on the shores of Laguna Caceres (often a destination in itself) just 3.7 miles/six km from Puerto Suarez on the road toward the border. This is the place to stay. The lake and property cover about 31 square miles/80 square km of reserve where the amount of wildlife is exceptional. The station charges $14 per person per night for a cabin that holds four people. There are six cabins in all and each has a modern bathroom complete with shower (hot is not needed). The place is clean and each room has mosquito netting over the bed. There are hammocks on the porch and lots of wildlife to be seen from the shore of the lagoon. The setting sun each day accents the beauty of the spot. The residence is operated by the NGO Hombre y Naturaleza of Bolivia and Amigos de Doñana of Spain. The volunteers working at El Tumbador can organize any tour you may want to take from a jaguar photo-hunt to a six-day trip upriver. There are numerous posters of the Pantanal for sale.

Hotel Sucre, *on the plaza,* ☎ *976-2069, $$$,* has small rooms with air conditioning (almost a must) set around a tended garden.

Hotel El Pantanal, ☎ *978-2020, www.elpantanalhotel.com, $$$$$,* is the luxury liner of the Pantanal. Resort rooms have tiled floors, matching décor, TV, fridge, air conditioning and room service. There are also tennis courts, palapa huts and a bar around the pool, volleyball court, soccer field, games room, karaoke bar, formal dining room, horses for rent and a tour office to help you get anything not included in the hotel services.

■ Tour Operator

 Hombre y Naturaleza, *at El Tumbador,* ☎ *716-28699, eltumbador@yahoo.com*, offers superb tours down Rio Paraguay with stops at different lakes to look for caimans, capybaras, iguanas, monkeys, tarantulas, birds and anacondas. The trip is done in a 23-ft/seven-m aluminum boat equipped with a small motor. A number of tours are offered. The half-day rate, depending on the number of people, is less than $10 per person. But you can go for a whole day or even numerous days. Some tours include stops at places along the river to enjoy fresh fish dinners with traditional side dishes.

If you have time and want to see wildlife, I can't think of a better tour agency. Prices are all dependent on time, services and number of people.

Puerto Quijarro

Puerto Quijarro is nine miles/15 km past Suarez and just as hot (in winter) as Suarez. Both towns have small places in which to eat.

■ Places to Stay

The Cascade, *Avenida Sucre,* ☎ *978-2099, $*, has basic rooms with fans and communal baths. **The Border**, *Avenida Rolello Gomez,* ☎ *978-0210, $*, is comparable to The Cascade.

Hotel Oasis, *Argentina #4,* ☎ *978-2159, $$*, is a two-star hotel that has clean rooms with private bath and fans.

The **Santa Cruz**, *Avenida Brazil,* ☎ *2113-2044 (cell), $$$*, has rooms with air conditioning and private baths. This hotel can also arrange tours on the Paraguay River.

San Matias

If you want to go into the farthest reaches of the Pantanal, see parts of the Brazilian side and be guided by a scientifically oriented organization, this station, 500 miles/815 km from Santa Cruz, is an amazing place to be. Some of the flora and fauna is different in this area than in the south due to the different climate. Birders have the greatest time here because it is so remote and there are so many migratory species passing through, along with a huge variety of resident birds. I have not visited this area so I am unable to recommend the best things for each outing. However, if you do come this way and want to do some trips, speak with the volunteers

The Pantanal

working at the station. They will be able to help. I have listed the trips below just as an introduction.

■ Getting Here

To get to San Matias you must either charter a plane ($500-$600 round-trip, four to six people) or book with **TAM** (☎ 244-3487, www.tam.com.br). They fly in on Mondays and Fridays for $60 per person. The adventurous can take a four-wheel-drive vehicle from San Rafael on the mission circuit. Under good conditions, San Matias is at least 12 hours from San Rafael or 24 hours from Santa Cruz. However, once in the boonies, the wildlife that you will see makes the difficult trip worthwhile.

■ Adventures in Nature

San Pedro is three miles/five km from San Matias through a forest that is rich in bird life, monkeys, capybaras, fish, crocodiles and lizards. The vegetation includes such plants as the cuchi and the motacu. It is possible to ride a horse both ways, to walk one way and be driven the other or to walk both ways. It takes about two hours to walk one way and 40 minutes to drive. This is not a big difference, which indicates that the road can be difficult to drive.

Mamon is a hill (odd in the Amazon) that peaks about 12 miles/20 km from San Matias. But within eight or nine kilometers from town you start hitting the lower reaches of the hill. You can visit here only in the driest season of July, August and September. The bird life includes some of the bigger birds like herons and vultures. You will also see a variety of fishes, martins, lizards and more capybaras. This trip takes four hours by vehicle. It can also be done as a full-day excursion on a horse.

San Antonio River is 24 miles/40 km from San Matias and it takes at least two hours during dry season to get as far as the vehicle can go and then another two hours to walk the final 3.7 miles/six km. Once there, you can fish for piraña and yiyu, or just swim with them. Whatever you catch will be cooked for your dinner. This is also a real birder's place.

If San Matias is not far enough into the jungle for you, there is a set of cabins farther in at **Cambara**. It takes two hours to get here during dry season and four in rainy. Once at the river, your transportation will be in a canoe, from which you can fish. The camp will provide a hammock for sleeping that has a mosquito net covering. The most important part of this trip is the bird life. Prices include all meals, cooked in traditional style. The cost is $144 during dry season and $168 during wet for the two days.

Laguna de la Totora is a half-day trip where you go part-way up the lake to the Bella Vista station. There, with binoculars, you can watch for birds that are found in the area, along with the migratory ones. You can walk into the forest where there are numerous species of plants like the zorro. Within 330 ft/100 m you will pass from one forest zone into another. For more about this area, see the section on Trinidad.

The above trips cost anywhere from $18 to $55 a day. This area is managed by Hombre y Naturaleza. Their main office is in Santa Cruz and they have another office in Trinidad at Banco Ganadero, ☎ 462-3331. Trip arrangements can be made at an office or via e-mail, reitenez@sauce.ben. entelnet.bo. Every station has someone who speaks some English.

■ Place to Stay

Hombre y Naturaleza has rooms at the ecological station. The place is rustic, but each room has four bunks equipped with mosquito nets, a table and chair and a private bath. The windows are also covered with mosquito netting. The cost is $10 per person with breakfast and if four rent one cabin the cost is $7 per person. The station has a reference library open for your use. The station workers will prepare a simple meal for $3-$5. However, should you want barbecued meat with yucca and salad, the cost goes up. This includes non-alcoholic drinks. To contact Humanos y Naturalesas in San Matias, you must contact the radio phone operator. Or reach them in Santa Cruz at ☎ 923-2239, hynb@bibosi.sca.entelnet.bo or prowames@cotas.com.bo. They speak good English and excellent Spanish.

There are other one-star hotels in the village, but I did not check them out.

■ Places to Eat

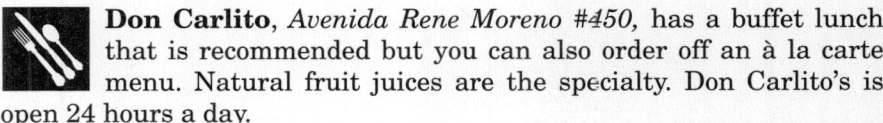

Don Carlito, *Avenida Rene Moreno #450,* has a buffet lunch that is recommended but you can also order off an à la carte menu. Natural fruit juices are the specialty. Don Carlito's is open 24 hours a day.

Restaurant El Pantanal, *main plaza*, has natural juices and will make just about any plate you could wish for in this outreach of Bolivia.

The Pantanal

The Amazon Basin

The Amazon region of Bolivia, also called the Beni by locals, covers about one third of the country's territory. A huge amount of the Amazon region remains unexplored. It is rich with wildlife – birds, plants, insects and amphibians – but low in human density. About a dozen indigenous groups inhabit the area.

The Amazon cannot be said to have a center. La Paz, really, is the trading center for the Beni and Madre de Dios drainage areas and Santa Cruz is the hub for the Mamore area. Trinidad is by far the largest city.

The Amazon has mysteries that reveal themselves in different ways. One example is the Llanos de Moxos, or earth mounds. It was an astute archeologist, who, while flying over the jungle, knew from experience that the lines of hillocks and canals that he could see from the plane were not natural. The area is now a major destination for researchers and tourists who are curious about the lives of the people who built these mounds of dry land in an ocean of swamp. An accessible, if not original, mound is on the outskirts of Trinidad, attached to a museum.

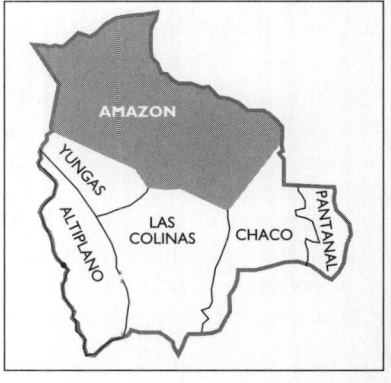

"AMAZON"

The word Amazon comes from Greek mythology and refers to a group of women who lived just beyond the known world. They fought on the Greek side in the Trojan War. Some stories claim that they removed their right breasts so that they could shoot a bow better. When the Spanish first came to the area and found bare-chested women (mostly with two breasts), they named the area after the mythological women.

There are hidden creatures too. While I was coming up the Madeira River from Brazil into Bolivia on a cargo boat, we stopped at a village so the boatmen could load rubber. I picked some guava that was ripe at the time for my husband who was sick with diarrhea (guava is thought to be a cure). Locals were picking the fruit off the ground, but I saw a lush one hanging in a tree. The fruit was beyond my reach so I climbed the tree and picked it. That night my skin looked like it had a serious case of smallpox and the itch was horrid. The doctor, a week later, informed me that I had been chewed alive by a tree parasite, invisible to the eye. It was all for nothing, too. My husband became ill from the guava and used Immodium instead.

The Amazon is isolated. The towns are small and I don't believe there is one, outside of Trinidad, that has a bank machine. In Riberalta and Guyaramirim, you can cash traveler's checks at some hotels, but only if you are a guest. Basically, you must carry cash. During rainy season, you must fly, or take a boat up and down the rivers. When flying, you will see below the people using canoes on flooded roads. You must learn to ride on the back of a moto-taxi and other small motorcycles. These are the most popular form of transportation.

But best of all, the beer tastes better in the Amazon than it does in any other part of Bolivia.

The Amazon is hot and humid, even during its coldest dry spell, and activities are often low key or delayed altogether until after dark. Pack loose cotton clothing, especially shorts and short-sleeved shirts. The dress code of the Altiplano, that wants people covered so no skin shows, doesn't apply in the Amazon. You must look after your feet. If there are cuts or sores on them, wear shoes or boots, rather than sandals, so that you don't get attacked by one of the ubiquitous parasites. Finding hotels with air conditioning or fans is a must or you will suffocate in your sleep.

Trinidad

Altitude: 513 ft / 156 m
Population: 275,000

Trinidad is a frontier town on the Mamore River, which flows north until it is joined by the Beni and the Madre de Dios. These three rivers merge at Villa Bella, north of Guayaramerin by about 31 miles/50 km, and flow into Brazil where they become the Madeira River.

Trinidad, the capital of Amazonia district, has clay roads that are used as canoe routes during rainy season. The upside is that the roads are flat.

In dry season, motorbikes, mule-carts, long-distance transport trucks and buses stir up dust that leaves an even film on everything.

In Trinidad, as in all Amazon towns, the favorite activity is riding around the plaza on a motorbike and howling at the opposite sex.

Walking in the town is almost as disagreeable, especially during rainy season when the above-ground sewers boil with disease, garbage and slime. These sewers are, in some places, covered with removable chunks of cement. The water in the sewers nurtures the microbes causing dengue fever and malaria, not to mention hepatitis, worms, lice and the tumbu fly. Don't fall in!

But there are some pleasant places to stay, some okay food (especially the ice cream) and a jungle that is fascinating no matter where you see it. The bird life is often the reason foreigners come to Trinidad. From the moment you arrive, the feathered ones are exotic enough to catch the attention of even untrained birders.

■ Getting Here & Around

Buses take a full 12 hours to reach Trinidad from Santa Cruz during good conditions. In rainy season, the trip can take 18 hours and may not get there at all. The buses pass through steaming jungle that you can't see most of the time during your nighttime journey. The timing is by choice. Daytime heat is unbearable when you are in a tin box that moves at 18 miles/30 km an hour.

Planes to Trinidad from Santa Cruz cost about $55 per person and take 1½ hours. If it is a clear day, you will get to see the impressive Lomos de Moxos (mounds believed to have been made by a society living here before the Spaniards arrived) from the air. Airlines going to Trinidad are **AeroSur**, ☎ 231-3233 or 336-7400, www.aerosur.com; **LAB**, ☎ 800-337-0918 (US), 800-10-3001 (Bolivia), www.labairlines.com; **SAVE**, ☎ 212-1548; and **TAM**, ☎ 244-3487, www.tam.com.br, and one flies every day.

Taxis at the airport are expensive, around $5 per person to town. The walk takes about half an hour. I walked it and saw some interesting birds along the road and a few flattened snakes. I enjoyed the walk.

You can also take a moto-taxi that means you and your luggage must perch on the back of a Honda 250 (or smaller). It is hardly worth the effort. The cost of one of these is $1 to town from the airport and 30¢ from place to place in town.

Boat travel around the Amazon Basin is by far the best way to go. Buy a hammock, and take lots of local currency and a thick book. Negotiate a ride on one of the barges collecting food or rubber from villages along the river. The Mamore flows down to the Brazilian border at Guayaramerin. This is a relaxing way to spend a week or so. The traveling time depends on how often the boat breaks down and how often the crew stops at a vil-

Amazon Basin

lage to party. The cost is about $10 a day, including your meals of beans and rice or rice and beans.

The port in Trinidad is actually 36 miles/15 km from the center of town at Puerto Almacen. If negotiating a ride, I suggest you avoid the large ocean freight barges heading for the Amazon River laden with train cars. They travel faster, but they are uncomfortable and the food is usually horrid.

■ History

 Father Cipriano Barace landed on the shores of the Mamore River in 1686 and built the first hut that later became the village of Trinidad. But in 1769 smallpox and floods wiped out most of the city and the remaining people moved about nine miles/15 km downstream to the city's present location on the Arrayo de San Juan, a river that rather resembles a creek.

After converting numerous indigenous groups to Catholicism, Father Barace was murdered on Rio Baures by some people who didn't really want conversion. Besides Catholicism, Barace is credited with introducing cattle farming to the area. This proved to be lucrative in the 1700s, but after the Jesuits with their exceptional managerial skills were expelled from Bolivia, prosperity declined. This resulted in farms being controlled by Spanish settlers and the indigenous people being forced to work as slaves.

It was during the struggles for independence that Trinidad became an industrial town and all traces of Jesuit influence were destroyed. However, within a hundred years of independence, the rubber trade became big and Trinidad prospered as a transportation center. This prosperity was again dependent on the labor of indigenous peoples. When they rose against the ill treatment, they were killed or driven off, leaving the rubber trade and the town to the Spaniards.

Once rubber was no longer a moneymaker, the men of the area turned back to cattle ranching. They interbred the half-wild cows that were brought in and then left by Jesuits with a breed from Brazil to form a line that is tolerant of the heat and also good for meat.

■ Services

The **Entel Office** is next door to the post office on Calle Antonio Vaca Diez.

The **post office** is on Calle Antonio Vaca Diez, between Cipriano Barace and Avenida Cochabamba.

There's a hidden **tourist office** on Calle Limpiaz. To get there, go into the parking lot next to Farmacia Beniana on Calle Limiaz and turn right

Trinidad

■ Archeological Museum

10
5 GANADERA

AV COMUNIDAD ECONOMICA EUROPEA

SERAFIN RIVERO

MARIA LUISA

COIMBRA

A I R P O R T

FELIX SATTORI

JOSE CHAVEZ

to Pt.
Bollivan

SUAREZ

FELIX PINTO

Pool ■

DEL MAR

CIPRIANO BARACE

COCHABAMBA

9 DE ABRIL

JOSE NATUSCH VELASCO

HORMANDO ORITZ CHAVEZ

RODOLFO ARAUZ

8

SIMON BOLIVAR

EJERCITO

TARIJA

VILLAVICENCIO

SANTA CRUZ

8 DE NOVIEMBRE

NICOLAS SUAREZ

ANTONIO JOSE DE SUCRE

CARMELO LOPEZ

FABIAN MONASTERIO CLAURE

HERMANO RIOJA

3

9

ANTONIO VACA DIEZ

7

6

2

PLAZA
BALLIVAN

1

AGOSTO

4

LA PAZ

MAMORE

to Laguna
Suarez

NOT TO SCALE

PLACES TO STAY & EAT
1. Hostal 18 de Noviembre
2. Hotel Paulista, Hotel Brazilia, Hotel Beni, Hotel Monte Verde
3. Hotel Sirari, Hotel Santa Cruz
4. Hotel Trinidad
5. Hotel La Hosteria
6. Hotel Gran Moxo
7. Mi Residencia
8. Hotel Jacaranda
9. Pollo Joel
10. Bambu Restaurant

N

HUNTER PUBLISHING

at the back of the lot. Go through the door at the end of the walkway. I found the people in the office pleasant and helpful. They have a map of the city for no charge; the tourist agency charged $1.50 for the same map.

The **police station** is on Calle Limpiaz and Cochabamba.

Cibermania Café and Internet on Calle Sucre and 18 de Noviembre, ☎ 462-1230, has good machines and they charge 75¢ an hour.

■ Sightseeing

The **cathedral** was built in 1931, replacing the old Jesuit mission that was previously there. Inside are some items of value like the embroidered linen, the statue of Jesus as a boy done by Guamaga, and some fine semi-precious stones. But the building itself is not very beautiful. The bishop of the area passed a law in 1916 stating that the old mission was to be replaced with this new, nondescript structure.

■ Adventures in Culture

Kenneth Lee Museum, Avenida Ganadera, 2,300 ft/700 m past the traffic circle, holds artifacts found by its namesake, an American geologist and archeology buff, who believed the lomas, when he first saw them as he flew over the area, were not natural mounds. To get there, walk up the east side of the square and continue along the road to the museum. There is no charge to enter.

After Lee started to explore in earnest, he found that the mounds, built on alluvial deposits that are about 10,000 ft/3,000 m deep started as burial mounds. He presented the theory that the people who had lived here buried their dead in jugs and buried the jugs in the ground. These indigenous people then lived on top of the burial sites. Other professionals disagree with Lee.

Lee found middens (full of pottery shards) on the mounds. The piles went as deep as 30 ft/10 m. These areas provided evidence that the people grew beans, squash, potato and manioc. In the canals between the *lomas*, they had fish farms stocked with both fish and shell fish. Lee believed that the societies lived on these mounds anywhere from 2,000 to 5,000 years ago.

The causeways between the mounds are 10-16 ft (three to five m) wide and three ft/one m above the highest water level. There are hundreds of *lomas* out on the Amazon savannah near Trinidad, but only a few have been excavated. A second excavated site is at Ibibate, 31 miles/50 km east of Trinidad. The hill they found here stood about 60 ft/18 m high and was actually two mounds connected by an earth wall.

A few other archeologists have worked on the *lomos*. William Denevan, who did his PhD thesis on the topic, believed that the mounds were pyramids and the canals were a means of transportation. He also claimed that the raised ridges were actually agricultural fields. It is a general belief that the mounds were abandoned between 1400 and 1700.

The museum is a tall, round, modern structure containing artifacts like vases, pestles for pounding chocolate and weights that are amazingly accurate. One section contains clay masks from the Moxos culture and the music section has a flute about 1½ inches long.

The money used by the Moxos people was in the form of imitation sand dollars similar to those found on some Pacific Ocean beaches. This is an indication that the Moxos traveled long distances in order to trade. Housing materials also came from far away – the wood, called cuta, is a dense, rot-resistant material.

The museum grounds have a mound surrounded on one side by a pool of water and on the other by a canal. This is a good example of the *lomos* found in the jungle just east of Trinidad.

Take insect repellent when you go to the museum as the mosquitoes are bad.

On the walk back, stop at the **Bambu Restaurant** for a drink. It is a clean and relatively quiet place, unlike the restaurants around the square.

Chuchini Lomos are 8.6 miles/14 km northeast of the city and have lagoons and man-made rivers that were built by the Paititis people about 5,000 years ago (according to some estimates). The waters of the lagoons flow into the Mamore River and there is an artificial lake where fish farms were once established. However, the main attraction is the pre-colonial mounds and canals, built so that the people could grow food, have fish and travel from place to place. Chuchini means "the tiger's guard."

There are trails through the jungle just back of the river where you can spot birds. The area is lush and Noel Kempff, who has a park named after him east of Santa Cruz, once wanted this area to become an ecological reserve. The downside of this reserve is that it is privately owned and the admission fee is $10. There are accommodations available and a full regalia of activities you can buy into. If interested in the *loma* only, go to the museum in Trinidad to see one.

■ Adventures on Water

 The **swimming pool** on Avenida Cipriano between Calle Felix Pinto and Felix Sattori costs 50¢ for the afternoon. It's large and clean, and surrounded with shaded tables. There is no loud music and there is a place to purchase drinks and snacks.

Laguna Suarez, formerly known as Socoreno, which means animal lagoon, is three miles/five km south of Trinidad and is a Bolivian and foreign tourist destination. The artificial lake is dotted with palapa palms and picnic tables. There are places to eat and you can get everything from fried fish to grilled steak or roasted chicken. There is also lots of *chicha*, beer, fruit drinks and sodas. If you don't want to swim in the lake itself, head to the Laguna Suarez Hotel. It is along the road by the lake. There, you can pay to swim in relatively clean water.

The main attraction (for me) is the abundant bird life. Some of the birds spotted near the lake are the great kiskadee, the white-tipped dove, the piratic flycatcher and the thornbird.

Puerto Almacen is five miles/eight km southwest of the city. This is where the Ibare River forms an estuary. It flows into a lake that, in turn, empties into the Mamore River. Just beyond Almacen is Puerto Barador. Tour operators in Trinidad offer one- and two-day trips from Puerto Almacen up the Ibare River in search of wildlife. You have a good chance of seeing the rare blue-throated macaw, of which there are only about 120 living in the wild. They nest in palm trees and eat palm nuts. This is one of the few places on the planet where the bird can be spotted. Other wildlife you could see are capybaras, caimans, pink dolphins, monkeys, turtles and snakes. If not doing a river trip anywhere else in the jungle, then do this one.

The ***Reina de Enin*** boat trip down the Mamore River is a first-class, five-day event starting and ending in Trinidad. The cost ($80 per person, per day) includes accommodations, transportation, meals and side tours with a guide. It goes through some primary forest growth to isolated villages before returning on the same river. You will ride in the jungle on a horse, swim in the river with the pink dolphins, hike through virgin forests, paddle a dugout canoe on a tributary river and do a night safari looking for nocturnal feeders. The river itself is busy. There are barges and canoes, triple-decker boats and private Sea Doos. For the most part, those on the boats are working, carrying freight up and down the river.

The *Reina de Enin* has rooms for singles or doubles, all with private bathrooms, hot water, air conditioning and fans. You should have light cotton clothing, including a long-sleeved shirt and long pants. Mosquito repellent is essential. Binoculars are recommended. There are not many places on the planet as remote as this, and the chances of seeing different and rare species of wildlife are great. If you are interested in this tour, see Fremen Tours, below.

■ Adventures in Nature

 Suarez Hill is seven miles/12 km northeast of Trinidad on Rio Ibare. The hill is artificial and has had many titles before this one. It was previously called Monovi Hill, but after the Suarez brothers bought the land, they renamed it the Ayacucho Hill. However, the people in the nearby village preferred the name Llamaron Suarez Hill, in honor of the owners. The river below the hill is good for watching wildlife. To get here, hire a motorbike (see below) or take a taxi. About 1.8 miles/three km before the hill along the river, is a spot where locals go to swim with the freshwater dolphins. This river flows into the Mamore. It is possible to fish or canoe if you have your own equipment (not likely for a traveler). Some of the birds spotted here are the blue-headed parrot and the chopi blackbird.

While near the river you will spot a mansion that belonged to the wealthy Suarez family. The property has a sugarcane plantation, a fruit orchard and an agricultural school. The family is no longer around.

■ Tour Operators

Paraiso Travel, 6 de Agosto #138, ☎ 462-0692, paraiso@sauce. ben.entelnet.bo, offers tours to Laguna Suarez and Rio Mamore. They also offer one-night camping trips in the jungle and a four-day birding tour. Rates vary from $25 per day to $110, depending on where you go and how many go with you. They will also accommodate you for festivals. Do not purchase a city map from them as they charge $1.50 for the map that is available free at the tourist office.

Freman Tours, Avenida Cipriano Barace #332, ☎ 462-2276, www. andes-amazonia.com or www.amazoncharters.com, offers the five-day river trip on a typical three-decker Amazonian boat. The cost is about $80 per day, all-inclusive.

Parais Travel, Avenida 6 de Agosto #138, ☎ 462-0692, offers many convenient half- and full-day trips in the area. The cost for one person to go to Laguna Suarez is $25, but if 10 go, the price drops to $10. They have a one-day Rio Mamore trip and an overnight jungle camping trip. Longer trips are available; negotiate particulars with them.

Moto Rental, 6 de Agosto #101, has small Suzukis and Hondas for rent at $1.50 per hour, $10 a day and $12 for 24 hours. The price includes gas. You must leave your passport as security and you must have a driver's license that allows you to drive a small motorbike. You can take these bikes to Laguna Suarez or Chuchini, but no farther, as you need special traveling papers to go beyond. These bikes will easily hold two people, and locals put as many as five on them. If you do rent one, you will see why motorcycles are so popular in the Amazon. They are the outdoor substitute for the fan in your room.

■ Places to Stay

Zᶻᶻᶻ It may be that when I checked these places they saw a *gringo* and raised the prices, but most places in Trinidad are just not worth the asking prices. Compared with Coroico, Sorata, Samaipata or Copacabana, Trinidad is expensive.

Also remember, no fan, no deal. There should be a fan in every room, preferably on the ceiling. With the ceiling fan, check to see if the lights are below the fan, especially if you suffer from epilepsy or motion sickness, or if you like to read.

HOTEL PRICES (US $)

Per person, per day, unless noted otherwise.

$. . . . . $2-$5
$$. . . . . $5-$10
$$$. . . . . $11-$17
$$$$. . . . . $18-$25
$$$$$. . . . . Over $25

Hostal 18 de Noviembre, ☎ *462-1272 $,* offers clean and basic rooms with or without private bath. The flowered courtyard is pleasant and dotted with hammocks.

Hotel Paulista, *Avenida 6 de Agosto,* ☎ *462-0018 or 462-0118, $,* has rooms on four levels around a central courtyard. The place is drab and the owner disinterested. Each room has a fan.

Hotel Brazilia, *6 de Agosto #46,* ☎ *462-1685, $,* is no different than the Paulista.

Hotel Sirari, *Avenida Santa Cruz, #526,* ☎ *462-4472, $$,* is a new place with a well-tended garden, clean rooms, tiled floors and bath, large windows and big rooms. All rooms have ceiling fans. This is the best deal in town. The lady who runs the hotel is pleasant, as are her staff.

Hotel Santa Cruz, *Avenida Santa Cruz,* ☎ *462-0711, $$,* is next best to the Sirari. The clean rooms have a TV and air conditioning and come with or without private bath. There is a courtyard. The owners are friendly.

Beni Hotel, *6 de Agosto #68,* ☎ *462-2788 or 462-2522, $$,* has large rooms with tile floors, private bath, TV and phone. Some have air conditioning. But the rooms are dark.

Hotel Monte Verde, *Avenida 6 de Agosto #76*, ☎ *462-2750 or 462-2738*, *$$$*. All rooms have private bath, air conditioning, fridge, cable TV and a small sitting area.

Hotel Trinidad, *Calle Pedro de la Rocha #80*, ☎ *462-1380, $$$$*, is just half a block from the central plaza, between the market and the square. Each room has private bath, cable TV, fridge and phone. It is a small hotel (10 rooms) with a small pool on premises. Although the owners were friendly, the hotel is quite drab.

Hotel La Hosteria, *Avenida Ganadera in front of Camp Ferial*, ☎ *462-2911, $$$$*, is the most comfortable place in town. It has a nice yard with trees and a pool. Large rooms come with TV, bar, phone and air conditioning, and there's a restaurant on site. La Hosteria comes highly recommended.

Chuchini Lodge, *8.7 miles / 14 km from Trinidad*, ☎ *462-4744, $$$$$*, is privately owned by Eferim Hinojasa and is located by Lomo Chuchini. Accommodations are in cabins with private bathrooms and meals are included. There is a plethora of things you can do while here, including night walks and fishing. Eferim offers a three-day, all-inclusive package for $210 per person, per day. If you visit no other jungle spot, then you may want to do it all here.

Hotel Gran Moxo, *Calle 6 de Agosto and Avenida Santa Cruz #146*, ☎ *462-2240 or 462-2462, moxostdd@sauce.ben.entelnet.bo, $$$$$*, has wide, tiled halls open to the outside, so there is a nice breeze. They have made an attempt at elegance, but have cut corners (for example, the floors in the rooms are linoleum, rather than ceramic). But the place is clean and the owners offer a 20% discount for stays of three days or longer. Rooms have a private bath with a separate shower stall, fridge, air conditioning and telephone. This hotel also has cabins two miles/3.4 km from town on the road to Santa Cruz. Each cabin holds one to four people. One has two floors, and they all have kitchens, safe deposits for valuables and private bathrooms. The rooms in town are large and have sitting areas with little eating tables. Rates: $50 single; $75 double.

Mi Residencia, *Manuel Limpias #76*, ☎ *292-2464, $$$$$, half a block from the plaza; and at Felix Pinto Saucedo #555*, ☎ *432-2535, www.hotelmiresidencia.com.bo, $$$$$*. They have clean, bright rooms with tiled floors and private bathrooms. There are wood ceilings and sitting areas and the air conditioning works very well. These hotels have been around for nine years. Again, the rates are far too high, even with the complimentary breakfast. Rates: $45 single; $67 double.

Hotel Jacaranda, *Calle Bolívar #229 between Nocals Suarez and Ciriano Barace*, ☎ *462-1659, $$$$$*, has rooms with private bathrooms, air conditioning and fans, phones, TVs and fridgobars. They also offer the use of their safe. There is a restaurant on site (breakfast is included in your room rate), private parking and laundry service. Rates: $35 single; $50 double.

■ Places to Eat

 Kivon Restaurant, *on the square*, is the local ice cream parlor. I sat there and watched as one couple came in after me, received a menu, placed an order and got the incorrect food. I still had not received a menu. If you look like a *gringo* and want what you order, I'd suggest trying elsewhere.

Heladoria Oriental, o*n the square up from Kivon*, is popular with locals in the morning and early evening. It is more of a bar than an ice cream parlor.

Pollo Joel, *on Vaca Diez,* charges $1.75 for chicken and fries, not the 75¢ that is on the sign. Although very popular with locals, the working conditions for the kitchen staff are the worst I have seen in Bolivia. The crowded kitchen is hot and the floors earthen. The food isn't all that good either.

La Casona, *on the square,* serves an excellent *almuerzo*. I thought it was better than Carlitos on the opposite side. The service is good, friendly and the fans work.

Carlitos, *on the square,* is popular and the food is okay but certainly not exceptional. The cost for one lunch is $1.75.

■ Nightlife

 Bar el Camion, Avenida Santa Cruz, just around the corner from Gran Moxos, has live entertainment on Friday night that is a huge improvement on watching the men whistle at the girls driving around the square on their motorbikes.

Cibermania Café and Internet on Calle Sucre and 18 de Noviembre, ☎ 462-1230, has good machines and charges 75¢ an hour. Next door to them is the **video shop** that has some English-language movies. Those staying at the Sirari can use the video machines that come with the TVs. It is great to lie under the fan and watch something like *Ghandi* in English. You must leave a $3 deposit for each video and the cost of the rental is 50¢ per movie. There is no problem getting your deposit back.

Noel Kempff
Mercado National Park

Although Noel Kempff is easiest reached from Santa Cruz, it is actually located in the Amazon Basin and the area is a wildlife viewers' paradise. Due to its isolation, the park is seething with animal and plant life.

■ About Preservation

 There are two major organizations in Bolivia trying to keep things in the backcountry under control. They are the elusive FAN and SERNAP. Another two that are less known but that offer a more scientific slant to the wildlife viewing, are Hombre y Naturaleza of Bolivia and Amigos de Doñana of Spain.

Fundacion de Amigos de Naturaleza's, or FAN, is in charge of Noel Kempff National Park. Their address at Calle Agreda #1100 and Bumberque in Santa Cruz is an abandoned building. We were also told by Tourism Bolivia that they might be found at the Museum of Natural History on Avenida Irala. That turned out to be untrue. The last address we found was on the highway going to Samaipata, Km 7, Casilla 2241, ☎ 352-4921, but we did not get there and their latest e-mail does not work. Good luck trying to reach them.

According to statistics, in the last five years 800 tourists have gone into the park. The cost is $1,000-2,000 whether you book through an agency or try to go in through FAN. This comes to a total of $1.6 million. I have no information on how much is being pumped back into the park. However, the park is accessible from the mission town of San Ignacio and the cost ends up being less than $200.

SERNAP (Natural Prot. Areas Systems) works with FAN looking after the parks of Bolivia; FAN seems to do most of the front line work. The two organizations are now involved with a climate-control/monitoring facility in Noel Kempff that, in turn, means more grant money for them.

Hombre y Naturaleza and Amigos de Doñana have biological stations in Puerto Suarez, Concepcion (east of Santa Cruz), San Matais (in the northern area of the Pantanal) and Charagua (close to Tarija and Villamontes). The stations offer tourists an ecological approach to the area and scientists a base from which to explore. They will also facilitate drivers and tour operators to take you into the backcountry. Their living quarters are simple but certainly adequate and the volunteers work hard to accommodate your needs. There is always a small reference library on site and some of the places have museums. Contact them in Santa Cruz at ☎ 923-2239, hynb@bibosi.sca.entelnet.bo or prowames@cotas.com.bo.

■ Animals & Land

Noel Kempff Mercado was first declared a park in 1979 and is one of the highlights of Bolivia's backcountry. It has tropical rainforests and flooded savannas, thorn scrub and dry forests, a huge area of wetland and the Caparu Plateau, 850,000 acres/345,000 hectares of Precambrian sandstone that has been carved by wind and water to create a fantasyland. Off this plateau, three dramatic waterfalls tumble over ancient red/brown rock that has roots of jungle vegetation clinging to every open space. The steam off the water forms a mist that acts like a filter and softens the view.

Because of the many environments, its isolation and its size (1.5 million acres/.6 million hectares), the wildlife of Noel Kempff is second to none in South America. About 700 species of resident and migratory birds have been spotted in the park and people on birding tours often see 400 in one 10-day visit. Some of the rarer birds are the starred wood quail, the snow-capped mannequin, Zimmer's toddy-tyrant, the tooth-billed wren and the blue finch. Park officials have also recorded 2,700 species of plants but biologists believe that there are about 4,000 all told. As for wild animals, there are believed to be about 300 species. The park seems to have an endless number of monkeys, jaguars, otters, caimans and, my favorite, capybaras.

Seldom do people talk about the symphony of sounds heard in the jungle. The water rushes down the rocks and the parrots screech across the sky, the cicadas scrape their musical legs together and the mosquitoes buzz. So as not to be outdone, the howlers announce their presence so loud that all other sounds are nullified, but just for a moment.

■ Getting Here & Around

To get into the park you can either join a tour ($600 to $2,000) or you can go to San Ignacio on the missions circuit (see page 454) by train and bus. From there, take a bus north to La Florida, at the edge of the park. The bus leaves San Ignacio at 10 am and, after passing through Piso Firme where the road branches, it arrives in La Florida at 4 pm. If you can, call FAN to arrange for a driver and a 4x4 to pick you up in Florida and take you into Campamento Los Fierros in the park. The most recent number I have for FAN is ☎ 591-3-355-6800 (in Santa Cruz) and the person to speak to is Zaira Duque. However, I see no reason why you can't arrive at La Florida and hire a local to take you in.

Once inside the park you must have a guide. I recommend Manuel, a La Florida resident. He charges $10 per day. There are basic places to stay in the village. If Flor de Oro is the destination of choice, you will have to fly in.

La Florida is a tiny community at the boundary of the park where there are roads going to Los Fierros. The village has three small hotels, all basic but clean enough. You can also, before entering the park, rent a dugout canoe and take a trip upriver to see freshwater dolphins, often referred to as pink dolphins.

■ Los Fierros Camp

 Los Fierros Camp is the lodge in the park that can be reached without flying. It is more rustic than Flor de Oro. It has a capacity to hold 16 people in double-occupancy huts or 25 people in a dorm. There is running water, a large kitchen/dining area and over 37 miles/60 km of developed and maintained trails that have interpretive signs posted at interesting spots. Some tour companies take in birding groups who are able to spot species common only to this area.

The **Caparu Plateau**, also called the Huanchaco Plateau, is a mesa or tupuy made of Precambrian sandstone that rises 2,000 ft/600 m straight up out of the ground. First described by Colonel Percy Fawcett (see *Sorata*, page 266) when he came across it in 1910, the plateau is one of the many places in South America given credit for inspiring Sir Arthur Conan Doyle to write *Lost Worlds* (another is Mount Roraima in Venezuela). The plateau is 850,000 acres/344,000 hectares of rock, jungle and wildlife that has three very dramatic waterfalls tumbling down its sides. From Los Fierros the plateau is five miles/eight km through steaming jungle. Five miles in the jungle is a long way. However, there is nothing in the park that is not worth the effort of getting to.

Accessible from Los Fierros is the **El Encanto** (The Charmer) waterfall. This is probably the most spectacular of the three. To get there you will go along a road to a second set of cabins and walk to the base of the plateau. But the waterfall is only the destination. The wildlife and plants you will see on the way could delay your progress by a full day. You may be lucky and spot plants not yet recorded by scientists.

■ Flor de Oro Camp

 Flor de Oro Camp, one of the camps under the care of FAN, is a renovated ranch on the banks of the Itenez River in the northern section of the park. It has the capacity to hold 35 people in double occupancy rooms, each with private bath and solar-generated electricity.

There is also a large kitchen/dining area, an observation deck and an interpretive center. Flor de Oro is accessible only by plane.

The waterfalls accessible from Flor de Oro are the **Ahlfeld** and **Arco Iris**. To get to the Ahlfeld Falls, you must travel by boat for five or six hours up the Paucerna River to a basic campsite and walk to the falls through the jungle. These falls drop about 100 ft/30 m and form a pool at the bottom in which you can (or should) swim. A trail that goes through the jungle to the top of the falls and the view of the water and surrounding jungle is just as impressive from the top as from the bottom. The hike up to the top of the falls takes about an hour.

The Arco Iris waterfall drops 80 ft/24 m and is the one seen in most of the advertising brochures about Noel Kempff Park. This waterfall is accessible by walking from the campsite for about five hours. The terrain is rough; often rocks and roots have to be navigated before you reach the view point. However, it is the jungle heat that is the most difficult obstruction.

Los Torres (The Towers) are two huge hunks of rock that jut up out of the landscape like towers. They can be climbed (no climbing equipment needed) and used as a vantage point for viewing birds and other wildlife. It is in this area that jaguars have been spotted – but they are nocturnal hunters so seeing one during the day would be an accident.

The towers are accessible by taking a boat trip up the Itenez River for about two hours. They will reward you with sightings of capybara, herons, storks, caimans and other river dwellers. From the river it is a half-hour walk to the rocks. Once you are on top, the views of the plateau make the climb worthwhile.

Caiman Bay and **Monkey Lookout** can be reached by walking along a jungle trail for four hours to an old scientific research station. From there it is an hour or two hike up the plateau to Monkey Lookout Point. From the edge of the escarpment, the chance of seeing monkeys is excellent, of course. Other wildlife is difficult to spot because most is nocturnal. Camping here would be both scary and exciting and would have to be negotiated with the tour leaders. A trail from Monkey Lookout Point leads across the plateau and ends at the Arco Iris waterfall. This is a long way and you would need a guide to take you across.

From Flor de Oro, you can take a boat to the Arco Iris waterfall and then walk to the top of the falls following the trail. If you are adventuresome, you can cross the plateau along an old jungle trail to the Monkey Lookout on the other side. From there it is another four-hour hike back to camp. You would have to leave Campamento Ahlfeld early in the morning, carry lots of water and be prepared to get into camp around dark. This hike is only for the experienced.

Bella Vista

Bella Vista is on the Brazil/Bolivia border and although the area is in the Amazon, just north of Noel Kempff National Park, the landscape is partly influenced by Chaco vegetation and wildlife. If you want remote and difficult-to-get-to wilderness, read on.

Bella Vista is managed by Hombre y Naturaleza, whose main office is in Santa Cruz, ☎ 923-2239. They have another office in Trinidad at Banco Ganadero, ☎ 462-3331. Arrangements can be made at either office or e-mail reitenez@sauce.ben.entelnet.bo. Every station has someone who speaks some English. You can get to this station by yourself, but that is not recommended. The best connection place is Asuncion, halfway between Trinidad and Santa Cruz. Bella Vista is another 110 miles/180 km from Asuncion, on Lake Algarañas, also called Lago Bella Vista. The lake is close to the Guapore River that eventually joins the Beni to flow into the Madeira and on down to the Amazon. If you hook up with Hombre y Naturaleza in Asuncion, you can travel upriver in a motor-powered boat to the station.

You also have the option of flying in to town. Discuss this with Hombre y Naturaleza. When planning activities, the organizers can also advise you as to the best excursions to meet your needs. For an example, there is a seven-day river trip around Bella Vista that is good for birding, animal viewing and plant life, or you can just go to the station to hang out for a few days before taking a boat into Brazil.

Hombre y Naturaleza also offer packages to this station that include all meals, lodgings during your stay, transportation and guides. Due to the isolation of the area, the meals are substantial in size, delicious in taste but certainly not gourmet.

■ Adventures in Nature

The most popular trip is four days long and possible only during the dry season from November to August. It includes four to six hours of hiking a day. This does not sound like much, but when the heat and humidity are factored in, the time is long. This particular trip is similar to their Rurrenabaque excursion, except that this area has fewer tourists and you get to do some birding.

The first day of the tour, after arrival at the station and dinner, centers on a night hike looking for caimans, lizards and other night feeders. The second day offers a visit to the *pampas* on foot or by horseback. If the *pampas* is too wet, the substitute is a boat trip down the Trinidacito River looking for wildlife and birds. The next day is spent taking a boat to San Martin, a tiny village with indigenous people living fairly traditional lives.

Prior to arriving at the village there is a hill from where the *pampas* can be seen. The climb takes about two hours. This is followed by a meal in the village. The meal is made, in part, from yucca flour. After lunch, you hike in the forest with a guide who can identify plants and birds. However, if the organizers know ahead of time that you have a special interest, they will be certain to send a guide knowledgeable, at least in part, about your topic. This trip also includes a visit to see how rubber is tapped from the trees. In the forest, you will spot the siringuero, a bird that has a "pico-tico" whistle and is always present where there are rubber trees. Later in the day, locals demonstrate the art of making bags and ponchos from the bark, roots and aerial roots of the rubber tree.

This tour can be adjusted so that you camp in the jungle for one or two nights, or it can become a seven-day river trip that includes five nights camping in the jungle. The river trip is more difficult between July and September because the sand bars are above the waterline and passengers must help push the boat across dry land.

These tours vary in price depending on the time you spend and the number of people in your group. If just staying at the station, the cost is $9 per person for a room with breakfast and $7 for a hammock. Lunch and dinner are generally $5 each. To rent a horse for the day costs between $10 and $36 over and above the cost of the trip. Two people going into the station for four nights and doing a simple river trip, some hiking and a horse trip would spend $366 per person. However, if three people go, the cost drops to $228, and if four go the cost is $188. Before going into Bella Vista, you should contact the organizers in Trinidad or Santa Cruz.

San Borja

Altitude: 700ft / 220 m
Population: Less than 5,000

San Borja is about 150 miles/250 km west of Trinidad. The area around the village is savannah and wetlands, dotted with tiny lakes and rimmed with forests, all teeming with bird life. If you are stuck in San Borja, take binoculars and head for the outskirts, away from the farming areas. Just out of town by 30 miles/50 km is the Beni Biosphere Reserve, which has a lodge and biological station. A trip to the biosphere is a must.

■ Getting Here & Away

 TAM (☎ 244-3487, www.tam.com.br) flies between La Paz and Santa Cruz twice a week with a stop in San Borja. They also have a direct flight here on Saturdays from La Paz. Check with your travel agent in La Paz or Santa Cruz for more information. In San Borja, you will find a travel agent just off the plaza.

The **buses** leave early every morning for La Paz. San Borja is 30 miles/ 50 km from Yacumo, which is on the way to Rurrenabaque. Buses to Yacumo leave every day around noon. Check with your hotel owner for exact times or see if you can arrange a shared taxi with locals. From Yacumo, catch the next bus heading to Rurrenabaque. These buses leave in the evenings. You can sometimes hitch a ride on a truck. If going toward Trinidad, 12 hours away, buses go every day and most travel at night.

If you're coming from Santa Cruz and going to the Beni Biosphere, get off the bus at El Porvenir and walk the third of a mile/half-kilometer into the station. Those coming from the other direction may have to overnight in San Borja and then catch a bus or *trufi* out in the morning.

■ Adventures in Nature

Beni Biosphere Reserve, www.madidi.com/reserves.html, was created in 1986 through an agreement between the Bolivian Government and Conservation International. It was the first debt-for-nature swap ever signed. In addition to putting the land into safe keeping, the agreement provided money for administrative costs. The reserve was first brought to the attention of the government when five large logging companies wanted to harvest the area's virgin forests. The Chimane Indians living there opposed this so strongly that they managed to get the attention of the government. Their main concern was the damage that would be caused from the construction of logging roads. Eventually, the logging companies were sent elsewhere and the Indians were allotted a large parcel of land.

The reserve encompasses 333,500 acres/135,000 hectares of subtropical and tropical grassland, savanna and shrub lands. About 75,000 acres/ 30,000 hectares is marked as Chimane traditional lands and is inhabited mainly by the Chimane. However, there is also a large pocket of Chinese settlers along the Maniqui River. These people live by fishing, gardening, harvesting medicinal plants and picking and selling the Jatata palm, which is used for roofing. El Porvenir is a tiny community within the reserve that offers a place to stay and eat, as well as locals willing to take you out on excursions.

The reserve has three geographical zones – the Amazon, the Chaco and the Cerrados (flooded savanna) – that have over 100 species of mammals, 500 species of birds, 2,000 species of plants (some of which are believed to be endemic), 200 species of fish and 45 kinds of amphibians. Of special interest is the black caiman and the river turtle, both endangered in the world, but whose numbers are on the rise in the biosphere. Because of its

Amazon Basin

diversity, the biosphere is of interest to zoologists, botanists, ecologists and anthropologists.

The reserve is sponsored by the Bolivian Academy of Sciences (☎ 235-2071 in Santa Cruz), which manages the finances and co-ordinates scientific research. There is a $6 fee for foreigners to enter the reserve. You pay this fee only once for each visit, no matter how many days you stay.

■ Adventures on Water

 LAGO NORMANDIA: This is the most popular destination from El Porvenir. The walk to the lake takes about two hours. Along the way, birding and looking at plants are the things to do. At the lake, canoes are provided so that you can paddle around and look for wildlife, such as the black caiman. This creature was once raised for its hide, which was used to make purses, shoes and belts. When that became illegal, the need for these animals died. Since they were bred in captivity, they were not able to return to the wild and survive. Their numbers became dangerously low, so the government moved a handful to Lago Normandia, where they have thrived (with the help of workers). There is an observation tower at the lake.

CURIRABA RIVER TRIP: This is a three-day excursion that starts with a jeep trip across the savannah to the river, where you board a motorized dugout canoe and travel upriver. The pink river dolphins you see along the way are so friendly and playful that you won't want to do anything else but watch them. However, I do suggest you go looking for the capybara, a 100-pound guinea pig that wallows in the mud and wiggles its ears. These, too, are so much fun that you'll want to adopt one. Just think what the neighbors would say. There are also hundreds of exotic water birds and, of course, the black caiman and the river turtle. In my experience, if a guide told me I was going to see something here, I almost always did.

You will overnight at the Marimono Jungle Camp on the river, where you can sleep to the calls of howler monkeys. The following day you will go on a three-hour hike through the forest to Anteojos Lakes (Eyeglass Lakes). Along the way you will again see monkeys and, probably, toucans. The guides will show you tracks left by jaguar, tapir and peccary. At the lakes you can fish or rest up for your three-hour hike back to camp and supper.

■ Adventure on Foot/Horseback

 RIDING THE PAMPAS: You can take a full day to ride horses along the pampas where there are three observatory towers, each 15 m/50 ft high, that allow for sightings of deer, wolves, monkeys and birds.

■ Tour Operators

All trip arrangements can be made at **El Porvenir Lodge**, ☎ 235-0612, www.madidi.com.

■ Places to Stay

HOTEL PRICES (US $)

Per person, per day, unless noted otherwise.

$..	$2-$5
$$.......................................	$5-$10
$$$......................................	$11-$17
$$$$.....................................	$18-$25
$$$$$....................................	Over $25

El Porvenir Lodge, *1,000 ft/300 m off the main road between Santa Cruz and San Borja,* ☎ *235-0612, www.madidi.com*, has dorm-styled rooms and excellent meals. The rate is $6 per person, per day. For another $6, you can get three meals a day.

Hotel San Borja, *on the plaza,* ☎ *848-3133, $$,* has rooms with or without baths. There is a restaurant and a pleasant courtyard around which the rooms are located. The rooms are big and bright and all have fans.

Hotel Tropico and **Hotel Victoria**, *$, (no phones),* sit across from each other two blocks past the plaza. The Victoria has rooms with private baths.

Casa Blaca, *Av. Sucre,* ☎ *895-3737, $$,* has bright rooms.

Jatata, *Calle Oruro, #249 and Cochabamba,* ☎ *895-3212, $$,* is just two blocks from the plaza. It has rooms with private baths, color TV, fridge and tiled floors. You can use the radio phone to call outlying areas. They have a laundry service and a snack bar.

Rurrenabaque

Altitude: 986 ft/300 m
Population: 9,600

The most popular reason to visit Rurrenabaque, called Rurre by the locals, is to take a river trip down the Yacuma River or a jungle trip to Chalalan. The area is hot and humid and the town is a dusty Amazonian river town-cum-resort. New hotels are constantly being opened and the restaurant services are excellent. The business people make foreigners welcome and hanging out is fun. Beer tastes best in the Amazon.

■ Getting Here & Around

To get to Rurre, you can take a jeep from La Paz for $35, a bus for $11 or a plane for $55. A bus takes 15 hours from La Paz, a plane takes 1½ hours and a jeep takes somewhere in between.

Amazonas Air (☎ 333-8263) has a small plane (holds 12) that flies from Rurre to La Paz for $50, Trinidad for $48 and Santa Cruz for $80. The schedules change depending on the season and weather. **TAM** (☎ 244-3487, www.tam.com.br) also flies into Rurre on Monday, Wednesday, Thursday, Friday and Saturday. Flying times change according to the weather. The planes cannot land in Rurre on a wet runway (it is a grass area spotted with mud potholes). There are four flights to Rurre from San Borja and Trinidad every week. The cost is less than $50 for a return flight.

Transportation at the airport costs about $1 per person for a ride into town. Airport tax out of Rurre is $2 for foreigners and 30¢ for locals.

Buses travel between Rurre and other destinations during dry season at reasonable speeds of under 30 miles/50 km an hour but over 10. During

Boat travel is common around Rurre.

wet season, a 12-hour bus trip between Riberalta and Rurre will take up to 24 hours, and in very wet times the buses don't go at all. On the other hand, in dry season, the trip to La Paz takes close to 18 hours, hardly worth the saving of $40 over taking the plane. Most buses travel at night due to the heat. The bus station is nine blocks from the central plaza. That is a fair walk in the heat.

Boats and rubber rafts come to Rurre from Guanay, down the Tuichi from the Apolo-bamba and a very few come up the Beni from Riberalta. During rainy season, travel along the rivers may be the only way to get in and out. The Guanay-to-Rurre trip can be arranged through Floating Bolivia Tours in Caravani (☎ 823-2396) and the Tuichi River trip can be booked through Explore Bolivia (☎ 303-545-5728; see *Outfitters Who Do All the Work*, page 82).

Moto-taxis (small motorcycles) are the norm in Rurre and they can be hired on the corner of Calle Comercio and Santa Cruz at 35¢ for a trip anywhere in town or $2 an hour. You will often see people carting things like ladders on their shoulders while being hauled around by one of these taxis.

!! WARNING !!

There have been women raped while on river trips out of Rurre. Although one culprit has been caught and imprisoned, he has also been released. His family lives in Rurre. The story is a sad/scary one. Do not travel in the jungle at night alone. Never take pills or drugs from anyone. One girl who was raped was offered some pills. They were a tranquilizer that put her into a heavy sleep. She woke up with the guy on top. Always be aware. The tours usually take six people. Try to pick the six you will go with and watch out for each other.

■ History

 Rurrenabaque was first made popular among tourists by **Yossi Ghinsberg**, an Israeli who was looking for adventure. In 1982, while roaming around South America, he met some other adventurers in La Paz and took a raft down the Tuichi River. Unprepared for that kind of jungle travel and after many misadventures, two of Ghinsberg's companions lost their lives. As the remaining two traveled through the jungle, they tipped their raft, became lost, without a knife or rifle, and encountered creatures like jaguars and anacondas. Ghinsberg was eventually rescued by his friend, who made it out and returned with Lulo, a man who lived in Rurrenabaque and knew the jungle well.

Ghinsberg wrote a book, *Back from Tuichi*, about his adventures. It was published in English by Random House and widely distributed both in Europe and America. As a result, Ghinsberg is now a cult-figure to young Israelis who come to Rurrenabaque specifically to follow in Ghinsberg's tracks. The first of these followers contacted Lulo, the man who rescued Ghinsberg, so that Lulo could take them into the jungle. Lulo saw the potential and opened Fluvial Tours. His success was copied by a plethora of entrepreneurs who now take visitors almost anywhere in the jungle around Rurre.

The book written by Ghinsberg is available in Rurre for $10 from Fluvial Tours. It is a spiral bound, photocopied version. There are no copyright laws being upheld in this little jungle town. According to Amazon.com the book is out of print but there are second-hand copies available.

Pre-Ghinsberg History

Rurre got its name from the Tacuna Indian words "seises es pato," which translates to "Royal de Partos" in Spanish, meaning royal birth in English. Eventually, this became bastardized into Rurrenabaque.

■ Services

The **telephone office** is on Calle Comercio and Santa Cruz.

An **Internet Café** next door to Camilas on Santa Cruz has four machines that are run off telephone lines. The cost is $2 per hour. The café is hot, but the machines are okay even if they are slow.

Lavanderia Rurrenabaque, Calle Vaca Diez next to Hotel Rurrenabaque, ☎ 892-2481, charges by weight. The laundry is open 9 am to 8 pm. Two other laundromats have varied times and comparable prices.

■ Adventures in Culture

The **Communities Tour** visits four Amazonian communities, each featuring a different aspect of their life. La Union is an Aymara village with families who migrated from Oruro when the economy fell. This new community uses local trees to mill lumber for construction. At Playa Ancha you will see a Quechua man from the Potosi area work in reforestation, fish farming, bee keeping and cattle ranching. His objective is to use the land in the most efficient manner. At Nuevos Horizontes you will view natural forest materials transformed into hats, bags and boxes. These items are for sale. At El Cebu, women make fruit wine, marmalades and drinks, while the men show how palm hearts are harvested. This tour starts at 7:30 am and returns to Rurre around 6 pm. It costs $40 per person if only two go, but dips to $22 per person when there are six or more. Although I didn't take this trip, everyone I spoke with was very happy with it. There was no sales pressure to buy items. See *Donato Tours*, below.

■ Adventures on Foot

MACUTI TRAIL: People live at the bottom of Mount Macuti, the mountain behind the church, and there is a trail leading to the top. This is a worthwhile walk on a nice day just for the views. It will take around 30 to 45 minutes to reach the top. Take water.

Rurrenabaque

PLACES TO STAY & EAT

1. Hostal Paraiso Tropical
2. Hostal Beni
3. Hostal El Balsero
4. Hotel Jasmin
5. Residencial Ballivan
6. Restaurant Playa Azul
7. Club Social
8. Hostal America
9. Moskitto Bar, Pizzeria Italia
10. Hotel Porteño
11. Café Motaco
12. Hotel Rurrenabaque
13. Hostal Tuichi
14. Camila's Restaurant
15. La Perlade Rurre
16. Hostal Santa Ana
17. Hotel Bella Vista, La Cabaña
18. Hotel Oriental
19. Hotel Eden

Amazon Basin

ETSAYA: Etsaya is a tiny village out of Rurre that takes 15 minutes to reach by motorbike taxi. The car taxi, found on Calle Comercio, will cost $1.25. Walking, by far the most interesting way to go, will take less than an hour. Along the way you will pass farms and see numerous birds (in the morning; afternoon is too hot). Etsaya has a few places offering snacks.

JUNGLE HIKE: This trip is similar to the river trip except you go to a camp in the jungle. It must be done using a tour agency as a guide and an established camp is needed. The first day of the hike is usually spent walking to a lookout. This can be dangerous as the wall that must be ascended is steep and no ropes or harnesses are provided. The trails show primary and secondary forests and one trek goes to a natural swimming pool. Treks in the jungle are mostly for those interested in plants since a lot of jungle animals are nocturnal feeders and are difficult to spot, especially during the day. Make certain if you take this hike, you have lamps that work for a night hike. The jungle is hot and humid and walking for long can be difficult

■ Adventures on Water

JUNGLE RIVER TRIP: One of the main reasons people come to Rurre is to get on a boat and go up a river to see things like anacondas, caimans, exotic birds, freshwater dolphins and capybaras. If you have not been in the jungle for an overnight trip, this is a must.

The most common tour consists of half a day in the jeep getting to the Yacuma River in Santa Rosa del Yacuma Nature Sanctuary and the other half going up the river to the camp. Each camp is a bit different but, in fact, they are of two classes. One class has wood beds covered with mosquito nets under a tarp and the other has the same beds inside a hut that has screening around it. They are all only a short walk from each other along the banks of the river. If the weather is very hot, you should choose a place that has the beds outside. Even a small breeze is a blessing. Sleeping under a net is hot. However, if there is lots of rain you may want to be inside. The companies will show photos of their camps.

There are lots of sand fleas here. Wear long-sleeved shirts and long pants in the evenings. The locals laugh at tourists who come as a ready meal for the bugs. Some bites can lead to serious infections that take months to heal. Do as the locals do.

A three-day tour is just enough. It takes half a day to get there and half a day to get back, so you have two days on the river and for a walk on the *pampas* to see snakes and birds. Getting to and from camp you will see every animal your tour operator has promised. Staying two days at the camp leaves a lot of time to explore, with some time on your own.

The big controversy is whether the animals (mostly anacondas) should be mauled by tourists or just left alone. I watched as a snake was almost choked to death by a tourist when he held it; when the snake was put down again it puked up a half-digested frog and a mouse. This handling was obviously traumatic to the snake, not to mention a waste of food. On the other hand, tour companies want so much to please their clients (and get their business) that they will take the chance on handling snakes This is where we, as people who have lost wildlife in our own countries, must encourage the no-touch style of eco-travel. With snakes, however, "no touch" is almost always "no see," as they must be dredged out of the mud to be examined.

The tour costs anywhere from $10 per day to $20, depending on the accommodations, time of year and extras like an anaconda hunter. Park fees are $6 for foreigners, $1.50 for locals. This is not included in the cost of the tour. See *Tour Operators*.

MOUNT BRUJO: When waters are low you can take a boat upriver to see some Tacana rock paintings on the far side of Mount Brujo, the second mountain in the village. Talk to the boat operators at the dock.

ISLAND BOAT TRIP: The islands on the Beni, across from Rurre, are occupied by locals who live in traditional houses and grow beans, yucca and plantains that they bring to the mainland to sell. The huts can be seen from the Bella Vista Restaurant. You can hire a dugout canoe ($3 per day) at the dock to go across and poke around.

SWIMMING POOL: The pool just off Calle Piscina is a great place to cool off and is popular with foreigners. To get there, walk along Piscina two blocks past the TAM office. It's open 9 am to noon and then again in the late afternoon.

■ Adventures in Nature

Chalalan Lodge in Madidi National Park, ☎ 3-892-2419, www. madidi.com/chalalan.html, chalalan_eco@yahoo.com, is an eco-lodge that was built after the Yossi Ghinsberg story came out. The people of the area realized that foreigners really wanted to experience life in the jungle, even if it was for just a couple of days. They also realized that it was better to bring money into their community through tourism than to take agricultural products eight hours downriver to market. With technical assistance from Conservation International and money from the InterAmerican Development Bank, the lodge was built.

Owned by shareholders who are permanent residents of San Jose de Uchupiamonas, a Quechua-Tacana village nearby, the cabins are built in traditional Tacana fashion with copa palm walls and woven jatata leaves on the roofs. There is solar power and a wastewater treatment disposal unit. Just outside the main hut is a tree with oropendula nests (and birds). Their song can be heard often. The males of this species have many mates.

Inside the cabins, each bed has a mosquito net. Outside is a porch with hammocks. Bathrooms and showers are in a separate unit. The main hall has an interpretive center and a small reference library. The kitchen has modern conveniences like refrigeration so that food can be safely cooked and kept.

To get here, travel from Rurre up the Beni and Tuichi rivers by wooden scow for six hours. You must then walk along the Wichi Trail for half an hour to the lodge. The property is situated just above Chalalan Lake, where there are 15 miles/25 km of trails for you to hike, looking for medicinal plants or exotic birds. The trails are named and each is specific for a particular subject. For example, the Sivador Trail is where you will find most of the medicinal plants, while the Chichilo Trail will take you to a lookout point where you can see the Chalalan Lake, Madidi Park and the Andes Mountains in the distance. Most trails take two to three hours to walk and you will likely see things like capuchin, howler and squirrel monkeys, tapirs, spiders, capybaras and, occasionally, a jaguar. There are also peccaries, agoutis, boa constrictors and numerous species of frogs. Over 340 species of birds have been spotted in the area, including the capped heron, wood stork, Orinoco goose, osprey, great-black hawk, pied lapwing and large-billed tern. Local guides are available to help you scout and to explain how the plants and animals play a part in everyday life. Some guides who specialize in birding can imitate a few of the calls. Some of the trails cut through others so that you can combine them to make your walk longer or shorter. Canoes are available for scouting around the lake.

Like the trails, each guide has a specialty. One may know medicinal plants, while another may be familiar with different insects. Night walks or a night canoe trip can be included in the itinerary. If staying longer than three days, your itinerary will include lessons in jungle survival and safety.

A cultural evening revolves around Tacana Indian traditions and includes food, music, dancing and Tacana stories.

The lodge also has carved masks or heads of animals for sale at $15 each. The wood used is from the Bibosi tree. The book *Chalalan*, by Hennessey, Rios and Perry, describes some of the animals and has drawings of their prints. It provides information on snakes and frogs and has sketches of the more common birds in the area. The price is $4.

This company hasn't figured out what a deal is or what cost-efficient trips would be. If you go for three nights, the cost is $280 and this includes transportation, guides and all meals. Four nights cost $380 and five nights run $480. This means that three nights cost $73 per night, four cost $97 and five cost $96. Considering the cost of travel, I suspect something has been miscalculated. However, if there are more than six people in your group, rates drop. You can also pay for additional days in Chalalan at a rate of $100 per person, per day. All profits go toward health services and education for the local people.

To make arrangements, you can either contact a tour office in La Paz or go directly to the office in Rurre. The ones handling tours in La Paz are American Tours, Crillon Tours, Magri Turismo, Transturin and Turismo Balsa. Explore Bolivia also takes rafting tours down the Tuichi, eventually landing at Chalalan.

If you want to do a custom trip farther into the jungles around Chalalan, contact biologist **Alan Perry**, who knows the area well. He is one of the authors of the book, *Chalalan*. For more information, go to www.madidi. com/chalalan.html or contact Alan direct at info@madidi.com.

MEET EMA NOVA, LONGTIME RESIDENT

Ema Nova, one of the oldest residents of Rurre, tends her flower garden next to the Oriental Hotel. She likes to talk about the past and remembers when Rurre was the hub on the Beni River. That was when it took seven hours by horse and cart to get to Reyes, two days to San Buenaventura and three or four days to Ixiamas. Born in 1923 and widowed in 1965 after birthing six kids, Ema remembers 1948, when the first car rolled into town. It wasn't long after that the airplane arrived. Then everything became different. Tourists came, but locals, who always stopped to chat and bring the news from downriver, stopped coming. They now shop in La Paz. And tourists don't seem to have the same gossipy nature as those living on the rivers had. Ema got her phone in 1981 and likes being able to contact her five children, who no longer live in the village. Like many young ones, they have left to find the opportunities that bigger centers are able to offer. If you see her working in her garden, stop and talk. I'm sure she will find you every bit as gossipy as the river dwellers who passed by long ago.

Mapajo Indigenous Lodge, www.madidi.com/mapajo.html or www. mapajo.com, is similar in nature to Chalalan, except the river trip is only three hours and you go up the Beni to Rio Quiquibey, and then east to the Pilon Lajas Bio Reserve. This lodge is run by the Moseten and (Chimane) Tsimane groups. It has four cabins that sleep two people each and share a bathroom with other cabins. They feature tables, chairs, bedside tables,

Amazon Basin

mosquito nets over the beds and balconies with hammocks. One of the cabins will hold six people and has a private bathroom.

The interpretive center is well stocked with a library, maps and a telescope. The group has published a large coffee table book called *Palabras Antigues y Nuevas del Rio Quiquibey*. It has numerous color photos depicting life in the Amazon in and near the river villages, plus it has stories and legends. However, the stories are all in Spanish. There are other books available about the area at the bookstore on their website.

Over 12 miles/20 km of hiking trails surround the lodge and walking them can take anywhere from an hour to three hours. Guided night walks are also included, as is a cultural night where dancing, music, food and stories are shared.

The cost of an all-inclusive trip is $60 per person, per day. To reach the lodge costs less than $60 at present, but it could change with rising gas prices. Although this lodge is less expensive and a little less advertised, it does not mean that the standard is any lower. If you are interested, talk to the operators in Rurre: Mapajo Ecoturismo, Calle Comercio, ☎ 892-2317, www.mapajo.com.

■ Tour Operators

As in La Paz, the tour agencies in Rurre will promise you anything just to get your business. Some jungle camps are good, while others are bad. Some cooks are clean, others are dirty, some guides practice the "touch" tour, while others prohibit any kind of touching. There is no way of knowing if the company you are going with will provide you with what they promise. Although I recommend some companies here, the best approach is to talk to as many travelers as possible and see what they say. As pressure for more consistent prices, cleaner camps and more ecologically sensitive tours increases, the companies will change so they can provide these things just to get your business.

Private guides can be hired if you do not want to join a tour group. **Obedio Valdez** is good for jungle trips. He has worked for some time at Chalalan as a guide and speaks working English. His price is $10 per day and he can be contacted at his office, ☎ 892-2419, or by cell phone at ☎ 10-2213 7391. For a more intense trip into the jungles around Chalalan, contact Alan Perry at info@madidi.com, PO Box 431, Hailey, ID 83333, ☎ 208-450-9010. Alan is a biologist who knows the area well and has written some books about the region, including the *Field Guide to Chalalan*.

Donato Tours, Avenida Comercio and Santa Cruz, ☎ 591-3892 or 591-2571, donato tours@hotmail.com. Donato takes groups of up to six people and his policy is to not traumatize the animals by touching. When I was there, workers kept the camp clean, carried out garbage, and located the toilet a long way from the river. However, they do put uneaten food into the river, not good ecological practice. Maybe a compost pit in town would be better. Donato has a low-impact camp without cabins, only beds under a tarp with mosquito nets over the beds (this is cooler than a cabin). During high water there are no trips to the *pampas* because much of the land is under water. Donato can also arrange horse trips into the jungle. We saw all the animals and birds we were told we'd see. Donato offers the one-day Communities Tour (see above).

Fluvial Tours, ☎ 892-2372, www.megalink.com/rurrenabaque, was first started when the owner, Lulo went out looking for the missing Yossi Ghinsberg. He now sells photocopied *Back from Tuichi* books to tourists for $10. Fluvial has five camps along the Yacuma River. Their tours are for groups of up to nine people and sometimes they join other groups on the river for evening activities. One of Fluvial's camps holds 20 people. This company started in 1986 and was the first tour company in Rurre. Their policy for touching animals is influenced by the group. The cost is $20 per person for three days and two nights. They also do the jungle tour for three days.

Mapajo Ecotourism Indegena, Calle Comercio, ☎ 892-2317, www. mapajo.com, offers a unique experience for the more adventuresome. See Mapajo Indigenous Lodge (above) for information.

Amazonico Travel, Calle Avaroa, is run and owned by the brothers who also run Fluvial. The cost, depending on the quality of the tour, is between $20 and $25 to go to the jungle and $25 to $30 to go to the pampas. Their camps have two buildings, one for eating and one for sleeping. Amazonico has five different camps in all, with varying prices. However, there are negligible differences between the camps themselves. In high season a group leaves every day. Their maximum number is nine to a group. During high water (low season) they go for only one night as there is far less to see. This company will also pick up clients from the airport or bus station.

Flecha Tours, Calle Avaroa, ☎ 7114-3529 (cell) cr 284-0221 (contact Oscar Huanto in La Paz), flechatours@hotmail.com. This company offers both *pampas* and jungle tours. The jungle tours can last for up to 20 days. These people are good and I recommend you talk with them first. The guide at Flecha spoke fairly good English.

PALM BONUS

There are many types of palms in the jungle and the bark of the chuchu-wasa palm is used by locals as an aphrodisiac. Have your guide point one out, but don't chew on it.

Amazonia Adventures, Calle Avaroia, ☎ 892-2333, amazoniaadventures@latinmail.com, will take only six people in each group to the jungle or the *pampas*. They have a "no touch, no feed" policy. The cost is $25 per person, per day. This company does not put vegetable matter into the river and their trips don't include fishing. The jungle trips travel on the Beni River. The camp is isolated and takes four hours to reach by boat. For an extra $3, horse travel can be included. This is good if you are unable or don't want to walk in the heat and the sometimes intense sunlight.

Indigena Tours, Calle Avaroa, ☎ 892-2091, mercadofreddy@hotmail.com, offer two classes of trips, one for $25 and the other for $30. They take between three and six people per trip and will go for up to 12 days. The wildlife common to these tours are caimans, turtles, pink dolphins, pirañas, capybaras, monkeys, anacondas, cobras, sloths, jabiru storks, hoatzin birds, and blue and yellow macaws. The *pampas* tour includes a spot for a shower. While looking through evaluation sheets I noticed great praise given to Victor Hugo and Freddy when they worked as guides on the trip. You may want to book with them.

Inca Land Tours, Calle Aniceto Arce between Bolívar and Avaroa, www.incalandtours.com, has the usual selection of tours to the *pampas*, the jungle or the Chalalan. They do either touch or no touch tours, depending on the group. However, when I last spoke with them, they were pushing toward the no-touch tour as the only option. You can book with Inca in La Paz and have everything ready for you when you arrive in Rurre. Inca Land is the only company that will take you up to Ixiamas if you are interested in jungle logging or in fishing. I found Inca Land very busy, often going far out of their way to provide good service. One day I noticed their agent, who speaks English well and is organized and thoughtful, seeing her customers onto the plane for the flight to Rurre.

■ Places to Stay

Hotel Rurrenebaque, *Calle Vaca Diez y Bolívar,* ☎ *892-2481 or (La Paz 279-5917), $,* has 11 rooms in all. The general manager, Mireya Luz is a fine lady who speaks some English. She is helpful and works hard to make her guests comfortable. The rooms are large, with tiled floors, fans, clean bathrooms, mirrors and towels. There is a garden, parking a safe, laundry service, a money exchange and a baggage deposit. A coffee shop and bakery are attached to the hotel. This is a good deal.

HOTEL PRICES (US $)

Per person, per day, unless noted otherwise.

$	$2-$5
$$	$5-$10
$$$	$11-$17
$$$$	$18-$25
$$$$$	Over $25

Tuichi Hostal, *Calle Avaroa*, ☎ *892-2326, $,* is next door to Fluvial Tours and is a hot spot in town, mostly because of Israelis following Yossi's path. It has dorms and private rooms as well as a small garden with hammocks that are constantly in use.

Hotel Eden, *at the back of the village just below the hill, (no phone), $,* has seven basic rooms but only one with a private bath. I found the staff friendly.

Hostal El Balsero, *Calle Comercio and Aniceto Arce*, ☎ *892-2042, $,* is just up from the Beni and is run by a friendly and helpful lady. The 12 rooms are large and have fans, TVs and shared bathrooms. The showers are clean and have hot water. A second-floor balcony overlooks the front street. This is not a bad deal.

Residencial Porteño, *Calle Comercio and Avenida Vaca Diez,* ☎ *892-2558 $,* is a well-run place. All rooms are clean and well maintained. The bathrooms have hot water as well as towels, soap, and toilet paper. The rooms are large and tastefully furnished with dressers, mirrors, and built-in cupboards. The cost is $4 per person. She also has a dorm that costs $2.50 per person. There are many repeat customers here.

Hotel Aquita, *is just past the square.* There was no one around when I was there. The rooms are small and basic, with cement floors and no fan.

Hotel Jasmin, *Calle Ceneseto Arse,* ☎ *892-2337, $,* has 24 basic rooms around a small garden. This is not a good deal.

Hostal America, *Avenida Mariscal Santa Cruz at La Playa,* ☎ *892-2413, $,* has 15 basic rooms that are scattered over three grotty floors. All rooms share baths.

Residencial Ballivian, *Calle Pando,* ☎ *892-2468, $,* is on a side street between the river and the main street. The rooms are basic and hot, with no fans, windows or bathrooms. The floors are unpainted cement and the bottom half of the walls are bamboo, while the tops are screen. The beds have mosquito nets. All this can be had for a mere $1.25 per person, which is a fair deal.

Amazon Basin

Hotel Santa Ana, *Calle Aboroa,* ☎ *892-2399, $$,* has 18 rooms around the most beautiful garden in Rurre. There is also a patio with hammocks under a palm-thatched hut. Each room is tiled and spotless and has a fan. There is a sink to do laundry, a baggage deposit and a car park. The hotel is managed by Domingo Agreado and he can arrange for a guide if you wish to go hiking in Madidi National Park. He is friendly and helpful. I highly recommend this hotel.

Hotel Oriental *on Plaza Principal,* ☎ *892-2401, $$,* is an excellent hotel with rooms around a spacious garden that is shaded with large mango trees. Breakfast is served in the garden. The rooms all have private bathrooms, with hot water and daily maid service. This clean, quiet and relaxing place is run by a friendly and helpful family.

Bella Vista, *Calle Comercio on the plaza,* ☎ *892-2328, $$,* is under new ownership. At present the owner has 20 rooms available, but once renovations are complete, he will have 40. The rooms have high ceilings, fans and large tiled bathrooms. When the new rooms are complete, prices will be raised. There is no single rate.

Hostal Beni, *Calle Comercio y Aniceto Arce,* ☎ *892-2408, $$/$$$.* This well-run establishment has rooms with tiled floors, built-in dressers, table and chairs, TV (local channel only) and air conditioning. The shower is sectioned off from the toilet and soap, toilet paper and fresh towels are provided. The place is spotless. Parking is available, and there is a small patio with hammocks. The walkway between the rooms overlooks the river. The staff at Hostal Beni will tell you that, in 1999, the Beni River came up 18 inches over the first level. Flooding like this happens about once every 20 years.

■ Places to Eat

Restaurant La Perla de Rurre, *Calle Vaca Diez,* has a large, attractive courtyard decorated with flowering plants and linen-covered tables. The place is welcoming. However, there is only one breakfast from which to choose and even scrambling the eggs rather than frying them is beyond the ability of the cook. The coffee is instant, but the papaya and milk are good. Breakfast costs $3.50. I did not try any other meals.

Camila's Restaurant, *Avenida Santa Cruz,* is popular for a reason. The meal I had was large, excellent, and not expensive, only $2.50 per plate. I recommend the fish with garlic sauce, a tasty white sauce that still makes my mouth water.

TASTY TUTUMA

Tutuma is a large round fruit, green in color, that resembles a melon. It hangs by a stem from a tree that grows more than 23 ft/seven m high. The pulp resembles cocoa in flavor and texture and is scraped out and cooked with wheat or rice.

Café Motacu, *Avenida Santa Cruz,* is an excellent coffee shop that also serves good food. It was opened by a Scot and a Peruvian in 1996. They were soon joined in the partnership by a Bolivian and an Argentinean. Besides selling food, they wanted a place for locals to sell their crafts, and over 100 artisans are now working through this shop, including Chimane (Tsimani), Moseten and Tacana artists. There are painted bowls carved from local trees, cards, bags, bows and arrows and designed t-shirts. The tea grown in the Beni region and available for sale here makes a great gift. In the book exchange I found an old Hunter Publication about Bolivia and Peru first published in 1987. At that time, Rurre was not a popular tourist destination. There is always someone sitting in the café scribbling in a journal or pouring over a novel. The café is open from 8:30 am till noon and 6:30 to 9:30 pm every day except Tuesday and Sunday. The restaurant will make a bag lunch for between $1 and $2.50.

Club Social, *Calle Comercio*, is a huge place that is popular with locals. The open-air restaurant overlooks the river. Although the service was good, my meat was tough and overcooked. I also found the room too big to be comfortable.

Restaurant Bella Vista, *Avenida Santa Cruz #1,* ☎ *790-6033,* is on the third floor overlooking the river. Part of the restaurant is under a thatch roof and part is open. Being high allows the place to catch a breeze and customers get a good sense of the landscape. The food is well prepared (the steak I had was tender) and the prices reasonable. A fish costs $2.50, a large beer was just over a dollar. For a romantic dinner watching the lights of boats on the Beni River, this place is second to none in Rurre.

When I was there I experienced one of those famous Amazon thunderstorms and downpours. The staff had to move stereo equipment out of the rain, and my table out of the flood that was spreading over the floor. They did this with elegance and good humor. They used umbrellas to bring my food from the kitchen to the table. The thunderstorm, seen from this level, was beautiful.

Restaurant La Cabaña, *below the Bella Vista,* is often patronized by upper-crust Bolivians. I thought the music was too loud, but the food is said to be good.

Restaurant Playa Azul, *on the beach under the Hostal America,* is run by someone who seems more interested in sprucing herself up than in providing good food and service. She did look good. The restaurant crew

Amazon Basin

seemed to be enjoying their beer as they served ours. I never saw foreigners in this place. There is a tree at the edge of the restaurant with a blue paint line showing where the river rose to during the last high water.

Restaurant Jatata, *Hotel Rurrenabaque on Calle Vaca Diez*, has a smorgasbord for under $5. Their à-la-carte dishes are good too. The restaurant is cosy and the service is excellent.

Pizzeria Italia, *Calle Comercio*, has a second location in Sorata. The pizza is thin-crusted and the toppings are thick. Excellent food. It is next door to Moskkito Jungle Bar and, if you are at the bar and do not want to abandon your beer, they will deliver. They also do not close during siesta as most places do, indicating that they are accustomed to *gringo* patterns.

■ Nightlife

Moskkito Jungle Bar, *Calle Comercio*, ☎ *892-2267, moskkito@ terra.com*, is the rockingest place in Rurre. The Pizzeria Italia, under the same thatch hut but on the other side of the games room (pool and darts), will deliver to the bar. A happy hour runs from 7 pm to 9 pm when mixed drinks are half-price. If you grow attached to the place, you can purchase a t-shirt as a reminder. I saw these shirts all over Bolivia.

■ Shopping

About 4,000 Tacana live in 20 communities just off the Beni River and its tributaries. They grow cotton and the fabric they design from this plant is like a language, rich in story. Numerous items made from this material – bags, skirts and blouses – are sold in shops throughout town. Café Motacu carries a good selection.

■ Around Rurre

Buena Ventura

Buena Ventura is a little outpost that sits across the Beni River from Rurre. A boat-ferry crosses about once every 15 minutes at the cost of 30¢ per person. In the village, toward the back and away from the river, is the **Centro Cultura de Tacana**. The museum costs $1.25 per person and has a few pieces of art like handmade baskets and natural seed necklaces. In 1986 the Tacana Indians received a land settlement that gave them more control over the hunting of animals and logging of trees. Part of the settlement resulted in funding for building the museum and promoting tourism. CARE Bolivia was also involved in funding.

Symbols used in weaving and pottery are explained in the museum and there's also a traditional log ladder, a large clay pot and a pestle and mortar. Actually, there is not much for the price here, but you can see what they are trying to do. If you are interested in indigenous cultures, support this museum so it can grow. There is a *baño* (bathroom) out back.

There are three hotels in town, with **Residencial Madidi** being the best. The seven rooms are basic but the floors are tiled and there is a fan, beds, and a chair. The cost is $1.25 per person. The second option is the **Florida**, on Calle Sucre and Palacio. The Florida is even more basic, with cement floors and no fans. It is the same price as the Madidi. The beds at the Florida were Inca, but the hotel is clean enough.

The Residencial La Paz at the dock should be left to its present patrons.

The Madidi National Park office is just up the street from Residencial La Paz. Don't waste your energy climbing the stairs to visit because information about the park is not available. A pamphlet cannot be handed out without the approval of the director, who is often in La Paz.

Reyes

Reyes is a small village nine miles/15 km in from the Beni River. It has the Hotel 6 de Enero where you can stay. There are also places to eat, and even more places to drink. The church on the plaza is fairly nice, but not spectacular.

The airport here is where TAM planes land if Rurre is wet. Should you land here, TAM will provide transportation to Rurre. If you happen to be staying in Reyes, you can take a local bus to Rurre, or catch a bus to Riberalta. The bus station, a basic and barely functional building, is on the road toward Santa Ana. There is a bus leaving for Riberalta every day. Time is dependent on road conditions, which depend in turn on the amount of rainfall.

Ixiamas

This small logging community of about 2,000 people was first occupied by Franciscan missionaries. There is one bus/truck leaving from La Paz every Saturday that can be caught in Rurre and that goes on to Ixiamas. The bus returns on Sunday. The village is close to Rio Madidi, where pacu and pintado fishing is the big draw. Madidi Park, a few miles away, has forests where jungle treks are exceptional. There is also a small airfield in Ixiamas. The hotel in the village is new. It's next to the airport and on Avenida La Paz. For reservations, call the Beni Hotel in Rurre, ☎ 892-2408.

Riberalta

Altitude: 557 ft / 175 m
Population: 52,000

Riberalta is fairly large as compared to most cities in the Bolivian Amazon. It was created in 1894 as a center for moving rubber and over the years has had three names. The first was La Cruz, named because it is at the crossroads of the Beni River and Rio de Madre. Next, it was called Barranca Colorada. A *barranca* is a gully or a ravine in Spanish. You'd have a hard time finding a substantial ravine in this town but there is one on a bluff overlooking the Madre de Dios River. Finally, the town was named Riberalta, which means high bank. Those living in Riberalta like to think that it really means the most beautiful high bank. I support that as being the most appropriate.

The city has a few things to do, great birding for example, and some good restaurants and coffee shops around the plaza. However, changing travelers' checks is not possible in this town. And remember, bank machines have not yet been introduced to the Amazon.

■ Getting Here & Around

 Flights from Santa Cruz, La Paz and Trinidad are offered by **SAVE**, ☎ 212-1548; **TAM**, ☎ 244-3487, www.tam.com.br; **Amaszonas Air**, ☎ 333-8263; and **LAB**, ☎ 800-337-0918 (US), 800-10-3001 (Bolivia), www.labairlines.com. The cost is about $115 from La Paz for a one-way ticket. There are also flights between Cobija, Cochabamba and Guayaramarin. The airport is a short walk from the center of town. If walking in the heat isn't to your liking, take a moto-taxi for 30¢.

Buses come from Guayaramarin each day during dry season, heading to Rurre. There is also transportation to the cities in the south via Trinidad. All trips are dependent on road conditions. I flew from Riberalta to Cochabamba and watched out the window with fascination as canoes paddled along the roads.

■ Adventures in Nature

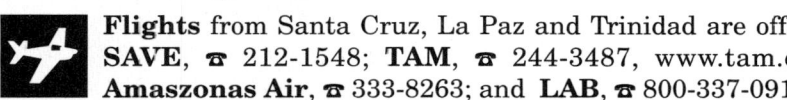 **Birding** is one of the big things around Riberalta. Because of the thick rubber-tree forests in the area, the bird population is high. But actually *seeing* the birds is a different matter.

In 1966, a birder by the name of Sjoerd Mayer sighted the rufous-sided pygmy-tyrant (previously found mostly in Noel Kempff Park) and the spotted antpitta. It was previously assumed that both birds did not range this far south. His discovery has sent a few birders to the area looking for these treasures.

The best places to see birds are in forest and scrub between the town and the Beni River. It is a half-hour walk or 10 minutes by moto-taxi to the banks of the river, where you can find birds like the chestnut jacamar, the spotted tody-tyrants and the tyrannulets. There's also good birding along the road to Guayaramerin and its tributary roads.

Parque Costanera in Riberalta overlooks the Beni River and has the last steamer ever to come up the Amazon into Bolivia, the *Tahuamanu*, sitting on cement. Built in 1899, this boat was used to haul rubber until the 1930s. You can tour the boat.

Iturralde Crater (also called the Araona Crater) is in the jungle southwest of Riberalta and southeast of Cobija. It was spotted in 1988 on a satellite photo but because of its inaccessibility no scientific team went in until 1998. The only way to reach the crater is to hire a helicopter. On the ground, you will find that the mosquitoes and sweat-sucking bees will drive you out before you can find anything of interest to see. Scientists believe that the meteor or comet entered the jungle 20,000 years ago at a speed of 43 miles/70 km per second. It landed in the silt with a splat. The depression it left is five miles/eight km wide and dips only 10 ft/three m into the landscape. The depression fills with water during rainy season.

A team led by Dr. Peter Wasilewski of NASA went into the crater in 2002 to get samples of rock and soil for laboratory examination. They also looked for glass that would indicate that a meteor rather than a comet landed on the spot. I don't know what the results were. The bedrock lies about 2.6 miles/four km below the surface sediment.

■ Places to Stay

 Hotel Los Reyes, *a block from the Riberalta airport*, ☎ 346-8018, *$*. They charge $4 per person for a large room without private bathroom and $6 for a room with.

Residencial Katita, *Avenida Martinez and Calle Natusch*, ☎ 346-8386, *$*, has basic rooms without private bathroom.

Hotel Amazonas, ☎ 346-8339, *$$*, has rooms with private bathrooms.

Hotel Colonial, *Avenida Baptista*, ☎ 346-8212, *$$*, is a colonial mansion that once belonged to a Bolivian rubber baron. The rooms have private bathrooms and are set around a central courtyard that is lush in vegetation. Rates include breakfast. The hotel's restaurant overlooks the courtyard.

Hotel Commercial Lazo *(no phone)*, *$$*, has clean, well-furnished rooms with private baths and fans. The staff is friendly. This is a good deal.

Hostal Tahuamanu, *a block from the plaza*, ☎ *346-8006, $$$*, has rooms with private bathrooms and air conditioning. Breakfast is complimentary. This is a pretty upscale choice for this area.

Guayaramerin

Elevation: 400 ft / 125 m
Population: 40,000

This little border town is a great introduction to Bolivia for those just entering from Brazil. The border guards are exceptionally fun and they welcome tourists. The river between Brazil and Bolivia is crossed on a ferry that runs 18 hours a day and costs about 50¢ per person. As you cross, you will be amazed at the colorful boats, flying the flags of their respective countries, buzzing back and forth.

There are money changers on both sides of the border. They will change American cash or Brazilian reales.

The town itself is spread across many blocks of dusty dry streets in the hot season and slippery muck in wet season. The main activity, as in many Amazonian towns, is to sit on the square, drink beer and howl at (or be howled at by) the opposite sex as they rod around the plaza on their motorbikes. When I was there, a couple of kids were going around the plaza singing songs for a penny or two. Of course, they were hard to hear above the motorbikes. One had a beautiful voice.

■ Getting Here & Around

Four airlines have small planes that will connect travelers from here to Riberalta, where you can catch a flight to other parts of Bolivia. The community is serviced by **TAM**, ☎ 244-3487, www.tam.com.br; **Amaszonas Air**, ☎ 855-3731; **LAB**, ☎ 800-337-0918 (US), 800-10-3001 (Bolivia), www.labairlines.com; and **SAVE**, ☎ 212-1548. At least one flight leaves daily from Guayaramerin, though it rarely runs on schedule. If a connecting flight is on your itinerary, be sure you have flex time because so much travel is weather-dependent in the Amazon area.

Buses will take you to Riberalta and from there you can go south to Trinidad or west to Rurrenabaque. Riberalta is only 60 miles/100 km away. During rainy season, the buses pass between Riberalta and Guayaramerin, but there are only a few that go beyond.

Boats take anywhere from four to six days to reach Trinidad and charge $30 per person. You must have a hammock, but food will be provided. To find a boat, go upriver from the border crossing.

Moto-taxis can be rented for the day at a cost of about $10. Be aware that passing the checkpoints at the edge of the city is a problem if you do not have your papers in order. Even if you do, there could be problems. You must have permission from the police to take the vehicle anywhere out of city limits. However, you may want to rent one and whirl around the plaza for an hour or two just to cool off.

■ Places to Stay

HOTEL PRICES (US $)
Per person, per day, unless noted otherwise.
$. . . . . $2-$5
$$. . . . . $5-$10
$$$. . . . . $11-$17
$$$$. . . . . $18-$25
$$$$$. . . . . Over $25

 Hotel Plaza Anexo, *on the plaza,* ☎ *346-2086, $,* is a popular place for travelers. It is basic but clean. Rooms have fans and private bathrooms.

Hotel Central, *Avenida Santa Cruz and 6 de Agosto,* ☎ *346-2042, $,* is just down from the San Carlos. They have basic rooms with fans for $5 per person.

Santa Ana Hotel, *near the airport,* ☎ *346-2206, $.* I didn't find the staff very friendly. Maybe it was the heat.

Hotel Esperanza, ☎ *346-2201, $$$.* This hotel can be booked through American Tours in La Paz. Rates include breakfast.

Hotel San Carlos, *Avenida Santa Cruz and 6 de Agosto,* ☎ *346-2419, $$$,* charges just a bit more than the Esperanza for a room with private bath, TV and air conditioning. This is the only hotel in town that will exchange travelers' checks, but only for paying guests.

Appendix

Recommended Reading

A Traveler's Guide to El Dorado and the Inca Empire, Lynn Meisch, Headlands Press, Penguin Books, 1977. This is a repository of cultural information rather than a travel guide.

Trekking in Bolivia, Yossi Brain, Andrew North, Isobel Stoddart, Mountaineers Books, Seattle, 1997.

Adventuring in the Andes, Charles Frasier with Donald Secreast, Sierra Club Books, San Francisco, 1985.

An Insider's Guide to Bolivia, Peter McFarren, Cultural Foundation of Quipus, La Paz, 2003. This fourth edition is full of cultural tidbits that give the traveler inside information on some of the activities one sees but does not understand while in Bolivia.

Bolivia: A Climbing Guide, Yossi Brain, Mountaineers Books, Seattle, 1999.

Bolivia: A Country Study, edited by RA Hudson, DM Hanratty, Library of Congress, 1991.

Ernesto, A Memoir of Che Guevara, Hilda Gadea, Doubleday, New York, 1972.

The Fat Man from La Paz, edited by Rosario Santos, Seven Stories Press, New York, NY, 2000. A collection of short stories written by contemporary writers. It is excellent.

Fire from the Andes, edited and translated by Susan E Benner and Kathy S Leonard, University of New Mexico Press, New Mexico, 1998. This is a collection of short stories written by women from Bolivia, Peru, and Ecuador.

Six Years in Bolivia, Anselm Verener Lee Guise, NotaBell Books, an imprint of Purdue University Press, West Lafayette, Indiana, 1998. A travel story written by a mining engineer.

Americas Before Columbus, EC Baity, Viking Press, New York, 1961.

Bolivian History, Charles Arnade, Los Amigos del Libro, La Paz, 1984.

Discovering Bolivia, Hugo Boero Rojo, Los Amigos del Libro, La Paz, 1994.

One River, Wade Davis, Simon & Schuster, New York, 1996. An ethnobotanist's story of exploring the Amazon.

The Mint of Potosi, 1997, published by the Cultural Foundation of Bolivia with the assistance of the Central Bank of Bolivia.

Baron de Estaño, is a hard-to-find, long biography of Patiño.

Memory of Fire – Genesis, Eduardo Galeano, Pantheon Books, New York, 1985. This is one book of a trilogy of collected folk tales from throughout the Spanish world.

Field Guide to Chalalan, A Bennett Hennessey, Boris Rios and Alan Perry, 1996. Available through the bookstore at www.madidi.com.

Consulates & Embassies

■ La Paz

ARGENTINA. Sanchez Lima & Aspiazu #497, ☎ 242-2912, 9-2 pm.

AUSTRALIA. Av. Arce & Montevideo, Edif. Montevideo Mezannine, ☎ 244-0459, 8:30 am-1:30 pm.

AUSTRIA. Av. 16 de Julio, #1616, Edif. Petrolero Mezz. office 11, ☎ 236-9863, 2:30-4 pm.

BELGIUM. Calle 9 #6, Achumani, ☎ 277-1480, 9 am-1 pm.

BRAZIL. Av. Arce, Edif. Multicentro P.B., ☎ 244-0202, 9 am-1 pm; 3-6:30 pm.

CANADA. Pl. España, Calle Victor Sanjinez #2678, Edif. Barcelona, ☎ 241-5021, 8:30 am-5 pm.

COLOMBIA. Calle 9 Calacoto #7835, ☎ 273-6841, 9 am-noon and 3-5 pm.

CHILE. Calacoto, Calle 14 #8024, ☎ 279-7331, 8 am-1 pm.

ECUADOR. Edificio Hermann, piso #14, ☎ 233-1588, 8:30 am-4 pm.

FRANCE. Calle 8 (Obrajes) & Hemando Siles #5390, ☎ 278-6189, 9 am-noon.

GERMANY. Av. Arce #2395, ☎ 244-0606, 9-noon.

GREAT BRITAIN. Av. Arce #2732 on Cordero & Campos, ☎ 243-3424, 9 am-noon and 2-4 pm.

HOLLAND. Av. 6 de Agosto # 2455, Edif. Hilda, ☎ 244-4040, 9 am-noon.

ISREAL. Av Mcal. Santa Cruz, Edif. Esperanza Piso 10, ☎ 237-4239, 9 am-4 pm.

ITALY. Av. 6 de Agosto #2575 on Salazar & Pinilla, ☎ 243-4955, 10:30 am-12:30 pm.

MEXICO. Sanchez Bustamante # 509 on 11 & 12 Calacoto, ☎ 277-1824, 8-11:30 am.

NORWAY. Calle Rene Moreno #1096 & San Miguel, ☎ 277-0009, 9 am-noon and 1:30-6:30 pm.

PARAGUAY. Av. 6 de Agosto, & Salazar, Edif. Illimani II, ☎ 243-3176, 8:30 am-4 pm.

PERU. Av. 6 de Agosto #2455, Edif. Hilda, Piso 4, office 402, ☎ 244-0631, 9 am-1 pm and 3-5 pm.

SPAIN. Av. 6 de Agosto #2827, ☎ 243-0118, 9 am-1:30 pm.

SWEDEN. Av. 14 de Septiembre #5080 & 5 Obrajes, ☎ 231-5617, 9 am-noon.

SWITZERLAND. Av. 16 de Julio, Edif. Petrolero, Piso 6, ☎ 231-5617, 9 am-noon.

UNITED STATES. Av. Arce #2780 & Cordero, ☎ 243-0251, 8 am-5 pm.

VENEZUELA. Edif. Illimani, Ave. Arce # 2678, Piso 5, ☎ 243-1365, 9 am-1 pm.

■ Cochabamba

ARGENTINA. Federico Blaco #929, ☎ 422-9347, 8:30 am-1 pm.

BRAZIL. Edif. Los Tiempos II, Piso 9, ☎ 425-5860, 8:30-11:30 am and 2:30-5:30 pm.

CHILE. Av. Heroinas, & Lanza #620, ☎ 425-3095, 8:30 am-1 pm.

GERMANY. Edif. La Promotora, Piso 6, Of. 602, ☎ 425-4024, 10 am-noon.

HOLLAND. Av. Oquendo #654 /tires Sofer, Piso 7, ☎ 425-7362, 8:30-noon and 2-4:30 pm.

ITALY. Calle Ayacucho Gal. Cochabamba, Piso 1, ☎ 423-8650, 6-7:30 pm.

MEXICO. 25 de Mayo, S-230, Piso 3, ☎ 425-671410, 10 am-12:30 pm.

NORWAY. Av. Guilemo Urquidi, E-2279, ☎ 423-1951, 8-9 am.

PARAGUAY. Edif. El Solar 16 de Julio # 211, ☎ 425-0183, 8:30 am-noon and 2-6:30 pm.

PERU. Av. Pando #1325, ☎ 424-0296, 8 am-noon and 2-6 pm.

SPAIN. Calle Los Molles & Paraiso Urb. Irlandes, ☎ 425-5733, 11 am-noon.

SWEDEN. Barquisimeto, Villa La Glorieta, ☎ 424-5358, 9 am-noon.

SWITZERLAND. Calle Miguel de Aquirre #1140, ☎ 424-2441, 8 am-noon.

UNITED STATES. Torres Sofer Bloque A, Off. 601, ☎ 425-6714, 9 am-noon.

VENEZUELA. Av. Blanco Galindo Km 7.5 (Duralit), ☎ 426-8311, 9 am-noon.

■ Santa Cruz

ARGENTINA. Calle Junin #22, ☎ 332-4153, 8 am-1 pm.

AUSTRIA. Pilcomayo #242, ☎ 352-5333, 2:30-5:30 pm.

BRAZIL. Av. Busch #330, ☎ 334-4400, 9 am-3 pm.

CHILE. Equipetrol C-5 Oeste # 224, ☎ 342-0051, 8 am-12:45 pm.

COLOMBIA. Edif. Santa Cruz, ☎ 333-8162, 9 am-noon, 3-6 pm.

ECUADOR. Velasco # 700, ☎ 336-9700, 9-noon and 3-6 pm.

FRANCE. Av. Alemana & Mutualista, 3rd *anillo*, ☎ 343-3434, 4:30-6 pm.

GERMAN. Calle Nuflo de Chavez # 241, ☎ 336-7585, 8:30 am-noon.

HOLLAND. Av. Roque Aquilera #300, 3rd *anillo*, ☎ 358-1866, 9 am-noon.

ITALY. Av. El Trompillo & Chaco, Edif. Honnen, ☎ 353-1796, 8:30 am-noon.

ISREAL. Calle Pailon Mercado #171 (Av. Banzer), ☎ 342-4777, 8:30 am-noon.

PARAGUAY. Manuel Ignacio Salvatierra # 99, Edif. Victoria, ☎ 336-6113, 7:30 am-2 pm.

PERU. Ed. Oriente,Ppiso 2, ☎ 336-8979, 8:30 am-1:30 pm.

SPAIN. Mons. Santiesteban #237, ☎ 332-8921, 9 am-noon.

SWITZERLAND. Av. Banzer #470, ☎ 343-5540, 8:30 am-noon and 2:30-5 pm.

UNITED STATES. Calle Guemes # 6 & Equipetrol, ☎ 333-0725, 9 to 11:30 am.

URUGUAY. Calle Moldes #436, ☎ 332-9317, 7:30 am-1:30 pm.

Glossary

■ THE CALENDAR

```
dia . . . . . . . . . . . . . . . . . . . . . . . . . . . . . . . . . . . . . . . . . . . . . . . . . . . day
semana . . . . . . . . . . . . . . . . . . . . . . . . . . . . . . . . . . . . . . . . . . . . . . . week
mes . . . . . . . . . . . . . . . . . . . . . . . . . . . . . . . . . . . . . . . . . . . . . . . . month
año . . . . . . . . . . . . . . . . . . . . . . . . . . . . . . . . . . . . . . . . . . . . . . . . . year
domingo. . . . . . . . . . . . . . . . . . . . . . . . . . . . . . . . . . . . . . . . . . . Sunday
lunes. . . . . . . . . . . . . . . . . . . . . . . . . . . . . . . . . . . . . . . . . . . . Monday
martes . . . . . . . . . . . . . . . . . . . . . . . . . . . . . . . . . . . . . . . . . . Tuesday
miercoles. . . . . . . . . . . . . . . . . . . . . . . . . . . . . . . . . . . . . . Wednesday
jueves. . . . . . . . . . . . . . . . . . . . . . . . . . . . . . . . . . . . . . . . . Thursday
viernes . . . . . . . . . . . . . . . . . . . . . . . . . . . . . . . . . . . . . . . . . . Friday
sabado . . . . . . . . . . . . . . . . . . . . . . . . . . . . . . . . . . . . . . . . Saturday
enero . . . . . . . . . . . . . . . . . . . . . . . . . . . . . . . . . . . . . . . . . January
```

febrero . . . . February
marzo . . . . March
abril . . . . April
mayo . . . . May
junio . . . . June
julio . . . . July
agosto . . . . August
septiembre . . . . September
octubre . . . . October
noviembre . . . . November
diciembre . . . . December

■ NUMBERS

uno . . . . one
dos . . . . two
tres . . . . three
cuatro . . . . four
cinco . . . . five
seis . . . . six
siete . . . . seven
ocho . . . . eight
nueve . . . . nine
diez . . . . ten
once . . . . eleven
doce . . . . twelve
trece . . . . thirteen
catorce . . . . fourteen
quince . . . . fifteen
dieciséis . . . . sixteen
diecisiete . . . . seventeen
dieciocho . . . . eighteen
diecinueve . . . . nineteen
veinte . . . . twenty
veintiuno . . . . twenty-one
veintidós . . . . twenty-two
treinta . . . . thirty
cuarenta . . . . forty
cincuenta . . . . fifty
sesenta . . . . sixty
setenta . . . . seventy
ochenta . . . . eighty
noventa . . . . ninety
cien . . . . hundred
ciento uno . . . . one hundred one
doscientos . . . . two hundred
quinientos . . . . five hundred
mil . . . . one thousand
mil uno . . . . one thousand one

dos mil. . . . . two thousand
millón . . . . one million
primero. . . . . first
segundo. . . . . second
tercero . . . . third
último . . . . last

■ CONVERSATION

¿Como esta? . . . . How are you?
¿Bien, gracias, y usted? . . . . Well, thanks, and you?
¿Que pasa?. . . . . What's happening?
Buenas dias. . . . . Good morning.
Buenas tardes. . . . . Good afternoon.
Buenas noches. . . . . Good evening/night.
Nos vemos. . . . . See you again.
¡Buena suerte!. . . . . Good luck!
Adios. . . . . Goodbye.
Que la vaya bien. . . . . Goodbye (used for someone special)
Mucho gusto. . . . . Glad to meet you.
Felicidades. . . . . Congratulations.
Feliz compleaños. . . . . Happy birthday.
Feliz Navidad. . . . . Merry Christmas.
Feliz Año Nuevo. . . . . Happy New Year.
Gracias.. . . . . Thank you.
Por favor. . . . . Please.
De nada/con mucho gusto. . . . . You're welcome.
Perdoneme. . . . . Pardon me (when bumping into someone).
Permitame. . . . . Pardon me (when passing in front of someone).
Desculpe . . . . Excuse me (when interrupting conversation).
¿Como se dice esto? . . . . What do you call this?
Lo siento. . . . . I'm sorry.
Quiero... . . . . I want/I like...
Adelante.. . . . . Come in.
Permitame presentarle... . . . . May I introduce...
¿Como se nombre?. . . . . What is your name?
Me nombre es... . . . . My name is...
No se. . . . . I don't know.
Tengo sed.. . . . . I am thirsty.
Tengo hambre.. . . . . I am hungry.
Soy gringa/gringo . . . . I am an American (female/male).
¿Donde hay...? . . . . Where is there/are there...?
Hay... . . . . There is/are
No hay. . . . . There is none
¿Que es esto? . . . . What is this?
¿Habla ingles? . . . . Do you speak English?
¿Hablan ingles?. . . . . Is there anyone here who speaks English?
Hablo/entiendo un poco . . . . I speak/understand a little Spanish.
  Español

Le entiendo. . . . . I understand you.
No entiendo. . . . . I don't understand.
Hable mas despacio por favor. . . . . Please speak more slowly.
Repita por favor. . . . . Please repeat.
¿Tiene...?. . . . . Do you have...?
Tengo.... . . . . I have...
Hecho... . . . . I make/made
¿Puedo? . . . . May I?
La cuenta por favor . . . . The bill, please.
bolsa. . . . . bag
muchila . . . . backpack

■ TIME

¿Que hora es? . . . . What time is it?
Son las.... . . . . It is...
... cinco. . . . . five o'clock.
... ocho y diez. . . . . ten past eight.
... seis y cuarto. . . . . quarter past six.
... cinco y media. . . . . half past five.
... siete y menos cinco. . . . . five of seven.
antes de ayer. . . . . the day before yesterday.
anoche. . . . . yesterday evening.
esta mañana. . . . . this morning.
a mediodia. . . . . at noon.
en la noche. . . . . in the evening.
de noche. . . . . at night.
mañana en la mañana. . . . . tomorrow morning.
mañana en la noche. tomorrow evening.

■ DIRECTIONS

Llevame alla ... por favor. . . . . Take me there please.
¿Cual es el mejor camino para...? . . . . . . Which is the best road to...?
Derecha. . . . . Right.
Izquierda.. . . . . Left.
Derecho/directo. . . . . Straight ahead.
¿A que distancia estamos de...? . . . . How far is it to...?
¿Es este el camino a...?. . . . . Is this the road to...?
¿Es cerca? . . . . Is it near?
¿Es largo? . . . . Is it a long way?
¿Donde hay...? . . . . Where is... ?
... el telefono. . . . . the telephone.
... el bano. . . . . the bathroom.
... el correos. . . . . the post office.
... el banco. . . . . the bank.
... el casa de cambio . . . . the money exchange office.
... estacion del policia. . . . . the police station.

■ ACCOMMODATIONS

¿Que quiere? . . . . What do you want?
Quiero un hotel... . . . . I want a hotel that's...

... buena. . . . . good.
... barato. . . . . cheap.
... limpio. . . . . clean.
¿Dónde hay un hotel buena?. . . . . Where is a good hotel?
¿Hay habitaciones libres? . . . . Do you have available rooms?
¿Dónde están los baños/servicios? . . . . Where are the bathrooms?
Quiero un habitacion. . . . . I would like a room.
habitacion sencillo. . . . . single room.
habitacion con baño privado. . . . . room with a private bath.
habitacion doble. . . . . double room.
baño comun . . . . without a private bath/with a shared bath
ducha . . . . shower
¿Esta incluido? . . . . Is that included?
¿Puedo verlo? . . . . May I see it?
cama. . . . . bed
cama matrimonial. . . . . double bed
¿Algo mas? . . . . Anything more?
¿Cuanto cuesta?. . . . . How much?
¡Es muy caro! . . . . It's too expensive!

■ FOOD

comer . . . . to eat
pan . . . . bread
carne . . . . meat
papas . . . . potatoes
leche . . . . milk
frutas . . . . fruit
jugo. . . . . juice
huevos . . . . eggs
mantequilla. . . . . butter
queso. . . . . cheese
agua mineral . . . . mineral water
cerveza . . . . beer
pescado . . . . fish
helado. . . . . ice cream
arroz. . . . . rice
ensalada . . . . salad
jamon . . . . ham
pollo. . . . . chicken
toronja. . . . . grapefruit
naranja . . . . orange (the fruit)
mariscos . . . . seafood
sopa . . . . soup
vino tinto. . . . . red wine
vino blanco . . . . white wine

Index

Index